ANALYTICAL PERSPECTIVES
BUDGET OF THE U.S. GOVERNMENT

FISCAL YEAR 2017
OFFICE OF MANAGEMENT AND BUDGET

Scan here to go to
our website.

THE BUDGET DOCUMENTS

Budget of the United States Government, Fiscal Year 2017 contains the Budget Message of the President, information on the President's priorities, and summary tables.

Analytical Perspectives, Budget of the United States Government, Fiscal Year 2017 contains analyses that are designed to highlight specified subject areas or provide other significant presentations of budget data that place the budget in perspective. This volume includes economic and accounting analyses; information on Federal receipts and collections; analyses of Federal spending; information on Federal borrowing and debt; baseline or current services estimates; and other technical presentations.

The *Analytical Perspectives* volume also has supplemental materials that are available on the internet at *www.budget.gov/budget/Analytical_Perspectives* and on the Budget CD-ROM. These supplemental materials include tables showing the budget by agency and account and by function, subfunction, and program.

Appendix, Budget of the United States Government, Fiscal Year 2017 contains detailed information on the various appropriations and funds that constitute the budget and is designed primarily for the use of the Appropriations Committees. The *Appendix* contains more detailed financial information on individual programs and appropriation accounts than any of the other budget documents. It includes for each agency: the proposed text of appropriations language; budget schedules for each account; legislative proposals; narrative explanations of each budget account; and proposed general provisions applicable to the appropriations of entire agencies or group of agencies. Information is also provided on certain activities whose transactions are not part of the budget totals.

ELECTRONIC SOURCES OF BUDGET INFORMATION

The information contained in these documents is available in electronic format from the following sources:

Internet. All budget documents, including documents that are released at a future date, spreadsheets of many of the budget tables, and a public use budget database are available for downloading in several formats from the internet at *www.budget.gov/budget*. Links to documents and materials from budgets of prior years are also provided.

Budget CD-ROM. The CD-ROM contains all of the printed budget documents in fully indexed PDF format along with the software required for viewing the documents.

The Internet and CD-ROM also include many of the budget tables in spreadsheet format, and supplemental materials that are part of the *Analytical Perspectives* volume. It also includes *Historical Tables* that provide data on budget receipts, outlays, surpluses or deficits, Federal debt, and Federal employment over an extended time period, generally from 1940 or earlier to 2017 or 2021.

For more information on access to electronic versions of the budget documents (except CD-ROMs), call (202) 512-1530 in the D.C. area or toll-free (888) 293-6498. To purchase the Budget CD-ROM or printed documents call (202) 512-1800.

GENERAL NOTES

1. All years referenced for budget data are fiscal years unless otherwise noted. All years referenced for economic data are calendar years unless otherwise noted.

2. Detail in this document may not add to the totals due to rounding.

ISBN 13: 978-1-59888-838-6

TABLE OF CONTENTS

Page

List of Charts and Tables ... iii

Introduction

   1. Introduction ...3

Economic Assumptions and Interactions with the Budget

   2. Economic Assumptions and Interactions with the Budget ...9

   3. Long-Term Budget Outlook ...21

   4. Federal Borrowing and Debt ...33

Performance and Management

   5. Social Indicators ...51

   6. Delivering A High-Performance Government ...61

   7. Building the Capacity to Produce and Use Evidence ...69

   8. Strengthening the Federal Workforce ...79

Budget Concepts and Budget Process

   9. Budget Concepts ...97

   10. Coverage of the Budget ...121

   11. Budget Process ...127

Federal Receipts

   12. Governmental Receipts ...153

   13. Offsetting Collections and Offsetting Receipts ...211

   14. Tax Expenditures ...225

Special Topics

   15. Aid to State and Local Governments ...269

   16. Strengthening Federal Statistics ...281

   17. Information Technology ...287

   18. Federal Investment ...293

   19. Research and Development ...299

   20. Credit and Insurance ...307

   21. Budgetary Effects of the Troubled Asset Relief Program ...335

   22. Homeland Security Funding Analysis ...347

		Page
23.	Federal Drug Control Funding	359
24.	Federal Budget Exposure to Climate Risk	361

Technical Budget Analyses

25.	Current Services Estimates	369
26.	Trust Funds and Federal Funds	381
27.	Comparison of Actual to Estimated Totals	395
Detailed Functional Tables		*
Federal Budget by Agency and Account		*

On the cover:
Denali National Park
Photo by Jacob Frank, National Park Service
Photograph has been reformatted from full color to monochrome

*Available on the Internet at *http://www.whitehouse.gov/omb/budget/Analytical_Perspectives/* and on the *Budget* CD-ROM

LIST OF CHARTS AND TABLES

LIST OF CHARTS AND TABLES

LIST OF CHARTS

Page

2–1. Range of Uncertainty for the Budget Deficit 19

3–1. Publicly Held Debt Under Continuation of Current Policies 22

3–2. Changes to Projected 2020 Deficit Under Continuation of Current Policies 23

3–3. Comparison of Publicly Held Debt 24

3–4. 2017 Budget Policies 25

3–5. Alternative Productivity and Interest Assumptions 26

3–6. Alternative Health Care Costs 27

3–7. Alternative Discretionary Projections 27

3–8. Alternative Revenue Projections 28

3–9. Long-Term Uncertainties 28

8–1. Changes Since 1975 in Employment/Population by Sector 80

8–2. Masters Degree or Above by Year for Federal and Private Sectors 83

8–3. High School Graduate or Less by Year for Federal and Private Sectors 84

8–4. Average Age by Year for Federal and Private Sectors 86

8–5. Pay Raises for Federal vs. Private Workforce, 1978–2017 87

9–1. Relationship of Budget Authority to Outlays for 2017 110

17–1. Trends in Federal IT Spending 288

20–1. Face Value of Federal Credit Outstanding 329

24–1. National Flood Insurance Program Paid Losses & Exposure 362

24–2. Crop Insurance Total Cost to Government 363

LIST OF TABLES

Page

Economic Assumptions and Interactions with the Budget

Economic Assumptions and Interactions with the Budget

2–1. Economic Assumptions 12

2–2. Comparison Of Economic Assumptions In The 2016 And 2017 Budgets 13

2–3. Comparison of Economic Assumptions 14

2–4. Sensitivity of the Budget to Economic Assumptions 17

2–5. Forecast Errors, January 1982-Present 18

2–6. Differences Between Estimated and Actual Surpluses or Deficits
for Five-Year Budget Estimates Since 1986 19

2–7. The Structural Balance 20

Long-Term Budget Outlook

3–1. 25-Year Fiscal Gap (–)/Surplus (+) Under Alternative Budget Scenarios 24

3–2. 25-Year Fiscal Gap (–)/Surplus (+) Under Alternative Budget Scenarios 26

3–3. Intermediate Actuarial Projections for OASDI And HI 30

Federal Borrowing and Debt

4–1. Trends in Federal Debt Held by the Public and Interest
on the Debt Held by the Public 34

4–2. Federal Government Financing and Debt 36

4–3. Debt Held by the Public Net of Financial Assets and Liabilities 39

4–4. Agency Debt 41

4–5. Debt Held by Government Accounts 43

4–6. Federal Funds Financing and Change in Debt Subject to Statutory Limit 46

4–7. Foreign Holdings of Federal Debt 47

Performance and Management

Social Indicators

5–1. Social Indicators 53

5–2. Sources for Social Indicators 57

Strengthening the Federal Workforce

8–1. Occupations of Federal and Private Sector Workforces 81

8–2. Federal Civilian Employment in the Executive Branch 82

8–3. Total Federal Employment 83

8–4. Personnel Compensation and Benefits 85

Budget Concepts and Budget Process

Budget Concepts

Budget Calendar 99

9–1. Totals for the Budget and the Federal Government 104

Coverage of the Budget

10–1. Comparison of Total, On-Budget, and Off-Budget Transactions 122

Budget Process

11–1. Enacted Cap Adjustments, Including Mandatory Savings 130

11–2. Proposals for Discretionary Program Integrity Base Funding and
Cap Adjustments, Including Mandatory and Receipts Savings 131

11–3. Mandatory and Receipt Savings from Other Program Integrity Initiatives 133

11–4. Size of Proposed Discretionary Cap Adjustment for 2020 Census 139

11–5. Budgetary Resources and Revenue for the 21st Century Clean
Transportation Plan 141

11–6. 10-Year PAYGO Analysis 21st Century Clean Transportation Plan 143

11–7. Effect of Student Aid Proposals on Discretionary Pell Funding Needs 145

Federal Receipts

Governmental Receipts

12–1. Receipts by Source—Summary 153

12–2. Effect of Budget Proposals 201

12–3. Receipts by Source 208

Offsetting Collections and Offsetting Receipts

13–1. Offsetting Collections and Offsetting Receipts from the Public 212

13–2. Offsetting Receipts by Type Summary 213

13–3. Gross Outlays, User Charges, Other Offsetting Collections and
Offsetting Receipts from the Public, and Net Outlays 214

13–4. User Charge Proposals in the FY 2017 Budget 222

13–5. Offsetting Receipts by Type .... *

Tax Expenditures

14–1. Estimates of Total Income Tax Expenditures for Fiscal Years 2015–2025 228

14–2A. Estimates of Total Corporate Income Tax Expenditures
for Fiscal Years 2015–2025 233

14–2B. Estimates of Total Individual Income Tax Expenditures
for Fiscal Years 2015–2025 238

14–3. Income Tax Expenditures Ranked by Total Fiscal Year 2016-2025
Projected Revenue Effect 243

14–4. Present Value of Selected Tax Expenditures for Activity in Calendar Year 2015 247

Special Topics

Aid to State and Local Governments

15–1. Trends in Federal Grants to State and Local Governments 271

15–2. Federal Grants to State and Local Governments—Budget Authority and Outlays ...... *

15–3. Summary of Programs by Agency, Bureau, and Program 278

15–4. Summary of Programs by State 279

15–5.—15–41. 2016 Budget State-by-State Tables .... *

Strengthening Federal Statistics

16–1. 2015-2017 Budget Authority for Principal Statistical Agencies 285

Information Technology

17–1. Federal IT Spending 287

*Available on the Internet at *http://www.budget.gov/budget/Analytical_Perspectives* and on the *Budget* CD-ROM

Federal Investment

  18–1. Composition of Federal Investment Outlays 294

  18–2. Federal Investment Budget Authority and Outlays: Grant
          and Direct Federal Programs 296

Research and Development

  19–1. Federal Research and Development Spending 305

Credit and Insurance

  20–1. Top 10 Firms Presenting Claims (1975-2014) 324

  20–2. Estimated Future Cost of Outstanding Direct Loans and Loan Guarantees 330

  20–3. Direct Loan Subsidy Rates, Budget Authority, and Loan Levels, 2015–2017 331

  20–4. Loan Guarantee Subsidy Rates, Budget Authority, and Loan Levels, 2015–2017 333

  20–5. Summary of Federal Direct Loans and Loan Guarantees 334

  20–6. Reestimates of Credit Subsidies on Loans Disbursed Between 1992-2013 .... *

  20–7. Face Value of Government-Sponsored Lending .... *

  20–8. Lending and Borrowing by Government-Sponsored Enterprises (GSEs) .... *

  20–9. Direct Loan Transactions of the Federal Government .... *

  20–10. Guaranteed Loan Transactions of the Federal Government .... *

Budgetary Effects of the Troubled Asset Relief Program

  21–1. Change in Programmatic Costs of Troubled Asset Relief Program 336

  21–2. Troubled Asset Relief Program Current Value 337

  21–3. Troubled Asset Relief Program Effects on the Deficit and Debt 338

  21–4. Troubled Asset Relief Program Effects on the Deficit and
          Debt Calculated on a Cash Basis 339

  21–5. Troubled Asset Relief Program Reestimates 340

  21–6. Detailed Tarp Program Levels and Costs 341

  21–7. Comparison of CBO and OMB TARP Costs 342

Homeland Security Funding Analysis

  22–1. Homeland Security Funding by Agency 350

  22–2. Prevent and Disrupt Terrorist Attacks 351

  22–3. Protect the American People, Our Critical Infrastructure, and Key Resources 352

  22–4. Respond and Recover from Incidents 353

  22–5. Discretionary Fee-Funded Homeland Security Activities by Agency 354

  22–6. Mandatory Homeland Security Activities by Agency 354

  22–7. Baseline Estimates—Total Homeland Security Funding by Agency 355

  22–8. Total Homeland Security Funding by Function 356

  22–9. Baseline Estimates—Total Homeland Security Funding by Function 357

  22–10. Department of Defense Homeland Security Reporting Adjustments 358

  Appendix—Homeland Security Mission Funding by Agency and Budget Account .... *

Federal Drug Control Funding

  23–1. Drug Control Funding FY 2015–FY 2017 359

*Available on the Internet at *http://www.budget.gov/budget/Analytical_Perspectives* and on the *Budget* CD-ROM

Technical Budget Analyses

Current Services Estimates

25–1.   Category Totals for the Adjusted Baseline 369

25–2.   Summary of Economic Assumptions 372

25–3.   Baseline Beneficiary Projections for Major Benefit Programs 373

25–4.   Impact of Regulations, Expiring Authorizations, and
        Other Assumptions in the Baseline .... *

25–5.   Receipts by Source in the Projection of Adjusted Baseline 374

25–6.   Effect on Receipts of Changes in the Social Security Taxable Earnings Base 374

25–7.   Change in Outlay Estimates by Category in the Adjusted Baseline 375

25–8.   Outlays by Function in the Adjusted Baseline 376

25–9.   Outlays by Agency in the Adjusted Baseline 377

25–10. Budget Authority by Function in the Adjusted Baseline 378

25–11. Budget Authority by Agency in the Adjusted Baseline 379

25–12   Current Services Budget Authority and Outlays by Function, Category, and Program ....*

Trust Funds and Federal Funds

26–1.   Receipts, Outlays and Surplus or Deficit by Fund Group 382

26–2.   Comparison of Total Federal Fund and Trust Fund Receipts to
        Unified Budget Receipts, Fiscal Year 2015 384

26–3.   Income, Outgo, and Balances of Trust Funds Group 385

26–4.   Income, Outgo, and Balance of Major Trust Funds 387

26–5.   Income, Outgo, and Balance of Selected Special Funds 394

Comparison of Actual to Estimated Totals

27–1.   Comparison of Actual 2015 Receipts with the Initial Current Services Estimates 395

27–2.   Comparison of Actual 2015 Outlays with the Initial Current Services Estimates 396

27–3.   Comparison of the Actual 2015 Deficit with the Initial Current Services Estimate 397

27–4.   Comparison of Actual and Estimated Outlays for Mandatory and
        Related Programs Under Current Law 398

27–5.   Reconciliation of Final Amounts for 2015 399

Detailed Functional Tables

28–1.   Budget Authority and Outlays by Function, Category and Program ....*

Federal Budget by Agency and Account

29–1.   Federal Budget by Agency and Account ....*

*Available on the Internet at *http://www.budget.gov/budget/Analytical_Perspectives* and on the *Budget* CD-ROM

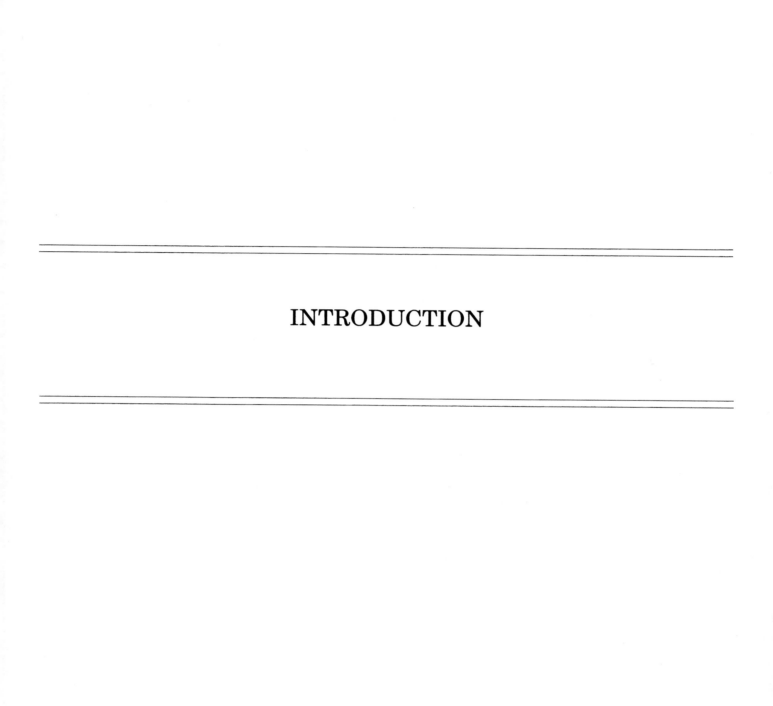

INTRODUCTION

1. INTRODUCTION

The *Analytical Perspectives* volume presents analyses that highlight specific subject areas or provide other significant data that place the President's 2017 Budget in context and assist the public, policymakers, the media, and researchers in better understanding the budget's effects on the Nation. This volume complements the main Budget volume, which presents the President's budget policies and priorities, and the Budget Appendix volume, which provides appropriations language, schedules for budget expenditure accounts, and schedules for selected receipt accounts.

Presidential budgets have included separate analytical presentations of this kind for many years. The 1947 Budget and subsequent budgets included a separate section entitled "Special Analyses and Tables" that covered four and sometimes more topics. For the 1952 Budget, the section was expanded to 10 analyses, including many subjects still covered today, such as receipts, investment, credit programs, and aid to State and local governments. With the 1967 Budget this material became a separate volume entitled "Special Analyses," and included 13 chapters. The material has remained a separate volume since then, with the exception of the Budgets for 1991–1994, when all of the budget material was included in one volume. Beginning with the 1995 Budget, the volume has been named *Analytical Perspectives*.

Several supplemental tables as well as several longer tables that were previously published within the volume are available at http://www.budget.gov/budget/ Analytical_Perspectives and on the Budget CD-ROM. These tables are shown in the List of Tables in the front of this volume with an asterisk instead of a page number.

OVERVIEW OF THE CHAPTERS

Economic and Budget Analyses

Economic Assumptions and Interactions Between the Economy and the Budget. This chapter reviews recent economic developments; presents the Administration's assessment of the economic situation and outlook, including the effects of macroeconomic policies; compares the economic assumptions on which the 2017 Budget is based with the assumptions for last year's Budget and those of other forecasters; provides sensitivity estimates for the effects on the Budget of changes in specified economic assumptions; and reviews past errors in economic projections. It also provides estimates of the cyclical and structural components of the budget deficit.

Long-Term Budget Outlook. This chapter assesses the long-term budget outlook under policies currently in effect and under the Budget's proposals as well as progress towards fiscal sustainability since 2010. It focuses on 25-year projections of Federal deficits, debt, and the fiscal gap, and shows how alternative long-term budget assumptions affect the results. It also discusses the long-term uncertainties of the budget projections over a 75-year horizon and discusses the actuarial status of the Social Security and Medicare programs.

Federal Borrowing and Debt. This chapter analyzes Federal borrowing and debt and explains the budget estimates. It includes sections on special topics such as trends in debt, debt held by the public net of financial assets and liabilities, investment by Government accounts, and the statutory debt limit.

Performance and Management

Social Indicators. This chapter presents a selection of statistics that offers a numerical picture of the United States and illustrates how this picture has changed over time. Included are economic, demographic and civic, socioeconomic and health statistics. There are also indicators covering security and safety, environment, and energy.

Delivering a High-Performance Government. This chapter describes the Administration's approach to performance management—the Federal Government's use of performance goals, measurement, regular data-driven reviews, and information dissemination to improve outcomes that matter to the American people and deliver returns on the taxpayers' investment. It explains why this approach was chosen, progress made, and future plans. It also discusses implementation of the Government Performance and Results Modernization Act.

Building the Capacity to Produce and Use Evidence. This chapter discusses evidence and its role in decision-making, articulates important principles and practices of agencies with strong evaluation functions, and highlights Administration efforts to build the capacity to produce and use evidence—particularly through the use of administrative data and the establishment of centralized evaluation functions. The chapter also provides examples of successes of the broader evidence agenda during this Administration.

Strengthening the Federal Workforce. Strengthening the Federal workforce is essential to building a high-performing Government. This chapter presents summary data on Federal employment and compensation; examines Federal workforce challenges; presents opportunities for strengthening the personnel system to achieve critical agency missions; and discusses progress in improving employee engagement, performance, and human capital management.

Budget Concepts and Budget Process

Budget Concepts. This chapter includes a basic description of the budget process, concepts, laws, and terminology, and includes a glossary of budget terms.

Coverage of the Budget. This chapter describes activities that are included in budget receipts and outlays (and are therefore classified as "budgetary") as well as those activities that are not included in the Budget (and are therefore classified as "non-budgetary"). The chapter also defines the terms "on-budget" and "off-budget" and includes illustrative examples.

Budget Process. This chapter discusses proposals to improve budgeting and fiscal sustainability within individual programs as well as across Government, describes the system of scoring mandatory and revenue legislation for purposes of the Statutory Pay-As-You-Go Act of 2010, and presents proposals to revise the budget baseline and improve budget presentation.

Federal Receipts

Governmental Receipts. This chapter presents information on estimates of governmental receipts, which consist of taxes and other compulsory collections. It includes detailed descriptions of tax legislation enacted in the last year and the receipts proposals in the Budget.

Offsetting Collections and Offsetting Receipts. This chapter presents information on collections that offset outlays, including collections from transactions with the public and intragovernmental transactions. In addition, this chapter presents information on "user fees," charges associated with market-oriented activities and regulatory fees. The user fee information includes a description of each of the user fee proposals in the Budget. A detailed table, "Table 13–5, Offsetting Receipts by Type" is available at the Internet address cited above and on the Budget CD-ROM.

Tax Expenditures. This chapter describes and presents estimates of tax expenditures, which are defined as revenue losses from special exemptions, credits, or other preferences in the tax code.

Special Topics

Aid to State and Local Governments. This chapter presents crosscutting information on Federal grants to State and local governments, including highlights of Administration proposals in the Budget. Detailed tables, including "Table 15–2, Federal Grants to State and Local Governments—Budget Authority and Outlays" and tables showing State-by-State spending for major grant programs, are available at the Internet address cited above and on the Budget CD-ROM.

Strengthening Federal Statistics. This chapter discusses 2017 Budget proposals for the Government's principal statistical programs.

Information Technology. This chapter gives an overview of Federal investments in information technology (IT), and the major Administration initiatives to improve the management of Federal data and IT by integrating modern technology solutions to enhance mission and service delivery and security. To achieve this, the Administration prioritizes four core objectives across the Federal IT portfolio discussed in the chapter: driving value in Federal IT investments; delivering world-class digital services, including opening Government data to fuel entrepreneurship and innovation; protecting Federal IT assets and information; and developing the next generation IT workforce.

Federal Investment. This chapter discusses Federally-financed spending that yields long-term benefits. It presents information on annual spending on physical capital, research and development, and education and training.

Research and Development. This chapter presents a crosscutting review of research and development funding in the Budget, including discussions about priorities and coordination across agencies.

Credit and Insurance. This chapter provides crosscutting analyses of the roles, risks, and performance of Federal credit and insurance programs and Government-sponsored enterprises (GSEs). The chapter covers the major categories of Federal credit (housing, education, small business and farming, energy and infrastructure, and international) and insurance programs (deposit insurance, pension guarantees, disaster insurance, and insurance against terrorism-related risks). Five additional tables address transactions including direct loans, guaranteed loans, and Government-sponsored enterprises. These tables are available at the Internet address cited above and on the Budget CD-ROM.

Budgetary Effects of the Troubled Asset Relief Program. The chapter provides special analyses of the Troubled Asset Relief Program (TARP) as described in Sections 202 and 203 of the Emergency Economic Stabilization Act of 2008, including information on the costs of TARP activity and its effects on the deficit and debt.

Homeland Security Funding Analysis. This chapter discusses homeland security funding and provides information on homeland security program requirements, performance, and priorities. Additional detailed information is available at the Internet address cited above and on the Budget CD-ROM.

Federal Drug Control Funding. This chapter displays enacted and proposed drug control funding for Federal departments and agencies.

Federal Budget Exposure to Climate Risk. This chapter discusses climate change-related risks for the Federal budget, including the potential for rising direct and indirect costs and lost revenue. The chapter presents estimates of costs incurred as a result of the types of extreme weather projected to grow in frequency and intensity as the climate changes, and discusses additional areas of vulnerability across the Federal budget.

Technical Budget Analyses

Current Services Estimates. This chapter presents estimates of what receipts, outlays, and the deficit would be if current policies remained in effect, using modified versions of baseline rules in the Balanced Budget and Emergency Deficit Control Act of 1985 (BBEDCA). Two detailed tables addressing factors that affect the baseline and provide details of the baseline budget authority and outlays are available at the Internet address cited above and on the Budget CD-ROM.

Trust Funds and Federal Funds. This chapter provides summary information about the two fund groups in the budget—Federal funds and trust funds. In addition, for the major trust funds and certain Federal fund programs, the chapter provides detailed information about income, outgo, and balances.

Comparison of Actual to Estimated Totals. This chapter compares the actual receipts, outlays, and deficit for 2015 with the estimates for that year published in the President's 2015 Budget.

The following materials are available at the Internet address cited above and on the Budget CD-ROM:

Detailed Functional Table

Detailed Functional Table. Table 28–1, "Budget Authority and Outlays by Function, Category, and Program," displays budget authority and outlays for major Federal program categories, organized by budget function (such as health care, transportation, or national defense), category, and program.

Federal Budget by Agency and Account

The Federal Budget by Agency and Account. Table 29–1, "Federal Budget by Agency and Account," displays budget authority and outlays for each account, organized by agency, bureau, fund type, and account.

ECONOMIC ASSUMPTIONS AND INTERACTIONS WITH THE BUDGET

2. ECONOMIC ASSUMPTIONS AND INTERACTIONS WITH THE BUDGET

This chapter presents the Administration's economic forecast and describes projections for important macroeconomic variables that inform the Administration's Fiscal Year 2017 Budget.[1] It also details the sensitivity of the Budget's estimates of receipts, outlays, and the deficit to the economic forecasts and gives a sense of the uncertainty associated with the forecast, based on historical experience.

When the President took office in 2009, the U.S. economy, along with that of much of the rest of the world, was in the midst of the deepest recession since the Great Depression. In response, the President and the entire Administration took unprecedented actions to mitigate the effects of this downturn, put people back to work, and bring the economy back on the road to recovery. To this end, the President worked with the Congress to enact the American Recovery and Reinvestment Act to boost spending on infrastructure, extend support to workers who had lost their jobs, provide tax credits to working families, and ease burdens on State and local governments so that they maintain essential services with minimal interruption. The Administration also took steps to reform the financial system and help prevent future financial crises by securing passage of the Dodd-Frank Wall Street Reform and Consumer Protection Act; and helped slow the growth of health care costs while providing quality, affordable insurance coverage to millions of Americans by fighting for passage of the Affordable Care Act (ACA). These, and other efforts, brought the economy back from the brink.

The avoidable and destructive effects of sequestration and repeated crises related to the threat of default and government shutdowns have at times, however, hampered economic recovery. Such episodes have occurred periodically over the last several years and have contributed to a slower rate of aggregate demand growth than might otherwise have been the case. Following the Government shutdown in October 2013, policymakers started to move away from manufactured crises and austerity budgeting, helping to lay the groundwork for job market gains and stronger growth. The President worked with Congress to secure a two-year budget agreement (the Bipartisan Budget Act of 2013) that replaced a portion of the harmful sequestration cuts and allowed for higher investment levels in 2014 and 2015. In 2015, the President worked with congressional leaders from both parties to secure agreements on aggregate targets for discretionary spending for fiscal years 2016 and 2017 with the passage of the Bipartisan Budget Act of 2015 and the Consolidated Appropriations Act of 2016. Based on analysis of the effects of full sequester relief by the Congressional Budget Office, it is estimated that these actions will add 340,000 jobs in 2016 and 500,000 job-years total over 2016 and 2017, while supporting middle-class families, investing in our long-term growth, protecting Social Security, and safeguarding our national security. In addition, the Bipartisan Budget Act of 2015 suspended the statutory debt limit until March 2017. Together, these two pieces of legislation ended yet another period of brinksmanship and uncertainty and put us on a path to continue creating jobs and promoting economic growth.

The United States right now has the strongest, most durable economy in the world. And while there is more work to do as the economy continues to grow, there are encouraging signs about the economy's future. Real GDP (gross domestic product) has grown steadily over the last few years. Driven by strong job growth in the private sector, the unemployment rate has dropped to its lowest level since early 2008 and it has been cut in half relative to its peak following the global financial crisis.

The Administration projects that real GDP will grow at a 2.6 percent rate in 2016, on a year-over-year basis, slightly faster than in 2014, and slightly faster than what is expected for 2015. This is expected to be followed by a further 2.6 percent gain in 2017. The unemployment rate is expected to continue falling to a trough of 4.5 percent in late 2016 and early 2017, after which it is expected to rise to 4.9 percent, the level that the Administration considers to be consistent with stable inflation and full employment.

The rest of this chapter proceeds as follows:

- The first section reviews the performance of the U.S. economy over the last year, across a wide range of indicators.

- The second section reports the Administration's projections for a number of macroeconomic variables over the next eleven years.

- The third section compares the Administration's forecasts with those of other prominent public and private sector forecasts.

- The fourth section illustrates the sensitivity of projections for Federal receipts and outlays (and implicitly the Federal budget balance) to deviations from the macroeconomic forecasts.

- The fifth section analyzes past forecasting errors on the part of the Administration, comparing them with the errors in forecasting made by the Congressional Budget Office and the Blue Chip Consensus of private professional forecasters.

- The sixth section combines the forecast errors and the sensitivity of budget projections to the economic assumptions to construct a probabilistic range for the values of the budget deficit over the next few years.

---

[1] Economic performance is discussed in terms of calendar years. Budget figures are discussed in terms of fiscal years. Economic growth figures are in real (inflation-adjusted) terms unless otherwise noted.

- The last section presents the cyclical budget balance, that part of the Federal budget deficit or surplus that can be ascribed to transitory factors associated with the economic cycle, and the structural budget balance, that part that would prevail even if the economy were operating at full employment.

Recent Economic Performance

In the past year, economic conditions in the United States have continued to improve, extending the recovery that began after the deep recession that began in 2007 and lasted into 2009. In the four quarters through the end of September 2015, real GDP growth was 2.1 percent. This was spurred by robust growth in consumer spending, which grew at a 3.1 percent rate during that time. Overall real GDP growth was held down, however, by weakness among our trading partners. The unemployment rate had decreased to 5.0 percent in the fall of 2015, the lowest rate since early 2008. Still, there is evidence that labor markets have room to improve further. The passage of the Bipartisan Budget Act of 2015 and the omnibus budget appropriations and tax bill, as well as the lifting of the Federal debt limit through March 2017, set the economy on a continued pace of recovery and resolved many of the uncertainties which might otherwise have impeded economic growth.

Labor Markets—The unemployment rate dropped to 5.0 percent in the fall of 2015. Creation of private nonfarm jobs remained strong, with an average monthly addition of over 200,000 jobs in 2015. This brought the string of consecutive months with positive private job creation to 70. These figures, however, do not fully reveal the scope of the recovery in the labor market. The proportion of the labor force that has been unemployed for more than 27 weeks declined to an average of 1.5 percent in 2015, down from an average of 2.9 percent over the years from 2008 to 2014. Still, the pre-crisis average was less than 1 percent, suggesting that there is yet further room for the labor market to improve. Similarly, the proportion that would like to be working full-time, but is working part-time for economic reasons, also declined to an average of 4.1 percent from an average of 5.1 percent from 2008 to 2014. The pre-crisis average was 3.6 percent, again signaling the potential for continued labor market improvements. Firmer labor markets contributed to inflation-adjusted median usual weekly earnings growth for full-time workers of 3.0 percent through the four quarters ending in December 2015, much faster than in comparable periods of recent years. The unemployment rate remained slightly above the Administration's estimate of 4.9 percent for the NAIRU (the so-called "non-accelerating inflation rate of unemployment"). This, combined with the still high number of people who were working part-time for economic reasons, the labor force participation rate having fallen faster than demographic fundamentals, and core inflation in the index for personal consumption expenditures (PCE) well below the Federal Reserve's target range, suggests scope for further above-trend growth of real GDP.

External Factors—In 2015, many large emerging economies experienced slower growth rates relative to what they had become accustomed to in recent years. Commonly, in the evaluation of emerging markets, analysts focus on the BRICS countries (Brazil, Russia, India, China, and South Africa) as a benchmark due to their size and diversity. The International Monetary Fund (IMF) estimates that the year-over-year growth rate of real GDP in China slowed by about half a percentage point in 2015, and it projects another drop in growth in 2016. Two other large emerging markets, Russia and Brazil, saw their GDP shrink in 2015, and the IMF expects continued declines for these countries in 2016 also. At the same time, South Africa saw positive but relatively slow growth. Weaker demand overseas has dampened foreign demand for American goods and services. It has also encouraged investors worldwide to shift to U.S. assets, continuing a trend that has developed over the last two to three years. Although this has helped to keep interest rates in the United States relatively low, it also has been a factor in strengthening the dollar (which has appreciated by about 11.8 percent in December 2015 relative to December 2014 on a nominal trade-weighted basis[2]), and this could make it more difficult for American firms to export to international markets going forward.

Oil Prices—Oil prices fell sharply over the second half of 2014 and have continued to decline through early 2016. The average price of a barrel of West Texas Intermediate crude (the U.S. benchmark) was a little under $50 in 2015, compared with an average over $90 in 2014. The lower price for oil is the result of a number of factors, including weaker demand abroad, the lack of production cuts in OPEC countries[3] in the face of low prices, and increased production in the United States. U.S. oil production grew by 10.1 percent in the first nine months through September 2015, the last month for which data was available, compared with the same period in 2014. This recent growth follows 16.8 percent growth in calendar year 2014 and 14.7 percent growth in calendar year 2013. For the second straight year, domestic oil production exceeded oil imports. Low oil prices have passed through to substantially lower gasoline prices for American consumers and, in turn, help to support consumer spending on other goods and services and also provide a competitive advantage to American firms, especially those that are energy-intensive.

House Prices—Housing prices (as measured by the Federal Housing Finance Agency (FHFA) purchase-only index) continued to recover from the sharp drop experienced leading into and following the most recent recession. In November 2015, the FHFA index was 5.9 percent higher than in the same month a year earlier. Up to a point, higher valuations of houses help the economy

---

[2] Specifically, this figure measures the appreciation of the dollar's value against a trade-weighted basket of major currencies, which include the euro, the Canadian dollar, the Japanese yen, the British pound, the Swiss franc, the Australian dollar, and the Swedish krona.

[3] OPEC stands for the Organization of Petroleum Exporting Countries and is an organization comprising many of the largest producers of crude oil in the world. In the past, OPEC has often responded to lower prices for oil by imposing tighter quotas on production by its members.

by enhancing household wealth, which, in turn, helps to support a higher level of consumption. Higher house prices can also encourage more home building, as appears to have happened in 2015 with an increase in the average monthly pace of housing starts. The average annual rate of housing starts rose to just over 1.1 million in the twelve months of 2015, up over ten percent from just over 1 million (at an average annual rate) in the same period a year earlier. Starts have trended steadily higher in the six years since bottoming out at an average annual rate of 554 thousand recorded at the depths of the recession in 2009. Despite this recent strength, housing starts are still well below the level commonly believed necessary to provide enough housing for a growing population with an expanding number of households, which is about 1.6 million per year. This suggests there is scope for continued growth in housing starts and increases in house prices in the near future.

Consumption—Consumption by private households is a major part of the country's economy, accounting for about 68.3 percent of annual output in 2014. Because of its large share of GDP, consumer spending growth is essential to economic growth in the United States. Since 2013, consumption growth has been faster than the rate of growth in the economy as a whole. Although growth in consumption in the first quarter of 2015 was fairly weak by the standards of the last few years, it picked up in the middle of the year. Consumer spending has been supported by rising wealth in the form of higher house prices and generally strong equity markets during the past several years. Growth in the consumption of services, such as health care and education, has been solid (2.8 percent growth in the year through the third quarter of 2015), as has been growth in spending on durable goods. Consumption of automobiles grew 3.3 percent in the four quarters ending in the third quarter of 2015, while that of furniture and other home equipment grew 6.1 percent in the same period.

Nonresidential Fixed Investment—Private nonresidential fixed investment tends to be one of the more volatile components of GDP. Year-over-year growth was quite rapid in 2011, 2012, and 2014, exceeding 6 percent, while it was more subdued in 2010, 2013, and 2015, when it was 3 percent or less. Despite being volatile, there is reason to believe that future growth in investment will be healthy. Strong growth in consumer spending ought to encourage firms to invest in new productive capacity to keep up with rising demand, and strong cash flows for nonfinancial firms ought to ensure adequate funding for investment.

The Government Sector—Federal consumption and gross investment has stabilized after several years of relatively sharp declines. Over the four quarters ending in the third quarter of 2015, Federal Government spending fell by 1.1 percent, but this compares with a decline of 4.0 percent in the year ending in the third quarter of 2011, a 1.4 percent drop in the year ending in the third quarter of 2012, and a 6.6 percent drop in the year ending in the third quarter of 2013. At the end of October, the Administration and the Congress came to an agreement

on a two-year budget deal (the Bipartisan Budget Act of 2015) that would help to offset some of the damaging fiscal cuts enacted in recent years and protect the economy from the dangers of an unnecessary default on the government's obligations in the near future due to failure to raise the statutory debt limit. These agreements help provide a degree of certainty that is essential to both consumers and firms when they are making decisions on how much to save or invest. Fiscal conditions at the State and local level have also improved after a four year period of spending cuts that finally ended in 2014. In the year ending in the third quarter of 2015, State and local government consumption and gross investment grew at a 1.9 percent clip, its fastest rate of increase since 2009.

Monetary Policy—At the beginning of the year, market expectations were that the Federal Reserve would finally begin returning to a more conventional policy stance, starting with raising the federal funds rate target from its zero lower bound. This process formally began when the Federal Open Market Committee raised its target for the federal funds rate, the rate that banks pay on their overnight loans, from a range of 0.00 percent to 0.25 percent to a range of 0.25 percent to 0.50 percent in mid-December 2015. Strength in the labor market and reasonable confidence that inflation would rise over the next few years were the rationale for this course of action by the Fed. This shift in policy, featuring the first increase in policy interest rates in nine years, is a signal of how far the economy has come since the depths of the financial crisis, when the Fed lowered interest rates to zero.

Economic Projections

In this section, the Administration's projections for a number of important macroeconomic variables are discussed. These projections are based on information available as of early November 2015 and they assume that all of the Administration's Budget proposals will be enacted. The current section discusses only the Administration's forecast, while the next section compares the Administration forecast with other major forecasts. The projections are shown in Table 2-1.

Real GDP—The Administration expects that real GDP growth will average about 2.5 percent annually over the three years from 2016 to 2018. After that, growth is projected to slow to 2.3 percent annually, the Administration's estimate of the economy's long-run rate of growth. Faster growth in the near term is possible, because a fair amount of slack in the economy is likely still left over from the very sharp downturn experienced from 2007 to 2009 and the steady recovery thereafter. This is partially reflected in the fact that the unemployment rate, which was 5.0 percent in November, is still above the assumed level of the NAIRU (4.9 percent), while the number of workers in part-time employment for economic reasons remains elevated.

On the other hand, despite residual economic slack, forecasted real GDP growth over the next three years is only slightly above what is believed to be its long-run rate. This can be explained by a number of factors. First, as in

Table 2–1. ECONOMIC ASSUMPTIONS[1]
(Calendar Years, Dollar Amounts in Billions)

	Actual	Projections											
	2014	2015	2016	2017	2018	2019	2020	2021	2022	2023	2024	2025	2026
Gross Domestic Product (GDP)													
Levels, Dollar Amounts in Billions:													
Current Dollars	17348	17948	18669	19510	20345	21237	22155	23121	24128	25179	26272	27413	28603
Real, Chained (2009) Dollars	15962	16351	16777	17209	17629	18041	18456	18880	19314	19759	20213	20678	21153
Chained Price Index (2009=100), Annual Average	108.7	109.8	111.3	113.4	115.4	117.7	120.0	122.5	124.9	127.4	130.0	132.6	135.2
Percent Change, Fourth Quarter over Fourth Quarter:													
Current Dollars	3.9	3.3	4.3	4.4	4.3	4.3	4.3	4.4	4.4	4.3	4.3	4.3	4.3
Real, Chained (2009) Dollars	2.5	2.2	2.7	2.5	2.4	2.3	2.3	2.3	2.3	2.3	2.3	2.3	2.3
Chained Price Index (2009=100)	1.3	1.1	1.6	1.8	1.9	2.0	2.0	2.0	2.0	2.0	2.0	2.0	2.0
Percent Change, Year over Year:													
Current Dollars	4.1	3.5	4.0	4.5	4.3	4.4	4.3	4.4	4.4	4.4	4.3	4.3	4.3
Real, Chained (2009) Dollars	2.4	2.4	2.6	2.6	2.4	2.3	2.3	2.3	2.3	2.3	2.3	2.3	2.3
Chained Price Index (2009=100)	1.6	1.0	1.4	1.9	1.8	2.0	2.0	2.0	2.0	2.0	2.0	2.0	2.0
Incomes, Billions of Current Dollars													
Domestic Corporate Profits	1655	1638	1636	1746	1858	1935	1988	2048	2105	2168	2227	2305	2404
Employee Compensation	9249	9606	9987	10369	10794	11261	11775	12322	12897	13496	14135	14780	15477
Wages and Salaries	7478	7777	8078	8400	8753	9132	9549	9983	10444	10926	11438	11963	12531
Other Taxable Income[2]	4075	4216	4282	4459	4638	4925	5209	5498	5767	6035	6286	6524	6759
Consumer Price Index (All Urban):[3]													
Level (1982-1984 = 100), Annual Average	236.7	237.0	240.7	245.9	250.9	256.6	262.3	268.3	274.4	280.6	287.0	293.4	300.1
Percent Change, Fourth Quarter over Fourth Quarter	1.2	0.5	1.9	2.1	2.2	2.3	2.3	2.3	2.3	2.3	2.3	2.3	2.3
Percent Change, Year over Year	1.6	0.1	1.5	2.1	2.1	2.3	2.2	2.3	2.3	2.3	2.3	2.3	2.3
Unemployment Rate, Civilian, Percent													
Fourth Quarter Level	5.7	5.0	4.5	4.6	4.6	4.6	4.7	4.8	4.8	4.9	4.9	4.9	4.9
Annual Average	6.2	5.3	4.7	4.5	4.6	4.6	4.7	4.7	4.8	4.9	4.9	4.9	4.9
Federal Pay Raises, January, Percent													
Military[4]	1.0	1.0	1.3	1.6	NA	NA	NA	NA	NA	NA	NA	NA	NA
Civilian[5]	1.0	1.0	1.3	1.6	NA	NA	NA	NA	NA	NA	NA	NA	NA
Interest Rates, Percent													
91-Day Treasury Bills[6]	*	*	0.7	1.8	2.6	3.1	3.3	3.4	3.4	3.3	3.3	3.2	3.2
10-Year Treasury Notes	2.5	2.1	2.9	3.5	3.9	4.1	4.2	4.2	4.2	4.2	4.2	4.2	4.2

[1] Based on information available as of mid-November 2015

[2] Rent, interest, dividend, and proprietors' income components of personal income

[3] Seasonally adjusted CPI for all urban consumers

[4] Percentages apply to basic pay only; percentages to be proposed for years after 2017 have not yet been determined.

[5] Overall average increase, including locality pay adjustments. Percentages to be proposed for years after 2017 have not yet been determined.

[6] Average rate, secondary market (bank discount basis)

* 0.05 percent or less

the case of the previous two expansions (1991 and 2001), the current expansion has generally featured steady, but fairly modest growth to this point. This is due in part to the special nature of the most recent recession, which was distinguished by a severe credit crunch that left a significant debt overhang for many households and firms. Also, weakness abroad, in Europe and in large emerging markets, is also likely to affect growth in the next couple of years. All of these factors are likely to restrain the rate of growth, especially when compared with what one might expect given that there is still scope for the economy to return to its pre-recession trend.

Long Run Growth—While it is difficult to project cyclical developments beyond the next few years, the Administration projects that after the economy returns to its trend rate of growth in the forecast, it will remain there for the duration of the forecast window. Real GDP growth is projected to be 2.3 percent at an average annual rate in the long run, below the average growth rate in the postwar period of 3.2 percent. The projected slower growth results from a decline in the growth rate of the working-age population and a decrease in the labor force participation rate caused by the retirement of the baby boom generation. The first cohort of the baby boom, born in

Table 2–2. COMPARISON OF ECONOMIC ASSUMPTIONS IN THE 2016 AND 2017 BUDGETS

(Calendar Years, Dollar Amounts in Billions)

	2015	2016	2017	2018	2019	2020	2021	2022	2023	2024	2025
Nominal GDP:											
2016 Budget Assumptions [1]	18123	18971	19862	20773	21692	22636	23620	24648	25720	26838	28005
2017 Budget Assumptions	17948	18669	19510	20345	21237	22155	23121	24128	25179	26272	27413
Real GDP (2009 Dollars):											
2016 Budget Assumptions [1]	16453	16947	17423	17872	18296	18717	19147	19588	20038	20499	20971
2017 Budget Assumptions	16351	16777	17209	17629	18041	18456	18880	19314	19759	20213	20678
Real GDP (Percent Change): [2]											
2016 Budget Assumptions [1]	3.1	3.0	2.8	2.6	2.4	2.3	2.3	2.3	2.3	2.3	2.3
2017 Budget Assumptions	2.4	2.6	2.6	2.4	2.3	2.3	2.3	2.3	2.3	2.3	2.3
GDP Price Index (Percent Change): [2]											
2016 Budget Assumptions [1]	1.3	1.6	1.8	2.0	2.0	2.0	2.0	2.0	2.0	2.0	2.0
2017 Budget Assumptions	1.0	1.4	1.9	1.8	2.0	2.0	2.0	2.0	2.0	2.0	2.0
Consumer Price Index (All-Urban; Percent Change): [2]											
2016 Budget Assumptions	1.4	1.9	2.1	2.2	2.3	2.3	2.3	2.3	2.3	2.3	2.3
2017 Budget Assumptions	0.1	1.5	2.1	2.1	2.3	2.2	2.3	2.3	2.3	2.3	2.3
Civilian Unemployment Rate (Percent): [3]											
2016 Budget Assumptions	5.4	5.1	4.9	4.9	5.0	5.1	5.2	5.2	5.2	5.2	5.2
2017 Budget Assumptions	5.3	4.7	4.5	4.6	4.6	4.7	4.7	4.8	4.9	4.9	4.9
91-Day Treasury Bill Rate (Percent): [3]											
2016 Budget Assumptions	0.4	1.5	2.4	2.9	3.2	3.3	3.4	3.4	3.5	3.5	3.5
2017 Budget Assumptions	*	0.7	1.8	2.6	3.1	3.3	3.4	3.4	3.3	3.3	3.2
10-Year Treasury Note Rate (Percent): [3]											
2016 Budget Assumptions	2.8	3.3	3.7	4.0	4.3	4.5	4.5	4.5	4.5	4.5	4.5
2017 Budget Assumptions	2.1	2.9	3.5	3.9	4.1	4.2	4.2	4.2	4.2	4.2	4.2

[1] Adjusted for July 2015 NIPA Revisions
[2] Calendar Year over Calendar Year
[3] Calendar Year Average
* 0.05 percent or less

1946, reached the early-retirement age for Social Security benefits (62 years old) in 2008. Since then, the number of individuals in cohorts entering their retirement years has increased, and retirements are projected to continue increasing for the next eight years. This phenomenon results in a lower projected long run growth rate.

Unemployment—For the 2016 Mid-Session Review, the Administration revised its estimate of the NAIRU down to 4.9 percent from 5.2 percent. The NAIRU is defined as the rate of unemployment consistent with a level of economic activity that is not placing either upward or downward pressure on the inflation rate. The unemployment rate stood at 5.0 percent in the fall of 2015. The Administration expects that the unemployment rate will actually dip below the NAIRU in coming years, with a low point of 4.5 percent in 2017. After that, unemployment is expected to rise gradually back to the NAIRU, reaching 4.9 percent in 2023. An unemployment rate below the NAIRU is made possible by the fact that inflation has generally run below the Federal Reserve's target in recent years, so that an unemployment rate below 4.9 percent is likely merely to push inflation back to a more normal level, rather than generate worryingly fast price increases.

Interest Rates—Since the onset of the most recent recession, both short-term and long-term interest rates have remained near historic lows. Although it is expected that the Federal Reserve will gradually raise short-term interest rates over the coming years as economic activity picks up and inflation moves closer to the Fed's target of 2 percent, the Administration expects that interest rates will remain substantially lower than the level of interest rates seen after past recoveries. The Administration projects the 91-day Treasury bill rate will reach a level of 3.3 percent by 2020 and settle at 3.2 percent by 2026. Similarly, the Administration expects the yield on the ten-year Treasury bond to rise gradually over the forecast window, eventually reaching 4.2 percent by 2020. Relatively subdued inflation is an important reason for the lower interest rate environment. It is also the case that the yield on ten-year government bonds (in both nominal and real terms) has been trending downward for several decades.[4]

Inflation—Consumer price inflation (as measured by the consumer price index for all urban consumers, or CPI-U) has been low in recent years. In fact, prices have risen at a pace of 2 percent or less annually since 2012, and they have been almost unchanged in 2015. The re-

---

[4] See the recent analysis by the Council of Economic Advisers (https://www.whitehouse.gov/sites/default/files/docs/interest_rate_report_final_v2.pdf).

Table 2–3. COMPARISON OF ECONOMIC ASSUMPTIONS
(Calendar Years)

	2015	2016	2017	2018	2019	2020	2021	2022	2023	2024	2025	2026
Nominal GDP:												
2017 Budget	17948	18669	19510	20345	21237	22155	23121	24128	25179	26272	27413	28603
CBO	17957	18689	19505	20326	21102	21923	22823	23766	24746	25764	26831	27942
Blue Chip	17955	18701	19553	20426	21313	22240	23207	24216	25268	26367	27512	28708
Real GDP (Year-over-Year):												
2017 Budget	2.4	2.6	2.6	2.4	2.3	2.3	2.3	2.3	2.3	2.3	2.3	2.3
CBO	2.4	2.5	2.6	2.3	1.8	1.9	2.1	2.1	2.1	2.0	2.0	2.0
Blue Chip	2.5	2.5	2.5	2.4	2.2	2.2	2.2	2.2	2.2	2.2	2.2	2.2
Real GDP (Fourth Quarter-over-Fourth Quarter):												
2017 Budget	2.2	2.7	2.5	2.4	2.3	2.3	2.3	2.3	2.3	2.3	2.3	2.3
CBO	2.0	2.7	2.5	2.1	1.8	1.9	2.1	2.1	2.0	2.0	2.0	2.0
Blue Chip	2.1	2.6	2.4	2.4	2.2	2.2	2.2	2.2	2.2	2.2	2.2	2.2
Federal Reserve Central Tendency[3]	2.1	2.3 - 2.5	2.0 - 2.3	1.8 to 2.2 longer run								
GDP Price Index:[1]												
2017 Budget	1.0	1.4	1.9	1.8	2.0	2.0	2.0	2.0	2.0	2.0	2.0	2.0
CBO	1.1	1.6	1.8	1.9	2.0	2.0	2.0	2.0	2.0	2.0	2.1	2.1
Blue Chip	1.0	1.7	2.0	2.1	2.1	2.1	2.1	2.1	2.1	2.1	2.1	2.1
Consumer Price Index (CPI-U):[1]												
2017 Budget	0.1	1.5	2.1	2.1	2.3	2.2	2.3	2.3	2.3	2.3	2.3	2.3
CBO	0.1	1.3	2.3	2.4	2.4	2.4	2.4	2.4	2.4	2.4	2.4	2.4
Blue Chip	0.1	1.6	2.3	2.4	2.4	2.3	2.3	2.3	2.3	2.3	2.3	2.3
Unemployment Rate:[2]												
2017 Budget	5.3	4.7	4.5	4.6	4.6	4.7	4.7	4.8	4.9	4.9	4.9	4.9
CBO	5.3	4.7	4.4	4.6	4.8	5.0	5.0	5.0	5.0	5.0	5.0	5.0
Blue Chip	5.3	4.8	4.6	4.7	4.7	4.8	4.9	5.0	5.0	5.0	5.0	5.0
Federal Reserve Central Tendency[3]	5.0	4.6 - 4.8	4.6 - 4.8	4.6 to 5.0 longer run								
Interest Rates:[2]												
91-Day Treasury Bills (discount basis):												
2017 Budget	*	0.7	1.8	2.6	3.1	3.3	3.4	3.4	3.3	3.3	3.2	3.2
CBO	0.1	0.7	1.6	2.5	3.2	3.2	3.2	3.2	3.2	3.2	3.2	3.2
Blue Chip	0.1	0.7	1.7	2.8	3.1	3.1	3.1	3.1	3.1	3.1	3.1	3.1
10-Year Treasury Notes												
2017 Budget	2.1	2.9	3.5	3.9	4.1	4.2	4.2	4.2	4.2	4.2	4.2	4.2
CBO	2.2	2.8	3.5	3.9	4.1	4.1	4.1	4.1	4.1	4.1	4.1	4.1
Blue Chip	2.1	2.6	3.2	3.8	4.0	4.0	4.0	4.1	4.1	4.1	4.1	4.1

Sources: Administration; CBO, The Budget and Economic Outlook: 2016 to 2026, January 2016; October 2015 and January 2016 Blue Chip Economic Indicators, Aspen Publishers, Inc.; Federal Reserve Open Market Committee, December 16, 2015

[1] Year-over-Year Percent Change
[2] Annual Averages, Percent
[3] Average of Fourth Quarter Values
* 0.05 percent or less
NA = Not Available

cent low level of inflation partly reflects the sharp drop in oil prices and nonpetroleum import prices in the last eighteen months. Stripping out the effects of energy and food prices, which tend to be volatile, the so-called core Consumer Price Index has also been relatively low over the last three years. Core prices were 2.0 percent higher in the fourth quarter of 2015 than in the fourth quarter of 2014. This followed fourth quarter-over-fourth quarter core inflation of 1.7 percent in 2013 and 2014. The Administration expects that the overall consumer price index will inch back to more normal rates of increase in the coming years, rising at an average pace of 2.0 percent over 2016-2018 and 2.3 percent after that. The Administration estimates that rates of increase in the CPI of 2.3 percent are consistent with the Federal Reserve's target of 2.0 percent for the price index for personal consumption expenditures.

Changes in Economic Assumptions from Last Year's Budget—There are a number of changes to the Administration's forecast relative to that published in the Budget last year, as reported in Table 2-2. For the years 2016 to 2018, the projection last year was for average annual growth of 2.7 percent, but this year's forecast calls for a 2.5 percent average growth rate. Still, the long-run trend growth rate of GDP is the same as forecast last year. The projected path of the unemployment rate has been revised down substantially compared with last year's forecast. It is now expected to reach a trough of 4.5 percent in 2016 and 2017, whereas last year, unemployment was not forecast to fall below 4.8 percent. In addition, as mentioned above, the Administration has revised down its assumption for the NAIRU to 4.9 percent from 5.2 percent and, consequently, the long run unemployment rate has also been revised downward. Expectations for the interest rate path, both at short- and long-run maturities, have also been lowered. The new forecasts for the 91-day Treasury bill rate and the yield on the ten-year Treasury note are lower in every year of the forecast window relative to last year. The expected level in the last year of the forecast is 30 basis points lower for the short rate and 30 basis points lower for the long rate.

Comparison with Other Forecasts

This section compares the Administration's forecast with those of the Congressional Budget Office (CBO), the Federal Reserve Open Market Committee (FOMC), and the Blue Chip Consensus, which aggregates the forecasts of about 50 private sector economists. The Administration's forecast is based on information available through mid-November 2015. The relevant CBO forecast was published in January of 2016. The Blue Chip figures presented here are from the October 2015 and January 2016 releases, and the FOMC projections are from December 2015. The FOMC projects a somewhat different set of variables than the others do. Table 2-3 presents all of these forecasts.

These forecasts have several features in common. For example, in all cases, real GDP growth is expected to pick up over the next two to three years before settling down again to its long run level. Analogously, the unemployment rate is forecast to dip over the next few years and then return to what each entity believes to be the equivalent of the NAIRU. All of the projections show interest rates slowly climbing throughout the forecast window, and all show inflation getting back to a steady rate of between 2.0 percent and 2.3 percent within the next couple of years. These forecasts differ, however, in several important ways.

Importantly, not all of the forecasts make the same assumptions about the extent to which the Administration's Budget proposals will be implemented. These include policies related to trade agreements, immigration reform (specifically its effect on total factor productivity), business tax reform, infrastructure investment, community college subsidies, and policies intended to boost labor supply. The Administration's forecast assumes that all of these policies will be fully implemented. CBO, on the other hand, constructs its forecast under current law, and it is unclear to what extent the FOMC or the Blue Chip take into account the Administration's policy proposals,

though it is unlikely that they are assuming full implementation of the proposals.

Real GDP—For real GDP growth, the Administration forecast differs from the rest of the forecasts in several ways. In the near term, the CBO and the Administration expect a faster rate of growth, calling for growth of 2.7 percent in 2016 and 2.5 percent in 2017, while the Blue Chip survey (2.6 percent in 2016 and 2.4 percent in 2017) and the FOMC (2.3 percent-2.5 percent and 2.0 percent-2.3 percent respectively) project slower growth rates. Also, in the later years of the forecast, the Administration currently expects a faster trend growth rate than any of the other forecasters at 2.3 percent, compared with 2.0 percent for CBO, 2.2 percent for the Blue Chip panel, and 2.0 percent for the FOMC median forecaster. There is also variation in when each forecast expects real GDP growth to return to its long-run pace. The FOMC projects that this will happen as soon as 2018, while the CBO does not see it happening until 2023. The Administration and the Blue Chip both expect growth to settle back down to its long run trend in 2019. While these differences are fairly small and likely within the margin of error for each, the Administration's forecast forms the upper bound of the range, probably due to the fact that it assumes that all of the Administration's Budget proposals, including trade expansion and the improvements in total factor productivity attributable to immigration reform, will be implemented.

Unemployment—The Administration's long-run unemployment rate forecast is 4.9 percent, which is at the low end of the range projected by other forecasters. The FOMC expects the long-run rate of unemployment to be within the range of 4.6 percent to 5.0 percent, which encompasses the Administration's forecast. The Blue Chip Consensus and CBO expect a slightly higher unemployment rate of 5.0 percent in the long run. In the short to medium term, the Administration's forecast projects that the unemployment rate will decline to a lower level than what is expected by most of the other forecasts (reaching a low of 4.5 percent while only CBO's forecast gets below 4.6 percent). Moreover, the Administration's projection takes longer than the other projections to get back to the NAIRU. For example, in the Administration's forecast, the unemployment rate returns to 4.9 percent, its long-run level, in 2023, but the FOMC projects it will return to its long-run level in 2018, the CBO in 2020, and the Blue Chip panel in 2022.

Interest Rates—The Administration's forecast for short-term interest rates is initially on the high end of the forecast range that includes only the CBO and the Blue Chip. It expects short-term rates to be at 1.8 percent in 2017, above the 1.7 percent forecast by Blue Chip and 1.6 percent forecast by CBO. The Administration projects a steady rise in interest rates after 2018, to 3.4 percent in 2021 and 2022 after which it forecasts a gradual decline to 3.2 percent by 2026. Blue Chip, on the other hand, expects no increase in the short-term rate after it reaches 3.1 percent in 2019, and CBO expects no change after reaching 3.2 percent in 2019. With regard to yields on ten-year government bonds, the Administration's projected path lies above those of the other two forecasters for nearly the entire forecast window. In the long run, the Administration's expected 4.2 percent interest rate is higher than the 4.1 percent forecast by both Blue Chip and CBO.

Inflation—In the near term, the Administration's forecast for consumer price inflation is below that of both the Blue Chip panel and the CBO. Even by 2020, the Administration expects an inflation rate of 2.2 percent, compared with the Blue Chip's expectation of 2.3 percent and CBO's expectation of 2.4 percent. By the end of the forecast window, both the Administration and Blue Chip project an annual inflation rate of 2.3 percent, but CBO projects a slightly higher 2.4 percent rate of inflation.

Sensitivity of the Budget to Economic Assumptions

Federal spending and tax collections are heavily influenced by developments in the economy. Receipts are a function of growth in incomes for households and firms. Spending on social assistance programs may rise when the economy enters a downturn, while increases in spending on Social Security and other programs are dependent on consumer price inflation. A robust set of projections for macroeconomic variables assists in budget planning, but unexpected developments in the economy have ripple effects for Federal spending and revenues. This section seeks to provide an understanding of the magnitude of the effects that unforeseen changes in the economy can have on the budget.

To make these assessments, the Administration relies on a set of rules of thumb that can predict how certain spending and revenue categories will react to a change in a given macroeconomic variable, holding everything else constant. These rules of thumb provide a sense of the broad changes one would expect after a given development, but they cannot anticipate how policy makers would react and potentially change course in such an event. For example, if the economy were to suffer an unexpected recession, the rules of thumb suggest that tax revenues would decline and that spending on programs such as unemployment insurance would go up. In such a situation, however, policy makers might cut taxes to stimulate the economy, and such behavior would not be accounted for by the historical relationships captured by the rules of thumb.

Another caveat is that it is often unrealistic to suppose that one macroeconomic variable might change but that others would remain constant. Most macroeconomic variables interact with each other in complex and subtle ways. For example, economists tend to believe that when the unemployment rate gets to very low levels, this will place upward pressure on wages, which will, in turn, push up the overall price level in the economy and lead to higher inflation. This relationship is known in the economics profession as the Phillips Curve. Thus, although in the exercises to follow, for example, results will be reported for an increase in the unemployment rate holding everything else constant, in practice, an increase in the unemployment rate might be likely to also entail a fall in inflation. These are important considerations to bear in mind when examining Table 2-4.

For real growth and employment:

- The first panel in the table illustrates the effect on the deficit resulting from a 1 percentage point reduction in GDP growth, relative to the Administration's forecast, in 2016 that is followed by a subsequent recovery in 2017 and 2018. The unemployment rate is assumed be 0.5 percentage point higher in 2016 before returning to the baseline level in 2017 and 2018. The table shows that receipts would temporarily be somewhat lower and outlays would temporarily be higher, but that the long run effect on the budget deficit would be fairly minor (an increase of just $110 billion over the eleven-year forecast horizon), due mostly to higher interest payments resulting from higher short-run deficits.

- The next panel in the table reports the effect of a reduction of 1 percentage point in GDP growth in 2016 that is not subsequently made up by faster growth in 2017 and 2018. In addition, the natural rate of unemployment is assumed to rise by half a percentage point relative to that assumed in the Administration's forecasts. Here, the effect on the Budget deficit is more substantial, as receipts are lowered in every year of the forecast, while outlays rise gradually over the forecast window. This is because unemployment will be higher, leading to lower tax revenues and higher outlays on unemployment insurance, as well as higher interest payments that follow from increased short-run deficits.

- The third panel in the table shows the impact of a GDP growth rate that is permanently reduced by 1 percentage point, while the unemployment rate is not affected. This is the sort of situation that would arise if, for example, the economy were hit by a permanent decline in productivity growth. In this case, the effect on the Budget deficit is quite large, with receipts being reduced substantially throughout the forecast window and outlays rising due to higher interest payments. The accumulated effect over the eleven-year horizon is an additional $3 trillion of deficits, reinforcing the need for productivity-enhancing investments.

For inflation and interest rates:

- The fourth panel in Table 2-4 shows the effect on the Budget in the case of a 1 percentage point higher rate of inflation and a 1 percentage point higher nominal interest rate in 2016. Both inflation and interest rates return to their assumed levels in 2017. This would result in a permanently higher price level and level of nominal GDP over the course of the forecast horizon. The effect on the Budget deficit would be fairly modest, although receipts would increase slightly more than outlays over the eleven years. This is because revenues would respond more quickly to price increases than outlays, which are set in advance. Over the years from 2016-2026, the Budget deficit would be smaller by about $54 billion. It is worth noting that higher inflation will not nec-

Table 2–4. SENSITIVITY OF THE BUDGET TO ECONOMIC ASSUMPTIONS
(Fiscal Years; In Billions of Dollars)

Budget Effect	2016	2017	2018	2019	2020	2021	2022	2023	2024	2025	2026	Total of Budget Effects: 2016-2026
Real Growth and Employment:												
Budgetary effects of 1 percent lower real GDP growth:												
(1) For calendar year 2016 only, with real GDP recovery in 2017–2018:[1]												
Receipts	−18.3	−26.2	−13.6	−1.4	1.0	0.9	0.9	0.9	0.8	0.8	0.7	−53.5
Outlays	6.7	16.7	8.9	3.0	2.9	3.1	3.1	3.1	3.1	3.2	3.3	57.1
Increase in deficit (+)	25.0	42.9	22.5	4.4	1.9	2.1	2.2	2.2	2.3	2.4	2.6	110.5
(2) For calendar year 2016 only, with no subsequent recovery:[1]												
Receipts	−18.3	−34.6	−40.9	−41.7	−43.2	−45.3	−47.4	−49.6	−53.4	−53.6	−56.0	−483.7
Outlays	6.7	20.3	23.3	26.5	29.6	32.7	35.8	39.0	42.4	46.3	50.4	353.0
Increase in deficit (+)	25.0	54.9	64.2	68.2	72.8	78.0	83.2	88.5	95.8	99.8	106.3	836.8
(3) Sustained during 2016–2026, with no change in unemployment:												
Receipts	−18.3	−51.4	−95.2	−139.5	−188.5	−242.5	−300.0	−361.5	−439.9	−493.3	−567.6	−2,897.7
Outlays	−0.1	0.3	1.9	5.8	11.2	17.6	24.9	33.1	42.6	54.1	67.7	259.2
Increase in deficit (+)	18.2	51.7	97.1	145.3	199.7	260.1	325.0	394.6	482.5	547.3	635.3	3,156.9
Inflation and Interest Rates:												
Budgetary effects of 1 percentage point higher rate of:												
(4) Inflation and interest rates during calendar year 2016 only:												
Receipts	30.5	45.6	41.4	41.0	42.5	43.9	45.3	46.9	49.6	49.5	51.3	487.6
Outlays	28.9	46.8	38.3	39.5	39.2	39.6	39.4	39.6	38.7	40.9	41.8	432.7
Decrease in deficit (−)	−1.6	1.2	−3.0	−1.5	−3.3	−4.4	−6.0	−7.3	−10.9	−8.6	−9.5	−54.9
(5) Inflation and interest rates, sustained during 2016–2026:												
Receipts	30.5	76.9	123.0	169.3	221.7	279.3	338.6	400.5	482.4	537.7	616.4	3,276.5
Outlays	26.7	80.9	127.7	176.5	226.6	278.9	336.8	392.1	446.6	515.7	584.1	3,192.5
Decrease in deficit (−)	−3.8	4.0	4.6	7.2	4.9	−0.5	−1.8	−8.4	−35.8	−22.0	−32.3	−84.0
(6) Interest rates only, sustained during 2016–2026:												
Receipts	12.3	26.4	31.5	36.5	42.7	49.0	52.0	54.1	56.6	59.0	61.4	481.5
Outlays	15.6	48.1	71.4	91.8	111.7	130.9	148.3	165.5	180.5	196.3	212.0	1,372.1
Increase in deficit (+)	3.4	21.7	39.9	55.3	69.0	81.9	96.3	111.4	123.9	137.3	150.6	890.7
(7) Inflation only, sustained during 2016–2026:												
Receipts	18.2	50.1	90.8	132.2	178.0	228.8	283.8	343.7	422.3	474.5	550.0	2,772.3
Outlays	3.7	21.7	45.7	74.9	105.9	140.3	182.2	222.2	263.8	319.9	375.1	1,755.5
Decrease in deficit (−)	−14.5	−28.4	−45.1	−57.3	−72.1	−88.4	−101.5	−121.5	−158.5	−154.6	−174.9	−1,016.8
Interest Cost of Higher Federal Borrowing:												
(8) Outlay effect of $100 billion increase in borrowing in 2016	0.3	1.5	2.5	3.3	3.8	4.1	4.2	4.3	4.4	4.5	4.6	37.5

[1] The unemployment rate is assumed to be 0.5 percentage point higher per 1 percent shortfall in the level of real GDP.

essarily help keep Budget deficits down, because it is likely that monetary policy makers will act to restrain excessive inflation.

- The fifth panel in the table illustrates the effects on the Budget deficit of an inflation rate and an interest rate 1 percentage point higher than projected in every year of the forecast. As in the previous case, the overall effect on the deficit over the forecast is modest (only $84 billion accumulated), and receipts rise faster than outlays because more spending decisions are determined in advance of price increases. It is still important to note, however, that faster in-

flation implies that the real value of Federal spending would be eroded.

- The next panel reports the effect on the deficit resulting from an increase in interest rates in every year of the forecast, with no accompanying increase in inflation. The result is a much higher accumulated deficit, as the Federal Government would have to make much higher interest payments on its debt. Receipts would be slightly higher as the Federal Reserve would earn more on its holdings of securities and households would pay higher taxes on interest income, but these increases would not offset the effect on outlays.

Table 2–5. FORECAST ERRORS, JANUARY 1982-PRESENT

REAL GDP ERRORS			
2-Year Average Annual Real GDP Growth	Administration	CBO	Blue Chip
Mean Error	0.1	–0.2	–0.2
Mean Absolute Error	1.2	1.0	1.1
Root Mean Square Error	1.6	1.4	1.4
6-Year Average Annual Real GDP Growth			
Mean Error	0.3	0.0	0.0
Mean Absolute Error	1.0	1.0	0.9
Root Mean Square Error	1.2	1.2	1.2
INFLATION ERRORS			
2-Year Average Annual Change in the GDP Price Index	Administration	CBO	Blue Chip
Mean Error	0.3	0.3	0.4
Mean Absolute Error	0.7	0.8	0.7
Root Mean Square Error	0.9	1.0	0.8
6-Year Average Annual Change in the GDP Index			
Mean Error	0.4	0.5	0.7
Mean Absolute Error	0.7	0.8	0.9
Root Mean Square Error	0.8	1.0	1.1
INTEREST RATE ERRORS			
2-Year Average 91-Day Treasury Bill Rate	Administration	CBO	Blue Chip
Mean Error	0.3	0.6	0.6
Mean Absolute Error	1.0	1.0	1.0
Root Mean Square Error	1.3	1.3	1.3
6-Year Average 91-Day Treasury Bill Rate			
Mean Error	0.7	1.3	1.4
Mean Absolute Error	1.3	1.5	1.5
Root Mean Square Error	1.6	1.8	1.9

• The seventh panel in the table reports the effect on the Budget deficit of an inflation rate 1 percentage point higher than projected in every year of the forecast window, while the interest rate remains as forecast. In this case, the result is a much smaller deficit over the eleven years of the forecast relative to the baseline. Permanently faster inflation results in much higher revenues over the next eleven years, which helps to reduce interest payments on debt. Outlays rise due to higher cost-of-living increases on items such as Social Security, though not so much as to offset the revenue increases.

• Finally, the table shows the effect on the budget deficit if the Federal government were to borrow an additional $100 billion in 2016, while all of the other projections remain constant. Outlays rise over the forecast window by an accumulated $37.5 billion, due to higher interest payments.

It is important to note that the rules of thumb that inform this sensitivity analysis are symmetric. This means that the effect of, for example, a 1 percentage point higher rate of growth over the forecast horizon would be of the same magnitude as a 1 percentage point reduction in growth, though with the opposite sign.

Forecast Errors for Growth, Inflation, and Interest Rates

Any economic forecast will invariably be subject to a great deal of uncertainty, because of unforeseeable developments of either an economic or political nature. The forecast prepared by the Administration is no different. Furthermore, as noted in the above section, projections for the path of the budget balance are highly sensitive to assumptions about the economy. Therefore, it is essential to take stock of past errors in the forecast for real GDP growth and other variables to provide a better understanding about possible budget balance outcomes. In this section, the Administration's forecast errors since the early 1980s are compared to those of the CBO and the Blue Chip panel. In particular, forecast errors are defined as the difference between actual average real GDP growth, actual average GDP price inflation, and the actual average three-month Treasury bill rate over two- and six-year horizons and the average level over the same horizons of the same variables forecasted by the Administration, the CBO, and the Blue Chip panel. Three metrics are used. These are the mean forecast error, the mean absolute value of the forecast error, and the square root of the mean squared value of the forecast error. These latter two metrics tend to punish forecasts that miss by wide margins. This comparison is reported in Table 2-5.

In the top panel of the table, the reader can see that for real GDP growth, the three forecasts are fairly compa-

Table 2–6. DIFFERENCES BETWEEN ESTIMATED AND ACTUAL SURPLUSES OR DEFICITS FOR FIVE-YEAR BUDGET ESTIMATES SINCE 1986

(As a Percent of GDP)

	Current Year Estimate	Budget Year Estimate	Estimate for Budget Year Plus:			
			One Year (BY + 1)	Two Years (BY + 2)	Three Years (BY + 3)	Four Years (BY + 4)
Average Difference [1]	–0.8	0.2	1.1	1.8	2.3	2.6
Average Absolute Difference [2]	1.1	1.4	2.2	2.9	3.5	3.8
Standard Deviation	1.0	2.0	2.9	3.3	3.5	3.5
Root Mean Squared Error	1.3	2.0	3.0	3.7	4.1	4.3

[1] A positive number represents an overestimate of the surplus or an underestimate of the deficit. A negative number represents an overestimate of the deficit or an underestimate of the surplus.

[2] Average absolute difference is the difference without regard to sign

rable, although the Administration's forecast has tended to be a little more optimistic than the other two in the past and, at the two-year horizon, has missed by a slightly larger margin on average. At the six-year horizon, however, the errors are attenuated somewhat. This is likely due to the fact that growth in real GDP tends to be mean-reverting over a longer span of time, thus making growth rates somewhat simpler to forecast in the medium term.

The middle panel of the table summarizes forecast errors in inflation, as measured by the GDP price index. All three forecasts have tended to project higher inflation than has actually transpired in this period, although on average, they have tended to miss by the same amount, at least at the two-year horizon. At the six-year horizon, the Administration's forecasts have tended to come closest to the actual inflation measure, while the Blue Chip panel, on average, has generally produced forecasts with much faster inflation than has actually occurred. The CBO's forecasts have generally fallen between the other two.

The bottom panel of the table provides a summary of forecast errors for the three-month Treasury bill interest rate. The average error of the Administration's forecast is smaller than that for CBO and the Blue Chip panel at both the two- and six-year horizons. In terms of the magnitude of absolute forecast errors at two years, the three forecasts have historically been comparable. In the medium term, the Administration's forecasts for interest rates have generally outperformed those of CBO and the Blue Chip panel, producing smaller errors by every metric.

Uncertainty and the Deficit Projections

The previous two sections demonstrate the sensitivity of the budget balance path to the actual realizations of macroeconomic variables and describe the uncertainty associated with the Administration's (and other) forecasts. It is helpful then to report the overall range of uncertainty surrounding the Administration's projections of the budget balance over the next few years. Table 2-6 summarizes past errors (since the 1986 budget year) in projecting the budget balance. The first column reports that past projections of the budget balance have tended to predict higher deficits (or lower surpluses) in the year the budget was published than actually occurred. That is, in the past, current year budget deficits have tended to be 0.8 percent of GDP lower than expected. This pattern reverses in subsequent years. Five years after the budget has been published, actual deficits have on average been 3 percentage points of GDP higher than expected

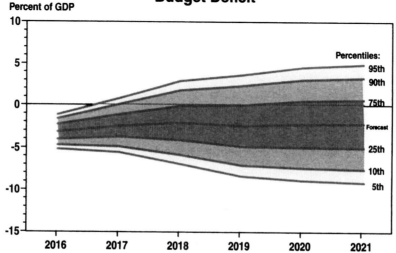

Chart 2-1. Range of Uncertainty for the Budget Deficit

at the time of publication. By taking the root mean squared errors of past budget forecasts at each horizon from the current year to five years later and assuming that these forecast errors are drawn from a normal distribution, it is possible to construct a probabilistic range of current year and future budget balances. Chart 2-1 contains this range. The middle line in the figure contains the Administration's projected budget balance. The other lines can be read in the following way. Consider the top line, which reports the 95th percentile outcome of the budget balance over the years 2016 to 2021. There is a 95 percent probability (based on past forecast errors) that the budget balance will be below this line in every year of the forecast window. That suggests that in 2016, there is a 95 percent chance of a deficit of magnitude greater than 1.2 percent of GDP. In 2021, there is a 95 percent chance that the budget surplus will be no greater than 4.7 percent. On the other hand, there is less than a 5 percent chance that the deficit will be greater than 9.5 percent percent in 2021.

Structural and Cyclical Deficits

The Federal Government's budget can act as a buffer for the U.S. economy in the face of both positive and negative deviations of growth from its trend. For example, when the economy is facing headwinds that impede economic activity, collections of tax receipts fall and spending on certain social insurance programs may rise. Specifically, if an especially large number of workers were to lose their jobs, overall spending on unemployment insurance benefits would increase, providing those unfortunate workers with the means to maintain a basic level of spending. On the other hand, during boom periods, government receipts will rise as firms and households earn more income and pay higher taxes. These budget functions are referred to in the economics profession as "automatic stabilizers," because they do not require special action on the part of policymakers to be implemented, being part of the natural reactions of the government's receipts and expenditures to macroeconomic changes. That is, they perform a smoothing role, ensuring that recessions do not become depressions and that expansions do not cause the economy to "overheat" and prices to rise excessively.

A side effect of these automatic stabilizers is that the headline budget surplus or deficit may not necessarily provide the best information on the overall fiscal stance of the Government. When the economy is in recession, tax receipts fall as households and businesses earn less and spending on social insurance rises to provide income smoothing, with the result being a larger fiscal deficit or smaller fiscal surplus than would have obtained had the economy been operating at full employment. Conversely, when the economy is very strong and growing faster than its potential, the deficit will look smaller or the surplus larger than it otherwise would. This part of the budget balance that fluctuates with the state of the economy is referred to as the cyclical component, while the part that does not is called the structural budget balance. It is this structural balance that provides greater information about the government's fiscal stance (i.e., whether it is operating an expansionary or contractionary fiscal policy).

Table 2-7 provides estimates of the structural and cyclical budget balances over the forecast window. These statistics are estimated by analyzing the historical relationships between indicators of the economy's health, such as the unemployment rate or the deviation of Gross Domestic Product from its potential level, and certain spending and revenue categories. Of course, the variables mentioned above are not the only influences on the cyclical response of the Federal Budget, and economists are still working to better identify the cyclical component of the budget balance. This incompleteness suggests that the cyclical portion of the budget balance might actually make up a larger share of the overall balance than reported in this table.

Notably, over the course of the forecast window, the cyclical component of the budget balance is projected to be fairly modest. This is because the unemployment rate is expected to be close to or below its natural rate over the next eleven years, indicating that the economy is likely to be operating near full employment and that the role of automatic stabilizers will be subdued. There is expected to be a cyclical deficit of about 0.1 percent of GDP in fiscal year 2016, followed by small cyclical surpluses from 2017 to 2021, as the unemployment rate dips below its natural rate. The Administration projects a gently fluctuating structural deficit until it reaches about 2.8 percent of GDP in 2026. For comparison, this is just slightly greater than the average fiscal deficit since World War II of about 2.1% of GDP and substantially lower than the deficit-to-GDP ratios averaging 9% seen in the aftermath of the global financial crisis. This suggests that the Administration's Budget will return the nation's fiscal balance to a broadly neutral and sustainable stance.

Table 2–7. THE STRUCTURAL BALANCE

(Fiscal Years; in Billions of Dollars)

	2014	2015	2016	2017	2018	2019	2020	2021	2022	2023	2024	2025	2026
Unadjusted Surplus (–) or Deficit (+)	483	438	616	504	454	549	534	552	660	677	650	741	793
Cyclical Component	164	53	12	–31	–17	–23	–14	–12	–4	–1	0	0	0
Structural Surplus (–) or Deficit (+)	319	385	604	535	471	572	548	564	664	678	650	741	793
(Fiscal Years; Percent of Gross Domestic Product)													
Unadjusted Surplus (–) or Deficit (+)	2.8	2.5	3.3	2.6	2.3	2.6	2.4	2.4	2.8	2.7	2.5	2.7	2.8
Cyclical Component	0.9	0.3	0.1	–0.2	–0.1	–0.1	–0.1	–0.1	0.0	0.0	0.0	0.0	0.0
Structural Surplus (–) or Deficit (+)	1.9	2.2	3.3	2.8	2.3	2.7	2.5	2.5	2.8	2.7	2.5	2.7	2.8
CHANGE IN STRUCTURAL DEFICIT (FISCAL DRAG)		0.3	1.1	–0.5	–0.4	0.4	–0.2	0.0	0.3	–0.1	–0.2	0.2	0.1

NOTE: The NAIRU is asssumed to be 4.9%. Sums may not add due to rounding.

3. LONG-TERM BUDGET OUTLOOK

When the current Administration took office, budget deficits and debt were rising sharply, primarily as a result of the Great Recession. Revenues as a share of Gross Domestic Product (GDP) were at their lowest level since 1950, and spending on countercyclical programs had also risen sharply.

As a result of both economic recovery and policy changes, deficits have since fallen rapidly. Last year's deficit (2.5 percent of GDP) was about three-quarters lower than the deficit the President inherited, reflecting the fastest sustained deficit reduction since just after World War II. However, with economic recovery well underway, and with the enactment of legislation extending a large number of expiring tax provisions at the end of the last congressional session, both the Administration and the Congressional Budget Office (CBO) project that, absent any changes in policy, the deficit will begin to rise this year and continue to rise over the following ten years. The ratio of debt to GDP will increase by about 10 percentage points over that period under current policy.

While the detailed estimates of receipts and outlays in the President's Budget extend only 10 years, this chapter reviews the longer-term budget outlook, both under a continuation of current policies and under the policies proposed in the Budget. The analysis finds:

- Legislation and other developments since 2010 have not only improved near-term projections, they have also substantially improved the medium- and long-term budget outlook.

- The most significant sources of progress are lower projected health spending (revised in light of slower health care cost growth rates of the last several years), discretionary policy changes, and revenue increases enacted in the American Taxpayer Relief Act of 2012 (ATRA).

- Enacted policy changes, while significant, are insufficient to stabilize debt over the next 10 or 25 years. Additional changes of about 1.7 percent of GDP are needed to achieve fiscal sustainability over the 25-year horizon.

- The deficit reduction proposed in the President's Budget puts the Nation on course towards fiscal sustainability, essentially closing the 25-year fiscal gap. With the Budget's proposals for health, tax, and immigration reforms and other policy changes, debt as a share of GDP declines modestly over the next decade and stabilizes after that.

The projections discussed in this chapter are highly uncertain. As highlighted below, small changes in economic or other assumptions can make a large difference to the results. This is even more relevant for projections over longer horizons. For this reason, the chapter focuses primarily on 25-year projections, although it also provides budget estimates for a 75-year period, as well as results under different economic assumptions and for different policy scenarios.

The chapter also discusses the status of the Social Security and Medicare Hospital Insurance (HI) trust funds, which are financed from dedicated revenue sources. The proposals contained in the 2017 Budget would extend the life of both the Social Security and HI trust funds. While immigration reform is primarily responsible for the improvements to Social Security trust fund solvency, the HI trust fund benefits from a robust package of health savings proposals, reforms to the net investment income tax (NIIT), and the dedication of NIIT tax revenues—which are currently deposited into the General Fund—to the HI trust fund. Still, additional measures would be needed to achieve 75-year trust fund solvency.

The Basis for the Long-Run Projections

For the 10-year budget window, the Administration produces both baseline projections, which show how deficits and debt would evolve under current policies, and projections showing the impact of proposed policy changes. Like the budget baseline more generally, long-term projections should provide policymakers with information about the Nation's expected fiscal trajectory in the absence of spending and tax changes. For this reason, the baseline long-term projections in this chapter assume that current policy continues for Social Security, Medicare, Medicaid, other mandatory programs, and revenues.[1] (See the appendix for details.)

In the case of discretionary spending, it is less clear how to project a continuation of current policy. After the period covered by the statutory caps, both the Administration's and CBO's 10-year baselines assume that discretionary funding levels generally grow slightly above the rate of inflation (about 2.4 percent per year). Long-run projections sometimes assume that discretionary funding remains constant as a share of the economy, implying long-run growth of a little over 4 percent per year. Meanwhile, over the past five years, discretionary funding has failed to even keep pace with inflation, falling by 13 percent in real terms.

The projections here adopt an intermediate approach, assuming that real per-person discretionary funding

---

[1] The long-run baseline projections are consistent with the Budget's adjusted baseline concept. The Budget's adjusted baseline concept is explained in more detail in Chapter 25, "Current Services Estimates," in this volume. The projections assume full payment of scheduled Social Security and Medicare benefits without regard to the projected depletion of the trust funds for these programs.

Chart 3-1. Publicly Held Debt Under Continuation of Current Policies

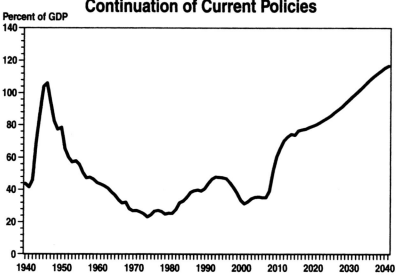

remains constant over the long run, which implies an annual growth rate of about 3 percent. For the many discretionary programs that provide services to individuals, it is reasonable to define current policy as maintaining the same level of services for the same share of the population, which can be approximated by holding real per-person discretionary funding constant. In contrast, holding discretionary spending constant as a share of GDP effectively assumes large increases in per-person service levels over time, as well as large increases in real funding levels for national defense, research, infrastructure, and other public goods.

Long-Run Projections Under Continuation of Current Policies

Chart 3-1 shows the path of debt as a share of GDP under continuation of current policies, *without* the policy changes proposed in the President's Budget. Over the next 10 years, debt rises from 74 percent of GDP last year to 88 percent of GDP in 2026. Beyond the 10-year horizon, debt increases more sharply, reaching 117 percent of GDP by 2041, the end of the 25-year projection window.

The key drivers of that increase are an aging population, health care cost growth, and insufficient revenues to keep pace with these trends.

Aging population. — Over the next 10 years, an aging population will put significant pressure on the budget. In 2008, when the oldest members of the baby boom generation became eligible for early retirement under Social Security, the ratio of workers to Social Security beneficiaries was 3.2. By the end of the 10-year budget window, that ratio will fall to 2.4, and it will reach about 2.1 in the early 2030s, at which point most of the baby boomers will have retired.

With fewer active workers paying taxes and more retired workers eligible for Social Security, Medicare, and Medicaid (including long-term care), budgetary pressures will increase. Social Security program costs will grow from 5.0 percent of GDP today to 5.9 percent of GDP by 2041, with most of that growth occurring within the 10-year budget window. Likewise, even if per-beneficiary health care costs grew at the same rate as GDP per capita, Medicare and Medicaid costs would still increase substantially as a share of GDP, due solely to the aging population.

Health costs. — Health care costs per capita have risen much faster than per-capita GDP growth for decades, leading both public and private spending on health care to increase as a share of the economy. However, the last few years have seen a sharp departure from long-term trends, with spending per enrollee growing in line with or more slowly than per-capita GDP in both the public and private sectors, and recent data indicate that slow growth in per-enrollee spending has continued through 2015. (Coverage expansions under the Affordable Care Act have temporarily increased growth in aggregate health care spending, but trends in per-enrollee costs, together with the demographic trends discussed above, are what matter for long-term fiscal projections.)

While some of the slowdown reflects the Great Recession and its aftermath, there is strong evidence that a portion of it is the result of structural changes. For example, since Medicare beneficiaries are typically retired or disabled, Medicare costs tend to be less sensitive to economic conditions than overall health spending. But Medicare cost growth has slowed in line with the overall slowdown in health care costs, suggesting that the recession was not the primary driver of the recent slowdown, particularly in public programs. The fact that growth in per-enrollee health care spending remains low more than five years into the economic recovery also implies that factors other than the recession are playing an important role.

Chart 3-2. Changes to Projected 2020 Deficit Under Continuation of Current Policies

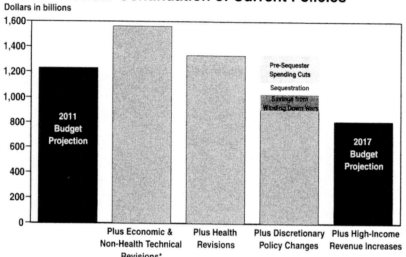

Dollars in billions

* Also includes modest policy changes (e.g. $25 billion in reduced outlays due to mandatory sequestration and $25 billion in lower revenues due to legislation enacted in December 2015).

Based on projections of Medicare enrollment and expenditures included in the 2015 Medicare Trustees Report, the projections here assume that Medicare per-beneficiary spending growth will accelerate over the next few years, with the growth rate averaging about 0.7 percentage points above the growth rate of per-capita GDP over the next 25 years.[2] (This average growth rate is still below the historical average for the last 25 years.) Under these assumptions, Medicare and Medicaid costs increase by a total of 2.4 percentage points as a share of GDP by 2041.

Revenues. — Without any further changes in tax laws, revenues will grow slightly faster than GDP over the long run, but not fast enough to keep pace with the increase in social insurance costs that results from an aging population. The increase in revenues as a share of GDP occurs primarily because individuals' real, inflation-adjusted incomes grow over time, and so a portion of their income falls into higher tax brackets. (Bracket thresholds are indexed for inflation but do not grow in real terms.)

Other programs. — Other mandatory programs are generally projected to decline relative to the size of the economy and to consume a smaller share of revenues over time. For example, spending on non-health safety net programs will decline as incomes grow. Likewise, pension benefits for Federal workers will shrink as a share of the economy as a result of reductions initiated in the 1980s. Overall, spending on mandatory programs outside of health care and Social Security equals 16.3 percent of revenues today, but is projected to equal 14.3 percent of revenues by 2041. Likewise, discretionary spending will consume a smaller share of revenues over time under current projections.

Fiscal Progress to Date

The deficit as a share of the economy began declining in 2010. Since then, deficits have fallen rapidly, sharply improving the near-term budget outlook. Taking 2010 as the point of departure, Charts 3-2 and 3-3 show that this progress extends to reducing medium- and long-term deficits and debt.

As Chart 3-2 shows, in the 2011 Mid-Session Review, published in July 2010, the Administration projected a 2020 deficit of $1,230 billion, or 5.1 percent of GDP, under continuation of current policies.[3] The 2017 Budget projects a baseline deficit of $814 billion, or 3.7 percent of GDP in 2020, a reduction of 1.4 percentage points or $416 billion (34 percent). As shown in the chart, one major contributor to the improvement is lower than expected Federal health spending. Revisions to health spending forecasts based on the slower growth of the past several years (and based on the assumption that only a portion of the slowdown will continue) will save the Federal government $231 billion in 2020, accounting for about half of the net improvement in the deficit.[4] Another important factor is the high-income revenue increases enacted in ATRA (about a fifth of the net improvement). Discretionary spending restraint has also played a large role, although the impact of sequestration (less than a quarter of the total discretionary contribution to deficit reduction) is much smaller than the impact of the pre-sequestration Budget Control Act cuts and less than the savings from winding down wars.[5]

---

[2] The projections in this year's Trustees report reflect the enactment of the Medicare Access and CHIP Reauthorization Act (MACRA) of 2015. This law repealed the sustainable growth rate formula that set physician fee schedule payments, which were usually modified.

[3] For comparability, this projection includes continuation of the 2001 and 2003 tax cuts and Alternative Minimum Tax Relief and assumes that the Medicare SGR reductions do not take effect.

[4] Aggregate projected Federal health care spending for 2020 has decreased by $185 billion when compared with the 2011 Mid-Session Review, excluding debt service and including premium tax credit revenues.

[5] To simplify the comparisons of projected health spending, these

Chart 3-3. Comparison of Publicly Held Debt

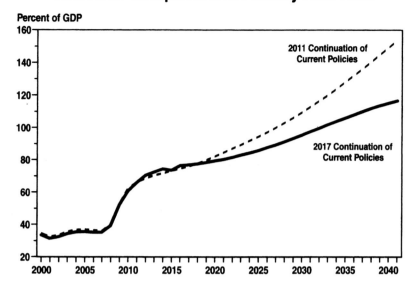

There has been a similar improvement in projected long-term deficits and debt. Chart 3-3 shows the projected path of debt as a share of GDP under the 2011 Budget (February 2010) current policy projection and as of the 2017 current policy projection.[6] A few years ago, debt in 2040 was projected to reach 149 percent of GDP. Today, it is projected to reach 115 percent of GDP. While it is difficult to precisely decompose the contributing factors over long periods, the major drivers behind the improvement

comparisons start from the 2011 Mid-Session Review, following the enactment of the Affordable Care Act. However, the ACA itself also reduced projected deficits. CBO estimated that the ACA would reduce the deficit by $25 billion in 2020 and by over $1 trillion in the decade starting in 2023. These direct, scored effects of the ACA are separate from any contributions to the broader health care cost growth slowdown, discussed below.

[6] The "2010 projections" are based on 2010 data and Trustees assumptions but—for comparability—use the Administration's current methodology for long-term projections, in particular assuming that discretionary funding grows with inflation plus population growth. While the Administration did not produce a comparable long-term projection for the 2011 Mid-Session Review, the long-term projections from the 2011 Budget projection of current policy can be used to illustrate the fiscal improvements achieved since 2010; the comparison relative to the 2011 Mid-Session Review would be qualitatively similar.

Table 3–1. 25-YEAR FISCAL GAP (–)/SURPLUS (+) UNDER ALTERNATIVE BUDGET SCENARIOS
(Percent of GDP)

2011 Budget Continuation of Current Policies	–2.4
2017 Budget Continuation of Current Policies	–1.7
2017 Budget policy	–0.1
Breakdown of changes in 2017 Budget Policy:	
Health reform	+0.3
High-income tax proposals	+0.4
Immigration reform	+0.2
Other policies	+0.8

are the same: lower projected health care costs, revenue increases from ATRA, and lower discretionary spending.

The Fiscal Gap

One way to quantify the size of the Nation's long-term fiscal challenges is the "fiscal gap." The fiscal gap is defined as the present value of the combined increase in taxes or reduction in non-interest spending needed to keep the debt-to-GDP ratio stable over a given period (more precisely, the present value adjustment required for the debt-to-GDP ratio at the end of the period to equal its level at the beginning of the period). If publicly held debt at the end of the period is projected to be lower than current debt, there is a fiscal surplus rather than a fiscal gap.

Table 3-1 shows the 25-year fiscal gap under the baseline projections, under the President's policies, and as of 2010. Under the base case current policy projections, the 25-year fiscal gap is 1.7 percent of GDP. This means that policy adjustments of about 1.7 percent of GDP would be needed each year to put the Nation on a sustainable fiscal course for the next two-and-a-half decades. In contrast, as of 2010, adjustments of 2.4 percent of GDP would have been needed to achieve the goal of stabilizing debt over 25 years. While the two values are not strictly comparable (due to the different 25-year time periods), the difference underscores the significant improvement in the fiscal outlook over the last few years.

The Impact of 2017 Budget Policies on the Long-Term Fiscal Outlook

The President's 2017 Budget proposes non-interest spending reductions and revenue increases equal to about 1.8 percent of GDP when fully in effect, nearly closing the 25-year fiscal gap and putting the Nation on a fiscally sustainable

Chart 3-4. 2017 Budget Policies

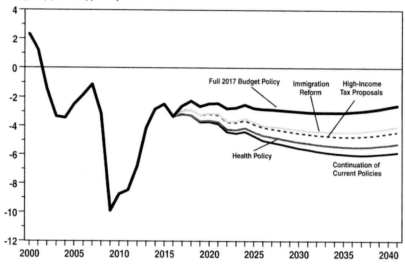

Surplus(+)/Deficit(-) as a percent of GDP

course over the next 75 years. As shown in Chart 3-4, over the 10-year budget window, the Budget stabilizes deficits around 2.8 percent of GDP and modestly reduces the debt-to-GDP ratio. Over the next decade and a half, the debt-to-GDP ratio reaches 78 percent of GDP and subsequently decreases. The Budget policies result in a small 25-year fiscal gap of 0.1 percent of GDP.

In addition to paying for all new investments, the 2017 Budget reduces deficits and debt through health, tax, and immigration reform.

Additional health reforms building on the ACA.— As discussed above, the last few years have seen slower growth in health care spending in both Medicare and the private market. While the slowdown reflects a variety of factors, there is evidence that the reforms enacted in the Affordable Care Act are already contributing to this slowdown, as discussed below.

The 2017 Budget builds on the ACA with a robust package of health savings proposals, estimated to reduce Medicare and Medicaid spending by about $380 billion, that will strengthen the Medicare trust fund, create incentives for both providers and beneficiaries to choose more cost-effective methods of care, and improve health care quality. The Budget also backstops these savings with a proposal to strengthen the Independent Payment Advisory Board (IPAB) by lowering its target growth rate to 0.5 percentage points above per-capita GDP growth.[7]

As shown in Chart 3-4 and Table 3-1, these reforms have a large effect on the long-run budget outlook, reducing the fiscal gap by 0.3 percent of GDP.

High-income tax proposals.—The Budget includes proposals to implement the Buffet Rule by imposing a new "Fair Share Tax," rationalize net investment income and Self-Employed Contributions Act taxes, and reduce the value of certain tax expenditures that increase revenues by about $955 billion over the first 10 years. These proposals to curb inefficient tax benefits for high-income households and close loopholes reduce the fiscal gap by an additional 0.4 percent of GDP.

Commonsense comprehensive immigration reform.— The 2017 Budget continues to propose commonsense, comprehensive immigration reform that would strengthen border security, modernize the legal immigration system, and provide a path to earned citizenship. By adding younger workers to the labor force, immigration reform would help balance an aging population as the baby boom generation retires. CBO estimates that the 2013 Senate-passed immigration bill would have reduced deficits by almost $1 trillion over 20 years. It would also boost economic growth and strengthen Social Security.

The Budget's 10-year projections include an allowance for deficit reduction from immigration reform based on the CBO estimate. The long-run projections are based on CBO's "second-decade" estimate extended as a constant share of GDP from 2035 to 2041. As shown in Chart 3-4 and Table 3-1, higher immigration has a positive effect on the budget, reducing the fiscal gap by an additional 0.2 percentage points.

Other 2017 Budget policies.— The remaining policies in the 2017 Budget reduce the fiscal gap by 0.8 percentage points. The Budget obtains these additional savings from additional spending reductions and tax changes beyond those needed to pay for its investments in education, infrastructure, research, and other areas.

---

[7] The ACA established an Independent Payment Advisory Board (IPAB) that is required to propose changes in Medicare should Medicare per beneficiary cost growth exceed target growth rates specified in law; such IPAB-proposed changes would take effect automatically, unless overridden by the Congress. The Budget includes a proposal that would strengthen the IPAB mechanism by lowering the target growth rate applicable for 2020 onward from GDP +1.0 percentage points to GDP +0.5 percentage points.

Chart 3-5. Alternative Productivity and Interest Assumptions

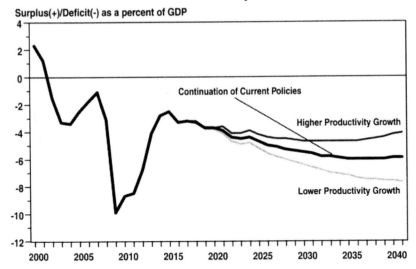

Uncertainty and Alternative Assumptions

Future budget outcomes depend on a host of unknowns: changing economic conditions, unforeseen international developments, unexpected demographic shifts, and unpredictable technological advances. These uncertainties make even short-run budget forecasting quite difficult. For example, the budget's projection of the deficit in five years is 2.4 percent of GDP, but a distribution of probable outcomes ranges from a deficit of 7.9 percent of GDP to a surplus of 3.1 percent of GDP, at the 10th and 90th percentiles, respectively.

The longer budget projections are extended, the more the uncertainties increase. Table 3-2 gives a sense of the degree of uncertainty in the 25-year projections under continuation of current policies. Under plausible alternative assumptions, the 25-year fiscal gap ranges from a gap of 2.5 percent of GDP to a gap of 0.9 percent of GDP. Alternative assumptions considered include:

Productivity and interest rates.—The rate of future productivity growth has a major effect on the long-run budget outlook (see Chart 3–5). Higher productivity growth improves the budget outlook, because it adds directly to the growth of the major tax bases while having a smaller effect on outlay growth. Meanwhile, productivity and interest rates tend to move together, but have opposite effects on the budget. Economic growth theory suggests that a 0.1 percentage point increase in productivity should be associated with a roughly equal increase in interest rates.

Productivity growth is also highly uncertain. For much of the last century, output per hour in nonfarm business grew at an average rate of around 2.2 percent per year, but there were long periods of sustained output growth at notably higher and lower rates than the long-term aver-age. The base case long-run projections assume that real GDP per hour worked will grow at an average annual rate of 1.7 percent per year, slower than the historical average, and assume interest rates on 10-year Treasury securities of 4.2 percent. The alternative scenarios illustrate the effect of raising and lowering the projected productivity growth rate by 0.25 percentage point and changing interest rates commensurately. The 25-year fiscal gap ranges from a fiscal gap of 0.9 percent of GDP in the high productivity scenario to a gap of 1.7 percent of GDP in the base case and 2.5 percent of GDP in the low productivity scenario. This variation highlights the importance of investments, like those in research and development, education, and training, and smarter tax policy, which can contribute to higher productivity.

Table 3–2.   25-YEAR FISCAL GAP (–)/SURPLUS (+) UNDER ALTERNATIVE BUDGET SCENARIOS
(Percent of GDP)

2017 Budget Continuation of Current Policies	–1.7
Health:	
Excess cost growth averages 1.5%	–2.3
Zero Excess cost growth	–0.9
Discretionary Outlays:	
Grow with inflation	–1.5
Grow with GDP	–1.9
Revenues:	
Income tax brackets are regularly increased	–1.8
Fixed as a percent of GDP	–2.1
Productivity and Interest:[1]	
Productivity grows by 0.25 percentage point per year faster than the base case	–0.9
Productivity grows by 0.25 percentage point per year slower than the base case	–2.5

[1] Interest rates adjust commensurately with increases or decreases in productivity.

Chart 3-6. Alternative Health Care Costs

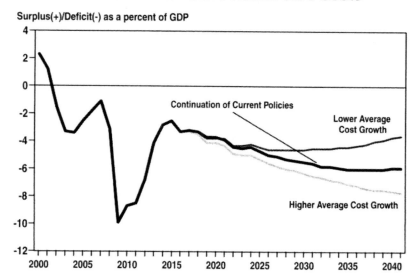

Health spending.—Health care cost growth represents another large source of uncertainty in the long-term budget projections (see Chart 3-6). As noted above, the baseline projections follow the Medicare Trustees in assuming that Medicare per-beneficiary costs grow an average of about 0.7 percentage points faster than per-capita GDP growth over the next 25 years. But historically, especially prior to 1990, health care costs grew even more rapidly. Conversely, over the last few years, per-enrollee health care costs have grown roughly in line with or more slowly than GDP per-capita, with particularly slow growth in Medicare and Medicaid.

As noted above, there is evidence that a significant portion of the recent decline in health care cost growth is structural (rather than related to the recession), and that the ACA is playing a contributing role, for example through Medicare provider payment reforms and incentives for hospitals to reduce readmissions. The ACA also enacted an array of more fundamental delivery system reforms that encourage efficient, high-quality care, including incentives for the creation of accountable care organizations and the launch of a wide variety of payment reform demonstrations. These reforms have generated promising early results and could have major effects on health care quality and cost going forward.

Table 3-2 shows the large impact that either slower or faster health care cost growth would have on the budget.

Chart 3-7. Alternative Discretionary Projections

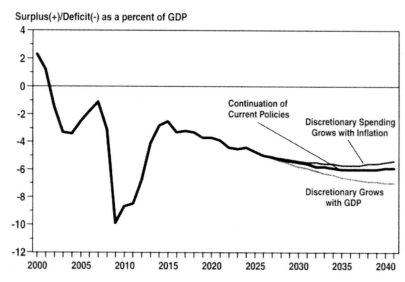

Chart 3-8. Alternative Revenue Projections

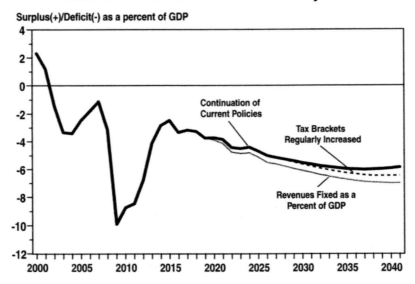

If health care cost growth averaged 1.5 percentage points, instead of roughly 0.7 percentage points, faster than per-capita GDP growth, the current policy 25-year fiscal gap would increase from 1.7 to 2.3 percent of GDP. If health care costs grew with GDP per capita, the 25-year fiscal gap would be 0.9 percent of GDP.

Policy assumptions.— As evident from the discussion of the 2017 Budget, policy choices will also have a large impact on long-term budget deficits and debt. The current base projection for discretionary spending assumes that after 2026, discretionary spending grows with inflation and population (see Chart 3–7). As discussed above, al-ternative assumptions are to grow discretionary spending with GDP or inflation. As shown in Table 3–2, the 25-year fiscal gap increases from 1.7 percent of GDP in the base case to 1.9 percent of GDP if discretionary spending grows with GDP, and falls to 1.5 percent of GDP if discretionary spending grows with inflation.

In the base case projection, tax receipts rise gradual-ly relative to GDP as real incomes rise, consistent with what would occur under current law. Chart 3–8 shows two alternative receipts assumptions. Cutting taxes to avoid the revenue increases associated with rising in-comes would bring about higher deficits and debt. The

Chart 3-9. Long-Term Uncertainties

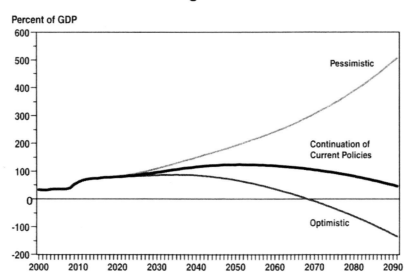

25-year fiscal gap rises from 1.7 percent of GDP in the base case to 1.8 percent of GDP in the alternative case where tax brackets are regularly increased after 2026. Further cutting taxes to keep revenues constant as a share of GDP at current levels results in a 25-year fiscal gap of 2.1 percent.

Finally, Chart 3-9 shows how uncertainties magnify over a 75-year forecast horizon. As the chart shows, under the baseline projections, without policy changes, debt exceeds 100 percent of GDP by 2033 before starting a slow decline in the very long run. Alternatively, assuming a combination of slower productivity growth and higher health care cost growth results in a debt explosion, with debt-to-GDP reaching over 500 percent by the end of the window. Meanwhile, assuming a combination of higher productivity growth and slower health care cost growth results in the debt being completely paid off by 2069.

Despite the striking uncertainties, long-term projections are helpful in highlighting some of the known budget challenges on the horizon, especially the impact of an aging population. In addition, the projections highlight the need for policy awareness and potential action to address drivers of future budgetary costs.

Actuarial Projections for Social Security and Medicare

While the Administration's long-run projections focus on the unified budget outlook, Social Security and Medicare Hospital Insurance benefits are paid out of trust funds financed by dedicated payroll tax revenue. Projected trust fund revenues fall short of the levels necessary to finance projected benefits over the next 75 years.

The Social Security and Medicare Trustees' reports feature the actuarial balance of the trust funds as a summary measure of their financial status. For each trust fund, the balance is calculated as the change in receipts or program benefits (expressed as a percentage of taxable payroll) that would be needed to preserve a small positive balance in the trust fund at the end of a specified time period. The estimates cover periods ranging in length from 25 to 75 years.

Table 3–3 shows the projected income rate, cost rate, and annual balance for the Medicare HI and combined OASDI trust funds at selected dates under the Trustees' intermediate assumptions. Data from the 2013 and the 2014 reports are shown along with the latest data from the 2015 reports. Following the passage of the ACA in 2010, there have been major improvements in trust fund solvency, although there is a continued imbalance in the long-run projections of the HI program due to demographic trends and continued high per-person costs. In the 2013 Trustees' report, Medicare HI trust fund costs as a percentage of Medicare covered payroll were projected to rise from 3.5 percent to 5.9 percent between 2014 and 2080 and the HI trust fund imbalance was projected to be -1.6 percent in 2080. In the 2014 report, costs rose from 3.4 percent of Medicare taxable payroll in 2014 to 5.6 percent in 2080 and the imbalance in the HI trust fund in 2080 was -1.4 percent. On average, the HI cost rate declined slightly in the 2015 report compared with 2014. In

the 2015 report, HI costs rise from 3.4 percent of Medicare taxable payroll in 2014 to 5.1 percent in 2080 and the imbalance in the HI trust fund in 2080 is -0.9 percent. The HI trust fund is projected to become insolvent in 2030, the same year projected in the 2014 report, versus 2017 in the last report before passage of the ACA.

Under the Medicare Modernization Act (MMA) of 2003, the Medicare Trustees must issue a "warning" when two consecutive Trustees' reports project that the share of Medicare funded by general revenues will exceed 45 percent in the current year or any of the subsequent six years. For the first time since 2007, the 2014 Trustees' Report did not include such a warning. The 2015 Trustees' Report also did not include this warning. The MMA requires that, if there is a Medicare funding warning, the President submit proposed legislation responding to that warning, within 15 days of submitting the Budget. In accordance with the Recommendations Clause of the Constitution and as the Executive Branch has noted in prior years, the Executive Branch considers a requirement to propose specific legislation to be advisory.

As a result of reforms legislated in 1983, Social Security had been running a cash surplus with taxes exceeding costs up until 2009. This surplus in the Social Security trust fund helped to hold down the unified budget deficit. The cash surplus ended in 2009, when the trust fund began using a portion of its interest earnings to cover benefit payments. The 2015 Social Security Trustees' report projects that the trust fund will not return to cash surplus, but the program will continue to experience an overall surplus for several more years because of the interest earnings. After that, however, Social Security will begin to draw on its trust fund balances to cover current expenditures. Over time, as the ratio of workers to retirees falls, costs are projected to rise further from 14.0 percent of Social Security covered payroll in 2014 to 14.2 percent of payroll in 2020, 16.1 percent of payroll in 2030 and 17.7 percent of payroll in 2080. Revenues excluding interest are projected to rise only slightly from 12.8 percent of payroll today to 13.3 percent in 2080. Thus the annual balance is projected to decline from -1.2 percent of payroll in 2014 to -1.3 percent of payroll in 2020, -2.9 percent of payroll in 2030, and -4.4 percent of payroll in 2080. On a 75-year basis, the actuarial deficit is projected to be -2.7 percent of payroll. In the process, the Social Security trust fund, which was built up since 1983, would be drawn down and eventually be exhausted in 2034. These projections assume that benefits would continue to be paid in full despite the projected exhaustion of the trust fund to show the long-run implications of current benefit formulas. Under current law, not all scheduled benefits would be paid after the trust funds are exhausted. However, benefits could still be partially funded from current revenues. According to the 2015 Trustees' report, beginning in 2034, 79 percent of projected Social Security scheduled benefits would be funded. This percentage would eventually decline to 73 percent by 2089.

Table 3–3. INTERMEDIATE ACTUARIAL PROJECTIONS FOR OASDI AND HI
(Percent of Payroll)

	2014	2020	2030	2040	2080
Medicare Hospital Insurance (HI)					
Income Rate					
2013 Trustees' Report	3.3	3.4	3.6	3.7	4.2
2014 Trustees' Report	3.3	3.4	3.6	3.7	4.2
2015 Trustees' Report	3.3	3.4	3.6	3.7	4.2
Cost Rate					
2013 Trustees' Report	3.5	3.5	4.4	5.2	5.9
2014 Trustees' Report	3.4	3.3	4.2	4.8	5.6
2015 Trustees' Report	3.4	3.3	4.2	4.7	5.1
Annual Balance					
2013 Trustees' Report	−0.2	−0.1	−0.8	−1.4	−1.6
2014 Trustees' Report	−0.1	*	−0.6	−1.1	−1.4
2015 Trustees' Report	−0.2	0.1	−0.6	−1.0	−0.9
Projection Interval:			25 years	50 years	75 years
Actuarial Balance: 2013 Trustees' Report			−0.6	−1.0	−1.1
Actuarial Balance: 2014 Trustees' Report			−0.4	−0.8	−0.9
Actuarial Balance: 2015 Trustees' Report			−0.4	−0.6	−0.7
Old Age Survivors and Disability Insurance (OASDI)					
Income Rate					
2013 Trustees' Report	12.8	13.0	13.1	13.2	13.2
2014 Trustees' Report	12.7	13.0	13.2	13.2	13.3
2015 Trustees' Report	12.8	13.0	13.2	13.2	13.3
Cost Rate					
2013 Trustees' Report	14.0	14.3	16.5	17.0	17.8
2014 Trustees' Report	14.0	14.3	16.6	17.1	17.9
2015 Trustees' Report	14.0	14.2	16.1	16.7	17.7
Annual Balance					
2013 Trustees' Report	−1.2	−1.3	−3.4	−3.8	−4.5
2014 Trustees' Report	−1.3	−1.4	−3.5	−3.9	−4.6
2015 Trustees' Report	−1.2	−1.3	−2.9	−3.5	−4.4
Projection Interval:			25 years	50 years	75 years
Actuarial Balance: 2013 Trustees' Report			−1.3	−2.2	−2.7
Actuarial Balance: 2014 Trustees' Report			−1.5	−2.4	−2.9
Actuarial Balance: 2015 Trustees' Report			−1.4	−2.2	−2.7

* 0.05 percent or less.

Note: Values from the 2014 Trustees' Report are not fully comparable to values for earlier years' reports, as 2014 Trustees Report numbers are based on a projected baseline rather than a current law baseline.

The 2017 Budget would improve the condition of both trust funds. The health savings proposed in the Budget and tax proposals directly affecting HI tax receipts, including transfers of revenue from the net investment income tax, would extend the life of the HI trust fund by more than 15 years. Meanwhile, the Social Security Actuary estimated the Senate-passed immigration bill would reduce the Social Security shortfall by 8 percent, extending the life of the trust fund by two years. Nonetheless, additional reforms will be needed to restore 75-year solvency in both programs.

TECHNICAL NOTE: SOURCES OF DATA AND METHODS OF ESTIMATING

The long-run budget projections are based on demographic and economic assumptions. A simplified model of the Federal budget, developed at OMB, is used to compute the budgetary implications of these assumptions.

Demographic and economic assumptions.—For the years 2016-2026, the assumptions are drawn from the Administration's economic projections used for the 2017 Budget. The economic assumptions are extended beyond this interval by holding inflation, interest rates, and the unemployment rate constant at the levels assumed in the final year of the budget forecast. Population growth and labor force growth are extended using the intermediate assumptions from the 2015 Social Security Trustees' report. The projected rate of growth for real GDP is built up from the labor force assumptions and an assumed rate of productivity growth. Productivity growth, measured as real GDP per hour, is assumed to equal its average rate of growth in the Budget's economic assumptions—1.7 percent per year.

CPI inflation holds stable at 2.3 percent per year, the unemployment rate is constant at 4.9 percent, the yield on 10-year Treasury notes is steady at 4.2 percent, and the 91-day Treasury bill rate is 3.3 percent. Consistent with the demographic assumptions in the Trustees' reports, U.S. population growth slows from around 1 percent per year to about two-thirds that rate by 2030, and slower rates of growth beyond that point. By the end of the 75-year projection period total population growth is slightly above 0.4 percent per year. Real GDP growth is projected to be less than its historical average of around 3.4 percent per year because the slowdown in population growth and the increase in the population over age 65 reduce labor supply growth. In these projections, real GDP growth averages between 2.1 percent and 2.3 percent per year for the period following the end of the 10-year budget window.

The economic and demographic projections described above are set by assumption and do not automatically change in response to changes in the budget outlook. This makes it easier to interpret the comparisons of alternative policies and is a reasonable simplification given the large uncertainties surrounding the long-run outlook.

Budget projections.—For the period through 2026, receipts and outlays in the baseline and policy projections follow the 2017 Budget's adjusted baseline and policy estimates respectively. After 2026, total tax receipts rise gradually relative to GDP as real incomes also rise. Discretionary spending grows at the rate of growth in inflation plus population afterwards. Long-run Social Security spending is projected by the Social Security actuaries using this chapter's long-run economic and demographic assumptions. Medicare benefits are projected based on a projection of beneficiary growth and excess health care cost growth from the 2015 Medicare Trustees' report current law baseline; for the policy projections, these assumptions are then also adjusted to account for the Budget's IPAB proposal. Medicaid outlays are based on the economic and demographic projections in the model, which assume average excess cost growth of approximately 1.2 percentage points above growth in GDP per capita after 2026. Other entitlement programs are projected based on rules of thumb linking program spending to elements of the economic and demographic projections such as the poverty rate.

4. FEDERAL BORROWING AND DEBT

Debt is the largest legally and contractually binding obligation of the Federal Government. At the end of 2015, the Government owed $13,117 billion of principal to the individuals and institutions who had loaned it the money to fund past deficits. During that year, the Government paid the public approximately $261 billion of interest on this debt. At the same time, the Government also held financial assets, net of financial liabilities other than debt, of $1,234 billion. Therefore, debt net of financial assets was $11,882 billion.

The $13,117 billion debt held by the public at the end of 2015 represents an increase of $337 billion over the level at the end of 2014. This increase is the result of the $438 billion deficit in 2015 and other financing transactions that reduced the need to borrow by $102 billion. Debt held by the public decreased from 74.4 percent of Gross Domestic Product (GDP) at the end of 2014 to 73.7 percent of GDP at the end of 2015. Meanwhile, financial assets net of liabilities fell by $90 billion in 2015, so that debt held by the public net of financial assets increased by $427 billion during 2015. Debt net of financial assets was 66.7 percent of GDP at the end of 2014 and at the end of 2015. The deficit is estimated to increase to $616 billion, or 3.3 percent of GDP, in 2016, and to fall below 3 percent of GDP starting in 2017. Debt held by the public is projected to reach 76.5 percent of GDP at the end of 2016 and then to generally decline gradually in subsequent years. Debt net of financial assets is expected to increase to 67.7 percent of GDP at the end of 2016, then slowly decline in the following years, falling to 65.7 percent of GDP at the end of 2026.

Trends in Debt Since World War II

Table 4–1 depicts trends in Federal debt held by the public from World War II to the present and estimates from the present through 2021. (It is supplemented for earlier years by Tables 7.1–7.3 in the Budget's historical tables, available as supplemental budget material.[1]) Federal debt peaked at 106.1 percent of GDP in 1946, just after the end of the war. From that point until the 1970s, Federal debt as a percentage of GDP decreased almost every year because of relatively small deficits, an expanding economy, and unanticipated inflation. With households borrowing large amounts to buy homes and consumer durables, and with businesses borrowing large amounts to buy plant and equipment, Federal debt also decreased almost every year as a percentage of total credit market debt outstanding. The cumulative effect was impressive. From 1950 to 1975, debt held by the public declined from 78.5 percent of GDP to 24.5 percent, and from 53.3 percent of credit market debt to 17.9 percent. Despite rising

interest rates, interest outlays became a smaller share of the budget and were roughly stable as a percentage of GDP.

Federal debt relative to GDP is a function of the Nation's fiscal policy as well as overall economic conditions. During the 1970s, large budget deficits emerged as spending grew faster than receipts and as the economy was disrupted by oil shocks and rising inflation. The nominal amount of Federal debt more than doubled, and Federal debt relative to GDP and credit market debt stopped declining after the middle of the decade. The growth of Federal debt accelerated at the beginning of the 1980s, due in large part to a deep recession, and the ratio of Federal debt to GDP grew sharply. It continued to grow throughout the 1980s as large tax cuts, enacted in 1981, and substantial increases in defense spending were only partially offset by reductions in domestic spending. The resulting deficits increased the debt to almost 48 percent of GDP by 1993. The ratio of Federal debt to credit market debt also rose, though to a lesser extent. Interest outlays on debt held by the public, calculated as a percentage of either total Federal outlays or GDP, increased as well.

The growth of Federal debt held by the public was slowing by the mid-1990s. In addition to a growing economy, three major budget agreements were enacted in the 1990s, implementing spending cuts and revenue increases and significantly reducing deficits. The debt declined markedly relative to both GDP and total credit market debt, from 1997 to 2001, as budget surpluses emerged. Debt fell from 47.8 percent of GDP in 1993 to 31.4 percent of GDP in 2001. Over that same period, debt fell from 26.3 percent of total credit market debt to 17.3 percent. Interest as a share of outlays peaked at 16.5 percent in 1989 and then fell to 8.9 percent by 2002; interest as a percentage of GDP fell by a similar proportion.

The impressive progress in reducing the debt burden stopped and then reversed course beginning in 2002. A decline in the stock market, a recession, and the initially slow recovery from that recession all reduced tax receipts. The tax cuts of 2001 and 2003 had a similarly large and longer-lasting effect, as did the costs of the wars in Iraq and Afghanistan. Deficits ensued and the debt began to rise, both in nominal terms and as a percentage of GDP. There was a small temporary improvement in 2006 and 2007 as economic growth led to a short-lived revival of receipt growth.

As a result of the most recent recession, which began in December 2007, and the massive financial and economic challenges it imposed on the Nation, the deficit began increasing rapidly in 2008. The deficit increased substantially in 2009 as the Government continued to take aggressive steps to restore the health of the Nation's economy and financial markets. The deficit fell somewhat

---

[1] The historical tables are available at https://www.whitehouse.gov/omb/budget/Historicals and on the Budget CD-ROM.

Table 4–1.   TRENDS IN FEDERAL DEBT HELD BY THE PUBLIC AND INTEREST ON THE DEBT HELD BY THE PUBLIC

(Dollar amounts in billions)

Fiscal Year	Debt held by the public:		Debt held by the public as a percent of:		Interest on the debt held by the public:[3]		Interest on the debt held by the public as a percent of:[3]	
	Current dollars	FY 2015 dollars[1]	GDP	Credit market debt[2]	Current dollars	FY 2015 dollars[1]	Total outlays	GDP
1946	241.9	2,416.9	106.1	N/A	4.2	41.8	7.6	1.8
1950	219.0	1,770.6	78.5	53.3	4.8	39.1	11.4	1.7
1955	226.6	1,610.1	55.7	42.1	5.2	36.9	7.6	1.3
1960	236.8	1,490.9	44.3	33.1	7.8	49.2	8.5	1.5
1965	260.8	1,537.5	36.7	26.4	9.6	56.5	8.1	1.3
1970	283.2	1,391.2	27.0	20.3	15.4	75.5	7.9	1.5
1975	394.7	1,429.0	24.5	17.9	25.0	90.5	7.5	1.6
1980	711.9	1,793.8	25.5	18.5	62.8	158.1	10.6	2.2
1985	1,507.3	2,898.7	35.3	22.2	152.9	294.1	16.2	3.6
1990	2,411.6	3,987.5	40.8	22.5	202.4	334.6	16.2	3.4
1995	3,604.4	5,259.4	47.5	26.3	239.2	349.0	15.8	3.2
2000	3,409.8	4,586.5	33.6	18.8	232.8	313.2	13.0	2.3
2005	4,592.2	5,510.9	35.6	17.1	191.4	229.6	7.7	1.5
2006	4,829.0	5,612.7	35.3	16.6	236.6	275.0	8.9	1.7
2007	5,035.1	5,697.3	35.2	15.9	252.0	285.1	9.2	1.8
2008	5,803.1	6,433.2	39.3	17.2	259.6	287.8	8.7	1.8
2009	7,544.7	8,267.4	52.3	21.8	201.5	220.8	5.7	1.4
2010	9,018.9	9,796.9	60.9	25.3	228.2	247.8	6.6	1.5
2011	10,128.2	10,783.0	65.9	27.7	266.0	283.2	7.4	1.7
2012	11,281.1	11,794.1	70.4	29.6	232.1	242.6	6.6	1.4
2013	11,982.7	12,316.1	72.6	30.3	259.0	266.2	7.5	1.6
2014	12,779.9	12,914.9	74.4	31.0	271.4	274.3	7.7	1.6
2015	13,116.7	13,116.7	73.7	30.6	260.6	260.6	7.1	1.5
2016 estimate	14,128.7	13,954.8	76.5	N/A	295.8	292.2	7.5	1.6
2017 estimate	14,763.2	14,320.2	76.5	N/A	364.3	353.4	8.8	1.9
2018 estimate	15,323.5	14,604.1	76.1	N/A	435.0	414.6	10.0	2.2
2019 estimate	15,982.2	14,936.5	76.1	N/A	514.1	480.5	11.1	2.4
2020 estimate	16,614.9	15,226.5	75.8	N/A	582.7	534.0	11.9	2.7
2021 estimate	17,263.5	15,509.9	75.5	N/A	639.8	574.8	12.5	2.8

N/A = Not available.

[1] Amounts in current dollars deflated by the GDP chain-type price index with fiscal year 2015 equal to 100.

[2] Total credit market debt owed by domestic nonfinancial sectors. Financial sectors are omitted to avoid double counting, since financial intermediaries borrow in the credit market primarily in order to finance lending in the credit market. Source: Federal Reserve Board flow of funds accounts. Projections are not available.

[3] Interest on debt held by the public is estimated as the interest on Treasury debt securities less the "interest received by trust funds" (subfunction 901 less subfunctions 902 and 903). The estimate of interest on debt held by the public does not include the comparatively small amount of interest paid on agency debt or the offsets for interest on Treasury debt received by other Government accounts (revolving funds and special funds).

in 2010, increased only slightly in 2011, and has decreased each year since 2012. Under the proposals in the Budget, the deficit is projected to increase in 2016 and then to fall below 3 percent of GDP starting in 2017. Debt held by the public as a percent of GDP is estimated to be 76.5 percent at the end of 2016, after which it declines gradually in subsequent years. Debt net of financial assets as a percent of GDP is estimated to increase to 67.7 percent at the end of 2016 and then fall to 67.4 percent at the end of 2017 and decline slowly in subsequent years.

Debt Held by the Public and Gross Federal Debt

The Federal Government issues debt securities for two main purposes. First, it borrows from the public to finance the Federal deficit.[2] Second, it issues debt to Federal Government accounts, primarily trust funds, that accumulate surpluses. By law, trust fund surpluses

---

[2] For the purposes of the Budget, "debt held by the public" is defined as debt held by investors outside of the Federal Government, both domestic and foreign, including U.S. State and local governments and foreign governments. It also includes debt held by the Federal Reserve.

must generally be invested in Federal securities. The gross Federal debt is defined to consist of both the debt held by the public and the debt held by Government accounts. Nearly all the Federal debt has been issued by the Treasury and is sometimes called "public debt," but a small portion has been issued by other Government agencies and is called "agency debt."[3]

Borrowing from the public, whether by the Treasury or by some other Federal agency, is important because it represents the Federal demand on credit markets. Regardless of whether the proceeds are used for tangible or intangible investments or to finance current consumption, the Federal demand on credit markets has to be financed out of the saving of households and businesses, the State and local sector, or the rest of the world. Federal borrowing thereby competes with the borrowing of other sectors of the domestic or international economy for financial resources in the credit market. Borrowing from the public thus affects the size and composition of assets held by the private sector and the amount of saving imported from abroad. It also increases the amount of future resources required to pay interest to the public on Federal debt. Borrowing from the public is therefore an important concern of Federal fiscal policy. Borrowing from the public, however, is an incomplete measure of the Federal impact on credit markets. Different types of Federal activities can affect the credit markets in different ways. For example, under its direct loan programs, the Government uses borrowed funds to acquire financial assets that might otherwise require financing in the credit markets directly. (For more information on other ways in which Federal activities impact the credit market, see the discussion at the end of this chapter.)

Issuing debt securities to Government accounts performs an essential function in accounting for the operation of these funds. The balances of debt represent the cumulative surpluses of these funds due to the excess of their tax receipts, interest receipts, and other collections over their spending. The interest on the debt that is credited to these funds accounts for the fact that some earmarked taxes and user charges will be spent at a later time than when the funds receive the monies. The debt securities are assets of those funds but are a liability of the general fund to the funds that hold the securities, and are a mechanism for crediting interest to those funds on their recorded balances. These balances generally provide the fund with authority to draw upon the U.S. Treasury in later years to make future payments on its behalf to the public. Public policy may result in the Government's running surpluses and accumulating debt in trust funds and other Government accounts in anticipation of future spending.

However, issuing debt to Government accounts does not have any of the credit market effects of borrowing from the public. It is an internal transaction of the Government, made between two accounts that are both within the Government itself. Issuing debt to a Government account is not a current transaction of the Government with the public; it is not financed by private saving and does not compete with the private sector for available funds in the credit market. While such issuance provides the account with assets—a binding claim against the Treasury—those assets are fully offset by the increased liability of the Treasury to pay the claims, which will ultimately be covered by the collection of revenues or by borrowing. Similarly, the current interest earned by the Government account on its Treasury securities does not need to be financed by other resources.

Furthermore, the debt held by Government accounts does not represent the estimated amount of the account's obligations or responsibilities to make future payments to the public. For example, if the account records the transactions of a social insurance program, the debt that it holds does not necessarily represent the actuarial present value of estimated future benefits (or future benefits less taxes) for the current participants in the program; nor does it necessarily represent the actuarial present value of estimated future benefits (or future benefits less taxes) for the current participants plus the estimated future participants over some stated time period. The future transactions of Federal social insurance and employee retirement programs, which own 92 percent of the debt held by Government accounts, are important in their own right and need to be analyzed separately. This can be done through information published in the actuarial and financial reports for these programs.[4]

This Budget uses a variety of information sources to analyze the condition of Social Security and Medicare, the Government's two largest social insurance programs. The excess of future Social Security and Medicare benefits relative to their dedicated income is very different in concept and much larger in size than the amount of Treasury securities that these programs hold.

For all these reasons, debt held by the public and debt net of financial assets are both better gauges of the effect of the budget on the credit markets than gross Federal debt.

Government Deficits or Surpluses and the Change in Debt

Table 4–2 summarizes Federal borrowing and debt from 2015 through 2026.[5] In 2015 the Government borrowed $337 billion, increasing the debt held by the public from $12,780 billion at the end of 2014 to $13,117 billion

---

[3] The term "agency debt" is defined more narrowly in the budget than customarily in the securities market, where it includes not only the debt of the Federal agencies listed in Table 4–4, but also certain Government-guaranteed securities and the debt of the Government-sponsored enterprises listed in Table 20–7 in the supplemental materials to the "Credit and Insurance" chapter. (Table 20-7 is available on the Internet at: https://www.whitehouse.gov/omb/budget/Analytical_Perspectives and on the Budget CD-ROM.)

[4] Extensive actuarial analyses of the Social Security and Medicare programs are published in the annual reports of the boards of trustees of these funds. The actuarial estimates for Social Security, Medicare, and the major Federal employee retirement programs are summarized in the *Financial Report of the United States Government*, prepared annually by the Department of the Treasury in coordination with the Office of Management and Budget.

[5] For projections of the debt beyond 2026, see Chapter 3, "Long-Term Budget Outlook."

Table 4–2. FEDERAL GOVERNMENT FINANCING AND DEBT
(In billions of dollars)

	Actual 2015	Estimate										
		2016	2017	2018	2019	2020	2021	2022	2023	2024	2025	2026
Financing:												
Unified budget deficit	438.4	615.8	503.5	453.6	549.3	534.1	552.3	659.6	676.9	650.1	740.7	793.1
Other transactions affecting borrowing from the public:												
Changes in financial assets and liabilities:[1]												
Change in Treasury operating cash balance	40.4	76.3	....	....	....	....	....	....	....	....	....	....
Net disbursements of credit financing accounts:												
Direct loan accounts	78.9	103.5	128.9	109.3	112.3	103.3	103.4	101.6	104.3	107.9	110.1	110.1
Guaranteed loan accounts	9.4	13.2	3.3	-1.4	-1.6	-3.6	-5.8	-7.0	-3.3	-2.5	-2.3	3.8
Troubled Asset Relief Program equity purchase accounts	-0.6	*	-*	-0.1	-0.1	-0.1	-*	-*	-*	-*	-*	-*
Subtotal, net disbursements	87.7	116.7	132.2	107.9	110.5	99.6	97.5	94.6	101.0	105.4	107.8	113.9
Net purchases of non-Federal securities by the National Railroad Retirement Investment Trust	-1.4	0.3	-0.9	-0.8	-0.7	-0.7	-0.8	-0.8	-0.5	-0.5	-0.5	-0.3
Net change in other financial assets and liabilities[2]	-227.8	203.2	....	....	....	....	....	....	....	....	....	....
Subtotal, changes in financial assets and liabilities	-101.1	396.6	131.3	107.1	109.9	98.9	96.8	93.8	100.5	104.9	107.3	113.5
Seigniorage on coins	-0.6	-0.4	-0.4	-0.4	-0.4	-0.4	-0.4	-0.4	-0.4	-0.4	-0.4	-0.5
Total, other transactions affecting borrowing from the public	-101.6	396.2	131.0	106.7	109.5	98.5	96.4	93.4	100.1	104.5	106.9	113.1
Total, requirement to borrow from the public (equals change in debt held by the public)	336.8	1,012.0	634.5	560.3	658.7	632.6	648.6	753.0	777.0	754.6	847.5	906.2
Changes in Debt Subject to Statutory Limitation:												
Change in debt held by the public	336.8	1,012.0	634.5	560.3	658.7	632.6	648.6	753.0	777.0	754.6	847.5	906.2
Change in debt held by Government accounts	-11.2	301.2	81.6	174.5	152.5	118.6	103.2	47.7	56.2	83.8	12.8	-11.5
Less: change in debt not subject to limit and other adjustments	6.2	-0.7	1.6	1.6	2.9	2.5	2.1	2.0	2.1	2.0	1.4	1.9
Total, change in debt subject to statutory limitation	331.9	1,312.5	717.7	736.5	814.1	753.8	753.9	802.6	835.2	840.5	861.7	896.6
Debt Subject to Statutory Limitation, End of Year:												
Debt issued by Treasury	18,093.8	19,406.5	20,122.6	20,858.0	21,670.5	22,422.8	23,175.5	23,976.9	24,810.9	25,650.5	26,512.2	27,408.5
Less: Treasury debt not subject to limitation (–)[3]	-13.3	-13.5	-11.9	-10.8	-9.3	-7.8	-6.5	-5.3	-4.1	-3.2	-3.2	-2.8
Agency debt subject to limitation	*	*	*	*	*	*	*	*	*	*	*	*
Adjustment for discount and premium[4]	32.5	32.5	32.5	32.5	32.5	32.5	32.5	32.5	32.5	32.5	32.5	32.5
Total, debt subject to statutory limitation[5]	18,113.0	19,425.5	20,143.2	20,879.7	21,693.7	22,447.6	23,201.5	24,004.1	24,839.3	25,679.8	26,541.5	27,438.2
Debt Outstanding, End of Year:												
Gross Federal debt:[6]												
Debt issued by Treasury	18,093.8	19,406.5	20,122.6	20,858.0	21,670.5	22,422.8	23,175.5	23,976.9	24,810.9	25,650.5	26,512.2	27,408.5
Debt issued by other agencies	26.3	26.8	26.8	26.3	24.9	23.9	23.0	22.3	21.4	20.3	19.0	17.4
Total, gross Federal debt	18,120.1	19,433.3	20,149.4	20,884.3	21,695.5	22,446.8	23,198.5	23,999.2	24,832.4	25,670.8	26,531.2	27,425.9
Held by:												
Debt held by Government accounts	5,003.4	5,304.6	5,386.2	5,560.8	5,713.2	5,831.9	5,935.0	5,982.7	6,038.9	6,122.7	6,135.5	6,124.0
Debt held by the public[7]	13,116.7	14,128.7	14,763.2	15,323.5	15,982.2	16,614.9	17,263.5	18,016.5	18,793.5	19,548.1	20,395.7	21,301.9
As a percent of GDP	73.7%	76.5%	76.5%	76.1%	76.1%	75.8%	75.5%	75.5%	75.4%	75.2%	75.2%	75.3%

*$50 million or less.

[1] A decrease in the Treasury operating cash balance (which is an asset) is a means of financing a deficit and therefore has a negative sign. An increase in checks outstanding (which is a liability) is also a means of financing a deficit and therefore also has a negative sign.

[2] Includes checks outstanding, accrued interest payable on Treasury debt, uninvested deposit fund balances, allocations of special drawing rights, and other liability accounts; and, as an offset, cash and monetary assets (other than the Treasury operating cash balance), other asset accounts, and profit on sale of gold.

[3] Consists primarily of debt issued by the Federal Financing Bank and Treasury securities held by the Federal Financing Bank.

[4] Consists mainly of unamortized discount (less premium) on public issues of Treasury notes and bonds (other than zero-coupon bonds) and unrealized discount on Government account series securities.

[5] Legislation enacted November 2, 2015 (P.L. 114-74), temporarily suspends the debt limit through March 15, 2017.

[6] Treasury securities held by the public and zero-coupon bonds held by Government accounts are almost all measured at sales price plus amortized discount or less amortized premium. Agency debt securities are almost all measured at face value. Treasury securities in the Government account series are otherwise measured at face value less unrealized discount (if any).

[7] At the end of 2015, the Federal Reserve Banks held $2,461.9 billion of Federal securities and the rest of the public held $10,654.8 billion. Debt held by the Federal Reserve Banks is not estimated for future years.

at the end of 2015. The debt held by Government accounts fell by $11 billion, and gross Federal debt increased by $326 billion to $18,120 billion.

Debt held by the public.—The Federal Government primarily finances deficits by borrowing from the public, and it primarily uses surpluses to repay debt held by the public.[6] Table 4–2 shows the relationship between the Federal deficit or surplus and the change in debt held by the public. The borrowing or debt repayment depends on the Government's expenditure programs and tax laws, on the economic conditions that influence tax receipts and outlays, and on debt management policy. The sensitivity of the budget to economic conditions is analyzed in Chapter 2, "Economic Assumptions and Interactions with the Budget," in this volume.

The total or unified budget deficit consists of two parts: the on-budget deficit; and the surplus of the off-budget Federal entities, which have been excluded from the budget by law. Under present law, the off-budget Federal entities are the two Social Security trust funds (Old-Age and Survivors Insurance and Disability Insurance) and the Postal Service Fund.[7] The on-budget and off-budget surpluses or deficits are added together to determine the Government's financing needs.

Over the long run, it is a good approximation to say that "the deficit is financed by borrowing from the public" or "the surplus is used to repay debt held by the public." However, the Government's need to borrow in any given year has always depended on several other factors besides the unified budget surplus or deficit, such as the change in the Treasury operating cash balance. These other factors—"other transactions affecting borrowing from the public"—can either increase or decrease the Government's need to borrow and can vary considerably in size from year to year. The other transactions affecting borrowing from the public are presented in Table 4–2 (where an increase in the need to borrow is represented by a positive sign, like the deficit).

In 2015 the deficit was $438 billion while these other factors reduced the need to borrow by $102 billion, or 30 percent of total borrowing from the public. As a result, the Government borrowed $337 billion from the public. The other factors are estimated to increase borrowing by $396 billion (39 percent of total borrowing from the public) in 2016, and $131 billion (21 percent) in 2017. In 2018–2026, these other factors are expected to increase borrowing by annual amounts ranging from $93 billion to $113 billion.

Three specific factors presented in Table 4–2 have historically been especially important.

Change in Treasury operating cash balance.—The cash balance increased by $70 billion, to $158 billion, in 2014 and increased by $40 billion, to $199 billion, in 2015. The operating cash balance is projected to increase by $76 billion, to $275 billion at the end of 2016. The increase in the cash balance reflects a number of factors. First, in 2015, Treasury announced that, for risk management purposes, it would seek to maintain a cash balance roughly equal to one week of Government outflows, with a minimum balance of about $150 billion. In addition, for debt management purposes, in November 2015 Treasury announced intentions to increase bill financing; because bills mature more frequently than other longer-dated debt, this financing decision effectively increases government outflows during any given week. Finally the timing of end-of-month auction settlements can often increase end-of-month cash balances dramatically. Changes in the operating cash balance, while occasionally large, are inherently limited over time. Decreases in cash—a means of financing the Government—are limited by the amount of past accumulations, which themselves required financing when they were built up. Increases are limited because it is generally more efficient to repay debt.

Net financing disbursements of the direct loan and guaranteed loan financing accounts.—Under the Federal Credit Reform Act of 1990 (FCRA), the budgetary program account for each credit program records the estimated subsidy costs—the present value of estimated net losses—at the time when the direct or guaranteed loans are disbursed. The individual cash flows to and from the public associated with the loans or guarantees, such as the disbursement and repayment of loans, the default payments on loan guarantees, the collection of interest and fees, and so forth, are recorded in the credit program's non-budgetary financing account. Although the non-budgetary financing account's cash flows to and from the public are not included in the deficit (except for their impact on subsidy costs), they affect Treasury's net borrowing requirements.[8]

In addition to the transactions with the public, the financing accounts include several types of intragovernmental transactions. They receive payment from the credit program accounts for the subsidy costs of new direct loans and loan guarantees and for any upward reestimate of the costs of outstanding direct and guaranteed loans. They also receive interest from Treasury on balances of uninvested funds. The financing accounts pay any negative subsidy collections or downward reestimate of costs to budgetary receipt accounts and pay interest on borrowings from Treasury. The total net collections and gross disbursements of the financing accounts, consisting of transactions with both the public and the budgetary accounts, are called "net financing disbursements." They occur in the same way as the "outlays" of a budgetary account, even though they do not represent budgetary costs, and therefore affect the requirement for borrowing from the public in the same way as the deficit.

---

[6] Treasury debt held by the public is measured as the sales price plus the amortized discount (or less the amortized premium). At the time of sale, the book value equals the sales price. Subsequently, it equals the sales price plus the amount of the discount that has been amortized up to that time. In equivalent terms, the book value of the debt equals the principal amount due at maturity (par or face value) less the unamortized discount. (For a security sold at a premium, the definition is symmetrical.) For inflation-indexed notes and bonds, the book value includes a periodic adjustment for inflation. Agency debt is generally recorded at par.

[7] For further explanation of the off-budget Federal entities, see Chapter 10, "Coverage of the Budget."

[8] The FCRA (sec. 505(b)) requires that the financing accounts be non-budgetary. They are non-budgetary in concept because they do not measure cost. For additional discussion of credit programs, see Chapter 20, "Credit and Insurance," and Chapter 9, "Budget Concepts."

The intragovernmental transactions of the credit program, financing, and downward reestimate receipt accounts do not affect Federal borrowing from the public. Although the deficit changes because of the budgetary account's outlay to, or receipt from, a financing account, the net financing disbursement changes in an equal amount with the opposite sign, so the effects are cancelled out. On the other hand, financing account disbursements to the public increase the requirement for borrowing from the public in the same way as an increase in budget outlays that are disbursed to the public in cash. Likewise, receipts from the public collected by the financing account can be used to finance the payment of the Government's obligations, and therefore they reduce the requirement for Federal borrowing from the public in the same way as an increase in budgetary receipts.

Borrowing due to credit financing accounts was $88 billion in 2015. In 2016 credit financing accounts are projected to increase borrowing by $117 billion. After 2016, the credit financing accounts are expected to increase borrowing by amounts ranging from $95 billion to $132 billion over the next 10 years.

In some years, large net upward or downward reestimates in the cost of outstanding direct and guaranteed loans may cause large swings in the net financing disbursements. In 2015, there was a net upward reestimate of $8.7 billion, due largely to direct student loans. In 2016, there is a net downward reestimate of $5.6 billion, due to a large downward reestimate for Federal Housing Administration (FHA) Mutual Mortgage Insurance guarantees, partly offset by an upward reestimate for direct student loans.

Net purchases of non-Federal securities by the National Railroad Retirement Investment Trust (NRRIT).— This trust fund, which was established by the Railroad Retirement and Survivors' Improvement Act of 2001, invests its assets primarily in private stocks and bonds. The Act required special treatment of the purchase or sale of non-Federal assets by the NRRIT trust fund, treating such purchases as a means of financing rather than as outlays. Therefore, the increased need to borrow from the public to finance NRRIT's purchases of non-Federal assets is part of the "other transactions affecting borrowing from the public" rather than included as an increase in the deficit. While net purchases and redemptions affect borrowing from the public, unrealized gains and losses on NRRIT's portfolio are included in both the "other transactions" and, with the opposite sign, in NRRIT's net outlays in the deficit, for no net impact on borrowing from the public. In 2015, net decreases, including redemptions and losses, were $1.4 billion. A $0.3 billion net increase is projected for 2016 and net annual decreases ranging from $0.3 billion to $0.9 billion are projected for 2017 and subsequent years.[9]

Net change in other financial assets and liabilities.— In addition to the three factors discussed above, in 2015 and 2016, the net change in other financial assets and liabilities is also particularly significant. Generally, the

amounts in this category are relatively small. For example, this category decreased the need to borrow by $1 billion in 2012 and increased the need to borrow by $5 billion in 2011. However, in 2015, this "other" category reduced the need to borrow by a net $228 billion. Of the net $228 billion, $203 billion was due to the temporary suspension of the daily reinvestment of the Thrift Savings Plan (TSP) Government Securities Investment Fund (G-Fund).[10] The Department of the Treasury is authorized to suspend the issuance of obligations to the TSP G-Fund as an "extraordinary measure" if issuances could not be made without causing the public debt of the United States to exceed the debt limit. The suspension of the daily reinvestment of the TSP G-Fund resulted in the amounts being moved from debt held by the public to deposit fund balances, an "other" financial liability. Once Treasury is able to do so without exceeding the debt limit, Treasury is required to fully reinvest the TSP G-Fund and restore any foregone interest. Accordingly, the TSP G-Fund was fully reinvested in November 2015. Table 4–2 reflects the $203 billion reinvestment in 2016, which returned the amount from deposit fund balances to debt held by the public. The debt ceiling and the use of the TSP G-Fund are discussed in further detail below.

Debt held by Government accounts.—The amount of Federal debt issued to Government accounts depends largely on the surpluses of the trust funds, both on-budget and off-budget, which owned 90 percent of the total Federal debt held by Government accounts at the end of 2015. Net investment may differ from the surplus due to changes in the amount of cash assets not currently invested. In 2015, the total trust fund surplus was $112 billion, while trust fund investment in Federal securities decreased by $54 billion. This $165 billion difference was primarily due to the Civil Service Retirement and Disability Fund (CSRDF), which had a surplus of $15 billion but net disinvestment of $126 billion, as a result of the extraordinary measures that the Treasury Department is authorized to take with the fund when the Government is at the debt ceiling. For further details on such measures, see the discussion below. The remainder of debt issued to Government accounts is owned by a number of special funds and revolving funds. The debt held in major accounts and the annual investments are shown in Table 4–5.

Debt Held by the Public Net of Financial Assets and Liabilities

While debt held by the public is a key measure for examining the role and impact of the Federal Government in the U.S. and international credit markets and for other purposes, it provides incomplete information on the Government's financial condition. The U.S. Government holds significant financial assets, which must be offset against debt held by the public and other financial liabilities to achieve a more complete understanding of the Government's financial condition. The acquisition of those financial assets represents a transaction with the

---

[9] The budget treatment of this fund is further discussed in Chapter 9, "Budget Concepts."

[10] The TSP is a defined contribution pension plan for Federal employees. The G-Fund is one of several components of the TSP.

Table 4–3. DEBT HELD BY THE PUBLIC NET OF FINANCIAL ASSETS AND LIABILITIES
(Dollar amounts in billions)

	Actual	Estimate										
	2015	2016	2017	2018	2019	2020	2021	2022	2023	2024	2025	2026
Debt Held by the Public:												
Debt held by the public	13,116.7	14,128.7	14,763.2	15,323.5	15,982.2	16,614.9	17,263.5	18,016.5	18,793.5	19,548.1	20,395.7	21,301.9
As a percent of GDP	73.7%	76.5%	76.5%	76.1%	76.1%	75.8%	75.5%	75.5%	75.4%	75.2%	75.2%	75.3%
Financial Assets Net of Liabilities:												
Treasury operating cash balance	198.7	275.0	275.0	275.0	275.0	275.0	275.0	275.0	275.0	275.0	275.0	275.0
Credit financing account balances:												
Direct loan accounts	1,144.1	1,247.6	1,376.6	1,485.9	1,598.1	1,701.4	1,804.8	1,906.4	2,010.7	2,118.6	2,228.7	2,338.7
Guaranteed loan accounts	11.4	24.6	27.9	26.6	25.0	21.4	15.5	8.5	5.2	2.7	0.4	4.3
Troubled Asset Relief Program equity purchase accounts	0.4	0.4	0.4	0.3	0.2	0.1	0.1	0.1	0.1	*	*	*
Subtotal, credit financing account balances	1,155.9	1,272.7	1,404.9	1,512.7	1,623.3	1,722.9	1,820.4	1,914.9	2,015.9	2,121.3	2,229.2	2,343.0
Government-sponsored enterprise preferred stock	106.3	106.3	106.3	106.3	106.3	106.3	106.3	106.3	106.3	106.3	106.3	106.3
Non-Federal securities held by NRRIT	23.7	24.0	23.1	22.4	21.7	21.0	20.3	19.5	19.1	18.5	18.0	17.7
Other assets net of liabilities	−250.3	−47.1	−47.1	−47.1	−47.1	−47.1	−47.1	−47.1	−47.1	−47.1	−47.1	−47.1
Total, financial assets net of liabilities	1,234.3	1,630.9	1,762.2	1,869.3	1,979.2	2,078.1	2,174.9	2,268.7	2,369.2	2,474.1	2,581.4	2,694.9
Debt Held by the Public Net of Financial Assets and Liabilities:												
Debt held by the public net of financial assets	11,882.4	12,497.9	13,001.0	13,454.2	14,003.1	14,536.8	15,088.6	15,747.8	16,424.3	17,074.0	17,814.2	18,606.9
As a percent of GDP	66.7%	67.7%	67.4%	66.8%	66.6%	66.3%	66.0%	66.0%	65.9%	65.7%	65.7%	65.7%

*$50 million or less.

credit markets, broadening those markets in a way that is analogous to the demand on credit markets that borrowing entails. For this reason, debt held by the public is also an incomplete measure of the impact of the Federal Government in the United States and international credit markets.

One transaction that can increase both borrowing and assets is an increase to the Treasury operating cash balance. When the Government borrows to increase the Treasury operating cash balance, that cash balance also represents an asset that is available to the Federal Government. Looking at both sides of this transaction—the borrowing to obtain the cash and the asset of the cash holdings—provides much more complete information about the Government's financial condition than looking at only the borrowing from the public. Another example of a transaction that simultaneously increases borrowing from the public and Federal assets is Government borrowing to issue direct loans to the public. When the direct loan is made, the Government is also acquiring an asset in the form of future payments of principal and interest, net of the Government's expected losses on the loan. Similarly, when NRRIT increases its holdings of non-Federal securities, the borrowing to purchase those securities is offset by the value of the asset holdings.

The acquisition or disposition of Federal financial assets very largely explains the difference between the deficit for a particular year and that year's increase in debt held by the public. Debt net of financial assets is a measure that is conceptually closer to the measurement of Federal deficits or surpluses; cumulative deficits and surpluses over time more closely equal the debt net of financial assets than they do the debt held by the public.

Table 4–3 presents debt held by the public net of the Government's financial assets and liabilities, or "net debt." Treasury debt is presented in the Budget at book value, with no adjustments for the change in economic value that results from fluctuations in interest rates. The balances of credit financing accounts are based on projections of future cash flows. For direct loan financing accounts, the balance generally represents the net present value of anticipated future inflows such as principal and interest payments from borrowers. For guaranteed loan financing accounts, the balance generally represents the net present value of anticipated future outflows, such as default claim payments net of recoveries, and other collections, such as program fees. NRRIT's holdings of non-Federal securities are marked to market on a monthly basis. Government-sponsored enterprise (GSE) preferred stock is measured at market value.

Net financial assets decreased by $90 billion, to $1,234 billion, in 2015. This $1,234 billion in net financial assets included a cash balance of $199 billion, net credit financing account balances of $1,156 billion, and other assets and liabilities that aggregated to a net liability of $120 billion. At the end of 2015, debt held by the public was $13,117 billion, or 73.7 percent of GDP. Therefore, debt net of financial assets was $11,882 billion, or 66.7 percent of GDP. As shown in Table 4–3, the value of the Government's net financial assets is projected to increase to $1,631 billion in 2016. While debt held by the public is expected to increase from 73.7 percent to 76.5 percent of GDP during 2016, net debt is expected to increase from 66.7 percent to 67.7 percent of GDP.

Debt securities and other financial assets and liabilities do not encompass all the assets and liabilities of the

Federal Government. For example, accounts payable occur in the normal course of buying goods and services; Social Security benefits are due and payable as of the end of the month but, according to statute, are paid during the next month; and Federal employee salaries are paid after they have been earned. Like debt securities sold in the credit market, these liabilities have their own distinctive effects on the economy. The Federal Government also has significant holdings of non-financial assets, such as land, mineral deposits, buildings, and equipment. A unique and important asset is the Government's sovereign power to tax. The different types of assets and liabilities are reported annually in the financial statements of Federal agencies and in the *Financial Report of the United States Government*, prepared by the Treasury Department in coordination with the Office of Management and Budget (OMB).

Treasury Debt

Nearly all Federal debt is issued by the Department of the Treasury. Treasury meets most of the Federal Government's financing needs by issuing marketable securities to the public. These financing needs include both the change in debt held by the public and the refinancing—or rollover—of any outstanding debt that matures during the year. Treasury marketable debt is sold at public auctions on a regular schedule and, because it is very liquid, can be bought and sold on the secondary market at narrow bid-offer spreads. Treasury also sells to the public a relatively small amount of nonmarketable securities, such as savings bonds and State and Local Government Series securities (SLGS).[11] Treasury nonmarketable debt cannot be bought or sold on the secondary market.

Treasury issues marketable securities in a wide range of maturities, and issues both nominal (non-inflation-indexed) and inflation-indexed securities. Treasury's marketable securities include:

Treasury Bills—Treasury bills have maturities of one year or less from their issue date. In addition to the regular auction calendar of bill issuance, Treasury issues cash management bills on an as-needed basis for various reasons such as to offset the seasonal patterns of the Government's receipts and outlays.

Treasury Notes—Treasury notes have maturities of more than one year and up to 10 years.

Treasury Bonds—Treasury bonds have maturities of more than 10 years. The longest-maturity securities issued by Treasury are 30-year bonds.

Treasury Inflation-Protected Securities (TIPS)—Treasury inflation-protected—or inflation-indexed—securities are coupon issues for which the par value of the security rises with inflation. The principal value is adjusted daily to reflect inflation as measured by changes in the Consumer Price Index (CPI-U-NSA, with a two-month lag). Although the principal value may be adjusted downward if inflation is negative, at maturity, the securities

will be redeemed at the greater of their inflation-adjusted principal or par amount at original issue.

Historically, the average maturity of outstanding debt issued by Treasury has been about five years. The average maturity of outstanding debt was 70 months at the end of 2015. Over the last several years there have been many changes in financial markets that have ultimately resulted in significant structural demand for high-quality, shorter-dated securities such as Treasury bills. At the same time, Treasury bills as a percent of outstanding issuance has fallen to historically low levels of around 10 percent. In recognition of these structural changes, in November 2015, the Treasury announced that it would increase issuance of shorter-dated Treasury securities.

Traditionally, Treasury has issued securities with a fixed interest rate. In 2014, Treasury began to issue floating rate securities, to complement its existing suite of securities and to support its broader debt management objectives. Floating rate securities have a fixed par value but bear interest rates that fluctuate based on movements in a specified benchmark market interest rate. Treasury's floating rate notes are benchmarked to the Treasury 13-week bill. Currently, Treasury is issuing floating rate securities with a maturity of two years.

In addition to quarterly announcements about the overall auction calendar, Treasury publicly announces in advance the auction of each security. Individuals can participate directly in Treasury auctions or can purchase securities through brokers, dealers, and other financial institutions. Treasury accepts two types of auction bids: competitive and noncompetitive. In a competitive bid, the bidder specifies the yield. A significant portion of competitive bids are submitted by primary dealers, which are banks and securities brokerages that have been designated to trade in Treasury securities with the Federal Reserve System. In a noncompetitive bid, the bidder agrees to accept the yield determined by the auction.[12] At the close of the auction, Treasury accepts all eligible noncompetitive bids and then accepts competitive bids in ascending order beginning with the lowest yield bid until the offering amount is reached. All winning bidders receive the highest accepted yield bid.

Treasury marketable securities are highly liquid and actively traded on the secondary market, which enhances the demand for Treasuries at initial auction. The demand for Treasury securities is reflected in the ratio of bids received to bids accepted in Treasury auctions; the demand for the securities is substantially greater than the level of issuance. Because they are backed by the full faith and credit of the United States Government, Treasury marketable securities are considered to be credit "risk-free." Therefore, the Treasury yield curve is commonly used as a benchmark for a wide variety of purposes in the financial markets.

Whereas Treasury issuance of marketable debt is based on the Government's financing needs, Treasury's issuance of nonmarketable debt is based on the public's demand for the specific types of investments. Increases in outstanding balances of nonmarketable debt reduce

---

[11] Under the SLGS program, the Treasury offers special low-yield securities to State and local governments and other entities for temporary investment of proceeds of tax-exempt bonds.

[12] Noncompetitive bids cannot exceed $5 million per bidder.

Table 4–4. AGENCY DEBT

(In millions of dollars)

	2015 Actual		2016 Estimate		2017 Estimate	
	Borrowing/ Repayment(–)	Debt, End-of-Year	Borrowing/ Repayment(–)	Debt, End-of-Year	Borrowing/ Repayment(–)	Debt, End-of-Year
Borrowing from the public:						
Housing and Urban Development:						
Federal Housing Administration	....	19	*	19	....	19
Architect of the Capitol	–8	107	–9	98	–9	89
National Archives	–20	97	–21	75	–23	52
Tennessee Valley Authority:						
Bonds and notes	256	23,872	688	24,561	248	24,809
Lease financing obligations	–109	1,932	–114	1,818	–120	1,698
Prepayment obligations	–100	310	–100	210	–100	110
Total, borrowing from the public	20	26,336	445	26,781	–3	26,777
Borrowing from other funds:						
Tennessee Valley Authority [1]	2	6	....	6	....	6
Total, borrowing from other funds	2	6	....	6	....	6
Total, agency borrowing	22	26,342	445	26,786	–3	26,783
Memorandum:						
Tennessee Valley Authority bonds and notes, total	258	23,878	688	24,567	248	24,815

* $500,000 or less.

[1] Represents open market purchases by the National Railroad Retirement Investment Trust.

the need for marketable borrowing. In 2015, there was net disinvestment in nonmarketables, necessitating additional marketable borrowing to finance the redemption of nonmarketable debt.[13]

Agency Debt

A few Federal agencies other than Treasury, shown in Table 4–4, sell or have sold debt securities to the public and, at times, to other Government accounts. Currently, new debt is issued only by the Tennessee Valley Authority (TVA) and the Federal Housing Administration; the remaining agencies are repaying past borrowing. Agency debt was $26.3 billion at the end of 2014 and at the end of 2015. Agency debt is less than one-quarter of one percent of Federal debt held by the public. Primarily as a result of TVA activity, agency debt is estimated to grow to $26.8 billion at the end of 2016 and to remain at that level in 2017.

The predominant agency borrower is TVA, which had borrowings of $26.1 billion from the public as of the end of 2015, or 99 percent of the total debt of all agencies other than Treasury. TVA issues debt primarily to finance capital projects.

TVA has traditionally financed its capital construction by selling bonds and notes to the public. Since 2000, it has also employed two types of alternative financing methods, lease financing obligations and prepayment obligations. Under the lease financing obligations method, TVA signs long-term contracts to lease some facilities and equipment. The lease payments under these contracts ultimately se-

cure the repayment of third party capital used to finance construction of the facility. TVA retains substantially all of the economic benefits and risks related to ownership of the assets.[14] Under the prepayment obligations method, TVA's power distributors may prepay a portion of the price of the power they plan to purchase in the future. In return, they obtain a discount on a specific quantity of the future power they buy from TVA. The quantity varies, depending on TVA's estimated cost of borrowing.

OMB determined that each of these alternative financing methods is a means of financing the acquisition of assets owned and used by the Government, or of refinancing debt previously incurred to finance such assets. They are equivalent in concept to other forms of borrowing from the public, although under different terms and conditions. The budget therefore records the upfront cash proceeds from these methods as borrowing from the public, not offsetting collections.[15] The budget presentation is consistent with the reporting of these obligations as li-

---

[13] Detail on the marketable and nonmarketable securities issued by Treasury is found in the *Monthly Statement of the Public Debt*, published on a monthly basis by the Department of the Treasury.

[14] This arrangement is at least as governmental as a "lease-purchase without substantial private risk." For further detail on the current budgetary treatment of lease-purchase without substantial private risk, see OMB Circular No. A–11, Appendix B.

[15] This budgetary treatment differs from the treatment in the *Monthly Treasury Statement of Receipts and Outlays of the United States Government* (Monthly Treasury Statement) Table 6 Schedule C, and the *Combined Statement of Receipts, Outlays, and Balances of the United States Government* Schedule 3, both published by the Department of the Treasury. These two schedules, which present debt issued by agencies other than Treasury, exclude the TVA alternative financing arrangements. This difference in treatment is one factor causing minor differences between debt figures reported in the Budget and debt figures reported by Treasury. The other factors are adjustments for the timing of the reporting of Federal debt held by NRRIT and treatment of the Federal debt held by the Securities Investor Protection Corporation.

abilities on TVA's balance sheet under generally accepted accounting principles. Table 4–4 presents these alternative financing methods separately from TVA bonds and notes to distinguish between the types of borrowing. At the end of 2015, lease financing obligations were $1.9 billion and obligations for prepayments were $0.3 billion.

Although the FHA generally makes direct disbursements to the public for default claims on FHA-insured mortgages, it may also pay claims by issuing debentures. Issuing debentures to pay the Government's bills is equivalent to selling securities to the public and then paying the bills by disbursing the cash borrowed, so the transaction is recorded as being simultaneously an outlay and borrowing. The debentures are therefore classified as agency debt.

A number of years ago, the Federal Government guaranteed the debt used to finance the construction of buildings for the National Archives and the Architect of the Capitol, and subsequently exercised full control over the design, construction, and operation of the buildings. These arrangements are equivalent to direct Federal construction financed by Federal borrowing. The construction expenditures and interest were therefore classified as Federal outlays, and the borrowing was classified as Federal agency borrowing from the public.

A number of Federal agencies borrow from the Bureau of the Fiscal Service (Fiscal Service) or the Federal Financing Bank (FFB), both within the Department of the Treasury. Agency borrowing from the FFB or the Fiscal Service is not included in gross Federal debt. It would be double counting to add together (a) the agency borrowing from the Fiscal Service or FFB and (b) the Treasury borrowing from the public that is needed to provide the Fiscal Service or FFB with the funds to lend to the agencies.

Debt Held by Government Accounts

Trust funds, and some special funds and public enterprise revolving funds, accumulate cash in excess of current needs in order to meet future obligations. These cash surpluses are generally invested in Treasury debt.

The total investment holdings of trust funds and other Government accounts decreased by $11 billion in 2015. Net investment by Government accounts is estimated to be $301 billion in 2016 and $82 billion in 2017, as shown in Table 4–5. The holdings of Federal securities by Government accounts are estimated to increase to $5,386 billion by the end of 2017, or 27 percent of the gross Federal debt. The percentage is estimated to decrease gradually over the next 10 years.

The Government account holdings of Federal securities are concentrated among a few funds: the Social Security Old-Age and Survivors Insurance (OASI) and Disability Insurance (DI) trust funds; the Medicare Hospital Insurance (HI) and Supplementary Medical Insurance (SMI) trust funds; and four Federal employee retirement funds. These Federal employee retirement funds include two trust funds, the Military Retirement Fund

and the Civil Service Retirement and Disability Fund, and two special funds, the uniformed services Medicare-Eligible Retiree Health Care Fund (MERHCF) and the Postal Service Retiree Health Benefits Fund (PSRHBF). At the end of 2017, these Social Security, Medicare, and Federal employee retirement funds are estimated to own 90 percent of the total debt held by Government accounts. During 2015–2017, the Military Retirement Fund has a large surplus and is estimated to invest a total of $173 billion, 47 percent of total net investment by Government accounts. CSRDF is projected to invest $47 billion, 13 percent of the net total. Some Government accounts are projected to have net disinvestment in Federal securities during 2015–2017.

Technical note on measurement.—The Treasury securities held by Government accounts consist almost entirely of the Government account series. Most were issued at par value (face value), and the securities issued at a discount or premium are traditionally recorded at par in the OMB and Treasury reports on Federal debt. However, there are two kinds of exceptions.

First, Treasury issues zero-coupon bonds to a very few Government accounts. Because the purchase price is a small fraction of par value and the amounts are large, the holdings are recorded in Table 4–5 at par value less unamortized discount. The only two Government accounts that held zero-coupon bonds during the period of this table are the Nuclear Waste Disposal Fund in the Department of Energy and the Pension Benefit Guaranty Corporation (PBGC). The total unamortized discount on zero-coupon bonds was $18.1 billion at the end of 2015.

Second, Treasury subtracts the unrealized discount on other Government account series securities in calculating "net Federal securities held as investments of Government accounts." Unlike the discount recorded for zero-coupon bonds and debt held by the public, the unrealized discount is the discount at the time of issue and is not amortized over the term of the security. In Table 4–5 it is shown as a separate item at the end of the table and not distributed by account. The amount was $7.5 billion at the end of 2015.

Debt Held by the Federal Reserve

The Federal Reserve acquires marketable Treasury securities as part of its exercise of monetary policy. For purposes of the Budget and reporting by the Department of the Treasury, the transactions of the Federal Reserve are considered to be non-budgetary, and accordingly the Federal Reserve's holdings of Treasury securities are included as part of debt held by the public.[16] Federal Reserve holdings were $2,462 billion (19 percent of debt held by the public) at the end of 2015. Over the last 10 years, the Federal Reserve holdings have averaged 15 percent of debt held by the public. The historical holdings of the Federal Reserve are presented in Table 7.1 in the Budget's historical tables. The Budget does not project Federal Reserve holdings for future years.

---

[16] For further detail on the monetary policy activities of the Federal Reserve and the treatment of the Federal Reserve in the Budget, see Chapter 10, "Coverage of the Budget."

Table 4–5.   DEBT HELD BY GOVERNMENT ACCOUNTS[1]

(In millions of dollars)

Description	Investment or Disinvestment (-)			Holdings, End of 2017 Estimate
	2015 Actual	2016 Estimate	2017 Estimate	
Investment in Treasury debt:				
Energy:				
Nuclear waste disposal fund [1]	1,428	296	41	34,236
Uranium enrichment decontamination fund	−161	−612	692	3,263
Health and Human Services:				
Federal hospital insurance trust fund	−6,750	−5,734	−2,028	187,696
Federal supplementary medical insurance trust fund	−2,263	12,216	−9,347	68,997
Vaccine injury compensation fund	93	162	195	3,810
Child enrollment contingency fund	−48	1,846	−2,743	1,156
Homeland Security:				
Aquatic resources trust fund	55	−51	58	1,949
Oil spill liability trust fund	541	702	715	5,660
Housing and Urban Development:				
Federal Housing Administration mutual mortgage fund	8,353	20,009	10,116	44,858
Guarantees of mortgage-backed securities	12,772	2,577	1,236	16,736
Interior:				
Abandoned mine reclamation fund	−4	6	−27	2,785
Federal aid in wildlife restoration fund	766	74	36	1,990
Environmental improvement and restoration fund	42	2	18	1,417
Justice: Assets forfeiture fund	−862	−1,001	−1,499	3,706
Labor:				
Unemployment trust fund	8,449	10,066	12,494	66,928
Pension Benefit Guaranty Corporation [1]	1,070	4,526	4,328	27,189
State: Foreign service retirement and disability trust fund	352	324	321	18,789
Transportation:				
Airport and airway trust fund	−43	−1,272	−1,145	10,299
Transportation trust fund	−3,029	57,581	−15,125	50,123
Aviation insurance revolving fund	−11	14	52	2,192
Treasury:				
Exchange stabilization fund	−1,876	1,881	30	22,684
Treasury forfeiture fund	4,132	−3,791	....	2,400
Comptroller of the Currency assessment fund	610	70	72	1,677
Veterans Affairs:				
National service life insurance trust fund	−726	−606	−682	3,615
Veterans special life insurance fund	−78	−107	−118	1,560
Corps of Engineers: Harbor maintenance trust fund	292	711	1,044	10,348
Other Defense-Civil:				
Military retirement trust fund	47,849	58,673	66,867	656,500
Medicare-eligible retiree health care fund	5,421	7,482	7,814	221,089
Education benefits fund	−192	−142	−185	1,049
Environmental Protection Agency: Hazardous substance trust fund	1,760	20	219	5,445
International Assistance Programs: Overseas Private Investment Corporation	92	74	99	5,792
Office of Personnel Management:				
Civil service retirement and disability trust fund	−125,902	157,257	15,784	904,308
Postal Service retiree health benefits fund	−3,231	5,843	3,892	54,972
Employees life insurance fund	745	−1,169	623	43,412
Employees and retired employees health benefits fund	−538	1,634	503	25,158
Social Security Administration:				
Federal old-age and survivors insurance trust fund [2]	53,844	−33,990	−77,687	2,654,972
Federal disability insurance trust fund [2]	−28,475	−1,593	56,173	96,218
District of Columbia: Federal pension fund	22	191	−57	3,857
Farm Credit System Insurance Corporation: Farm Credit System Insurance fund	284	315	292	4,334

Table 4–5.   DEBT HELD BY GOVERNMENT ACCOUNTS [1]—Continued

(In millions of dollars)

Description	Investment or Disinvestment (-)			Holdings, End of 2017 Estimate
	2015 Actual	2016 Estimate	2017 Estimate	
Federal Communications Commission: Universal service fund	466	–819	–999	6,304
Federal Deposit Insurance Corporation: Deposit insurance fund	11,346	7,455	10,912	78,463
National Credit Union Administration: Share insurance fund	559	400	513	12,497
Postal Service fund [2]	1,713	28	–1,861	5,330
Railroad Retirement Board trust funds	–58	–134	56	2,466
Securities Investor Protection Corporation [3]	300	183	70	2,613
United States Enrichment Corporation fund	2	2	–470	1,146
Other Federal funds	–64	–742	169	5,753
Other trust funds	–126	311	178	6,006
Unrealized discount [1]	–94	....	....	–7,533
Total, investment in Treasury debt [1]	**–11,172**	**301,167**	**81,639**	**5,386,214**
Investment in agency debt:				
Railroad Retirement Board:				
National Railroad Retirement Investment Trust	2	....	....	6
Total, investment in agency debt [1]	**2**	**.........**	**.........**	**6**
Total, investment in Federal debt [1]	**–11,169**	**301,167**	**81,639**	**5,386,220**
Memorandum:				
Investment by Federal funds (on-budget)	40,799	46,212	34,515	561,432
Investment by Federal funds (off-budget)	1,713	28	–1,861	5,330
Investment by trust funds (on-budget)	–78,956	290,510	70,499	2,075,801
Investment by trust funds (off-budget)	25,369	–35,583	–21,514	2,751,190
Unrealized discount [1]	–94	....	....	–7,533

[1] Debt held by Government accounts is measured at face value except for the Treasury zero-coupon bonds held by the Nuclear Waste Disposal Fund and the Pension Benefit Guaranty Corporation (PBGC), which are recorded at market or redemption price; and the unrealized discount on Government account series, which is not distributed by account. Changes are not estimated in the unrealized discount. If recorded at face value, at the end of 2015 the debt figures would be $17.9 billion higher for the Nuclear Waste Disposal Fund and $0.2 billion higher for PBGC than recorded in this table.

[2] Off-budget Federal entity.

[3] Amounts on calendar-year basis.

Limitations on Federal Debt

Definition of debt subject to limit.—Statutory limitations have usually been placed on Federal debt. Until World War I, the Congress ordinarily authorized a specific amount of debt for each separate issue. Beginning with the Second Liberty Bond Act of 1917, however, the nature of the limitation was modified in several steps until it developed into a ceiling on the total amount of most Federal debt outstanding. This last type of limitation has been in effect since 1941. The limit currently applies to most debt issued by the Treasury since September 1917, whether held by the public or by Government accounts; and other debt issued by Federal agencies that, according to explicit statute, is guaranteed as to principal and interest by the U.S. Government.

The third part of Table 4–2 compares total Treasury debt with the amount of Federal debt that is subject to the limit. Nearly all Treasury debt is subject to the debt limit.

A large portion of the Treasury debt not subject to the general statutory limit was issued by the Federal Financing Bank. The FFB is authorized to have outstanding up to $15 billion of publicly issued debt. The FFB has on occasion issued this debt to CSRDF in exchange for equal amounts of regular Treasury securities. The FFB securities have the same interest rates and maturities as the Treasury securities for which they were exchanged. The FFB issued $14 billion of securities to the CSRDF on November 15, 2004, with maturity dates ranging from June 30, 2009, through June 30, 2019, and issued $9 billion to the CSRDF on October 1, 2013, with maturity dates from June 30, 2015, through June 30, 2024. At the end of 2015, a total of $12 billion of this FFB borrowing remained outstanding. On October 15, 2015, FFB issued $3 billion of securities to the CSRDF, with maturity dates from June 30, 2026, through June 30, 2029, bringing this category of debt to its statutory limit. The outstanding balance of FFB debt held by CSRDF is projected to be $13 billion at the end of 2016 and $11 billion at the end of 2017.

The Housing and Economic Recovery Act of 2008 created another type of debt not subject to limit. This debt, termed "Hope Bonds," has been issued by Treasury to the FFB for the HOPE for Homeowners program. The outstanding balance of Hope Bonds was $494 million at the end of 2015 and is projected to fall to $7 million by the end of 2016 and then to increase gradually in subsequent years.

The other Treasury debt not subject to the general limit consists almost entirely of silver certificates and other currencies no longer being issued. It was $483 million at the end of 2015 and is projected to gradually decline over time.

The sole agency debt currently subject to the general limit, $209 thousand at the end of 2015, is certain debentures issued by the Federal Housing Administration.[17]

Some of the other agency debt, however, is subject to its own statutory limit. For example, the Tennessee Valley Authority is limited to $30 billion of bonds and notes outstanding.

The comparison between Treasury debt and debt subject to limit also includes an adjustment for measurement differences in the treatment of discounts and premiums. As explained earlier in this chapter, debt securities may be sold at a discount or premium, and the measurement of debt may take this into account rather than recording the face value of the securities. However, the measurement differs between gross Federal debt (and its components) and the statutory definition of debt subject to limit. An adjustment is needed to derive debt subject to limit (as defined by law) from Treasury debt. The amount of the adjustment was $32.5 billion at the end of 2015 compared with the total unamortized discount (less premium) of $56.9 billion on all Treasury securities.

Changes in the debt limit.—The statutory debt limit has been changed many times. Since 1960, the Congress has passed 82 separate acts to raise the limit, revise the definition, extend the duration of a temporary increase, or temporarily suspend the limit.[18]

The four most recent laws addressing the debt limit have each provided for a temporary suspension followed by an increase in an amount equivalent to the debt that was issued during that suspension period in order to fund commitments requiring payment through the specified end date. The No Budget, No Pay Act of 2013 suspended the debt limit from February 4, 2013, through May 18, 2013, and then raised the debt limit on May 19, 2013, by $305 billion, from $16,394 billion to $16,699 billion. The Continuing Appropriations Act, 2014, suspended the $16,699 billion debt ceiling from October 17, 2013, through February 7, 2014, and then raised the debt limit on February 8, 2014, by $512 billion to $17,212 billion. The Temporary Debt Limit Extension Act suspended the $17,212 billion debt ceiling from February 15, 2014, through March 15, 2015, and then raised the debt limit on March 16, 2015, by $901 billion to $18,113 billion. The Bipartisan Budget Act of 2015 suspended the $18,113 billion debt ceiling from November 2, 2015, through March 15, 2017.

At many times in the past several decades, including 2013, 2014, and 2015, the Government has reached the statutory debt limit before an increase has been enacted. When this has occurred, it has been necessary for the Department of the Treasury to take extraordinary measures to meet the Government's obligation to pay its bills and invest its trust funds while remaining below the statutory limit. As mentioned above, one such measure is the partial or full suspension of the daily reinvestment of the

Thrift Savings Plan G-Fund. The Treasury Secretary has statutory authority to suspend investment of the G-Fund in Treasury securities as needed to prevent the debt from exceeding the debt limit. Treasury determines each day the amount of investments that would allow the fund to be invested as fully as possible without exceeding the debt limit. At the end of December 2015, the TSP G-Fund had an outstanding balance of $207 billion. The Secretary is also authorized to suspend investments in the CSRDF and to declare a debt issuance suspension period, which allows him or her to redeem a limited amount of securities held by the CSRDF. The Postal Accountability and Enhancement Act of 2006 provides that investments in the Postal Service Retiree Health Benefits Fund shall be made in the same manner as investments in the CSRDF.[19] Therefore, Treasury is able to take similar administrative actions with the PSRHBF. The law requires that when any such actions are taken with the G-Fund, the CSRDF, or the PSRHBF, the Secretary is required to make the fund whole after the debt limit has been raised by restoring the forgone interest and investing the fund fully. Another measure for staying below the debt limit is disinvestment of the Exchange Stabilization Fund. The outstanding balance in the Exchange Stabilization Fund was $23 billion at the end of December 2015.

As the debt has neared the limit, including in 2013, 2014, and 2015, Treasury has also suspended the issuance of SLGS to reduce unanticipated fluctuations in the level of the debt.

In October 2015, as Treasury neared the exhaustion of its extraordinary measures, Treasury also postponed the 2-year note auction originally scheduled for Tuesday, October 27. After the November 2nd enactment of the Bipartisan Budget Act of 2015, Treasury rescheduled the auction for Wednesday, November 4.

In addition to these steps, Treasury has previously exchanged Treasury securities held by the CSRDF with borrowing by the FFB, which, as explained above, is not subject to the debt limit. This measure was most recently taken in November 2004, October 2013, and October 2015.

The debt limit has always been increased prior to the exhaustion of Treasury's limited available administrative actions to continue to finance Government operations when the statutory ceiling has been reached. Failure to enact a debt limit increase before these actions were exhausted would have significant and long-term negative consequences. Without an increase, Treasury would be unable to make timely interest payments or redeem maturing securities. Investors would cease to view U.S. Treasury securities as free of credit risk and Treasury's interest costs would increase. Because interest rates throughout the economy are benchmarked to the Treasury rates, interest rates for State and local governments, businesses, and individuals would also rise. Foreign investors would likely shift out of dollar-denominated assets, driving down the value of the dollar and further increasing interest rates on non-Federal, as well as Treasury, debt. In addition, the Federal Government would be forced to

---

[17] At the end of 2015, there were also $18 million of FHA debentures not subject to limit.

[18] The Acts and the statutory limits since 1940 are listed in Table 7.3 of the Budget's historical tables, available at https://www.whitehouse.gov/omb/budget/Historicals.

[19] Both the CSRDF and the PSRHBF are administered by the Office of Personnel Management.

Table 4–6.   FEDERAL FUNDS FINANCING AND CHANGE IN DEBT SUBJECT TO STATUTORY LIMIT

(In billions of dollars)

Description	Actual 2015	Estimate										
		2016	2017	2018	2019	2020	2021	2022	2023	2024	2025	2026
Change in Gross Federal Debt:												
Federal funds deficit (+)	550.0	802.6	613.9	588.6	659.4	609.5	615.4	666.8	691.9	689.1	703.1	742.2
Other transactions affecting borrowing from the public—Federal funds[1]	−100.2	395.9	131.8	107.5	110.1	99.2	97.1	94.1	100.6	105.0	107.4	113.4
Increase (+) or decrease (−) in Federal debt held by Federal funds	42.5	46.2	32.7	39.5	42.3	43.3	40.0	40.4	41.2	44.9	50.4	39.4
Adjustments for trust fund surplus/deficit not invested/disinvested in Federal securities[2]	−166.6	68.5	−62.3	−0.8	−0.7	−0.7	−0.8	−0.8	−0.5	−0.5	−0.5	−0.3
Change in unrealized discount on Federal debt held by Government accounts	−0.1	....	....	....	....	....	....	....	....	....	....	....
Total financing requirements	325.6	1,313.2	716.1	734.9	811.2	751.3	751.8	800.7	833.2	838.5	860.3	894.8
Change in Debt Subject to Limit:												
Change in gross Federal debt	325.6	1,313.2	716.1	734.9	811.2	751.3	751.8	800.7	833.2	838.5	860.3	894.8
Less: increase (+) or decrease (−) in Federal debt not subject to limit	−1.3	0.7	−1.6	−1.6	−2.9	−2.5	−2.1	−2.0	−2.1	−2.0	−1.4	−1.9
Less: change in adjustment for discount and premium[3]	−5.0	....	....	....	....	....	....	....	....	....	....	....
Total, change in debt subject to limit	331.9	1,312.5	717.7	736.5	814.1	753.8	753.9	802.6	835.2	840.5	861.7	896.6
Memorandum:												
Debt subject to statutory limit[4]	18,113.0	19,425.5	20,143.2	20,879.7	21,693.7	22,447.6	23,201.5	24,004.1	24,839.3	25,679.8	26,541.5	27,438.2

[1] Includes Federal fund transactions that correspond to those presented in Table 4-2, but that are for Federal funds alone with respect to the public and trust funds.

[2] Includes trust fund holdings in other cash assets and changes in the investments of the National Railroad Retirement Investment Trust in non-Federal securities.

[3] Consists of unamortized discount (less premium) on public issues of Treasury notes and bonds (other than zero-coupon bonds).

[4] Legislation enacted November 2, 2015 (P.L. 114-74), temporarily suspends the debt limit through March 15, 2017.

delay or discontinue payments on its broad range of obligations, including Social Security and other payments to individuals, Medicaid and other grant payments to States, individual and corporate tax refunds, Federal employee salaries, payments to vendors and contractors, and other obligations.

The debt subject to limit is estimated to increase to $19,426 billion by the end of 2016 and to $20,143 billion by the end of 2017. The Budget anticipates prompt Congressional action to increase the statutory limit as necessary after the suspension period ends on March 16, 2017, so that Treasury is able to finance the Government's payments without the need to employ extraordinary measures.

Federal funds financing and the change in debt subject to limit.—The change in debt held by the public, as shown in Table 4–2, and the change in debt net of financial assets are determined primarily by the total Government deficit or surplus. The debt subject to limit, however, includes not only debt held by the public but also debt held by Government accounts. The change in debt subject to limit is therefore determined both by the factors that determine the total Government deficit or surplus and by the factors that determine the change in debt held by Government accounts. The effect of debt held by Government accounts on the total debt subject to limit can be seen in the second part of Table 4–2. The change in debt held by Government accounts results in 12 percent of the estimated total increase in debt subject to limit from 2016 through 2026.

The budget is composed of two groups of funds, Federal funds and trust funds. The Federal funds, in the main, are derived from tax receipts and borrowing and are used for the general purposes of the Government. The trust funds, on the other hand, are financed by taxes or other receipts dedicated by law for specified purposes, such as for paying Social Security benefits or making grants to State governments for highway construction.[20]

A Federal funds deficit must generally be financed by borrowing, which can be done either by selling securities to the public or by issuing securities to Government accounts that are not within the Federal funds group. Federal funds borrowing consists almost entirely of Treasury securities that are subject to the statutory debt limit. Very little debt subject to statutory limit has been issued for reasons except to finance the Federal funds deficit. The change in debt subject to limit is therefore determined primarily by the Federal funds deficit, which is equal to the difference between the total Government deficit or surplus and the trust fund surplus. Trust fund surpluses are almost entirely invested in securities subject to the debt limit, and trust funds hold most of the debt held by Government accounts. The trust fund surplus reduces the total budget deficit or increases the total budget surplus, decreasing the need to borrow from the public or increasing the ability to repay borrowing from the public. When the trust fund surplus is invested in Federal securities, the debt held by Government accounts increases, offsetting the decrease in debt held by the public by an equal amount. Thus, there is no net effect on gross Federal debt.

Table 4–6 derives the change in debt subject to limit. In 2015 the Federal funds deficit was $550 billion, and other

---

[20] For further discussion of the trust funds and Federal funds groups, see Chapter 26, "Trust Funds and Federal Funds."

factors reduced financing requirements by $100 billion. While the change in the Treasury operating cash balance increased financing requirements by $40 billion and the net financing disbursements of credit financing accounts increased financing requirements by $88 billion, other factors decreased financing requirements by $228 billion. As discussed earlier in this chapter, this net $228 billion in other factors was mainly due to the disinvestment of the TSP G-Fund. In addition, special funds and revolving funds, which are part of the Federal funds group, invested a net of $43 billion in Treasury securities. A -$167 billion adjustment is also made for the difference between the trust fund surplus or deficit and the trust funds' investment or disinvestment in Federal securities (including the changes in NRRIT's investments in non-Federal securities). As discussed above, this unusually large adjustment amount is due primarily to the extraordinary measures taken with the CSRDF. As a net result of all these factors, $326 billion in financing was required, increasing gross Federal debt by that amount. Since Federal debt not subject to limit fell by $1 billion and the adjustment for discount and premium changed by $5 billion, the debt

subject to limit increased by $332 billion, while debt held by the public increased by $337 billion.

Debt subject to limit is estimated to increase by $1,313 billion in 2016 and by $718 billion in 2017. The projected increases in the debt subject to limit are caused by the continued Federal funds deficit, supplemented by the other factors shown in Table 4–6. While debt held by the public increases by $8,185 billion from the end of 2015 through 2026, debt subject to limit increases by $9,325 billion.

Foreign Holdings of Federal Debt

During most of American history, the Federal debt was held almost entirely by individuals and institutions within the United States. In the late 1960s, foreign holdings were just over $10 billion, less than 5 percent of the total Federal debt held by the public. Foreign holdings began to grow significantly starting in the 1970s and now represent almost half of outstanding debt. This increase has been almost entirely due to decisions by foreign central banks, corporations, and individuals, rather than the direct marketing of these securities to foreign investors.

Table 4–7. FOREIGN HOLDINGS OF FEDERAL DEBT
(Dollar amounts in billions)

Fiscal Year	Debt held by the public			Change in debt held by the public [2]	
	Total	Foreign [1]	Percentage foreign	Total	Foreign
1965	260.8	12.2	4.7	3.9	0.3
1970	283.2	14.0	4.9	5.1	3.7
1975	394.7	66.0	16.7	51.0	9.1
1980	711.9	126.4	17.8	71.6	1.3
1985	1,507.3	222.9	14.8	200.3	47.3
1990	2,411.6	463.8	19.2	220.8	72.0
1995	3,604.4	820.4	22.8	171.3	138.4
2000	3,409.8	1,038.8	30.5	-222.6	-242.6
2005	4,592.2	1,929.6	42.0	296.7	135.1
2006	4,829.0	2,025.3	41.9	236.8	95.7
2007	5,035.1	2,235.3	44.4	206.2	210.0
2008	5,803.1	2,802.4	48.3	767.9	567.1
2009	7,544.7	3,570.6	47.3	1,741.7	768.2
2010	9,018.9	4,324.2	47.9	1,474.2	753.6
2011	10,128.2	4,912.1	48.5	1,109.3	587.9
2012	11,281.1	5,476.1	48.5	1,152.9	564.0
2013	11,982.7	5,652.8	47.2	701.6	176.7
2014	12,779.9	6,069.2	47.5	797.2	416.4
2015	13,116.7	6,103.1	46.5	336.8	33.9

[1] Estimated by Treasury Department. These estimates exclude agency debt, the holdings of which are believed to be small. The data on foreign holdings are recorded by methods that are not fully comparable with the data on debt held by the public. Projections of foreign holdings are not available. The estimates include the effects of benchmark revisions in 1984, 1989, 1994, and 2000, annual June benchmark revisions for 2002-2010, and additional revisions.

[2] Change in debt held by the public is defined as equal to the change in debt held by the public from the beginning of the year to the end of the year.

Foreign holdings of Federal debt are presented in Table 4–7. At the end of 2015, foreign holdings of Treasury debt were $6,103 billion, which was 47 percent of the total debt held by the public.[21] Foreign central banks and other foreign official institutions owned 68 percent of the foreign holdings of Federal debt; private investors owned nearly all the rest. At the end of 2015, the nations holding the largest shares of U.S. Federal debt were China, which held 21 percent of all foreign holdings, and Japan, which held 19 percent. All of the foreign holdings of Federal debt are denominated in dollars.

Although the amount of foreign holdings of Federal debt has grown greatly over this period, the proportion that foreign entities and individuals own, after increasing abruptly in the very early 1970s, remained about 15–20 percent until the mid-1990s. During 1995–97, however, growth in foreign holdings accelerated, reaching 33 percent by the end of 1997. Foreign holdings of Federal debt resumed growth in the following decade, increasing from 34 percent at the end of 2002 to 42 percent at the end of 2004 and to 48 percent at the end of 2008. Since 2008, foreign holdings have remained relatively stable as a percentage of Federal debt. As a percent of total Federal borrowing from the public, foreign holdings were 47 percent at the end of 2014 and 2015. The dollar increase in foreign holdings was about 10 percent of total Federal borrowing from the public in 2015 and 43 percent over the last five years.

Foreign holdings of Federal debt are around 20-25 percent of the foreign-owned assets in the United States, depending on the method of measuring total assets. The foreign purchases of Federal debt securities do not measure the full impact of the capital inflow from abroad on the market for Federal debt securities. The capital inflow supplies additional funds to the credit market generally, and thus affects the market for Federal debt. For example, the capital inflow includes deposits in U.S. financial intermediaries that themselves buy Federal debt.

Federal, Federally Guaranteed, and Other Federally Assisted Borrowing

The Government's effects on the credit markets arise not only from its own borrowing but also from the direct loans that it makes to the public and the provision of assistance to certain borrowing by the public. The Government guarantees various types of borrowing by individuals, businesses, and other non-Federal entities, thereby providing assistance to private credit markets. The Government is also assisting borrowing by States through the Build America Bonds program, which subsidizes the interest that States pay on such borrowing. In addition, the Government has established private corporations—Government-sponsored enterprises—to provide financial intermediation for specified public purposes; it exempts the interest on most State and local government debt from income tax; it permits mortgage interest to be deducted in calculating taxable income; and it insures the deposits of banks and thrift institutions, which themselves make loans.

Federal credit programs and other forms of assistance are discussed in Chapter 20, "Credit and Insurance," in this volume. Detailed data are presented in tables accompanying that chapter.

---

[21] The debt calculated by the Bureau of Economic Analysis is different, though similar in size, because of a different method of valuing securities.

PERFORMANCE AND MANAGEMENT

5. SOCIAL INDICATORS

The social indicators presented in this chapter illustrate in broad terms how the Nation is faring in selected areas in which the Federal Government has significant responsibilities. Indicators are drawn from six selected domains: economic, demographic and civic, socioeconomic, health, security and safety, and environment and energy. The indicators shown in the tables in this chapter were chosen in consultation with statistical and data experts from across the Federal Government. These indicators are only a subset of the vast array of available data on conditions in the United States. In choosing indicators for these tables, priority was given to measures that are broadly relevant to Americans and consistently available over an extended period. Such indicators provide a current snapshot while also making it easier to draw comparisons and establish trends.

The measures in these tables are influenced to varying degrees by many Government policies and programs, as well as by external factors beyond the Government's control. They do not measure the impacts of Government policies. However, they do provide a quantitative picture of the progress (or lack of progress) toward some of the ultimate ends that Government policy is intended to promote, and of the baseline on which future policies are set. Subsequent chapters in the Performance and Management section of this volume discuss approaches to assessing the impacts of Government programs and improving their quality.

The President has made it clear that policy decisions should be based upon evidence—evidence that identifies the Nation's greatest needs and challenges and evidence about which strategies are working to overcome those challenges. The social indicators in this chapter provide useful context both for prioritizing budgetary and policy-making resources and for evaluating how well existing approaches are working.

Economic: The 2008-2009 economic downturn produced the worst labor market since the Great Depression. The employment-population ratio dropped sharply from its pre-recession level, and real GDP per person also declined. The economy has steadily recovered since then. The unemployment rate stood at 5 percent in December 2015, down from a high of 10 percent in October 2009, and job growth continued in 2015. However, there remains room for further recovery. For example, rates of marginally attached and underemployed workers are still above pre-recession levels.

Over the entire period from 1960 to 2015, the primary pattern has been one of economic growth and rising living standards. Real GDP per person has nearly tripled as technological progress and the accumulation of human and physical capital have increased the Nation's productive capacity. The stock of physical capital including consumer durable goods like cars and appliances amounted to nearly $53 trillion in 2014, more than four times the size of the capital stock in 1960, after accounting for inflation.

National saving, a key determinant of future prosperity because it supports capital accumulation, fell from 5.8 percent in 2000 to 2.7 percent in 2005 as Federal budget surpluses turned to deficits, and fell even further in the recession that followed, turning negative in 2010. Since then, national saving has increased to 3.1 percent in 2015. Meanwhile, the labor force participation rate, also critical for growth, has declined for more than a decade, in large part reflecting the beginning of a trend in which the baby boom generation retires.

The United States continues to be a leader in innovation. From 1970 to 2014, the rate of patents for invention by U.S. inventors increased from 231 to 454 per million population. National Research and Development (R&D) spending has hovered between 2.2 percent and 2.8 percent of GDP for the past 50 years, and currently stands at 2.7 percent of GDP.

Demographic and Civic: The U.S. population has steadily increased from 1970, when it numbered 204 million, to 321 million in 2015. The foreign born population has increased rapidly since 1970, quadrupling from about 10 million in 1970 to 42 million in 2014. The U.S. population is getting older, due in part to the aging of the baby boomers, improvements in medical technology, and declining birth rates. From 1970 to 2014, the percent of the population over age 65 increased from 9.8 to 14.5, and the percent over age 85 increased from 0.7 to 1.9.

The composition of American households and families has evolved considerably over time. The percent of Americans who have ever married continues to decline as it has over the last five decades. Average family sizes have also fallen over this period, a pattern that is typical among developed countries. After increasing for over three decades, births to unmarried women age 15-17 and the fraction of single parent households reached a turning point in 1995. From 1995 to 2014, the number of births per 1,000 unmarried women age 15-17 fell from 30 to 11, the lowest level on record. Meanwhile, the fraction of single parent households stopped increasing in 1995, stabilizing at about 9 percent of all households.

Charitable giving among Americans, measured by the average charitable contribution per itemized tax return, has generally increased over the past 50 years.[1] The effects of the 2008-2009 recession are evident in the sharp drop in charitable giving from 2005 to 2010, but much of that decline was reversed in 2012. More Americans are

---

[1] This measure includes charitable giving only among those who claim itemized deductions. It is therefore influenced by changes in tax laws and in the characteristics of those who itemize.

volunteering. In 1990, 20 percent of Americans volunteered at least once over the course of a year; in 2014, 25 percent volunteered. The political participation of Americans, measured by the voting rate in Presidential elections, declined from about 63 percent in 1964 to 57 percent in 1972. It fell further in the 1996 and 2000 elections, reaching a low of only 50 percent in 1996. However, the Presidential election voting rate rebounded in the past three elections, averaging close to 57 percent. The cultural engagement of Americans has changed over time. The percentage of adults attending visual or performing arts activities, including movie going, decreased from 72 percent in 1980 to 65 percent in 2013. The percentage of Americans engaging in leisure reading of novels, short stories, poetry, or plays decreased from 56 percent in 1980 to 45 percent in 2013. However, new modes of cultural engagement have emerged, such as consumption of entertainment and new kinds of media via the internet and electronic devices.

Socioeconomic: Education is a critical component of the Nation's economic growth and competitiveness, while also benefiting society in areas such as health, crime, and civic engagement. Between 1960 and 1980, the percentage of 25- to 34-year olds who have graduated from high school increased from 58 percent to 84 percent, a gain of 13 percentage points per decade. Progress has slowed since then with a five percentage point gain over the past 34 years. But the percentage of 25- to 34-year olds who have graduated from college continues to rise, from only 11 percent in 1960 to 34 percent in 2014. Reading and mathematics achievement show little if any improvement for American 17-year olds over the period from 1970 to 2012. However, achievement in these areas has improved among 9- and 13-year olds, especially for mathematics and particularly since the 2004 assessment. While the percentage of the population with a graduate degree has risen over time, the percentage of graduate degrees in science and engineering fell by half in the period between 1960 to 1980, from 22 percent to 11 percent, and stood at 14 percent in 2014.

Although national prosperity has grown considerably over the past 50 years, these gains have not been shared equally. Real disposable income per capita more than tripled since 1960, but real income for the median household increased only 21 percent from 1970 to 2000, and has declined by 7 percent since 2000. The income share of the top 1 percent of taxpayers, approximately 9 percent in 1980, rose to 19 percent in 2013. In contrast, the income share of the bottom 50 percent of taxpayers declined from 18 percent in 1980 to 12 percent in 2013. From 2000 to 2012, the poverty rate, the percentage of food-insecure households, and the percentage of Americans receiving benefits from the Supplemental Nutrition Assistance Program (formerly known as the Food Stamp Program), increased as Americans struggled with the economic downturn. These measures have declined over the past several years as the economy continued to strengthen, but still remain high compared with levels prior to the 2008-2009 economic downturn.

After increasing from 1990 to 2005, homeownership rates have fallen since the 2008 housing crisis. The share of families with children and severe housing cost burdens more than doubled from 8 percent in 1980 to 18 percent in 2011, before falling to 16 percent in 2013. In contrast, the share of families with children and inadequate housing steadily decreased from a high of 9 percent in 1980 to a low of 5 percent in 2013.

Health: America has by far the most expensive health care system in the world, yet has historically had much higher rates of uninsured than many other countries with comparable wealth. National health expenditures as a share of GDP have increased from about 5 percent in 1960 to over 17 percent in 2014. This increase in health care spending has coincided with improvements in medical technology that have improved health, but the level of per capita spending in the United States is far greater than that in other Organization for Economic Cooperation and Development (OECD) countries that have experienced comparable health improvements. In recent years, however, health care spending as a share of GDP has grown more slowly, reflecting some combination of structural changes and economic conditions. In addition, the uninsured rate, at 16 percent in 2010, has declined substantially as the coverage provisions of the Affordable Care Act have taken effect and is now below 10 percent for the first time in history.

Some key indicators of national health have improved since 1960. Life expectancy at birth increased by nine years, from 69.7 in 1960 to 78.8 in 2014. Infant mortality fell from 26 to approximately 6 per 1,000 live births, with a rapid decline occurring in the 1970s.

Improvement in health-related behaviors among Americans has been mixed. Although the percent of adults who smoke cigarettes in 2014 was less than half of what it was in 1970, rates of obesity have soared. In 1980, 15 percent of adults and 6 percent of children were obese; in 2013, 39 percent of adults and 17 percent of children were obese. Adult obesity continued to rise even as the share of adults engaging in regular physical activity increased from 15 percent in 2000 to 22 percent in 2014.

Security and Safety: The last three decades have witnessed a remarkable decline in crime. From 1980 to 2014, the property crime rate dropped by 76 percent while the murder rate fell by 59 percent. Road transportation has also become safer. Safety belt use increased by 16 percentage points from 2000 to 2014, and the annual number of highway fatalities fell by 38 percent from 1970 to 2014 despite the increase in the population.

The number of military personnel on active duty has declined for several years, reflecting the withdrawal of U.S. troops from Iraq and Afghanistan. In 2015 the active duty count fell to its lowest level since at least 1960. The highest count of active duty military personnel was 3.07 million in 1970, reached during the Vietnam War. The number of veterans has declined from 29 million in 1980 to 22 million in 2015.

Environment and Energy: The Nation's future well-being and prosperity depend on stewardship of our natural resources, the environment, and on our ability to grow a clean energy economy. Substantial progress has been made on air quality in the United States, with the concentration of particulate matter falling 35 percent from 2000 to 2014.

Although technological advances and a shift in production patterns mean that Americans now use less than half as much energy per real dollar of GDP as they did 50 years ago, rising income levels have contributed to a level of per capita consumption that has remained relatively constant over the last 40 years. The percent of U.S. electricity production from renewable sources grew from 8.8 percent in 2005 to 13.2 percent in 2014.

Moving forward, the greatest environmental challenge is reducing greenhouse gas emissions. In 2014, the President announced a target reduction in the range of 26-28 percent of 2005 net greenhouse gas emissions by 2025.[2] From 2005 to 2013, gross greenhouse gas emis-

sions fell by 10 percent. Gross greenhouse gas emissions per capita and per unit of GDP fell by 15 and 18 percent, respectively. Annual mean atmospheric carbon dioxide (CO_2) concentration, a global measure of climate change, continues to rise. In 1960 the level of CO_2 concentration was 13 percent above its pre-industrial level of 280 ppm; in 2015 it was 43 percent above the pre-industrial level. However, the December 2015 Paris Agreement, involving more than 190 countries, sets a goal of keeping warming well below 2 degrees Celsius and aspires to limit the increase in temperatures to 1.5 degrees Celsius. The Agreement includes commitments to post-2020 climate action targets by countries representing roughly 95 percent of global greenhouse gas emissions, and establishes a framework to ratchet up the ambition of those commitments over time.[3]

[2] http://www.whitehouse.gov/the-press-office/2014/11/11/fact-sheet-us-china-joint-announcement-climate-change-and-clean-energy-c

[3] https://www.whitehouse.gov/the-press-office/2015/12/12/us-leadership-and-historic-paris-agreement-combat-climate-change

Table 5–1. SOCIAL INDICATORS

Calendar Years	1960	1970	1980	1990	1995	2000	2005	2010	2012	2013	2014	2015
Economic												
General Economic Conditions												
1 Real GDP per person (chained 2009 dollars) [1]	17,198	23,024	28,325	35,794	38,167	44,475	48,090	47,719	48,822	49,184	50,010	50,777
2 Real GDP per person change, 5-year annual average [1]	0.8	2.4	2.6	2.4	1.3	3.1	1.6	−0.1	−0.2	0.2	1.3	1.3
3 Consumer Price Index [2]	12.5	16.4	34.8	55.2	64.4	72.7	82.5	92.1	97.0	98.4	100.0	N/A
4 Private goods producing (%)	N/A	N/A	N/A	N/A	N/A	24.9	23.9	22.3	22.7	22.9	22.8	N/A
5 Private services producing (%)	N/A	N/A	N/A	N/A	N/A	75.1	76.1	77.7	77.3	77.1	77.2	N/A
Jobs and Unemployment												
6 Labor force participation rate (%)	59.4	60.4	63.8	66.5	66.6	67.1	66.0	64.7	63.7	63.2	62.9	62.7
7 Employment (millions)	65.8	78.7	99.3	118.8	124.9	136.9	141.7	139.1	142.5	143.9	146.3	148.8
8 Employment-population ratio (%)	56.1	57.4	59.2	62.8	62.9	64.4	62.7	58.5	58.6	58.6	59.0	59.3
9 Payroll employment change - December to December, SA (millions)	−0.4	−0.5	0.3	0.3	2.2	1.9	2.5	1.1	2.3	2.4	3.1	2.7
10 Payroll employment change - 5-year annual average, NSA (millions)	0.7	2.0	2.7	2.4	1.6	2.9	0.4	−0.7	−0.8	−0.2	1.6	2.0
11 Civilian unemployment rate (%)	5.5	4.9	7.1	5.6	5.6	4.0	5.1	9.6	8.1	7.4	6.2	5.3
12 Unemployment plus marginally attached and underemployed (%)	N/A	N/A	N/A	N/A	10.1	7.0	8.9	16.7	14.7	13.8	12.0	10.4
13 Receiving Social Security disabled-worker benefits (% of population) [3]	0.9	2.0	2.8	2.5	3.3	3.7	4.5	5.5	5.9	5.9	5.9	N/A
Infrastructure, Innovation, and Capital Investment												
14 Nonfarm business output per hour (average 5 year % change) [4]	1.8	2.1	1.2	1.6	1.6	2.8	3.2	2.0	1.7	1.5	1.0	N/A
15 Corn for grain production (million bushels)	3,907	4,152	6,639	7,934	7,400	9,915	11,112	12,425	10,755	13,829	14,216	13,654
16 Real net stock of fixed assets and consumer durable goods (billions of chained 2009 dollars)	11,383	16,921	23,265	30,870	34,246	40,217	46,305	50,332	51,438	52,117	52,866	N/A
17 Population served by secondary wastewater treatment or better (%) [5]	N/A	41.6	56.4	63.7	61.1	71.4	74.3	72.0	N/A	N/A	N/A	N/A
18 Electricity net generation (kWh per capita)	4,202	7,486	10,076	12,170	12,594	13,475	13,723	13,335	12,886	12,847	12,838	N/A
19 Patents for invention, U.S. origin (per million population) [6]	N/A	231	164	190	209	301	253	348	385	422	454	N/A
20 Net national saving rate (% of GDP) [1]	10.8	8.5	7.2	3.9	4.0	5.8	2.7	−0.9	1.8	2.4	2.9	3.1
21 R&D spending (% of GDP) [7]	2.52	2.44	2.21	2.54	2.40	2.61	2.50	2.73	2.69	2.72	N/A	N/A
Demographic and Civic												
Population												
22 Total population (millions) [8]	N/A	204.0	227.2	249.6	266.3	282.2	295.5	309.3	314.1	316.5	318.9	321.4
23 Foreign born population (millions) [9]	9.7	9.6	14.1	19.8	N/A	31.1	37.5	40.0	40.8	41.3	42.4	N/A
24 17 years and younger (%) [8]	N/A	N/A	28.0	25.7	26.1	25.7	24.9	24.0	23.5	23.3	23.1	22.9
25 65 years and older (%) [8]	N/A	9.8	11.3	12.5	12.7	12.4	12.4	13.1	13.7	14.1	14.5	N/A

Table 5–1. SOCIAL INDICATORS—Continued

Calendar Years	1960	1970	1980	1990	1995	2000	2005	2010	2012	2013	2014	2015
26 85 years and older (%) [8]	N/A	0.7	1.0	1.2	1.4	1.5	1.6	1.8	1.9	1.9	1.9	N/A
Household Composition												
27 Ever married (% of age 15 and older) [10]	78.0	75.1	74.1	73.8	72.9	71.9	70.9	69.3	68.8	68.6	68.3	68.2
28 Average family size [11]	3.7	3.6	3.3	3.2	3.2	3.2	3.1	3.2	3.1	3.1	3.1	3.1
29 Births to unmarried women age 15–17 (per 1,000 unmarried women age 15–17)	N/A	17.1	20.6	29.6	30.1	23.9	19.4	16.8	13.7	11.9	10.6	N/A
30 Single parent households (%)	4.4	5.2	7.5	8.3	9.1	8.9	8.9	9.1	9.3	9.1	8.9	8.8
Civic and Cultural Engagement												
31 Average charitable contribution per itemized tax return (2012 dollars) [12]	2,204	2,187	2,522	3,171	3,371	4,474	4,580	3,899	4,436	4,391	N/A	N/A
32 Voting for President (% of voting age population) [13]	63.4	57.0	55.1	56.4	49.8	52.1	56.7	58.3	54.9	N/A	N/A	N/A
33 Persons volunteering (% age 16 and older) [14]	N/A	N/A	N/A	20.4	N/A	N/A	28.8	26.3	26.5	25.4	25.3	N/A
34 Attendance at visual or performing arts activity, including movie-going (% age 18 and older) [15]	N/A	N/A	71.7	72.1	N/A	70.1	N/A	63.9	63.5	65.4	N/A	N/A
35 Reading: Novels or short stories, poetry, or plays (not required for work or school; % age 18 and older) [15]	N/A	N/A	56.4	54.2	N/A	46.6	N/A	50.2	47.0	45.0	N/A	N/A
Socioeconomic												
Education												
36 High school graduates (% of age 25–34) [16]	58.1	71.5	84.2	84.1	N/A	83.9	86.4	87.2	88.4	88.6	89.1	N/A
37 College graduates (% of age 25–34) [17]	11.0	15.5	23.3	22.7	N/A	27.5	29.9	31.1	32.2	32.9	33.5	N/A
38 Reading achievement score (age 17) [18]	N/A	285	285	290	288	288	283	286	287	N/A	N/A	N/A
39 Math achievement score (age 17) [19]	N/A	304	298	305	306	308	305	306	306	N/A	N/A	N/A
40 Science and engineering graduate degrees (% of total graduate degrees)	22.0	17.2	11.2	14.7	14.2	12.6	12.7	12.1	12.6	13.2	13.7	N/A
41 Receiving special education services (% of age 3–21 public school students)	N/A	N/A	10.1	11.4	12.4	13.3	13.7	13.0	12.9	12.9	N/A	N/A
Income, Savings, and Inequality												
42 Real median income: all households (2014 dollars) [20]	N/A	47,538	48,462	52,623	52,604	57,724	56,160	53,507	52,605	54,462	53,657	N/A
43 Real disposable income per capita (chained 2009 dollars) [1]	11,877	16,643	20,158	25,555	27,180	31,524	34,424	35,684	37,156	36,369	37,084	38,004
44 Adjusted gross income share of top 1% of all taxpayers	N/A	N/A	8.5	14.0	14.6	20.8	21.2	18.9	21.9	19.0	N/A	N/A
45 Adjusted gross income share of lower 50% of all taxpayers	N/A	N/A	17.7	15.0	14.5	13.0	12.9	11.7	11.1	11.5	N/A	N/A
46 Personal saving rate (% of disposable personal income) [1]	10.0	12.6	10.6	7.8	6.4	4.2	2.6	5.6	7.6	4.8	4.8	5.1
47 Poverty rate (%) [21]	22.2	12.6	13.0	13.5	13.8	11.3	12.6	15.1	15.0	14.8	14.8	N/A
48 Food-insecure households (% of all households) [22]	N/A	N/A	N/A	N/A	11.9	10.5	11.0	14.5	14.5	14.3	14.0	N/A
49 Supplemental Nutrition Assistance Program (% of population on SNAP) [23]	N/A	3.3	9.5	8.2	9.9	6.1	8.9	13.5	15.0	15.0	14.6	14.2
50 Median wealth of households, age 55–64 (in thousands of 2013 dollars) [24]	78	N/A	153	177	175	243	311	192	N/A	166	N/A	N/A
Housing												
51 Homeownership among households with children (%) [25]	N/A	N/A	N/A	63.6	65.1	67.5	68.4	65.5	62.9	62.5	N/A	N/A
52 Families with children and severe housing cost burden (%) [26]	N/A	N/A	8	10	12	11	14.5	17.9	17.0	15.7	N/A	N/A
53 Families with children and inadequate housing (%) [27]	N/A	N/A	9	9	7	7	5.4	5.3	5.2	5.0	N/A	N/A
Health												
Health Status												
54 Life expectancy at birth (years)	69.7	70.8	73.7	75.4	75.8	76.8	77.6	78.7	78.8	78.8	78.8	N/A
55 Infant mortality (per 1,000 live births)	26.0	20.0	12.6	9.2	7.6	6.9	6.9	6.1	6.0	6.0	5.8	N/A
56 Low birthweight [<2,500 gms] (% of babies)	7.7	7.9	6.8	7.0	7.3	7.6	8.2	8.2	8.0	8.0	8.0	N/A
57 Activity limitation (% of age 5–17) [28]	N/A	N/A	N/A	N/A	N/A	7.0	8.0	9.2	9.4	9.2	N/A	N/A
58 Activity limitation (% of age 18 and over) [29]	N/A	N/A	N/A	N/A	N/A	27.9	29.1	29.9	28.4	29.5	28.9	N/A
59 Difficulties with activities of daily living (% of age 65 and over) [30]	N/A	N/A	N/A	N/A	N/A	6.3	6.2	6.8	6.5	7.3	6.2	N/A
Health Behavior												
60 Engaged in regular physical activity (% of age 18 and older) [31]	N/A	N/A	N/A	N/A	N/A	15.0	16.6	20.7	20.8	21.0	21.5	N/A
61 Obesity (% of age 20–74 with BMI 30 or greater) [32]	13.4	N/A	15.0	23.2	N/A	30.9	35.1	36.1	N/A	38.6	N/A	N/A
62 Obesity (% of age 2–19) [33]	N/A	N/A	5.5	10.0	N/A	13.9	15.4	16.9	N/A	17.2	N/A	N/A
63 Cigarette smokers (% of age 18 and older)	N/A	37.1	33.1	25.3	24.6	23.1	20.8	19.3	18.2	17.9	17.0	N/A
64 Heavier drinker (% of age 18 and older) [34]	N/A	N/A	N/A	N/A	N/A	4.3	4.8	5.2	5.0	5.3	5.3	N/A
Access to Health Care												
65 Total national health expenditures (% of GDP)	5.0	6.9	8.9	12.1	13.3	13.3	15.5	17.3	17.3	17.3	17.5	N/A

Table 5–1. SOCIAL INDICATORS—Continued

Calendar Years		1960	1970	1980	1990	1995	2000	2005	2010	2012	2013	2014	2015
66	Persons without health insurance (% of age 18–64) [35]	N/A	N/A	N/A	N/A	16.9	18.9	19.3	22.3	20.9	20.5	16.3	N/A
67	Persons without health insurance (% of age 17 and younger) [35]	N/A	N/A	N/A	N/A	13.0	12.6	9.3	7.8	6.6	6.6	5.4	N/A
68	Children age 19–35 months with recommended vaccinations (%) [36]	N/A	N/A	N/A	N/A	N/A	N/A	N/A	56.6	68.4	70.4	71.6	N/A
	Security and Safety												
	Crime												
69	Property crimes (per 100,000 households) [37]	N/A	N/A	49,610	34,890	31,547	19,043	15,947	12,541	15,584	13,144	11,806	N/A
70	Violent crime victimizations (per 100,000 population age 12 or older) [38]	N/A	N/A	4,940	4,410	7,068	3,749	2,842	1,928	2,612	2,317	2,010	N/A
71	Murder rate (per 100,000 persons)	5.1	7.9	10.2	9.4	8.2	5.5	5.6	4.8	4.7	4.5	4.5	N/A
	National Security												
72	Military personnel on active duty (thousands) [39]	2,475	3,065	2,051	2,044	1,518	1,384	1,389	1,431	1,400	1,382	1,338	1,314
73	Veterans (thousands)	22,534	26,976	28,640	27,320	26,198	26,551	24,521	23,032	22,328	22,299	21,999	21,681
	Transportation Safety												
74	Safety belt use (%)	N/A	N/A	N/A	N/A	N/A	71	82	85	86	87	87	N/A
75	Highway fatalities	36,399	52,627	51,091	44,599	41,817	41,945	43,510	32,999	33,782	32,894	32,675	N/A
	Environment and Energy												
	Air Quality and Greenhouse Gases												
76	Ground level ozone (ppm) [40]	N/A	N/A	0.101	0.090	0.091	0.082	0.080	0.073	0.076	0.068	0.068	N/A
77	Particulate matter 2.5 (ug/m3) [41]	N/A	N/A	N/A	N/A	N/A	13.5	12.8	9.9	9.1	8.9	8.8	N/A
78	Annual mean atmospheric CO_2 concentration (Mauna Lao, Hawaii; ppm) [42]	316.9	325.7	338.7	354.4	360.8	369.5	379.8	389.9	393.8	396.5	398.6	400.8
79	Gross greenhouse gas emissions (teragrams CO_2 equivalent) [43]	N/A	N/A	N/A	6,301	6,695	7,213	7,350	6,899	6,545	6,673	N/A	N/A
80	Net greenhouse gas emissions, including sinks (teragrams CO_2 equivalent)	N/A	N/A	N/A	5,525	5,940	6,571	6,438	6,027	5,665	5,791	N/A	N/A
81	Gross greenhouse gas emissions per capita (metric tons CO_2 equivalent)	N/A	N/A	N/A	24.9	24.8	25.2	24.5	22.0	20.6	20.8	N/A	N/A
82	Gross greenhouse gas emissions per 2009$ of GDP (kilograms CO_2 equivalent)	N/A	N/A	N/A	0.704	0.658	0.574	0.516	0.467	0.426	0.425	N/A	N/A
	Energy												
83	Energy consumption per capita (million Btu)	250	331	344	338	342	350	339	315	301	307	309	N/A
84	Energy consumption per 2009$ GDP (thousand Btu per 2009$)	14.5	14.4	12.1	9.4	8.9	7.9	7.0	6.6	6.2	6.2	6.2	N/A
85	Electricity net generation from renewable sources, all sectors (% of total)	19.7	16.4	12.4	11.8	11.5	9.4	8.8	10.4	12.2	12.8	13.2	N/A

N/A=Number is not available.

[1] Data for 2015 are averages of the first 3 quarters.

[2] Adjusted CPI-U. 2014=100.

[3] Gross prevalence rate for persons receiving Social Security disabled-worker benefits among the estimated population insured in the event of disability at end of year. Gross rates do not account for changes in the age and sex composition of the insured population over time.

[4] Values for prior years have been revised from the prior version of this publication.

[5] Data correspond to years 1972, 1982, 1992, 1996, 2000, 2004, 2008.

[6] Patent data adjusted by OMB to incorporate total population estimates from U.S. Census Bureau.

[7] The R&D to GDP ratio data are now revised to reflect the new methodology introduced in the 2013 comprehensive revision of the GDP and other National Income and Product Accounts by the U.S. Bureau of Economic Analysis (BEA). In late July 2013, BEA reported GDP and related statistics that were revised back to 1929. The new GDP methodology treats R&D as investment in all sectors of the economy, among other methodological changes. The net effects of these changes are somewhat higher levels of GDP year to year and corresponding decreases in the R&D to GDP ratios reported annually by the National Science Foundation (NSF). For further details see NSF's InfoBrief "R&D Recognized as Investment in U.S. Gross Domestic Product Statistics: GDP Increase Slightly Lowers R&D-to-GDP Ratio" at *http://www.nsf.gov/statistics2015 nsf15315 nsf15315.pdf*.

[8] Data source and values for 2010 to 2014 have been updated relative to the prior version of this publication.

[9] Data source for 1960 to 2000 is the decennial census; data source for 2006, 2010, 2012, 2013, and 2014 is the American Community Survey.

[10] For 1960, age 14 and older.

[11] Average size of family households. Family households are those in which there is someone present who is related to the householder by birth, marriage, or adoption.

[12] Charitable giving reported as itemized deductions on Schedule A.

[13] Data correspond to years 1964, 1972, 1980, 1992, 1996, 2000, 2004, 2008, and 2012. The voting statistics in this table are presented as ratios of official voting tallies, as reported by the U.S. Clerk of the House, to population estimates from the Current Population Survey.

[14] Refers to those who volunteered at least once during a one-year period, from September of the previous year to September of the year specified. For 1990, refers to 1989 estimate from the CPS Supplement on volunteers.

[15] The 1980, 1990, 2000, and 2010 data come from the 1982, 1992, 2002, and 2008 waves of the Survey of Public Participation in the Arts, respectively.

[16] For 1960, includes those who have completed 4 years of high school or beyond. For 1970 and 1980, includes those who have completed 12 years of school or beyond. For 1990 onward, includes those who have completed a high school diploma or the equivalent.

[17] For 1960 to 1980, includes those who have completed 4 or more years of college. From 1990 onward, includes those who have completed a bachelor's degree or higher.

Table 5–1. SOCIAL INDICATORS—Continued

[18] Data correspond to years 1971, 1980, 1990, 1994, 1999, 2004, 2008, and 2012.

[19] Data correspond to years 1973, 1982, 1990, 1994, 1999, 2004, 2008, and 2012.

[20] Beginning with 2013, data are based on redesigned income questions. The source of the 2013 data is a portion of the CPS ASEC sample which received the redesigned income questions, approximately 30,000 addresses. For more information, please see the report Income and Poverty in the United States: 2014, U.S. Census Bureau, Current Population Reports, P60–252.

[21] The poverty rate does not reflect noncash government transfers. Beginning with 2013, data are based on redesigned income questions. The source of the 2013 data is a portion of the CPS ASEC sample which received the redesigned income questions, approximately 30,000 addresses. For more information, please see the report Income and Poverty in the United States: 2014, U.S. Census Bureau, Current Population Reports, P60–252.

[22] Food-insecure classification is based on reports of three or more conditions that characterize households when they are having difficulty obtaining adequate food, out of a total of 10 such conditions.

[23] 2015 reflects average monthly participation from January through August 2015 due to lags in data availability.

[24] Data values shown are 1962, 1983, 1989, 1995, 2001, 2004, 2010, and 2013. For 1962, the data source is the SFCC; for subsequent years, the data source is the SCF.

[25] Some data interpolated.

[26] Expenditures for housing and utilities exceed 50 percent of reported income. Some data interpolated.

[27] Inadequate housing has moderate to severe problems, usually poor plumbing, or heating or upkeep problems. Some data interpolated.

[28] Total activity limitation includes receipt of special education services; assistance with personal care needs; limitations related to the child's ability to walk; difficulty remembering or periods of confusion; limitations in any activities because of physical, mental, or emotional problems.

[29] Activity limitation among adults aged 18 and over is defined as having a basic action difficulty in one or more of the following: movement, emotional, sensory (seeing or hearing), or cognitive.

[30] Activities of daily living include personal care activities: bathing or showering, dressing, getting on or out of bed or a chair, using the toilet, and eating. Persons are considered to have an ADL limitation if any condition(s) causing the respondent to need help with the specific activities was chronic.

[31] Participation in leisure-time aerobic and muscle-strengthening activities that meet 2008 Federal physical activity guidelines.

[32] BMI refers to body mass index. The 1960, 1980, 1990, 2000, 2005, 2010, 2013 data correspond to survey years 1960–1962, 1976–1980, 1988–1994, 1999–2000, 2005–2006, 2009–2010, 2013–2014 respectively.

[33] Percentage at or above the sex-and age-specific 95th percentile BMI cutoff points from the 2000 CDC growth charts. The 1980, 1990, 2000, 2005, 2010, 2013 data correspond to survey years 1976–1980, 1988–1994, 1999–2000, 2005–2006, 2013–2014 respectively.

[34] Heavier drinking is based on self-reported responses to questions about average alcohol consumption and is defined as more than 14 drinks per week for men and more than 7 drinks per week for women on average.

[35] A person was defined as uninsured if he or she did not have any private health insurance, Medicare, Medicaid, CHIP (1999–2014), state-sponsored, other government-sponsored health plan (1997–2014), or military plan. Beginning in 2014, a person with health insurance coverage through the Health Insurance Marketplace or state-based exchanges was considered to have private coverage. A person was also defined as uninsured if he or she had only Indian Health Service coverage or had only a private plan that paid for one type of service such as accidents or dental care. In 1993–1996 Medicaid coverage is estimated through a survey question about having Medicaid in the past month and through participation in Aid to Families with Dependent Children (AFDC) or Supplemental Security Income (SSI) programs. In 1997 to 2014, Medicaid coverage is estimated through a question about current Medicaid coverage. Beginning in the third quarter of 2004, a Medicaid probe question was added to reduce potential errors in reporting Medicaid status. Persons under age 65 with no reported coverage were asked explicitly about Medicaid coverage.

[36] Recommended vaccine series consists of 4 or more doses of diphtheria and tetanus toxoids and pertussis vaccine (DTP), diphtheria and tetanus toxoids vaccine (DT), or diphtheria and tetanus toxoids and acellular pertussis vaccine (DTaP); 3 or more doses of any poliovirus vaccine; 1 or more doses of a measles-containing vaccine (MCV); 3 or more doses or 4 or more doses of Haemophilus influenzae type b vaccine (Hib) depending on Hib vaccine product type (full series Hib); 3 or more doses of hepatitis B vaccine; 1 or more doses of varicella vaccine; and 4 or more doses of pneumococcal conjugate vaccine (PCV).

[37] Property crimes, including burglary, motor vehicle theft, and property theft, reported by a sample of households. Includes property crimes both reported and not reported to law enforcement.

[38] Violent crimes include rape, robbery, aggravated assault, and simple assault. Includes crimes both reported and not reported to law enforcement. Due to methodological changes in the enumeration method for NCVS estimates from 1993 to present, use caution when comparing 1980 and 1990 criminal victimization estimates to future years. Estimates from 1995 and beyond include a small number of victimizations, referred to as series victimizations, using a new counting strategy. High-frequency repeat victimizations, or series victimizations, are six or more similar but separate victimizations that occur with such frequency that the victim is unable to recall each individual event or describe each event in detail. Including series victimizations in national estimates can substantially increase the number and rate of violent victimization; however, trends in violence are generally similar regardless of whether series victimizations are included. See Methods for Counting High-Frequency Repeat Victimizations in the National Crime Victimization Survey, NCJ 237308, BJS web, April 2012 for further discussion of the new counting strategy and supporting research.

[39] For all years, the actuals reflect Active Component only excluding full-time Reserve Component members and RC mobilized to active duty. End Strength for 2015 is preliminary.

[40] Ambient ozone concentrations based on 218 monitoring sites meeting minimum completeness criteria.

[41] Ambient PM2.5 concentrations based on 505 monitoring sites meeting minimum completeness criteria.

[42] Data for 2015 are preliminary.

[43] The gross emissions indicator does not include sinks, which are processes (sometimes naturally occurring) that remove greenhouse gases from the atmosphere. Gross emissions are therefore more indicative of trends in energy consumption and efficiency than are net emissions.

Table 5–2.   SOURCES FOR SOCIAL INDICATORS

	Indicator	Source
	Economic	
	General Economic Conditions	
1	Real GDP per person (chained 2009 dollars)	Bureau of Economic Analysis, National Economic Accounts Data. *http://www.bea.gov/national/*
2	Real GDP per person change, 5-year annual average	Bureau of Economic Analysis, National Economic Accounts Data. *http://www.bea.gov/national/*
3	Consumer Price Index	Bureau of Labor Statistics, BLS Consumer Price Index Program. *http://www.bls.gov/cpi/*
4	Private goods producing (%)	Bureau of Economic Analysis, National Economic Accounts Data. *http://www.bea.gov/national/*
5	Private services producing (%)	Bureau of Economic Analysis, National Economic Accounts Data. *http://www.bea.gov/national/*
	Jobs and Unemployment	
6	Labor force participation rate (%)	Bureau of Labor Statistics, Current Population Survey. *http://www.bls.gov/cps*
7	Employment (millions)	Bureau of Labor Statistics, Current Population Survey. *http://www.bls.gov/cps*
8	Employment-population ratio (%)	Bureau of Labor Statistics, Current Population Survey. *http://www.bls.gov/cps*
9	Payroll employment change - December to December, SA (millions)	Bureau of Labor Statistics, Current Employment Statistics program. *http://www.bls.gov/ces/*
10	Payroll employment change - 5-year annual average, NSA (millions)	Bureau of Labor Statistics, Current Employment Statistics program. *http://www.bls.gov/ces/*
11	Civilian unemployment rate (%)	Bureau of Labor Statistics, Current Population Survey. *http://www.bls.gov/cps*
12	Unemployment plus marginally attached and underemployed (%)	Bureau of Labor Statistics, Current Population Survey. *http://www.bls.gov/cps*
13	Receiving Social Security disabled-worker benefits (% of population)	Social Security Administration, Office of Research, Evaluation, and Statistics, Annual Statistical Supplement to the Social Security Bulletin, tables 4.C1 5.A4. *http://www.ssa.gov/policy/docs/statcomps/supplement/*
	Infrastructure, Innovation, and Capital Investment	
14	Nonfarm business output per hour (average 5 year % change)	Bureau of Labor Statistics, Major Sector Productivity Program. *http://www.bls.gov/lpc/*
15	Corn for grain production (million bushels)	National Agricultural Statistics Service, Agricultural Estimates Program. *http://www.nass.usda.gov/*
16	Real net stock of fixed assets and consumer durable goods (billions of chained 2009 dollars)	Bureau of Economic Analysis, National Economic Accounts Data. *http://www.bea.gov/national/*
17	Population served by secondary wastewater treatment or better (%)	U.S. Environmental Protection Agency, Clean Watersheds Needs Survey. *http://www.epa.gov/cwns*
18	Electricity net generation (kWh per capita)	U.S. Energy Information Administration (EIA) calculation from: EIA, Monthly Energy Review (December 2015), Table 7.2a *http://www.eia.gov/totalenergy/data/monthly/index.cfm*; and U.S. Census Bureau, Population Division, Vintage 2014 Population Estimates (2010-2014) *http://www.census.gov/popest/data/national/asrh/2014/index.html*
19	Patents for invention, U.S. origin (per million population)	U.S. Patent and Trademark Office, Patent Technology Monitoring Team, U.S. Patent Statistics Chart, Calendar Years 1963-2013. *http://www.uspto.gov/web/offices/ac/ido/oeip/taf/us_stat.htm*; and, U.S. Census Bureau, Population Division.
20	Net national saving rate (% of GDP)	Bureau of Economic Analysis, National Economic Accounts Data. *http://www.bea.gov/national/*
21	R&D spending (% of GDP)	National Science Foundation, National Patterns of R&D Resources. *http://www.nsf.gov/statistics/natlpatterns/*
	Demographic and Civic	
	Population	
22	Total population (millions)	U.S. Census Bureau, Population Division, Vintage 2015 Population Estimates (2015), Vintage 2014 Population Estimates (2010-2014), 2000-2010 Intercensal Estimates (2000-2005), 1990-1999 Intercensal Estimates (1990-1995), 1980-1990 Intercensal Estimates (1980), 1970-1980 Intercensal Estimates (1970).
23	Foreign born population (millions)	U.S. Census Bureau, Population Division, Decennial Census and American Community Survey. *http://www.census.gov/prod/www/abs/decennial/* and *http://www.census.gov/acs*
24	17 years and younger (%)	U.S. Census Bureau, Population Division, Vintage 2015 Population Estimates (2015), Vintage 2014 Population Estimates (2010-2014), 2000-2010 Intercensal Estimates (2000-2005), 1990-1999 Intercensal Estimates (1990-1995), 1980-1990 Intercensal Estimates (1980), 1970-1980 Intercensal Estimates (1970).
25	65 years and older (%)	U.S. Census Bureau, Population Division, Vintage 2015 Population Estimates (2015), Vintage 2014 Population Estimates (2010-2014), 2000-2010 Intercensal Estimates (2000-2005), 1990-1999 Intercensal Estimates (1990-1995), 1980-1990 Intercensal Estimates (1980), 1970-1980 Intercensal Estimates (1970).
26	85 years and older (%)	U.S. Census Bureau, Population Division, Vintage 2015 Population Estimates (2015), Vintage 2014 Population Estimates (2010-2014), 2000-2010 Intercensal Estimates (2000-2005), 1990-1999 Intercensal Estimates (1990-1995), 1980-1990 Intercensal Estimates (1980), 1970-1980 Intercensal Estimates (1970).
	Household Composition	
27	Ever married (% of age 15 and older)	U.S. Census Bureau, Current Population Survey. *http://www.census.gov/hhes/families/*
28	Average family size	U.S. Census Bureau, Current Population Survey. *http://www.census.gov/hhes/families/*
29	Births to unmarried women age 15-17 (per 1,000 unmarried women age 15-17)	Centers for Disease Control and Prevention, National Center for Health Statistics, National Vital Statistics System (natality); Births: Final data for 2014: *http://www.cdc.gov/nchs/data/nvsr/nvsr64/nvsr64_12.pdf.*

Table 5–2.   SOURCES FOR SOCIAL INDICATORS—Continued

	Indicator	Source
30	Single parent households (%)	U.S. Census Bureau, Current Population Survey. *http://www.census.gov/hhes/families/*
	Civic and Cultural Engagement	
31	Average charitable contribution per itemized tax return (2012 dollars)	U.S. Internal Revenue Service, Statistics of Income - Individual Income Tax Returns (IRS Publication 1304). *http://www.irs.gov/uac/SOI-Tax-Stats-Individual-Income-Tax-Returns-Publication-1304-(Complete-Report)*
32	Voting for President (% of voting age population)	The Office of the Clerk of the U.S. House of Representatives and the U.S. Census Bureau, Current Population Survey. *http://www.census.gov/cps/*
33	Persons volunteering (% age 16 and older)	Bureau of Labor Statistics, Current Population Survey. *http://www.bls.gov/cps*
34	Attendance at visual or performing arts activity, including movie-going (% age 18 and older)	The National Endowment for the Arts, Survey of Public Participation in the Arts & Annual Arts Benchmarking Survey.
35	Reading: Novels or short stories, poetry, or plays (not required for work or school; % age 18 and older)	The National Endowment for the Arts, Survey of Public Participation in the Arts & Annual Arts Benchmarking Survey.
	Socioeconomic	
	Education	
36	High school graduates (% of age 25-34)	U.S. Census Bureau, Decennial Census and American Community Survey. *http://www.census.gov/prod/www/decennial.html* and *http://www.census.gov/acs*
37	College graduates (% of age 25-34)	U.S. Census Bureau, Decennial Census and American Community Survey. *http://www.census.gov/prod/www/decennial.html* and *http://www.census.gov/acs*
38	Reading achievement score (age 17)	National Center for Education Statistics, National Assessment of Educational Progress. *http://nces.ed.gov/nationsreportcard/*
39	Math achievement score (age 17)	National Center for Education Statistics, National Assessment of Educational Progress. *http://nces.ed.gov/nationsreportcard/*
40	Science and engineering graduate degrees (% of total graduate degrees)	National Center for Education Statistics, Integrated Postsecondary Education Data System. *http://nces.ed.gov/ipeds/*
41	Receiving special education services (% of age 3-21 public school students)	National Center for Education Statistics, Digest of Education Statistics, 2012. *http://nces.ed.gov/programs/digest/d12/tables/dt12_046.asp*
	Income, Savings, and Inequality	
42	Real median income: all households (2014 dollars)	U.S. Census Bureau, Current Population Survey, Annual Social and Economic Supplements. *http://www.census.gov/hhes/www/income/data/historical/household/*
43	Real disposable income per capita (chained 2009 dollars)	Bureau of Economic Analysis, National Economic Accounts Data. *http://www.bea.gov/national/*
44	Adjusted gross income share of top 1% of all taxpayers	U.S. Internal Revenue Service, Statistics of Income. *http://www.irs.gov/uac/SOI-Tax-Stats-Individual-Statistical-Tables-by-Tax-Rate-and-Income-Percentile*
45	Adjusted gross income share of lower 50% of all taxpayers	U.S. Internal Revenue Service, Statistics of Income. *http://www.irs.gov/uac/SOI-Tax-Stats-Individual-Statistical-Tables-by-Tax-Rate-and-Income-Percentile*
46	Personal saving rate (% of disposable personal income)	Bureau of Economic Analysis, National Economic Accounts Data. *http://www.bea.gov/national/*
47	Poverty rate (%)	U.S. Census Bureau, Current Population Survey, Annual Social and Economic Supplements. *http://www.census.gov/hhes/www/poverty/publications/pubs-cps.html*
48	Food-insecure households (% of all households)	Economic Research Service, Household Food Security in the United States report series. *http://www.ers.usda.gov/topics/food-nutrition-assistance/food-security-in-the-us/readings.aspx*
49	Supplemental Nutrition Assistance Program (% of population on SNAP)	Food and Nutrition Service, USDA
50	Median wealth of households, age 55-64 (in thousands of 2013 dollars)	Board of Governors of the Federal Reserve System, Survey of Consumer Finances 2013 Estimates inflation-adjusted to 2013 dollars (Internal Data) *http://www.federalreserve.gov/econresdata/scf/scfindex.htm*
	Housing	
51	Homeownership among households with children (%)	U.S. Census Bureau, American Housing Survey (Current Housing Report). Estimated by Housing and Urban Development's Office of Policy Development and Research. *http://www.census.gov/housing/ahs*
52	Families with children and severe housing cost burden (%)	U.S. Census Bureau, American Housing Survey. Tabulated by Housing and Urban Development's Office of Policy Development and Research. *http://www.census.gov/housing/ahs*
53	Families with children and inadequate housing (%)	U.S. Census Bureau, American Housing Survey. Tabulated by Housing and Urban Development's Office of Policy Development and Research. *http://www.census.gov/housing/ahs*
	Health	
	Health Status	
54	Life expectancy at birth (years)	Centers for Disease Control and Prevention, National Center for Health Statistics, Health, United States 2015 forthcoming, Table 15.
55	Infant mortality (per 1,000 live births)	Centers for Disease Control and Prevention, National Center for Health Statistics, Health, United States, 2015 forthcoming, Table 11.
56	Low birthweight [<2,500 gms] (% of babies)	Centers for Disease Control and Prevention, National Center for Health Statistics, National Vital Statistics System (natality); Births: Final data for 2014: *http://www.cdc.gov/nchs/data/nvsr/nvsr64/nvsr64_12.pdf.*

Table 5–2. SOURCES FOR SOCIAL INDICATORS—Continued

	Indicator	Source
57	Activity limitation (% of age 5-17)	Centers for Disease Control and Prevention, National Center for Health Statistics, National Health Interview Survey; America's Children in Brief: Key National Indicators of Well-Being, Table HEALTH5, crude percentages; http://www.childstats.gov/americaschildren/tables/health5.asp?popup=true.
58	Activity limitation (% of age 18 and over)	Centers for Disease Control and Prevention, National Center for Health Statistics, National Health Interview Survey, http://www.cdc.gov/nchs/nhis.htm, Health, United States, 2015 forthcoming, Table 42, age-adjusted.
59	Difficulties with activities of daily living (% of age 65 and over)	Center for Disease Control and Prevention, National Center for Health Statistics, National Health Interview Survey: http://www.cdc.gov/nchs/nhis.htm (unpublished data).
	Health Behavior	
60	Engaged in regular physical activity (% of age 18 and older)	Centers for Disease Control and Prevention, National Center for Health Statistics, National Health Interview Survey, http://www.cdc.gov/nchs/nhis.htm, Health, United States, 2015 forthcoming, Table 57, age adjusted.
61	Obesity (% of age 20-74 with BMI 30 or greater)	Centers for Disease Control and Prevention, National Center for Health Statistics, National Health and Nutrition Examination Survey, http://www.cdc.gov/nchs/nhanes.htm. Health E-stat: http://www.cdc.gov/nchs/data/hestat/obesity_adult_11_12/obesity_adult_11_12.pdf and unpublished data (2013).
62	Obesity (% of age 2-19)	Centers for Disease Control and Prevention, National Center for Health Statistics, National Health and Nutrition Examination Survey, http://www.cdc.gov/nchs/nhanes.htm. Health E-stat: http://www.cdc.gov/nchs/data/hestat/obesity_child_11_12/obesity_child_11_12.pdf and unpublished data (2013).
63	Cigarette smokers (% of age 18 and older)	Centers for Disease Control and Prevention, National Center for Health Statistics, National Health Interview Survey, http://www.cdc.gov/nchs/nhis.htm, Health, United States, 2015 forthcoming, Table 47 and unpublished data (1970 and 1980), age adjusted.
64	Heavier drinker (% of age 18 and older)	Centers for Disease Control and Prevention, National Center for Health Statistics, National Health Interview Survey, http://www.cdc.gov/nchs/nhis.htm, Health, United States, 2014, Table 58 and unpublished data (2014), age adjusted.
	Access to Health Care	
65	Total national health expenditures (% of GDP)	Centers for Medicare and Medicaid Services, National Health Expenditures Data. http://www.cms.gov/Research-Statistics-Data-and-Systems/Statistics-Trends-and-Reports/NationalHealthExpendData/index.html
66	Persons without health insurance (% of age 18-64)	Centers for Disease Control and Prevention, National Center for Health Statistics, National Health Interview Survey.
67	Persons without health insurance (% of age 17 and younger)	Centers for Disease Control and Prevention, National Center for Health Statistics, National Health Interview Survey.
68	Children age 19-35 months with recommended vaccinations (%)	Centers for Disease Control and Prevention, National Center for Health Statistics, National Immunization Survey: http://www.cdc.gov/vaccines/imz-managers/coverage/nis/child/index.html, Health, United States, 2015 forthcoming, Table 66.
	Security and Safety	
	Crime	
69	Property crimes (per 100,000 households)	Bureau of Justice Statistics, National Crime Victimization Survey. http://www.bjs.gov/index.cfm?ty=dcdetail&iid=245
70	Violent crime victimizations (per 100,000 population age 12 or older)	Bureau of Justice Statistics, National Crime Victimization Survey. http://www.bjs.gov/index.cfm?ty=dcdetail&iid=245
71	Murder rate (per 100,000 persons)	Federal Bureau of Investigation, Uniform Crime Reports, Crime in the United States. http://www.fbi.gov/about-us/cjis/ucr/ucr
	National Security	
72	Military personnel on active duty (thousands)	ES actuals for 1960 and 1970 as reported in Table 2-11 of the DoD Selected Manpower Statistics for FY 1997 (DoD WHS, Directorate for Information Operations and Reports). The source for the remaining fiscal year actuals are the Service budget justification books.
73	Veterans (thousands)	U.S. Department of Veterans Affairs. 1960-1999 (Annual Report of the Secretary of Veterans Affairs); 2000-2009 (VetPop07); 2010-2012 (VetPop11); 2013-2015 (VetPop2014), Office of the Actuary. http://www.va.gov/vetdata/Veteran_Population.asp
	Transportation Safety	
74	Safety belt use (%)	National Highway Traffic Safety Administration, National Center for Statistics and Analysis. http://www-nrd.nhtsa.dot.gov/Pubs/811875.pdf
75	Highway fatalities	National Highway Traffic Safety Administration, National Center for Statistics and Analysis. http://www-nrd.nhtsa.dot.gov/Pubs/812032.pdf
	Environment and Energy	
	Air Quality and Greenhouse Gases	
76	Ground level ozone (ppm)	U.S. Environmental Protection Agency, AirTrends Website. http://www.epa.gov/airtrends/ozone.html
77	Particulate matter 2.5 (ug/m3)	U.S. Environmental Protection Agency, AirTrends Website. http://www.epa.gov/airtrends/pm.html
78	Annual mean atmospheric CO_2 concentration (Mauna Lao, Hawaii; ppm)	National Oceanic and Atmospheric Administration. http://www.esrl.noaa.gov/gmd/ccgg/trends/

Table 5–2.   SOURCES FOR SOCIAL INDICATORS—Continued

	Indicator	Source
79	Gross greenhouse gas emissions (teragrams CO2 equivalent)	U.S. Environmental Protection Agency, Inventory of U.S. Greenhouse Gas Emissions and Sinks: 1990-2013. *http://epa.gov/climatechange/ghgemissions/usinventoryreport.html*
80	Net greenhouse gas emissions, including sinks (teragrams CO2 equivalent)	U.S. Environmental Protection Agency, Inventory of U.S. Greenhouse Gas Emissions and Sinks: 1990-2013. *http://epa.gov/climatechange/ghgemissions/usinventoryreport.html*
81	Gross greenhouse gas emissions per capita (metric tons CO2 equivalent)	U.S. Environmental Protection Agency, Inventory of U.S. Greenhouse Gas Emissions and Sinks: 1990-2013. *http://epa.gov/climatechange/ghgemissions/usinventoryreport.html*
82	Gross greenhouse gas emissions per 2009$ of GDP (kilograms CO2 equivalent)	U.S. Environmental Protection Agency, Inventory of U.S. Greenhouse Gas Emissions and Sinks: 1990-2013. *http://epa.gov/climatechange/ghgemissions/usinventoryreport.html*
	Energy	
83	Energy consumption per capita (million Btu)	U.S. Energy Information Administration, Monthly Energy Review (December 2015), Table 1.7 *http://www.eia.gov/totalenergy/data/monthly/index.cfm*
84	Energy consumption per 2009$ GDP (thousand Btu per 2009$)	U.S. Energy Information Administration, Monthly Energy Review (December 2015), Table 1.7 *http://www.eia.gov/totalenergy/data/monthly/index.cfm*
85	Electricity net generation from renewable sources, all sectors (% of total)	U.S. Energy Information Administration, Monthly Energy Review (December 2015), Table 7.2a *http://www.eia.gov/totalenergy/data/monthly/index.cfm*

6. DELIVERING A HIGH-PERFORMANCE GOVERNMENT

Building a government that works smarter, better, and more efficiently to deliver results for the American people is a cornerstone of this Administration. Since taking office, the President has challenged Federal leaders and managers to build a Government that is leaner, smarter, and more effective, while delivering the best results for the American taxpayer.

The Administration has continued to shift the emphasis from simply publishing performance information to focus on increasing its use to inform decision-making and deliver greater impact for the American public. Looking to incorporate successful practices from both private and public organizations, the Administration designed its performance management framework to recognize the critical role senior leadership plays in driving agency results.

In 2010, the Administration worked with the Congress to enact the Government Performance and Results (GPRA) Modernization Act, incorporating performance management best practices while also ensuring reforms and lessons learned were institutionalized to ensure stability. The approach to delivering more effective and efficient Government rests on the following proven management practices:

- Engaging Leaders

- Focusing on Clear Goals and Data-Driven Performance Reviews that Incorporate a Broad Range of Qualitative and Quantitative inputs

- Expanding Impact through Strategic Planning and Strategic Reviews

- Strengthening Agency Capabilities, Collaboration, and Knowledge

- Communicating Performance Results Effectively

Working in conjunction with agencies, the Administration continues to build upon and ingrain these proven management practices in the operations of the Federal Government. This chapter reviews the Federal Government's progress to date as well as looks ahead to efforts to further embed these practices within the Federal performance management framework.

Engaging Leaders

Frequent and sustained leadership engagement is a key ingredient of an effective performance management system. It fosters a high-performance culture by helping to facilitate dialogue across different parts of the organization that must work together to achieve shared outcomes, empowers employees at all levels by establishing a results-oriented culture, enables the organization to change existing processes to solve problems, and ensure

accountability. Management and leadership engagement are central to government performance, leading organization commitment to performance management through the linkage between resources and results.

Several key leadership roles have been established within the Administration's performance management framework to lead and focus performance management efforts in each agency:

- Chief Operating Officer (COO),

- Performance Improvement Officer (PIO), and

- Goal Leader.

Agency Secretaries or equivalents name a Chief Operating Officer (COO). Often the Deputy Secretary, agency COOs perform a number of specific roles and responsibilities which are outlined by OMB, serving to both elevate accountability as well as drive agency performance. From conducting quarterly data-driven performance reviews to setting clear and ambitious goals to improve results and reduce costs, COOs provide the organizational leadership to improve performance by bringing a broader set of players together to overcome challenges across the organization while empowering accountable officials to lead and make data-driven decisions. Each COO names a Performance Improvement Officer (PIO) to support agency heads and COOs by leading efforts to drive coordinated performance improvement practices across the organization, amongst program managers, and with other agencies.

Agency heads and COOs identify Goal Leaders for each Strategic Objective and Agency Priority Goal (APG), which are implementation-focused two-year priorities set by agencies to accelerate progress towards achieving ambitious goals. Accountable for implementation efforts, Goal Leaders are agency officials that lead an agency's collective strategy for realizing strategic objectives and APG outcomes. From determining implementation strategies to managing execution toward goal objectives, engaging team members, and making course corrections as appropriate, Goal Leader responsibilities often bridge traditional organizational boundaries to ensure all programs and components needed to deliver against a specified goal are engaged throughout planning, implementation, and evaluation. Over 90 Goal Leaders led agency performance management practices during the Federal Government's most recently completed two-year APG cycle covering Fiscal Years (FY) 2014-2015, and have already begun executing strategies across agencies for achieving results during the current FY 2016-2017 APG performance period.

While efforts to build capabilities on the part of agency performance officials and staff continue, preliminary research has nonetheless validated early successes regarding the Administration's integration of leader engagement in its performance management framework. A 2013 Government Accountability Office (GAO) survey of PIOs at all 24 CFO Act Federal agencies found that most agency COOs, PIOs, Deputy PIOs, Goal Leaders, and other senior-level officials were to a "large extent" involved in processes central to improving agency performance management, such as strategic planning and goal setting, performance measurement and analysis, quarterly data-driven performance reviews, and the communication of agency progress towards performance goals.[1] GAO notes that "PIOs who reported large involvement for themselves generally reported larger involvement for other officials, suggesting that agencies with a strong commitment to performance management were following this philosophy." The designation of senior officials responsible for goal performance and progress has served to not only elevate accountability for performance, but also reinforce the role of leader engagement throughout the performance cycle, further strengthening performance management practices within agencies.

Focusing on Clear Goals and Data-Driven Performance Reviews that Incorporate a Broad Range of Qualitative and Quantitative Inputs

Goal-setting provides agencies an opportunity to outline a clear expectation of the level of success to be achieved during a set period of time. Goals clarify what success is, motivate people, communicate priorities, and mobilize agency resources to tackle challenges while improving the Federal Government's performance, transparency, and accountability to the American people. Through a combination of near-term and longer-term goal-setting, the Administration has focused on implementing a limited number of actionable goal strategies to advance the well-being of the American people, stimulate economic growth and job creation, and cut the costs of service delivery.

Cross-Agency Priority Goals

The Administration uses the CAP Goals to overcome organizational barriers and achieve better performance than one agency can achieve on its own. Moreover, CAP Goals are a key mechanism by which we implement the four pillars of the President's Management Agenda–Effectiveness, Efficiency, Economic Growth, and People and Culture–with eight of the 15 CAP Goals being used to execute that agenda. Specifically, the eight management CAP Goals have been set to achieve some of the most pressing priorities within the Federal Government, including delivering world-class customer service to the American people, smarter IT, expanding shared services across Federal agencies, and modernizing the Federal infrastructure permitting and review process for major infrastructure projects, to name a few. The remaining seven CAP Goals are focused on key mission areas for

the Administration such as improving veterans' mental health and furthering the outcomes of STEM education programs.

For each CAP Goal, Goal Leaders are identified, action plans are developed, and goal teams track performance and discuss results using quarterly data-driven reviews. Progress updates and results are published quarterly on *Performance.gov*. OMB, the Performance Improvement Council (PIC), and agencies have worked together to support progress on CAP Goals. The end of 2015 marks the half-way point in delivery of the CAP Goals, with real progress and successes being realized as agencies work together and break down silos. The following examples are illustrative of the progress being made.

- To achieve the *Customer Service* goal, the General Services Administration launched the Feedback USA customer experience initiative, a simple tool that allows customers to rate their transactional experience by tapping a button at a kiosk. Agencies can use FeedbackUSA to solicit, aggregate, and analyze customer service feedback in real time to quickly act to resolve any issues and improve services to the public. Feedback USA is currently being piloted in two Federal agencies, with individuals registering their customer service experience at 27 Department of State passport processing centers and 14 Social Security Administration card centers. The success of this pilot has led to the initiative being expanded to other agencies, including its planned launch by the Transportation Security Administration in Spring 2016 at four of the nation's busiest airports.

- Positive work has occurred on the part of agencies to achieve the goal of *Improved Mental Health Outcomes for Service Members, Veterans, and their Families*. The inTransition program supports Service Members with behavioral health care as they transition to the VA system. Since the program began tracking cases in the third quarter of FY 2015, over 3,200 new coaching cases have been opened and over 1,400 coaching cases closed. Survey respondents have expressed high levels of satisfaction with inTransition, with 94% indicating the assistance received from the inTransition program increased the likelihood of continuing treatment at the new location, and 95% stating the products and services offered by inTransition met their needs. Newly available data also showed that for those Service members completing a Post-Deployment Health Reassessment (PDHRA) in 2013, who screened positive for PTSD, depression, or alcohol abuse and received a referral to a mental health specialty or behavioral health in primary care, 55% received care at the Department of Veterans Affairs or Department of Defense (FY 2013), up from 46% in 2011 and performing well against a target of 56% by FY 2016.

- Efforts to *Modernize the Federal Infrastructure Permitting and Review Process* have also returned promising results, with the Administration's permitting team working closely with Congress to establish

---

[1] Agencies Have Elevated Performance Management Leadership Roles, but Additional Training is Needed. Through the results of GAO's PIO survey, GAO found most key officials were "greatly involved in central aspects of performance management." April 2013. *www.gao.gov/products/GAO-13-356.*

a Federal Permitting Improvement Council as part of the FAST ("Fixing America's Surface Transportation") Act. The Federal Permitting Improvement Council will provide technical assistance on infrastructure permitting, including developing model performance timelines for commonly required infrastructure project permits and reviews, maintaining a public dashboard to increase transparency and accountability for coordinated permitting timetables, and supporting new fee structures for project proponents to reimburse the Federal Government for reasonable permitting and review costs. In 2015, the U.S. Army Corps of Engineers, Department of Transportation, U.S. Coast Guard and three other agencies also released the first update in nearly 30 years to the Synchronizing Environmental Reviews for Transportation and Other Infrastructure Projects handbook (known as the Red Book). The Red Book provides practical, real-world guidance to Federal agencies, applicants, project sponsors, and consultants on how to improve the efficiency and effectiveness of key permits and reviews required for these project.

• To achieve the *Shared Services* goal the Administration announced the establishment of the first-ever, government-wide shared services management and oversight operation model for delivering mission support functions such as financial management, human resources, and acquisition. A new cross-governmental Shared Services Governance Board, led by OMB, was launched to serve as the decision-making body for the shared services ecosystem. A Unified Shared Services Management (USSM) office is also being established within the General Services Administration (GSA) to serve as an integration body for the ecosystem, working across functions, providers and consumers to improve shared service delivery and increase agency adoption. This new model will expand shared services to acquisitions, grants, and information technology by leveraging lessons learned from prior successes in financial management and human resources, such as the consolidation of government-wide payroll operations, or the Department of Housing and Urban Development's (HUD) successful transition of many of its core financial management and human resource functions to the Department of the Treasury in October 2015.

Though these examples do not encapsulate the entirety of performance accomplishments made in pursuit of CAP goals, they nonetheless offer a brief glimpse into the hard work and promising initiatives being launched by agencies to strengthen the way Government works. And while the results on CAP Goal progress are encouraging, challenges nonetheless remain on program and service delivery across agency boundaries. Often few resources are dedicated to identifying and solving interagency challenges. In many instances, significant management improvements require investments that cut across agencies. Towards this end, the Administration has taken steps to institutionalize capacity to address cross-cutting challenges.

First, consistent with authority granted in FY 2016, the President's FY 2017 Budget includes authority for agencies, with prior notification to Congress from the Director of OMB, to transfer up to $15 million from agency budgets to support these cross-cutting management initiatives. This institutionalizes a capability to fund cross-agency efforts, rather than handling them on a case-by-case basis, and provides a powerful tool to turn management reforms ideas into real and lasting results for the American people. Absent this continued authority, CAP Goal leaders are constrained in their ability to implement effective solutions across agencies, leaving various Federal programs and activities to address shared issues in a duplicative, siloed, and ad hoc way.

Second, in November 2015, the inaugural class of 16 White House Leadership Development Program (WHLDP) fellows began their one-year rotations providing additional support to implement the CAP Goals. Originally announced by the President in December 2014, the WHLDP is an initiative to deliver on the President's Management Agenda, representing a continued commitment to developing and strengthening the next generation of Federal career leaders while increasing our capacity to make progress on issues that cut across multiple agencies. Program fellows are comprised of emerging leaders and Senior Executive Service (SES) candidates, and through a one-year rotational assignment, are assigned to work on the Federal Government's highest priority and highest impact challenges that require the coordination of multiple Federal agencies to succeed. Through the WHLDP, the Administration is focused on developing and unlocking the full potential of the Federal workforce to drive greater effectiveness and efficiency within government and better harness taxpayer resources. Over the course of the next year, these emerging leaders will play a key role in addressing the government's critical management challenges with participants gaining valuable experience as they take on leadership roles in their agency.

Agency Priority Goals

Agency Priority Goals are used to achieve an agency's near-term, implementation-focused priorities. Agencies establish Priority Goals every two years and use clearly-identified Goal Leaders and Deputy Goal Leaders and quarterly metrics and milestones to manage progress. COOs lead quarterly data-driven performance reviews to overcome barriers and accelerate performance results. Progress on APGs is updated publicly on a quarterly basis with data and progress reported on *Performance.gov*. Agency leaders have set goals for improving access to capital to enhance job creation, reducing foodborne illness through targeted inspections, coordinating multiple agency services to reduce veteran homelessness, and reducing hospital acquired infections.

Since 2009, the Administration has seen measurable progress from the use of Agency Priority Goals. Illustrative examples of performance results achieved this past year include:

- *Restoring Vitality to Contaminated Sites.* The Environmental Protection Agency's Superfund, Resource Conservation and Recovery Act (RCRA) corrective action (CA), leaking underground storage tank (LUST), and Brownfields cleanup programs reduce risks to human health and the environment by assessing and cleaning up contaminated sites to enhance the livability and economic vitality of neighborhoods. Since the EPA began collecting the number of sites ready for anticipated use (RAU) in FY 2008, the cumulative number of sites RAU has increased. As of the end of FY 2015, more than 463,500 sites were made ready for anticipated use with the EPA adding 21,836 RAU sites over the course of the FY 2014-2015 APG cycle and exceeding the agency's goal of 18,970 RAU sites by 15%.

- *Reduce the Federal Footprint.* The General Services Administration established a goal of reducing the amount of Federal leased office space by 5% for replacement leases by the end of FY 2015. GSA reduced federally leased office space by a half-million square feet which far exceeds its target throughout the FY 2014-2015 goal cycle.

- *Decreasing Veterans' Disability Claims Backlog.* Improving customer service and reducing the length of time it takes to process disability claims are integral to the Department of Veterans' Affairs (VA) mission of providing benefits to eligible Veterans in a timely and efficient manner. Between March 2013 and September 30, 2015, the claims backlog (defined as claims that have been pending over 125 days) was reduced from 611,073 to 71,352 claims, a decrease of 88.3%. Moreover, while decreasing the disability claims backlog, the VA also increased the accuracy of processing the claims, with nearly 98% accuracy across all categories.

- *Access to Capital and Disaster Loan Application Rate.* Providing access to capital, particularly to survivors of natural disasters, has been one of the Small Business Administration's critical strategies in meeting its objective to drive business formation, job growth and economic expansion. Helping expand the agency's footprint to increase small businesses access to capital, the SBA added 292 new and returning lenders to its flagship lending program as these lenders made 752 loans totaling over $260 million in capital funding in FY 2015. Additionally, the agency has sought to increase the return rate for disaster survivor applications by the end of September, 2015. Since implementing a new process for issuing applications to disaster survivors in Presidential disaster declarations for Individual Assistance (IA), SBA has attained a disaster loan application return rate of 98% at the end of FY 2015. SBA's new process for issuing applications in Presidential-IA declarations helped increase the application return rate and im-

proves customer service by adding multiple touch points with disaster survivors.

Fiscal Year 2016 marked both the end of the FY 2014-2015 APG cycle as well as the beginning of an updated round of APGs covering FY 2016-2017. At the start of FY 2016, major Federal agencies working in conjunction with OMB announced 99 APGs for the new two-year cycle covering FY 2016-2017. This is the fourth cohort of APGs of this Administration, and included the continuation of approximately sixty percent of the APGs from the FY 2014-2015 cohort. Progress to date on APGs is encouraging and leading to measurable improvements on the ground. Over eighty percent of APGs able to be assessed in the FY 2014-2015 cycle saw improved performance during the course of the goal period. The 99 APGs announced for the FY 2016-2017 cycle will focus agencies over the next two years to improve near-term outcomes that at the same time advance progress towards longer-term, outcome-focused strategic goals and objectives within each agency's four-year strategic plan.

With this Budget, agencies have identified action plans for each of these goals, ranging from the Department of Housing and Urban Development's goal to end homelessness by reducing the total number of homeless families, youth and children, and people experiencing chronic homelessness, to Department of Justice efforts to protect the most vulnerable within society, including victims and survivors of human trafficking, and the Department of the Interior's initiatives to improve the graduation rate of tribal high school students and facilitate tribal self-determination in shaping the educational curriculum for students. Looking ahead, agencies continue to build upon the successes and performance outcomes achieved over the past two years while charting new and even more ambitious priority performance goals. Agencies and their Goal Leaders have announced their plans for achieving targets outlined in the FY 2016-2017 APGs, and as with prior APG cycles, updates will continue to be published to *Performance.gov*.

Studies on implementation of the Administration's new performance management approach point towards a broader, more measureable impact across agencies through the use of performance measures in the budget process. Results of recent research have yielded promising insights in terms of CAP Goals, APGs, and the quarterly data-driven review process leading to greater rates of performance information use by agency leadership to assess progress and inform decisions surrounding resource allocations. Using data from nationwide surveys[2] conducted over the last decade by GAO in the major 24 agencies, researchers have found evidence that mid- and upper-level Federal managers engaged in the implementation of the priority goals, and exposed to data-driven reviews, were significantly more likely to "use performance data to

---

[2] Agencies' Trends in the Use of Performance Information to Make Decisions. GAO measured agency use of performance information by creating an index from manager survey data collected in 2007 and 2013. The index reflected the extent to which managers reported that their agencies used performance information for various management activities. September 2014. *http://www.gao.gov/products/GAO-14-747*.

manage programs and employees, and identify and solve problems," suggesting "success...where prior [Federal] reforms have struggled".[3] Such early successes regarding performance information use have been further expanded beyond the context of priority goals and data-driven reviews, incorporating strategic planning and reviews to further inform strategic decision-making, budget formulation, and near-term agency actions in addition to initiatives for strengthening the resources of performance management staff within agencies.

Expanding Impact Through Strategic Plans and Strategic Reviews

New agency strategic plans were published in February 2014 on *Performance.gov* and agency websites concurrent with the President's FY 2015 Budget. Agencies are now in the 3rd year of these strategic plans, which serve to chart a course for long-term agency performance over a five-year time horizon, define agency missions, long-term goals and objectives, and strategies planned for achieving these objectives. Outcomes are advanced by strategic objectives, which are supported by specific performance goals and indicators. As part of their strategic plans, Federal agencies have identified more than 350 strategic objectives, reflecting the scope of each agency mission as well as the breadth of Federal activities and outcomes.[4]

To expand proven performance management practices further and ensure that agency strategic plans are being implemented and assessed, the Administration established annual strategic reviews. The strategic reviews provide a comprehensive framework at each agency to make informed strategic, budget, legislative, and management decisions based on evidence in alignment with the agency strategic plan. The annual assessments are expected to incorporate not only performance measures, but also evaluation results, challenges, risks, and external factors to inform the decision-making at the agency and OMB. Incentivizing organizations to develop a culture focused on learning and improving performance, strategic reviews help leadership in identifying opportunities for reform proposals and executive actions.

To date, agencies have conducted two rounds of strategic reviews. The 2015 strategic reviews were intended to build upon the successes and gains made by agencies during the first round in 2014. OMB's approach reflects an embrace of a multi-year maturity model, recognizing that effective reviews would take multiple years to establish as part of a planning and review process that adds value to agency's strategic and performance planning activities. As such, agencies are provided flexibility to tailor their reviews to the uniqueness of agency missions and capabilities. OMB has also encouraged agencies to use proven management principles for their implementation, such as leveraging existing business processes, engaging the ap-

propriate stakeholders, and balancing a focus on learning from the reviews with a focus on accountability. Progress updates for each major agency's strategic objectives are available on *Performance.gov*, and also in annual agency Performance Reports.

Reflecting on 2015 Reviews, Looking Ahead to 2016

In 2015, the Administration established "FedStat," which combined Strategic Reviews with two other data-driven reviews–PortfolioStat and Benchmarking–in order to facilitate one integrated review among senior Administration and agency leadership. In preparing for the 2015 strategic review, agencies focused their assessments on providing a snapshot of mission performance with a prioritized focus on mission support functions to achieve performance gains in efficiency and effectiveness. To facilitate management decisions, agencies also made meaningful distinctions in performance across strategic objective assessments, identifying areas of noteworthy progress as well as where significant challenges existed. Agencies were asked to identify only a limited number of areas where the agency made noteworthy progress and a limited number as focus areas for improvement. Areas demonstrating noteworthy progress could be identified as a result of new innovations in strategy, program design, or operations that have led to notable improvements in outcomes or cost reductions. Focus areas for improvement could be the result of challenges during program execution, for example, or when a problem the strategic objective seeks to address is growing more quickly than current actions or resources can address it.

Across the strategic objectives analyzed in 2015, agencies identified approximately 15% as making noteworthy progress, and 10% as focus area for improvement, a slight improvement over 2014's assessments. The validity and implications of these findings will continue to be reviewed annually for refinement as agency's strategic review and performance management capabilities continue to mature and strengthen. More information is available in the progress updates provided for each major agency's strategic objectives on *Performance.gov*, and in the 2015 Annual Performance Reports. Agencies have summarized proposed next steps in their 2017 Annual Performance Plans.

Based on feedback, the Administration's strategic review policy confers a range of benefits, including improved interagency collaboration, a chance to identify evidence gaps and opportunities to improve data quality to inform better resource allocation decisions, and further institutionalizing a strategic review policy framework that uses data-driven performance reviews to improve decision-making as part of the budget formulation process. The Department of the Interior offers an example of such an approach. The agency makes funding allocations related to each of the strategic objectives based on its department-wide strategic plan and an assessment of its performance measures. Past performance and future targets are discussed in the context of the accompanying trends in funding, including past allocated funding and future corresponding budget projections. This is especially useful for those programmatic areas where performance

---

[3] Moynihan, Donald, & Kroll, Alexander. "Performance Management Routines that Work? An Early Assessment of the GPRA Modernization Act." Public Administration Review, DOI: *10.1111/puar*.12434. *http://onlinelibrary.wiley.com/doi/10.1111/puar.12434/abstract.*

[4] The 350 objectives do not include all government corporations and independent establishments. Rather, this number consists of the 24 CFO Act Agencies excluding the Nuclear Regulatory Commission.

takes more than one year of funding and effort to realize results. While the Department of the Interior's strategic plan integrates across the various bureaus to show how the different programmatic efforts in the different bureaus contribute to related goals, funding allocations are provided by individual bureaus and the budget activity or program supporting each strategic objective. This approach at the Department of the Interior illustrates the performance and budget link, based on evidence and evaluation, which the strategic review process is intended to inform within agencies.

Looking ahead to 2016, the upcoming round of strategic reviews will look to cement gains made in agencies' capacity for conducting effective reviews, advancing them further along the maturity model by providing an appropriate policy structure and framework to anchor their strategic plans and review processes. OMB guidance largely aligns with and complements several practices for conducting effective agency strategic reviews recently identified by GAO,[5] underscoring the importance of providing a strong policy framework in which to institutionalize this critical component of performance management. As OMB, the PIC, and agencies share best practices and lessons learned from previous rounds of strategic reviews, the Administration anticipates they will play an expanded role in informing budget development and operational decisions, facilitating a broader improvement in the use of evidence for decision-making by managers across the Federal Government.

Strengthening Agency Capabilities, Collaboration, and Knowledge

Since its establishment, the Performance Improvement Council (PIC) continues to play an important role in sharpening and broadening the application of performance management tools throughout the Federal Government by providing opportunities for Federal program managers and performance professionals to share practices and build their own capabilities.

The PIC offers a number of ways for agencies to collaborate and build capabilities. Most recently the PIC released the results from a working group involving individuals from across Law Enforcement entities in the Federal Government. This working group explored some of the challenges of performance measurement in their particular work. In the lead-up to the 2014 strategic review sessions, the PIC hosted several strategic review-themed summits for agencies, and published a training guide on leading an effective strategic review as a follow-up to agency's initial experiences. The PIC holds a speaker series on performance issues and convenes a number of larger-scale government-wide events for employees to work together to solve common challenges around implementation of the Government Performance and Results Modernization Act. These collaboration opportunities have brought together hundreds of people across two dozen agencies and will continue in 2016.

In addition to ongoing working groups, summits, and speaker series, the PIC has launched two websites in recent years, expanding its reach and impact to the larger government performance community through a strengthened online presence. Their namesake website, *PIC.gov*, provides news about the Federal performance management and improvement community. The Performance Learning Center at *LearnPerformance.gov* has been operating in beta form but will be updated in 2016, and promises to be a one-stop-shop for online training, resources, and career development for federal performance measurement and management. *LearnPerformance.gov* will provide users with a variety of learning resources and training course information, and is designed for multiple audiences, including performance analysts, program managers, and others contributing to government performance management.

The PIC has also led in establishing innovative, cross-agency initiatives focused on strengthening agency performance management capabilities that move agency progress on performance goals. The PIC engages in building capacity for those new to the performance field through an established training program offered at no charge to Federal employees three-times per year, as well as a professional development program called the Performance Enthusiast and Ambassador Program. These programs invest in community members through building their knowledge and skills in performance management and measurement, ultimately transferring that knowledge back to their agency.

Supporting a facilitative approach to cross-agency collaboration, the PIC's Collaboration Studio team successfully delivered 65 engagements during FY 2015, with a focus ranging from cross-agency and agency priority goals to supporting agency and policy council teams in building better clarity on goals and outcomes. In one illustrative example, the Collaboration Studio team led the design and implementation of the IT Solutions Challenge Initiative for the Federal CIO, finding innovative solutions based on the fresh perspectives of Federal IT staff. In 2016, the Collaboration Studio will continue to focus on using action-based approaches to help teams solve leadership and cross-cutting government challenges.

And lastly, the Leaders Delivery Network (LDN) is a leadership and cross-agency networking program designed for APG deputy goal leaders across the Federal Government. Throughout the FY 2016-2017 APG cycle, a cohort of approximately 25 leaders from 17 major agencies will meet bi-monthly to engage with high profile speakers, discuss challenges, and share best practices in program management and implementation. LDN participants are also offered several additional opportunities throughout the two-year cycle, including coaching, individualized managerial consultations, and self-assessments that help target opportunities for professional growth and results.

Through efforts like the LDN and Collaboration Studio, the PIC and OMB continue to strengthen the performance management framework, spark targeted improvements, and most importantly, expand agency capabilities and capacity for performance management. Collaboration

---

[5] Practices for Effective Agency Strategic Reviews. July 2015. *http://www.gao.gov/products/GAO-15-602.*

across the PIC and OMB will continue to be a priority in order to promote learning and innovation in performance management in 2016 and beyond.

Communicating Performance Results Effectively

Performance.gov offers an online portal to Federal performance management efforts, helping to improve accountability by providing one, centralized reporting location for the public to find information on agency programs, goals, and regular progress updates towards achieving APGs and CAP Goals. In support of the President's commitment to transparency and implementation of the GPRA Modernization Act, the Administration continues to develop *Performance.gov* to inform stakeholders on performance improvement on the part of major Federal agencies.

Formal, cross-collaborative structures have been created to assist in this endeavor and make continued advancements in this important aspect of Federal performance management policy. Chartered in 2013, the Performance Management Line of Business (PMLOB) was founded with a charge to take a lead role in overseeing future development of *Performance.gov*. An interagency effort comprised of representatives from major Federal agencies, OMB, and the PIC, the PMLOB works collaboratively to develop government-wide performance management capabilities to help meet the transparency requirements of the GPRAMA. PMLOB continues to support the evolution of *Performance.gov* from a site that is not just a GPRAMA-compliant tool, but to one that communicates performance results effectively and offers a cohesive, comprehensive view of Federal performance.

Performance Agenda Looking Ahead

The work of the Federal Government has a tangible effect on people's lives – on small business-owners who need loans, on young people who want to go to college,

on the men and women in our Armed Forces who need the best resources when in uniform and who, after they have served, deserve the benefits they earned. Whether protecting individuals and communities, modernizing infrastructure, investing in our children, or taking care of the most vulnerable, the American people deserve a highly effective government. Delivering high-performing Federal programs for the American people is not the exception, but the norm. Building a government that works smarter, better, and more efficiently to deliver results for the American people is a cornerstone of this Administration. The five management practices outlined in this chapter inform the Administration's approach to delivering on the goal of a high performing Federal Government, and offer descriptive insight into the progress that has been achieved by agencies to date.

These practices provide the framework to shape future initiatives in Federal performance management. As work continues on agency internal controls and enterprise risk management, 2016 offers an opportunity to integrate risk management profiles around mission and mission support functions in agency strategic planning and reviews. Opportunities also exist for collaboration and integration across evidence, evaluation, and performance teams.

The Administration is strongly committed to the President's charge to deliver a government that works, a government that is smarter, leaner, and more effective, one that produces tangible results all around us – in a small business opening its doors, more homes becoming energy-efficient, new wind turbines generating clean renewable energy, healthier children, better served veterans, and falling crime rates. Leadership engagement, clear goals, measurement, analysis of progress, and frequent progress reviews to find and promote what works and fix or eliminate what does not are keys to improving the lives of the American people.

7. BUILDING THE CAPACITY TO PRODUCE AND USE EVIDENCE

> *"We usually do better when we're on the side of facts and evidence and science. Just as a general rule, that's proved to be our strength as Americans."*
>
> —President Obama, *"Remarks by the President to the Business Roundtable"* September 16, 2015

The President has made it clear that policy decisions should be driven by evidence—evidence about what works and what does not, and evidence that identifies the greatest needs and opportunities to solve great challenges. The Administration is committed to living up to this principle through a broad-based set of activities to better integrate evidence and rigorous evaluation in budget, management, and policy decisions, including through: (1) making better use of data already collected by government agencies; (2) promoting the use of high-quality, low-cost evaluations and rapid, iterative experimentation in addition to larger evaluations examining long-term outcomes; (3) adopting more evidence-based structures for grant programs; and (4) strengthening agency evidence-building capacity and developing tools to better communicate what works.[1]

There is a growing momentum for these evidence-based approaches at all levels of government, as well as among nonprofits, foundations, faith-based institutions, and community-based organizations. The Administration's embrace of these approaches has resulted in important gains in areas ranging from reducing veterans' homelessness, to improving educational outcomes, to enhancing the effectiveness of international development programs. The 2017 Budget advances these approaches through a range of investments in evidence building, as well as by increasing investment in programs with strong evidence of effectiveness. These proposals are described in the main budget volume and accompanying documents.[2]

All of these efforts embody the simple guiding principle that: "Where evidence is strong, we should act on it. Where evidence is suggestive, we should consider it. Where evidence is weak, we should build the knowledge to support better decisions in the future."[3] In order to integrate this guiding principle in all aspects of government

decision-making, it is essential that Federal agencies develop the capacity to credibly build and use evidence and implement a culture that supports doing so—and many agencies are making progress in doing so. Given the centrality of agency capacity to these efforts, this chapter focuses on a few specific components of capacity, especially the principles and practices that support credible evaluation functions.

What is Evidence and How Should it be Used?

The best government programs use a broad range of analytical and management tools, which collectively comprise an "evidence infrastructure," to learn what works (and what does not) for whom and under what circumstances, as well as improve results. Broadly speaking, "evidence" is the available body of facts or information indicating whether a belief or proposition is true or valid. Evidence can be quantitative or qualitative and may come from a variety of sources, including performance measurement, evaluations, statistical series, retrospective reviews, and other data analytics and research.

Evidence cannot be separated from the purposes for which it is being used, and the credible use of evidence in decision-making requires an understanding of what conclusions can and, equally important, cannot be drawn from the information. For example:

- Multiple rigorous impact evaluations, in particular randomized experiments, may provide strong evidence that a particular intervention is effective with a particular population in a particular setting. However, they may be less definitive on how effective that intervention may be in other settings or with other populations.

- Quasi-experimental evidence from large, diverse samples of administrative data may make it easier to generalize across a range of circumstances, but they could lack definitive evidence on causality or be silent on important outcomes not captured in the administrative data.

- Descriptive analyses from Federal statistical series provide context to examine societal and economic trends over time.

- Studies of the observed behavior of individuals, groups, businesses, and other entities can provide

---

[1] Several Administration documents lay out this "evidence agenda," including previous versions of this chapter, the *"Evaluation as a Tool for Improving Federal Programs"* chapter of the Council of Economic Advisers' 2014 Economic Report to the President, and the OMB Memorandum M-13-17, *"Next Steps in the Evidence and Innovation Agenda,"* May 2012, jointly signed by the Office of Management and Budget, the Domestic Policy Council, the Office of Science and Technology Policy, and the Council of Economic Advisers. Many of these documents are available on the OMB website at *http://www.whitehouse.gov/omb/evidence.* In addition, note that *OMB Circular A-11* has been updated to be consistent with many of these principles.

[2] See *http://www.whitehouse.gov/omb/evidence.*

[3] See OMB Memorandum M-12-14, *"Use of Evidence and Evaluation in the 2014 Budget,"* May 2012.

important insights into the dynamics that policies and programs may be designed to address, whether through the use of administrative, survey, or linked datasets. However, they do not provide direct tests of specific policies, nor account for the exigencies of program administration.

- Qualitative and quantitative implementation studies can complement other evidence by providing insight into how programs and practices can be successfully implemented.

- High-quality performance measures can provide valid, reliable, and useful information on program inputs and/or outputs.

Evidence has varying degrees of credibility, and the strongest evidence generally comes from a portfolio of high-quality evidence rather than a single study or data point, i.e., from multiple sources and/or multiple studies covering different aspects and nuances of the topic. While many of these forms of evidence are complementary, some evidence that is useful for one purpose may not be useful for another. For example, performance measures are an essential resource for agencies to understand ongoing, real-time program performance so they can use that information to build a culture of continuous improvement, but they often do not tell us a lot about some key questions, including the effects of programs. Evaluations provide context for the performance measures and help us better understand what can and cannot be learned from them. In particular, rigorous impact evaluations, particularly randomized experiments, can provide the most credible information on the impact of the program on outcomes, isolated from the effects of other factors. Thus combining both performance and evaluation information, and using the results of one to inform the design of the other, can be very powerful in understanding program performance and ensuring that the program is maximizing performance and impact on an ongoing basis.

Examples of Progress

The Administration encourages agencies to generate more high quality evaluations, place greater attention on goal-setting and measuring performance through the implementation of the Government Performance and Results Modernization Action of 2010, increase the use of existing "administrative" data for evidence building, and strengthen the capacity of statistical agencies to build objective and quality evidence. The Administration is committed to acting on available evidence and has proposed to invest in, scale up, or change a variety of programs on the basis of strong evidence that they are effective. These proposals cover a broad range of policy areas including ending homelessness, improving employment outcomes, reducing crime and recidivism, and reducing global poverty and improving global health.

The Administration has also introduced a number of grant program innovations that embed evidence more fundamentally into their structures. Among the most notable advances in this area are "tiered-evidence" or "innovation fund" grant designs that focus resources on practices with strong evidence while also promoting innovation and further evaluation. The Administration has adopted "tiered evidence" grant programs in multiple areas, such as K-12 education interventions, teenage pregnancy prevention, social innovations for communities, voluntary home visitations for parents, and international assistance efforts.

The Administration is also promoting the Pay for Success financing model in a wide range of programs, including for workforce, education, recidivism, housing, and environmental interventions. Pay for Success financing leverages philanthropic and private dollars to fund preventive services and other interventions, which are provided by nonprofits and other non-governmental entities up front, with the Government paying only after the interventions generate sufficient measurable results. Since as early as 2012, agencies including the Departments of Education (ED), Housing and Urban Development (HUD), Justice (DOJ), and Labor (DOL) as well as the Corporation for National and Community Service (CNCS) have been working to implement Pay for Success. So far, Federal agencies have made awards supporting roughly 50 efforts, and still more agencies continue to explore possible applications of this model.

In addition, the Administration created Performance Partnership Pilots for Disconnected Youth that allow States, tribes, and localities to blend funding from various programs and receive waivers under multiple youth-serving programs in order to improve education, employment, and other key outcomes and build evidence about more effective ways to help vulnerable youth. In FY 2015, a consortium of six agencies awarded the first cohort of nine pilots to give State, local, and tribal communities customized flexibility to make a difference in the lives of local youth. Each pilot is conducting a site-specific evaluation of local outcomes, and the Department of Labor is leading an evaluation to look at cross-site implementation of the initiative overall. In FY 2016, the interagency consortium has grown to include HUD alongside ED, DOL, DOJ, the Department of Health and Human Services (HHS), CNCS, and the Institute for Museum and Library Services. In the coming year, this consortium expects to select up to 20 new pilots under two competitions.

At the same time, the Administration has pursued innovative approaches to improve federal capacity to identify more effective strategies. For example, the Administration established the Social and Behavioral Sciences Team (SBST)—a cross-agency group of experts in applied behavioral science—to help agencies translate findings and methods from the social and behavioral sciences into improvements in Federal policies and programs. Due to SBST projects, more military service members are saving for retirement, more students are going to college and better managing their student loans, more Veterans are taking advantage of education and career counseling benefits, more small farms are gaining access to credit, and more families are securing health insurance coverage.[4]

---

[4] For additional information on SBST's work please see their website (*https://sbst.gov/*) and their *2015 Annual Report*.

One common component of SBST's work is making better use of the administrative data that government already collects in order to learn which approaches work best. The Administration encourages all Federal agencies to make better use of these data to identify effective practices, facilitate day-to-day performance measurement, and inform the public about how society and the economy are faring. As discussed in the *"Building Evidence with Administrative Data"* chapter in the *2016 Analytical Perspectives* volume,[5] the ability to access and make better use of these data—while protecting privacy and confidentiality—has played a pivotal role in a range of policy areas, including some of the most innovative grant reforms and increased accountability and transparency across a range of programs. For example, multiple studies on student aid simplification showed the feasibility and importance of simplifying the Free Application for Federal Student Aid (FAFSA), using Federal administrative records as well as survey data. This research influenced the steps the Administration has already taken to simplify the FAFSA and motivated both Administration and Congressional proposals to make further legislative progress.

Principles and Practices that Support Credible Evidence Development

In order for government to make credible use of evidence, the evidence itself must be credible—meaning that it must be objective and of sufficient quality, utility, and integrity. Informed by national and international professional practice, the Federal Government has taken a number of steps to foster the credibility of evidence. For example, pursuant to the Information Quality Act[6] and OMB guidelines,[7] agencies are required to establish procedures to ensure the objectivity, utility, and integrity of information provided to the public, and to match the quality of the study with its intended use.

Similarly, a central theme of the Presidential Memorandum on the Preservation and Promotion of Scientific Integrity[8] and the associated implementation guidance[9] is that the public must be able to trust the science and scientific processes informing public policy decisions. These documents articulate and provide guidance on principles and procedures integral to the preservation and promotion of scientific integrity, including those related to strengthening the actual and perceived credibility of Government research, communicating scientific and technological information to the public, and the importance of shielding scientific data and analysis from undue political influence.

Most recently, OMB issued Statistical Policy Directive 1, Fundamental Responsibilities of Federal Statistical Agencies and Recognized Statistical Units,[10] which affirms the Federal Statistical System's responsibility to produce and disseminate relevant and timely information; conduct credible, accurate, and objective statistical activities; and protect the trust of information providers by ensuring confidentiality and exclusive statistical use of their responses. The framework articulates principles and practices that support these responsibilities and requires Federal statistical agencies and recognized statistical units to adopt policies, best practices, and appropriate procedures to implement these responsibilities. These guidelines and policies provide a common foundation for core statistical agency functions to ensure that the information they provide adheres to a high standard of quality and utility to evidence based decision making.

Under this Administration, several evaluation offices have also established agency-specific statements of evaluation policy—for example *The Administration for Children & Families (ACF) Evaluation Policy* (in the Department of Health and Human Services) and *The Department of Labor Evaluation Policy*. These resources have generated useful conversations and agreements within agencies about their evaluation-related practices and principles.

Many Federal evaluators believe that establishing a common set of government-wide principles and practices for evaluation offices could help to ensure that Federal program evaluations meet scientific standards, are designed to be useful, and are conducted and the results disseminated without bias or undue influence. Establishing these standards is an important building block in furthering agencies' capacity to routinely build and use high-quality evidence to improve program performance, and help evaluation offices maintain standards for their programs across administrations and changes in personnel.

While the process for developing such a set of standards is ongoing, a few fundamental principles emerge as common themes in the established U.S. frameworks discussed above as well as in international frameworks. These principles include: Rigor, Relevance, Independence, Transparency, and Ethics.

Rigor

The accuracy and quality of evaluation results are dependent on the design and implementation of the underlying studies. All forms of evaluation should use the most rigorous methods as appropriate, and should use the most appropriate type of evaluation to answer the specific question(s) being asked. Rigor is not restricted to impact evaluations. It is also necessary in implementation or process evaluations, assessments, descriptive studies, outcome evaluations, and formative evaluations, as well as in both qualitative and quantitative approaches.

There are several practices that agencies use to support the rigor of evaluations. One of the most important is recruiting and maintaining an evaluation workforce with

---

[5] See *"Building Evidence with Administrative Data,"* chapter 7 in the *2016 Analytical Perspectives* volume.

[6] See Section 515 of the Treasury and General Government Appropriations Act, 2001 (Pub. L. No. 106-554, 44 U.S.C. § 3516 note).

[7] See *Guidelines for Ensuring and Maximizing the Quality, Objectivity, Utility, and Integrity of Information Disseminated by Federal Agencies*, February 22, 2002 (67 FR 8452).

[8] See *Memorandum for the Heads of Executive Departments and Agencies 3-9-09*, May 2009.

[9] See OSTP Memorandum, *"Memorandum for the Heads of Executive Departments and Agencies,"* December 2010.

[10] See *Federal Register*, Volume 79, Number 231, Part III, *"Statistical Policy Directive 1, Fundamental Responsibilities of Federal Statistical Agencies and Recognized Statistical Units,"* December 2014

training and experience appropriate for planning and overseeing a rigorous evaluation portfolio. To accomplish this, agencies seeking to maintain or increase the rigor of their evaluation functions recruit staff with advanced degrees and experience in a range of relevant disciplines and provide professional developmental opportunities so that staff can keep their skills current. Agencies have cited hiring and retaining a skilled evaluation workforce as an area of difficulty. The Administration is working on how best to address these issues.

Another practice that helps agencies ensure rigor is the development and implementation of quality review and control procedures. Examples of strong procedures that maintain the integrity of evaluations include technical reviews of all aspects of evaluation designs (methodological design, data collection instruments and procedures, statistical and analytic plans); minimization of the burden of data collection; and external peer reviews by third-party independent technical experts and technical working groups.

Finally, evaluation guidelines and/or frameworks that indicate the standards for high quality evaluations—and how different types of evaluations and studies contribute to the evidence base—facilitate both the production and use of rigorous evidence. OMB encourages agencies to establish such frameworks and make them available as a technical resource for in-house and external evaluators when designing evaluations. These guidelines are also useful when assessing the quality of the evaluation as it was actually implemented.

These guidelines can be particularly powerful when they apply to more than one agency. For example, ED and National Science Foundation (NSF) issued Common

Guidelines for Education Research and Development in 2013.[11] These guidelines clarify how different types of studies contribute to the evidence base, including basic research and impact evaluations, and set expectations for the evidence that different types of studies seek to generate. Other agencies, such as DOL and components of HHS, are using the same guidelines for their evaluation activities. Research experts from Federal agencies, States, and academia are working with the National Academy of Sciences on ways to build consensus on standards for benefit-cost analysis of preventive interventions for children, youth, and families that would help government compare the benefits and costs of multiple strategies focused on similar target populations and outcomes. Common research standards and evidence frameworks across agencies can facilitate evaluation contracting, information collection clearance, and the strengthening or creation of research clearinghouses and repositories about "what works."

Relevance

Evaluations that do not inform decision-making have little applied value. For that reason this Administration has made integrating evidence into all types of budget, management, and policy decision-making a priority. Performance, evaluation, and other research evidence plays an important role in annual agency strategic review processes. Agencies seeking to increase the relevance and eventual use of evaluation findings take into account the viewpoints of a variety of stakeholders when establishing their research agendas, including

_____

[11] See Institute of Education Sciences, Department of Education and the National Science Foundation, "*Common Guide-lines for Education Research and Development*," August 2013.

INCREASING RELEVANCE: THE "LEARNING AGENDA" APPROACH

The Administration encourages agencies to adopt "learning agenda" approaches in which agencies collaboratively identify the critical questions that, when answered, will help their programs work more effectively and develop a plan to answer those questions using the most appropriate tools. The key components of this learning agenda approach are that agencies:

- Identify the most important questions that need to be answered in order to improve program implementation and performance. These questions should reflect the interests and needs of a large group of stakeholders, including program office staff and leadership, agency and Administrative leadership, program partners at state and local levels, and researchers, as well as legislative requirements and Congressional interests.

- Strategically prioritize which of those questions to answer within available resources, including which studies or analyses will help the agency make the most informed decisions.

- Identify the most appropriate tools and methods (e.g. evaluations, research, analytics, and/or performance measures) to answer each question.

- Implement studies, evaluations, and analysis using the most rigorous methods appropriate to the context.

- Develop plans to disseminate findings in ways that are accessible and useful to program officials, policy-makers, practitioners, and other key stakeholders—including integrating results into performance measurement and strategic planning activities.

Several agencies have successfully implemented learning agendas. For example, the Department of Housing and Urban Development (HUD) has been a leader in integrating its performance measurement, evaluation, and research efforts into a HUD-Stat process that engages its leadership in evidence-driven discussions of key priorities. These HUDStat processes not only discuss evidence but identify areas where more evidence is needed. The Millennium Challenge Corporation (MCC) organizes itself around its learning agenda. Its decisions to enter into compacts with developing countries are based upon evidence on the effectiveness of particular types of interventions in particular types of countries and typically embed evaluations into those compacts in order to inform future decisions.

Congress, Administration leadership, agency leadership, the implementing program, and other partners and stakeholders. While evaluations can be expensive and lengthy undertakings, taking these viewpoints into account when developing evaluations or research agendas increases the likelihood that the eventual results will be relevant to those implementing programs and making important policy decisions. Taking these viewpoints into consideration also ensures that federal evaluation offices continue to be connected to programs as they are implemented, and ensures that they are addressing the most pressing questions, rather than those that may be of interest academically but have little practical impact. Such an approach requires agencies to develop strong partnerships and collaborations among evaluation staff, program staff, policy makers and service providers. It also requires agencies to effectively disseminate evaluation findings in formats that are easier to interpret and apply.

Credibility and Independence

Actively engaging stakeholders in identifying evaluation priorities and questions and assessing the implications of findings increases relevance. However, developing and maintaining a widely acknowledged position of independence from political or other undue external influences is critical in order for evaluation offices and their work to be credible. Credible evaluations are not constructed or intended to deliver a predetermined or politically expedient result—rather they seek to develop the most accurate evidence practicable to answer a specific question. Just as federal statistics, such as the calculation of the unemployment rate, do not change based on which political party is in power, credible evaluation methods are not be altered due to undue external influences. Credible evaluation offices produce products that are methodologically sound, impartial, clear, and readily perceived to be so by the users of their products and the general public. Through demonstration of rigor, these offices establish their authority to determine the appropriate designs, data, and methods to use to conduct their work. They establish the capacity to make persuasive arguments for their chosen methods based on scientific principles and not by fiat. This capacity requires assurance that the selection and promotion of candidates for evaluation positions is based primarily on each candidate's scientific and technical knowledge, credentials, experience, and integrity.

Given the potential for political or other undue pressures, credible evaluation offices must demonstrate that their efforts can withstand critical review. Any personal or professional biases are stated and made transparent through the scientific testing of hypotheses, and both significant and null results are made transparent so that users understand the full array of hypotheses that were tested. The objectivity of the information released to the public is maximized by making information available on an equitable, policy neutral, transparent, and timely basis. As such, directors of credible evaluation offices have the authority to approve the design of evaluation projects and analysis plans, and the authority to approve, release, and disseminate evaluation reports, subject to legal, judicial, and security restrictions.

In this way, evaluation offices can demonstrate their independence from undue influences that may attempt to sway their work. The credibility that comes from independence and the independence that comes from credibility are both essential for users to maintain confidence in the accuracy and objectivity of evaluation results and for programs to be willing to cooperate with evaluation entities' requests.

Transparency

This Administration has placed a particular emphasis on increasing the transparency of federal evaluation

---

INCREASING THE TRANSPARENCY AND RELEVANCE OF EVALUATIONS THROUGH RESEARCH CLEARINGHOUSES

At the Federal level, many agencies have moved to increase the transparency and relevance of their evaluation findings by making them publicly available through "what works" repositories, sometimes referred to as research clearinghouses. "What works" repositories synthesize evaluation findings in ways that make research useful to decision-makers, researchers, and practitioners in the field. They also make evaluation results easily accessible to the public, and improve the transparency of evaluation results. Information in the repositories also indicates the implementation contexts of programs and strategies evaluated, and areas where more innovation or more evaluation is needed. Examples of Agency "what works" repositories include the:

- Administration for Children and Families (HHS) *Home Visiting Evidence of Effectiveness* (HomVEE),

- Administration for Children and Families (HHS) *Employment Strategies for Low-Income Adults* (ESER),

- Office of the Assistant Secretary for Planning and Evaluation (HHS) *Teen Pregnancy Prevention Evidence Review*,

- Substance Abuse and Mental Health Services Administration (HHS) *National Registry of Evidenced-based Programs and Practices* (NREPP),

- Department of Justice *CrimeSolutions.gov*,

- Department of Justice *What Works in Reentry Clearinghouse*,

- Department of Education *What Works Clearinghouse*, and

- Department of Labor *Clearinghouse for Labor Evaluation and Research* (CLEAR).

activities.[12] Transparency increases public awareness of ongoing and planned evaluation work, and of evaluation results, regardless of their findings. Public awareness of evaluation findings increases the likelihood that evaluation results will be used to inform a wide range of decision making; thus transparency is related to relevance.

Transparent evaluation offices make information about planned and ongoing evaluations/assessments easily accessible, typically through posting online information about the contractor or grantee conducting the work, descriptions of the evaluation/assessment questions, methods to be used, and the expected timeline for reporting results.

In addition, except in cases where there are legal, judicial, or security restrictions, transparent evaluation offices make evaluation plans, progress on ongoing evaluation work, and evaluation findings easily accessible to the public and release them in a timely way regardless of the findings. When these evaluations are released, the reports describe the methods used, including strengths and weaknesses, and discuss the generalizability of the findings. The released reports present comprehensive results, including favorable, unfavorable, and null findings.

Ethics

Evaluations/assessments should be conducted in an ethical manner and safeguard the dignity, rights, safety, and privacy of participants. Individuals and entities that participate in evaluations and the custodians of administrative data that may be used in support of evaluations must be able to trust that the information they provide as a part of an evaluation will be used only for the purposes that the agency has described. Thus, they must be able to trust that information collected for evaluation purposes will not be used for another purpose, such as law enforcement or regulation, directed at specific individuals or organizations. Evaluation offices should further build trust by minimizing the intrusiveness of questions and the time and effort required to respond to such questions, consistent with the agency's requirements for information. This can be accomplished through informing respondents of the expected time required to participate in the data collection, whether the collection is mandatory or voluntary, and any additional uses of the information. Multiple laws are in place in order to protect the rights, safety, and privacy of participants, and evaluations should comply with both the spirit and the letter of the relevant requirements.

Operationalizing an Effective Evidence Infrastructure

Operationalizing an effective evidence infrastructure requires a wide variety of capacities in addition to the principles and practices for evaluation offices articulated above. Developing and supporting the use of evidence and evaluation in decision-making requires a coordinated effort between those charged with managing the operations of a program, including administrative data collection and maintenance, and those responsible for using data and evaluation to understand a program's effectiveness. It requires consistent messages from leaders at different levels of an agency—policy officials, program and performance managers, strategic planning and budget staff, evaluators, and statistical staff—to ensure that data and evidence are collected or built, analyzed, understood, and appropriately acted upon.

No one individual in an agency has the knowledge and skills necessary to develop research designs that address actionable questions; collect, maintain, curate, and analyze administrative data; understand different types of evidence; interpret evidence; and develop and implement effective, evidence-based practices. Rather, it takes an agency leadership team to oversee these efforts and to build and sustain a commitment to learning. It also takes a team of "implementers" at the program level to encourage the use of evidence and data so that it reaches program management.

This section highlights two of the many capacities that support an effective evidence infrastructure: making better use of administrative data, and the establishment of centralized evaluation offices.

Building Evidence with Administrative Data

As described in last year's version of this chapter,[13] making better use of the "administrative data" that the government already collects to build evidence is an incredibly promising strategy. Administrative data are data collected by government entities for program administration, regulatory, or law enforcement purposes. Federal and state administrative data include rich information on labor market outcomes, health care, criminal justice, housing, and other important topics, but they are often greatly underutilized in evaluating programs' effects as well as in day-to-day performance measurement and for informing the public about how society and the economy are faring.

Over the course of this and previous Administrations, Federal agencies have steadily made progress improving the use of administrative data for evidence building. Some agencies are creating capacity to support research and evaluation in a particular policy area. For example, since 1995, the Bureau of Justice Statistics (BJS) has administered the National Criminal History Improvement Program which, among other accomplishments, helped all states achieve full participation in the Federal Bureau of Investigation's Interstate Identification Index. This critical operational network allows criminal justice agencies in the United States to exchange automated criminal history records (records which chronicle offenders' contacts with the justice system —i.e., "rapsheets"). Recently, BJS constructed an automated process which standardizes these variable federal and state records and creates unified researchable databases which can support a variety of research and evaluation of recidivism patterns and sentencing.

Similarly, ED has improved public understanding of how well colleges serve their students by matching administrative federal student loan and grant data to Department of

---

[12] See, for example, OMB Memorandum M-10-01, *"Increased Emphasis on Program Evaluation,"* October 2009.

[13] See *"Building Evidence with Administrative Data,"* chapter 7 in the *2016 Analytical Perspectives* volume.

Treasury tax data to create the new College Scorecard. The new College Scorecard provides students with the clearest, most accessible, and most reliable national data on college cost, graduation, debt, and post-college earnings to enable them to make better informed choices about colleges that fit their educational and career aspirations. The matched administrative data are also integrated into an open API that allows researchers and policymakers to customize analysis of college performance and allows other organizations to build tools to help students make more informed college choices.

However, most Federal agencies could make greater use of administrative data to build evidence. In addition, many agencies have data that would be useful to other agencies, other levels of government, or outside researchers for these same purposes. At the same time, not all agencies have the technological infrastructure or the expertise needed to utilize, share, or link data themselves, nor does it make sense to fully duplicate these capacities at every agency.

Federal statistical agencies already play a leading role in bringing together data from multiple sources, protecting privacy and confidentiality and ensuring data security, using data to create a wide variety of statistical products, and providing secure access to researchers inside and outside of government to conduct a broad array of policy- and program-relevant analyses. There are several examples where high-capacity statistical agencies have partnered with other Federal agencies to link and analyze administrative and survey data for evidence building purposes. Such partnerships build on the critical capacities that statistical agencies already have in order to make better use of existing data without creating unnecessary duplication.

Some agencies are leveraging capacity across the statistical system to build evidence in a particular policy area. For example, HUD has collaborated with the Census Bureau, the Centers for Medicare and Medicaid Services, and most recently National Center for Health Statistics to combine data and expertise to study relationships between housing, health risk behaviors, and health in order to use housing as a platform to improve quality of life. One outcome of these collaborations is new availability of linked survey and administrative datasets for researchers. Similarly, the Census Bureau and the Bureau of Labor Statistics are leading a multiagency effort to improve the Supplemental Poverty Measure (SPM). The SPM is designed to complement the official poverty measure, which is based on outdated assumptions and does not take into account most government transfer programs, and hence, cannot be used to evaluate their impact. In order to estimate the effectiveness of targeting resources toward the disadvantaged, the SPM integrates household income and expenditure information from national survey data with administrative data from a variety of Federal programs that help families, households, and individuals meet their basic needs.

The Budget proposes to expand this successful collaborative model. The Census Bureau is a leader for the often highly technical work of bringing together data from multiple sources, protecting privacy and confidentiality and ensuring data security, using data to create a wide variety of statistical products, and providing secure access to researchers inside and outside of government to conduct a broad array of policy- and program-relevant analyses. The Budget requests $10 million in funding for the Census Bureau to build on these existing strengths and start developing a more comprehensive infrastructure to prepare and share administrative data. This investment would help the Census Bureau work with States to obtain access to data from State-administered programs, such as the Supplemental Nutrition Assistance Program or the Special Supplemental Nutrition Program for Women, Infants, and Children, allowing new analysis of how these programs are used and their effects. Census would also improve its infrastructure for processing and linking data sets, as well as for providing data to researchers outside the Census Bureau.

Administrative Data Legislative Proposals

The above examples illustrate some of the exciting progress that agencies have made to better use administrative data. However, some significant barriers remain, including legislative barriers. The Budget continues many of the Administrative data legislative proposals included in the 2016 Budget, including the package of proposals designed to facilitate greater use of employment and earnings information and ease implementation of the Workforce Innovation and Opportunity Act. Employment and earnings data are among the most valuable Federal administrative data. Because many Federal (as well as State and local) programs are intended, in whole or in part, to increase employment and earnings, accurate employment and earnings data are needed to measure performance or conduct rigorous evaluations across a range of programs. The National Directory of New Hires (NDNH) is a database of employment and Unemployment Insurance information administered by the Office of Child Support Enforcement within HHS. Access to this data is tightly controlled by statute, and HHS implements strong privacy, confidentiality, and security protections to protect the data from unauthorized use or disclosure—there has never been a breach of the national NDNH data. Currently several programs are successfully using this data for program integrity, implementation, and research purposes.

The Budget proposes to build on this strong history of data stewardship and protection and allow additional programs and agencies to access this valuable data to learn what works and improve program implementation, while continuing to protect the privacy, security and confidentiality of that data. Specifically, the Budget proposes a package of proposals,[14] each of which is designed to clearly specify the purpose for which the data may be used, require that the minimum data necessary be used to achieve the purpose, and include strong penalties for the unauthorized access, use, disclosure, or re-disclosure of the data. In order to streamline access to the data by authorized agencies for program integrity purposes, the package includes a proposal which would allow the authorized agencies to access the NDNH data through the Do Not Pay Business Center at the Department of the Treasury.

---

[14] See Budget Chapter 5, "A Government of the Future," and HHS's Administration for Children and Families Congressional Justification for additional information on the full package of NDNH access proposals and the criteria for considering access to NDNH data.

In addition, each component of the package is designed to satisfy the Administration's criteria for when authority to access NDNH data should be considered. The package also requires HHS to review each agency's data security before allowing that agency to access the data, prohibits HHS from granting access to the data for any purpose not authorized in statute, and requires HHS to publicly report on the use of NDNH data.

Centralized Evaluation Offices

Centralized or chief evaluation offices play an important role in developing and sustaining agency capacity to build and use evidence. A recent General Accountability Office (GAO) report[15] found that Federal agencies with a centralized evaluation authority reported greater evaluation coverage of their performance goals and were more likely to use evaluation results in decision making. However, the GAO report also found that only half of the existing centralized evaluation offices reported having a stable source of funding.

Centralized or chief evaluation offices are often a key component of implementing evaluation policies reflective of the core principles discussed above. Indeed the establishment of a centralized evaluation function and an evaluation policy re-

---

[15] Government Accountability Office Publication No. 15-25, "*Program Evaluation: Some Agencies Reported that Networking, Hiring, and Involving Program Staff Help Build Capacity*," November 2014.

flective of these core principles is a particularly strong and mutually reinforcing combination. Establishing a centralized office allows the agency to credibly establish the independence and transparency of its evaluation work, develop the specialized expertise required to implement rigorous evaluations, and creates a centralized entity responsible for coordinating and disseminating research findings.

These offices also play a central role in implementing effective learning agendas. Learning agendas cross program and agency boundaries and thus are difficult to implement well without an office with the responsibility to look across programs and work across agencies. Often data from one program may be useful in the learning agenda for another program; centralized evaluation offices can play an important role in that cross-program and cross-agency collaboration. Centralized evaluation offices also develop expertise about evaluation, about how to integrate evaluation and other research evidence with performance measurement and strategic review processes, and about how to help decision-makers use evidence. In several cases these offices, working in partnership with other evaluation offices and statistical agencies, also play a crucial role in using administrative data to build evidence about what works. Several agencies have successfully implemented centralized or chief evaluation offices. CNCS has successfully used its centralized evaluation office to coordinate its learning agenda across

---

CHIEF EVALUATION OFFICE AT THE DEPARTMENT OF LABOR

Over the last six years, the Department of Labor (DOL) has made significant progress in institutionalizing a culture of evidence and learning. The Chief Evaluation Office (CEO), established in 2010, plays a critical role in developing and maintaining this culture within DOL. As a part of its primary responsibility to manage DOL's evaluation program, CEO maintains a strong commitment to conducting rigorous, relevant, and independent evaluations. CEO is also committed to identifying and funding research and evaluation priorities established through a collaborative learning agenda process with DOL's various agencies. These agencies cover a broad range of topics, from employment and training programs to worker protection and enforcement activities. CEO plays an important role in initiating research that cuts across these agency and program silos.

CEO also serves as an "honest broker" on evidence issues within DOL, and its work is not limited to implementing evaluations. CEO actively participates in the performance management and strategic planning processes of the Department, and disseminates the results of their evaluations in formats that enable use by programs and policy makers.

Some of the key capacities that DOL developed to support this important work include:

- **Hiring staff with sufficient expertise** for CEO to manage rigorous evaluations of various methodologies. For example, using behavioral insights, CEO worked with Occupational Safety and Health Administration to implement a large random assignment study that identified an effective way to support establishments that have injury and illness rates above the national average.

- Launching the *Clearinghouse for Labor Research and Evaluation* (CLEAR), which makes research on labor topics more accessible to practitioners, policymakers, researchers, and the public more broadly, thus increasing the transparency and relevance of the Department's evaluation efforts.

- Implementing a **learning agenda process** for the Department, in which CEO collaborates with each agency to identify key evaluation and research priorities.

- Securing the budget authority to **set aside a portion of specified program funds** (.75% in 2016) to support these evaluations.

- Creating a **data analytics unit** to support and complement agencies on their analytic needs and work; build data, statistical, and analytical expertise and capacity for the Department; and promote and innovate DOL administrative and public use data.

- Establishing a *Departmental of Labor Evaluation Policy* to institutionalize and guide the Department's evaluation efforts.

programs and to work with other agencies. NSF has recently instituted a centralized evaluation office that is in the process of developing a learning agenda for the first time. The Chief Evaluation Office at DOL has become a leader both at DOL and across the Federal government in advancing the role of evidence in decision-making. See the box above for more on DOL's Chief Evaluation Office.

Conclusion

The evidence capacity building efforts outlined in this chapter fit into the Budget's broader emphasis on tackling challenging but important issues that are integral to making government work better. This chapter articulates common principles that support the development of credible evidence, as well as the capacity required to operationalize an effective evidence infrastructure. This Budget makes substantial investments in programs based on evidence in addition to further building the capacity to produce and use evidence.

8. STRENGTHENING THE FEDERAL WORKFORCE

In President Obama's Public Service Recognition Week Proclamation, issued on May 2, 2015, he reflected:

"With more than 2 million civilian workers and more than 1 million active duty service members, our Federal workforce represents extraordinary possibility. Our Government can and must be a force for good, and together, we can make sure our democracy works for all Americans. We know there are some things we do better when we join in common purpose, and with hard work and a commitment worthy of our Nation's potential, we can keep our country safe, guarantee basic security, and ensure everyone has a shot at success."

Historically, this sentiment has had bipartisan support. President Ronald Reagan stated, "Government employees, with their commitment to excellence and diversity of skills, contribute significantly to the leadership of the United States in the world. These dedicated men and women are a valuable national resource, serving in the Executive, Legislative, and Judicial branches at all levels of government, and dealing with nearly every aspect of national life."[1]

Investing in a strong Federal workforce is integral to the competitiveness and security of the United States. The workforce needs to be hired based on merit, trained to be prepared for tomorrow, engaged to improve performance, and compensated on the basis of results. Personnel rules must support the type of work the Government does today and tomorrow, balancing flexibility and consistency.

The Federal Workforce Today

Investments to strengthen the workforce have far-reaching implications. The Federal Government is America's largest employer, with more than 2.1 million civilian workers and 1.3 million active duty military serving throughout the country and the world. About 85 percent of Federal employees work outside of the Washington, D.C. metropolitan area. Federal Employees are our neighbors, civic leaders, and tax-payers. The Federal Government is the Nation's largest employer of doctors and employs individuals responsible for protecting our natural resources, waterways and historic landmarks, providing grants for research, housing, and education. Federal employees are also called into action in the event of a disaster, whether that means stopping Ebola or out-of-control forest fires.

Every day Federal employees actively collaborate with the private and nonprofit sectors, as well as state and local governments to advance our national priorities.

During the years of delayed budgets, sequestration, pay freezes and award caps, Federal employees have continued to serve their country. In 2015 alone, Federal employees addressed a wide range of national priorities – including modernizing the military by opening all combat positions to women, negotiating complex trade and political treaties and determining a way to rate college's return on investment. Thanks in part to the efforts of Federal employees, the Nation's economy and fiscal outlook continued to improve in 2015, with unemployment falling to 5 percent and annual deficits continuing a historic decline.

Reflecting the importance of the workforce, one of the four pillars of the President's Management Agenda (PMA) is People & Culture, focused on unlocking the full potential of today's Federal workforce and building the workforce we need in the future. This Cross-Agency Priority (CAP) Goal is improving how we hire, engage and lead our workforce. Removing frustrating barriers will allow us to achieve the breakthroughs and daily operational success that the American public expects. Fixing broken human capital processes will help agencies concentrate on performance and results.

This chapter discusses four broad areas related to the Federal workforce. First, it describes trends in Federal employment levels over the past several decades and includes estimates for the FY 2017 Budget. Second, it outlines the shifts in composition of the Federal workforce over the past decades. Third, the chapter lays out some of the challenges the Federal workforce has faced, such as pay freezes, sequester and furloughs. Finally, it discusses the Administration's recent accomplishments and future plans to fully capitalize on the talents in the Federal workforce today, and recruit and develop the capabilities we need to serve the American people tomorrow.

Trends in Federal Workforce Size

The size of the Federal civilian workforce relative to the country's population has declined dramatically over the past several decades, with occasional upticks due, for example, to military conflicts and the administration of the Census. Since the 1960s, the U.S. population increased by 67 percent, the private sector workforce increased by 136 percent, and State and local government workforces (excluding education workers) increased by 127 percent, while the size of the Federal workforce rose about 10 percent.[2]

---

[1] Proclamation 5813 - Public Service Recognition Week, 1988, May 5, 1988

[2] Teachers, professors, and workers in schools, colleges, and universities make up almost half of the State and local workforce. To make the State and local workforce more comparable to the Federal workforce, those educational workers are excluded from these comparisons.

Chart 8-1. Changes Since 1975 in Employment/Population by Sector

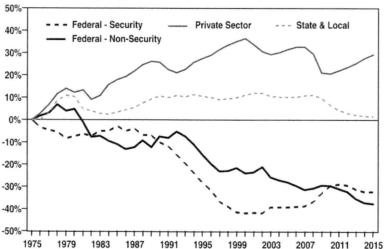

Source: Office of Personnel Management and the Bureau of Labor Statistics.
Notes: Federal excludes the military and Postal Service. Security agencies include the Department of Defense, the Department of Homeland Security, the Department of State, and the Department of Veterans Affairs. Non-Security agencies include the remainder of the Executive Branch. State & Local excludes educational workers.

Chart 8-1 highlights the sharp drops, relative to population, in both the security and non-security parts of the Federal workforce since 1975 (the end of the Vietnam War), compared to increases in the private sector and State and local governments (excluding education). Since 1975, the security and non-security parts of the Federal workforce have declined 32 and 38 percent, respectively, relative to the population, but the patterns in the declines differ. The Federal security workforce (63 percent of the current Federal civilian workforce) has largely tracked the history of U.S. engagement in conflicts overseas. The non-security workforced decreased drastically in the 1980s. While the 1990s reversed some of that decline, the non-security Federal workforce has declined by about 18 percent since 1992 (during a period of time when the private sector workforce has increased 34 percent). The reasons for the decline in the non-security Federal workforce are less clear than for the security workforce, particularly given increasing responsibilities at many Federal agencies.

Explanations for the relative decline of the non-security Federal workforce include: (1) relative increases in efficiency in the Federal sector; (2) an increase in the contract workforce (which likely also plays a role on the security side); and (3) shifting of some duties of the Federal Government to State and local governments. Both an increased reliance on a contract workforce and shifting responsibilities to State and local governments have required the Federal workforce to take on greater management roles over time.

Table 8-2 shows actual Federal civilian full-time equivalent (FTE) levels in the Executive Branch by agency for fiscal years 2014 and 2015, with estimates for 2016 and 2017. Estimated employment levels for 2017 result in

an estimated 1.5 percent increase compared to 2016, or approximately 30,000 Federal jobs. This increase is primarily driven by growth at the Departments of Veterans Affairs, Homeland Security and Treasury. Table 8-3 shows actual 2015 total and estimated 2016 and 2017 total Federal employment, including the Uniformed Military, Postal Service, Judicial and Legislative branches. The total growth of .1 percent is a result of decreases in the Uniformed Services and Postal Service, but increases in the Executive, Legislative and Judicial Branches. Total compensation is summarized in Table 8-4, with an increase of 1.9 percent between the estimates for 2016 and 2017.

Attributes of the Federal Workforce

The previous section describes the long-term decline in the size of the Federal workforce relative to the U.S. population, the private sector workforce, and State and local government workforces. That relative reduction in size in the face of a Federal mission that has only grown more complex, along with an historical trend of greater reliance on contractors and State and local partners in many areas, results in Federal jobs that have become increasingly complex and require greater levels of skill. It is equally important to consider how the Federal workforce differs from the private sector and how it has changed over time. As discussed in more detail below, in comparison to private sector jobs, Federal jobs are concentrated in higher paying professions and are based in higher cost metropolitan areas.

Type of occupation. The last half century has seen significant shifts in the composition of the Federal work-

Table 8–1. OCCUPATIONS OF FEDERAL AND PRIVATE SECTOR WORKFORCES
(Grouped by Average Private Sector Salary)

Occupational Groups	Percent	
	Federal Workers	Private Sector Workers
Highest Paid Occupations Ranked by Private Sector Salary		
Lawyers and judges	2.0%	0.6%
Engineers	4.3%	1.9%
Scientists and social scientists	5.2%	0.7%
Managers	11.8%	13.8%
Pilots, conductors, and related mechanics	2.0%	0.5%
Doctors, nurses, psychologists, etc.	7.7%	6.3%
Miscellaneous professionals	15.4%	8.8%
Administrators, accountants, HR personnel	6.1%	2.7%
Inspectors	1.3%	0.3%
Total Percentage	**55.8%**	**35.6%**
Medium Paid Occupations Ranked by Private Sector Salary		
Sales including real estate, insurance agents	1.3%	6.2%
Other miscellaneous occupations	3.4%	4.5%
Automobile and other mechanics	1.7%	3.0%
Law enforcement and related occupations	9.4%	0.8%
Office workers	2.5%	6.0%
Social workers	1.4%	0.5%
Drivers of trucks and taxis	0.8%	3.2%
Laborers and construction workers	3.4%	9.5%
Clerks and administrative assistants	13.4%	10.9%
Manufacturing	2.8%	7.6%
Total Percentage	**40.0%**	**52.0%**
Lowest Paid Occupations Ranked by Private Sector Salary		
Other miscellaneous service workers	2.2%	5.9%
Janitors and housekeepers	1.1%	2.4%
Cooks, bartenders, bakers, and wait staff	0.8%	4.0%
Total Percentage	**4.2%**	**12.3%**

Source: 2011-2015 Current Population Survey, Integrated Public Use Microdata Series.

Notes: Federal workers exclude the military and Postal Service, but include all other Federal workers in the Executive, Legislative, and Judicial Branches. However, the vast majority of these employees are civil servants in the Executive Branch. Private sector workers exclude the self-employed. Neither category includes state and local government workers. This analysis is limited to full-time, full-year workers, i.e. those with at least 1,500 annual hours of work.

force. Fifty years ago, most professional Federal employees performed clerical tasks, such as filing or data entry. Today their jobs are vastly different, requiring advanced skills to serve a knowledge-based economy. For example, the IRS previously required thousands of employees in warehouses to print and sort hard-copy tax returns, while thousands more manually adjudicated the returns. With the majority of tax returns now electronically filed, the IRS today requires more forensic accountants and analysts rather than warehouse clerks. Federal employees must manage highly sensitive tasks that require great skill, experience, and judgment. Many need sophisticated management and negotiation skills to effect change, not just across the Federal Government, but also with other levels of government and the private sector.

Using data from the Bureau of Labor Statistics on full-time, full-year workers, Table 8-1 breaks all Federal and private sector jobs into 22 occupation groups to demonstrate the differences in composition between the Federal and private workforces. Professionals such as doctors, engineers, scientists, statisticians, and lawyers now make up a large and growing portion of the Federal workforce. For example, the Federal STEM workforce has increased by about 10 percent from FY 2008 to FY 2015, with all other occupations growing 6 percent. More than half (56 percent) of Federal workers are employed in the nine highest-paying private sector occupation groups, such as judges and lawyers, engineers, and scientists, compared to a little over a third (36 percent) of private sector workers. In contrast, 12 percent of private sector workers are employed in the three lowest-paying occupation groups, as cooks, janitors, service workers, etc. Only about 4 percent of Federal workers are employed in those three lowest-paying occupation groups.

Education level. The complexity of much Federal work – whether that work is analyzing security or financial risk, forecasting weather, planning bridges to withstand

Table 8–2.   FEDERAL CIVILIAN EMPLOYMENT IN THE EXECUTIVE BRANCH
(Civilian employment as measured by full-time equivalents (FTE) in thousands, excluding the Postal Service)

Agency	Actual		Estimate		Change: 2016 to 2017	
	2014	2015	2016	2017	FTE	Percent
Cabinet agencies:						
Agriculture	86.1	85.9	90.1	90.5	0.4	0.4%
Commerce	39.5	40.4	44.1	45.6	1.5	3.4%
Defense	723.9	725.0	738.1	732.9	-5.2	-0.7%
Education	4.0	4.1	4.3	4.5	0.2	4.7%
Energy	15.0	14.7	16.0	16.1	0.1	0.6%
Health and Human Services	69.9	70.6	72.6	74.4	1.8	2.5%
Homeland Security	183.2	179.3	184.0	188.1	4.1	2.2%
Housing and Urban Development	8.4	8.3	8.3	8.4	0.1	1.2%
Interior	64.4	63.5	65.6	66.7	1.1	1.7%
Justice	112.4	113.6	118.3	119.8	1.5	1.3%
Labor	16.7	16.6	16.9	17.7	0.8	4.7%
State	33.1	34.0	34.2	34.5	0.3	0.9%
Transportation	54.1	54.3	55.7	56.2	0.5	0.9%
Treasury	99.2	95.1	99.0	103.0	4.0	4.0%
Veterans Affairs	323.0	335.3	349.8	366.5	16.7	4.8%
Other agencies—excluding Postal Service:						
Broadcasting Board of Governors	1.7	1.7	1.9	1.9	0.0	0.0%
Corps of Engineers—Civil Works	21.8	21.6	22.2	22.2	0.0	0.0%
Environmental Protection Agency	15.3	14.7	15.5	15.6	0.1	0.6%
Equal Employment Opportunity Comm	2.1	2.2	2.3	2.4	0.1	4.3%
Federal Deposit Insurance Corporation	7.3	6.8	7.1	6.8	-0.3	-4.2%
General Services Administration	11.5	11.1	11.7	11.9	0.2	1.7%
International Assistance Programs	5.5	5.6	5.7	5.8	0.1	1.8%
National Aeronautics and Space Admin	17.7	17.3	17.4	17.4	0.0	0.0%
National Archives and Records Administration ...	2.9	2.8	2.9	2.9	0.0	0.0%
National Labor Relations Board	1.5	1.6	1.6	1.6	0.0	0.0%
National Science Foundation	1.4	1.4	1.4	1.4	0.0	0.0%
Nuclear Regulatory Commission	3.8	3.7	3.6	3.5	-0.1	-2.8%
Office of Personnel Management	5.0	5.0	5.6	5.8	0.2	3.6%
Railroad Retirement Board	0.9	0.9	0.9	0.9	0.0	0.0%
Securities and Exchange Commission	4.2	4.3	4.6	4.9	0.3	6.5%
Small Business Administration	3.3	3.1	3.3	3.3	0.0	0.0%
Smithsonian Institution	4.9	4.9	5.4	5.6	0.2	3.7%
Social Security Administration	60.8	63.9	65.5	67.0	1.5	2.3%
Tennessee Valley Authority	11.3	10.9	11.5	11.5	0.0	0.0%
All other small agencies	17.6	17.8	18.8	19.3	0.5	2.7%
Total, Executive Branch civilian employment * ...	**2,033.4**	**2,042.0**	**2,105.9**	**2,136.6**	**30.7**	**1.5%**

* Totals may not add due to rounding.

extreme events, conducting research to advance human health or energy efficiency, or pursuing scientific advancements in a laboratory – necessitates a workforce with education requirements and licensures. Charts 8-2 and 8-3 present trends in educational levels for the Federal and private sector workforces over the past two decades. In 1992 there were only about half as many highly-educated Federal workers (masters degrees or above) compared to less-educated workers (high school degrees or less); by 2015 there were almost twice as many highly-educated Federal workers than less educated workers. The private sector has also experienced increases in educational level, but the increases in highly educated workers have been slower than in the Federal sector. Even in large firms, the percentage of highly educated workers is less than half that of the Federal sector and the rate of growth over the last decade is only about half as fast.

Size of organization and responsibilities. Another important difference between Federal workers and private sector workers is the average size of the organization in which they work. Federal agencies are large and often face challenges of enormous scale – distributing benefit payments to over 66 million Social Security and Supplemental Security Income beneficiaries each year, providing medical care to 8.9 million veterans, or managing defense contracts costing billions of dollars. Most

Chart 8-2. Masters Degree or Above by Year for Federal and Private Sectors

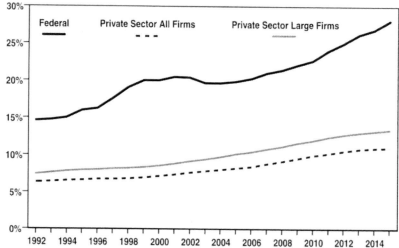

Source: 1992-2015 Current Population Survey, Integrated Public Use Microdata Series.

Notes: Federal excludes the military and Postal Service, but includes all other Federal workers. Private Sector excludes the self-employed. Neither category includes State and local government workers. Large firms have at least 1,000 workers. This analysis is limited to full-time, full-yea workers, i.e. those with at least 1,500 annual hours of work and presents five-year averages

Federal employees work in large organizations more comparable to the largest firms. Data shows that workers from large firms (those with 1,000 or more employees) are paid about 16 percent more than workers from small firms (those with fewer than 100 employees), even after accounting for occupational type, level of education, and other characteristics. However, even large private sector firms may not be ideal comparisons to the Federal sector, because the Federal sector is larger and more highly educated (see Charts 8-2 and 8-3).

Demographic characteristics. Federal workers tend to have demographic characteristics associated with higher pay in the private sector. They are more experienced, older, and live in higher cost metropolitan areas. For example, Federal workers, on average, are 45.4 years old – up 2.6 years from 20 years ago and higher than the average age of 42.1 years old in the private sector (even in large firms). Chart 8-4 shows the trends in average age in both the Federal and private sectors over the past two decades.

Table 8–3. TOTAL FEDERAL EMPLOYMENT
(As measured by Full-Time Equivalents)

Description	2015 Actual	2016 Estimate	2017 Estimate	Change: 2016 to 2017 FTE	Change: 2016 to 2017 Percent
Executive Branch Civilian:					
All Agencies, Except Postal Service	2,041,974	2,105,915	2,136,590	30,675	1.5%
Postal Service [1]	575,906	574,122	562,024	-12,098	-2.1%
Subtotal, Executive Branch Civilian	2,617,880	2,680,037	2,698,614	18,577	0.7%
Executive Branch Uniformed Military:					
Department of Defense [2]	1,356,612	1,340,473	1,327,007	-13,466	-1.0%
Department of Homeland Security (USCG)	40,025	41,777	42,054	277	0.7%
Commissioned Corps (DOC, EPA, HHS)	7,004	7,100	7,112	12	0.2%
Subtotal, Uniformed Military	1,403,641	1,389,350	1,376,173	-13,177	-0.9%
Subtotal, Executive Branch	4,021,521	4,069,387	4,074,787	5,400	0.1%
Legislative Branch [3]	29,825	33,953	34,256	303	0.9%
Judicial Branch	32,467	33,101	33,343	242	0.7%
Grand total	**4,083,813**	**4,136,441**	**4,142,386**	**5,945**	**0.1%**

[1] Includes Postal Rate Commission.

[2] Includes activated Guard and Reserve members on active duty. Does not include Full-Time Support (Active Guard & Reserve (AGRs)) paid from Reserve Component appropriations.

[3] FTE data not available for the Senate (positions filled were used).

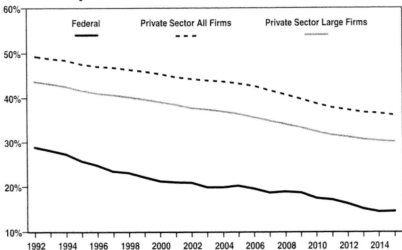

Chart 8-3. High School Graduate or Less by Year for Federal and Private Sectors

Source: 1992-2015 Current Population Survey, Integrated Public Use Microdata Series.

Notes: Federal excludes the military and Postal Service, but includes all other Federal workers. Private Sector excludes the self-employed. Neither category includes State and local government workers. Large firms have at least 1,000 workers. This analysis is limited to full-time, full-year workers, i.e. those with at least 1,500 annual hours of work and presents five-year averages

In FY 2015 (as of September 2015), the percentage of minorities in the Federal workforce increased by 0.5 percent from 34.9 percent in FY 2014 to 35.4 percent in FY 2015. The Federal workforce is 17.7 percent Black, 8.4 percent Hispanic, 5.7 percent Asian, 0.5 percent Native Hawaiian/Pacific Islander, 1.7 percent American Indian/ Alaska Native, 1.3 percent Non-Hispanic/Multi-Racial, and 64.6 percent White. Men comprised 56.8 percent of all Federal permanent employees and women 43.2 percent. The SES is 11.3 percent Black, 4.4 percent Hispanic, 3.3 percent Asian, 0.2 percent Native Hawaiian/Pacific Islander, 1.2 percent American Indian/Alaska Native, and 0.7 percent Non-Hispanic/Multi-Racial. In addition, women now make up 34 percent of the SES, which is a 0.5 percent increase from FY 2014. Federal employment for people with disabilities increased from 239,615 in FY 2014 to 258,001, representing an increase from 11.7 percent to 12.5 percent. Overall, the percentage of minority employment increased 1.4% from 2009 to 2015.

Veteran hiring. In recent years, the Executive Branch has had made considerable progress hiring veterans, and the Federal Government continues to benefit from retaining the dedication, leadership, and skills these veterans have honed. In November 2009, President Obama signed Executive Order 13518, establishing the Veterans Employment Initiative and the Council on Veterans Employment. In FY 2011, the first full year of the President's Veteran Employment Initiative, veterans made up 28.3 percent of the total new hires in the Federal Government and veterans were 47.1 percent of new hires at DOD (highest) and 4.1 percent of new hires

at NSF (lowest). By the end of FY 2014, veterans were 33.2 percent of new hires Government-wide, and 47.1 percent of new hires at DOD (highest) and 8.1 percent of new hires at NSF (lowest). The total number of veterans employed by the Government also increased. In FY 2011, there were 567,314 veterans in the Federal Government, or 27.3 percent of the workforce. By the end of FY 2014 (the most recent available data), the number of veterans had grown to over 612,661, or 30.8 percent of the entire Federal workforce, and veterans represented 46.9 percent of the workforce at DOD (highest) and 7.2 percent of the workforce at HHS (lowest). By comparison, veterans comprise approximately 6 percent of the private sector non-agricultural workforce.

Federal Compensation Trends

Chart 8-5 shows how increases in the Federal pay scale have compared to increases in private sector wages since 1978. After more than a decade when the percentage increases in annual Federal pay raises did not keep pace with the percentage increase in private sector pay raises, Congress passed the Federal Employees Pay Comparability Act of 1990 (FEPCA) pegging Federal pay raises, as a default, to changes in the Employment Cost Index (ECI). The law gives the President the authority to propose alternative pay adjustments for both base and locality pay, and Presidents have regularly supported alternative pay plans. A civilian pay raise less than 2.1 percent in FY 2017 would result in the eighth consecutive below-ECI increase, resulting in a relative decrease in civilian pay compared to the private sector of about 9 per-

Table 8–4. PERSONNEL COMPENSATION AND BENEFITS

(In millions of dollars)

Description	2015 Actual	2016 Estimate	2017 Estimate	Change: 2016 to 2017	
				Dollars	Percent
Civilian Personnel Costs:					
Executive Branch (excluding Postal Service):					
Direct compensation	181,206	189,584	195,929	6,345	3.3%
Personnel Benefits	74,580	77,809	79,908	2,099	2.7%
Subtotal	255,786	267,393	275,837	8,444	3.2%
Postal Service:					
Direct compensation	36,208	35,853	35,768	-85	-0.2%
Personnel benefits	19,051	18,967	18,177	-790	-4.2%
Subtotal	55,259	54,820	53,945	-875	-1.6%
Legislative Branch: [1]					
Direct compensation	2,036	2,147	2,228	81	3.8%
Personnel benefits	614	680	709	29	4.3%
Subtotal	2,650	2,827	2,937	110	3.9%
Judicial Branch:					
Direct compensation	3,095	3,375	3,418	43	1.3%
Personnel benefits	988	1,047	1,073	26	2.5%
Subtotal	4,083	4,422	4,491	69	1.6%
Total, Civilian Personnel Costs	317,778	329,462	337,210	7,748	2.4%
Military personnel costs:					
Department of Defense					
Direct compensation	96,160	96,118	97,856	1,738	1.8%
Personnel benefits	44,135	44,261	43,693	-568	-1.3%
Subtotal	140,295	140,379	141,549	1,170	0.8%
All other Executive Branch, uniformed personnel:					
Direct compensation	3,294	3,317	3,358	41	1.2%
Personnel benefits	720	698	698	0	0.0%
Subtotal	4,014	4,015	4,056	41	1.0%
Total, Military Personnel Costs [2]	144,309	144,394	145,605	1,211	0.8%
Grand total, personnel costs	**462,087**	**473,856**	**482,815**	**8,959**	**1.9%**
ADDENDUM					
Former Civilian Personnel:					
Retired pay for former personnel					
Government payment for Annuitants:	83,864	84,820	86,983	2,163	2.6%
Employee health benefits	11,695	12,004	12,984	980	8.2%
Employee life insurance	45	47	48	1	2.1%
Former Military personnel:					
Retired pay for former personnel	56,829	57,334	58,256	922	1.6%
Military annuitants health benefits	9,508	9,770	10,272	502	5.1%

[1] Excludes members and officers of the Senate.

[2] Amounts in this table for military compensation reflect direct pay and benefits for all service members, including active duty, guard, and reserve members.

cent since 2009. This would be the largest relative pay cut over an eight year period since the passage of FEPCA by a significant margin (the second largest eight year drop, from 1990 to 1997, was roughly 2 percent).

While increases in Federal and private sector pay remained fairly even during the early 1990s, private sector pay incrementally rose in comparison to the public sector in the mid-1990s. That trend reversed itself in the 2000s when the Federal pay scale rose relative to private sector wages. Other factors have also eroded relative compensation for civilian Federal employees. For example, the Bipartisan Budget Act of 2013 requires Federal employees hired after January 2014 to pay an additional 3.6 percent of their salaries, 4.4 percent in total, into the Federal Employees Retirement System (FERS) compared to those hired before 2013. The Office of Personnel Management (OPM) also reports that budgetary constraints have created an impediment for agencies in funding discretionary civilian recruitment and retention programs, one of the most popular being student loan repayments.

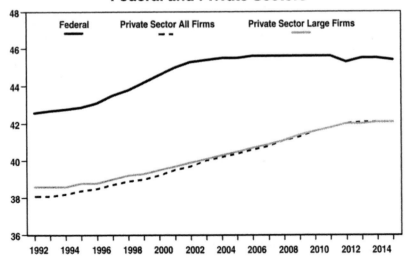

Chart 8-4. Average Age by Year for Federal and Private Sectors

Source: 1992-2015 Current Population Survey, Integrated Public Use Microdata Series.

Notes: Federal excludes the military and Postal Service, but includes all other Federal workers. Private Sector excludes the self-employed. Neither category includes State and local government workers. Large firms have at least 1,000 workers. This analysis is limited to full-time, full-year workers, i.e. those with at least 1,500 annual hours of work and presents five-year averages.

Comparisons of Federal and Private Sector Compensation

Federal worker compensation receives a great deal of attention, particularly in comparison to that of private sector workers. Comparisons of the pay and benefits of Federal employees and private sector employees must account for factors affecting pay, such as differences in skill levels, complexity of work, scope of responsibility, size of the organization, location, experience level, and exposure to personal danger, and should account for all types of compensation, including pay and bonuses, health benefits, retirement benefits, flexibility of work schedules, job security, training opportunities, and profit sharing.

Taking into account both the pay freezes in place in 2011 through 2013 and the changes in retirement contributions that started in 2014, earnings for new Federal employees have fallen more than 10 percentage points relative to the private sector between 2009 and 2015. The President's Pay Agent Report, which is unique in basing its findings on Federal employee job descriptions, rather than the characteristics of the employees filling the jobs, concludes that Federal jobs are severely underpaid, relative to a salary that would be needed to attract a truly qualified candidate for a similar job in the private sector. While the average gap is currently 35 percent, it varies considerably by grade level with higher GS levels showing a 70 percent gap or more with their private sector counterparts and lower grade levels being closer to zero in some areas. Following the 3-year pay freeze, a one percent pay increase for General Schedule employees was implemented in 2014 and 2015, a 1.3 percent increase

was enacted in 2016 and a 1.6 percent increase is proposed in 2017.

A series of reports released in January 2012 by the Congressional Budget Office (CBO) that accounted for some, but not all, of the factors described above, found that prior to the three-year Federal pay freeze, Federal pay, on average, was slightly higher (2.0 percent) than comparable private sector pay. CBO reported that overall Federal sector compensation (including benefits) was on average substantially higher, but noted that its findings about comparative benefits relied on far more assumptions and were less definitive than its pay findings. The CBO study also excluded forms of compensation, such as job security, that favor the Federal sector, and factors such as training opportunities and profit sharing that favor the private sector.

CBO emphasized that focusing on averages is misleading, because the Federal/private sector differentials vary dramatically by education and complexity of job. Compensation for highly educated Federal workers (or those in more complex jobs) is lower than for comparable workers in the private sector, whereas CBO found the opposite for less educated workers. These findings suggest that across-the-board compensation increases or cuts may not be the most efficient use of Federal resources.

The CBO reports focus on workers and ask what employees with the educational backgrounds and other characteristics of Federal workers earn in the private sector. The President's Pay Agent Report, mentioned above, focuses on jobs and asks what the private sector would pay people with the same roles and responsibilities as

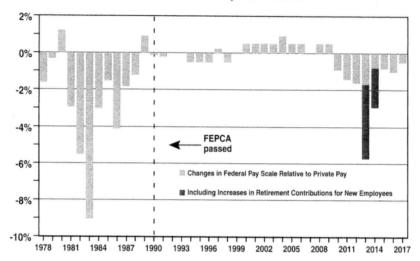

Chart 8-5. Pay Raises for Federal vs. Private Workforce, 1978-2017

Source: Public Laws, Executive Orders, and the Bureau of Labor Statistics.

Notes: Federal pay is for civilians and includes base and locality pay. Private pay is measured by the Employment Cost Index wages and salaries, private industry workers series, lagged 15 months.

Federal workers. Unlike CBO, which found that Federal pay is (on average) roughly in line with private sector pay, the Pay Agent Report found that in 2015 Federal jobs paid 35 percent less than comparable non-Federal jobs.

There are possible explanations for the discrepancy in the CBO versus the Pay Agent Report findings. First, methodological issues around the classification of Federal and private sector jobs introduce considerable uncertainty into the Pay Agent Report approach. It is significantly easier to compare college graduates in Federal versus private sector jobs than it is to determine what private sector job is most comparable to a given Federal job. Second, the studies ask fundamentally different questions that are not necessarily in conflict. It could be the case that Federal and private sector workers with similar characteristics are paid about the same, but that jobs in the Federal sector are underpaid relative to their private sector counterparts. That would imply that, at least in some jobs, the Federal Government could have difficulty hiring and retaining workers with the same skills or managerial experience as their counterparts in equivalent private sector jobs. This could be a reason for concern, given the decline in the size of the Federal workforce relative to the population and the increasingly supervisory role it plays (e.g., supervising contractors and State and local governments).

Finally, differences in non-salary compensation such as student loan repayment, transportation subsidies, travel funds to attend professional development conferences or site visits, training and professional certifications, as well as sabbaticals and other incentives common in the private sector can also affect an employee's choice of employer. While the Federal Government is a leader in telework and alternative work schedules, those benefit only a subsection of employees whose positions do not require either onsite performance or 24/7 coverage.

Workforce Challenges

The Federal Government faces unique human capital challenges, including a personnel system that requires further modernization, an aging and retiring workforce, and the need to engage a future generation of Federal workers. According to the Partnership for Public Service, individuals younger than 30 years of age make up 23 percent of the U.S. workforce, but account for only 7 percent of permanent, full-time Federal employees. If the Government loses top talent, experience, and institutional memory through retirements, but cannot recruit, retain, and train highly qualified workers, performance suffers. While the current Federal age distribution and potential for a large number of retiring workers poses a challenge, it also creates an opportunity to reshape the workforce and to infuse it with new workers excited about government service and equipped with strong management skills, problem-solving ability, technology skills, and fresh perspectives. A national climate of criticism of service in the Federal Government makes it difficult to recruit the needed workforce and convince them to commit their talents and develop into future leaders.

Modernizing the Federal Personnel System

In the past sixty years, the workplace and workforce have changed dramatically, and approaches to personnel management in the private sector have continued to adapt to reflect this evolution. While the Federal personnel system is founded on core principles and requirements that necessarily distinguish it from other employment sectors (e.g., providing hiring preference to veterans, or ensuring fair and open competition so that every citizen who is interested in a Federal job has a fair opportunity to apply), in many ways, the Federal personnel system can also benefit from modernization. Recent hiring reform efforts are showing some progress in simplifying hiring, however, additional reforms are needed to ensure that hiring, pay, classification, benefits systems, and the performance management process (including how to reward top performers and address low performers) meet today's needs and demands. The General Schedule (GS) pay system has been in effect since 1949. Enacted in 1951, aspects of the current benefit and leave laws do not always reflect today's employee and family structures. The Administration is committed to developing modern, cost-effective systems that will allow the Government to compete for and reward top talent, incentivize performance, and encourage adequate flexibility to family caregivers, among other requirements.

To that end, the Administration proposed to the Joint Select Committee on Deficit Reduction that the Congress establish a Commission on Federal Public Service Reform comprised of Members of Congress, representatives from the President's National Council on Federal Labor-Management Relations, members of the private sector, and academic experts. The purpose of a Congressionally-chartered Commission would be to develop recommendations on reforms to modernize Federal personnel policies and practices within fiscal constraints and core principles, including – but not limited to – compensation, staff development and mobility, and personnel performance and motivation.

One clear manifestation of the challenges of the GS system is the continued requests for additional flexibilities, exceptions, and authorities that the agencies need to effectively manage their workforce. While a fragmented personnel system provides needed customization, today's personnel strategy and oversight must strike a balance between flexibility and consistency to continue to reflect and uphold longstanding core merit principles. Quite simply, a 21st Century Government must be supported by a 21st Century personnel system.

Retirement-Eligible Workforce

Between FY 2009 and FY 2013, the annual number of Federal retirements steadily increased, rising from 87,907 to 116,039, leveling at 99,710 in 2014. The 99,864 Federal retirements in 2015 represent approximately 3.6 percent of the total workforce, including Postal, Judiciary and Congressional workers. Consistent with 2014 levels, twenty-five percent of respondents to the 2015 Employee Viewpoint Survey (EVS) expressed intent to retire during the next five years, with four percent intending to retire in the next year. Given these demographics, the Federal Government faces a few immediate challenges: preparing for retirements by maximizing knowledge transfer from one generation to the next; succession planning to assure needed leadership; and hiring and developing the next generation of the Government workforce to accomplish the varied and challenging missions the Federal Government must deliver.

Employee Engagement

OPM administers the Government-wide Employee Viewpoint Survey (EVS) to gather employee perceptions about whether, and to what extent, their agencies share the characteristics of successful organizations. The EVS measures employee engagement, defined as employees' sense of purpose, evident in their display of dedication, persistence, and effort in their work or overall attachment to their organization and its mission. The commitment of the Federal workforce is evident in the 2015 EVS results. Federal employees continue to be engaged in their work, with a one percent increase in the Employee Engagement Index (EEI) reported since the 2014 survey. Additionally, 53 items showed increases of at least one percentage point, and for the first time ever, no items decreased Government-wide. While these changes are modest, they are in the right direction and consistent across the survey results.

One well-documented challenge in any organization is managing a workforce so it is engaged, innovative, and committed to continuous improvement. Federal employees are extremely positive about the importance of their work and repeatedly express a willingness to put in extra effort to accomplish the goals of their agencies. Consistent with the 2014 results, the 2015 EVS indicates that 96 percent of respondents answer positively to the statement "When needed I am willing to put in the extra effort to get the job done." Addressing training needs has increased two percentage points to 52 percent positive, approaching the 2012 level of 53 percent. Also a one percentage point increase was noted for whether employees "feel encouraged to come up with new and better ways of doing things."

The Employee Engagement Index is an important tool to measure the conditions likely to lead to employee engagement. There are three subfactors that make up the index – Leaders Lead, Supervisors and Intrinsic Work Experiences. Ratings of Leaders Lead and Intrinsic Work Experience each improved by one percentage point Government-wide, and supervisors maintained a score of 71 percent positive. Given the focus in the President's Management Agenda on engaging agency leaders and managers, these results provide some evidence that the Federal workforce is responding to these initiatives.

Budgetary Constraints

Throughout the Administration, relative reductions in Federal employee compensation have contributed significant Federal savings during a period of rapidly declining federal deficits. Cuts in salaries and benefits over the past six years have already saved the Government tens of billions of dollars. Using the current pay assumptions for 2017 and assuming ECI-level pay increases in FY2018 and later, these reductions in benefits will save the Government an additional $260 billion over the next decade. This equals more than $100,000 per FTE, the equivalent of an entire year of the civilian payroll.

Addressing Federal Workforce Challenges

The Administration is committed to accelerating employee performance and human capital management. These initiatives are a core component of the President's Management Agenda, as discussed in the main Budget volume. Multiple efforts are underway, including: building a workforce with the skills necessary to meet agency missions, developing and using personnel analytics to drive decision making, new programs to infuse talent into agencies, heightened attention to a diverse and inclusive workforce, continued focus on the Senior Executive Service (SES) hiring and performance appraisal systems, and strengthened labor-management partnerships.

Mission Focused and Data-Driven Personnel Management

The Administration is committed to strengthening Federal agencies' capacity to analyze human resources data to address workplace problems, improve productivity, and cut costs. OPM, in conjunction with OMB, is implementing several key initiatives that will lead to better evaluation and management of Federal employees. These efforts include using the EVS as a diagnostic tool to guide management of our Federal workers, expanding implementation of data-driven review sessions, greater alignment between human capital and mission performance, and quarterly updates of key HR performance indicators on Performance.gov.

As discussed earlier, OPM's EVS is a valuable management tool that helps agencies identify areas of strength and weakness and informs the implementation of targeted action plans to help improve employee engagement and agency performance. Notably, OPM has worked with agencies in recent years to increase the number of components within agencies for which office-specific results are available. Whereas only 1,687 components received results in 2011, more than 26,000 offices received results in 2015. The increased response and reporting granularity enables agencies to identify areas of strength, offering possible models for others, and areas of weakness needing attention. Agencies across Government are using EVS data to develop and implement targeted, mission-driven action plans to address identified challenges. With the 2014 release of UnlockTalent.Gov, an innovative, data visualization tool, OPM is providing managers across Government the ability to review their own results on engagement and satisfaction indices in comparison to the rest of Government. In addition, while previously only Federal managers and leaders were able to access Unlocktalent.gov, with the release of the 2015 EVS results, members of the public can view agency-level data on the website and Federal employees can register to see their agency-specific dashboards with more granular data. This broadening of access to the results provides transparency to Federal employees, who share their views through the survey, and to the taxpayer, who wants accountability. The Administration continues its investment in OPM's data analytics to increase the number of data sets available to Federal managers.

Since 2012, Chief Human Capital Officer (CHCO) level agencies have utilized HRstat reviews. These quarterly data-driven reviews, which are led by the agency CHCOs in collaboration with the designated agency Performance Improvement Officer (PIO), focus on agency-specific human capital performance and key human resources management metrics. Agencies have the flexibility to focus on areas critical to their mission and use metrics to understand issues such as performance management, succession planning, recruitment timeliness, and strategic workforce planning. The HRstat reviews are intended to enable quick course correction, if needed, to help ensure progress is being made on key human resources issues. For example, through HRstat, the Treasury Department matched up different bureaus as partners to collaborate on veterans hiring and in one year more than doubled the rate of new veterans hires.

Creating a Culture of Excellence and Engagement to Enable Higher Performance

Leadership, organizational culture, and employee engagement are critical factors in the success of private and public institutions. While employee engagement is linked to everything from higher earnings per share, to lower workplace accidents and turnover, and overall high performance in the private sector[3], the Administration's focus on employee engagement and mission performance are critical to supporting a Culture of Excellence that can improve all Federal services, and are important components of the Management Agenda. As the President said in his remarks to the SES on December 9, 2014: "One of the things that we know in the private sector about continuous improvement is you've got to have the folks right there on the front lines able to make suggestions and know that they're heard, and to not simply be rewarded for doing an outstanding job, but to see their ideas implemented in ways that really make a difference."

Elevating employee engagement is a top priority for the Administration. In December 2014, the Director and Deputy Director of OMB, Director of OPM and Deputy Director of the White House Presidential Personnel Office co-signed a memorandum to the Heads of all Agencies that outlined the linkage between strengthening employee engagement and organizational performance. Building on strong evidence from the private sector and case studies within the Federal Government, Senior Leaders will be held accountable for ensuring that employee engagement is a priority and becomes an integral part of the performance-management system.

Following the signing of the memorandum, OPM and OMB staff met with each of the 24 Senior Accountable Officials (SAO) designated by agency heads to lead employee engagement initiatives. These meetings included candid discussions on the challenges individual agencies and the Federal Government are facing. Throughout the year, the agencies collaborated to share best practices and

---

[3] Heskett, J. L., T. O. Jones, G. W.Loveman, W. Earl Sasser, and L. A. Schlesinger."Putting the Service-Profit Chain to Work." Harvard Business Review 72, no. 2 (March-April 1994): 164-174; Heskett, J., W. E. Sasser Jr., and L. Schlesinger. The Service Profit Chain. N.Y.: Free Press, 1997

refine their engagement efforts. The results are promising as no EVS questions showed a decline in 2015.

There are also effective tools available for managers and supervisors to address employee performance challenges. OPM offers periodic classroom training sessions; on-line training on HR University; and an OPM desk guide for supervisors to assist them in addressing and resolving poor performance of employees they supervise. Consistent with recommendations from the President's Management Council (PMC), OPM will help agencies understand the authorities they have and how to use them effectively to spread best practices to deal with poor performers who fail to improve as needed or are ill suited to their current positions.

One other promising development is a new way to permit part-time details, allowing employees to work on agency projects for different managers. "GovConnect" is helping agencies deploy a more mobile, agile, and innovative Federal workforce through testing and adopting new workforce models. The Environmental Protection Agency (EPA), General Services Administration (GSA), Housing and Urban Development (HUD), and OPM collaborated to develop GovConnect. The proposal was approved by President's Management Council (PMC) and the GovConnect initiative was launched at a PMC meeting in March 2014. Agencies are already seeing success with manager-initiated micro-projects, employee suggested projects and cloud-based skills deployment systems.

As capabilities are enhanced and credibility is built, these efforts will incorporate continuous improvement in learning and development opportunities and tools available to Federal managers and employees. As part of the Government Performance and Results Act implementation, agencies are aligning strategic human capital planning, with mission planning – specifically strategic and performance plans.

Building a World-Class Federal Management Team Starting with Enhancements to the Senior Executive Service

One of the key pillars of the President's Management Agenda is building a world-class Federal workforce, starting with the Senior Executive Service. The Administration is committed to investing in and supporting the thousands of hard working and dedicated leaders in the SES and ensuring the Federal government remains competitive in attracting and retaining top talent for leadership positions.

On December 9th, 2014 the President announced the creation of a White House Advisory Group (WHAG) to Strengthen the Senior Executive Service. The WHAG, comprised of 24 leaders from across the Federal Government, was charged with making recommendations to the Administration on how to improve the way the Federal Government recruits, hires, develops, manages, retains, and ensures accountability for its senior career leaders. Over the past year, OMB and OPM, working collaboratively with the WHAG, sought the viewpoints of many agencies and stakeholder groups and incorporated feedback and input on proposals that have led to the rec-

ommendations issued as part of an Executive Order in December 2015. The Executive Order, along with a series of actions the administration is undertaking, focus on three key themes – hiring the best talent, strengthening SES development and improving SES accountability, recognition and rewards. Many of these recommendations will be implemented immediately, while some will be phased in over three years.

To improve the hiring process, agency leadership will track and monitor SES vacancies and recruiting efforts on a regular basis. OPM will review the Qualifications Review Board (QRB) process and determine new materials acceptable for QRB consideration and agencies will streamline their hiring process accordingly. Building on successful models currently employed at the Department of Defense and in the Intelligence Community, agencies will establish an annual talent and succession management process to inform decisions about promotions, career development, and executive rotations.

To strengthen SES development, agencies will implement robust onboarding programs, capitalizing on the success of onboarding pilots in six agencies. Agencies are required to develop plans to facilitate the rotation of their SES based on the needs of the agency and the developmental needs and growth opportunities of the executive. In addition, executives are required to participate in regular professional development opportunities, including a multi-rater assessment, such as a 360 degree review, every three years.

The Administration is also taking steps to improve performance and accountability. In October, 2015, OPM issued a final rule to help standardize a common framework for the performance management of all SES members across the Federal Government, ensuring agencies have a consistent approach to SES performance management and hold leaders accountable for individual and agency performance. While the new rules only took effect on October 26, 2015, many agencies are already meeting these new requirements under the basic SES performance appraisal system that they have voluntarily adopted. Executive reviews will also include performance factors that address customer and employee perspectives, leadership effectiveness in promoting diversity, inclusion and engagement in their organizations, and the productivity and effectiveness of their employees.

In 2016, OPM plans to launch an education campaign on SES performance and accountability. OPM will develop a short summary of the rules and processes that govern SES performance and will host quarterly webinars to provide information, training, and sharing of successful practices. Furthermore, OPM is establishing an expert team to consult two or three agencies to address SES conduct and performance challenges. OPM will help agencies assess SES performance management systems and programs, prepare action plans, and provide technical assistance.

The Executive Order creates a subcommittee of the PMC to advise OPM, members of the PMC, and the President on implementation of the order and additional ways to strengthen and improve the SES workforce. The

Deputy Director for Management for OMB, the Director of OPM and three other members of the PMC will serve on the Subcommittee. The Subcommittee will select at least two career members of the SES to advise them and will collaborate with the Chief Human Capital Officers Council.

The White House Leadership Development Fellows

Announced in December 2014, the Administration launched the White House Leadership Development Program. Through this program, GS-15 (and equivalent) emerging leaders participate in rotational assignments to drive progress on Cross-Agency Priority (CAP) Goals and lead change across Departments and programs. Agencies nominated dozens of their top-performing leads who then were assessed by panels comprised of existing executives across Government. The initial class of 16 Fellows entered on duty in November 2015 and are now working on cross-agency priorities such as shared service centers, veterans mental health, climate change and human capital. The cadre meets weekly for executive development sessions. Participants in the program will gain valuable cross-agency experience by playing a key role in addressing critical management challenges facing the Federal Government while building networks and best practices to bring back to their agencies. Upon completion of the program many of the Fellows will be better prepared to enter senior leadership roles with a whole-of-government perspective.

Enabling Agencies to Hire the Best Talent

The Administration is committed to working with labor groups, universities, nonprofits and the private sector to improve hiring outcomes by exploring flexible approaches to recruit, hire, and retain individuals with high-demand talents and skills to fill our most critical positions. As part of the President's Management Agenda, the Administration will continue to engage with agencies in 2016 to identify promising practices in recruiting, hiring, onboarding, and deploying talent across agencies. The goal remains to increase the quality of new Federal hires, foster diversity and inclusion throughout the hiring process, and improve organizational outcomes. OPM is working individually with agencies to "untie the knots" that previously hindered the ability to hire the best talent from all segments of society. Also in FY 2015, OPM completed the design and development of a web-based Hiring Toolkit that will provide a wide variety of resources and information related to hiring authorities, hiring process, mythbusters, and technical support/information for hiring managers and HR practitioners. In FY 2016, OPM will be building upon the 2010 Hiring Reform efforts but with a focus on Hiring Excellence, ensuring the Government can attract applicants and hire highly qualified and diverse talent, achieved through engaged and empowered hiring managers, and supported by highly skilled HR staff. In FY 2016, OPM will launch a Hiring Excellence Campaign for outreach and education to human resources professionals, managers and supervisors supported by robust tools and guidance.

Family Friendly Workplace Policies

The Federal Government has also made progress towards pay equality. Based on recent studies, the gap between average male and female salaries in the Federal Government is about half the gap in the private sector. A growing number of working Americans – both men and women – struggle to balance the needs of their families with the responsibilities of their jobs. Leading companies in the private sector are working to develop new tools to redesign their workplaces to provide greater flexibility to workers. While the Federal leave system has been enhanced over the years and is generally regarded as providing good benefits and flexibilities, there is room for further enhancements that would help the Federal Government in its efforts to recruit and retain a quality workforce.

On June 23, 2014, the President issued a broadly focused Presidential Memorandum (PM) on Enhancing Workplace Flexibilities and Work-Life Programs that directs agency heads to ensure that various workplace flexibilities are available 'to the maximum extent practicable,' including the advancement of leave for employee and family care situations. The June PM requires that agencies review and assess the efficacy of existing workplace flexibilities and work-life programs in meeting employee needs.

While Federal workers already have access to paid sick leave and vacation time, the Government has fallen behind industry-leading companies and offers no paid time off specifically for family or parental leave. In order to recruit and retain the best possible workforce to provide outstanding service to American taxpayers, OPM is proposing legislation, with the President's support, that would provide Federal employees with six weeks of paid administrative leave for the birth, adoption, or foster placement of a child. In addition, the proposal would allow parents to use sick days to care for a new child. In doing so, the proposals will strengthen Federal recruitment and retention, and make significant progress in bringing Federal parental leave policies in line with benefit programs already provided by many companies, while also encouraging wider adoption of such standards in the private sector. The costs of providing this benefit would be covered within agency budget requests for salaries and expenses.

The President also signed a Presidential Memorandum, Modernizing Federal Leave Policies for Childbirth, Adoption and Foster Care to Recruit and Retain Talent and Improve Productivity on January 15, 2015, directing agencies to allow for the advance of 30 days of paid sick leave for parents with a new child, employees caring for ill family members, and other sick leave-eligible uses. This allows new mothers the opportunity to recuperate after child birth, even if they have not yet accrued enough sick leave. It allows spouses and partners to care for a new mother during her recuperation period and both parents to attend proceedings relating to the adoption of a new child. Finally, it directs agencies to consider a benefit some agencies already provide—help finding, and in some cases subsidizing, emergency backup child care (as well as backup care for seniors and adults with disabilities) that parents can use for a limited numbers of days per year when they need to go to work but their regular care is not available. Some agencies provide this benefit through their Employee Assistance Program and it can help parents with a temporary need for safe care for their children.

The Federal Government should be a model employer and has already aggressively increased the use of telework and other policies to promote family-friendly policies. The 2015 EVS indicated that teleworkers are more likely to feel empowered (47 percent versus 41 percent), and more likely to be satisfied with their jobs (69 percent compared to 63 percent of non-teleworkers). Finally, employees who telework are more likely to want to stay with their agencies (67 percent compared to 64 percent of non-teleworkers) and to recommend their agencies to others (67 percent compared to 61 percent of non-teleworkers). As documented by OPM's 2013 report on the status of telework (the most recent available), the percentage of eligible Federal employees who participated in routine telework grew to 21 percent as of September 2012, compared to 10 percent during calendar year 2009. Equally important, the number of employees deemed eligible to telework increased by nearly 50 percent from 2011 to 2012. However, there is still more work to be done in breaking down barriers to the effective use of telework.

Closing Skills Gaps in the Workforce

The demands of the workplace necessitate new and agile skill sets in the Federal workforce. OPM's mission is to ensure that the Federal Government recruits, retains, and honors the talent agencies require to serve the American people. In 2011, OPM partnered with the CHCO Council to take on the challenge of closing skills gaps across the Government. This initiative was launched in response to the President's 2012-2013 CAP Goal to close skills gaps, as well as GAO's designation of human capital as a Government-wide high risk area. The Department of Defense joined OPM in chairing an interagency workgroup that designed a sustainable strategic workforce planning method to identify and close skills gaps in mission-critical occupations. Based on rigorous data analysis, the workgroup identified the following mission-critical occupations: IT-Cybersecurity Specialists, Acquisition Specialists, Economists, Human Resources Specialists, and Auditors. In addition, the workgroup identified STEM (science, technology, engineering, and mathematics) as a sixth functional area covering multiple occupations which requires sustained strategic attention across Government. In 2016, the workgroup is expanding its work to more broadly involve subject matter experts and examine more series.

To close skills gaps in these areas, OPM designated sub-goal leaders from agencies whose missions critically depend on these occupations. Together with these sub-goal leaders, OPM is developing and executing strategies to close skills gaps in these occupations. The sub-goal leaders meet quarterly with the OPM Director to apprise her of their progress by providing updated metrics that will be reported on Performance.gov.

OPM will continue to work with these occupations' leaders to close skill gaps. In Cybersecurity, OPM has completed a major initiative to populate the Enterprise Human Resources Integration (EHRI) database with a Cybersecurity data code that designates which Federal positions work in the Cybersecurity function, and in which specialty area. In FY 2014, all agencies met their targets to add a Cybersecurity identifier to all relevant positions. In FY 2015, OPM validated and analyzed the data to identify tools that can be applied to workforce planning for this occupation, which poses high risk to the Federal Government if the positions are not filled. As part of the Office of the Federal CIO's Cybersecurity Strategy Implementation Plan, OPM is partnering with several agencies to map the current cybersecurity workforce and identify strategies to close critical skills gaps in this area in 2016. In the STEM functional area, a specific Pathways Program was developed for attracting STEM applicants for the Presidential Management Fellows opportunity. The PMF-STEM Pathways track was piloted during FY 2014. The Acquisition area has begun to increase efficiencies in training, development, and management of the workforce. Interagency workgroups are exploring possible pilots to test special hiring and compensation authorities for several occupations, including Economist, STEM, and Cybersecurity roles. OPM is assisting the Auditor occupational area in studying what changes are needed to the classification and qualification requirements to increase the talent brought into that workforce. Individual agencies are also identifying and targeting critical skills gaps as a priority, and are piloting innovative approaches to competency gap closure. OPM is helping agencies share promising practices and lessons learned from these pilot projects, and will drive replication of best practices upon completion of the pilots.

Successful skills gap closure is particularly dependent on a strong HR workforce that can provide strategies, programs, and tools that help occupational leaders design and implement skills gaps closure efforts. For this reason, OPM has been focusing heavily on this workforce and designated HR Skills Gaps as an Agency Priority Goal. One of the ways OPM is addressing skills gaps among human resources professionals is through HR University. Developed in 2011 by the CHCO Council, HR University provides an excellent training foundation for human resources professionals to become more effective. HR University is a source of centralized training that takes courses and resources Federal agencies have already developed and provides a platform for cross-agency sharing. HR University realizes savings through the sharing of resources (agencies no longer need to independently develop courses that already exist) and economies of scale. In addition, HR University ensures that courses meet OPM's high standards by vetting each course through a very rigorous quality review.

In partnership with the CHCO Council, OPM will continue to expand HR University's offerings. This effort may include more partnerships with colleges and universities, development of HR certifications, accreditation of courses, greater use of social media, website enhancements, and more courses on key topics that will close identified skill and competency gaps in the human resources field. OPM registered 98 percent of the human resources workforce onto HR University by September 30, 2015. In FY 2015, OPM added 10 courses to HR University. In FY 2016, OPM will continue to engage agencies to register and expand the course offerings.

Developing an Agile Workforce

To maximize effectiveness and potential, the Federal Government must continue to prepare its talent for challenges on the horizon. New cost-effective programs are being implemented to develop current employees, foster collaboration with innovators from the private sector, and enhance institutional knowledge transfer. For example, OPM has implemented a phased retirement program that provides employees who once had a financial incentive to retire fully, to work part time while mentoring and training new employees. Several agencies have implemented phased retirement, and others are currently developing policies to fully implement and leverage this important tool. These efforts are essential for developing a nimble, efficient 21st Century workforce that can help ensure agencies achieve their important missions under a tightening fiscal climate.

Informing Our Work with a Diversity of Experiences

A rich diversity of experiences and talents inform the abilities of Federal applicants and everyday work of Federal employees. Opportunities exist both in employee hiring and throughout employment experiences to leverage this diversity. In recent years, OPM has been focusing on improving the way agencies use Federal applicant and applicant flow data to improve the hiring process. OPM continues to increase the accessibility and use of this data by hiring managers, so they can determine whether outreach, recruitment, and hiring strategies have been successful in attracting and retaining a workforce that reflects the diversity of our country and the many talents of its people.

Leveraging the diversity of our workforce also requires that we measure and improve the extent to which diversity and inclusion are supported in work units. To that end, and mirroring the aforementioned efforts to measure and target improvements in employee engagement, OPM developed an index based on 20 EVS items called the New Inclusion Quotient (New IQ) that represents each work unit's inclusive intelligence and provides feedback to executive leadership, program managers, and supervisors on how well work units are leveraging the unique experiences, perspectives, and viewpoints of their employees to improve program delivery.

Importantly, the Budget recognizes that increased availability of this data is not sufficient. Fostering inclusive work environments and realizing the full potential of our workforce's diversity requires agencies to employ effective management practices. OPM's change manage-

ment tools supplement the inclusion index. The index and tools, referred to jointly as the New Inclusion Quotient Plus, arm agencies with instruments and practices necessary to support diversity and inclusion more fully. In addition, OPM will continue to promote proven practices in using all workforce data to inform everyday support for diversity and inclusion in the workplace.

Strengthening Labor-Management Relations

In early FY 2015, OPM released a report on "Labor Management Relations in the Executive Branch," describing how labor-management relations are structured and how they operate in the Federal Government. This report detailed examples of the benefits that can result from strengthening labor-management relationships. Specifically, improving labor-management relations facilitates opportunities for agencies to improve their performance. This report is expected to be updated in early FY 2017.

The Administration continues to fulfill the robust vision laid out in Executive Order 13522, Creating Labor-Management Forums to Improve Delivery of Government Services. Issued in 2009, this Executive Order created a National Council, which meets regularly to coordinate Government-wide efforts, and a multitude of labor-management forums around Government where agency management and union representatives work collaboratively to improve service delivery to the public. In 2016, Labor-Management Forums will continue to use metrics to track progress.

At the Council's meetings, representatives from both management and labor regularly provide details about their efforts to improve performance and productivity at their agencies by working together. Recently, the Council heard from participants in the General Services Administration, Region 5, the American Federation of Government Employees, and the National Federation of Federal Employees on their formation of a Space Council, a joint, collaborative body formed to facilitate sharing information about how to handle office relocations early and often to avoid the disagreements that occur when employees are not involved in these major changes. The Council also allowed them to reduce the need for formal bargaining. They were able to establish a consistent, known, participatory process that encouraged pre-decisional involvement (PDI) even outside of the space issues. The Council also heard from participants in the forum between the EPA and the National Treasury Employees Union. This group worked together to implement the Skills Marketplace at EPA, which was the first large scale use of PDI for an initiative at the agency. The Skills Marketplace is a program that gives employees the opportunity to work on a program 20 percent of the time anywhere else in the agency without leaving their home office. In the past year, they have done 340 projects. EPA employees who participate bring new skills back, and are provided an opportunity for staff career growth without them leaving permanently or going on full time detail.

The Council will continue to seek ways to spread these and other labor-management successes to other agencies in 2016 and 2017. One method employed by the Council has been to develop training and guidance to assist forums with successfully engaging in PDI and with using metrics to track their activities. The Council is currently gathering lessons-learned narratives which are based upon the many success stories that the Council has heard about labor-management cooperation and PDI. The narratives will allow the parties to share their experiences and how they succeeded with regard to PDI. The information gleaned from the narratives will be compiled and posted on the Council website as a series of lessons learned that can be used by other parties. Additionally, the Council is exploring the measurement and reporting of PDI outcomes, PDI awards and recognition, and PDI barriers and accountability. The Council is also working to identify common contract language in collective bargaining agreements and make it available to agencies and unions in contract negotiations. The goal is to find contract language that could serve as a template for agencies and labor unions in order to reduce time and resources spent by parties in the negotiation process. Recently, the Council supported the work of the Federal Labor Relations Authority (FLRA), Federal Mediation and Conciliation Service (FMCS), and the GSA on their collaborative effort to present a live two day pilot training program to labor and management participants about the labor relations aspects of space management and the potential use of PDI in office moves and space allocation. The pilot program will lead to additional training opportunities, including a webinar. The Council will continue working in 2016 to ensure that additional labor-management forums transition into effective partnerships with a focus on improving the productivity and effectiveness of the Federal Government.

Honoring a World-Class Workforce

Federal Employees make a difference every single day in the lives of millions of people across the country and around the world. As President Obama said in his Public Service Recognition Proclamation:

"In the face of difficult challenges, public servants give new life to the values that bind our Nation together... Public service is a calling which has meant so much to so many. It embodies our sense of shared values and reflects our drive to serve a cause beyond our own—to give back to our Nation, leave our mark, and nudge history forward. There is no greater opportunity to help more people or to make a bigger difference."

BUDGET CONCEPTS AND BUDGET PROCESS

9. BUDGET CONCEPTS

The budget system of the United States Government provides the means for the President and the Congress to decide how much money to spend, what to spend it on, and how to raise the money they have decided to spend. Through the budget system, they determine the allocation of resources among the agencies of the Federal Government and between the Federal Government and the private sector. The budget system focuses primarily on dollars, but it also allocates other resources, such as Federal employment. The decisions made in the budget process affect the Nation as a whole, State and local governments, and individual Americans. Many budget decisions have worldwide significance. The Congress and the President enact budget decisions into law. The budget system ensures that these laws are carried out.

This chapter provides an overview of the budget system and explains some of the more important budget concepts. It includes summary dollar amounts to illustrate major concepts. Other chapters of the budget documents discuss these amounts and more detailed amounts in greater depth.

The following section discusses the budget process, covering formulation of the President's Budget, action by the Congress, and execution of enacted budget laws. The next section provides information on budget coverage, including a discussion of on-budget and off-budget amounts, functional classification, presentation of budget data, types of funds, and full-cost budgeting. Subsequent sections discuss the concepts of receipts and collections, budget authority, and outlays. These sections are followed by discussions of Federal credit; surpluses, deficits, and means of financing; Federal employment; and the basis for the budget figures. A glossary of budget terms appears at the end of the chapter.

Various laws, enacted to carry out requirements of the Constitution, govern the budget system. The chapter refers to the principal ones by title throughout the text and gives complete citations in the section just preceding the glossary.

THE BUDGET PROCESS

The budget process has three main phases, each of which is related to the others:

1. Formulation of the President's Budget;

2. Action by the Congress; and

3. Execution of enacted budget laws.

Formulation of the President's Budget

The Budget of the United States Government consists of several volumes that set forth the President's fiscal policy goals and priorities for the allocation of resources by the Government. The primary focus of the Budget is on the budget year—the next fiscal year for which the Congress needs to make appropriations, in this case 2017. (Fiscal year 2017 will begin on October 1, 2016, and end on September 30, 2017.) The Budget also covers the nine years following the budget year in order to reflect the effect of budget decisions over the longer term. It includes the funding levels provided for the current year, in this case 2016, which allows the reader to compare the President's Budget proposals with the most recently enacted levels. The Budget also includes data on the most recently completed fiscal year, in this case 2015, so that the reader can compare budget estimates to actual accounting data.

In a normal year, the President begins the process of formulating the budget by establishing general budget and fiscal policy guidelines, usually by the spring of each year, at least nine months before the President transmits the budget to the Congress and at least 18 months before the fiscal year begins. (See the "Budget Calendar" later in this chapter.) Based on these guidelines, the Office of Management and Budget (OMB) works with the Federal agencies to establish specific policy directions and planning levels, both for the budget year and for at least the following four years, and in this case, the following nine years, to guide the preparation of their budget requests.

During the formulation of the budget, the President, the Director of OMB, and other officials in the Executive Office of the President continually exchange information, proposals, and evaluations bearing on policy decisions with the Secretaries of the departments and the heads of the other Government agencies. Decisions reflected in previously enacted budgets, including the one for the fiscal year in progress, reactions to the last proposed budget (which the Congress is considering at the same time the process of preparing the forthcoming budget begins), and evaluations of program performance all influence decisions concerning the forthcoming budget, as do projections of the economic outlook, prepared jointly by the Council of Economic Advisers, OMB, and the Treasury Department.

In early fall, agencies submit their budget requests to OMB, where analysts review them and identify issues that OMB officials need to discuss with the agencies. OMB and the agencies resolve many issues themselves. Others require the involvement of White House policy officials and the President. This decision-making process is usually completed by late December. At that time, the final stage of developing detailed budget data and the preparation of the budget documents begins.

The decision-makers must consider the effects of economic and technical assumptions on the budget estimates. Interest rates, economic growth, the rate of inflation, the unemployment rate, and the number of people eligible for various benefit programs, among other factors, affect Government spending and receipts. Small changes in these assumptions can alter budget estimates by many billions of dollars. (Chapter 2 "Economic Assumptions and Interactions with the Budget," provides more information on this subject.)

Thus, the budget formulation process involves the simultaneous consideration of the resource needs of individual programs, the allocation of resources among the agencies and functions of the Federal Government, and the total outlays and receipts that are appropriate in light of current and prospective economic conditions.

The law governing the President's budget requires its transmittal to the Congress on or after the first Monday in January but not later than the first Monday in February of each year for the following fiscal year, which begins on October 1. The budget is routinely sent to the Congress on the first Monday in February, giving the Congress eight months to act on the budget before the fiscal year begins.

Congressional Action[1]

The Congress considers the President's budget proposals and approves, modifies, or disapproves them. It can change funding levels, eliminate programs, or add programs not requested by the President. It can add or eliminate taxes and other sources of receipts or make other changes that affect the amount of receipts collected.

The Congress does not enact a budget as such. Through the process of adopting a planning document called a budget resolution (described below), the Congress agrees on targets for total spending and receipts, the size of the deficit or surplus, and the debt limit. The budget resolution provides the framework within which individual congressional committees prepare appropriations bills and other spending and receipts legislation. The Congress provides spending authority—funding—for specified purposes in appropriations acts each year. It also enacts changes each year in other laws that affect spending and receipts. Both appropriations acts and these other laws are discussed in the following paragraphs.

In making appropriations, the Congress does not vote on the level of outlays (spending) directly, but rather on budget authority, or funding, which is the authority provided by law to incur financial obligations that will result in outlays. In a separate process, prior to making appropriations, the Congress usually enacts legislation that authorizes an agency to carry out particular programs, authorizes the appropriation of funds to carry out those

---

[1] For a fuller discussion of the congressional budget process, see Bill Heniff Jr., Introduction to the Federal Budget Process (Congressional Research Service Report 98–721), and Robert Keith and Allen Schick, Manual on the Federal Budget Process (Congressional Research Service Report 98–720, archived).

programs, and, in some cases, limits the amount that can be appropriated for the programs. Some authorizing legislation expires after one year, some expires after a specified number of years, and some is permanent. The Congress may enact appropriations for a program even though there is no specific authorization for it or its authorization has expired.

The Congress begins its work on its budget resolution shortly after it receives the President's budget. Under the procedures established by the Congressional Budget Act of 1974, the Congress decides on budget targets before commencing action on individual appropriations. The Act requires each standing committee of the House and Senate to recommend budget levels and report legislative plans concerning matters within the committee's jurisdiction to the Budget Committee in each body. The House and Senate Budget Committees then each design and report, and each body then considers, a concurrent resolution on the budget—a congressional budget plan, or budget resolution. The budget resolution sets targets for total receipts and for budget authority and outlays, both in total and by functional category (see "Functional Classification" later in this chapter). It also sets targets for the budget deficit or surplus and for Federal debt subject to statutory limit.

The congressional timetable calls for the House and Senate to resolve differences between their respective versions of the congressional budget resolution and adopt a single budget resolution by April 15 of each year.

In the report on the budget resolution, the Budget Committees allocate the total on-budget budget authority and outlays set forth in the resolution to the Appropriations Committees and the other committees that have jurisdiction over spending. (See "Coverage of the Budget," later in this chapter, for more information on on-budget and off-budget amounts.) Now that statutory limits on discretionary budget authority have been reinstated, as discussed below, the budget resolution allocation to the Appropriations Committees will equal those limits. Once the Congress resolves differences between the House and Senate and agrees on a budget resolution, the Appropriations Committees are required to divide their allocations of budget authority and outlays among their subcommittees. There are procedural hurdles associated with considering appropriations bills ("discretionary" spending) that would breach or further breach an Appropriations subcommittee's target. Similar procedural hurdles exist for considering legislation that would cause the overall spending target for any such committee to be breached or further breached. The Budget Committees' reports may discuss assumptions about the level of funding for major programs. While these assumptions do not bind the other committees and subcommittees, they may influence their decisions.

The budget resolution may also contain "reconciliation directives" (discussed below) to the committees responsible for tax laws and for mandatory spending—programs not controlled by annual appropriation acts—in order to conform the level of receipts and this type of spending to the targets in the budget resolution.

Since the concurrent resolution on the budget is not a law, it does not require the President's approval. However, the Congress considers the President's views in preparing budget resolutions, because legislation developed to meet congressional budget allocations does require the President's approval. In some years, the President and the joint leadership of Congress have formally agreed on plans to reduce the deficit or balance the budget. These agreements were then reflected in the budget resolution and legislation passed for those years.

Once the Congress approves the budget resolution, it turns its attention to enacting appropriations bills and authorizing legislation. Appropriations bills are initiated in the House. They provide the budgetary resources for the majority of Federal programs, but only a minority of Federal spending. The Appropriations Committee in each body has jurisdiction over annual appropriations. These committees are divided into subcommittees that hold hearings and review detailed budget justification materials prepared by the Executive Branch agencies within the subcommittee's jurisdiction. After a bill has been drafted by a subcommittee, the full committee and the whole House, in turn, must approve the bill, sometimes with amendments to the original version. The House then forwards the bill to the Senate, where a similar review follows. If the Senate disagrees with the House on particular matters in the bill, which is often the case, the two bodies form a conference committee (consisting of some Members of each body) to resolve the differences. The conference committee revises the bill and returns it to both bodies for approval. When the revised bill is agreed to, first in the House and then in the Senate, the Congress sends it to the President for approval or veto.

Since 1977, when the start of the fiscal year was established as October 1, there have been only three fiscal years (1989, 1995, and 1997) for which the Congress agreed to and enacted every regular appropriations bill by that date. When one or more appropriations bills has not been agreed to by this date, Congress usually enacts a joint resolution called a "continuing resolution," (CR) which is an interim or stop-gap appropriations bill that provides authority for the affected agencies to continue operations at some specified level until a specific date or until the regular appropriations are enacted. Occasionally, a CR has funded a portion or all of the Government for the entire year.

The Congress must present these CRs to the President for approval or veto. In some cases, Presidents have rejected CRs because they contained unacceptable provisions. Left without funds, Government agencies were required by law to shut down operations—with exceptions for some limited activities—until the Congress passed a CR the President would approve. Shutdowns have lasted for periods of a day to several weeks.

The Congress also provides budget authority in laws other than appropriations acts. In fact, while annual appropriations acts fund the majority of Federal programs, they account for only about a third of the total spending in a typical year. Authorizing legislation controls the rest of the spending, which is commonly called "mandatory spending." A distinctive feature of these authorizing laws is that they provide agencies with the authority or requirement to spend money without first requiring the Appropriations Committees to enact funding. This category of spending includes interest the Government pays on the public debt and the spending of several major programs, such as Social Security, Medicare, Medicaid, unemployment insurance, and Federal employee retirement. This chapter discusses the control of budget authority and outlays in greater detail under "Budget Authority and Other Budgetary Resources, Obligations, and Outlays." Almost all taxes and most other receipts also result from authorizing laws. Article I, Section 7, of the Constitution provides that all bills for raising revenue shall originate in the House of Representatives. In the House, the Ways and Means Committee initiates tax bills; in the Senate, the Finance Committee has jurisdiction over tax laws.

The budget resolution often includes reconciliation directives, which require authorizing committees to recommend changes in laws that affect receipts or mandatory spending. They direct each designated committee to report amendments to the laws under the committee's

BUDGET CALENDAR

The following timetable highlights the scheduled dates for significant budget events during a normal budget year:

Between the 1st Monday in January and the 1st Monday in February	President transmits the budget
Six weeks later	Congressional committees report budget estimates to Budget Committees
April 15	Action to be completed on congressional budget resolution
May 15	House consideration of annual appropriations bills may begin even if the budget resolution has not been agreed to.
June 10	House Appropriations Committee to report the last of its annual appropriations bills.
June 15	Action to be completed on "reconciliation bill" by the Congress.
June 30	Action on appropriations to be completed by House
July 15	President transmits Mid-Session Review of the Budget
October 1	Fiscal year begins

jurisdiction that would achieve changes in the levels of receipts or reductions in mandatory spending controlled by those laws. These directives specify the dollar amount of changes that each designated committee is expected to achieve, but do not specify which laws are to be changed or the changes to be made. However, the Budget Committees' reports on the budget resolution frequently discuss assumptions about how the laws would be changed. Like other assumptions in the report, they do not bind the committees of jurisdiction but may influence their decisions. A reconciliation instruction may also specify the total amount by which the statutory limit on the public debt is to be changed.

The committees subject to reconciliation directives draft the implementing legislation. Such legislation may, for example, change the tax code, revise benefit formulas or eligibility requirements for benefit programs, or authorize Government agencies to charge fees to cover some of their costs. Reconciliation bills are typically omnibus legislation, combining the legislation submitted by each reconciled committee in a single act.

Such a large and complicated bill would be difficult to enact under normal legislative procedures because it usually involves changes to tax rates or to popular social programs, generally to reduce projected deficits. The Senate considers such omnibus reconciliation acts under expedited procedures that limit total debate on the bill. To offset the procedural advantage gained by expedited procedures, the Senate places significant restrictions on the substantive content of the reconciliation measure itself, as well as on amendments to the measure. Any material in the bill that is extraneous or that contains changes to the Federal Old-Age and Survivors Insurance and the Federal Disability Insurance programs is not in order under the Senate's expedited reconciliation procedures. Non-germane amendments are also prohibited. In addition, the Senate does not allow reconciliation bills as a whole to increase projected deficits or reduce projected surpluses. This Senate prohibition complements the Statutory Pay-As-You-Go Act of 2010, discussed below. The House does not allow reconciliation bills to increase mandatory spending in net, but does allow such bills to increase deficits by reducing revenues.

Reconciliation acts, together with appropriations acts for the year, are usually used to implement broad agreements between the President and the Congress on those occasions where the two branches have negotiated a comprehensive budget plan. Reconciliation acts have sometimes included other matters, such as laws providing the means for enforcing these agreements, as described under "Budget Enforcement."

Budget Enforcement

The Federal Government uses three primary enforcement mechanisms to control revenues, spending, and deficits. First, the Statutory Pay-As-You-Go Act of 2010, enacted on February 12, 2010, reestablished a statutory procedure to enforce a rule of deficit neutrality on new revenue and mandatory spending legislation. Second, the Budget Control Act of 2011 (BCA), enacted on August 2, 2011, amended the Balanced Budget and Emergency Deficit Control Act of 1985 (BBEDCA) by reinstating limits ("caps") on the amount of discretionary budget authority that can be provided through the annual appropriations process. Third, the BCA also created a Joint Select Committee on Deficit Reduction that was instructed to develop a bill to reduce the Federal deficit by at least $1.5 trillion over a 10-year period and imposed automatic spending cuts to achieve $1.2 trillion of deficit reduction over 9 years after the Joint Committee process failed to achieve its deficit reduction goal.

BBEDCA divides spending into two types—discretionary spending and direct or mandatory spending. Discretionary spending is controlled through annual appropriations acts. Funding for salaries and other operating expenses of government agencies, for example, is generally discretionary because it is usually provided by appropriations acts. Direct spending is more commonly called mandatory spending. Mandatory spending is controlled by permanent laws. Medicare and Medicaid payments, unemployment insurance benefits, and farm price supports are examples of mandatory spending, because permanent laws authorize payments for those purposes. Receipts are included under the same statutory enforcement rules that apply to mandatory spending because permanent laws generally control receipts.

Discretionary cap enforcement. BBEDCA specifies spending limits ("caps") on discretionary budget authority for 2012 through 2021. Similar enforcement mechanisms were established by the Budget Enforcement Act of 1990 and were extended in 1993 and 1997, but expired at the end of 2002. The caps originally established by the BCA were divided between security and nonsecurity categories for 2012 and 2013, with a single cap for all discretionary spending established for 2014 through 2021. The security category included discretionary budget authority for the Departments of Defense, Homeland Security, and Veterans Affairs, the National Nuclear Security Administration, the Intelligence Community Management account, and all budget accounts in the international affairs budget function (budget function 150). The nonsecurity category includes all discretionary budget authority not included in the security category. As part of the enforcement mechanisms triggered by the failure of the BCA's Joint Committee process, the security and nonsecurity categories were redefined and established for all years through 2021. The "revised security category" included discretionary budget authority in the defense budget function 050, which primarily consists of the Department of Defense. The "revised nonsecurity category" includes all discretionary budget authority not included in the defense budget function 050. The redefined categories are commonly referred to as the "defense" and "non-defense" categories, respectively, to distinguish them from the original categories.

Since the Joint Committee sequestration that was ordered on March 1, 2013, the Congress and the President have enacted two agreements to provide more resources to discretionary programs than would have been available under the Joint Committee enforcement mechanisms. These increases to the caps were paid for largely with savings in mandatory spending. The Bipartisan Budget Act (BBA) of 2013 set new discretionary caps for 2014 at $520.5 billion for the defense category and $491.8 billion for the non-defense category and for 2015 at $521.3 billion for the defense category and $492.4 billion for the non-defense category. The BBA of 2015 set new discretionary caps for 2016 at $548.1 billion for the defense category and $518.5 for the non-defense category and for 2017 at $551.1 billion for the defense category and $518.5 billion for the non-defense category. In addition, the BBA of 2013 reaffirmed the defense and non-defense category limits through 2021 and the BBA of 2015 left these in place after 2017. However, these limits are still subject to Joint Committee reductions if those procedures remain in place.

BBEDCA requires OMB to adjust the caps each year for: changes in concepts and definitions; appropriations designated by the Congress and the President as emergency requirements; and appropriations designated by the Congress and the President for Overseas Contingency Operations/Global War on Terrorism. BBEDCA also specifies cap adjustments (which are limited to fixed amounts) for: appropriations for continuing disability reviews and redeterminations by the Social Security Administration; the health care fraud and abuse control program at the Department of Health and Human Services; and appropriations designated by Congress as being for disaster relief.

BBEDCA requires OMB to provide cost estimates of each appropriations act in a report to the Congress within 7 business days after enactment of such act and to publish three discretionary sequestration reports: a "preview" report when the President submits the budget; an "update" report in August, and a "final" report within 15 days after the end of a session of the Congress.

The preview report explains the adjustments that are required by law to the discretionary caps, including any changes in concepts and definitions, and publishes the revised caps. The preview report may also provide a summary of policy changes, if any, proposed by the President in the Budget to those caps. The update and final reports revise the preview report estimates to reflect the effects of newly enacted discretionary laws. In addition, the update report must contain a preview estimate of the adjustment for disaster funding for the upcoming fiscal year.

If OMB's final sequestration report for a given fiscal year indicates that the amount of discretionary budget authority provided in appropriations acts for that year exceeds the cap for that category in that year, the President must issue a sequestration order canceling budgetary resources in nonexempt accounts within that category by the amount necessary to eliminate the breach. Under sequestration, each nonexempt account within a category is reduced by a dollar amount calculated by multiplying the enacted level of sequestrable budgetary resources in that account by the uniform percentage necessary to eliminate a breach within that category. BBEDCA specifies special rules for reducing some programs and exempts some

programs from sequestration entirely. For example, any sequestration of certain health and medical care accounts is limited to 2 percent. Also, if a continuing resolution is in effect when OMB issues its final sequestration report, the sequestration calculations will be based on the annualized amount provided by that continuing resolution. During the 1990s and so far under the BCA caps, the threat of sequestration proved sufficient to ensure compliance with the discretionary spending limits. In that respect, discretionary sequestration can be viewed first as an incentive for compliance and second as a remedy for noncompliance. This is also true for mandatory sequestration under PAYGO, as discussed below.

Supplemental appropriations can also trigger spending reductions. From the end of a session of the Congress through the following June 30th, a within-session discretionary sequestration of current-year spending is imposed if appropriations for the current year cause a cap to be breached. In contrast, if supplemental appropriations enacted in the last quarter of a fiscal year (i.e., July 1 through September 30) cause the caps to be breached, the required reduction is instead achieved by reducing the applicable spending limit for the following fiscal year by the amount of the breach, because the size of the potential sequestration in relation to the unused funding remaining for the current year could severely disrupt agencies' operations.

Direct spending enforcement. The Statutory Pay-As-You-Go Act of 2010 requires that new legislation changing mandatory spending or revenue must be enacted on a "pay-as-you-go" (PAYGO) basis; that is, that the cumulative effects of such legislation must not increase projected on-budget deficits. Unlike the budget enforcement mechanism for discretionary programs, PAYGO is a permanent requirement, and it does not impose a cap on spending or a floor on revenues. Instead, PAYGO requires that legislation reducing revenues must be fully offset by cuts in mandatory programs or by revenue increases, and that any bills increasing mandatory spending must be fully offset by revenue increases or cuts in mandatory spending.

This requirement of deficit neutrality is not enforced on a bill-by-bill basis, but is based on two cumulative scorecards that tally the cumulative budgetary effects of PAYGO legislation as averaged over rolling 5- and 10-year periods starting with the budget year. Any impacts of PAYGO legislation on the current year deficit are counted as budget year impacts when placed on the scorecard. Like the discretionary caps, PAYGO is enforced by sequestration. Within 14 business days after a congressional session ends, OMB issues an annual PAYGO report and determines whether a violation of the PAYGO requirement has occurred. If either the 5- or 10-year scorecard shows net costs in the budget year column, the President is required to issue a sequestration order implementing across-the-board cuts to nonexempt mandatory programs by an amount sufficient to offset those net costs. The PAYGO effects of legislation may be directed in legislation by reference to statements inserted into the *Congressional Record* by the chairmen of the House and

Senate Budget Committees. Any such estimates are determined by the Budget Committees and are informed by, but not required to match, the cost estimates prepared by the Congressional Budget Office (CBO). If this procedure is not followed, then the PAYGO effects of the legislation are determined by OMB. During the first year of statutory PAYGO, nearly half the bills included congressional estimates. In the subsequent five years, OMB estimates were used for all but one of the enacted bills due to the absence of a congressional estimate. Provisions of mandatory spending or receipts legislation that are designated in that legislation as an emergency requirement are not scored as PAYGO budgetary effects.

The PAYGO rules apply to the outlays resulting from outyear changes in mandatory programs made in appropriations acts and to all revenue changes made in appropriations acts. However, outyear changes to mandatory programs as part of provisions that have zero net outlay effects over the sum of the current year and the next five fiscal years are not considered PAYGO.

The PAYGO rules do not apply to increases in mandatory spending or decreases in receipts that result automatically under existing law. For example, mandatory spending for benefit programs, such as unemployment insurance, rises when the number of beneficiaries rises, and many benefit payments are automatically increased for inflation under existing laws. Additional information on the Statutory Pay-As-You-Go Act of 2010 can be found on OMB's website at *https://www.whitehouse.gov/omb/paygo_description.*

The Senate imposes points of order against consideration of tax or mandatory spending legislation that would violate the PAYGO principle, although the time periods covered by the Senate's rule and the treatment of previously enacted costs or savings may differ in some respects from the requirements of the Statutory Pay-As-You-Go Act of 2010.

The House, in contrast, imposes points of order on legislation increasing mandatory spending in net, whether or not those costs are offset by revenue increases, but the House rule does not constrain the size of tax cuts or require them to be offset.

For the 114th Congress, House rules require the official cost estimates of major legislation that are used for enforcing the budget resolution and other House rules to incorporate the budgetary effects of changes in economic output, employment, capital stock and other macroeconomic variables. This is known as dynamic scoring and involves estimating the impact of policy changes on the overall economy as well as secondary "feedback" effects.

Joint Committee reductions. The failure of the Joint Select Committee on Deficit Reduction to propose, and the Congress to enact, legislation to reduce the deficit by at least $1.2 trillion triggered automatic reductions to discretionary and mandatory spending in fiscal years 2013 through 2021. The reductions are implemented through a combination of sequestration and reductions in the discretionary caps. These reductions have already been ordered to take effect for 2013 through 2017, with some modifications as provided for in the American Taxpayer

Relief Act of 2012, the BBA of 2013, and the BBA of 2015. Unless the Congress acts, further reductions will be implemented by pro rata reductions to the discretionary caps from 2018 through 2021, which would be reflected in OMB's discretionary sequestration preview report for those years, and by a sequestration of non-exempt mandatory spending for 2018 onward, which would be ordered when the President's Budget is transmitted to Congress and would take effect beginning October 1 of the upcoming fiscal year.

OMB is required to calculate the amount of the deficit reduction required for 2018 onward as follows:

- The $1.2 trillion savings target is reduced by 18 percent to account for debt service.

- The resulting net savings of $984 billion is divided by nine to spread the reductions in equal amounts across the nine years, 2013 through 2021.

- The annual spending reduction of $109.3 billion is divided equally between the defense and non-defense functions.

- The annual reduction of $54.7 billion for each functional category of spending is divided proportionally between discretionary and direct spending programs, using as the base the discretionary cap, redefined as outlined in the discretionary cap enforcement section above, and the most recent baseline estimate of non-exempt mandatory outlays.

- The resulting reductions in defense and non-defense direct spending are implemented through a sequestration order released with the President's Budget and taking effect the following October 1st. The reductions in discretionary spending are applied as reductions in the discretionary caps, and are enforced through the discretionary cap enforcement procedures discussed earlier in this section.

Subsequent to the enactment of the BCA, the mandatory sequestration provisions were extended beyond 2021 by the BBA of 2013, which extended sequestration through 2023, P.L. 113-82, commonly referred to as the Military Retired Pay Restoration Act, which extended sequestration through 2024, and the BBA of 2015, which extended mandatory sequestration through 2025. Sequestration in these four years is to be applied using the same percentage reductions for defense and nondefense as calculated for 2021 under the procedures outlined above.[2]

The BBA of 2013 and the BBA of 2015 took important steps in moving away from manufactured crises and austerity budgeting by replacing a portion of the Joint Committee reductions with sensible long-term reforms, including a number of reforms proposed in previous President's Budgets. The 2017 Budget builds on the achievements secured for 2016 and adheres to the agreement's funding levels. However, failing to fully replace

---

[2] The BBA of 2015 specified that, notwithstanding the 2 percent limit on Medicare sequestration in the BCA, in extending sequestration into 2025 the reduction in the Medicare program should be 4.0 percent for the first half of the sequestration period and zero for the second half of the period.

the Joint Committee reductions has consequences. To further the goal of building durable economic growth in the future, the Budget also includes a series of investments using mandatory funding.

The 2017 Budget also recognizes that without further Congressional action, Joint Committee enforcement will return in full in 2018. Therefore, starting in 2018, the Budget once again proposes to support a range of investments to move the Nation forward by ending the Joint Committee reductions and replacing the savings by cutting inefficient spending and closing tax loopholes, while putting the Nation on a sustainable fiscal path.

Budget Execution

Government agencies may not spend or obligate more than the Congress has appropriated, and they may use funds only for purposes specified in law. The Antideficiency Act prohibits them from spending or obligating the Government to spend in advance of an appropriation, unless specific authority to do so has been provided in law. Additionally, the Act requires the President to apportion the budgetary resources available for most executive branch agencies. The President has delegated this authority to OMB. Some apportionments are by time periods (usually by quarter of the fiscal year), some are by projects or activities, and others are by a combination of both. Agencies may request OMB to reapportion funds during the year to accommodate changing circumstances. This system helps to ensure that funds do not run out before the end of the fiscal year.

During the budget execution phase, the Government sometimes finds that it needs more funding than the Congress has appropriated for the fiscal year because of unanticipated circumstances. For example, more might be needed to respond to a severe natural disaster. Under such circumstances, the Congress may enact a supplemental appropriation.

On the other hand, the President may propose to reduce a previously enacted appropriation. The President may propose to either "cancel" or "rescind" the amount. If the President initiates the withholding of funds while the Congress considers his request, the amounts are apportioned as "deferred" or "withheld pending rescission" on the OMB-approved apportionment form. Agencies are instructed not to withhold funds without the prior approval of OMB. When OMB approves a withholding, the Impoundment Control Act requires that the President transmit a "special message" to the Congress. The historical reason for the special message is to inform the Congress that the President has unilaterally withheld funds that were enacted in regular appropriations acts. The notification allows the Congress to consider the proposed rescission in a timely way. The last time the President initiated the withholding of funds was in fiscal year 2000.

COVERAGE OF THE BUDGET

Federal Government and Budget Totals

The budget documents provide information on all Federal agencies and programs. However, because the laws governing Social Security (the Federal Old-Age and Survivors Insurance and the Federal Disability Insurance trust funds) and the Postal Service Fund require that the receipts and outlays for those activities be excluded from the budget totals and from the calculation of the deficit or surplus, the budget presents on-budget and off-budget totals. The off-budget totals include the Federal transactions excluded by law from the budget totals. The on-budget and off-budget amounts are added together to derive the totals for the Federal Government. These are sometimes referred to as the unified or consolidated budget totals.

It is not always obvious whether a transaction or activity should be included in the budget. Where there is a question, OMB normally follows the recommendation of the 1967 President's Commission on Budget Concepts to be comprehensive of the full range of Federal agencies, programs, and activities. In recent years, for example, the budget has included the transactions of the Affordable Housing Program funds, the Universal Service Fund, the Public Company Accounting Oversight Board, the Securities Investor Protection Corporation, Guaranty Agencies Reserves, the National Railroad Retirement Investment Trust, the United Mine Workers Combined Benefits Fund, the Federal Financial Institutions Examination Council, Electric Reliability Organizations (EROs) established pursuant to the Energy Policy Act of 2005, the Corporation for Travel Promotion, and the National Association of Registered Agents and Brokers.

In contrast, the budget excludes tribal trust funds that are owned by Indian tribes and held and managed by the Government in a fiduciary capacity on the tribes' behalf. These funds are not owned by the Government, the Government is not the source of their capital, and the Government's control is limited to the exercise of fiduciary duties. Similarly, the transactions of Government-sponsored enterprises, such as the Federal Home Loan Banks, are not included in the on-budget or off-budget totals. Federal laws established these enterprises for public policy purposes, but they are privately owned and operated corporations. Nevertheless, because of their public charters, the budget discusses them and reports summary financial data in the budget *Appendix* and in some detailed tables.

The budget also excludes the revenues from copyright royalties and spending for subsequent payments to copyright holders where (1) the law allows copyright owners and users to voluntarily set the rate paid for the use of protected material, and (2) the amount paid by users of copyrighted material to copyright owners is related to the frequency or quantity of the material used. The budget excludes license royalties collected and paid out by the

Copyright Office for the retransmission of network broadcasts via cable collected under 17 U.S.C. 111 because these revenues meet both of these conditions. The budget includes the royalties collected and paid out for license fees for digital audio recording technology under 17 U.S.C. 1004, since the amount of license fees paid is unrelated to usage of the material.

The *Appendix* includes a presentation for the Board of Governors of the Federal Reserve System for information only. The amounts are not included in either the on-budget or off-budget totals because of the independent status of the System within the Government. However, the Federal Reserve System transfers its net earnings to the Treasury, and the budget records them as receipts. Chapter 10 of this volume, "Coverage of the Budget," provides more information on this subject.

Table 9–1. TOTALS FOR THE BUDGET AND THE FEDERAL GOVERNMENT
(In billions of dollars)

	2015 Actual	Estimate	
		2016	2017
Budget authority			
Unified	3,773	3,991	4,235
On-budget	3,024	3,198	3,403
Off-budget	749	792	832
Receipts:			
Unified	3,250	3,336	3,644
On-budget	2,480	2,538	2,817
Off-budget	770	798	827
Outlays:			
Unified	3,688	3,951	4,147
On-budget	2,945	3,162	3,319
Off-budget	743	790	829
Deficit (–) / Surplus (+):			
Unified	–438	–616	–503
On-budget	–466	–624	–502
Off-budget	27	8	–2

Functional Classification

The functional classification is used to organize budget authority, outlays, and other budget data according to the major purpose served—such as agriculture, transportation, income security, and national defense. There are 20 major functions, 17 of which are concerned with broad areas of national need and are further divided into subfunctions. For example, the Agriculture function comprises the subfunctions Farm Income Stabilization and Agricultural Research and Services. The functional classification meets the Congressional Budget Act requirement for a presentation in the budget by national needs and agency missions and programs. The remaining three functions—Net Interest, Undistributed Offsetting Receipts, and Allowances—enable the functional classification system to cover the entire Federal budget.

The following criteria are used in establishing functional categories and assigning activities to them:

- A function encompasses activities with similar purposes, emphasizing what the Federal Government seeks to accomplish rather than the means of accomplishment, the objects purchased, the clientele or geographic area served (except in the cases of functions 450 for Community and Regional Development, 570 for Medicare, 650 for Social Security, and 700 for Veterans Benefits and Services), or the Federal agency conducting the activity (except in the case of subfunction 051 in the National Defense function, which is used only for defense activities under the Department of Defense—Military).

- A function must be of continuing national importance, and the amounts attributable to it must be significant.

- Each basic unit being classified (generally the appropriation or fund account) usually is classified according to its primary purpose and assigned to only one subfunction. However, some large accounts that serve more than one major purpose are subdivided into two or more functions or subfunctions.

In consultation with the Congress, the functional classification is adjusted from time to time as warranted. Detailed functional tables, which provide information on Government activities by function and subfunction, are available online at *www.budget.gov/budget/Analytical_Perspectives* and on the *Budget CD-ROM*.

Agencies, Accounts, Programs, Projects, and Activities

Various summary tables in the *Analytical Perspectives* volume of the Budget provide information on budget authority, outlays, and offsetting collections and receipts arrayed by Federal agency. A table that lists budget authority and outlays by budget account within each agency and the totals for each agency of budget authority, outlays, and receipts that offset the agency spending totals is available online at: *www.budget.gov/budget/Analytical_Perspectives* and on the *Budget CD-ROM*. The *Appendix* provides budgetary, financial, and descriptive information about programs, projects, and activities by account within each agency.

Types of Funds

Agency activities are financed through Federal funds and trust funds.

Federal funds comprise several types of funds. Receipt accounts of the ***general fund***, which is the greater part of the budget, record receipts not earmarked by law for a specific purpose, such as income tax receipts. The general fund also includes the proceeds of general borrowing. General fund appropriations accounts record general fund expenditures. General fund appropriations draw from general fund receipts and borrowing collectively and, therefore, are not specifically linked to receipt accounts.

Special funds consist of receipt accounts for Federal fund receipts that laws have designated for specific purposes and the associated appropriation accounts for the expenditure of those receipts.

Public enterprise funds are revolving funds used for programs authorized by law to conduct a cycle of business-type operations, primarily with the public, in which outlays generate collections.

Intragovernmental funds are revolving funds that conduct business-type operations primarily within and between Government agencies. The collections and the outlays of revolving funds are recorded in the same budget account.

Trust funds account for the receipt and expenditure of monies by the Government for carrying out specific purposes and programs in accordance with the terms of a statute that designates the fund as a trust fund (such as the Highway Trust Fund) or for carrying out the stipulations of a trust where the Government itself is the beneficiary (such as any of several trust funds for gifts and donations for specific purposes). *Trust revolving funds* are trust funds credited with collections earmarked by law to carry out a cycle of business-type operations.

The Federal budget meaning of the term "trust," as applied to trust fund accounts, differs significantly from its private-sector usage. In the private sector, the beneficiary of a trust usually owns the trust's assets, which are managed by a trustee who must follow the stipulations of the trust. In contrast, the Federal Government owns the assets of most Federal trust funds, and it can raise or lower future trust fund collections and payments, or change the purposes for which the collections are used, by changing existing laws. There is no substantive difference between a trust fund and a special fund or between a trust revolving fund and a public enterprise revolving fund.

However, in some instances, the Government does act as a true trustee of assets that are owned or held for the benefit of others. For example, it maintains accounts on behalf of individual Federal employees in the Thrift Savings Fund, investing them as directed by the individual employee. The Government accounts for such funds in *deposit funds*, which are not included in the budget.

(Chapter 26 of this volume, "Trust Funds and Federal Funds," provides more information on this subject.)

Budgeting for Full Costs

A budget is a financial plan for allocating resources—deciding how much the Federal Government should spend in total, program by program, and for the parts of each program and deciding how to finance the spending. The budgetary system provides a process for proposing policies, making decisions, implementing them, and reporting the results. The budget needs to measure costs accurately so that decision makers can compare the cost of a program with its benefits, the cost of one program with another, and the cost of one method of reaching a specified goal with another. These costs need to be fully included in the budget up front, when the spending decision is made, so that executive and congressional decision makers have the information and the incentive to take the total costs into account when setting priorities.

The budget includes all types of spending, including both current operating expenditures and capital investment, and to the extent possible, both are measured on the basis of full cost. Questions are often raised about the measure of capital investment. The present budget provides policymakers the necessary information regarding investment spending. It records investment on a cash basis, and it requires the Congress to provide budget authority before an agency can obligate the Government to make a cash outlay. However, the budget measures only costs, and the benefits with which these costs are compared, based on policy makers' judgment, must be presented in supplementary materials. By these means, the budget allows the total cost of capital investment to be compared up front in a rough way with the total expected future net benefits. Such a comparison of total costs with benefits is consistent with the formal method of cost-benefit analysis of capital projects in government, in which the full cost of a capital asset as the cash is paid out is compared with the full stream of future benefits (all in terms of present values). (Chapter 18 of this volume, "Federal Investment," provides more information on capital investment.)

RECEIPTS, OFFSETTING COLLECTIONS, AND OFFSETTING RECEIPTS

In General

The budget records amounts collected by Government agencies two different ways. Depending on the nature of the activity generating the collection and the law that established the collection, they are recorded as either:

- *Governmental receipts*, which are compared in total to outlays (net of offsetting collections and offsetting receipts) in calculating the surplus or deficit; or

- *Offsetting collections* or *offsetting receipts*, which are deducted from gross outlays to calculate net outlay figures.

Governmental Receipts

Governmental receipts are collections that result from the Government's exercise of its sovereign power to tax or otherwise compel payment. Sometimes they are called receipts, budget receipts, Federal receipts, or Federal revenues. They consist mostly of individual and corporation income taxes and social insurance taxes, but also include excise taxes, compulsory user charges, regulatory fees, customs duties, court fines, certain license fees, and deposits of earnings by the Federal Reserve System. Total receipts for the Federal Government include both on-budget and off-budget receipts (see Table 9–1, "Totals for the Budget and the Federal Government," which appears earlier in this chapter.) Chapter 12 of this volume,

"Governmental Receipts," provides more information on governmental receipts.

Offsetting Collections and Offsetting Receipts

Offsetting collections and offsetting receipts are recorded as offsets to (deductions from) spending, not as additions on the receipt side of the budget. These amounts are recorded as offsets to outlays so that the budget totals represent governmental rather than market activity and reflect the Government's net transactions with the public. They are recorded in one of two ways, based on interpretation of laws and longstanding budget concepts and practice. They are offsetting collections when the collections are authorized by law to be credited to expenditure accounts and are generally available for expenditure without further legislation. Otherwise, they are deposited in receipt accounts and called offsetting receipts.

Offsetting collections and offsetting receipts result from any of the following types of transactions:

- *Business-like transactions or market-oriented activities with the public*—these include voluntary collections from the public in exchange for goods or services, such as the proceeds from the sale of postage stamps, the fees charged for admittance to recreation areas, and the proceeds from the sale of Government-owned land; and reimbursements for damages. The budget records these amounts as *offsetting collections from non-Federal sources* (for offsetting collections) or as *proprietary receipts* (for offsetting receipts).

- *Intragovernmental transactions*—collections from other Federal Government accounts. The budget records collections by one Government account from another as *offsetting collections from Federal sources* (for offsetting collections) or as *intragovernmental receipts* (for offsetting receipts). For example, the General Services Administration rents office space to other Government agencies and records their rental payments as offsetting collections from Federal sources in the Federal Buildings Fund. These transactions are exactly offsetting and do not affect the surplus or deficit. However, they are an important accounting mechanism for allocating costs to the programs and activities that cause the Government to incur the costs.

- *Voluntary gifts and donations*—gifts and donations of money to the Government, which are treated as offsets to budget authority and outlays.

- *Offsetting governmental transactions*—collections from the public that are governmental in nature and should conceptually be treated like Federal revenues and compared in total to outlays (e.g., tax receipts, regulatory fees, compulsory user charges, custom duties, license fees) but required by law or longstanding practice to be misclassified as offsetting. The budget records amounts from non-Federal sources that are governmental in nature as *offset-ting governmental collections* (for offsetting collections) or as *offsetting governmental receipts* (for offsetting receipts).

Offsetting Collections

Some laws authorize agencies to credit collections directly to the account from which they will be spent and, usually, to spend the collections for the purpose of the account without further action by the Congress. Most revolving funds operate with such authority. For example, a permanent law authorizes the Postal Service to use collections from the sale of stamps to finance its operations without a requirement for annual appropriations. The budget records these collections in the Postal Service Fund (a revolving fund) and records budget authority in an amount equal to the collections. In addition to revolving funds, some agencies are authorized to charge fees to defray a portion of costs for a program that are otherwise financed by appropriations from the general fund and usually to spend the collections without further action by the Congress. In such cases, the budget records the offsetting collections and resulting budget authority in the program's general fund expenditure account. Similarly, intragovernmental collections authorized by some laws may be recorded as offsetting collections and budget authority in revolving funds or in general fund expenditure accounts.

Sometimes appropriations acts or provisions in other laws limit the obligations that can be financed by offsetting collections. In those cases, the budget records budget authority in the amount available to incur obligations, not in the amount of the collections.

Offsetting collections credited to expenditure accounts automatically offset the outlays at the expenditure account level. Where accounts have offsetting collections, the budget shows the budget authority and outlays of the account both gross (before deducting offsetting collections) and net (after deducting offsetting collections). Totals for the agency, subfunction, and overall budget are net of offsetting collections.

Offsetting Receipts

Collections that are offset against gross outlays but are not authorized to be credited to expenditure accounts are credited to receipt accounts and are called offsetting receipts. Offsetting receipts are deducted from budget authority and outlays in arriving at total net budget authority and outlays. However, unlike offsetting collections credited to expenditure accounts, offsetting receipts do not offset budget authority and outlays at the account level. In most cases, they offset budget authority and outlays at the agency and subfunction levels.

Proprietary receipts from a few sources, however, are not offset against any specific agency or function and are classified as undistributed offsetting receipts. They are deducted from the Government-wide totals for net budget authority and outlays. For example, the collections of rents and royalties from outer continental shelf lands are undistributed because the amounts are large and for the most part are not related to the spending of the agency that administers the transactions and the subfunction that records the administrative expenses.

Similarly, two kinds of intragovernmental transactions—agencies' payments as employers into Federal employee retirement trust funds and interest received by trust funds—are classified as undistributed offsetting receipts. They appear instead as special deductions in computing total net budget authority and outlays for the Government rather than as offsets at the agency level. This special treatment is necessary because the amounts are so large they would distort measures of the agency's activities if they were attributed to the agency.

User Charges

User charges are fees assessed on individuals or organizations for the provision of Government services and for the sale or use of Government goods or resources. The payers of the user charge must be limited in the authoriz-ing legislation to those receiving special benefits from, or subject to regulation by, the program or activity beyond the benefits received by the general public or broad segments of the public (such as those who pay income taxes or customs duties). Policy regarding user charges is established in OMB Circular A–25, "User Charges." The term encompasses proceeds from the sale or use of Government goods and services, including the sale of natural resources (such as timber, oil, and minerals) and proceeds from asset sales (such as property, plant, and equipment). User charges are not necessarily dedicated to the activity they finance and may be credited to the general fund of the Treasury.

The term "user charge" does not refer to a separate budget category for collections. User charges are classified in the budget as receipts, offsetting receipts, or offsetting collections according to the principles explained previously.

See Chapter 13, "Offsetting Collections and Offsetting Receipts," for more information on the classification of user charges.

BUDGET AUTHORITY, OBLIGATIONS, AND OUTLAYS

Budget authority, obligations, and outlays are the primary benchmarks and measures of the budget control system. The Congress enacts laws that provide agencies with spending authority in the form of budget authority. Before agencies can use these resources—obligate this budget authority—OMB must approve their spending plans. After the plans are approved, agencies can enter into binding agreements to purchase items or services or to make grants or other payments. These agreements are recorded as obligations of the United States and deducted from the amount of budgetary resources available to the agency. When payments are made, the obligations are liquidated and outlays recorded. These concepts are discussed more fully below.

Budget Authority and Other Budgetary Resources

Budget authority is the authority provided in law to enter into legal obligations that will result in immediate or future outlays of the Government. In other words, it is the amount of money that agencies are allowed to commit to be spent in current or future years. Government officials may obligate the Government to make outlays only to the extent they have been granted budget authority.

The budget records new budget authority as a dollar amount in the year when it first becomes available for obligation. When permitted by law, unobligated balances of budget authority may be carried over and used in the next year. The budget does not record these balances as budget authority again. They do, however, constitute a budgetary resource that is available for obligation. In some cases, a provision of law (such as a limitation on obligations or a benefit formula) precludes the obligation of funds that would otherwise be available for obligation. In such cases, the budget records budget authority equal to the amount of obligations that can be incurred. A major exception to this rule is for the highway and mass transit programs financed by the Highway Trust Fund, where budget authority is measured as the amount of contract authority (described later in this chapter) provided in authorizing statutes, even though the obligation limitations enacted in annual appropriations acts restrict the amount of contract authority that can be obligated.

In deciding the amount of budget authority to request for a program, project, or activity, agency officials estimate the total amount of obligations they will need to incur to achieve desired goals and subtract the unobligated balances available for these purposes. The amount of budget authority requested is influenced by the nature of the programs, projects, or activities being financed. For current operating expenditures, the amount requested usually covers the needs for the fiscal year. For major procurement programs and construction projects, agencies generally must request sufficient budget authority in the first year to fully fund an economically useful segment of a procurement or project, even though it may be obligated over several years. This full funding policy is intended to ensure that the decision-makers take into account all costs and benefits fully at the time decisions are made to provide resources. It also avoids sinking money into a procurement or project without being certain if or when future funding will be available to complete the procurement or project.

Budget authority takes several forms:

- **Appropriations**, provided in annual appropriations acts or authorizing laws, permit agencies to incur obligations and make payment;

- **Borrowing authority**, usually provided in permanent laws, permits agencies to incur obligations but requires them to borrow funds, usually from the general fund of the Treasury, to make payment;

- **Contract authority**, usually provided in permanent law, permits agencies to incur obligations in advance of a separate appropriation of the cash for payment or in anticipation of the collection of receipts that can be used for payment; and

- **Spending authority from offsetting collections**, usually provided in permanent law, permits agencies to credit offsetting collections to an expenditure account, incur obligations, and make payment using the offsetting collections.

Because offsetting collections and offsetting receipts are deducted from gross budget authority, they are referred to as negative budget authority for some purposes, such as Congressional Budget Act provisions that pertain to budget authority.

Authorizing statutes usually determine the form of budget authority for a program. The authorizing statute may authorize a particular type of budget authority to be provided in annual appropriations acts, or it may provide one of the forms of budget authority directly, without the need for further appropriations.

An appropriation may make funds available from the general fund, special funds, or trust funds, or authorize the spending of offsetting collections credited to expenditure accounts, including revolving funds. Borrowing authority is usually authorized for business-like activities where the activity being financed is expected to produce income over time with which to repay the borrowing with interest. The use of contract authority is traditionally limited to transportation programs.

New budget authority for most Federal programs is normally provided in annual appropriations acts. However, new budget authority is also made available through permanent appropriations under existing laws and does not require current action by the Congress. Much of the permanent budget authority is for trust funds, interest on the public debt, and the authority to spend offsetting collections credited to appropriation or fund accounts. For most trust funds, the budget authority is appropriated automatically under existing law from the available balance of the fund and equals the estimated annual obligations of the funds. For interest on the public debt, budget authority is provided automatically under a permanent appropriation enacted in 1847 and equals interest outlays.

Annual appropriations acts generally make budget authority available for obligation only during the fiscal year to which the act applies. However, they frequently allow budget authority for a particular purpose to remain available for obligation for a longer period or indefinitely (that is, until expended or until the program objectives have been attained). Typically, budget authority for current operations is made available for only one year, and budget authority for construction and some research projects is available for a specified number of years or indefinitely. Most budget authority provided in authorizing statutes, such as for most trust funds, is available indefinitely. If

budget authority is initially provided for a limited period of availability, an extension of availability would require enactment of another law (see "Reappropriation" later in this chapter).

Budget authority that is available for more than one year and not obligated in the year it becomes available is carried forward for obligation in a following year. In some cases, an account may carry forward unobligated budget authority from more than one prior year. The sum of such amounts constitutes the account's **unobligated balance**. Most of these balances had been provided for specific uses such as the multi-year construction of a major project and so are not available for new programs. A small part may never be obligated or spent, primarily amounts provided for contingencies that do not occur or reserves that never have to be used.

Amounts of budget authority that have been obligated but not yet paid constitute the account's **unpaid obligations**. For example, in the case of salaries and wages, one to three weeks elapse between the time of obligation and the time of payment. In the case of major procurement and construction, payments may occur over a period of several years after the obligation is made. Unpaid obligations (which are made up of accounts payable and undelivered orders) net of the accounts receivable and unfilled customers' orders are defined by law as the **obligated balances**. Obligated balances of budget authority at the end of the year are carried forward until the obligations are paid or the balances are canceled. (A general law provides that the obligated balances of budget authority that was made available for a definite period is automatically cancelled five years after the end of the period.) Due to such flows, a change in the amount of budget authority available in any one year may change the level of obligations and outlays for several years to come. Conversely, a change in the amount of obligations incurred from one year to the next does not necessarily result from an equal change in the amount of budget authority available for that year and will not necessarily result in an equal change in the level of outlays in that year.

The Congress usually makes budget authority available on the first day of the fiscal year for which the appropriations act is passed. Occasionally, the appropriations language specifies a different timing. The language may provide an **advance appropriation**—budget authority that does not become available until one year or more beyond the fiscal year for which the appropriations act is passed. **Forward funding** is budget authority that is made available for obligation beginning in the last quarter of the fiscal year (beginning on July 1) for the financing of ongoing grant programs during the next fiscal year. This kind of funding is used mostly for education programs, so that obligations for education grants can be made prior to the beginning of the next school year. For certain benefit programs funded by annual appropriations, the appropriation provides for **advance funding**—budget authority that is to be charged to the appropriation in the succeeding year, but which authorizes obligations to be incurred in the last quarter of the current fiscal year if necessary to meet benefit payments in excess of the specific amount appropriated for the year. When such authority is used, an adjustment is made to increase the budget authority for the fiscal year in which it is used and to reduce the budget authority of the succeeding fiscal year.

Provisions of law that extend into a new fiscal year the availability of unobligated amounts that have expired or would otherwise expire are called reappropriations. Reappropriations of expired balances that are newly available for obligation in the current or budget year count as new budget authority in the fiscal year in which the balances become newly available. For example, if a 2015 appropriations act extends the availability of unobligated budget authority that expired at the end of 2014, new budget authority would be recorded for 2015. This scorekeeping is used because a reappropriation has exactly the same effect as allowing the earlier appropriation to expire at the end of 2014 and enacting a new appropriation for 2015.

For purposes of BBEDCA and the Statutory Pay-As-You-Go Act of 2010 (discussed earlier under "Budget Enforcement"), the budget classifies budget authority as *discretionary* or *mandatory*. This classification indicates whether an appropriations act or authorizing legislation controls the amount of budget authority that is available. Generally, budget authority is discretionary if provided in an annual appropriations act and mandatory if provided in authorizing legislation. However, the budget authority provided in annual appropriations acts for certain specifically identified programs is also classified as mandatory by OMB and the congressional scorekeepers. This is because the authorizing legislation for these programs entitles beneficiaries—persons, households, or other levels of government—to receive payment, or otherwise legally obligates the Government to make payment and thereby effectively determines the amount of budget authority required, even though the payments are funded by a subsequent appropriation.

Sometimes, budget authority is characterized as current or permanent. Current authority requires the Congress to act on the request for new budget authority for the year involved. Permanent authority becomes available pursuant to standing provisions of law without appropriations action by the Congress for the year involved. Generally, budget authority is current if an annual appropriations act provides it and permanent if authorizing legislation provides it. By and large, the current/permanent distinction has been replaced by the discretionary/mandatory distinction, which is similar but not identical. Outlays are also classified as discretionary or mandatory according to the classification of the budget authority from which they flow (see "Outlays" later in this chapter).

The amount of budget authority recorded in the budget depends on whether the law provides a specific amount or employs a variable factor that determines the amount. It is considered *definite* if the law specifies a dollar amount (which may be stated as an upper limit, for example, "shall not exceed ..."). It is considered *indefinite* if, instead of specifying an amount, the law permits the amount to be determined by subsequent circumstances. For example, indefinite budget authority is provided for interest on the public debt, payment of claims and judgments awarded by the courts against the United States, and many entitlement programs. Many of the laws that authorize collections to be credited to revolving, special, and trust funds make all of the collections available for expenditure for the authorized purposes of the fund, and such authority is considered to be indefinite budget authority because the amount of collections is not known in advance of their collection.

Obligations

Following the enactment of budget authority and the completion of required apportionment action, Government agencies incur obligations to make payments (see earlier discussion under "Budget Execution"). Agencies must record obligations when they enter into binding agreements that will result in immediate or future outlays. Such obligations include the current liabilities for salaries, wages, and interest; and contracts for the purchase of supplies and equipment, construction, and the acquisition of office space, buildings, and land. For Federal credit programs, obligations are recorded in an amount equal to the estimated subsidy cost of direct loans and loan guarantees (see "Federal Credit" later in this chapter).

Outlays

Outlays are the measure of Government spending. They are payments that liquidate obligations (other than most exchanges of financial instruments, of which the repayment of debt is the prime example). The budget records outlays when obligations are paid, in the amount that is paid.

Agency, function and subfunction, and Government-wide outlay totals are stated net of offsetting collections and offsetting receipts for most budget presentations. (Offsetting receipts from a few sources do not offset any specific function, subfunction, or agency, as explained previously, but only offset Government-wide totals.) Outlay totals for accounts with offsetting collections are stated both gross and net of the offsetting collections credited to the account. However, the outlay totals for special and trust funds with offsetting receipts are not stated net of the offsetting receipts. In most cases, these receipts offset the agency, function, and subfunction totals but do not offset account-level outlays. However, when general fund payments are used to finance trust fund outlays to the public, the associated trust fund receipts are netted against the bureau totals to prevent double-counting budget authority and outlays at the bureau level

The Government usually makes outlays in the form of cash (currency, checks, or electronic fund transfers). However, in some cases agencies pay obligations without disbursing cash, and the budget nevertheless records outlays for the equivalent method. For example, the budget records outlays for the full amount of Federal employees' salaries, even though the cash disbursed to employees is net of Federal and State income taxes withheld, retirement contributions, life and health insurance premiums,

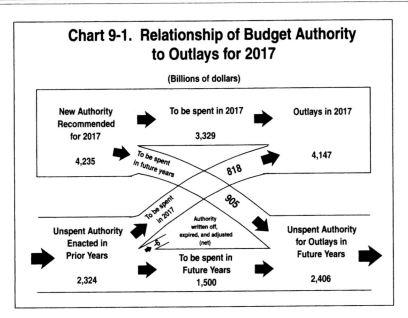

Chart 9-1. Relationship of Budget Authority to Outlays for 2017

(Billions of dollars)

and other deductions. (The budget also records receipts for the amounts withheld from Federal employee paychecks for Federal income taxes and other payments to the Government.) When debt instruments (bonds, debentures, notes, or monetary credits) are used in place of cash to pay obligations, the budget records outlays financed by an increase in agency debt. For example, the budget records the acquisition of physical assets through certain types of lease-purchase arrangements as though a cash disbursement were made for an outright purchase. The transaction creates a Government debt, and the cash lease payments are treated as repayments of principal and interest.

The budget records outlays for the interest on the public issues of Treasury debt securities as the interest accrues, not when the cash is paid. A small portion of Treasury debt consists of inflation-indexed securities, which feature monthly adjustments to principal for inflation and semiannual payments of interest on the inflation-adjusted principal. As with fixed-rate securities, the budget records interest outlays as the interest accrues. The monthly adjustment to principal is recorded, simultaneously, as an increase in debt outstanding and an outlay of interest.

Most Treasury debt securities held by trust funds and other Government accounts are in the Government account series. The budget normally states the interest on these securities on a cash basis. When a Government account is invested in Federal debt securities, the purchase price is usually close or identical to the par (face) value of the security. The budget generally records the investment at par value and adjusts the interest paid by Treasury and collected by the account by the difference between purchase price and par, if any.

For Federal credit programs, outlays are equal to the subsidy cost of direct loans and loan guarantees and are recorded as the underlying loans are disbursed (see "Federal Credit" later in this chapter).

The budget records refunds of receipts that result from overpayments by the public (such as income taxes withheld in excess of tax liabilities) as reductions of receipts, rather than as outlays. However, the budget records payments to taxpayers for refundable tax credits (such as earned income tax credits) that exceed the taxpayer's tax liability as outlays. Similarly, when the Government makes overpayments that are later returned to the Government, those refunds to the Government are recorded as offsetting collections or offsetting receipts, not as governmental receipts.

Not all of the new budget authority for 2017 will be obligated or spent in 2017. Outlays during a fiscal year may liquidate obligations incurred in the same year or in prior years. Obligations, in turn, may be incurred against budget authority provided in the same year or against unobligated balances of budget authority provided in prior years. Outlays, therefore, flow in part from budget authority provided for the year in which the money is spent and in part from budget authority provided for prior years. The ratio of a given year's outlays resulting from budget authority enacted in that or a prior year to the original amount of that budget authority is referred to as the spendout rate for that year.

As shown in the accompanying chart, $3,329 billion of outlays in 2017 (80 percent of the outlay total) will be made from that year's $4,235 billion total of proposed new budget authority (a first-year spendout rate of 79 percent). Thus, the remaining $818 billion of outlays in 2017 (20 percent of the outlay total) will be made from budget authority enacted in previous years. At the same time, $905 billion of the new budget authority proposed for 2017 (21 percent of the total amount proposed) will not lead to outlays until future years.

As described earlier, the budget classifies budget authority and outlays as discretionary or mandatory. This classification of outlays measures the extent to which actual spending is controlled through the annual appropriations process. About 32 percent of total outlays in 2015 ($1,165 billion) were discretionary and the remaining 68 percent ($2,524 billion in 2015) were mandatory spending and net interest. Such a large portion of total spending is mandatory because authorizing rather than appropriations legislation determines net interest ($223 billion in 2015) and the spending for a few programs with large amounts of spending each year, such as Social Security ($882 billion in 2015) and Medicare ($540 billion in 2015).

The bulk of mandatory outlays flow from budget authority recorded in the same fiscal year. This is not necessarily the case for discretionary budget authority and outlays. For most major construction and procurement projects and long-term contracts, for example, the budget authority covers the entire cost estimated when the projects are initiated even though the work will take place and outlays will be made over a period extending beyond the year for which the budget authority is enacted. Similarly, discretionary budget authority for most education and job training activities is appropriated for school or program years that begin in the fourth quarter of the fiscal year. Most of these funds result in outlays in the year after the appropriation.

FEDERAL CREDIT

Some Government programs provide assistance through direct loans or loan guarantees. A **direct loan** is a disbursement of funds by the Government to a non-Federal borrower under a contract that requires repayment of such funds with or without interest and includes economically equivalent transactions, such as the sale of Federal assets on credit terms. A **loan guarantee** is any guarantee, insurance, or other pledge with respect to the payment of all or a part of the principal or interest on any debt obligation of a non-Federal borrower to a non-Federal lender. The Federal Credit Reform Act of 1990, as amended (FCRA), prescribes the budgetary treatment for Federal credit programs. Under this treatment, the budget records obligations and outlays up front, for the net cost to the Government (subsidy cost), rather than recording the cash flows year by year over the term of the loan. FCRA treatment allows the comparison of direct loans and loan guarantees to each other, and to other methods of delivering assistance, such as grants.

The cost of direct loans and loan guarantees, sometimes called the "subsidy cost," is estimated as the present value of expected payments to and from the public over the term of the loan, discounted using appropriate Treasury interest rates.[3] Similar to most other kinds of programs, agencies can make loans or guarantee loans only if the Congress has appropriated funds sufficient to cover the subsidy costs, or provided a limitation in an appropriations act on the amount of direct loans or loan guarantees that can be made.

The budget records the subsidy cost to the Government arising from direct loans and loan guarantees—the budget authority and outlays—in **credit program accounts**. When a Federal agency disburses a direct loan or when a non-Federal lender disburses a loan guaranteed by a Federal agency, the program account disburses or outlays an amount equal to the estimated present value cost, or subsidy, to a non-budgetary credit **financing account**. The financing accounts record the actual transactions with the public. For a few programs, the estimated subsidy cost is negative because the present value of expected Government collections exceeds the present value of expected payments to the public over the term of the loan. In such cases, the financing account pays the estimated subsidy cost to the program's negative subsidy receipt account, where it is recorded as an offsetting receipt. In a few cases, the offsetting receipts of credit accounts are dedicated to a special fund established for the program and are available for appropriation for the program.

The agencies responsible for credit programs must reestimate the subsidy cost of the outstanding portfolio of direct loans and loan guarantees each year. If the estimated cost increases, the program account makes an additional payment to the financing account equal to the change in cost. If the estimated cost decreases, the financing account pays the difference to the program's downward reestimate receipt account, where it is recorded as an offsetting receipt. The FCRA provides permanent indefinite appropriations to pay for upward reestimates.

If the Government modifies the terms of an outstanding direct loan or loan guarantee in a way that increases the cost as the result of a law or the exercise of administrative discretion under existing law, the program account records obligations for the increased cost and outlays the amount to the financing account. As with the original subsidy cost, agencies may incur modification costs only if the Congress has appropriated funds to cover them. A modification may also reduce costs, in which case the amounts are generally returned to the general fund, as the financing account makes a payment to the program's negative subsidy receipt account.

Credit financing accounts record all cash flows arising from direct loan obligations and loan guarantee commitments. Such cash flows include all cash flows to and from the public, including direct loan disbursements and repayments, loan guarantee default payments, fees, and recoveries on defaults. Financing accounts also record intragovernmental transactions, such as the receipt of subsidy cost payments from program accounts, borrowing and repayments of Treasury debt to finance program activities, and interest paid to or received from the Treasury. The cash flows of direct loans and of loan guarantees are recorded in separate financing accounts for programs that provide both types of credit. The budget totals exclude the transactions of the financing accounts because they are not a cost to the Government. However, since financing accounts record all credit cash flows to and from the public, they affect the means of financing a budget surplus or deficit (see "Credit Financing Accounts" in the next section). The budget documents display the transactions of

---

[3] Present value is a standard financial concept that considers the time-value of money. That is, it accounts for the fact that a given sum of money is worth more today than the same sum would be worth in the future because interest can be earned.

the financing accounts, together with the related program accounts, for information and analytical purposes.

The FCRA grandfathered the budgetary treatment of direct loan obligations and loan guarantee commitments made prior to 1992. The budget records these on a cash basis in *credit liquidating accounts*, the same as they were recorded before FCRA was enacted. However, this exception ceases to apply if the direct loans or loan guarantees are modified as described above. In that case, the budget records the subsidy cost or savings of the modification, as appropriate, and begins to account for the associated transactions under FCRA treatment for direct loan obligations and loan guarantee commitments made in 1992 or later.

Under the authority provided in various acts, certain activities that do not meet the definition in FCRA of a direct loan or loan guarantee are reflected pursuant to FCRA. For example, the Emergency Economic Stabilization Act of 2008 (EESA) created the Troubled Asset Relief Program (TARP) under the Department of the Treasury, and authorized Treasury to purchase or guarantee troubled assets until October 3, 2010. Under the TARP, Treasury has purchased equity interests in financial institutions. Section 123 of the EESA provides the Administration the authority to treat these equity investments on a FCRA basis, recording outlays for the subsidy as is done for direct loans and loan guarantees. The budget reflects the cost to the Government of TARP direct loans, loan guarantees, and equity investments consistent with the FCRA and Section 123 of EESA, which requires an adjustment to the FCRA discount rate for market risks. Treasury equity purchases under the Small Business Lending Fund are treated pursuant to the FCRA, as provided by the Small Business Jobs Act of 2010. The 2009 increases to the International Monetary Fund (IMF) quota and New Arrangements to Borrow (NAB) enacted in the Supplemental Appropriations Act of 2009 were treated on a FCRA basis through 2015, with a risk adjustment to the discount rate, as directed in that Act. However, pursuant to Title IX of the Department of State, Foreign Operations, and Related Programs Appropriations Act, 2016, these transactions have been restated on a present value basis with a risk adjustment to the discount rate, and the associated FCRA accounts have been closed.

BUDGET DEFICIT OR SURPLUS AND MEANS OF FINANCING

When outlays exceed receipts, the difference is a deficit, which the Government finances primarily by borrowing. When receipts exceed outlays, the difference is a surplus, and the Government automatically uses the surplus primarily to reduce debt. The Federal debt held by the public is approximately the cumulative amount of borrowing to finance deficits, less repayments from surpluses, over the Nation's history.

Borrowing is not exactly equal to the deficit, and debt repayment is not exactly equal to the surplus, because of the other transactions affecting borrowing from the public, or other means of financing, such as those discussed in this section. The factors included in the other means of financing can either increase or decrease the Government's borrowing needs (or decrease or increase its ability to repay debt). For example, the change in the Treasury operating cash balance is a factor included in other means of financing. Holding receipts and outlays constant, increases in the cash balance increase the Government's need to borrow or reduce the Government's ability to repay debt, and decreases in the cash balance decrease the need to borrow or increase the ability to repay debt. In some years, the net effect of the other means of financing is minor relative to the borrowing or debt repayment; in other years, the net effect may be significant.

Borrowing and Debt Repayment

The budget treats borrowing and debt repayment as a means of financing, not as receipts and outlays. If borrowing were defined as receipts and debt repayment as outlays, the budget would always be virtually balanced by definition. This rule applies both to borrowing in the form of Treasury securities and to specialized borrowing in the form of agency securities. The rule reflects the common-sense understanding that lending or borrowing is just an exchange of financial assets of equal value—cash for Treasury securities—and so is fundamentally different from, say, paying taxes.

In 2015, the Government borrowed $337 billion from the public, bringing debt held by the public to $13,117 billion. This borrowing financed the $438 billion deficit in that year, partly offset by the net impacts of the other means of financing, such as changes in cash balances and other accounts discussed below.

In addition to selling debt to the public, the Treasury Department issues debt to Government accounts, primarily trust funds that are required by law to invest in Treasury securities. Issuing and redeeming this debt does not affect the means of financing, because these transactions occur between one Government account and another and thus do not raise or use any cash for the Government as a whole.

(See Chapter 4 of this volume, "Federal Borrowing and Debt," for a fuller discussion of this topic.)

Exercise of Monetary Power

Seigniorage is the profit from coining money. It is the difference between the value of coins as money and their cost of production. Seigniorage reduces the Government's need to borrow. Unlike the payment of taxes or other receipts, it does not involve a transfer of financial assets from the public. Instead, it arises from the exercise of the Government's power to create money and the public's desire to hold financial assets in the form of coins. Therefore, the budget excludes seigniorage from receipts and treats it as a means of financing other than borrowing from the public. The budget also treats proceeds from the sale of gold as a means of financing, since the value of gold is determined by its value as a monetary asset rather than as a commodity.

Credit Financing Accounts

The budget records the net cash flows of credit programs in credit financing accounts. These accounts include the transactions for direct loan and loan guarantee programs, as well as the equity purchase programs under TARP that are recorded on a credit basis consistent with Section 123 of EESA. Financing accounts also record equity purchases under the Small Business Lending Fund consistent with the Small Business Jobs Act of 2010. Credit financing accounts are excluded from the budget because they are not allocations of resources by the Government (see "Federal Credit" earlier in this chapter). However, even though they do not affect the surplus or deficit, they can either increase or decrease the Government's need to borrow. Therefore, they are recorded as a means of financing.

Financing account disbursements to the public increase the requirement for Treasury borrowing in the same way as an increase in budget outlays. Financing account receipts from the public can be used to finance the payment of the Government's obligations and therefore reduce the requirement for Treasury borrowing from the public in the same way as an increase in budget receipts.

Deposit Fund Account Balances

The Treasury uses non-budgetary accounts, called deposit funds, to record cash held temporarily until ownership is determined (for example, earnest money paid by bidders for mineral leases) or cash held by the Government as agent for others (for example, State and local income taxes withheld from Federal employees' salaries and not yet paid to the State or local government or amounts held in the Thrift Savings Fund, a defined contribution pension fund held and managed in a fiduciary capacity by the Government). Deposit fund balances may be held in the form of either invested or uninvested balances. To the extent that they are not invested, changes in the balances are available to finance expenditures and are recorded as a means of financing other than borrowing from the public. To the extent that they are invested in Federal debt, changes in the balances are reflected as borrowing from the public (in lieu of borrowing from other parts of the public) and are not reflected as a separate means of financing.

United States Quota Subscriptions to the International Monetary Fund (IMF)

The United States participates in the IMF through a quota subscription.[4] Financial transactions with the IMF

are exchanges of monetary assets. When the IMF draws dollars from the U.S. quota, the United States simultaneously receives an equal, offsetting, interest-bearing, Special Drawing Right (SDR)-denominated claim in the form of an increase in the U.S. reserve position in the IMF. The U.S. reserve position in the IMF increases when the United States transfers dollars to the IMF and decreases when the United States is repaid and the cash flows return to the Treasury.

The budgetary treatment of appropriations for the IMF quota has changed over time. Prior to 1981, the transactions were not included in the budget because they are exchanges of cash for monetary assets (SDRs) of the same value. This was consistent with the scoring of other exchanges of monetary assets, such as deposits of cash in Treasury accounts at commercial banks.[5] As a result of an agreement reached with the Congress in 1980 to allow appropriators to have jurisdiction over changes to the IMF quota (and later the NAB), the budget began to record budget authority for the quotas, but did not record outlays because of the continuing view that the transactions are exchanges of monetary assets of equal value. This scoring convention continued to be applied through 2008.[6] The 2010 Budget proposed to change the scoring back to the pre-1981 practice of showing zero budget authority and outlays for proposed increases in the U.S. quota subscriptions to the IMF.

In 2009, Congress enacted increases in the U.S. participation in the quota and the NAB in the Supplemental Appropriations Act of 2009 (Public Law 111–32, Title XIV, International Monetary Programs) and directed that the increases in this Act be scored under the requirements of the Federal Credit Reform Act of 1990, with an adjustment to the discount rate for market risk. Accordingly, in the budget execution of the quota and the NAB increases provided by the Supplemental Appropriations Act of 2009, the Budget through 2015 reflected obligations and outlays for the estimated present value cost to Government as if these transactions were direct loans under credit reform, plus an additional risk premium.

Pursuant to Title IX of the Department of State, Foreign Operations, and Related Programs Appropriations Act, 2016, the estimated cost of the 2009 increases as well as the rescission of the NAB and the IMF quota authorized by the Act are recorded on a present value basis with a fair value premium added to the discount rate, and the credit accounts associated with the 2009 increases have been closed.

The methods for estimating present value are similar to the methods used under FCRA, and the adjustment to the discount rate for fair value is also similar. The Budget records budget authority and outlays equal to the estimated present value, including the fair value adjustment to the discount rate, in 2016, the year that the quota increase was enacted.

---

[4] For a more detailed discussion of the history of the budgetary treatment of U.S. participation in the quota and NAB, see pages 139-141 in the Analytical Perspectives volume of the 2016 Budget As discussed in that volume, the budgetary treatment of the U.S. participation in the NAB is similar to the quota.

[5] The Report of the 1967 President's Commission on Budget Concepts notes that the IMF "is more like a bank in which funds are deposited and from which funds in the form of needed foreign currencies can be withdrawn."

[6] This budgetary treatment was also proposed again in the 2014 Budget, after the Supplemental Appropriations Act of 2009 was enacted.

As a result of this directed change in the budgetary accounting of the cost, the deficit is affected by the present value estimate of the cost adjusted for the fair value discount rate, and the nominal cash flows between the U.S. Treasury and the IMF are treated as a means of financing (see "Credit Financing Accounts" earlier in this chapter), and do not affect the deficit. In contrast, for increases to the U.S. quota subscriptions made prior to the Supplemental Appropriations Act of 2009, the 2017 Budget records interest received from the IMF on U.S. deposits as an offsetting receipt in the general fund of the Treasury. Treasury records outlays in the prior year for financial transactions with the IMF to the extent there is an unrealized loss in dollar terms and offsetting receipts to the extent there is an unrealized gain in dollar terms on the SDR-denominated interest-bearing portion of the U.S. reserve position—the amount of the quota actually being used by the IMF for its lending programs. Changes in the value of the portion of the U.S. quota held at Treasury in a letter of credit are recorded as a change in obligations.

FEDERAL EMPLOYMENT

The budget includes information on civilian and military employment. It also includes information on related personnel compensation and benefits and on staffing requirements at overseas missions. Chapter 8 of this volume, "Strengthening the Federal Workforce," provides employment levels measured in full-time equivalents (FTE). Agency FTEs are the measure of total hours worked by an agency's Federal employees divided by the total number of one person's compensable work hours in a fiscal year.

BASIS FOR BUDGET FIGURES

Data for the Past Year

The past year column (2015) generally presents the actual transactions and balances as recorded in agency accounts and as summarized in the central financial reports prepared by the Treasury Department for the most recently completed fiscal year. Occasionally, the budget reports corrections to data reported erroneously to Treasury but not discovered in time to be reflected in Treasury's published data. In addition, in certain cases the Budget has a broader scope and includes financial transactions that are not reported to Treasury (see Chapter 27 of this volume, "Comparison of Actual to Estimated Totals," for a summary of these differences).

Data for the Current Year

The current year column (2016) includes estimates of transactions and balances based on the amounts of budgetary resources that were available when the budget was prepared. In cases where the budget proposes policy changes effective in the current year, the data will also reflect the budgetary effect of those proposed changes.

Data for the Budget Year

The budget year column (2017) includes estimates of transactions and balances based on the amounts of budgetary resources that are estimated to be available, including new budget authority requested under current authorizing legislation, and amounts estimated to result from changes in authorizing legislation and tax laws.

The budget *Appendix* generally includes the appropriations language for the amounts proposed to be appropriated under current authorizing legislation. In a few cases, this language is transmitted later because the exact requirements are unknown when the budget is transmitted. The *Appendix* generally does not include appropriations language for the amounts that will be requested under proposed legislation; that language is usually transmitted later, after the legislation is enacted. Some tables in the budget identify the items for later transmittal and the related outlays separately. Estimates of the total requirements for the budget year include both the amounts requested with the transmittal of the budget and the amounts planned for later transmittal.

Data for the Outyears

The budget presents estimates for each of the nine years beyond the budget year (2018 through 2026) in order to reflect the effect of budget decisions on objectives and plans over a longer period.

Allowances

The budget may include lump-sum allowances to cover certain transactions that are expected to increase or decrease budget authority, outlays, or receipts but are not, for various reasons, reflected in the program details. For example, the budget might include an allowance to show the effect on the budget totals of a proposal that would affect many accounts by relatively small amounts, in order to avoid unnecessary detail in the presentations for the individual accounts.

This year's Budget, like last year's, includes an allowance for the costs of possible future natural disasters.

Baseline

The budget baseline is an estimate of the receipts, outlays, and deficits or surpluses that would occur if no changes were made to current laws and policies during the period covered by the budget. The baseline assumes that receipts and mandatory spending, which generally are authorized on a permanent basis, will continue in the future consistent with current law and policy. The baseline assumes that the future funding for most discretionary programs, which generally are funded annually, will equal the most recently enacted appropriation, adjusted for inflation.

Baseline outlays represent the amount of resources that would be used by the Government over the period covered by the budget on the basis of laws currently enacted.

The baseline serves several useful purposes:

- It may warn of future problems, either for Government fiscal policy as a whole or for individual tax and spending programs.

- It may provide a starting point for formulating the President's Budget.

- It may provide a "policy-neutral" benchmark against which the President's Budget and alternative proposals can be compared to assess the magnitude of proposed changes.

A number of significant changes in policies are embedded in the baseline rules specified in BBEDCA. For example, the BBEDCA baseline rules for discretionary programs would inflate discretionary spending for future years above the statutory caps that limit such spending. Because the inflation of discretionary spending above the statutory caps would create significant differences between the BBEDCA baseline and policies in effect this year, the Administration also issues an adjusted baseline that, unlike the BBEDCA baseline, assumes such changes in policy will not occur. (Chapter 25 of this volume, "Current Services Estimates," provides more information on the baseline, including the differences between the baseline as calculated under the rules of BBEDCA and the adjusted baseline used in this Budget.)

PRINCIPAL BUDGET LAWS

The following basic laws govern the Federal budget process:

Article 1, section 8, clause 1 of the Constitution, which empowers the Congress to collect taxes.

Article 1, section 9, clause 7 of the Constitution, which requires appropriations in law before money may be spent from the Treasury and the publication of a regular statement of the receipts and expenditures of all public money.

Antideficiency Act (codified in Chapters 13 and 15 of Title 31, United States Code), which prescribes rules and procedures for budget execution.

Balanced Budget and Emergency Deficit Control Act of 1985, as amended, which establishes limits on discretionary spending and provides mechanisms for enforcing discretionary spending limits.

Chapter 11 of Title 31, United States Code, which prescribes procedures for submission of the President's budget and information to be contained in it.

Congressional Budget and Impoundment Control Act of 1974 (Public Law 93–344), as amended. This Act comprises the:

- ***Congressional Budget Act of 1974***, as amended, which prescribes the congressional budget process; and

- ***Impoundment Control Act of 1974***, which controls certain aspects of budget execution.

- ***Federal Credit Reform Act of 1990, as amended (2 USC 661–661f)***, which the Budget Enforcement Act of 1990 included as an amendment to the Congressional Budget Act to prescribe the budget treatment for Federal credit programs.

Government Performance and Results Act of 1993 (Public Law 103–62, as amended) which emphasizes managing for results. It requires agencies to prepare strategic plans, annual performance plans, and annual performance reports.

Statutory Pay-As-You-Go Act of 2010, which establishes a budget enforcement mechanism generally requiring that direct spending and revenue legislation enacted into law not increase the deficit.

GLOSSARY OF BUDGET TERMS

Account refers to a separate financial reporting unit used by the Federal Government to record budget authority, outlays and income for budgeting or management information purposes as well as for accounting purposes. All budget (and off-budget) accounts are classified as being either expenditure or receipt accounts and by fund group. Budget (and off-budget) transactions fall within either of two fund group: (1) Federal funds and (2) trust funds. (Cf. Federal funds group and trust funds group.)

Accrual method of measuring cost means an accounting method that records cost when the liability is incurred. As applied to Federal employee retirement benefits, accrual costs are recorded when the benefits are earned rather than when they are paid at some time in the future. The accrual method is used in part to provide data that assists in agency policymaking, but not used in presenting the overall budget of the United States Government.

Advance appropriation means appropriations of new budget authority that become available one or more fiscal years beyond the fiscal year for which the appropriation act was passed.

Advance funding means appropriations of budget authority provided in an appropriations act to be used, if necessary, to cover obligations incurred late in the fiscal year for benefit payments in excess of the amount specifically appropriated in the act for that year, where the budget authority is charged to the appropriation for the program for the fiscal year following the fiscal year for which the appropriations act is passed.

Agency means a department or other establishment of the Government.

Allowance means a lump-sum included in the budget to represent certain transactions that are expected to increase or decrease budget authority, outlays, or receipts but that are not, for various reasons, reflected in the program details.

Balanced Budget and Emergency Deficit Control Act of 1985 (BBEDCA) refers to legislation that altered the budget process, primarily by replacing the earlier fixed targets for annual deficits with a Pay-As-You-Go requirement for new tax or mandatory spending legislation and with caps on annual discretionary funding. The Statutory Pay-As-You-Go Act of 2010, which is a standalone piece of legislation that did not directly amend the BBEDCA, reinstated a statutory pay-as-you-go rule for revenues and mandatory spending legislation, and the Budget Control Act of 2011, which did amend BBEDCA, reinstated discretionary caps on budget authority.

Balances of budget authority means the amounts of budget authority provided in previous years that have not been outlayed.

Baseline means a projection of the estimated receipts, outlays, and deficit or surplus that would result from continuing current law or current policies through the period covered by the budget.

Budget means the Budget of the United States Government, which sets forth the President's comprehensive financial plan for allocating resources and indicates the President's priorities for the Federal Government.

Budget authority (BA) means the authority provided by law to incur financial obligations that will result in outlays. (For a description of the several forms of budget authority, see "Budget Authority and Other Budgetary Resources" earlier in this chapter.)

Budget Control Act of 2011 refers to legislation that, among other things, amended BBEDCA to reinstate discretionary spending limits on budget authority through 2021 and restored the process for enforcing those spending limits. The legislation also increased the statutory debt ceiling; created a Joint Select Committee on Deficit Reduction that was instructed to develop a bill to reduce the Federal deficit by at least $1.5 trillion over a 10-year period. It also provided a process to implement alternative spending reductions in the event that legislation achieving at least $1.2 trillion of deficit reduction was not enacted.

Budget resolution—see concurrent resolution on the budget.

Budget totals mean the totals included in the budget for budget authority, outlays, receipts, and the surplus or deficit. Some presentations in the budget distinguish on-budget totals from off-budget totals. On-budget totals reflect the transactions of all Federal Government entities except those excluded from the budget totals by law. Off-budget totals reflect the transactions of Government entities that are excluded from the on-budget totals by law. Under current law, the off-budget totals include the Social Security trust funds (Federal Old-Age and Survivors Insurance and Federal Disability Insurance Trust Funds) and the Postal Service Fund. The budget combines the on- and off-budget totals to derive unified (i.e. consolidated) totals for Federal activity.

Budget year refers to the fiscal year for which the budget is being considered, that is, with respect to a session of Congress, the fiscal year of the government that starts on October 1 of the calendar year in which that session of Congress begins.

Budgetary resources mean amounts available to incur obligations in a given year. The term comprises new budget authority and unobligated balances of budget authority provided in previous years.

Cap means the legal limits for each fiscal year under BBEDCA on the budget authority and outlays (only if applicable) provided by discretionary appropriations.

Cap adjustment means either an increase or a decrease that is permitted to the statutory cap limits for each fiscal year under BBEDCA on the budget authority and outlays (only if applicable) provided by discretionary appropriations only if certain conditions are met. These conditions may include providing for a base level of funding, a designation of the increase or decrease by the Congress, (and in some circumstances, the President) pursuant to a section of the BBEDCA, or a change in concepts and definitions of funding under the cap. Changes in concepts and definitions require consultation with the Congressional Appropriations and Budget Committees.

Cash equivalent transaction means a transaction in which the Government makes outlays or receives collections in a form other than cash or the cash does not accurately measure the cost of the transaction. (For examples, see the section on "Outlays" earlier in this chapter.)

Collections mean money collected by the Government that the budget records as a governmental receipt, an offsetting collection, or an offsetting receipt.

Concurrent resolution on the budget refers to the concurrent resolution adopted by the Congress to set budgetary targets for appropriations, mandatory spending legislation, and tax legislation. These concurrent resolutions are required by the Congressional Budget Act of 1974, and are generally adopted annually.

Continuing resolution means an appropriations act that provides for the ongoing operation of the Government in the absence of enacted appropriations.

Cost refers to legislation or administrative actions that increase outlays or decrease receipts. (Cf. savings.)

Credit program account means a budget account that receives and obligates appropriations to cover the subsidy cost of a direct loan or loan guarantee and disburses the subsidy cost to a financing account.

Current services estimate—see Baseline.

Debt held by the public means the cumulative amount of money the Federal Government has borrowed from the public and not repaid.

Debt held by the public net of financial assets means the cumulative amount of money the Federal Government has borrowed from the public and not repaid, minus the current value of financial assets such as loan assets, bank deposits, or private-sector securities or equities held by the Government and plus the current value of financial liabilities other than debt.

Debt held by Government accounts means the debt the Treasury Department owes to accounts within the Federal Government. Most of it results from the surpluses of the Social Security and other trust funds, which are required by law to be invested in Federal securities.

Debt limit means the maximum amount of Federal debt that may legally be outstanding at any time. It includes both the debt held by the public and the debt held by Government accounts, but without accounting for offsetting financial assets. When the debt limit is reached, the Government cannot borrow more money until the Congress has enacted a law to increase the limit.

Deficit means the amount by which outlays exceed receipts in a fiscal year. It may refer to the on-budget, off-budget, or unified budget deficit.

Direct loan means a disbursement of funds by the Government to a non-Federal borrower under a contract that requires the repayment of such funds with or without interest. The term includes the purchase of, or participation in, a loan made by another lender. The term also includes the sale of a Government asset on credit terms of more than 90 days duration as well as financing arrangements for other transactions that defer payment for more than 90 days. It also includes loans financed by the Federal Financing Bank (FFB) pursuant to agency loan guarantee authority. The term does not include the acquisition of a federally guaranteed loan in satisfaction of default or other guarantee claims or the price support "loans" of the Commodity Credit Corporation. (Cf. loan guarantee.)

Direct spending—see mandatory spending.

Disaster funding means a discretionary appropriation that is enacted that the Congress designates as being for disaster relief. Such amounts are a cap adjustment to the limits on discretionary spending under BBEDCA. The total adjustment for this purpose cannot exceed a ceiling for a particular year that is defined as the total of the average funding provided for disaster relief over the previous 10 years (excluding the highest and lowest years) and the unused amount of the prior year's ceiling (excluding the portion of the prior year's ceiling that was itself due to any unused amount from the year before). Disaster relief is defined as activities carried out pursuant to a determination under section 102(2) of the Robert T. Stafford Disaster Relief and Emergency Assistance Act.

Discretionary spending means budgetary resources (except those provided to fund mandatory spending programs) provided in appropriations acts. (Cf. mandatory spending.)

Emergency requirement means an amount that the Congress has designated as an emergency requirement. Such amounts are not included in the estimated budgetary effects of PAYGO legislation under the requirements of the Statutory Pay-As-You-Go Act of 2010, if they are mandatory or receipts. Such a discretionary appropriation that is subsequently designated by the President as an emergency requirement results in a cap adjustment to the limits on discretionary spending under BBEDCA.

Entitlement refers to a program in which the Federal Government is legally obligated to make payments or provide aid to any person who, or State or local government that, meets the legal criteria for eligibility. Examples include Social Security, Medicare, Medicaid, and Food Stamps.

Federal funds group refers to the moneys collected and spent by the Government through accounts other than those designated as trust funds. Federal funds include general, special, public enterprise, and intragovernmental funds. (Cf. trust funds group.)

Financing account means a non-budgetary account (an account whose transactions are excluded from the budget totals) that records all of the cash flows resulting from post-1991 direct loan obligations or loan guarantee commitments. At least one financing account is associated with each credit program account. For programs that make both direct loans and loan guarantees, separate financing accounts are required for direct loan cash flows and for loan guarantee cash flows. (Cf. liquidating account.)

Fiscal year means the Government's accounting period. It begins on October 1st and ends on September 30th, and is designated by the calendar year in which it ends.

Forward funding means appropriations of budget authority that are made for obligation starting in the last quarter of the fiscal year for the financing of ongoing grant programs during the next fiscal year.

General fund means the accounts in which are recorded governmental receipts not earmarked by law for a specific purpose, the proceeds of general borrowing, and the expenditure of these moneys.

Government sponsored enterprises mean private enterprises that were established and chartered by the Federal Government for public policy purposes. They are classified as non-budgetary and not included in the Federal budget because they are private companies, and their securities are not backed by the full faith and credit of the Federal Government. However, the budget presents statements of financial condition for certain Government sponsored enterprises such as the Federal National Mortgage Association. (Cf. off-budget.)

Intragovernmental fund —see Revolving fund.

Liquidating account means a budget account that records all cash flows to and from the Government resulting from pre-1992 direct loan obligations or loan guarantee commitments. (Cf. financing account.)

Loan guarantee means any guarantee, insurance, or other pledge with respect to the payment of all or a part of the principal or interest on any debt obligation of a non-Federal borrower to a non-Federal lender. The term does not include the insurance of deposits, shares, or other withdrawable accounts in financial institutions. (Cf. direct loan.)

Mandatory spending means spending controlled by laws other than appropriations acts (including spending for entitlement programs) and spending for the food stamp program. Although the Statutory Pay-As-You-Go Act of 2010 uses the term direct spending to mean this, mandatory spending is commonly used instead. (Cf. discretionary spending.)

Means of financing refers to borrowing, the change in cash balances, and certain other transactions involved in financing a deficit. The term is also used to refer to the debt repayment, the change in cash balances, and certain other transactions involved in using a surplus. By definition, the means of financing are not treated as receipts or outlays and so are non-budgetary.

Obligated balance means the cumulative amount of budget authority that has been obligated but not yet outlayed. (Cf. unobligated balance.)

Obligation means a binding agreement that will result in outlays, immediately or in the future. Budgetary resources must be available before obligations can be incurred legally.

Off-budget refers to transactions of the Federal Government that would be treated as budgetary had the Congress not designated them by statute as "off-budget." Currently, transactions of the Social Security trust funds and the Postal Service are the only sets of transactions that are so designated. The term is sometimes used more broadly to refer to the transactions of private enterprises that were established and sponsored by the Government, most especially "Government sponsored enterprises" such as the Federal Home Loan Banks. (Cf. budget totals.)

Offsetting collections mean collections that, by law, are credited directly to expenditure accounts and deducted from gross budget authority and outlays of the expenditure account, rather than added to receipts. Usually, they are authorized to be spent for the purposes of the account without further action by the Congress. They result from business-like transactions with the public, including payments from the public in exchange for goods and services, reimbursements for damages, and gifts or donations of money to the Government and from intragovernmental transactions with other Government accounts. The authority to spend offsetting collections is a form of budget authority. (Cf. receipts and offsetting receipts.)

Offsetting receipts mean collections that are credited to offsetting receipt accounts and deducted from gross budget authority and outlays, rather than added to receipts. They are not authorized to be credited to expenditure accounts. The legislation that authorizes the offsetting receipts may earmark them for a specific purpose and either appropriate them for expenditure for that purpose or require them to be appropriated in annual appropriation acts before they can be spent. Like offsetting collections, they result from business-like transactions or market-oriented activities with the public, including payments from the public in exchange for goods and services, reimbursements for damages, and gifts or donations of

money to the Government and from intragovernmental transactions with other Government accounts. (Cf. receipts, undistributed offsetting receipts, and offsetting collections.)

On-budget refers to all budgetary transactions other than those designated by statute as off-budget (Cf. budget totals.)

Outlay means a payment to liquidate an obligation (other than the repayment of debt principal or other disbursements that are "means of financing" transactions). Outlays generally are equal to cash disbursements, but also are recorded for cash-equivalent transactions, such as the issuance of debentures to pay insurance claims, and in a few cases are recorded on an accrual basis such as interest on public issues of the public debt. Outlays are the measure of Government spending.

Outyear estimates mean estimates presented in the budget for the years beyond the budget year of budget authority, outlays, receipts, and other items (such as debt).

Overseas Contingency Operations/Global War on Terrorism (OCO/GWOT) means a discretionary appropriation that is enacted that the Congress and, subsequently, the President have so designated on an account by account basis. Such a discretionary appropriation that is designated as OCO/GWOT results in a cap adjustment to the limits on discretionary spending under BBEDCA. Funding for these purposes has most recently been associated with the wars in Iraq and Afghanistan.

Pay-as-you-go (PAYGO) refers to requirements of the Statutory Pay-As-You-Go Act of 2010 that result in a sequestration if the estimated combined result of new legislation affecting direct spending or revenue increases the on-budget deficit relative to the baseline, as of the end of a congressional session.

Public enterprise fund —see Revolving fund.

Reappropriation means a provision of law that extends into a new fiscal year the availability of unobligated amounts that have expired or would otherwise expire.

Receipts mean collections that result from the Government's exercise of its sovereign power to tax or otherwise compel payment. They are compared to outlays in calculating a surplus or deficit. (Cf. offsetting collections and offsetting receipts.)

Revolving fund means a fund that conducts continuing cycles of business-like activity, in which the fund charges for the sale of products or services and uses the proceeds to finance its spending, usually without requirement for annual appropriations. There are two types of revolving funds: Public enterprise funds, which conduct business-like operations mainly with the public, and intragovernmental revolving funds, which conduct business-like operations mainly within and between Government agencies. (Cf. special fund and trust fund.)

Savings refers to legislation or administrative actions that decrease outlays or increase receipts. (Cf. cost.)

Scorekeeping means measuring the budget effects of legislation, generally in terms of budget authority, receipts, and outlays, for purposes of measuring adherence to the Budget or to budget targets established by the Congress, as through agreement to a Budget Resolution.

Sequestration means the cancellation of budgetary resources. The Statutory Pay-As-You-Go Act of 2010 requires such cancellations if revenue or direct spending legislation is enacted that, in total, increases projected deficits or reduces projected surpluses relative to the baseline. The Balanced Budget and Emergency Deficit Control Act of 1985, as amended, requires such cancellations if discretionary appropriations exceed the statutory limits on discretionary spending.

Special fund means a Federal fund account for receipts or offsetting receipts earmarked for specific purposes and the expenditure of these receipts. (Cf. revolving fund and trust fund.)

Statutory Pay-As-You-Go Act of 2010 refers to legislation that reinstated a statutory pay-as-you-go requirement for new tax or mandatory spending legislation. The law is a standalone piece of legislation that cross-references BBEDCA but does not directly amend that legislation. This is a permanent law and does not expire.

Subsidy means the estimated long-term cost to the Government of a direct loan or loan guarantee, calculated on a net present value basis, excluding administrative costs and any incidental effects on governmental receipts or outlays.

Surplus means the amount by which receipts exceed outlays in a fiscal year. It may refer to the on-budget, off-budget, or unified budget surplus.

Supplemental appropriation means an appropriation enacted subsequent to a regular annual appropriations act, when the need for additional funds is too urgent to be postponed until the next regular annual appropriations act.

Trust fund refers to a type of account, designated by law as a trust fund, for receipts or offsetting receipts dedicated to specific purposes and the expenditure of these receipts. Some revolving funds are designated as trust funds, and these are called trust revolving funds. (Cf. special fund and revolving fund.)

Trust funds group refers to the moneys collected and spent by the Government through trust fund accounts. (Cf. Federal funds group.)

Undistributed offsetting receipts mean offsetting receipts that are deducted from the Government-wide totals for budget authority and outlays instead of being offset against a specific agency and function. (Cf. offsetting receipts.)

Unified budget includes receipts from all sources and outlays for all programs of the Federal Government, including both on- and off-budget programs. It is the most comprehensive measure of the Government's annual finances.

Unobligated balance means the cumulative amount of budget authority that remains available for obligation under law in unexpired accounts. The term "expired balances available for adjustment only" refers to unobligated amounts in expired accounts.

User charges are charges assessed for the provision of Government services and for the sale or use of Government goods or resources. The payers of the user charge must be limited in the authorizing legislation to those receiving special benefits from, or subject to regulation by, the program or activity beyond the benefits received by the general public or broad segments of the public (such as those who pay income taxes or custom duties).

10. COVERAGE OF THE BUDGET

The Federal budget is the central instrument of national policy making. It is the Government's financial plan for proposing and deciding the allocation of resources to serve national objectives. The budget provides information on the cost and scope of Federal activities to inform decisions and to serve as a means to control the allocation of resources. When enacted it establishes the level of public goods and services provided by the Government.

Federal Government activities can be characterized as either "budgetary" or "non-budgetary." Those Federal Government activities that involve direct and measurable allocation of Federal resources are characterized as budgetary. The payments to and from the public resulting from budgetary activities are included in the budget's accounting of outlays and receipts. Federal activities that do not involve direct and measurable allocation of Federal resources are characterized as non-budgetary and are not included in the budget's accounting of outlays and receipts. For more detailed information about outlays and receipts, see Chapter 9 "Budget Concepts," in this volume.

The budget documents include information on some non-budgetary activities because they can be important instruments of Federal policy and provide insight into the scope and nature of Federal activities. For example, as discussed in more detail later, the budget documents show the transactions of the Thrift Savings Fund (TSP), a collection of investment funds managed by the Federal Retirement Thrift Investment Board. Despite the fact that one of the TSP investment funds is invested entirely in Federal securities, the transactions of these funds are non-budgetary because the funds are owned by current and retired Federal employees. The Government manages these funds only in a fiduciary capacity.

The budget also includes information on cash flows that are a means of financing Federal activity, such as for credit financing accounts. However, means of financing amounts are not included in the estimates of outlays or receipts to avoid double-counting; the costs of the underlying Federal activities are already reflected in the deficit.[1] Similarly, while budget totals of outlays and receipts do not include non-Federal costs resulting from Federal regulation, the Office of Management and Budget (OMB) annually reports on the costs and benefits of Federal regulation to non-Federal entities.[2] This chapter provides details about the budgetary and non-budgetary activities of the Federal Government

Budgetary Activities

The Federal Government has used the unified budget concept—which consolidates outlays and receipts from federal funds and trust funds, including the Social Security trust funds—since 1968, starting with the 1969 Budget. This change was based on a recommendation made by the 1967 President's Commission on Budget Concepts (the Commission) to include the financial transactions of all of the Federal Government's programs and agencies. Thus, the budget includes information on the financial transactions of all 15 Executive departments, all independent agencies (from all three branches of Government), and all Government corporations.[3]

The budget reflects the legal distinction between on-budget activities and off-budget activities by showing outlays and receipts for both types of activities separately. Although there is a legal distinction between on-budget and off-budget activities, conceptually there is no difference between the two. Off-budget Federal activities reflect the same kinds of governmental roles as on-budget activities and result in outlays and receipts. Like on-budget activities, off-budget activities are funded and controlled by the Government. The "unified budget" reflects the conceptual similarity between on-budget and off-budget activities by showing combined totals of outlays and receipts for both.

Many Government corporations are entities with business-type operations that charge the public for services at prices intended to allow the entity to be self-sustaining although some operate at a loss in order to provide subsidies to specific recipients. Often these entities are more independent than other agencies and have limited exemptions from certain Federal personnel requirements to allow for flexibility.

All accounts in Table 29-1, "Federal Budget by Agency and Account," in the supplemental materials to this volume are budgetary.[4] The majority of budgetary accounts are associated with the departments or other entities that are clearly Federal agencies. Some budgetary accounts reflect Government payments to entities that were created or chartered by the Government as private or non-Federal entities. Some of these entities receive

---

[1] For more information on means of financing, see the "Budget Deficit or Surplus and Means of Financing" section of Chapter 9, "Budget Concepts," in this volume.

[2] For the 2015 draft of the "Report to Congress on the Benefits and Costs of Federal Regulation and Unfunded Mandates on State, Local and Tribal Entities," see *https://www.whitehouse.gov/sites/default/files/omb/inforeg/2015_cb/draft_2015_cost_benefit_report.pdf*.

[3] Government corporations are Government entities that are defined as corporations pursuant to the Government Corporation Control Act, as amended (31 U.S.C. 9101), or elsewhere in law. Examples include the Commodity Credit Corporation, the Export-Import Bank of the United States, the Federal Crop Insurance Corporation, the Federal Deposit Insurance Corporation, the Millennium Challenge Corporation, the Overseas Private Investment Corporation, the Pension Benefit Guaranty Corporation, the Tennessee Valley Authority, the African Development Foundation (22 U.S.C. 290h-6), the Inter-American Foundation (22 U.S.C. 290f), the Presidio Trust (16 U.S.C. 460bb note), and the Valles Caldera Trust (16 U.S.C. 698v-4).

[4] Table 29-1 can be found at: http://www.budget.gov/budget/analytical_perspectives.

Table 10–1. COMPARISON OF TOTAL, ON-BUDGET, AND OFF-BUDGET TRANSACTIONS[1]

(In billions of dollars)

Fiscal Year	Receipts			Outlays			Surplus or deficit (–)		
	Total	On-budget	Off-budget	Total	On-budget	Off-budget	Total	On-budget	Off-budget
1980	517.1	403.9	113.2	590.9	477.0	113.9	–73.8	–73.1	–0.7
1981	599.3	469.1	130.2	678.2	543.0	135.3	–79.0	–73.9	–5.1
1982	617.8	474.3	143.5	745.7	594.9	150.9	–128.0	–120.6	–7.4
1983	600.6	453.2	147.3	808.4	660.9	147.4	–207.8	–207.7	–0.1
1984	666.4	500.4	166.1	851.8	685.6	166.2	–185.4	–185.3	–0.1
1985	734.0	547.9	186.2	946.3	769.4	176.9	–212.3	–221.5	9.2
1986	769.2	568.9	200.2	990.4	806.8	183.5	–221.2	–237.9	16.7
1987	854.3	640.9	213.4	1,004.0	809.2	194.8	–149.7	–168.4	18.6
1988	909.2	667.7	241.5	1,064.4	860.0	204.4	–155.2	–192.3	37.1
1989	991.1	727.4	263.7	1,143.7	932.8	210.9	–152.6	–205.4	52.8
1990	1,032.0	750.3	281.7	1,253.0	1,027.9	225.1	–221.0	–277.6	56.6
1991	1,055.0	761.1	293.9	1,324.2	1,082.5	241.7	–269.2	–321.4	52.2
1992	1,091.2	788.8	302.4	1,381.5	1,129.2	252.3	–290.3	–340.4	50.1
1993	1,154.3	842.4	311.9	1,409.4	1,142.8	266.6	–255.1	–300.4	45.3
1994	1,258.6	923.5	335.0	1,461.8	1,182.4	279.4	–203.2	–258.8	55.7
1995	1,351.8	1,000.7	351.1	1,515.7	1,227.1	288.7	–164.0	–226.4	62.4
1996	1,453.1	1,085.6	367.5	1,560.5	1,259.6	300.9	–107.4	–174.0	66.6
1997	1,579.2	1,187.2	392.0	1,601.1	1,290.5	310.6	–21.9	–103.2	81.4
1998	1,721.7	1,305.9	415.8	1,652.5	1,335.9	316.6	69.3	–29.9	99.2
1999	1,827.5	1,383.0	444.5	1,701.8	1,381.1	320.8	125.6	1.9	123.7
2000	2,025.2	1,544.6	480.6	1,789.0	1,458.2	330.8	236.2	86.4	149.8
2001	1,991.1	1,483.6	507.5	1,862.8	1,516.0	346.8	128.2	–32.4	160.7
2002	1,853.1	1,337.8	515.3	2,010.9	1,655.2	355.7	–157.8	–317.4	159.7
2003	1,782.3	1,258.5	523.8	2,159.9	1,796.9	363.0	–377.6	–538.4	160.8
2004	1,880.1	1,345.4	534.7	2,292.8	1,913.3	379.5	–412.7	–568.0	155.2
2005	2,153.6	1,576.1	577.5	2,472.0	2,069.7	402.2	–318.3	–493.6	175.3
2006	2,406.9	1,798.5	608.4	2,655.0	2,233.0	422.1	–248.2	–434.5	186.3
2007	2,568.0	1,932.9	635.1	2,728.7	2,275.0	453.6	–160.7	–342.2	181.5
2008	2,524.0	1,865.9	658.0	2,982.5	2,507.8	474.8	–458.6	–641.8	183.3
2009	2,105.0	1,451.0	654.0	3,517.7	3,000.7	517.0	–1,412.7	–1,549.7	137.0
2010	2,162.7	1,531.0	631.7	3,457.1	2,902.4	554.7	–1,294.4	–1,371.4	77.0
2011	2,303.5	1,737.7	565.8	3,603.1	3,104.4	498.6	–1,299.6	–1,366.8	67.2
2012	2,450.0	1,880.5	569.5	3,537.0	3,029.4	507.6	–1,087.0	–1,148.9	61.9
2013	2,775.1	2,101.8	673.3	3,454.6	2,820.8	633.8	–679.5	–719.0	39.5
2014	3,021.5	2,285.9	735.6	3,506.1	2,800.1	706.1	–484.6	–514.1	29.5
2015	3,249.9	2,479.5	770.4	3,688.3	2,945.2	743.1	–438.4	–465.7	27.3
2016 estimate	3,335.5	2,537.8	797.7	3,951.3	3,161.6	789.7	–615.8	–623.8	8.0
2017 estimate	3,643.7	2,816.9	826.9	4,147.2	3,318.6	828.6	–503.5	–501.8	–1.7
2018 estimate	3,898.6	3,035.4	863.3	4,352.2	3,467.9	884.3	–453.6	–432.5	–21.1
2019 estimate	4,095.1	3,196.8	898.2	4,644.3	3,702.4	941.9	–549.3	–505.5	–43.7
2020 estimate	4,345.7	3,413.8	931.9	4,879.8	3,871.7	1,008.2	–534.1	–457.8	–76.3
2021 estimate	4,572.0	3,591.8	980.2	5,124.2	4,052.1	1,072.2	–552.3	–460.3	–91.9

[1] Off-budget transactions consist of the Social Security trust funds and the Postal Service fund.

all or a majority of their funding from the Government. These include the Corporation for Public Broadcasting, Gallaudet University, Howard University, the Legal Services Corporation, the National Railroad Passenger Corporation (Amtrak), the Smithsonian Institution, the State Justice Institute, and the United States Institute of Peace. A related example is the Standard Setting Board, which is not a Federally-created entity but since 2003 has received a majority of funding through a Federally-mandated assessment on public companies under the Sarbanes-Oxley Act. Although the Federal payments to these entities are budgetary, the entities themselves are non-budgetary.

Whether an entity was created or chartered by the Government does not alone determine its budgetary status. The Commission recommended that the budget be comprehensive but it also recognized that proper budgetary classification required weighing all relevant factors regarding establishment, ownership, and control of an entity while erring on the side of inclusiveness. Generally, entities that are primarily owned or controlled by the Government are classified as budgetary. Determinations regarding the budgetary classification of entities are made by consultation between the OMB, the Congressional Budget Office (CBO), and the Budget Committees of the Congress.

One example of a recent budgetary classification involved the National Association of Registered Agents and Brokers (NARAB). NARAB allows insurance licensing, continuing education, and other nonresident producer qualification requirements to be adopted and applied on a multi-state basis. In other words, NARAB streamlines the ability of a nonresident insurer to become a licensed agent in another State. In exchange for providing enhanced market access NARAB will collect fees from its members beginning in 2017. The association was established by the Terrorism Risk Insurance Reauthorization Act of 2015. In addition to being established by statute, which in itself is an indication that the entity is governmental, NARAB has a board of directors appointed by the President and confirmed by the Senate. It must also submit bylaws and an annual report to the Department of the Treasury and its primary function involves exercising a regulatory function. For these reasons, it is classified as budgetary.

Off-budget Federal activities.—Despite the Commission's recommendation that the budget be comprehensive, every year since 1971 at least one Federal program or agency has been presented as off-budget because of a legal requirement.[5] Such off-budget Federal activities are funded by the Government and administered according to Federal legal requirements but their net costs are excluded, by law, from the rest of the budget totals, which are also known as the "on-budget" totals.

Off-budget Federal activities currently consist of the U.S. Postal Service and the two Social Security trust funds: Old-Age and Survivors Insurance and Disability Insurance. Social Security has been classified as off-budget since 1986 and the Postal Service has been classified as off-budget since 1990.[6] Other activities that had been designated in law as off-budget at various times before 1986

have been classified as on-budget by law since at least 1985 as a result of the Balanced Budget and Emergency Deficit Control Act of 1985 (Public Law 99–177). Activities that were off-budget at one time but that are now on-budget are classified as on-budget for all years in historical budget data.

Social Security is the largest single program in the unified budget and it is classified by law as off-budget; as a result, the off-budget accounts constitute a significant part of total Federal spending and receipts. Table 10–1 divides total Federal Government outlays, receipts, and the surplus or deficit between on-budget and off-budget amounts. Within this table, the Social Security and Postal Service transactions are classified as off-budget for all years to provide a consistent comparison over time.

Non-Budgetary Activities

Some important Government activities are characterized as non-budgetary because they do not involve the direct allocation of resources by the Government.[7] These activities can affect budget outlays or receipts even though they have components that are non-budgetary.

Federal credit programs: budgetary and non-budgetary transactions.—Federal credit programs make direct loans or guarantee private loans to non-Federal borrowers. The Federal Credit Reform Act of 1990 (FCRA), as amended by the Balanced Budget Act of 1997, established the current budgetary treatment for credit programs. Under FCRA, the budgetary cost of a credit program is known as the "subsidy cost." The subsidy cost is the estimated lifetime cost to the Government of a loan or a loan guarantee on a net present value basis, excluding administrative costs.

Outlays equal to the subsidy cost are recorded in the budget up front as they are incurred—for example, when a loan is made or guaranteed. Credit program cash flows to and from the public are recorded in non-budgetary financing accounts and the information is included in budget documents to provide insight into the program size and costs. For more information, the mechanisms of credit programs are discussed in more detail in Chapter 9 of this volume, "Budget Concepts," and credit programs are discussed in more detail in Chapter 20 of this volume, "Credit and Insurance."

Deposit funds.—Deposit funds are non-budgetary accounts that record amounts held by the Government temporarily until ownership is determined (such as earnest money paid by bidders for mineral leases) or held by the Government as an agent for others (such as State income taxes withheld from Federal employees' salaries and not yet paid to the States). The largest deposit fund

---

[5] While the term "off-budget" is sometimes used colloquially to mean non-budgetary, the term has a meaning distinct from non-budgetary. Off-budget activities would be considered budgetary, absent legal requirement to exclude these activities from the budget totals.

[6] See 42 U.S.C. 911, and 39 U.S.C. 2009a, respectively. The off-budget Postal Service accounts consist of the Postal Service Fund, which is classified as a mandatory account, and the Office of the Inspector General and the Postal Regulatory Commission, both of which are classified as discretionary accounts. The Postal Service Retiree Health Benefits Fund is an on-budget mandatory account with the Office of Personnel Management. The off-budget Social Security accounts consist of the Federal Old-Age and Survivors Insurance trust fund and the Federal Disability Insurance trust fund, both of which have mandatory and discretionary funding.

[7] Tax expenditures, which are discussed in Chapter 14 of this volume, are an example of Government activities that could be characterized as either budgetary or non-budgetary. Tax expenditures refer to the reduction in tax receipts resulting from the special tax treatment accorded certain private activities. Because tax expenditures reduce tax receipts and receipts are budgetary, tax expenditures clearly have budgetary effects. However, the size and composition of tax expenditures are not explicitly recorded in the budget as outlays or as negative receipts and, for this reason, tax expenditures might be considered a special case of non-budgetary transactions.

is the Government Securities Investment Fund, which is also known as the G-Fund. It is one of several investment funds managed by the Federal Retirement Thrift Investment Board for Federal employees who participate in the Government's defined contribution retirement plan, the TSP (which is similar to private-sector 401(k) plans). The G-Fund assets, which are held by the Department of the Treasury, are the property of Federal employees and are held by the Government only in a fiduciary capacity; the transactions of the Fund are not resource allocations by the Government and are therefore non-budgetary.[8] For similar reasons, the budget excludes funds that are owned by Native American Indians but held and managed by the Government in a fiduciary capacity.

Government-Sponsored Enterprises (GSEs).— Government-Sponsored Enterprises are privately owned and therefore distinct from government corporations. The Federal Government has chartered GSEs such as the Federal National Mortgage Association (Fannie Mae), the Federal Home Loan Mortgage Corporation (Freddie Mac), the Federal Home Loan Banks, the Farm Credit System, and the Federal Agricultural Mortgage Corporation to provide financial intermediation for specified public purposes. Although federally-chartered to serve public-policy purposes, the GSEs are classified as non-budgetary. This is because they are intended to be privately owned and controlled, with any public benefits accruing indirectly from the GSEs' business transactions. Estimates of the GSEs' activities are reported in a separate chapter of the Budget *Appendix*, and their activities are discussed in Chapter 20 of this volume, "Credit and Insurance."

In September 2008, in response to the financial market crisis, the director of the Federal Housing Finance Agency (FHFA)[9] placed Fannie Mae and Freddie Mac into conservatorship for the purpose of preserving the assets and restoring the solvency of these two GSEs. As conservator, FHFA has broad authority to direct the operations of these GSEs. However, these GSEs remain private companies with board of directors and management responsible for their day-to-day operations. This Budget continues to treat these two GSEs as non-budgetary private entities in conservatorship rather than as Government agencies. By contrast, CBO treats these GSEs as budgetary Federal agencies. Both treatments include budgetary and non-budgetary amounts.

While all of the GSEs' transactions with the public are reflected as non-budgetary, the payments from the Treasury to the GSEs are recorded as budgetary outlays and dividends received by the Treasury are recorded as budgetary receipts. Under CBO's approach, the subsidy costs—or expected losses over time—of Fannie Mae's and Freddie Mac's past credit activities have already been recorded in the budget estimates; the subsidy costs of future credit activities will be recorded when the activities occur. Lending and borrowing activities between the GSEs

and the public apart from the subsidy costs are treated as non-budgetary by CBO, and Treasury payments to the GSEs are intragovernmental transfers (from Treasury to the GSEs) that net to zero in CBO's budget estimates.

Overall, both the Budget's accounting and CBO's accounting present Fannie Mae's and Freddie Mac's losses as Government outlays—which increase Government deficits. The two approaches, however, reflect the losses as budgetary costs at different times.

Other federally-created non-budgetary entities.— In addition to the GSEs, the Federal Government has created a number of other entities that are classified as non-budgetary. These include federally-funded research and development centers (FFRDCs), non-appropriated fund instrumentalities (NAFIs), and other entities; some of these are incorporated as non-profit entities and some are incorporated as for-profit entities.[10]

FFRDCs are entities that conduct agency-specific research under contract or cooperative agreement. Some FFRDCs were created by and conduct research for the Department of Defense and are administered by colleges, universities, or other non-profit entities. Despite being classified as non-budgetary, many FFRDCs do receive direct resource allocation from the Government and are included as budget lines in various agencies. Examples of FFRDCs include the Center for Naval Analysis and the Jet Propulsion Laboratory.[11] Even though FFRDCs are non-budgetary, Federal payments to the FFRDC are recorded as budget outlays. In addition to Federal funding, FFRDCs may receive funding from non-Federal sources.

Non-appropriated fund instrumentalities (NAFIs) are entities that support an agency's current and retired personnel. Nearly all NAFIs are associated with the Departments of Defense, Homeland Security (Coast Guard), and Veterans Affairs. Most NAFIs are located on

---

[8] The administrative functions of the Federal Retirement Thrift Investment Board are carried out by Government employees and included in the budget totals.

[9] FHFA is the regulator of Fannie Mae, Freddie Mac, and the Federal Home Loans Banks.

[10] Although most entities created by the Federal Government are budgetary, as discussed in this section, the GSEs and the Federal Reserve System were created by the Federal Government, but are classified as non-budgetary. In addition, Congress and the President have chartered, but not necessarily created, approximately 100 non-profit entities that are non-budgetary. These include patriotic, charitable, and educational organizations under Title 36 of the U.S. Code and foundations and trusts chartered under other titles of the Code. Title 36 corporations include the American Legion, the American National Red Cross, Big Brothers—Big Sisters of America, Boy Scouts of America, Future Farmers of America, Girl Scouts of the United States of America, the National Academy of Public Administration, the National Academy of Sciences, and Veterans of Foreign Wars of the United States. Virtually all of the non-profit entities chartered by the Government existed under State law prior to the granting of a Government charter, making the Government charter an honorary rather than governing charter. A major exception to this is the American National Red Cross. Its Government charter requires it to provide disaster relief and to ensure compliance with treaty obligations under the Geneva Convention. Although any Government payments (whether made as direct appropriations or through agency appropriations) to these chartered non-profits, including the Red Cross, would be budgetary, the non-profits themselves are classified as non-budgetary. On April 29, 2015, the Subcommittee on Immigration and Border Security of the Committee on the Judiciary in the U.S. House of Representatives adopted a policy prohibiting Congress from granting new Federal charters to private, non-profit organizations. This policy has been adopted by every subcommittee with jurisdiction over charters since the 101st Congress.

[11] The National Science Foundation maintains a list of FFRDCs at *www.nsf.gov/statistics/ffrdc*.

military bases and include the armed forces exchanges (which sell goods to military personnel and their families), recreational facilities, and child care centers. NAFIs are financed by proceeds from the sale of goods or services and do not receive direct appropriations. As a result they have been characterized as non-budgetary but any agency payments to the NAFIs are recorded as budget outlays.

A number of entities created by the Government receive a significant amount of non-Federal funding. Certain of these entities are significantly controlled by non-Federal individuals or organizations. These entities include Gallaudet University, Howard University, and the Universal Services Administrative Company, among others.[12] Most of these entities receive direct appropriations or other recurring payments from the Government. The appropriations or other payments are budgetary and included in Table 29-1. However, many of these entities are themselves non-budgetary. Generally, entities that receive a significant portion of funding from non-Federal sources and that are not controlled by the Government are treated as non-budgetary.

Regulation.—Federal Government regulations often require the private sector or other levels of government to make expenditures for specified purposes that are intended to have public benefits, such as workplace safety and pollution control. Although the budget reflects the Government's cost of conducting regulatory activities, the costs imposed on the private sector as a result of regulation are treated as non-budgetary and not included in the budget. The Government's regulatory priorities and plans are described in the annual Regulatory Plan and the semi-annual Unified Agenda of Federal Regulatory and Deregulatory Actions.[13] The estimated costs and benefits of Federal regulation have been published annually by OMB since 1997.[14]

Monetary policy.— As a fiscal policy tool, the budget is used by elected Government officials to promote economic growth and achieve other public policy objectives. Monetary policy is another tool that governments use to promote economic policy objectives. In the United States, monetary policy is conducted by the Federal Reserve System, which is composed of a Board of Governors and 12 regional Federal Reserve Banks. The Federal Reserve Act provides that the goal of monetary policy is to "maintain long-run growth of the monetary and credit aggregates commensurate with the economy's long run potential to increase production, so as to promote effectively the goals of maximum employment, stable prices, and mod-

erate long-term interest rates."[15] The dual goals of full employment and price stability were reaffirmed by the Full Employment and Balanced Growth Act of 1978, also known as the Humphrey-Hawkins Act.[16]

By law, the Federal Reserve System is a self-financing entity that is independent of the Executive Branch and subject only to broad oversight by the Congress. Consistent with the recommendations of the Commission, the effects of monetary policy and the actions of the Federal Reserve System are non-budgetary, with exceptions for the transfer to the Treasury of excess income generated through its operations. The Federal Reserve System earns income from a variety of sources including interest on Government securities, foreign currency investments and loans to depository institutions, and fees for services (e.g., check clearing services) provided to depository institutions. The Federal Reserve System remits to Treasury any excess income over expenses annually. For the fiscal year ending September 2015, Treasury recorded $96.4 billion in receipts from the Federal Reserve System. In addition to remitting excess income to Treasury, the Federal Reserve is required by law to transfer a portion of its excess earnings to the Consumer Financial Protection Bureau (CFPB).[17]

The Board of Governors of the Federal Reserve is a Federal Government agency, but because of its independent status, its budget is not subject to Executive Branch review and is included in the Budget *Appendix* for informational purposes only. The Federal Reserve Banks are subject to Board oversight and managed by boards of directors chosen by the Board of Governors and member banks, which include all national banks and State banks that choose to become members. The budgets of the regional Banks are subject to approval by the Board of Governors and are not included in the Budget *Appendix*.

---

[15] See 12 U.S.C. 225a.

[16] See 15 U.S.C. 3101 et seq.

[17] See section 1011 of Public Law 111-203 (12 U.S.C. 5491), (2010). The CFPB is an executive agency, led by a director appointed by the President and reliant on Federal funding, that serves the governmental function of regulating Federal consumer financial laws. Accordingly, it is included in the Budget.

---

[12] Under section 415(b) of the Amtrak Reform and Accountability Act of 1997, (49 U.S.C. 24304 and note), Amtrak was required to redeem all of its outstanding common stock. Once all outstanding common stock is redeemed, Amtrak will be wholly-owned by the Government and, at that point, its non-budgetary status may need to be reassessed.

[13] The most recent Regulatory Plan and introduction to the Unified Agenda issued by the General Services Administration's Regulatory Information Service Center are available at *www.reginfo.gov* and at *www. gpoaccess.gov*.

[14] In the most recent report, OMB indicates that the estimated annual benefits of Federal regulations it reviewed from October 1, 2004, to September 30, 2014, range from $216 billion to $812 billion, while the estimated annual costs range from $57 billion to $85 billion.

11. BUDGET PROCESS

Since taking office, the Administration has sought to present budget figures that accurately reflect the present and future course of the Nation's finances, and to make improvements in budget process and enforcement. An honest and transparent accounting of the Nation's finances is critical to making decisions about key fiscal policies, and effective budget enforcement mechanisms are necessary to promote budget discipline.

This chapter begins with a description of three broad categories of budget reform. First, the chapter discusses proposals to improve budgeting and fiscal sustainability with respect to individual programs as well as across Government. These proposals include: legislation that exceeds the remaining savings required for the Joint Select Committee on Deficit Reduction, repeals the Joint Committee reductions, and restores amounts that would be reduced by the 2017 mandatory sequestration order; various initiatives to reduce improper payments; funding requested for disaster relief; a proposed cap adjustment for the decennial census; limits on advance appropriations; structural reforms for surface transportation programs; proposals for the Pell Grant program;

Postal Service reforms; reclassification for contract support costs; and a fast-track procedure for the Congress to consider certain rescission requests. Second, the chapter describes the system under the Statutory Pay-As-You-Go Act of 2010 (PAYGO) of scoring legislation affecting receipts and mandatory spending, and it summarizes the Administration's commitment to applying a PAYGO requirement to administrative actions affecting mandatory spending. Finally, the chapter presents proposals to revise the budget baseline and to improve budget presentation, for example, by including an allowance for the costs of potential future natural disasters. This revised baseline better captures the likely future costs of operating the Federal Government. This section also discusses the use of debt net of financial assets, instead of debt held by the public, as a better measure of the Government's demand on private credit markets.

Taken together, these reforms generate a Budget that is more transparent, comprehensive, accurate, and realistic, and is thus a better guidepost for citizens and their representatives in making decisions about the key fiscal policy issues that face the Nation.

I. BUDGET REFORM PROPOSALS

Joint Committee Enforcement

In August 2011, as part of the Budget Control Act of 2011 (BCA), bipartisan majorities in both the House and Senate voted to establish the Joint Select Committee for Deficit Reduction to recommend legislation to achieve at least $1.2 trillion of deficit reduction over the period of fiscal years 2012 through 2021. The BCA included automatic reductions as a mechanism to encourage the Congress to enact legislation to achieve this goal. On multiple occasions, the President has presented comprehensive plans to replace these reductions with a mix of specific spending cuts and revenue proposals. The failure of the Congress to enact such comprehensive deficit reduction legislation to achieve the $1.2 trillion goal has already triggered a sequestration of discretionary and mandatory spending in 2013, led to reductions in the discretionary caps for 2014 through 2017, and forced additional sequestrations of mandatory spending in each of fiscal years 2014 through 2016. A further sequestration of mandatory spending is scheduled to take effect beginning on October 1 based on the order released with the 2017 Budget.

To date, legislation has been enacted to partially address the annual reductions required to the discretionary spending limits set in the BCA through 2017. The American Taxpayer Relief Act of 2012 reduced the sequestration required of 2013 discretionary and mandatory spending by $24 billion. The Bipartisan Budget Act of 2013 (BBA of 2013) (P.L. 113-67)

decreased the reductions otherwise required to the 2014 discretionary caps by $44.8 billion and set new discretionary caps in 2015 that were approximately $18.5 billion more than the Congressional Budget Office's (CBO) estimate of the post-reduction discretionary spending limits in that year. The Bipartisan Budget Act of 2015 (BBA of 2015) (P.L. 114-74) decreased the reductions to the 2016 discretionary caps by $50 billion and replaced the reductions for the 2017 discretionary caps that would have been required with smaller reductions of $61.4 billion from the original caps agreed to in the BCA. The smaller reduction for 2017 was approximately $30 billion more than the March 2015 CBO estimate of the post-reduction discretionary spending limits. All of these revisions were paid for by enacting alternative deficit reduction.

In addition to the mandatory sequestration for 2017 noted above, damaging annual reductions of $109 billion will continue to be required for each of fiscal years 2018 through 2021, unless the Congress enacts balanced deficit reduction legislation that replaces and repeals the Joint Committee reductions. Further, legislation enacted subsequent to the BCA has extended the sequestration of mandatory spending through 2025 at the percentage reduction required for 2021.[1] The reductions to discre-

---

[1] The BBA of 2015, which extended sequestration into 2025, required that the reduction in the Medicare program be 4.0 percent for the first half of the sequestration period and zero for the second half of the period.

tionary spending for fiscal years 2018 through 2021 are to be implemented in the sequestration preview report for each year by reducing the discretionary caps. The reductions to mandatory programs are to be implemented by a sequestration of non-exempt mandatory budgetary resources in each of fiscal years 2017 through 2025, which is triggered by the transmittal of the President's Budget for each year and takes effect on the first day of the fiscal year.

The budget agreements of 2013 and 2015 took important steps in moving away from manufactured crises and austerity budgeting by replacing a portion of the Joint Committee reductions with sensible long-term reforms, including a number of reforms proposed in previous President's Budgets. The 2017 Budget builds on the achievements secured for 2016 and adheres to the agreement's funding levels. However, failing to fully replace sequestration has consequences. To further the goal of building durable economic growth in the future, the Budget also includes a series of investments using mandatory funding.

The 2017 Budget also recognizes that without further Congressional action, sequestration will re-turn in full in 2018. Therefore, starting in 2018, the Budget once again proposes to support a range of investments to move the Nation forward by ending sequestration and replacing the savings by cutting inefficient spending and closing tax loopholes, while putting the Nation on a sustainable fiscal path.

Program Integrity Funding

Critical programs such as Social Security, Unemployment Insurance, Medicare, and Medicaid, should be run efficiently and effectively. Therefore, the Administration proposes to make significant investments in activities to ensure that taxpayer dollars are spent correctly, by expanding oversight activities in the largest benefit programs and increasing investments in tax compliance and enforcement activities. In addition, the Administration supports a number of legislative and administrative reforms in order to reduce improper payments and improve debt collection. Many of these proposals will provide savings for the Government and taxpayers, and will support Government-wide efforts to improve the management and oversight of Federal resources.

The Administration supports efforts to provide Federal agencies with the necessary resources and incentives to prevent, reduce, or recover improper payments. With the enactment of the Improper Payments Elimination and Recovery Act of 2010 (P.L. 111-204) and the Improper Payments Elimination and Recovery Improvement Act of 2012 (P.L. 112-248), and the release of three Presidential directives on improper payments under this Administration, agencies are well positioned to utilize these new tools and techniques to prevent, reduce, and recover improper payments. The Administration will continue to identify areas—in addition to those outlined in the Budget—where it can work with the Congress to further improve agency efforts.

Administrative Funding for Program Integrity.— There is compelling evidence that investments in administrative resources can significantly decrease the rate of improper payments and recoup many times their initial investment. The Social Security Administration (SSA) estimates that medical continuing disability reviews conducted in 2017 will yield net Federal program savings over the next 10 years of roughly $8 on average per $1 budgeted for dedicated program integrity funding, including the Old Age, Survivors, and Disability Insurance Program (OASDI), Supplemental Security Income (SSI), Medicare and Medicaid program effects. Similarly, for Health Care Fraud and Abuse Control (HCFAC) program integrity efforts, CMS actuaries conservatively estimate approximately $2 is saved or payments averted for every additional $1 spent. The Internal Revenue Service (IRS) enforcement activities recoup roughly $6 for every $1 spent.

Enacted Adjustments Pursuant to BBEDCA.—The Balanced Budget and Emergency Deficit Control Act of 1985, as amended (BBEDCA) recognized that a multi-year strategy of agencies focusing attention and resources on reducing the rate of improper payments, commensurate with the large and growing costs of the programs administered by that agency, is a laudable goal. To support that goal, BBEDCA provided for adjustments to the discretionary spending limits to allow for additional funding for specific program integrity activities to reduce improper payments in the Social Security programs and in the Medicare and Medicaid programs. These adjustments are increases in the discretionary caps on budget authority through 2021 and are made only if appropriations bills increase funding for the specified program integrity purposes above specified minimum, or base levels. Recently, recognizing the significant benefits to program integrity activities, the BBA of 2015 increased such adjustments for Social Security programs by a net $484 million over the 2017-2021 period. The BBA of 2015 also expanded the uses of cap adjustment funds to include cooperative disability investigation units, and special attorneys for fraud prosecutions. This budget mechanism was intended to ensure that the additional funding did not supplant other Federal spending on these activities and that such spending was not diverted to other purposes.

The Consolidated Appropriations Act, 2016 (P.L. 114-113) did not provide full funding of the adjustment to the discretionary spending limit for HCFAC and SSA. Although the final levels in 2016 increased from 2015 in nominal terms for both SSA and HCFAC, the final levels for both accounts were less than the Administration's request for the full allowable cap adjustments by $13 million and $25 million, respectively. Both were fully funded at the levels specified in BBEDCA for 2015. Tens of billions of dollars in deficit savings over the next 10 years from curtailing improper payments will be realized if the levels of administrative expenses for program integrity envisioned by BBEDCA continue to be provided. To ensure these important program integrity investments are made, the Budget proposes to continue the full discretionary cap adjustment for SSA and for HCFAC through 2026.

These proposals will produce new net deficit savings of $38.6 billion over 10 years.

Social Security Administration Medical Continuing Disability Reviews and Non-Medical Redeterminations of SSI Eligibility.—For the Social Security Administration, the Budget's proposed $1,819 million in discretionary funding in 2017 ($273 million in base funding and $1,546 million in cap adjustment funding) will allow SSA to conduct 1.1 million full medical CDRs and approximately 2.8 million SSI non-medical redeterminations of eligibility. Medical CDRs are periodic reevaluations to determine whether disabled OASDI or SSI beneficiaries continue to meet SSA's standards for disability. The funding provided will enable the agency to work down a backlog of medical CDRs. As a result of the discretionary funding requested in 2017, as well as the fully funded base and cap adjustment amounts in 2018 through 2026, the OASDI, SSI, Medicare and Medicaid programs would recoup almost $48 billion in gross Federal savings with additional savings after the 10-year period, according to estimates from SSA's Office of the Chief Actuary. Access to increased cap adjustment amounts and SSA's commitment to fund the fully loaded costs of performing the requested CDR and redetermination volumes would produce new net deficit savings of $34 billion in the 10-year window, and additional savings in the out-years. These costs and savings are reflected in Table 11-1.

SSA is required by law to conduct medical CDRs for all beneficiaries who are receiving disability benefits under the OASDI program, as well as all children under age 18 who are receiving SSI. SSI redeterminations are also required by law. However, the frequency of CDRs and redeterminations is constrained by the availability of funds to support these activities. As noted above, for 2016, the base amounts, as well as an additional $1,153 million in discretionary cap adjustment funding pursuant to section 251(b)(2)(B) of BBEDCA were enacted in the annual appropriations bill. The mandatory savings from the base funding in every year and the enacted discretionary cap adjustment funding in 2016 are included in the BBEDCA baseline, consistent with the levels amended by the BBA of 2015, because the baseline assumes the continued funding of program integrity activities. The Budget shows the savings that would result from the increase in CDRs and redeterminations made possible by the discretionary funding requested in 2017 through 2026. With enactment of the new cap adjustment amounts in the BBA of 2015 and full funding of the cap adjustment amounts through 2026, SSA should eliminate the backlog of CDRs by the end of 2019 and prevent a new backlog from developing during the budget window.

As stated above, current estimates indicate that medical CDRs conducted in 2017 will yield a return on investment (ROI) of about $8 on average in net Federal program savings over 10 years per $1 budgeted for dedicated program integrity funding, including OASDI, SSI, Medicare and Medicaid program effects. Similarly, SSA estimates indicate that non-medical redeterminations conducted in 2017 will yield a ROI of about $3 on average

of net Federal program savings over 10 years per $1 budgeted for dedicated program integrity funding, including SSI and Medicaid program effects. The Budget assumes the full cost of performing CDRs in 2017 and beyond to ensure that sufficient resources are available to account for spending on these activities. The savings from one year of program integrity activities are realized over multiple years because some results find that beneficiaries are no longer eligible to receive OASDI or SSI benefits.

Redeterminations are periodic reviews of non-medical eligibility factors, such as income and resources, for the means-tested SSI program and can result in a revision of the individual's benefit level. However, the schedule of savings resulting from redeterminations will be different for the base funding and the cap adjustment funding in 2017 through 2026. This is because redeterminations of eligibility can uncover underpayment errors as well as overpayment errors. SSI recipients are more likely to initiate a redetermination of eligibility if they believe there are underpayments, and these recipient-initiated redeterminations are included in the base. The estimated savings per dollar spent on medical CDRs and non-medical redeterminations reflects an interaction with a provision in the Affordable Care Act (ACA) that allows States to expand Medicaid coverage beginning January 2014 for individuals under age 65 with income less than 133 percent of poverty. As a result of this provision, some SSI beneficiaries, who would otherwise lose Medicaid coverage due to a medical CDR or non-medical redetermination, would continue to be covered. In addition, some of the coverage costs for these individuals will be eligible for the Medicaid ACA enhanced Federal matching rate, resulting in higher Federal Medicaid costs in those states.

Health Care Fraud and Abuse Program.—The 2017 Budget proposes base and cap adjustment funding levels over the next 10 years and continues the program integrity cap adjustment through 2026.

The discretionary base funding of $311 million and cap adjustment of $414 million for HCFAC activities in 2017 are designed to reduce the Medicare improper payment rate, support the Health Care Fraud Prevention & Enforcement Action Team (HEAT) initiative, reduce Medicaid improper payment rates, and monitor and prevent fraud, waste, and abuse in the private health insurance market including the Health Insurance Marketplace. The investment will also allow CMS to deploy innovative efforts that focus on improving the analysis and application of data, including state-of-the-art predictive modeling capabilities, in order to prevent potentially wasteful, abusive, or fraudulent payments before they occur. The funding is to be allocated among CMS, the Health and Human Services Office of Inspector General, and the Department of Justice (DOJ). Over 2017 through 2026, as reflected in Table 11-1, this $5.1 billion investment in HCFAC cap adjustment funding will generate approximately $10.2 billion in savings to Medicare and Medicaid, for new net deficit reduction of $5.1 billion over the 10-year period, reflecting prevention and recoupment of improper payments made to providers, as well as recoveries related to civil and criminal penalties. The

Table 11-1. ENACTED CAP ADJUSTMENTS, INCLUDING MANDATORY SAVINGS

(Outlays in millions of dollars)

	2017	2018	2019	2020	2021	2022	2023	2024	2025	2026	2017-2026 Total
SSA Program Integrity											
Discretionary Costs [1]	1,546	1,462	1,410	1,309	1,302	1,341	1,382	1,423	1,466	1,509	14,150
Mandatory Savings [2]	−106	−2,140	−3,331	−4,100	−4,825	−5,756	−6,105	−6,350	−7,218	−7,779	−47,710
Net Savings	1,440	−678	−1,921	−2,791	−3,523	−4,415	−4,723	−4,927	−5,752	−6,270	−33,560
Health Care Fraud and Abuse Control Program											
Discretionary Costs	414	434	454	475	496	518	541	565	590	616	5,103
Mandatory Savings [3]	−795	−844	−894	−947	−991	−1,036	−1,085	−1,135	−1,187	−1,241	−10,155
Net Savings	−381	−410	−440	−472	−495	−518	−544	−570	−597	−625	−5,052

[1] The annual discretionary cost includes the amounts newly enacted in the Bipartisan Budget Act of 2015 for 2017 through 2021, pursuant to section 251(b)(2)(B) of BBEDCA. Amounts from 2022 through 2026 are the requested adjustment to the Administration's proposed caps. For 2016 the base amount was enacted in the annual appropriations bill and an additional $1,153 million was provided as a discretionary cap adjustment pursuant to section 251(b)(2)(B) of BBEDCA. The mandatory savings from the base funding in every year and the 2016 enacted discretionary cap adjustment funding continues to be included in the BBEDCA baseline.

[2] This is based on SSA's Office of the Actuary estimates of savings.

[3] These savings are based on estimates from the HHS Office of the Actuary for return on investment (ROI) from program integrity activities.

mandatory savings from base funding, assuming that amount is to continue in future years, are included in the BBEDCA baseline, as are the savings from the 2016 enacted cap adjustment funding of $370 million.

Proposed Adjustments to BBEDCA Discretionary Spending Limits.—The Administration also proposes to amend BBEDCA to enact adjustments to the discretionary spending limits for tax code enforcement at the IRS and Treasury's Alcohol and Tobacco Tax and Trade Bureau (TTB) over the 2017 to 2026 period and for the Department of Labor (DOL) to reduce improper payments in the Unemployment Insurance (UI) program in 2017. Beginning in 2018, the Administration proposes to fund these activities with mandatory funding. As shown in Table 11-2, the new spending is estimated to result in more than $64 billion in lower spending and additional tax revenue over the next 10 years, with further savings after the ten-year period. The base level of funding and the additional funding that would trigger cap adjustments, as well as mandatory funding requests for UI are also listed in Table 11-2.

Internal Revenue Service and Treasury's Alcohol and Tobacco Tax and Trade Bureau.—For the IRS and TTB, the base funds current tax administration activities, including all tax enforcement and compliance program activities, in the Enforcement and Operations Support accounts at IRS and the Salaries and Expenses account at TTB. The additional $514 million cap adjustment funds new and continuing investments in expanding and improving the effectiveness and efficiency of the IRS's and TTB's overall tax enforcement program. As a result of base tax enforcement and compliance activities, the Government will collect roughly $54 billion in 2017 in

direct enforcement revenue. The IRS estimates that the proposed new 2017 enforcement initiatives will yield an additional $278 million in revenue from the work done in 2017. Furthermore, once the new staff are trained and become fully operational in 2019, the additional annual revenue generated by these initiatives is expected to be $2.6 billion, or roughly $6 in additional revenue for every $1 in IRS expenses. The activities through 2026 will generate $63.6 billion in additional revenue over 10 years and will cost $17.4 billion for an estimated net savings of $46.2 billion. Notably, the ROI is likely understated because it only includes amounts received; it does not reflect the effect enhanced enforcement has on deterring noncompliance. This indirect deterrence helps to ensure the continued payment of over $3 trillion in taxes paid each year without direct enforcement measures.

Unemployment Insurance.—The Budget proposes a cap adjustment in 2017, which would be a transition year to dedicated mandatory funding in 2018 and beyond for the Department of Labor's (DOL) Unemployment Insurance (UI) State administrative grants program to reduce UI improper payments, a top management challenge identified by GAO and DOL's Inspector General. The proposal would expand what is now a $115 million initiative to conduct Reemployment Services and Eligibility Assessments (RESEA).

The REA initiative was begun in 2005 to finance in-person interviews at American Job Centers (also known as "One-Stop Career Centers"), to assess UI beneficiaries' need for job finding services and their continued eligibility for benefits. Research, including a random-assignment evaluation, shows that a combination of eligibility reviews and reemployment services reduces the time on

UI, increases earnings, and reduces improper payments to claimants who are not eligible for benefits. Based on this research, the Budget proposes to expand funding for the RESEA initiative to allow States to conduct robust reemployment services along with REAs. These reemployment services, which may include the development of reemployment and work search plans, provision of skills assessments, career counseling, job matching and referrals, and referrals to training as appropriate.

The funding proposed in the Budget would allow States to provide RESEA services to focus on UI claimants identified as most likely to exhaust their UI benefits and on newly separated veterans claiming unemployment compensation for ex-service members (UCX). The proposed mandatory program would result in savings in UI benefit payments of an estimated $5.1 billion. These benefit savings would allow States to reduce their UI taxes by $1.5 billion, reducing the burden on employers.

Because most unemployment claims are now filed by telephone or online, in-person assessments conducted in the Centers can help determine the continued eligibility for benefits and the adequacy of work search, verify the identity of beneficiaries where there is suspicion of possible identity theft, and provide a referral to reemployment assistance for those who need additional help. The benefit savings from this initiative are short-term because the maximum UI benefit period is limited, typically 26 weeks for regular State UI programs. The proposed amount to be spent in 2017 would be $35 million through a cap adjustment, while the out years would request total funding of $1.7 billion on the mandatory side of the Budget through 2026. Of that amount, $228 million is requested as new funding. Overall, the new mandatory funding would result in total deficit savings estimated at $669 million. The 2017 cap adjustment would result in total outlay savings of $134 million. These deficit savings from the cap adjust-

Table 11–2. PROPOSALS FOR DISCRETIONARY PROGRAM INTEGRITY BASE FUNDING AND CAP ADJUSTMENTS, INCLUDING MANDATORY AND RECEIPTS SAVINGS

(Budget authority/outlays in millions of dollars)

	2017	2018	2019	2020	2021	2022	2023	2024	2025	2026	2017-2026 Total
IRS Tax Enforcement											
Proposed Adjustments Pursuant to the Balanced Budget and Emergency Deficit Control Act of 1985, as Amended:											
Enforcement Base	8,854	9,057	9,265	9,477	9,696	9,918	10,145	10,379	12,846	13,118	102,755
Cap Adjustments:											
BA	514	938	1,300	1,667	2,042	2,141	2,160	2,185	2,211	2,237	17,395
Outlays	458	890	1,255	1,622	1,996	2,124	2,153	2,180	2,206	2,231	17,115
Receipt Savings from Discretionary Program Integrity Base Funding and Cap Adjustments: [1]											
Enforcement Base [2]	–54,000	–54,000	–54,000	–54,000	–54,000	–54,000	–54,000	–54,000	–54,000	–54,000	–540,000
Cap Adjustment [3]	–278	–1,585	–3,263	–5,008	–6,763	–8,327	–9,264	–9,590	–9,737	–9,814	–63,629
Unemployment Insurance Improper Payments											
Proposed Adjustments Pursuant to the Balanced Budget and Emergency Deficit Control Act of 1985, as Amended/Proposed Increase in Mandatory Funding:											
Discretionary Costs (BA) [4]	35	0	0	0	0	0	0	0	0	0	35
Mandatory Costs	0	23	24	24	25	26	25	27	26	28	228
Mandatory Savings from Program Integrity Cap Adjustment, and UI Mandatory Proposal: [5]											
Cap Adjustment	–76	–58	0	0	0	0	0	0	0	0	–134
UI Mandatory Funding Increase	0	–27	–67	–70	–75	–80	–79	–88	–87	–96	–669

[1] Savings for IRS are revenue increases rather than spending reductions. They are shown as negatives for consistency in presentation.

[2] No official estimate for 2017 enforcement revenue has been produced, so this figure is an approximation and included only for illustrative purposes.

[3] The Internal Revenue Service (IRS) cap adjustment funds increases for existing enforcement initiatives and activities and new initiatives. The IRS enforcement program helps maintain the more than $2 trillion in taxes paid each year without direct enforcement measures. The cost increases will help maintain the base revenue while generating additional revenue through targeted program investments. The activities and new initiatives funded out of the cap adjustment will yield more than $46 billion in savings over ten years. Aside from direct enforcement revenue, the deterrence impact of these activities suggests the potential for even greater savings.

[4] The cost of shifting the current UI base funding ($151 million in 2017, adjusted annually for inflation) from discretionary to mandatory is not reflected above in 2018 through 2026 because it is offset with and annual reduction to the discretionary spending limits in section 251(c) of the Balanced Budget and Emergency Deficit Control Act of 1985. For 2017, the Budget requests base UI program integrity funding of $151 million through discretionary appropriations, as well as $35 million through an adjustment to the 2017 discretionary cap. The mandatory savings from the base funding every year continue to be included in the BBEDCA baseline. The mandatory cost is the incerse requested above the inflation adjusted baseline.

[5] The maximum UI benefit period is typically 26 weeks unless temporary extended benefits programs are in effect. As a result, preventing an ineligible individual from collecting UI benefits would save at most a half year of benefits in the absence of extended benefits. The savings estimates are based on regular UI benefits and spread over two years, reflecting the fact that reemployment and eligibility assessments conducted late in the year affect individuals whose benefits would have continued into the subsequent fiscal year. As a result of the benefit savings, many States will be able to reduce their unemployment taxes. The reduction in State UI taxes from the cap adjustment is $85 million. The estimated reduction in State UI taxes from mandatory funding is $204 million.

ment and additional mandatory spending would result in some States reducing their UI taxes, which would result in an estimated revenue loss of $289 million. Net savings for the proposal, including the cost of the cap adjustment, the mandatory outlay savings, and the revenue declines, totals $251 million. The cost of shifting UI base funding from discretionary to mandatory in 2018 through 2026 is not reflected in the new net deficit savings because it is being offset with an annual reduction to the discretionary spending limits in section 251(c) of BBEDCA, if the mandatory funding proposal is enacted.

Partnership Fund for Program Integrity Innovation.—Funded from 2010 through 2013, the Partnership Fund invested over $29 million in eleven pilot projects estimated to lead to total savings of $200 million or more annually if the pilots are taken to scale. The Partnership Fund's focus on program integrity expanded to include increased cost-effectiveness in the delivery of federally funded services with State and local partners. As evaluations are completed and results finalized, OMB will work with Federal agencies, States and local governments, and other stakeholders to disseminate lessons learned and apply the tools and methods tested more broadly across programs and levels of government.

In the past year, the Administration for Children and Families at HHS awarded $3.6 million to scale the successful pilot National Electronic Interstate Compact Enterprise (NEICE) System to a national level. Formerly known as Supporting Permanent Placements of Foster Care Children through Electronic Records Exchange, this effort has helped States implement a real-time, on-line data exchange to share records and other information to support permanent placements of children and youth in foster care when they are placed in homes across State lines. By increasing efficiency, NEICE helps to reduce the time that youth in foster care spend waiting for an interstate placement. The award will support efforts over the next three years by the Association of Administrators of the Interstate Compact on the Placement of Children (AAICPC), which governs the placement of children across State lines for purposes of foster care, adoption and residential placements, to improve the administrative efficiency of interstate placements.

Additionally, some pilots are close to having results. The Food and Nutrition Service (FNS) at the Department of Agriculture completed the National Accuracy Clearinghouse pilot. FNS worked with States to test an interstate database of program information to support the Supplemental Nutrition Assistance Program (SNAP) and Disaster SNAP (D-SNAP) eligibility determinations by allowing States to determine whether an applicant is already receiving benefits in a different participating State. A pilot evaluation is being finalized. The Trusted On-Line Credentials pilot, in which Commerce is working with States to develop effective and secure identity verification solutions to support convenient customer access and program integrity across different services and agencies, has completed implementation and is producing its evaluation for one of the two participating States.

In 2016, early results are expected for the Identifying State Innovations for Improving Temporary Assistance for Needy Families (TANF) Program Administration pilot. ACF is working with States to develop cost-effective approaches and best practices to maximize TANF block grants by reducing improper payments and directing cash assistance payments to eligible families not participating.

In 2017, the DOJ's Juvenile Justice Reinvestment and Realignment Initiative (JJRRI) pilot is expected to produce preliminary results. Under JJRRI, DOJ is working with State and local youth-serving agencies as well as community service providers to develop and implement an integrated set of evidence-based and cost-measurement tools that will enable them to make informed decisions about resources and services for justice-involved youth. Pilot partners are collecting and analyzing local data on recidivism, cost, and other factors to implement a practical "ground up" solution to the challenges of local and State service quality.

Mandatory Program Integrity Initiatives.—Table 11-3 presents the mandatory and receipt savings from other program integrity initiatives that are included in the 2017 Budget, beyond the expansion in resources resulting from the increases in administrative funding discussed above. These savings total almost $15.8 billion over 10 years. These mandatory proposals to reduce improper payments and ensure agencies recover debt owed to the Federal Government reflect the importance of these issues to the Administration. Through these and other initiatives outlined in the Budget, the Administration can improve management efforts across the Federal Government.

Cut Waste, Fraud, and Abuse in Medicare and Medicaid.—The Budget includes a robust package of Medicare and Medicaid program integrity proposals to help prevent fraud and abuse before they occur; detect fraud and abuse as early as possible; more comprehensively enforce penalties and other sanctions when fraud and abuse occur; provide greater flexibility to the Secretary of Health and Human Services to implement program integrity activities that allow for efficient use of resources and achieve high returns-on-investment; and promote integrity in Federal-State financing. For example, the Budget proposes to authorize civil monetary penalties or other intermediate sanctions for providers who do not update enrollment records, permit exclusion of individuals affiliated with entities sanctioned for fraudulent or other prohibited action from Federal health care programs, and strengthens Medicaid and the Children's Health Insurance Program (CHIP) by providing tools to States, Territories, and the Federal Government to fight fraud, waste, and abuse. Together, the CMS program integrity authority would net approximately $3.4 billion over 10 years PAYGO and non-PAYGO savings.

Unemployment Insurance Integrity.—The Budget includes a package aimed at improving integrity in the Unemployment Insurance program. The package would result in $79 million in PAYGO outlay costs over 10 years, but would result in $2 billion in non-PAYGO outlay sav-

Table 11–3. MANDATORY AND RECEIPT SAVINGS FROM OTHER PROGRAM INTEGRITY INITIATIVES

(Receipts and outlays in millions of dollars)

	2017	2018	2019	2020	2021	2022	2023	2024	2025	2026	10-year total
Department of Health and Human Services:											
Cut Waste, Fraud, and Abuse in Medicare and Medicaid [1]	104	79	93	88	98	123	132	152	172	192	1,233
Cut Waste, Fraud, and Abuse in Medicare and Medicaid (non-PAYGO) [1]	-111	-156	-256	-362	-482	-552	-608	-658	-703	-759	-4,647
Department of Labor:											
Unemployment Insurance Integrity Package	-12	-25	-6	22	24	27	30	36	31	39	166
Unemployment Insurance Integrity Package (non-PAYGO)	-57	-83	-134	-202	-194	-186	-182	-147	-194	-168	-1,547
Department of the Treasury:											
Authorize Treasury to locate and recover assets of the United States and to retain a portion of amounts collected to pay for the cost of recovery	-8	-8	-8	-8	-8	-9	-9	-9	-9	-9	-85
Increase delinquent Federal non-tax debt collection	-32	-32	-32	-32	-32	-32	-32	-32	-32	-32	-320
Social Security Administration:											
Windfall Elimination Provision/Government Pension Offset Enforcement Provision (non-PAYGO)	18	28	24	-433	-1002	-1350	-1421	-1318	-1246	-1142	-7,842
Hold Fraud Facilitators Liable for Overpayments [3] (non-PAYGO)	....	....	-1	-1	-1	-1	-1	-1	-1	-1	-8
Government Wide Use of CBP Entry/Exit Data to Prevent Improper Payment	....	....	-1	-4	-9	-18	-24	-28	-36	-39	-159
Government Wide Use of CBP Entry/Exit Data to Prevent Improper Payment (non-PAYGO)	....	....	....	-1	-2	-2	-2	-3	-3	-5	-18
Allow SSA to Use Commercial Databases to Verify Real Property Data in the SSI Program	-12	-28	-44	-53	-60	-69	-70	-68	-76	-79	-559
Increase the Minimum Monthly OASDI Overpayment Collection from $10 a Month to 10% (non-PAYGO)	-8	-26	-43	-59	-77	-93	-107	-135	-144	-156	-848
Authorize SSA to Use All Collection Tools to Recover Funds in Certain Scenarios (non-PAYGO)		-2	-2	-3	-4	-4	-5	-5	-5	-5	-35
Move from Annual to Quarterly Wage Reporting	20	30	90	-119	-125	-136	-149	-172	-201	-253	-1,015
Move from Annual to Quarterly Wage Reporting (non-PAYGO)	....	....	....	....	-1	-12	-29	-31	-24	-17	-114
Total, Mandatory and Receipt Savings	**-98**	**-223**	**-320**	**-1,167**	**-1,875**	**-2,314**	**-2,477**	**-2,419**	**-2,471**	**-2,434**	**-15,798**
PAYGO Savings	*60*	*16*	*92*	*-106*	*-112*	*-114*	*-122*	*-121*	*-151*	*-181*	*-739*
Non-PAYGO Savings	*-158*	*-239*	*-412*	*-1,061*	*-1,763*	*-2,200*	*-2,355*	*-2,298*	*-2,320*	*-2,253*	*-15,059*

[1] Savings estimates may not include all interactions.

ings. In addition, these proposals would allow States to reduce their unemployment taxes by $516 million. The total package would result in $1.4 billion in deficit reduction.

Included in this package are proposals to: allow for data disclosure to contractors for the Treasury Offset Program; expand State use of the Separation Information Data Exchange System (SIDES), which already improves program integrity by allowing States and employers to exchange information on reasons for a claimant's separation from employment and thereby helping States to determine UI eligibility; mandate the use of the National Directory of New Hires to conduct cross-matches for program integrity purposes; allow the Secretary to set corrective action measures for poor State performance; require States to cross-match claimants against the Prisoner Update Processing System (PUPS), which is currently used by some States; and allow States to retain five percent of overpayment and tax investigation recoveries to fund program integrity activities.

Improve Treasury Debt Collection.—The Budget includes two proposals that would increase collections of delinquent debt:

- *Authorize Treasury to locate and recover assets of the United States and to retain a portion of amounts collected to pay for the cost of recovery.*—States and other entities hold assets in the name of the United States or in the name of departments, agencies and other subdivisions of the Federal Government. Many agencies are not recovering these assets due to lack of expertise and funding. Under current authority, Treasury collects delinquent debts owed to the United States and retains a portion of collections, which is the sole source of funding for its debt collection operations. While unclaimed Federal assets are generally not considered to be delinquent debts, Treasury's debt collection operations personnel have the skills and training to recover these assets. The Budget proposes to authorize Treasury to use its resources to recover assets of the United States. This proposal would result in PAYGO savings of $85 million over 10 years.

- *Increase delinquent Federal non-tax debt collections. Authorize administrative bank garnishment for non-tax debts of commercial entities.*—Allow Federal agencies to collect non-tax debt by garnishing the bank and other financial institution accounts of delinquent commercial debtors without a court order and after providing full administrative due process. The Budget proposes to direct the Secretary of the Treasury to issue Government-wide regulations implementing the authority of bank garnishment for non-tax debts of commercial entities. Bank garnishment orders under this authority would be subject to Treasury's rule (31 CFR 212) protecting exempt benefit payments from garnishment. To reach income of commercial entities and other non-wage income and funds available to commercial debtors owing delinquent non-tax obligations to the United States, this proposal would authorize agencies to issue garnishment orders to financial institutions without a court order. Agencies would be required to provide debtors with appropriate administrative due process and other protections to ensure that debtors have had the full opportunity to contest the debts and/or enter into repayment agreements to avoid issuance of an order. The Internal Revenue Service currently has similar authority to collect Federal tax debts. The Debt Collection Improvement Act of 1996 (DCIA) authorized Federal agencies to collect delinquent non-tax debt by garnishing the wages of debtors without the need to first obtain a court order. Since July 2001, the U.S. Department of the Treasury's Bureau of the Fiscal Service has collected $279.3 million in garnished wages (as of November 30, 2015) on behalf of Federal agencies. This proposal would result in estimated savings of $320 million over 10 years in commercial non-tax debts.

Preventing Improper Payments in Social Security.—Overall, the Budget proposes legislation that would avert close to $9 billion in improper payments in Social Security over 10 years. While much of this savings is considered off-budget and would be non-PAYGO, about $2 billion from various proposals would be PAYGO savings.

- ***Improve Collection of Pension Information and Transition after 10 Years to an Alternative Approach based on Years of Non-Covered Earnings.***—The Budget proposes legislation that would improve reporting for non-covered pensions by including up to $70 million for administrative expenses, $50 million of which would be available to the States, to develop a mechanism so that the Social Security Administration could enforce the offsets for the Windfall Elimination Provision (WEP), and Government Pension Offset (GPO). The proposal would require State and local governments to provide information on their non-covered pension payments to SSA so that the agency can apply the WEP and GPO adjustments. Under current law, the WEP and GPO adjustments are dependent on self-reported pension data and cannot be independently verified. This proposal would result in savings in the Old-Age, Survivors, and Disability Insurance program of almost $7.9

billion over 10 years, which would be scored as non-PAYGO savings because the program is off-budget. In addition, the Budget proposes to transition after 10 years to an alternative approach, which would adjust Social Security benefits based on the extent to which workers have non-covered earnings. SSA now collects data on non-covered employment and could calculate the offset without any disclosure from the individual.

- ***Hold Fraud Facilitators Liable for Overpayments.***—The Budget proposes to hold fraud facilitators liable for overpayments by allowing SSA to recover the overpayment from a third party if the third party was responsible for making fraudulent statements or providing false evidence that allowed the beneficiary to receive payments that should not have been paid. This proposal would result in an estimated $8 million in savings over 10 years.

- ***Government-wide Use of Custom and Border Patrol (CBP) Entry/Exit Data to Prevent Improper Payments.***—The Budget will provide for the use of CBP Entry/Exit data to prevent improper OASDI and Supplemental Security Insurance (SSI) payments. Generally, U.S. citizens can receive benefits regardless of residence. Noncitizens may be subject to additional residence requirements depending on the country of residence and benefit type. However, an SSI beneficiary who is outside the United States for 30 consecutive days is not eligible for benefits for that month. These data have the potential to be useful across the Government to prevent improper payments. This proposal would result in an estimated $178 million in savings over 10 years.

- ***Allow SSA to Use Commercial Databases to Verify Real Property Data in the SSI Program.***—The Budget proposes to reduce improper payments and lessen recipients' reporting burden by authorizing SSA to use private commercial databases to check for ownership of real property (i.e. land and buildings), which could affect SSI eligibility. Consent to allow SSA to access these databases would be a condition of benefit receipt for new beneficiaries and current beneficiaries who complete a determination. All other current due process and appeal rights would be preserved. This proposal would result in savings of $559 million over 10 years.

- ***Increase the Minimum Monthly OASDI Overpayment Collection from $10 a Month to 10%.***—The Budget would change the minimum monthly withholding amount for recovery of Social Security benefit overpayments to reflect the increase in the average monthly benefit since the Agency established the current minimum of $10 in 1960. By changing this amount from $10 to 10% of the monthly benefit payable, SSA would recover overpayments more quickly and better fulfill its stewardship obligations to the combined Social Security Trust Funds. The SSI program already utilizes the 10% rule. This proposal would result in savings of $848 million over 10 years.

- *Authorize SSA to Use All Collection Tools to Recover Funds in Certain Scenarios.*—The Budget also proposes to allow SSA a broader range of collection tools when someone improperly receives a benefit after the beneficiary has died. Currently, if a spouse cashes a benefit payment (or does not return a directly deposited benefit) for an individual who has died and the spouse is also not receiving benefits on that individual's record, SSA has more limited collection tools available than would be the case if the spouse also receives benefits on the deceased individual's earning record. The Budget proposal would end this disparate treatment of similar types of improper payments and results in an estimated $35 million in savings over 10 years.

- *Move from Annual to Quarterly Wage Reporting.*—The Budget re-proposes moving from annual to quarterly employer reporting of wages to the Social Security Administration. This would provide more accurate and timely wage data which would further program integrity efforts and facilitate tax administration. This proposal would result in savings of $1.129 billion over 10 years.

Other Program Integrity Initiatives.—

Data Analytics to Reduce Improper Payments.— Under this Administration, the Federal Government has focused on increased use of technology to address improper payments. Pursuant to Executive Order 13520 (issued November 20, 2009), work groups were created to analyze the role that cutting-edge forensic technologies could play in identifying and preventing fraud and other improper payments, as well as efforts that could be undertaken to improve data sharing between agencies.

On June 18, 2010, a Presidential Memorandum on Enhancing Payment Accuracy Through a "Do Not Pay List" required Federal agencies to review current pre-payment and pre-award procedures and ensure that a thorough review of available databases with relevant information on eligibility occurs before the release of any Federal funds. The "Do Not Pay" list established a single portal, the Department of the Treasury's (Treasury) Do Not Pay Business Center, through which agencies could check multiple eligibility databases before making an award or payment. The 2012 Budget requested (and the Consolidated Appropriations Act, 2012 appropriated) $10 million to the Treasury Department to support expansion of the "Do Not Pay" list and to add forensic fraud detection capabilities to the basic Do Not Pay Business Center. Specifically, the funding helped to:

1. Expand the number of databases and infrastructure of the "Do Not Pay" list;

2. Procure the detection technology and staff an operations center to analyze fraud patterns using available public and private sector information; and

3. Refer potential improper payment issues to the relevant agency management and Inspector General.

The Improper Payments and Elimination and Recovery Improvement Act of 2012 (IPERIA; P.L. 112-248) reinforced the Administration's "Do Not Pay" initiative, by codifying the efforts underway to improve payment accuracy. Through OMB Memorandum M-13-20, Protecting Privacy while Reducing Improper Payments with the Do Not Pay Initiative, OMB designated the Department of the Treasury to spearhead the Do Not Pay working system with the five databases specified by IPERIA, enabled Treasury to publish a System of Records Notification in accordance with the Privacy Act of 1974, and provided substantial guidance for Federal agencies to ensure that individual privacy is fully protected in the program. Given the increasing range of sensitive information available about individuals through commercial sources, this guidance was a significant step to ensure privacy protections when data is used to inform government decision-making. The Treasury Do Not Pay Business Center has established a working system that enables agencies to identify, prevent, capture, and recover payments at different phases of the payments life cycle using available databases, and Do Not Pay analytics specialists work one-on-one with agencies to review payment data to identify and address internal control weaknesses that resulted in improper payments. Treasury's team also provides business process review services to support this work.

Treasury initiated the system in a phased approach to meet IPERIA's requirement for agencies to begin reviewing all payments and awards with Do Not Pay by June 1, 2013. The effective use of data analytics has provided insight into methods of reducing costs and improving performance and decision-making capabilities. Collectively, agency reports indicated to OMB after the first year of reviewing payments under the Initiative resulted in over $2 billion of stopped payments with additional operational efficiencies identified.

The Do Not Pay initiative has continued to expand and incorporate other agency best practices and activities that further promote program integrity and benefits to the taxpayer. The Bipartisan Budget Act of 2013 expanded the Do Not Pay initiative to include additional information collected by the Social Security Administration's Prisoner Updates Processing System (PUPS) to prevent the improper payment of Federal funds to incarcerated individuals, and in 2015, the Do Not Pay Business Center began facilitating the Internal Revenue Service use of these data to prevent fraud committed by prisoners. Additional examples of agencies using data to improve payment accuracy include the Centers for Medicare & Medicaid Services' (CMS) Fraud Prevention System (FPS), a state-of-the-art predictive analytics technology used to identify and prevent fraud in the program; the Department of Defense Business Activity Monitoring tool; and the Department of Labor's Unemployment Insurance (UI) Integrity Center for Excellence, a Federal-State partnership which facilitates the development and implementation of integrity tools that help detect and reduce improper payments in state run programs.

Agencies need available data to be timely, accurate, and relevant to their programs to improve their payment accuracy, and additional authorities will enhance data sharing on death, prisoners, and employment for payment accuracy, while maintaining privacy.

Use of the Death Master File to Prevent Federal Improper Payments.—The Administration is continuing to pursue opportunities to improve information sharing by developing or enhancing policy guidance, ensuring privacy protection, and developing legislative proposals to leverage available information and technology in determining benefit eligibility and other opportunities to prevent improper payments.

The Budget proposes to improve payment accuracy further by sharing available death data across Government agencies to prevent improper payments. This proposal would amend the Social Security Act to provide the Do Not Pay system at Treasury and agencies that use the system access to the full death data at SSA to prevent, identify, or recover improper payments. This proposal would include information received from a State, or any other source, about the deceased.

Efficient use of Employment Data to Streamline Processes.—The Budget also proposes to allow programs that are statutorily authorized to access HHS's National Directory of New Hires data the option to do so via the Do Not Pay system at Treasury, providing them a centralized portal of information. This proposal will increase efficiency and effectiveness of data matching, while ensuring robust privacy protections are maintained.

Social Security Workers' Compensation Enforcement Provision.—The Budget proposes the improvement of data collection on the receipt of Workers' Compensation benefits. Similar to non-covered pension information (see description in the mandatory program integrity initiatives section above), this information is self-reported to SSA and is used to offset benefit amounts in the Social Security Disability Insurance and Supplemental Security Income programs. This proposal would develop a process to collect this information in a timely manner from States and private insurers to correctly offset Disability Insurance benefits and reduce SSI payments. The proposal includes $10 million to help fund States' implementation costs and would reduce program overpayments and underpayments.

Using Rigorous Evidence to Develop Cost Estimates.—OMB works with Federal agencies and CBO to develop PAYGO estimates for mandatory programs. OMB has issued guidance to agencies for scoring legislation under the PAYGO. This guidance states that agencies must score the effects of program legislation on other programs if the programs are linked by statute.

(For example, effects on Medicaid spending that are due to statutory linkages in eligibility for Supplemental Security Income benefits must be scored.) In addition, even when programs are not linked by statute, agencies may score effects on other programs if those effects are significant and well documented. Specifically, the guidance states: "Under certain circumstances, estimates may also include effects in programs not linked by statute where such effects are significant and well documented. For example, such effects may be estimated where rigorous experimental research or past program experience has established a high probability that changes in eligibility or terms of one program will have significant effects on participation in another program."

Rigorous evidence can help policy makers identify policies that reduce Government spending overall. Because PAYGO accounts for long-term mandatory savings, it creates an incentive to invest in relatively cost-effective programs. Discretionary programs can save money too, but discretionary scoring typically does not capture these savings. For example, research shows investments in the Special Supplemental Nutrition Program for Women, Infants, and Children (WIC) reduce Medicaid costs for the mother and child. Although the interventions can reduce Federal costs, the appropriations bills are scored with the discretionary costs but are not credited with the savings in mandatory spending. As discussed earlier in this chapter, one exception to this is the program integrity cap adjustments, which allow the appropriators to provide money above the discretionary caps for activities that have been shown to generate cost savings. OMB would like to work with the Congress and CBO to develop options to provide similar incentives to use rigorous evidence to reward discretionary program investments in interventions that reduce government spending in other areas. In addition to promoting better use of limited discretionary funding, such incentives would also stimulate better data collection and evaluation about the impacts of Federal spending.

Disaster Relief Funding

Section 251(b)(2)(D) of BBEDCA includes a provision to adjust the discretionary caps for appropriations that the Congress designates as being for disaster relief in statute. The law allows for the discretionary cap to be increased by no more than the average funding provided for disaster relief over the previous 10 years, excluding the highest and lowest years. The ceiling for each year's adjustment (as determined by the 10 year average) is then increased by the unused amount of the prior year's ceiling (excluding the portion of the prior year's ceiling that was itself due to any unused amount from the year before). Disaster relief is defined as activities carried out pursuant to a determination under section 102(2) of the Robert T. Stafford Disaster Relief and Emergency Assistance Act (42 U.S.C. 5122(2)) for major disasters declared by the President. The request amends BBEDCA to extend the discretionary cap adjustment for disaster funding through 2026.

As required by law, OMB included in its Sequestration Update Report for FY 2016 a preview estimate of the 2016 adjustment for disaster relief. The ceiling for the disaster relief adjustment in 2016 was calculated to be $14,125 million. In the Consolidated Appropriations Act, 2016 (P.L. 114-113), the Congress provided $6,713 million designated for disaster relief in the Federal Emergency Management Agency's Disaster Relief Fund (DRF); $300 million in the Department of Housing and Urban Development's Community Development Fund; $91 million in the Farm Service Agency's Emergency Conservation Program and $2 million in its Emergency Forest Restorations Program; and $37 million in the Natural Resources Conservation Service's Watershed and Flood Prevention Operations account, for a total of $7,143 million.

OMB must include in its Sequestration Update Report for FY 2017 a preview estimate of the ceiling on the adjustment for disaster relief funding for 2017. This estimate will contain an average funding calculation that incorporates five years (2007 through 2011) using the definition of disaster relief from OMB's September 1, 2011 report and five years using the funding the Congress designated in 2012 through 2016 for disaster relief pursuant to BBEDCA excluding the highest and lowest years. The amounts enacted as appropriations for disaster relief in 2016 are $6,982 million below the preview adjustment estimate of $14,125 million. However, pursuant to section 251(b)(2)(D)(i)(II) of BBEDCA, any unused carryover from 2015 cannot carry forward into the calculation of the 2017 preview estimate. As a result, only $1,598 million of this total underage will carry forward into the calculation of the 2017 preview adjustment in OMB's August 2016 Sequestration Update Report for Fiscal Year 2017 if no further appropriations are enacted in 2016 that are designated for disaster relief.

At this time, the Administration is requesting $6,868 million in funding in two accounts to be designated for disaster relief by the Congress: more than $6.7 billion in FEMA's DRF to cover the costs of Presidentially declared major disasters, including identified costs for previously declared catastrophic events (defined by FEMA as events with expected costs that total more than $500 million) and the predictable annual cost of non-catastrophic events expected to obligate in 2017, and $159 million in the Small Business Administration's Disaster Loans Program Account for administrative expenses. For these two programs, the Budget requests funding for both known needs based on expected costs of prior declared disasters and the typical average expenditures in these programs. This is consistent with past practice of requesting and funding these as part of regular appropriations bills. Also consistent with past practice, the 2017 request level does not seek to pre-fund anticipated needs in other programs arising out of disasters that have yet to occur, nor does the Budget seek funding for potential catastrophic needs. As additional information about the need to fund prior or future disasters becomes available, additional requests, in the form of either 2016 supplemental appropriations (designated as either disaster relief or emergency requirements pursuant to BBEDCA) or budget amendments to the Budget, may be transmitted.

Under the principles outlined above, since the Administration does not have the adequate information about known or estimated needs that is necessary to state the total amount that will be requested in future years to be designated by the Congress for disaster relief, the Budget does not explicitly request to use the BBEDCA disaster designation in any year after the budget year. Instead, a placeholder for disaster relief is included in the current year, the budget year, and each of the outyears. See the discussion of this placeholder allowance later in this chapter in Section III (Improved Definition of Baseline) under the heading titled "Adjustments for Emergency and Disaster Costs."

Proposed Adjustment to the Discretionary Spending Limits for Wildfire Suppression Operations at the Departments of Agriculture and the Interior

On December 19, 2013, Senator Ron Wyden and Senator Mike Crapo introduced the Wildfire Disaster Funding Act of 2013 (S. 1875). On February 5, 2014, Representative Mike Simpson and Representative Kurt Schrader introduced a companion bill in the House (H.R. 3992), with Representative Peter DeFazio and Representative Raul Labrador as cosponsors. This legislation would have amended section 251(b)(2) of BBEDCA to add an adjustment to the discretionary spending limits for wildfire suppression operations. The adjustment allowed for an increase in the discretionary caps for each of fiscal years 2014 through 2021 of up to $2.7 billion if appropriations bills provide funding for wildfire suppression operations at specified base levels. The $2.7 billion permissible adjustment is a ceiling, rather than a target. It is intended to give flexibility to respond to severe, complex, and threatening fires or a severe fire season that is not captured by the historical averages. In addition, it does not increase overall discretionary spending, since it would reduce the ceiling for the existing disaster relief cap adjustment by an equivalent amount as is provided for wildfire suppression operations.

The base levels are defined in the legislation as 70 percent of the average costs for wildfire suppression operations over the previous 10 years. These base levels ensure that the cap adjustment would only be used for the most severe fire activity, since it is 1 percent of fires that cause 30 percent of costs. Only extreme fires that require emergency response or are near urban areas or activities during abnormally active fire seasons including large fires that require emergency response, which rightly should be considered disasters, would be permitted to be funded through the adjustment to the discretionary spending limits.

Wildfire suppression operations are defined by the legislation as the emergency and unpredictable aspects of wildland firefighting including support, response, and emergency stabilization activities, other emergency management activities, and funds necessary to repay any transfers needed for those costs. This means that related activities, such as fire preparedness, must continue to be funded from base appropriations and are not considered when determining if the cap adjustment is triggered.

As described above, the legislation does not allow for an increase in total discretionary spending. Rather, by its design, total funding for disasters is not expected to increase above currently estimated levels because the bill allocates funding for wildfire suppression operations from within the existing disaster relief funding cap adjustment described under the previous heading. Specifically, the ceiling for the disaster relief adjustment would be reduced by the amount provided for wildfire suppression operations under the cap adjustment for the preceding fiscal year.

The two introduced Wildfire Disaster Funding Acts and the two most recent Senate Appropriations committee markups of the Department of the Interior, Environment, and Related Agencies Appropriations Act, which included similar language, attempt to create a more responsible way to budget for wildfire suppression operations that allows for improved agency planning and management. The reality is that the Government has historically fully funded wildfire suppression operations and will continue to do so in the future. It is inefficient and ineffective to provide those resources on an ad hoc basis and to raid other critical land management operations to pay for suppression operation needs. The practice of doing so in prior years led to destabilizing transfers from other accounts, and ultimately to underinvesting in other areas that are critical to long-term forest health and resilience.

The Budget assumes that the cap adjustment will begin in 2017 and will remain in effect through 2026. The only significant departure from the two introduced Wildfire Disaster Funding Acts is that the Budget proposes to phase in the size of the cap adjustment, beginning with a maximum permissible adjustment of $1.4 billion in 2017 that increases slowly to $2.7 billion by 2023 and remains at that level thereafter. At this time, the Administration is requesting to fund only $1.2 billion through the wildfire suppression operations cap adjustment in 2017 ($864 million in the Department of Agriculture and $290 million in the Department of the Interior). If the cap adjustment were to be enacted, additional requests, in the form of amendments to the Budget, might be transmitted as additional information about the severity of the fire season becomes known.

Proposed Adjustment to the Discretionary Spending Limits for Decennial Census at the Department of Commerce

The decennial census is one of the oldest, most influential programs in the history of the U.S. government. Its mission is simple while its execution is complex: to count everyone in the U.S. once, and only once, and in the right place. Its impacts are fundamental and far-reaching: drawing official local geographical boundaries, determining each state's allocation in the U.S. House of Representatives and drawing congressional districts, and providing the bedrock data that forms the framework for government and private sector decision-making. Demographic and technological changes have increased

the cost of the decennial census per household in each decade since 1980. The Administration is committed to working with the Congress toward a 2020 Census that:

- Keeps pace with significant technological advancements since the last decennial census;
- Maintains focus on the core mission to count everyone in the U.S. once, and only once; and
- Keeps costs at or below the per-household cost of the 2010 decennial census, adjusted for inflation, allowing for lifecycle cost savings of at least $5.2 billion relative to the costs of repeating 2010 methodologies.

To meet those goals, the Budget proposes to amend BBEDCA to allow an adjustment to the discretionary spending limits for the cyclical increase in decennial census operations. An adjustment to the caps would:

- Provide the Census Bureau the funding certainty to confidently invest in cost saving technology that will lower the life cycle cost of the 2020 Census and future decennial censuses;
- Avoid either a large emergency appropriation for a predictable funding need in 2020 or unnecessary trade-offs in other discretionary programs as Census needs squeeze out other spending;
- Comply with the 2020 Census operational plan provided to Congress in October 2015 for the rest of the cycle;
- In future decades, when applicable, provide sufficient funding to implement and test innovations early enough to allow for successful implementation with lower risk of cost overrun or degradation of data accuracy; and
- Avoid inefficient and possibly wasteful spending due to a 'starvation/gluttony' cycle, which would be caused by cutting other programs in order to afford peak decennial census funding under the discretionary caps in 2020, followed by $5.5 billion in 'surplus' funds to spread around in 2021.

The discretionary spending limits enacted in the Budget Control Act of 2011 and put into place through 2021 did not incorporate an increase for the cyclical decennial census spending that occurs in the second half of every decade. Without adequate funding in the decade's middle years, the Census Bureau is less able to test and implement cost-saving innovations; the result is an increase in any potential costs that might occur in later years from operational failures due to lack of sufficient testing. Adequate funding in the later years of the decade is imperative, where shortfalls would destroy the quality, accuracy, and efficiency of the 2020 Census. This predictable and cyclical spike in decennial census funding should not crowd out baseline levels of ongoing domestic discretionary budget priorities. Nor should the cyclical spikes be considered part of the baseline domestic discretionary spending. In 2000, when discretionary caps were last in place and decennial census funding competed with other

Table 11–4. SIZE OF PROPOSED DISCRETIONARY CAP ADJUSTMENT FOR 2020 CENSUS
(In millions of dollars)

Fiscal Year	2020 Census Funding Needs	Start in 2018 (Base: 2015) [1]		
		Base Spending	Size of cap adjustment	Adjustment as % of non-def. disc. cap growth
2012	67	67	....	....
2013	94	94	....	....
2014	233	233	....	....
2015	345	345	....	....
2016	600	600	....	....
2017	781	781	....	....
2018	912	365	548	5%
2019	2,054	373	1,682	13%
2020	6,154	381	5,772	48%
2021	650	390	260	2%
Total	**11,891**	**3,629**	**8,262**	

[1] If this cap adjustment is employed in future applicable decades, the adjustment would begin in Year 6 rather than in Year 8, as shown above for the 2020 Census.

programs, the Congress provided emergency funding to avoid both of these problems.

A discretionary cap adjustment for the decennial census establishes a permanent and cyclical adjustment that would accommodate prudent, cost efficient spending and reduce total lifecycle costs in any decade in which caps are in law. It establishes a funding base sufficient to cover the early research years of the decade, and a cap adjustment that allows additional funding during the years of significant implementation, scale-up, and operationalization in the second half of the decade. Using this method, base spending levels for the decennial census for each year's cap adjustment will be established using the appropriation received in Year 5 (i.e., 2015) of the decade, adjusted for inflation measured by the CPI-U. The size of the cap adjustments will be determined early in Year 5 of the decade when the Census Bureau releases its initial operational plan and funding needs for each year of the next six years of the cycle as was done in 2015. The size of each year's cap adjustment, starting in Year 6, will be derived from this estimate less the base spending for that year. This structure will provide the Census Bureau an incentive to innovate and keep costs down while providing funding certainty to allow for a low risk and high quality decennial census. It allows for the execution of multi-year plans from a lifecycle rather than annual perspective, which will bring down life-cycle costs. A cyclical cap adjustment also allows Congressional appropriators funding flexibility late in the decade without having to sacrifice key priorities or a streamlined, effective, and cost efficient decennial census.

Since the opportunity has passed to enact the cap adjustment at the ideal point in 2016 when the major costs for implementing and refining technology and methods

for the decennial census begin, the proposal assumes for this decade that the cap adjustment would begin no later than 2018, as costs begin to rise to their peak levels. Enacting and utilizing the adjustment as early as Year 6 of future applicable decades would allow the Census Bureau even greater cost certainty in the critical testing and implementation years prior to the final end-to-end test of all systems and process interoperability in Year 8 of each decade. Doing so will strengthen the quality and efficiency and significantly reduce the risk of cost overruns of future decennial censuses, without burdening the rest of the domestic priorities.

This proposal is not included as an adjustment to the proposed 2017 Budget caps at this time in order to present its merits first; Table 11-4 shows how the discretionary cap adjustments would be structured using the parameters delineated above for the 2020 Census using the decennial census cost baseline submitted to the Congress in October 2015. The first cap adjustment estimate is $548 million in 2018, in addition to $365 million in base funding (the inflation-adjusted pre-operational funding need), to meet the anticipated total funding need of $912 million. This shifts some cyclical funding that was funded in the base in 2016 and 2017 to the cap adjustment, as these amounts would have been funded through this mechanism in those years if it had been enacted then. The cap adjustment expands to its peak level in 2020, representing the magnitude of other core discretionary program spending enabled by this proposal, totaling $8.2 billion. The last column of Table 11-4 shows the amount the proposed cap adjustment would take up as a percentage of annual growth in the original non-defense discretionary caps passed in the Budget Control Act of 2011, reaching 48 percent, or almost half, of the increase that would have occurred in 2020. While total discretionary spending would rise, paired with a full regular appropriation in 2017 this more stable and predictable funding mechanism for 2018-2021 would also support the full realization of $5.2 billion in lifecycle cost savings for the 2020 Census relative to repeating 2010 methods.

Limit on Discretionary Advance Appropriations

An advance appropriation first becomes available for obligation one or more fiscal years beyond the year for which the appropriations act is passed. Budget authority is recorded in the year the funds become available for obligation, not in the year the appropriation is enacted.

There are legitimate policy reasons to use advance appropriations to fund programs. For example, funding for the Corporation for Public Broadcasting is customarily appropriated two years in advance. This gives the beneficiaries of this funding time to plan their broadcasting budgets before the broadcast season starts.

However, advance appropriations can also be used in situations that lack a programmatic justification, as a gimmick to make room for expanded funding within the discretionary spending limits on budget authority for a given year under BBEDCA. For example, some education grants are forward funded (available beginning July 1 of the fiscal year) to provide certainty of funding for an entire school year, since school years straddle Federal fiscal years. This funding is recorded in the budget year because the funding is first legally available in that fiscal year. However, $22.6 billion of this funding is advance appropriated (available beginning three months later, on October 1) rather than forward funded. Prior Congresses increased advance appropriations and decreased the amounts of forward funding as a gimmick to free up room in the budget year without affecting the total amount available for a coming school year. This gimmick works because the advance appropriation is not recorded in the budget year but rather the following fiscal year. But it works only in the year in which funds are switched from forward funding to advance appropriations; that is, it works only in years in which the amounts of advance appropriations for such "straddle" programs are increased.

To curtail this gimmick, which allows over-budget funding in the budget year and exerts pressure for increased funding in future years by committing upfront a portion of the total budget authority limits under the discretionary caps in BBEDCA, in those years, congressional budget resolutions since 2001 have set limits on the amount of advance appropriations. When the congressional limit equals the amount that had been advance appropriated in the most recent appropriations bill, there is no additional room to switch forward funding to advance appropriations, and so no room for this particular gimmick to operate in that year's budget.

The Budget includes $28,768 million in advance appropriations for 2018 and freezes them at this level in subsequent years. In this way, the Budget does not employ this potential gimmick. Moreover, the Administration supports limiting advance appropriations to the proposed level for 2018, similar to the limits included in sections 3202 and 3304 for the Senate and the House, respectively, of the Concurrent Resolution on the Budget for Fiscal Year 2016 (S. Con. Res. 11). Those limits apply only to the accounts explicitly specified in the joint explanatory statement of managers accompanying S. Con. Res. 11.

In addition, the Administration would allow advance appropriations for the Corporation for Public Broadcasting, which is typically enacted two years in advance, and for Veterans Medical Care, as is required by the Veterans Health Care Budget Reform and Transparency Act (P.L. 111-81). The veterans medical care accounts currently comprise Medical Services, Medical Support and Compliance, and Medical Facilities. Consistent with section 4003 of the Surface Transportation and Veterans Health Care Choice Improvement Act of 2015 (P.L. 114-41), the Administration is also including the new Medical Community Care account in its advance appropriations request for veterans medical care for 2018. The level of advance appropriation funding for veterans medical care is largely determined by the Enrollee Health Care Projection Model of the Department of Veterans Affairs (VA). This actuarial model projects the funding requirement for over 80 types of health care services, including primary care, specialty care, and mental health. The remaining funding requirement is estimated based on other models and assumptions for services such as readjustment counseling and special activities. VA has included detailed information in its Congressional Budget Justifications about the overall 2018 veterans medical care funding request.

The Administration also proposes to allow advance appropriations for the spending and collections of the payments in the General Services Administration (GSA) Federal Buildings Fund. This net zero proposal supports capital requirements as well as operating expenses. This would provide greater certainty to support capital projects and ensure that the funds that agencies pay to GSA are used promptly to construct, maintain, and operate GSA facilities.

For a detailed table of accounts that have received discretionary and mandatory advance appropriations since 2015 or for which the Budget requests advance appropriations for 2018 and beyond, please refer to the Advance Appropriations chapter in the *Appendix*.

Budgetary Treatment of Surface Transportation Infrastructure Funding

Overview.—Currently, surface transportation programs financed from the Highway Trust Fund (HTF) are treated as hybrids: contract authority is classified as mandatory, while outlays are classified as discretionary. Broadly speaking, this framework evolved as a mechanism to ensure that collections into the HTF (e.g., motor fuel taxes) were used to pay only for programs that benefit surface transportation users, and that funding for those programs would generally be commensurate with collections. Recent passage of the Fixing America's Surface Transportation Act, or the FAST Act, shored up the Highway Trust Fund and maintained this hybrid funding structure through 2020. The Administration reflects this bipartisan agreement in the Budget.

Table 11–5. BUDGETARY RESOURCES AND REVENUE FOR THE 21ST CENTURY CLEAN TRANSPORTATION PLAN

(In billions of dollars)

Budgetary Resources	
Department of Transportation	303
Clean Transportation Plan Funding - Other Agencies (DOE, NASA, EPA)	16
Family Emergency Assistance Fund	65
Total, Proposed Resources, New Programs	**385**
Projected Trust Fund Gap, 2021–2026	110
Total, Proposed Resources	**495**
Revenue	
Gross Oil Fee Receipts	–436
Impact on Other Receipts	117
Total, Net Impact of Oil Fee	**–319**
Business Tax Reform Transition Revenue	–176
Total, Proposed Revenues	**–495**

The Administration's 21st Century Clean Transportation Initiative provides resources for DOT programs over and above those included in the FAST Act. To encourage movement toward a more unified and consistent scorekeeping regime, the Budget presents those programs as exclusively mandatory rather than as hybrids. Furthermore, the Administration's proposal would broaden the scope of programs included under the Trust Fund umbrella: the HTF is renamed the Transportation Trust Fund (TTF), and supports additional highway safety and transit programs, as well as passenger rail programs and multimodal programs administered by the Department of Transportation, all of which are focused on investing in surface transportation infrastructure and aimed at reducing emissions from the transportation sector. The initiative also includes funding for select programs outside of DOT, though not through a trust fund.

The mechanics of the 2017 Clean Transportation Initiative are described in greater detail below. Generally speaking, within DOT:

- FAST Act accounts remain at authorized levels through the Budget window.

- New TTF accounts supporting transportation-related clean infrastructure activities receive mandatory contract authority and mandatory outlays, with discretionary obligation limitations.

- $4.4 billion of surface transportation spending from the general fund is reclassified from discretionary budget authority and outlays to mandatory contract authority and outlays, with annual obligation limitations continuing to be established by the Appropriations Committee and funded through the TTF.

- For the sake of comparability, the current law general fund accounts reclassified in the Budget are presented as reclassified to mandatory spending in 2015 and 2016. This is intended to allow policy makers to transparently calculate the difference between baseline levels and the President's proposal.

As proposed by the Administration, this unified scoring framework for clean transportation funding does not radically alter traditional roles and jurisdictional relationships as they are conceived of under current law and scorekeeping practice.

The budget process reform associated with the Clean Transportation Initiative is only one element of the Administration's comprehensive plan to make investments in a transportation initiative that is geared toward the Nation's 21st Century demands. The *Budget* and *Appendix* volumes discuss the broader policy in more detail.

Account-by-Account Budgetary Treatment.—As part of the Clean Transportation Plan, the Budget proposes the enactment of mandatory contract authority for the Transportation Trust Fund for each year, 2017-2026, totaling $303 billion over ten years.

Under the Budget, outlays flowing from contract authority for the clean transportation initiative will also be treated as mandatory. The same treatment is applied to outlays flowing from previous accounts funded from the General Fund of the Treasury, which will now be attributed to the Transportation Trust Fund; this is a departure from current law. As is the case for other mandatory programs, this aligns outlays with budget authority. By placing outlays on the mandatory side of the Budget, increases above the baseline go on the PAYGO scorecard, giving real scoring effect to funding increases for these programs. Accounts funded through the FAST Act continue the hybrid treatment of mandatory contract authority and discretionary outlays.

For all of the resources in the 21st Century Clean Transportation Initiative proposal, the Budget proposes that the reauthorization contain annual obligation limits at the same level as the contract authority, and that annual appropriations bills include obligation limits at those levels. The obligation limits enacted by the appropriators enable the Administration and the Congress to review TTF policies and resource levels on an annual basis, but under a framework that will continue to give external stakeholders a high level of certainty regarding the multi-year resource trajectory for highways, transit, passenger rail, and multimodal activities.

The Budget modifies individual accounts to conform to the proposed budgetary treatment in all years. Specifically:

- For accounts that are presently classified as having discretionary budget authority and outlays, but that the Administration proposes to incorporate into the TTF (for example, the Federal Transit Administration's Capital Investment Grants account), the Budget includes separate schedules that:

    o Show baseline budget authority and outlays as discretionary, consistent with current classifications.

    o Reclassify baseline budget authority and outlays as mandatory in all years, including 2015 and 2016, for comparability purposes (i.e., to enable a comparison of funding levels across years in an account).

    o Show adjustments (subject to PAYGO) to the reclassified mandatory amounts so that the proposal properly accounts for requested program growth in the five new trust fund accounts.

- For the proposed new account supported by the TTF, the 21st Century Clean Transportation Plan Investment Initiative, the Budget includes a schedule that includes new mandatory contract authority and outlays requested to support those programs.

The discretionary accounts that are incorporated into the TTF construct are:

- Office of the Secretary: National Infrastructure Investments.

- Federal Railroad Administration (FRA): Operating Subsidy Grants to the National Railroad Passenger Corporation; Capital and Debt Service Grants to the National Railroad Passenger Corporation; and Northeast Corridor Improvement Program.

- National Highway Traffic Safety Administration (NHTSA): Operations and Research.

- Federal Transit Administration (FTA): Administrative Expenses; Capital Investment Grants; and Job Access and Reverse Commute Grants.

Amounts in these accounts total $4.3 billion in discretionary budget authority for 2016. The 2017 baseline levels for these amounts are what constitute the discretionary cap adjustment noted in the *OMB Sequestration Preview Report to the President and Congress for Fiscal Year 2017*. Note that in a number of cases, activities captured in these accounts are requested under a new account supported by the TTF in the Administration's 21st Century Clean Transportation Plan proposal. For example, activities under the two existing Amtrak accounts are requested as part of the Federal Railroad Administration's new Current Passenger Rail Service

account. In those instances, the PAYGO impact of the Administration's proposal must be calculated at the aggregate level rather than the individual account level (i.e., the change between the reclassified baseline amounts in the existing general fund accounts and the proposed levels in the successor account).

Transportation Trust Fund Mechanics.—As discussed earlier, the Budget proposes a successor to the Highway Trust Fund, the Transportation Trust Fund, which continues all activities currently supported in the FAST Act. Additionally, it includes funding to support the 21st Century Clean Transportation proposal, which includes each of the accounts formerly funded through the general fund.

The goal of a broader Trust Fund is to allow policymakers to review and consider surface transportation policy and spending in a more comprehensive way.

Offsets.—The 21st Century Clean Transportation Plan ("the Plan") is fully paid for by two sources:

- A new fee of $10.25 per barrel on oil paid by oil companies, which would be phased in over five years, and

- One-time transition revenues from business tax reform that ensure that:

    o Transportation Trust Fund solvency is not impacted as the Plan's investments ramp up and the oil fee is phased in;

    o The proposal is fully paid for over time (i.e., oil fees plus business tax reform revenue covers the total outlays from the proposal over the full life of the initiative, including outlays outside the ten year window); and

    o The Transportation Trust Fund solvency gap in years 5-10 of the budget window is eliminated and the Plan generates a sustainable revenue level for the TTF going forward.

The Plan is envisioned as a surge in transportation investment that would not only improve infrastructure condition and performance, but catalyze a broad shift in the way Americans use the transportation system. Also, the Plan dedicates 15 percent of gross oil fee revenues over ten years to assist families with burdensome energy costs, including a focus on supporting households in the Northeast as they transition from fuel oil for heating to cleaner forms of energy. At the end of the ten-year window, Transportation Trust Fund revenue sources—current law and the proposed oil fee (which is indexed to inflation)—are estimated to raise just over $100 billion per year. Current law receipts account for around 40 percent of that total. The Plan is therefore designed to support surface transportation spending over the long-term at levels well above current law spending.

Table 11-5 illustrates the financing structure of the initiative in broad terms. All DOT budgetary resources run through the Transportation Trust Fund; spending outside DOT runs through separate special funds.

Table 11–6. 10-YEAR PAYGO ANALYSIS
21ST CENTURY CLEAN TRANSPORTATION PLAN
(In billions of dollars)

Outlays	
Department of Transportation	231
Family Emergency Assistance Fund	65
Other Agencies (DOE, NASA, EPA)	16
Total, New Program Outlays	**312**
New General Fund Transfers to Offset Current Law Trust Fund Revenue Gap	59
Total New Outlays, 21st Century Clean Transportation Plan	**371**
Revenue	
Net Oil Receipts	–319
Business Tax Reform Transition Revenue	–176
Total, Proposed Revenues	**–495**
Net PAYGO Cost/Savings (+/–)	**–124**

Table 11-5 does not depict the proposal's PAYGO impact, however. The differences are:

- The PAYGO scorecard only counts new outlays and receipts inside the 10-year window.

- PAYGO scorekeeping must accommodate the initial shift of general fund accounts from discretionary budget authority and outlays to the mandatory side of the Budget. The activities that the Administration proposes to incorporate in the TTF as mandatory outlays would generate discretionary outlays under current law totaling an estimated $41 billion over 10 years. If those amounts are reclassified, they should not be added to the PAYGO cost of any legislation by virtue of the fact that they are new to the mandatory side of the Budget. Rather, the mandatory baseline should be adjusted to include those outlays that would occur under current law—as the 2017 Budget does—and calculate any changes from that baseline. Without this initial accommodation, scorekeeping rules would overstate the cost of legislation. An adjustment to the discretionary caps is shown in the preview report to comply with section 251(b) of BBEDCA that requires an adjustment for these types of shifts in the baseline.

- Under the proposal, revenue raised from oil fees and business tax reform is sufficient to cover both the new outlays associated with the proposal and the gap between current law spending and current law receipts. Under current law, that gap is estimated to begin in 2021 and total $110 billion over the remainder of the ten-year window. Because of the timing associated with the new spending and revenues under the 21st Century Transportation Plan, within the 10-year window, $59 billion is transferred from the general fund to TTF, rather than the full $110 billion.

Table 11-6 reflects those adjustments and depicts the PAYGO cost of the proposal.

Pell Grants

The Pell Grant program includes features that make it unlike other discretionary programs including that Pell Grants are awarded to all applicants who meet income and other eligibility criteria. From the start of the Great Recession through 2011, when many Americans returned to school to improve their skills while their own job prospects were not strong, the number of students receiving Pell Grants increased by 3.8 million. This increase in participation, coupled with greater average financial need, resulted in a significant rise in Pell program costs. Since this peak, the economy improved significantly, the number of Pell recipients has slowly decreased, and program costs that were once growing have declined. This section provides some background on the unique nature of the Pell Grant program and explains how the Budget accommodates these changes in discretionary costs.

Under current law, the Pell program has several notable features:

- The Pell Grant program acts like an entitlement program, such as the Supplemental Nutrition Assistance Program or Supplemental Security Income, in which everyone who meets specific eligibility requirements and applies for the program receives a benefit. Specifically, Pell Grant costs in a given year are determined by the maximum award set in statute, the number of eligible applicants, and the award for which those applicants are eligible based on their needs and costs of attendance. The maximum Pell award for the academic year 2016-2017 is $5,815, of which $4,860 was established in the annual appropriations act and the remaining $955 is provided automatically by the College Cost Reduction and Access Act (CCRAA), as amended. Under the CCRAA as amended, the amount needed to index the Pell Grant for inflation is provided through the mandatory funds through the 2017-18 award year.

- The cost of each Pell Grant is funded by discretionary budget authority provided in annual appropriations acts, along with mandatory budget authority provided not only by the CCRAA, as amended, and the BCA, but also by amendments to the Higher Education Act of 1965 contained in the 2011 and 2012 appropriations acts. There is no programmatic difference between the mandatory and discretionary funding.

- If valid applicants are more numerous than expected, or if these applicants are eligible for higher awards than anticipated, the Pell Grant program will cost more than the appropriations provided. If the costs during one academic year are higher than provided for in that year's appropriation, the Department of Education funds the extra costs with the subsequent year's appropriation.[2]

- To prevent deliberate underfunding of Pell costs, in 2006 the congressional and Executive Branch scorekeepers agreed to a special scorekeeping rule for Pell. Under this rule, the annual appropriations bill is charged with the full Congressional Budget Office estimated cost of the Pell Grant program for the budget year, plus or minus any cumulative shortfalls or surpluses from prior years. This scorekeeping rule was adopted by the Congress as §406(b) of the Concurrent Resolution on the Budget for Fiscal Year 2006 (H. Con. Res. 95, 109th Congress).

Given the nature of the program, it is reasonable to consider Pell Grants an individual entitlement for purposes of budget analysis and enforcement, and in the 2010 and 2011 Budgets, the Administration requested that Pell Grants be converted into a mandatory program. The Congress has chosen to continue treating the portion funded in annual appropriations acts as discretionary, counting that budget authority for Pell Grants against the discretionary spending caps pursuant to section 251 of BBEDCA and appropriations allocations established annually under §302 of the Congressional Budget Act. The 2017 Budget maintains this discretionary treatment.

The total cost of Pell Grants can fluctuate from year to year, even with no change in the maximum Pell Grant award, because of changes in enrollment, college costs, and family resources. In addition, since 2009 the program has relied on temporary mandatory or emergency appropriations to fund the program well above the level that could have been provided as a practical matter by the regular discretionary appropriation. The 2017 Budget expects program costs to stay within available resources,

which include the discretionary level, carried forward budget authority, and extra mandatory funds, until 2025. While the 2016 Budget expected these resources to run out before 2018, Pell program costs and student enrollment have continued to decline since a 2010 peak, and the funding has lasted longer than anticipated. Under current law, the Budget now projects a ten year funding shortfall of $4.1 billion, $25.6 billion less than the 10-year forecast from the 2016 Budget (see Table 11-7). These estimates have changed significantly from year to year, which illustrates continuing uncertainty about the amount of the Pell shortfall, and the year in which the shortfall will reemerge.

Administration policy is to ensure that students have access to the maximum Pell award, and that the Pell Grant keeps up with inflation. As in prior years, the Budget provides sufficient resources to fully fund Pell Grants in the award years covered by the budget year, and subsequent years. The Budget provides $22.5 billion in discretionary budget authority in 2017, the same level of discretionary budget authority provided in 2016. Level-funding Pell in 2017, combined with carried forward budget authority and mandatory funding provided in previous legislation, provides $8.5 billion more than is needed to fully fund the program in the 2017-18 award year. Ensuring that carried forward budget authority remains available in the Pell Grant program will help guarantee that sufficient resources are available to support the program in future years. Cutting the budget authority in Pell to only the level needed to fund the program in 2017 would have a doubly detrimental impact on the future cliff; it would reduce the budget authority carried forward from 2017, while simultaneously reducing the discretionary base funding level in the program.

Since 2013, the Pell maximum award has increased annually to account for inflation. Under current law, these adjustments are set to expire in 2017, and students will no longer benefit from annual aid increases designed to offset rises in student costs. The Budget proposes to provide mandatory funding to continue indexing Pell for inflation beyond 2017. It also proposes to expand and reform the Perkins loan program and to make legislative changes to the Pay As You Earn plan for student loan borrowers that would complement administrative actions announced last year that extend Pay As You Earn to all borrowers.

With significant budget authority expected to be carried forward into 2017, the Budget proposes several new student aid policies to help make college more affordable for students. In addition, the Budget continues to propose student aid reforms proposed in the 2016 Budget that impact Pell Grant program costs:

- First, the Budget proposes to support "Pell for Accelerated Completion," allowing students to earn a third semester of Pell Grants in an academic year so they can take courses continuously throughout the year, accumulate credits, and graduate more quickly. Students will now be eligible for a third semester of Pell during a year if they have already completed 24 credits; this policy is an effort to ensure that the third semester eligibility is assisting students who

---

[2] This ability to "borrow" from a subsequent appropriation is unique to the Pell program. It comes about for two reasons. First, like many education programs, Pell is "forward-funded"—the budget authority enacted in the fall of one year is intended for the subsequent academic year, which begins in the following July. Second, even though the amount of funding is predicated on the expected cost of Pell during one academic year, the money is made legally available for the full 24-month period covering the current fiscal year and the subsequent fiscal year. This means that, if the funding for an academic year proves inadequate, the following year's appropriation will legally be available to cover the funding shortage for the first academic year. The 2017 appropriation, for instance, will support the 2017-2018 academic year beginning in July 2017 but will become available in October 2016 and can therefore help cover any shortages that may arise in funding for the 2016-2017 academic year.

Table 11–7. EFFECT OF STUDENT AID PROPOSALS ON DISCRETIONARY PELL FUNDING NEEDS

(In billions of dollars)

	2016	2017	2018	2019	2020	2021	2022	2023	2024	2025	2026
Discretionary Pell Funding Needs (Baseline)											
Full Funding, Discretionary Pell		15.6	23.4	24.0	24.3	24.7	25.0	25.5	26.0	26.5	26.7
Previously Provided Mandatory Funding		(1.6)	(1.4)	(1.4)	(1.4)	(1.1)	(1.1)	(1.1)	(1.1)	(1.1)	(1.1)
Discretionary Need	22.5	14.0	22.0	22.5	22.8	23.5	23.9	24.4	24.9	25.4	25.6
Fund Pell at 2017 Full Funding Estimate	22.5	14.0	14.0	14.0	14.0	14.0	14.0	14.0	14.0	14.0	14.0
Surplus/Funding Gap from Prior Year			....	(8.0)	(16.5)	(25.3)	(34.9)	(44.8)	(55.1)	(66.0)	(77.3)
Cumulative Surplus/Discretionary Funding Gap		....	(8.0)	(16.5)	(25.3)	(34.9)	(44.8)	(55.1)	(66.0)	(77.3)	(88.9)
Fund Pell at 2016 Enacted Level		8.5	8.5	8.5	8.5	8.5	8.5	8.5	8.5	8.5	8.5
Surplus/Funding Gap from Prior Year			8.5	9.0	8.9	8.6	7.5	6.1	4.2	1.8	(1.0)
Cumulative Surplus/Discretionary Funding Gap		8.5	9.0	8.9	8.6	7.5	6.1	4.2	1.8	(1.0)	(4.1)
Effect of 2017 Student Aid Proposals											
Enact 2017 Student Aid Proposals		(1.7)	(1.7)	(1.7)	(1.8)	(1.8)	(2.0)	(2.0)	(2.1)	(2.1)	(2.2)
Mandatory Funding Shift*		(0.3)	(0.2)	(0.2)	(0.3)	(0.3)	(0.3)	(0.3)	(0.3)	(0.3)	(0.4)
Surplus/Funding Gap from Prior Year			6.6	5.1	3.1	0.7	(2.5)	(6.1)	(10.4)	(15.1)	(20.5)
Cumulative Surplus/Discretionary Funding Gap		6.6	5.1	3.1	0.7	(2.5)	(6.1)	(10.4)	(15.1)	(20.5)	(26.1)

* Some budget authority, provided in previous legislation and classified as mandatory, but used to meet discretionary Pell Grant program funding needs, will be shifted to instead fund new outlays for the mandatory add-on.

are utilizing the additional semester to help ensure on-time completion.

- Second, to further incentivize students to enroll in enough credits to complete degree programs on time, the Budget proposes to increase the Pell Grant by $300 for students taking at least 15 credit hours per semester in an academic year, the number of credits typically required for on-time completion. This feature will be treated as discretionary and funded through annual appropriations and carry-over funding.

- Third, the Budget will lift the restriction on providing Pell Grants to individuals incarcerated in Federal or State penal institutions.

- Fourth, the Budget will strengthen academic progress requirements in the Pell Grant program to encourage students to complete their studies on time.

- Fifth, the Budget will limit the receipt of additional Pell disbursements by recipients who are not advancing academically.

- Sixth, the Budget proposes to reduce the share of a college's or university's revenue that can come from Federal student aid programs from 90 percent to 85 percent and to include Federal student aid programs outside of the Department of Education, such as the Department of Defense Tuition Assistance and GI Bill Benefits, in the 85 percent portion of the 85/15 calculation.

- Seventh, the Budget would move Iraq Afghanistan Service Grants to the Pell Grant program to ensure our veterans' children receive a full, non-sequestered Pell award.

- Eighth, the Administration also supports the simplification of the Free Application for Federal Student Aid (FAFSA). The Budget proposes eliminating questions related to assets, non-IRS untaxed income, non-IRS income exclusions, and other income adjustments, which have been shown to confuse students. To prevent resulting decreases in Pell Grant awards, the Budget also proposes slight adjustments to Expected Family Contributions.

Together, these student aid reforms increase future discretionary Pell program costs by $22 billion over 10 years (see Table 11-7). However, even with these increases, the shortfall will not be expected to arrive until 2021.

Postal Service Reforms

The Administration proposes reform of the Postal Service, necessitated by the serious financial condition of the Postal Service Fund. The policy proposals are discussed in the Postal Service and Office of Personnel Management sections of the *Appendix*.

As a matter of law, the Postal Service is designated as an off-budget independent establishment of the Executive Branch. This designation and budgetary treatment was most recently mandated in 1989, in part to reflect the policy agreement that the Postal Service should pay for its own costs through its own revenues and should operate more like an independent business entity. Statutory requirements on Postal Service expenses and restrictions that impede the Postal Service's ability to adapt to the ongoing evolution to paperless written communications have made this goal increasingly difficult to achieve. To address its current financial and structural challenges, the Administration proposes specific financial relief and reform measures to ensure that the Postal Service can continue to operate in the short term and work toward viability in the long run. The Administration also proposes PAYGO scoring of Postal legislation on a unified budget basis to better reflect how and when such legislation will affect overall deficits and debt. That is, for the purposes of entering amounts on the statutory PAYGO scorecards, the applicable estimates should include both the off-budget and the on-budget costs and savings produced by the legislation. This scorekeeping change would be accomplished by a provision contained within Postal reform legislation.

In addition to scoring Postal reform on a unified basis, the Administration's baseline now reflects probable defaults to on-budget accounts at the Office of Personnel Management. This treatment allows for a clearer presentation of the Postal Service's likely actions in the absence of reform and more realistic scoring of reform proposals with improvements in the Postal Service's finances reflected through lower defaults and added costs for the Postal Service reflected as higher defaults.

Contract Support Costs Reclassification

The Budget proposes a reclassification of the Bureau of Indian Affairs' (BIA) and Indian Health Service's (IHS) Contract Support Costs from a discretionary to a mandatory appropriation beginning in 2018. The Contract Support Costs proposal would reduce the discretionary spending limits in section 251(c) of BBEDCA beginning in 2018, to offset the cost of shifting the base funding from discretionary to mandatory. In addition, the mandatory appropriation includes a three-year program expansion to fully fund Contract Support Costs as well as a new investment to ensure program integrity. Through a reauthorization process for 2021 and beyond, updated Contract Support Costs estimates will be provided to set funding levels every three years.

Expedited Rescission

The Administration continues to support enactment of the President's proposal for expedited rescission, transmitted May 24, 2010. That legislation would create an important tool for reducing unneeded funding. In short, the bill would provide the President with additional authority to propose a package of rescissions that would then receive expedited consideration in the Congress and a guaranteed up-or-down vote. The proposal is crafted in a way that preserves the constitutional balance of power between the President and the Congress while providing the President with important, but limited, powers that would allow the President and the Congress to work together more effectively to eliminate unnecessary funding that could be deployed more effectively in other areas.

II. STATUTORY PAYGO

The Statutory Pay-As-You-Go Act of 2010 (PAYGO, or "the Act") was enacted on February 12, 2010. The Act strengthens the rules of budget discipline, which is a key priority for the Administration.

Drawing upon the PAYGO provisions enacted as part of the Budget Enforcement Act, the Act requires that, subject to specific exceptions, all legislation enacted during each session of the Congress changing taxes or mandatory expenditures and collections not increase projected deficits. Mandatory spending encompasses any spending except that controlled by the annual appropriations process.[3]

The Act established 5- and 10-year scorecards to record the budgetary effects of legislation; these scorecards are maintained by OMB and are published on the OMB web site (*http://www.whitehouse.gov/omb/paygo_default*). The Act also established special scorekeeping rules that affect whether all estimated budgetary effects of PAYGO bills are entered on the scorecards. Off-budget programs do not have budgetary effects for the purposes of PAYGO and are not counted. Provisions designated by the Congress in law as emergencies appear on the scorecards, but the effects are subtracted before computing the scorecard totals.

In addition to the exemptions in the PAYGO Act itself, the Congress has enacted laws affecting revenues or direct spending with a provision directing that the budgetary effects of all or part of the law be held off of the PAYGO scorecards. In the most recently completed Congressional session, four pieces of legislation were enacted with such provisions. For more information, see the 2015 Annual PAYGO Report on the OMB web site (*http://www.whitehouse.gov/omb/paygo_default*).

The requirement of budget neutrality is enforced by an accompanying requirement of automatic across-the-board cuts in selected mandatory programs if enacted legislation, taken as a whole, does not meet that standard. If the Congress adjourns at the end of a session with net costs—that is, more costs than savings—in the budget-year column of either the 5- or 10-year scorecard, OMB is required to prepare, and the President is required to issue, a sequestration order implementing across-the-board cuts to non-exempt mandatory programs in an amount sufficient to offset the net costs on the PAYGO scorecards.

Exemptions from a PAYGO sequestration order generally include Social Security; most unemployment benefits; veterans' benefits; interest on the debt; Federal retirement; and the low-income entitlements such as Medicaid, the Supplemental Nutrition Assistance Program (SNAP, formerly known as food stamps), and SSI.[4] The major remaining mandatory programs, which are subject to sequestration, include most Medicare payments (limited to a maximum sequestration of 4 percent), farm price supports, vocational rehabilitation basic State grants, mineral leasing payments to States, the Social Services

---

[3] Mandatory spending is termed direct spending in the PAYGO Act. The term mandatory encompasses entitlement programs, e.g., Medicare and Medicaid, and any funding not controlled by annual appropriations bills, such as the automatic availability of immigration examination fees to the Department of Homeland Security.

[4] Although many programs are exempt from sequestration, those programs are rarely exempt from PAYGO. For example, a bill to increase veterans' disability benefits or Medicaid benefits must be offset, even though a sequestration, if it is required, will not reduce those benefits.

Block Grant, and many smaller programs. The list of exempt programs and the special sequestration rules for certain programs are contained in sections 255 and 256 of BBEDCA, and the exemptions and special rules generally apply to the following sequestrations: the sequestration pursuant to the PAYGO Act, the sequestration to eliminate excess spending above discretionary caps specified in section 251 of BBEDCA, and the mandatory sequestration currently required by the BCA as a result of the failure of the Joint Committee process.

Even though sequestration is calculated to fully offset any net costs on the PAYGO scorecard, it historically has acted as a successful deterrent to enacting legislation with net costs, and so, has not been implemented. During the 1990s, under the first statutory PAYGO law, the sequestration rules and exemptions were almost identical to those in the current Act. The Congress complied with PAYGO throughout that decade. As a result, no PAYGO sequestration ever occurred.

As was the case during the 1990s, the PAYGO sequestration has not been required during the six Congressional sessions since the PAYGO Act reinstated the statutory PAYGO requirement. For each of those sessions, OMB's annual PAYGO reports showed net savings in the budget year column of both the 5- and 10-year scorecards. For the first session of the 114th Congress, the most recent session, enacted legislation added net savings of $3,456 million in each year of the 5-year scorecard and $5,718 million in each year of the 10-year scorecard. Including net savings and costs from prior sessions of the Congress, balances in 2016, the budget year column, showed total net savings of $3,016 million on the 5-year scorecard and $15,448 million on the 10-year scorecard, so no sequestration was required.[5]

Administrative PAYGO

The Administration continues to review potential administrative actions by Executive Branch agencies affecting entitlement programs, as stated in a memorandum issued on May 23, 2005, by the Director of the Office of Management and Budget. This effectively establishes a PAYGO requirement for administrative actions involving mandatory spending programs. Exceptions to this requirement are only provided in extraordinary or compelling circumstances.[6]

---

[5] OMB's annual PAYGO reports and other explanatory material about the PAYGO Act are available at www.whitehouse.gov/omb/paygo_default.

[6] For a review of the application of Administrative PAYGO, see *USDA's Application of Administrative PAYGO to Its Mandatory Spending Programs*, GAO, October 31, 2011, GAO-11-921R.

III. IMPROVED BASELINE AND BUDGET PRESENTATION

Improved Definition of Baseline

In each of its Budgets, this Administration has depicted its budget proposals relative to a baseline that is designed to reflect the budget outlook under current policy and to serve as a realistic basis for evaluating the effects of policy changes. The Administration recommends that the Congress, the Congressional Budget Office, and the public use such a baseline in their own analyses as well.

Section 257 of BBEDCA provides rules for constructing a baseline that were used by the Congress for many years. In recent years, however, these rules have become less useful because they do not provide guidance to address major changes in policy, including the reestablishment of the discretionary spending limits and the enactment of Joint Committee enforcement procedures. The rules also fall short in their approach to one-time emergency appropriations, which are extended permanently in the BBEDCA baseline along with regular agency appropriations.

This section describes the Administration's adjustments to the BBEDCA baseline to make it more useful. The deficit impacts of these adjustments are summarized in Summary Table S-8 of the *Budget*. Further detail about the adjusted baseline is provided in Chapter 25, "Current Services Estimates," in this volume.

While the adjusted baseline provides a more realistic basis for analyzing budgets, it is not intended to replace the BBEDCA baseline with respect to mandatory programs and revenues, either for legal purposes or to alter the application of the Statutory PAYGO Act of 2010. Specifically, the costs or savings from legislation affecting mandatory spending or revenues are measured relative to the BBEDCA baseline for purpose of entries on the PAYGO scorecards, discussed earlier in the chapter.

Adjustments for Emergency and Disaster Costs.— Because the BBEDCA baseline extends all appropriations already enacted for the year in progress, it can be subject to huge swings as a result of funding enacted as an emergency requirement or as disaster relief funding pursuant to the cap adjustments for these items permitted by section 251(b)(2) of BBEDCA. At times, the BBEDCA baseline could extend large one-time emergency or disaster appropriations for the next 10 years; at other times it might extend very little. The Administration's baseline includes adjustments to account for these swings. Specifically, for the 2017 Budget, the Administration's adjusted baseline removes the extension of $7.6 billion in enacted 2016 appropriations that were designated as emergency requirements or as disaster relief funding. In addition, the adjusted baseline substitutes an allowance for disaster costs in the current year, the budget year, and future fiscal years. This allowance reflects the fact that major natural or man-made disasters may occur in the near future and are highly likely to occur at some point in subsequent years. Obviously, both the timing and amounts are unknowable in advance. In addition to the inclusion of this entry in the baseline, the Administration includes the same allowance in its Budget.

The baseline and Budget figures are not a "reserve fund," nor are they a request for discretionary budget authority or congressional legislation of any kind. Instead, they are placeholders that represent a meaningful down payment on potential future disaster relief requirements that are not for known needs in the budget year. For more information, see the discussion of disaster relief funding earlier in this chapter in Section I (Budget Reform Proposals) under the heading titled "Disaster Relief Funding." Including a meaningful down payment for the future costs of potential disaster relief funding makes the budget totals more honest and realistic.

Discretionary spending limits and Joint Committee enforcement.—The BBEDCA baseline extends enacted appropriations without regard to the discretionary spending limits imposed by BBEDCA. The adjusted baseline includes an allowance to reduce the discretionary spending levels in the baseline to comply with the limits for the defense and non-defense categories. These adjustments assume that the limits remain in place after their statutory expiration in 2021, growing with inflation in each subsequent year through the end of the budget window. In addition, appropriations for program integrity activities of the Social Security Administration and the Health Care Fraud and Abuse Control account are adjusted to the levels of cap adjustments permitted under BBEDCA. No adjustment is made for appropriations designated as Overseas Contingency Operations because this category of appropriations is not subject to spending limits.

The adjusted baseline also reflects the future operation of Joint Committee enforcement procedures, under which the discretionary spending limits would be further reduced for 2018 through 2021, and mandatory spending sequestered for 2018 through 2025, according to the procedures of BBEDCA.

Reclassification of surface transportation spending.—The adjusted baseline includes a reclassification of certain surface transportation accounts from discretionary to mandatory. This reclassification allows the Administration's surface transportation proposal to be portrayed more clearly, as discussed in more detail earlier in this chapter.

Former current policy extensions of Medicare physician payment relief and Recovery Act tax credits.—In the 2016 Budget, the adjusted baseline assumed extension of the policies in place to provide relief from the large cuts in Medicare physician payments required under the Sustainable Growth Rate (SGR) mechanism. In April 2015, the Medicare Access and CHIP Reauthorization Act replaced the SGR system with a new system of physician payments that does not include the large, unrealistic reductions embedded in prior law. As a result, the Budget no longer includes policy extensions to maintain Medicare physician payment levels in the adjusted baseline. Likewise, the adjusted baseline assumed extension of certain tax credits for individuals and families enacted in the American Recovery and Reinvestment Act of 2009, and subsequently extended through tax year 2017. In December 2015, the Protecting Americans from Tax Hikes Act made these tax credits permanent, so an adjustment is no longer necessary to continue current policy for these provisions.

Fannie Mae and Freddie Mac

The Budget continues to present Fannie Mae and Freddie Mac, the housing Government-sponsored enterprises (GSEs) currently in Federal conservatorship, as non-Federal entities. However, Treasury equity investments in the GSEs are recorded as budgetary outlays, and the dividends on those investments are recorded as offsetting receipts. In addition, the budget estimates reflect collections from the 10 basis point increase in GSE guarantee fees that was enacted under the Temporary Payroll Tax Cut Continuation Act of 2011 (P.L. 112-78), and collections from the 4.2 basis point set-aside on each dollar of unpaid principal balance of new business purchases authorized under the Housing and Economic Recovery Act of 2008 (P.L. 111-289) to be remitted to several Federal affordable housing funds. The GSEs are discussed in more detail in Chapter 20, "Credit and Insurance."

Fair Value for Credit Programs

In recent years, some analysts have argued that Federal direct loan and loan guarantee programs impose costs on taxpayers that are not reflected under the current budgeting rules, such as the risk that assets may not perform as expected, and propose to require that the Budget use "fair value" estimates for these credit programs. Under fair value, comparable market interest rates would be used to discount expected cash flows, instead of the Federal Government's cost of borrowing. While fair value may offer some useful insights and inform decision-making in some cases, using fair value for budgetary cost estimates of credit programs raises serious conceptual and implementation problems. Most importantly, it would compromise the central objective of current budgeting rules for credit, which are designed to put credit program estimates on a comparable basis to other forms of Federal spending and improve the allocation of resources. In addition, many of the factors reflected in fair value pricing are irrelevant or less relevant to taxpayers than to private investors; including these factors in budgetary cost estimates would overstate the cost of credit assistance and introduce a bias relative to other forms of Federal assistance. On top of these and other conceptual issues, implementing fair value may require significant increases in the costs of administering credit programs and introduce inconsistencies in how credit subsidy costs are estimated across programs, reducing the consistency and transparency of the Budget. For a detailed discussion of the conceptual and implementation issues raised by fair value estimates, see the "Credit and Insurance" chapter of the *Analytical Perspectives* volume of the 2015 Budget.

Debt Net of Financial Assets

In the Summary Tables included in the main *Budget* volume, Tables S-1 and S-13 display both debt held by the public and debt held by the public net of financial assets. Borrowing from the public is normally a good approximation of the Federal demand on credit markets. However, it provides an incomplete picture of the financial condition of the Government and under some circumstances may misrepresent the net effect of Federal activity on credit markets. Some transactions that increase the Federal debt also increase the financial assets held by the Government. For example, when the Government lends money to a private firm or individual, the Government acquires a financial asset that provides a stream of future payments of principal and interest, net of the Government's expected losses on the loan. At the time the loan is made, debt held by the public reflects only Treasury's borrowing to finance the loan, failing to reflect the value of the loan asset acquired by the Government. Similarly, the estimate of debt held by the public does not reflect estimated liabilities on loan guarantees. In contrast, debt held by the public net of financial assets provides a more accurate measure of the Government's net financial position by including the value of loans and other financial assets held by the Government. While Federal borrowing reduces the amount of private saving that is available through financial markets for private-sector investment, Federal acquisition of financial assets has the opposite effect—it injects cash into financial markets. Thus, the change in debt net of financial assets can also better indicate the effect of the Federal Government on the financial markets. For further discussion of debt net of financial assets, see Chapter 4, "Federal Borrowing and Debt."

FEDERAL RECEIPTS

12. GOVERNMENTAL RECEIPTS

A simpler, fairer, and more efficient tax system is critical to achieving many of the President's fiscal and economic goals. At a time when middle-class and working parents remain anxious about how they will meet their families' needs, the tax system does not do enough to reward hard work, support working families, or create opportunity. After decades of rising income and wealth inequality, the tax system continues to favor unearned over earned income, and a porous capital gains tax system lets the wealthy shelter hundreds of billions of dollars from taxes each year. In a period where an aging population will put increasing pressure on the Federal budget, a wide range of inefficient tax breaks prevents the tax system from raising the level of revenue the Nation needs. The U.S. needs to invest in building an American transportation system that supports a competitive 21st Century economy -- innovative, sustainable, and capable of integrating new technologies and speeding goods to market -- while reducing reliance on oil, cutting carbon pollution, and strengthening resilience to the impacts of climate change. And while commerce around the world is increasingly interconnected, an out-of-date, loophole-ridden business tax system puts U.S. companies at a disadvantage relative to their competitors, while also failing to encourage investment in the United States.

The tax proposals outlined in this chapter address each of these challenges. The Budget would reform and simplify tax incentives that help families afford child care, pay for college, and save for retirement, while expanding tax benefits that support and reward work. It would pay for these changes by reforming the system of capital gains taxation and by imposing a new fee on large, heavily-leveraged financial firms, and it would raise revenue for deficit reduction by curbing high-income tax benefits and closing loopholes. The Budget also supports sustained investment in a 21st Century Clean Transportation Plan while providing for the long-term solvency of the new Transportation Trust Fund by levying a new fee on oil, paid by oil companies. Finally, the Budget includes proposals to broaden the business tax base, strengthen incentives for research and clean energy, grow and create innovative small businesses, and reform the international tax system.

Going forward, the President is committed to working with the Congress and other stakeholders to build on the foundation laid by the Budget to create a tax system that is fair, simple, and efficient—one that is right for the 21st Century American economy.

ESTIMATES OF GOVERNMENTAL RECEIPTS

Governmental receipts (on-budget and off-budget) are taxes and other collections from the public that result from the exercise of the Federal Government's sovereign or governmental powers. The difference between governmental receipts and outlays is the surplus or deficit.

Table 12–1. RECEIPTS BY SOURCE—SUMMARY
(In billions of dollars)

	2015 Actual	Estimate										
		2016	2017	2018	2019	2020	2021	2022	2023	2024	2025	2026
Individual income taxes	1,540.8	1,627.8	1,788.0	1,891.3	1,985.0	2,106.3	2,221.9	2,339.1	2,460.7	2,585.9	2,716.4	2,853.4
Corporation income taxes	343.8	292.6	418.7	492.8	525.2	574.7	582.4	554.1	537.0	545.9	556.4	567.8
Social insurance and retirement receipts	1,065.3	1,100.8	1,141.2	1,191.1	1,239.7	1,286.5	1,351.8	1,416.5	1,478.6	1,546.4	1,614.0	1,694.7
(On-budget)	(294.9)	(303.1)	(314.3)	(327.9)	(341.5)	(354.6)	(371.6)	(388.9)	(406.5)	(422.9)	(440.7)	(462.3)
(Off-budget)	(770.4)	(797.7)	(826.9)	(863.3)	(898.2)	(931.9)	(980.2)	(1,027.5)	(1,072.0)	(1,123.5)	(1,173.3)	(1,232.4)
Excise taxes	98.3	96.8	110.1	142.9	152.6	164.6	178.2	189.0	192.7	196.5	201.0	206.1
Estate and gift taxes	19.2	21.1	22.4	31.5	34.0	36.7	39.8	43.0	46.7	50.9	55.5	60.2
Customs duties	35.0	36.7	39.5	39.9	41.0	42.4	43.8	45.2	46.5	47.7	48.9	50.3
Miscellaneous receipts	147.5	159.7	122.8	102.1	97.6	104.6	114.0	123.8	131.6	139.2	145.1	152.8
Allowance for immigration reform	....	....	....	1.0	7.0	20.0	30.0	40.0	45.0	55.0	64.0	84.0
Total, receipts	**3,249.9**	**3,335.5**	**3,643.7**	**3,898.6**	**4,095.1**	**4,345.7**	**4,572.0**	**4,755.8**	**4,948.9**	**5,176.5**	**5,411.2**	**5,669.3**
(On-budget)	(2,479.5)	(2,537.8)	(2,816.9)	(3,035.4)	(3,196.8)	(3,413.8)	(3,591.8)	(3,728.3)	(3,876.8)	(4,053.0)	(4,237.9)	(4,436.9)
(Off-budget)	(770.4)	(797.7)	(826.9)	(863.3)	(898.2)	(931.9)	(980.2)	(1,027.5)	(1,072.0)	(1,123.5)	(1,173.3)	(1,232.4)
Total receipts as a percentage of GDP	18.3	18.1	18.9	19.4	19.5	19.8	20.0	19.9	19.9	19.9	20.0	20.0

The Federal Government also collects income from the public from market-oriented activities. Collections from these activities, which are subtracted from gross outlays, rather than added to taxes and other governmental receipts, are discussed in the next Chapter.

Total governmental receipts (hereafter referred to as "receipts") are estimated to be $3,335.5 billion in 2016, an increase of $85.6 billion or 2.6 percent from 2015. The estimated increase in 2016 is largely due to increases in payroll taxes and individual income taxes. Receipts in 2016 are estimated to be 18.1 percent of Gross Domestic Product (GDP), which is lower than in 2015, when receipts were 18.3 percent of GDP.

Receipts are estimated to rise to $3,643.7 billion in 2017, an increase of $308.2 billion or 9.2 percent relative to 2016. Receipts are projected to grow at an average annual rate of 5.8 percent between 2017 and 2021, rising to $4,572.0 billion. Receipts are projected to rise to $5,669.3 billion in 2026, growing at an average annual rate of 4.4 percent between 2021 and 2026. This growth is largely due to assumed increases in incomes resulting from both real economic growth and inflation, as well as the effect of the Budget's receipt proposals.

As a share of GDP, receipts are projected to increase from 18.1 percent in 2016 to 18.9 percent in 2017, and to rise to 20.0 percent in 2026.

LEGISLATION ENACTED IN 2015 THAT AFFECTS GOVERNMENTAL RECEIPTS

Several laws were enacted during 2015 that affect receipts. The major provisions of those laws that have a significant impact on receipts are described below.[1]

TERRORISM RISK INSURANCE PROGRAM REAUTHORIZATION ACT OF 2015 (PUBLIC LAW 114-1)

This Act, which was signed into law by President Obama on January 12, 2015, extended the Terrorism Risk Insurance Program for six years through December 31, 2020, and made major reforms to the program. These reforms reduced taxpayer exposure, increased private sector contributions, and better positioned the Program for future transition to the private sector. The Act also established a National Association of Registered Agents and Brokers (NARAB) as a mechanism for insurance producers to be licensed to sell insurance in States other than their home State without having to be separately licensed in each State.

MEDICARE ACCESS AND CHIP REAUTHORIZATION ACT OF 2015 (PUBLIC LAW 114-10)

This Act was signed into law by President Obama on April 16, 2015. The major provisions of this Act that affect receipts are described below.

Permanently extend the work-related transitional medical assistance (TMA) program.—This Act permanently extended the TMA program, which requires States to provide continued medical coverage for certain families who would otherwise become ineligible for Medicaid because of increased earnings. Some of those families would no longer be enrolled in employment-based health insurance or Marketplace qualified health plans. This will increase tax revenues and reduce outlays associated with the premium tax credit.

Extend the Children's Health Insurance Program (CHIP).—This Act extended CHIP through 2017, which would reduce enrollment in employment-based health insurance and Marketplace qualified health plans. This

will increase tax revenues and reduce outlays associated with the premium tax credit.

Increase levy authority for payments to Medicare providers with delinquent tax debt.—Under prior law, the Department of the Treasury was authorized to continuously levy up to 30 percent of a payment to a Medicare provider to collect delinquent tax debt. This Act increased this authority to 100 percent, effective for payments made more than 180 days after the date of enactment.

TRADE PREFERENCES EXTENSION ACT OF 2015 (PUBLIC LAW 114-27)

This Act was signed into law by President Obama on June 29, 2015. The major provisions of this Act that affect receipts are described below.

Extend the Generalized System of Preferences (GSP).—Under GSP, which expired under prior law on July 31, 2013, the United States provided nonreciprocal elimination of duties on up to 5,000 products from 122 developing countries. Generally, duty-free treatment of imported goods from GSP-designated developing countries applied to products that are not considered import-sensitive, with many used as inputs by U.S. companies to manufacture goods in the United States. Under this Act, GSP was renewed retroactively to August 1, 2013, and extended through December 31, 2017.

Extend the African Growth and Opportunity Act (AGOA).—Under AGOA, the United States provides nonreciprocal tariff reductions to roughly 40 eligible sub-Saharan African countries for certain goods that the United States imports. This Act extended the authority for reduced tariffs under AGOA, which were set to expire at the end of September 30, 2015, through September 30, 2025. This Act also extended the special rule that would apply to certain lesser-developed sub-Saharan countries under AGOA. Under this rule, a lesser-developed country may export duty-free to the United States any apparel good that is assembled within the country, regardless of the origin of the fabric or yarn. In addition, this Act revised the rules of origin for AGOA beneficiary countries under GSP and provided the Executive Branch more flexibility to withdraw, suspend, or limit benefits under

---

[1] In the discussions of enacted legislation, years referred to are calendar years, unless otherwise noted.

AGOA and undertake an out-of-cycle review of a country's AGOA eligibility.

Extend preferential duty treatment for Haiti.— Under the Haitian Hemispheric Opportunity through Partnership Encouragement Act (HOPE) and related programs, certain textile and apparel goods that the United States imports from Haiti are eligible for duty-free treatment if restrictions regarding the source of the yarns and fabrics used in the imported goods are met. Under prior law, some of these trade benefits for Haiti were scheduled to expire beginning in 2016. This Act extended the duty-free status for qualifying goods from Haiti through September 30, 2025. Special rules regarding the duty-free entry of apparel articles, including woven articles and certain knit articles assembled in Haiti and imported by the United States from Haiti or the Dominican Republic were extended through December 19, 2025.

Reinstate, extend, and modify the health coverage tax credit (HCTC).—Under prior law, the HCTC was provided to eligible individuals for a portion of the cost of qualified health insurance for the individual and qualifying family members. Qualified individuals included those eligible for Trade Adjustment Assistance (TAA) or alternative TAA, and certain retired workers whose pensions were paid by the Pension Benefit Guaranty Corporation (PBGC) and who were not eligible for Medicare. This refundable tax credit, which expired on December 31, 2013, was advanced to eligible individuals and families for health coverage on a monthly basis applied to their health plan premium or paid as a credit on their Federal tax returns. Under this Act the HCTC was reinstated retroactively to January 1, 2014, and extended through December 31, 2019. The credit rate was set at 72.5 percent of premiums paid for qualifying health insurance (the last rate in effect under prior law). The Act also provided that an eligible individual could not claim both the HCTC and the premium tax credit provided under the Affordable Care Act (ACA) for the same coverage for the same month and that individual health insurance coverage purchased through the Health Insurance Marketplace is qualified coverage for coverage months in 2014 and 2015.

Modify tariff classification of certain articles.— This Act established new categories in the Harmonized Tariff Schedule of the United States for recreational performance outerwear, effective for such articles entering the United States or withdrawn from warehouse for consumption 180 days after the date of enactment. This Act also modified the definition of protective active footwear and reduced the duty rate on such articles effective for such articles entering the United States or withdrawn from warehouse for consumption 15 days after the date of enactment.

Modify the timing of estimated tax payments by corporations.—Corporations generally are required to pay their income tax liability in quarterly estimated payments. For corporations that keep their accounts on a calendar year basis, these payments are due on or before April 15, June 15, September 15 and December 15. If these dates fall on a holiday or weekend, payment is due on the next business day. This Act increased the estimated

tax payments due in July through September by corporations with assets of at least $1 billion to 108 percent of the amount otherwise due in 2020. For corporations affected by this provision, the next required estimated tax payment is reduced accordingly.

Require payee statement to claim certain education tax benefits.—Under this Act, except as otherwise provided by the Secretary of the Treasury, a taxpayer may not claim the American Opportunity tax credit (AOTC), the Hope Scholarship tax credit, the Lifetime Learning tax credit, or a tax deduction for qualified tuition and related expenses unless the taxpayer or the taxpayer's dependent receives a payee statement containing the student's taxpayer identification number (TIN) and other information. This provision is effective for taxable years beginning after the date of enactment.

Establish special rule for educational institutions unable to collect TINs of individuals with respect to higher education tuition and related expenses.—Under this Act, information reporting penalties are not imposed on eligible educational institutions for failure to provide the student's TIN on Form 1098-T if the institution contemporaneously certifies under penalties of perjury that it has complied with standards promulgated by the Secretary of the Treasury for obtaining the TIN. This provision is effective for returns required to be made and statements required to be furnished after December 31, 2015.

Increase penalty for failure to file correct information returns and provide payee statements.—This Act increased penalties for failure to file correct information returns and correct payee statements, and for the intentional disregard of such requirements. This provision is effective for returns and statements required to be filed after December 31, 2015.

Disallow refundable child tax credit for taxpayers electing to exclude foreign earned income from tax.—This Act disallowed any taxpayer who elects to exclude from gross income any amount of foreign earned income or foreign housing costs from claiming the refundable portion of the child tax credit for the taxable year. This change is effective for taxable years beginning after December 31, 2014.

SURFACE TRANSPORTATION AND VETERANS HEALTH CARE CHOICE IMPROVEMENT ACT OF 2015 (PUBLIC LAW 114-41)

This Act was signed into law by President Obama on July 31, 2015. The major provisions of this Act that affect receipts are described below.

Modify mortgage reporting requirements.—Under prior law, mortgage lenders who received interest from a borrower of $600 or more on any mortgage for any calendar year were required to include on their information returns the following items: (1) the name and address of the borrower; (2) the amount of interest received; and (3) the amount of points received. Effective for returns required to be filed and statements required to be furnished after December 31, 2016, this Act required mortgage lenders to include the following additional information: (1) the outstanding principal on the mortgage as of the beginning of the calendar year; (2) the mortgage origination date; and (3) the address (or other description in the case of property without an address) of the property that secures the mortgage.

Require consistency between estate tax value and income tax basis of assets acquired from a decedent.—This Act imposes a consistency requirement on the recipient of property inherited from a decedent if that property increases the estate's Federal estate tax liability: the recipient's initial basis in that inherited property may not exceed the final value of that property for federal estate tax purposes. A penalty is imposed on any underpayment of tax attributable to any inconsistent estate basis. In addition, the Act requires the executor of any estate subject to Federal estate tax to furnish the Department of the Treasury and each person acquiring any interest in property included in the decedent's gross estate a statement identifying the estate tax value of the person's interest in such property. This statute is intended to ensure that beneficiaries do not overstate the basis of an inherited property, and thus understate the tax liability, at the time of sale and applies to property with respect to which an estate tax return is filed after July 31, 2015.

Clarify six-year statute of limitations in the case of overstatement of basis.—In general, the amount of any tax imposed under the Internal Revenue Code must be assessed within three years after the return is filed by the taxpayer. However, among other exceptions to this general rule, if a taxpayer omits from gross income an amount properly includible that is in excess of 25 percent of the amount of gross income stated in the return, the tax may be assessed at any time within six years after the return was filed. Under this Act, "an understatement of gross income by reason of an overstatement of unrecovered cost or other basis" is to be included as an omission in determining the amount of the understatement of gross income for purposes of applying the six-year statute of limitations. This provision applies to returns filed after July 31, 2015 and returns filed on or before that date if the period of limitations on assessment with respect to such return has not expired as of that date.

Modify certain due dates.—Under this Act, the tax return due date for filing tax returns of partnerships and S corporations is March 15 following the close of the calendar year (or the fifteenth day of the third month following the close of the fiscal year, in the case of a fiscal-year filer) and the tax return due date for filing tax returns of C corporations is April 15 following the close of the calendar year (or the fifteenth day of the fourth month following the close of the fiscal year). This Act also increased the automatic three-month extension for filing a tax return for a corporation to six months, except in the case of C corporations with a taxable year that ends on December 31 and begins before January 1, 2026: (1) there is a five-month automatic extension; and (2) C corporations with a taxable year that ends on June 30 and begins before January 1, 2026, the automatic extension is seven

months. These changes are generally effective for returns for taxable years beginning after December 31, 2015. For C corporations with a year that ends on June 30, the change in the tax return due date is effective for taxable years beginning after December 31, 2025.

Extend the ability of employers to transfer excess pension assets to retiree health accounts.—This Act extended the ability of employers to transfer excess assets of a defined benefit pension plan to a retiree medical account for four years to apply to such transfers made after December 31, 2021, and before January 1, 2026.

Equalize excise taxes on liquefied natural gas, liquefied petroleum gas, and compressed natural gas.—This Act adjusted the excise taxes on a gallon of liquefied natural gas, liquefied petroleum gas, and compressed natural gas on an energy-equivalent basis with a gallon of gasoline or diesel. These changes apply to any sale or use of such fuel after December 31, 2015.

Modify Internal Revenue Code with regard to health care for veterans.—Under this Act, effective for months beginning after December 31, 2015, a veteran receiving medical care under any law administered by the Secretary of Veterans Affairs for a service-connected disability cannot be denied eligibility for a health savings account merely because the individual receives such care. In addition, effective for months beginning after December 31, 2013, an individual with medical coverage under TRICARE or a Department of Veterans Affairs health program for a month shall not be taken into account for such month as an employee solely for purposes of determining whether an employer is large enough to be subject to the employer shared responsibility provisions under the Affordable Care Act (ACA).

AIRPORT AND AIRWAY EXTENSION ACT OF 2015 (PUBLIC LAW 114-55)

This Act, which was signed into law by President Obama on September 30, 2015, extended the authority to collect taxes that fund the Airport and Airway Trust Fund through March 31, 2016. The prior law exemption from domestic and international air passenger ticket taxes provided for aircraft in fractional ownership aircraft programs was also extended through that date. These taxes had been scheduled to expire after September 30, 2015, under prior law.

BIPARTISAN BUDGET ACT OF 2015 (PUBLIC LAW 114-74)

This Act was signed into law by President Obama on November 2, 2015. The major provisions of this Act that affect receipts are described below.

Allow adjustments to mortality tables used by defined benefit pension plans.—Under prior law, private sector-defined benefit pension plans generally had to use mortality tables prescribed by the Department of the Treasury for purposes of calculating pension liabilities. Plans could apply to use a separate mortality table only under certain conditions. Under this Act, effective for plan years beginning after December 31, 2015, the determination of whether a plan has credible mortality information shall be made in accordance with established actuarial credibility theory, which is materially different from prior law rules. A plan will be allowed to use mortality tables that are adjusted from the tables provided by the Department of the Treasury tables if such adjustments are based on a plan's experience.

Extend current funding stabilization percentages for single-employer pension funding rules.—Under prior law, the interest rates for valuing single-employer defined benefit pension plan liabilities for plan years 2012 through 2017 were deemed not to vary more than 10 percent from the average interest rates over the prior 25 years. That interest rate corridor increased by five percent per year through 2021, and remained permanently at 30 percent in each subsequent year. Under this Act, the corridor on interest rates will remain at 10 percent through 2019 and will increase by five percent per year through 2023, at which point the corridor will remain permanently at 30 percent.

Repeal automatic enrollment in health plans by large employers.—This Act repealed the prior-law requirement that employers with more than 200 full-time employees automatically enroll new full-time employees in a health plan if one is offered by that employer, and continue the enrollment of current employees in a health plan offered by the employer. Prior to repeal, employers had not been required to comply with this provision, as regulations had not been issued.

Adjust civil monetary penalties for inflation.— This Act amended the Federal Civil Penalties Inflation Adjustment Act of 1990 by requiring that no later than July 1, 2016, all Federal agencies with civil monetary penalties covered by the statute update penalties based on their value in the last update prior to 1996 and the change in the consumer price index (CPI) between that date and October 2015. This initial "catch up adjustment" would be capped at 150 percent. This Act also required annual adjustments in such penalties not later than January 15th of each subsequent year, replaced prior law rounding rules with a simple rule that penalties be rounded to the nearest dollar, and expanded these inflation adjustments to apply to civil penalties assessed under the Occupational Safety and Health Act and under the Social Security Act. The Act also provided for increasing a penalty by less than the required amount if increasing the penalty by the full amount would have a negative economic impact or the social costs outweighed the benefits.

Extend reserve depletion date for Social Security's Disability Insurance program.—This Act provided a temporary reallocation of payroll taxes from the Social Security Administration's Old-Age and Survivors Insurance (OASI) Trust Fund to the Disability Insurance (DI) Trust Fund, effective for wages paid in calendar years 2016 through 2018, and self-employment earnings reported in taxable years beginning after December 31 2015, and before January 1, 2019. Under this reallocation the combined OASDI payroll tax rate will remain at 12.4 percent; however, 10.03 percent will be allocated to OASI and 2.37 percent will be allocated to DI, compared to the 10.6 percent and 1.8 percent allocations, respectively, in prior years. This reallocation is expected to allow the DI Trust Fund to pay full disability benefits until calendar year 2022.

Modify partnership audit rules.—This Act replaced existing partnership audit rules with a centralized system for audit, adjustment, and collection of tax at the partnership level, unless a partnership makes a valid election to opt out of application of these rules (generally available to partnerships with no more than 100 partners). Under these rules any adjustment to items of partnership income, gain, loss, deductions, credits, or partnership distribution as a result of such adjustments is determined at the partnership level and any tax resulting from an imputed underpayment attributable to these adjustments is generally imputed to the partnership and assessed and collected at the partnership level in the year the adjustment becomes final. As an alternative to payment at the partnership level, the partnership may elect to push the partnership adjustments out to the partners for the reviewed year and have them pay in the current year the tax attributable to their allocable portion of the adjustments. The partners are generally bound by the final determination of partnership adjustments and any action taken by the partnership's designated representative who may be a partner or other person with a substantial presence in the United States. These new rules generally apply to returns filed for partnership taxable years beginning after December 31, 2017.

Clarify rules for partnership interests created by gift.—This Act clarified that in the case of a capital interest in a partnership in which capital is a material income-producing factor, the determination of whether a person is a partner with respect to such interest must be made under the generally applicable rules defining a partner and a partnership, without regard to whether such interest was derived by gift from any other person. This clarification applies to partnership taxable years beginning on or after January 1, 2015.

NATIONAL DEFENSE AUTHORIZATION ACT FOR FISCAL YEAR 2016 (PUBLIC LAW 114-92)

This Act was signed into law by President Obama on November 25, 2015. The provision of this Act that affects receipts is described below.

Establish a Thrift Savings Plan (TSP) benefit for all uniformed servicemembers.—This Act established a TSP benefit for all uniformed servicemembers who enter on or after October 1, 2017, or current eligible servicemembers who make a voluntary election to opt-in to the new plan. Under this Act, the Department of Defense would provide an automatic TSP contribution of one percent to all uniformed servicemembers upon reaching 60 days of service, which would continue through the second year of service. After the second year of service, the Department of Defense would begin matching TSP contributions by servicemembers up to five percent of that servicemember's base pay. Both the automatic and matching TSP contributions would end on the day the servicemember reaches 26 years of service.

FIXING AMERICA'S SURFACE TRANSPORTATION ACT OF 2015 (PUBLIC LAW 114-94)

This Act was signed into law by President Obama on December 4, 2015. The major provisions of this Act that affect receipts are described below.

Extend highway-related taxes.—This Act extended the authority to collect taxes that fund the Highway Trust Fund, the Leaking Underground Storage Tank (LUST) Trust Fund, and the Sport Fish Restoration and Boating Trust Fund, which were scheduled to expire on September 30, 2016, through September 30, 2022. This Act also extended the annual use tax on heavy vehicles, which is deposited in the Highway Trust Fund and was scheduled to expire on September 30, 2017, through September 30, 2023.

Revoke or deny passport in case of certain unpaid taxes.—This Act provided for the denial, revocation or limitation of passports by the Department of State for persons with seriously delinquent tax debts (generally individuals who owe more than $50,000 and who are not on a payment plan), effective on December 4, 2015.

Reform rules relating to qualified tax collection contracts.—Under this Act, the Secretary of the Treasury is required to enter into qualified tax collection contracts for the collection of outstanding inactive tax receivables. Inactive tax receivables are defined as any tax receivable 1) removed from the active inventory for lack of resources or inability to locate the taxpayer, 2) for which more than one-third of the applicable limitations period has lapsed and no Internal Revenue Service (IRS) employee has been assigned to collect the receivable, or 3) for which a receivable has been assigned for collection but more than 365 days have passed without interaction with the taxpayer or a third party for purposes of furthering the collection. Tax receivables are defined as any outstanding assessment that the IRS includes in potentially collectible inventory. The provision designates certain tax receivables as not eligible for collection under qualified tax collection contracts and requires the Secretary of the Treasury to give priority to private collection contractors and debt collection centers currently approved by the Treasury Department's Bureau of the Fiscal Service. The provision generally applies to tax receivables identified by the Secretary after the date of enactment.

Limit surplus funds of Federal Reserve banks.—This Act capped the Federal Reserve surplus account at $10 billion and required any amounts that exceed the cap to be remitted to the U.S. Treasury.

Reduce dividends of certain Federal Reserve member banks.—For member banks with assets in excess of $10 billion, this Act reduced the dividend paid by the Federal Reserve to the lower of six percent or the high yield of the 10-year Treasury note auctioned at the last auction held prior to the payment of a dividend. For member banks with assets of $10 billion or less, the Act retained the six-percent dividend consistent with prior law, indexed to inflation.

CONSOLIDATED APPROPRIATIONS ACT, 2016 (PUBLIC LAW 114-113)

This Act was signed into law by President Obama on December 18, 2015. The major provisions that affect receipts are included in Division Q of this Act, which may be cited as the "Protecting Americans from Tax Hikes Act of 2015." These provisions, as well as those included in Division P of this Act, "Tax Related Provisions," are described below.

PROTECTING AMERICANS FROM TAX HIKES ACT OF 2015

Tax Relief for Families and Individuals

Permanently extend increased refundability of the child tax credit (CTC).—The American Recovery and Reinvestment Act of 2009 (ARRA) increased the refundability of the CTC by reducing the earnings threshold for refundability to $3,000 (unindexed) from $10,000 (indexed after 2001), effective for taxable years 2009 and 2010. The Tax Relief, Unemployment Insurance Reauthorization and Job Creation Act of 2010 (TRUIRJCA) extended this provision through 2012 and the American Taxpayer Relief Act of 2012 (ATRA) extended the provision through 2017. This Act permanently extended the $3,000 earnings threshold.

Permanently extend Earned Income Tax Credit (EITC) marriage penalty relief.—ARRA, as extended by TRUIRJCA and ATRA, provided tax relief through 2017 to married couples filing a joint return (regardless of the number of qualifying children) by increasing the amount by which the income thresholds for the phaseout of the EITC exceed the thresholds for other taxpayers from $3,000 (indexed for inflation after 2008) to $5,000 (indexed for inflation after 2009). This Act permanently extended the indexed $5,000 increase in the EITC phaseout threshold for married couples.

Permanently extend EITC for larger families.—ARRA, as extended by TRUIRJCA and ATRA, added a fourth credit schedule to the EITC through 2017 to provide a larger credit for families with more than two qualifying children. This Act permanently extended the fourth schedule.

Permanently extend AOTC.—The AOTC, which was created under ARRA and extended through 2017 by TRUIRJCA and ATRA, provided taxpayers a credit of up to $2,500 per eligible student per year for qualified tuition and related expenses paid for each of the first four years of the student's post-secondary education in a degree or certification program. The student must be enrolled at least half-time to receive the credit, which is partially refundable and phased out above specified income thresholds. This Act permanently extended the AOTC.

Modify and permanently extend the above-the-line deduction for qualified out-of-pocket classroom expenses.—Certain teachers and other elementary and secondary school professionals are permitted to deduct up to $250 in annual qualified out-of-pocket classroom expenses. Under prior law, the deduction expired for taxable years beginning before January 1, 2015. This Act reinstated and permanently extended this above-the-line deduction, effective for such expenses incurred after December 31, 2014, and provided for the annual indexation of the $250 deduction limit, effective for taxable years beginning after 2015. In addition, this Act expanded the deduction to apply to professional development expenses, effective for such expenses incurred after December 31, 2015.

Permanently extend parity for exclusion from income for employer-provided mass transit and parking benefits.—Qualified transportation fringe benefits provided by an employer through transit passes and vanpooling can be excluded from an employee's income up to a statutory maximum of $100 per month in combined transit pass and vanpool benefits and $175 per month in qualified parking benefits. Both statutory limits are adjusted annually for inflation after 1999. Prior law temporarily provided parity in these benefits by increasing the monthly exclusion for combined employer-provided transit pass and vanpool benefits to the same level as the exclusion for employer-provided parking benefits. This Act reinstated and permanently extended that parity, effective for benefits provided after December 31, 2014.

Permanently extend optional deduction for State and local general sales taxes.—Under prior law, a taxpayer was allowed to elect to take an itemized deduction for State and local general sales taxes in lieu of the itemized deduction for State and local income taxes for taxable years beginning before January 1, 2015. This Act reinstated and permanently extended this deduction, effective for taxable years beginning after December 31, 2014.

Modify and extend the ability to exclude discharges of indebtedness on principal residences from gross income.—Up to $2 million (or up to $1 million per spouse for married taxpayers filing separate returns) of discharges of certain indebtedness on a principal residence may be excluded from gross income for indebtedness discharged before January 1, 2015. This Act reinstated and extended the exclusion for two years, to apply to indebtedness discharged after December 31, 2014, and before January 1, 2017. The exclusion will also apply to indebtedness discharged after December 31, 2016, if the discharge is pursuant to a written arrangement entered into before 2017.

Extend deduction for mortgage insurance premiums.—Certain premiums paid or accrued for qualified mortgage insurance by a taxpayer in connection with acquisition indebtedness on a qualified residence are deductible for income tax purposes, for amounts paid or accrued before 2015. This Act reinstated and extended the deduction for two years, to apply to amounts paid or accrued in 2015 and 2016 that are not properly allocable to any period after December 31, 2016.

Extend deduction for qualified tuition and related expenses.—An above-the-line deduction of up to $4,000 is provided for qualified higher education expenses paid by a qualified taxpayer during the taxable year. For a given taxable year, the deduction may not be claimed: (1) if an education tax credit is claimed for the same student; (2) for amounts taken into account in determining the amount excludable from income due to a distribution from a Coverdell education savings account or the amount of interest excludable from income with respect to education savings bonds; and (3) for the amount of a distribution from a qualified tuition plan that is excludable from income, except that the deduction may be claimed for the amount not attributable to earnings. Under prior law, the deduction expired for expenses incurred in taxable years after December 31, 2014. This Act reinstated and extended the deduction for two years, to apply to expenses incurred in taxable years beginning after December 31, 2014, and before January 1, 2017.

Tax Incentives for Charitable Giving

Modify and permanently extend increased limits on contributions of partial interest in real property for conservation purposes.—Special rules for the deductibility of qualified conservation contributions were temporarily enhanced, applicable for qualified conservation contributions made in taxable years beginning after December 31, 2005, and before January 1, 2015. These enhancements: (1) increased the cap on deductions for qualified conservation contributions from 30 percent to 50 percent of the excess of the donor's contribution base over the amount of all other allowable charitable contributions; (2) increased the cap on deductions for qualified conservation contributions applicable to qualified ranchers and farmers to 100 percent of the excess of the donor's contribution base over the amount of all other allowable charitable contributions in the case of individuals and to 100 percent of the excess of taxable income over the amount of all other allowable charitable contributions in the case of corporations; and (3) increased the number of years qualified conservation contributions in excess of the 50- and 100-percent caps may be carried forward from five to 15 years. This Act reinstated and permanently extended these enhanced special rules, applicable for qualified conservation contributions made in taxable years beginning after December 31, 2014. In addition, Alaska Native Corporations will be allowed to deduct donations of conservation easements of up to 100 percent of taxable income, effective for such donations made after December 31, 2015.

Permanently extend tax-free distributions from Individual Retirement Accounts (IRAs) for charitable contributions.—An exclusion from gross income was provided for otherwise taxable distributions from a traditional or a Roth IRA made directly to a qualified charitable organization in taxable years beginning after December 31, 2005, and before January 1, 2015. The exclusion for these qualified charitable distributions may not exceed $100,000 per taxpayer per taxable year and is applicable only to distributions made on or after the date the IRA owner attains age 70 1/2. This Act reinstated and permanently extended the exclusion to apply to distributions made in taxable years beginning after December 31, 2014.

Modify and permanently extend the enhanced charitable deduction for contributions of food inventory.—A taxpayer's deduction for charitable contributions of inventory generally is limited to the taxpayer's basis (typically cost) in the inventory or, if less, the fair market value of the inventory. For certain contributions of inventory, C corporations may claim an enhanced deduction equal to the lesser of: (1) basis plus one-half of the item's appreciation; or (2) two times basis. However, under a special temporary provision, any taxpayer (not just a C corporation) engaged in a trade or business was eligible to claim the enhanced deduction for donations of food inventory in taxable years beginning after August 28, 2005, and before January 1, 2015. To qualify for the enhanced deduction, the donated food inventory must meet certain quality standards and cannot exceed 10 percent of the taxpayer's net income from the related trade or business. This Act reinstated and permanently extended the enhanced charitable deduction for contributions of food inventory, to apply to contributions made after December 31, 2014. In addition, this Act increased the limitation from 10 percent to 15 percent of the taxpayer's net income from the related trade or business and modified the deduction to provide special rules for valuing food inventory, effective for taxable years beginning after December 31, 2015.

Permanently extend special rule regarding tax treatment of certain payments to controlling exempt organizations.—Interest, rents, royalties, and income from annuities generally are excluded from the tax on unrelated business income of tax-exempt organizations, unless such income is received from a taxable or tax-exempt subsidiary that is more than 50-percent controlled by the parent tax-exempt organization. However, under a special temporary provision, such income received by a tax-exempt parent organization from a controlled subsidiary before January 1, 2015, and pursuant to a binding written contract that was in effect on August 17, 2006, is taxable only to the extent that it exceeds amounts that would have been received if such payments had been determined under the arm's length principles of section 482 of the Internal Revenue Code. This Act reinstated and permanently extended this provision, to apply to such income received after December 31, 2014.

Extend basis adjustment to stock of S corporations contributing appreciated property.—Each shareholder of an S corporation must take into account his or her pro rata share of a charitable contribution by the S corporation in determining his or her income tax liability. For donations of property, this generally is the pro rata share of the property's fair market value; the shareholder's basis in the stock of the company is reduced by the amount of the charitable contribution that flows through to the shareholder. However, effective for charitable contributions made by an S corporation in taxable years beginning after December 31, 2005, and before

January 1, 2015, shareholders were allowed to adjust their basis in the stock of the company by their pro rata share of the adjusted basis of the contributed property instead of by their pro rata share of the market value of the contributed property. This Act reinstated and permanently extended this provision, to apply to charitable contributions made by an S corporation in taxable years beginning after December 31, 2014.

Tax Incentives for Growth, Jobs, Investment, and Innovation

Modify and permanently extend research and experimentation (R&E) tax credit.—A tax credit of 20 percent is provided for qualified research and experimentation expenditures above a base amount. An alternative simplified credit (ASC) of 14 percent is also provided. Under prior law, these credits expired for amounts paid or incurred after December 31, 2014. This Act reinstated and permanently extended these tax credits, to apply to expenditures paid or incurred after December 31, 2014. In addition, effective for taxable years beginning after December 31, 2015, eligible small businesses ($50 million or less in gross receipts) will be allowed to claim the credit against their alternative minimum tax (AMT) liability, and certain qualified small businesses will be able to claim the credit against their Social Security payroll tax liability.

Permanently extend employer wage credit for employees who are active duty members of the uniformed services.—Some employers voluntarily pay their employees who are called to active duty in the armed forces of the United States the difference between the compensation that they would have paid the employee during the period of military service and the amount of pay received by the employee from the military. This payment by the employer is often referred to as "differential pay." Eligible small business employers are provided a tax credit equal to 20 percent of up to $20,000 in annual eligible differential wage payments made to each qualified employee. Under prior law, this credit expired for amounts paid after December 31, 2014. This Act reinstated and permanently extended the credit, making it available for eligible differential wage payments made to a qualified employee after December 31, 2014, and expanded the credit to apply to all employers, effective for such payments made after December 31, 2015.

Permanently extend modified recovery period for qualified leasehold improvement property, qualified restaurant property, and qualified retail improvement property.—This Act reinstated and permanently extended the 15-year recovery period for qualified leasehold improvement property, qualified restaurant property, and qualified retail improvement property, effective for such property placed in service after December 31, 2014.

Modify and permanently extend increased expensing for small business.—Taxpayers were allowed to expense up to $500,000 in annual investment expenditures for qualifying depreciable property used in an active trade or business (including off-the-shelf computer software and up to $250,000 of certain qualified real property) placed in service in taxable years beginning after 2009 and before 2015. The maximum amount that could be expensed was reduced by the amount by which the taxpayer's cost of qualifying property exceeded $2 million. This Act reinstated and permanently extended the annual expensing limit and the phase-out threshold amount that were in effect in 2010 through 2014, effective for qualifying property placed in service in taxable years beginning after December 31, 2014. Qualifying property will continue to include off-the-shelf computer software and certain real property. Effective for taxable years beginning after December 31, 2015, both the $500,000 and $2 million amounts will be indexed annually for inflation; the $250,000 cap on annual expensing of certain real property will be eliminated; and the definition of qualifying property will be expanded to include air conditioning and heating units.

Permanently extend special tax rules applicable to regulated investment companies (RICs).—This Act reinstated and permanently extended, effective for taxable years beginning after December 31, 2014, the following special tax rules applicable to RICs: (1) the exemption from U.S. withholding tax for certain interest-related dividends and short-term capital gain dividends paid by a RIC to a foreign shareholder; and (2) the treatment of RICs as "qualified investment entities" for purposes of the provisions regarding foreign investment in U.S. real property interests.

Permanently extend exclusion of 100 percent of gain on certain small business stock.—Capital gains realized on the sale of certain small business stock held by an individual for more than five years are excluded from tax, effective for stock issued after September 27, 2010, and before January 1, 2015. This Act reinstated and permanently extended the 100-percent exclusion and eliminated the treatment of a percentage of the exclusion as a preference for the AMT, to apply to qualified small business stock issued after December 31, 2014.

Permanently extend reduction in recognition period for S corporation built-in gains tax.—A "small business corporation" may elect to be treated as an S corporation. Unlike C corporations, S corporations generally pay no corporate-level tax; instead, items of income and loss of an S corporation pass through to its shareholders. A corporate level tax, at the highest marginal tax rate applicable to corporations (currently 35 percent), is imposed on the net recognized built-in gain of an S corporation that arose prior to the conversion of a C corporation to the S corporation and that is recognized by the S corporation during the "recognition period." The "recognition period" is the 10-year period beginning with the first day of the first taxable year for which the election to be treated as an S corporation is in effect; however, the "recognition period" was reduced to five years for dispositions of property in taxable years beginning in 2011, 2012, 2013, and 2014. This Act reinstated and permanently extended the five-year recognition period, to apply to dispositions of property in taxable years beginning in 2015

Extend subpart F "active financing" and "look-through" exceptions.—Under the rules contained in subpart F of the Internal Revenue Code, U.S. shareholders of a controlled foreign corporation (CFC) are subject to U.S. tax currently on certain income earned by the CFC, whether or not such income is distributed. Exceptions from subpart F are provided for: (1) certain income derived in the active conduct of a banking, financing, insurance, or similar business (active financing exception); and (2) dividends, interest, rents, and royalties received by one CFC from a related CFC to the extent attributable or properly allocable to income of the related CFC that is neither subpart F income nor income treated as effectively connected with the conduct of a trade or business in the United States (look-through exception). Under prior law, these exceptions expired for taxable years beginning after December 31, 2014. This Act reinstated and permanently extended the exception under subpart F for active financing income to apply to taxable years of foreign corporations beginning after December 31, 2014, and reinstated and extended the look-through exception for five years, to apply to taxable years of foreign corporations beginning after December 31, 2014, and before January 1, 2020.

Extend the New Markets tax credit (NMTC).—The NMTC is a 39-percent credit for qualified equity investments made in qualified community development entities that are held for a period of seven years. This Act reinstated and extended the NMTC, which expired at the end of 2014, for five years, authorizing up to $3.5 billion in qualifying investment for each year, 2015 through 2019.

Modify and extend the work opportunity tax credit (WOTC).—The WOTC provides incentives to employers for hiring individuals from one or more of nine targeted groups. The credit available for qualified wages paid to members of all targeted groups (except for long-term family assistance recipients and qualified summer youth employees) is equal to 40 percent (25 percent for employment of 400 hours or less) of the first $6,000 of qualified first-year wages attributable to service rendered during the one-year period beginning with the day the individual began work for the employer. With respect to qualified summer youth employees, the maximum credit is $1,200 (40 percent of the first $3,000 of qualified first-year wages). In the case of long-term family assistance recipients, the credit is equal to 40 percent (25 percent for employment of 400 hours or less) of the first $10,000 in qualified first-year wages and 50 percent of the first $10,000 of qualified second-year wages. Under prior law, this credit expired for individuals who begin work for an employer after December 31, 2014. This Act reinstated and extended the credit for five years, to apply to wages paid to qualified individuals who begin work for the employer after December 31, 2014, and before January 1, 2020. This Act also modified the credit to apply to wages paid to qualified long-term unemployed individuals (those who have been unemployed for 27 weeks or more) who begin work for the employer after December 31, 2015, and before January 1, 2020.

Extend first-year depreciation deduction for certain property.—This Act reinstated and extended for five years the additional first-year depreciation deduction to apply to qualifying property acquired and placed in service in calendar years 2015 through 2019. The placed-in-service deadline was extended through 2020 for certain longer-lived property, transportation property, and certain aircraft. The deduction is 50 percent of the adjusted basis of the property for qualifying property acquired and placed in service in calendar years 2015 through 2017, 40 percent for property placed in service in 2018, and 30 percent for property placed in service in 2019. For certain longer-lived property, transportation property, and certain aircraft, the deduction percentage is 50 percent for 2016 through 2018, 40 percent for 2019, and 30 percent for 2020. Under this Act, corporations may continue to elect to claim additional AMT credits in lieu of claiming the additional first-year depreciation for property placed in service in 2015. The Act increased the amount of unused AMT credits that may be claimed in lieu of bonus depreciation for taxable years beginning after December 31, 2015. This Act expanded the definition of qualified property to include qualified improvement property for property placed in service after December 31, 2015, in taxable years beginning after such date. After December 31, 2015, and before January 1, 2020, it also altered the treatment for certain trees, vines, and plants bearing fruit or nuts that are planted or grafted to a plant that has already been planted. The additional first-year depreciation deduction is allowed when such plants are planted or grafted, rather than when they are placed in service.

Extend tax incentives for employment on Indian reservations.—This Act reinstated and extended for two years, for taxable years beginning before January 1, 2017, the employment tax credit for qualified workers employed on an Indian reservation. The employment tax credit is not available for employees involved in certain gaming activities or who work in a building that houses certain gaming activities.

Modify and extend railroad track maintenance credit.—A 50-percent business tax credit is provided for qualified railroad track maintenance expenditures paid or incurred by an eligible taxpayer in taxable years beginning after December 31, 2004, and before January 1, 2015. The credit was limited to the product of $3,500 times the number of miles of railroad track owned or leased by, or assigned to, an eligible taxpayer as of the close of the taxable year. In general, an eligible taxpayer is a Class II or Class III railroad. This Act reinstated and extended the credit for two years, to apply to qualified expenses incurred in taxable years beginning after December 31, 2014, and before January 1, 2017. This Act also modified the credit to apply to expenditures for maintaining railroad track owned or leased as of January 1, 2015, rather than as of January 1, 2005, as provided under prior law.

Extend credit for mine rescue training.—An eligible taxpayer may claim a general business tax credit with respect to each qualified mine rescue team employee equal to the lesser of: (1) 20 percent of the amount paid or incurred by the taxpayer during the taxable year with respect to the training program costs of the qualified mine rescue team employee; or (2) $10,000. Under prior law, this credit expired for taxable years beginning after December 31, 2014. This Act reinstated and extended the credit for two years, to apply to costs incurred in taxable years beginning after December 31, 2014, and before January 1, 2017.

Extend the issuance of qualified zone academy bonds.—This Act reinstated and extended the qualified zone academy bond program for two years, authorizing the issuance of $400 million in such bonds in calendar years 2015 and 2016.

Extend classification of certain race horses as three-year property.—Under this Act, the three-year recovery period applicable to any race horse placed in service after December 31, 2008, and before January 1, 2015, was reinstated and extended for two years, to apply to race horses placed in service before January 1, 2017.

Extend seven-year recovery period for motorsports entertainment complexes.—Under this Act, the seven-year recovery period applicable to motorsports entertainment complexes placed in service before January 1, 2015, was reinstated and extended for two years, to apply to such facilities placed in service before January 1, 2017.

Modify and extend accelerated depreciation for business property on Indian reservations.—This Act reinstated and extended for two years, through December 31, 2016, the accelerated depreciation rules for qualified property used in the active conduct of a trade or business within an Indian reservation. Property used to conduct or house certain gaming activities is not eligible for the accelerated depreciation rules. This Act also modified the deduction for taxable years beginning after December 31, 2015, allowing taxpayers to elect out of the accelerated depreciation rules.

Extend expensing of advanced mine safety equipment.—Under prior law, taxpayers were allowed to immediately expense 50 percent of the cost of underground mine safety equipment that is above and beyond existing safety equipment requirements for property placed in service before January 1, 2015. This Act reinstated and extended this provision for two years, to apply to property placed in service after December 31, 2014, and before January 1, 2017.

Extend expensing for certain qualified film and television productions.—Taxpayers could elect to deduct up to $15 million ($20 million for productions in certain areas) of the aggregate costs of any qualifying film and television production in the year in which the expenses were incurred, in lieu of capitalizing the cost and recovering it through depreciation allowances. Under prior law, this deduction expired for qualifying film and television production, commencing after December 31, 2014. This Act reinstated and extended this provision for two years, to apply to qualified film and television productions commencing after December 31, 2014, and before January 1, 2017. The Act also extended this expensing provision to qualified live theatrical productions commencing after December 31, 2015.

Extend the domestic production activities deduction for activities in Puerto Rico.—A deduction is provided for a portion of a taxpayer's qualified production activities income. Qualified production activities income generally is equal to domestic production gross receipts reduced by the sum of the costs of goods sold and other expenses, losses, or deductions that are properly allocable to those receipts. Domestic production gross receipts generally only include receipts from activities performed within the United States, and do not include receipts from activities performed in Puerto Rico. For taxable years beginning after May 17, 2006, the amount of the deduction for a taxable year is limited to 50 percent of the wages paid by the taxpayer and properly allocable to domestic production gross receipts during the calendar year that ends in such taxable year. Wages paid to bona fide residents of Puerto Rico generally are not included in the wage limitation amounts. However, effective for the first nine taxable years of a taxpayer beginning after December 31, 2005, and before January 1, 2015, a taxpayer with gross receipts from sources within the Commonwealth of Puerto Rico can treat production activities performed in Puerto Rico as performed in the United States for purposes of determining qualified production activities income, and can take into account wages paid to bona fide residents of Puerto Rico for services performed in Puerto Rico in computing the 50-percent wage limitation, provided all of the taxpayer's gross receipts are subject to the Federal income tax. This Act reinstated and extended this provision for two years, to apply to the first eleven taxable years of a taxpayer beginning after December 31, 2005, and before January 1, 2017.

Modify and extend tax incentives for empowerment zones.—This Act reinstated and extended the tax incentives (including employment credits and low-cost loans) that are provided to businesses located in the 40 Federally-designated empowerment zones (30 in urban areas and 10 in rural areas) for two years, through December 31, 2016. In addition, beginning in 2016, employees will be allowed to meet the enterprise zone facility bond employment requirement if they are residents of the empowerment zone, an enterprise community, or a qualified low-income community within an applicable nominating jurisdiction.

Extend temporary increase in limit on cover over of rum excise taxes to Puerto Rico and the Virgin Islands.—A $13.50-per-proof-gallon excise tax is imposed on distilled spirits produced in or imported into the United States. Under current law, $10.50 per proof gallon of the tax imposed on rum imported into the United States is covered over (paid) to Puerto Rico and the Virgin Islands. A temporary increase in the amount covered over to Puerto Rico and the Virgin Islands to $13.25 per proof gallon expired with respect to rum imported into the United States after December 31, 2014. This Act reinstated and extended the $13.25-per-proof-gallon cover over amount for two years, to apply to rum imported into the United States after December 31, 2014, and before January 1, 2017.

Extend the economic development credit for American Samoa.—Under prior law, a domestic corporation that was an existing possession tax credit claimant with respect to American Samoa and elected the application of the tax credit for its last taxable year beginning before January 1, 2006, was allowed to claim a possession tax credit based on the economic activity-based limitation rules for the first nine taxable years beginning after December 31, 2005, and before January 1, 2015. A domestic corporation that was an existing possession tax credit claimant and did not elect the application of the tax credit for its last taxable year beginning before January 1, 2006, was allowed to claim a possession tax credit based on the economic activity-based limitation rules for the first three taxable years beginning after December 31, 2011, and before January 1, 2015. This Act reinstated and extended the ability of domestic corporations to claim a possession tax credit based on the economic activity-based limitation rules for two years, to apply to taxable years beginning after December 31, 2014, and before January 1, 2017.

Suspend tax on manufacturers of medical devices for two years.—This Act suspended the 2.3-percent excise tax imposed on the sale of any taxable medical device by the manufacturer, producer, or importer of the device, effective for sales after December 31, 2015, and before January 1, 2018.

Tax Incentives for Real Estate Investment

Permanently extend temporary minimum Low-Income Housing tax credit (LIHTC) rate for non-Federally subsidized new buildings.—The LIHTC is provided to owners of qualified low-income rental units. The credit may be claimed over a 10-year period for a portion of the cost of rental housing occupied by tenants having incomes below specified levels. Under prior law, a temporary minimum credit percentage of nine percent was provided for newly constructed non-Federally subsidized buildings that received an allocation of a housing credit dollar amount before January 1, 2015. This Act reinstated and permanently extended the nine-percent rate, effective January 1, 2015.

Permanently extend treatment of basic housing allowances for the purpose of LIHTC income eligibility rules.—In general, to be eligible for the LIHTC, a qualified low-income housing project must satisfy one of two tests at the election of the taxpayer: (1) 20 percent or more of the residential units in the project are both rent-restricted, and occupied by individuals whose income is 50 percent or less of area median gross income; or (2) 40 percent or more of the residential units in the project are both rent-restricted, and occupied by individuals whose income is 60 percent or less of area median gross income. These income requirements are adjusted for family size. Effective for income determinations made after July 30, 2008, and before January 1, 2015, for buildings that are located in certain counties, the basic housing allowance (payments provided under section 403 of title 37, United States Code) provided to military personnel was not included in income for the purpose of LIHTC income eligibility rules. This Act reinstated and permanently extended the disregard of basic housing allowances for purposes of LIHTC income eligibility rules for buildings in those counties, effective for income determinations made after December 31, 2014.

Permanently extend special tax rules applicable to RICs provided under the Foreign Investment in Real Property Tax Act (FIRPTA).—This Act reinstated and permanently extended the following special tax rules applicable to RICs: (1) the exemption from U.S. withholding tax for certain interest-related dividends and short-term capital gain dividends paid by a RIC to a foreign shareholder; and (2) the treatment of RICs as "qualified investment entities" for purposes of the provisions regarding foreign investment in U.S. real property interests.

Tax Incentives for Energy Production and Conservation

Extend credit for nonbusiness energy property.—A tax credit is provided for the purchase of qualified energy efficient improvements to existing homes located in the United States and owned and used by the taxpayer as the taxpayer's principal residence. Under prior law, this credit expired for qualified property placed in service after December 31, 2014. This Act reinstated and extended the credit for two years, to apply to property purchased and placed in service after December 31, 2014, and before January 1, 2017.

Extend credit for alternative fuel vehicle refueling property.—A tax credit is provided for the cost of qualified clean-fuel vehicle refueling property to be used in a trade or business of the taxpayer or installed at the principal residence of the taxpayer. Under prior law, the credit is available for hydrogen and non-hydrogen refueling property placed in service before January 1, 2015. This Act reinstated and extended the credit for hydrogen and non-hydrogen refueling property for two years, to apply to property placed in service after December 31, 2014, and before January 1, 2017.

Extend the credit for two-wheeled plug-in electric vehicles.—Under prior law, a ten-percent credit (capped at $2,500) was available for qualifying two-wheeled plug-in electric vehicles acquired after December 31, 2011, and before January 1, 2014. This Act reinstated and extended the credit for a few years, to apply to such vehicles acquired after December 31, 2014, and before January 1, 2017.

Extend second generation biofuel producer credit.—An income tax credit (generally equal to $1.01 per gallon) is provided to producers of second generation biofuel for fuel produced before January 1, 2015. This Act reinstated and extended the credit for two years, to apply to fuel produced after December 31, 2014, and before January 1, 2017.

Extend credits for renewable diesel and biodiesel fuels.—An excise tax credit (or a payment) of $1.00 is provided for each gallon of biodiesel and agri-biodiesel used by a taxpayer in producing a biodiesel mixture for sale or use in a trade or business. An income tax credit for biodiesel fuels (the biodiesel fuels credit) is also provided. The biodiesel fuels income tax credit is the sum of three credits: (1) the biodiesel mixture credit, which is $1.00 for each gallon of biodiesel and agri-biodiesel used by the taxpayer in the production of a qualified biodiesel mixture; (2) the biodiesel credit, which is $1.00 for each gallon of biodiesel and agri-biodiesel that is not in a mixture with diesel when used as a fuel or sold at retail; and (3) the small agri-biodiesel producer credit, which is a 10-cents-per-gallon credit for up to 15 million gallons of agri-biodiesel produced by small producers. Renewable diesel is eligible for the excise tax credit (or payment) and the income tax credit provided to biodiesel fuels at a rate of $1.00 per gallon. Under prior law, these credits and payments expired with respect to fuel sold or used after December 31, 2014. This Act reinstated and extended for two years, through December 31, 2016, these credits and payments for biodiesel and renewable diesel fuels.

Modify and extend credit for the production of Indian coal.—A credit is available for the production of coal from reserves owned by Indian tribes at a qualified facility (a facility placed in service before January 1, 2009) for the nine-year period beginning January 1, 2006, through December 31, 2014. This Act reinstated and extended the credit for two years, to apply to production for the eleven-year period beginning January 1, 2006, through December 31, 2016. This Act also modified the credit beginning in 2016 by removing the placed-in-service date limitation and allowing the credit to be claimed against the AMT.

Extend tax credit with respect to facilities producing energy from certain renewable sources.—Taxpayers are allowed a tax credit for electricity produced from wind, closed-loop biomass, open-loop biomass, geothermal energy, solar energy, small irrigation power, municipal solid waste, qualified hydropower, and marine and hydrokinetic renewable energy at qualified facilities (the renewable electricity production credit). To qualify for the credit, electricity generally must be sold by the taxpayer to an unrelated person and must be produced at a qualified facility. For the production of electricity from solar energy or small irrigation power, a facility is qualified if it was placed in service before January 1, 2006, and October 3, 2008, respectively. For the production of electricity from wind, closed-loop biomass, open-loop biomass, geothermal energy, municipal solid waste, qualified hydropower, and marine and hydrokinetic renewable energy, a facility is qualified if construction began before January 1, 2015. This Act reinstated and extended for two years, through December 31, 2016, the date on which construction must commence for a facility that produces electricity from closed-loop biomass, open-loop biomass, geothermal energy, municipal solid waste, qualified hydropower, and marine and hydrokinetic renewable energy to be a qualified facility. This Act also extended for two years, through December 31, 2016, the election to treat qualified facilities as energy property eligible for the 30-percent energy production credit, in lieu of the renewable electricity production credit.

Extend credit for the construction of energy-efficient new homes.—An eligible contractor is provided a tax credit for each qualified new energy-efficient home that is constructed and acquired from the contractor by a person for use as a residence for homes purchased before January 1, 2015. This Act reinstated and extended the credit for two years, to apply to homes purchased after December 31, 2014, and before January 1, 2017.

Extend special allowance for second generation biofuel plant property.—This Act reinstated and extended the additional first-year depreciation deduction, equal to 50 percent of the adjusted basis of qualified second generation biofuel plant property, for two years, to apply to such property placed in service before January 1, 2017.

Extend deduction for energy-efficient commercial building property.—A deduction is provided for the cost of energy-efficient commercial building property placed in service before January 1, 2015. This Act reinstated and extended the deduction for two years, to apply to such property placed in service after December 31, 2014, and before January 1, 2017. This Act also updated the standard against which energy savings are measured in the definition of energy efficient commercial building property.

Extend special rules for sales or dispositions to implement Federal Energy Regulatory Commission (FERC) or State electric restructuring rules for qualified electric utilities.—Under a special provision of prior law, taxpayers were allowed to elect to recognize gain from the sale or disposition of qualifying electric transmission property before January 1, 2015 ratably over an eight-year period beginning in the year of sale if the amount realized from such sale was used to purchase exempt utility property (reinvestment property) within the applicable period. Any gain realized in excess of the amount used to purchase the reinvestment property was recognized as income in the year of the qualifying electric transmission transaction. This Act reinstated and extended this special rule for two years, to apply to the sale or disposition of qualifying electric transmission property after December 31, 2014, and before January 1, 2017.

Extend alternative fuels excise tax credits.—Two per-gallon excise tax credits are available for the production of alternative fuel: the alternative fuel credit and the alternative fuel mixture credit. Alternative fuel means liquefied petroleum gas, P Series fuels, compressed or liquefied natural gas, liquefied hydrogen, liquid fuel derived from coal through the Fischer-Tropsch process, compressed or liquefied gas derived from biomass, or liquefied fuel derived from biomass. The alternative fuel credit is 50 cents per gallon of alternative fuel or gasoline gallon equivalents of nonliquid alternative fuel sold by the taxpayer for use as a motor fuel in a motor vehicle or motorboat, sold for use in aviation or so used by the taxpayer. The alternative fuel mixture credit is 50 cents per gallon of alternative fuel used in producing an alternative fuel mixture for sale or use in a trade or business of the taxpayer. A taxpayer is also allowed to file a claim for payment equal to the amount of the alternative fuel credit. Under prior law, these credits and payments expired with respect to fuel used or sold after December 31, 2014. This Act reinstated and extended the alternative fuel credit, the alternative fuel mixture credit, and related payments, to apply to fuel sold or used before January 1, 2017. In light of the retroactive nature of the provision as it relates to fuel sold or used in 2015, a special rule is provided to address claims regarding credits and payments associated with that year.

Extend credit for new qualified fuel cell motor vehicles.—A credit is provided for the purchase of new fuel cell vehicles. The amount of the credit ranges from $4,000 to $40,000, depending on the weight of the vehicle. Under prior law, the credit expired for vehicles purchased after December 31, 2014. This Act reinstated and extended the credit for two years, to apply to vehicles purchased after December 31, 2014 and before January 1, 2017.

Program Integrity

This Act included a number of provisions that could increase program integrity within the tax system by: (1) accelerating the filing due date for Forms W-2, W-3, and returns and statements reporting nonemployee compensation to January 31 and removing the extended March 31 due date for these electronically filed forms; and prohibiting the payment of credits or refunds to taxpayers receiving the refundable CTC or EITC prior to February 15; (2) establishing a safe harbor from penalties for certain de minimis errors on information returns and payee statements; (3) modifying the rules relating to the issuance, renewal, and expiration of an individual taxpayer identification number (ITIN); (4) prohibiting the filing of retroactive claims for the EITC, CTC or AOTC by requiring that the required TIN be issued on or before the filing due date of the return; (5) extending the paid-preparer due diligence requirements with respect to the EITC to returns claiming the CTC and the AOTC; (6) extending the rules that bar a taxpayer from claiming the EITC for 10 years if convicted of fraud and for two years if found to have recklessly or intentionally disregarded the rules, to apply to the CTC and the AOTC; (7) applying the penalty for erroneous refunds and credits to the EITC and providing reasonable cause relief from the penalty, and applying the accuracy-related penalty to the refundable portion of erroneously claimed refundable credits; (8) increasing the penalty for tax preparers who engage in willful or reckless conduct; (9) requiring that a taxpayer claiming the AOTC provide the employer identification number (EIN) of the educational institution to which the taxpayer makes qualified payments under the credit; and (10) requiring that educational institutions report only qualified tuition and related expenses actually paid on Form 1098-T.

Miscellaneous Provisions

This Act included a number of miscellaneous provisions that modify tax relief provided to families, modify the taxation of real estate investment trusts (REITs), and make other changes to prior tax law. The major miscellaneous provisions that affect receipts are described below.

Modify tax relief provided to families.—This Act included a number of provisions that provided tax relief to families by: (1) excluding payments received under a comprehensive student work-learning-service program operated by a work college (as defined under the Higher Education Act of 1965) from gross income; (2) expanding the definition of qualified higher education expenses eligible for tax-preferred distributions from a qualified tuition program (section 529 account); (3) eliminating the residency requirement for qualified Achieving a Better Life Experience (ABLE) accounts; and (4) excluding from gross income civil damages, restitution, or other monetary awards received by a taxpayer as compensation for a wrongful incarceration.

Modify taxation of REITs and other provisions.— This Act included a number of provisions that modified the taxation of REITs by (1) placing restrictions on tax-free spinoffs involving REITs; (2) increasing the maximum stock ownership a shareholder may have held during the applicable period in a publicly traded REIT (from 5 to 10 percent) to avoid having that stock treated as a U.S. real property interest under FIRPTA or to avoid having a distribution from a publicly traded REIT being subject to FIRPTA; (3) providing that stock of a REIT owned by certain publicly traded foreign entities is not treated as a U.S. real property interest, and, therefore, can be disposed of without triggering FIRPTA withholding, except to the extent the REIT stock owned by such a publicly traded foreign entity is attributable to an investor that owns more than 10 percent of the publicly traded foreign entity; (4) exempting any U.S. real property interest held by, or any distribution received from a REIT by, a foreign pension fund from the application of FIRPTA, including FIRPTA withholding; (5) increasing the rate of withholding of tax on dispositions of most U.S. real property interests (from 10 to 15 percent) for dispositions occurring 60 days after the date of enactment; (6) providing that the "cleansing rule" (applicable to interests in corporations that generally have disposed of all U.S. real property interests during the prior five-year period in fully taxable transactions) applies only to interests in a corporation that has not been a RIC or a REIT during the five-year period ending on the date of the disposition of stock of the corporation; (7) providing new rules and presumptions for purposes of determining whether a RIC or a REIT is domestically controlled; and (8) making dividends derived by a foreign corporation from RICs and REITs ineligible for treatment as dividends from domestic corporations for purposes of determining whether dividends from the foreign corporation that owns shares in the RIC or REIT are eligible for a dividend received deduction.

Prevent transfer of certain losses from tax indifferent parties.—This Act modified the related-party loss rules to prevent losses from being shifted from a tax-indifferent party to another party in whose hands any gain or loss with respect to the property would be subject to U.S. tax. This change is effective for sales and other dispositions of property acquired after December 31, 2015.

Treat certain persons as employers with respect to motion picture projects.—Employment taxes imposed on employers and employees include the Social Security or old age, survivors, and disability insurance (OASDI) tax, equal to 6.2 percent of covered wages up to the OASDI wage base ($118,500 for 2015) and taxes under the Federal Unemployment Tax Act (FUTA), equal to six percent of wages up to the FUTA wage base of $7,000. In each case, wages that exceed the applicable wage base are not subject to the otherwise applicable employment tax. A separate wage base applies to each employer that employs an individual during the calendar year. This Act modifies the application of the wage base to remuneration paid by a motion picture employer to a motion picture worker by treating all such remuneration as paid by a single employer without regard to whether the worker is a common law employee of multiple clients of the motion picture employer during the year. As a result, a single OASDI wage base and a single FUTA wage base will apply to all such remuneration paid during a calendar year.

Expand and modify the alternative tax for certain small non-life insurance companies.—This Act increased the maximum amount of annual premiums from $1.2 million to $2.2 million that a small non-life insurance company may receive and still elect to be taxed only on its taxable investment income. The $2.2 million amount refers to a company's net written premiums (or, if greater, its direct written premiums) for a taxable year. This threshold amount is indexed for inflation beginning in 2016. The Act also added a diversification requirement for electing companies, effective for taxable years beginning after December 31, 2016. No more than 20 percent of premiums for a taxable year be attributable to a single policyholder, where all related policyholders are treated as one. If this requirement is not met, then a company may still qualify as long as each owner of an interest in the insurance company that is a spouse or lineal descendant of an owner of the business or assets being insured by the insurance company does not own a greater (direct or indirect) percentage interest in the insurance company than he or she has in the insured business or insured assets.

Tax Administration

This Act included a number of provisions related to tax administration, including a number of IRS reforms that: (1) require the Commissioner to ensure that IRS employees are familiar with and act in accordance with certain taxpayer rights; (2) prohibit IRS employees from using personal e-mail accounts for official business; (3) permit the IRS to disclosure to the taxpayer the status of an investigation regarding a claim of unauthorized disclosure or inspection of the taxpayer's return or return information or unlawful acts by revenue officers or agents: (4) require the establishment of procedures under which a 501(c) organization may request an administrative appeal of an adverse determination; (5) require the establishment of a notification process for organizations claiming tax-exemption under section 501(c)(4); (6)

provide for the termination of IRS employees who take official actions for political purposes; and (7) extend IRS authority to permit truncated social security numbers on Forms W-2 furnished to employees. This Act also provides that the gift tax is not to apply to contributions to certain exempt organizations that are described in section 501(c)(4), (5) or)(6).

Trade-Related Provisions

Modify effective date of provisions relating to tariff classification of recreational performance outer wear.—This Act delayed implementation of changes in the classification of certain recreation performance outerwear products that would inadvertently increase tariffs on some of those products. The implementation is delayed from the 180th day after the enactment of the Trade Preferences Extension Act of 2015 on June 29, 2015, to March 31, 2016.

Reduce rates of duty on certain environmental goods to fulfill an agreement by Asia-Pacific Economic Cooperation members.—This Act ensured that the reduction of tariffs on certain environmental goods to fulfill an agreement by members of the Asia-Pacific Economic Cooperation (APEC) forum is implemented in accordance with the Bipartisan Congressional Trade Priorities and Accountability Act of 2015.

TAX RELATED PROVISIONS (DIVISION P)

Delay tax on high-cost employer-sponsored health insurance coverage.—This Act delayed the excise tax on high-cost employer-sponsored health insurance coverage for two years, making the tax effective for taxable years beginning after December 31, 2019. This Act also provided for the deductibility of the tax by taxpayers.

Place a one-year moratorium on tax levied on health insurance providers.—This Act placed a one-year moratorium on the excise tax levied on health insurance providers under section 9010 of the ACA, effective for calendar year 2017.

Modify and extend tax credit with respect to facilities producing energy from wind.—This Act extended through December 31, 2019, the date by which construction must commence for a facility that produces electricity from wind to qualify for the renewable electricity production tax credit, and included annual reductions in the credit rate for facilities that begin construction after 2016. This Act also extended through December 31, 2019, the election to treat qualified facilities as energy property eligible for the energy property investment credit, in lieu of the renewable electricity production credit and phased out the energy percentage for facilities that begin construction after 2016.

Modify and extend investment tax credit for solar energy property.—This Act extended for five years the 30 percent business investment tax credit for solar energy property (equipment) used to generate electricity, to heat or cool a structure, or to provide solar process heat (except for the purpose of heating a swimming pool), effective for property on which construction commences after December 31, 2016, and before January 1, 2022. This Act reduced the rate of the credit from 30 percent to 26 percent for property on which construction commences after December 31, 2019, and before January 1, 2021, and to 22 percent for property on which construction commences after December 31, 2020 and before January 1, 2022. The energy percentage is 10 percent for eligible property on which construction begins before January 1, 2022, that is not placed in service before January 1, 2024. A permanent 10 percent credit is available to property on which construction begins on or after January 1, 2022.

Modify and extend tax credit for residential energy efficient solar property.—This Act extended for five years the tax credit provided to individuals for expenditures made on qualified solar electric property and qualified solar water heating property, to apply to purchases made by the taxpayer after December 31, 2016, and before January 1, 2022. A qualified solar electric property expenditure is an expenditure for property that uses solar energy to generate electricity for use in a dwelling unit located in the United States and used as a residence by the taxpayer. A qualified solar water heating property expenditure is an expenditure for property to heat water for use in a dwelling unit located in the United States and used as a residence by the taxpayer, if at least half of the energy used by the property for that purpose is derived from the sun. This Act also reduced the rate of the credit from 30 percent to 26 percent, effective for property placed in service after December 31, 2019, and before January 1, 2021, and to 22 percent, effective for property placed in service after December 31, 2020, and before January 1, 2022.

Modify treatment of transportation costs of independent refiners.—This Act temporarily exempted 75 percent of qualified transportation costs of certain independent refiners from the calculation of their domestic production activities, effective for taxable years beginning after December 31, 2021, and before January 1, 2022.

BUDGET PROPOSALS

The number of special deductions, credits, and other tax preferences provided to businesses in the Internal Revenue Code has expanded significantly since the last comprehensive tax reform effort nearly three decades ago. Such tax preferences help well-connected special interests, but do little for economic growth. To be successful in an increasingly competitive global economy, the Nation cannot afford to maintain a tax code burdened with such tax breaks; instead, the tax code needs to ensure that the United States is the most attractive place for entrepreneurship and business growth. Therefore, the President's Budget includes a detailed set of business tax reform proposals to achieve the following five goals: (1) cut the corporate tax rate and pay for it by making structural reforms and eliminating loopholes and subsidies; (2) strengthen American manufacturing and innovation; (3) strengthen the international tax system; (4) simplify and cut taxes for small businesses; and (5) avoid adding to deficits in the short-term or the long-term.

The Administration's receipt proposals begin the process of comprehensively reforming the Internal Revenue Code to help address the challenges faced by working families. These proposals: (1) help make work pay by expanding the EITC for workers without qualifying children and creating a new second-earner credit; (2) reform and simplify tax incentives that help families save for retirement and pay for college and child care; and (3) reform' capital gains taxation to eliminate a loophole that lets substantial capital gains income escape tax forever. They also reduce the deficit and make the tax system fairer by eliminating a number of tax loopholes and reducing tax benefits for higher-income taxpayers. The Administration's proposals that affect receipts are described below.

ELEMENTS OF BUSINESS TAX REFORM

Reform the U.S. International Tax System

Restrict deductions for excessive interest of members of financial reporting groups.—Section 163(j) of the Internal Revenue Code generally places a cap on the amount of interest expense paid to related parties (and to unrelated parties on debt guaranteed by a related party) that a corporation can deduct relative to its U.S. earnings, but does not consider whether a foreign-parented group's U.S. operations are more leveraged than the rest of the group's operations. In lieu of applying section 163(j), the Administration's proposal would limit the interest expense deduction of an entity that is a member of a group that prepares consolidated financial statements if the member's net interest expense for financial statement purposes exceeds the member's proportionate share of the group's financial statement net interest expense (excess financial statement net interest expense). The member's share of the groups' financial statement net interest expense would be determined based on the member's proportionate share of the group's reported earnings. If a member has excess financial statement net interest expense, that member will have excess net interest expense for tax purposes for which a deduction is disallowed in the same proportion that the member's net interest expense for financial statement purposes is excess financial statement net interest expense. Alternatively, if a member fails to substantiate its share of the group's net interest expense, or a member so elects, the member's interest deduction would be limited to 10 percent of the member's U.S. adjusted taxable income. The proposal would not apply to financial services entities or financial reporting groups that would otherwise report less than $5 million of net U.S. interest expense for a taxable year. The proposal would be effective for taxable years beginning after December 31, 2016.

Provide tax incentives for locating jobs and business activity in the United States and remove tax deductions for shipping jobs overseas.—To provide a tax incentive for U.S. companies to move jobs into the United States from offshore, the Administration proposes to create a credit against income tax equal to 20 percent of the expenses paid or incurred in connection with insourcing a U.S. trade or business. In addition, to reduce incentives for U.S. companies to move jobs offshore, the proposal would disallow deductions for expenses paid or incurred in connection with outsourcing a U.S. trade or business. For this purpose, insourcing (outsourcing) a U.S. trade or business means reducing or eliminating a trade or business or line of business currently conducted outside (inside) the United States and starting up, expanding, or otherwise moving the same trade or business within (outside) the United States. Also for this purpose, expenses paid or incurred in connection with insourcing or outsourcing a U.S. trade or business are limited solely to expenses associated with the relocation of the trade or business and do not include capital expenditures, severance pay, or other assistance to displaced workers. The proposal would be effective for expenses paid or incurred after the date of enactment.

Repeal delay in the implementation of worldwide interest allocation.—The rules for allocating and apportioning interest expense between U.S. and foreign source income are based on the theory that money is fungible and, therefore, interest expense is properly attributable to all investments of a taxpayer. Under current law, however, interest expense of the domestic members of a worldwide group of companies is allocated by treating only the domestic members as a single corporation. Consequently, U.S. members are required to allocate their U.S. interest expense to their U.S. and foreign investments without taking into account any third party interest expense incurred by foreign members of the group. Under current law, an election is available for taxable years beginning after December 31, 2020, to allow members of an affiliated group of U.S. corporations to allocate interest on a worldwide group basis under which interest expense incurred in the United States would be allocated against foreign-source income only to the extent that the debt-to-asset ratio is higher for U.S. than for foreign investments. Under the Administration's proposal, this election would be permitted for taxable years beginning after December 31, 2016.

Impose a 19-percent minimum tax on foreign income.—Subject to certain limited exceptions under subpart F, U.S. companies are able to defer paying U.S. tax on the profits earned by their CFCs until the profits are repatriated. This ability to defer U.S. tax creates an incentive for U.S. multinationals to locate production overseas and shift profits abroad, eroding the U.S. tax base. In addition, the current system discourages these companies from bringing low-taxed foreign earnings back to the United States. To address these problems, the Administration proposes to supplement the existing subpart F regime with a per-country minimum tax on foreign earnings.

Under the Administration's proposal, foreign earnings, other than subpart F income, would be subject to current U.S. taxation at a rate of 19 percent less 85 percent of the per-country foreign effective tax rate. The tentative minimum tax base for each country would be the total earnings of all business units that are tax resident in that country under foreign law, net of dividends received. The tentative minimum tax base would be reduced by an allowance for corporate equity that would provide a risk-free return on equity invested in active assets. The minimum tax would be imposed on foreign earnings regardless of whether they are repatriated to the United States, and all foreign earnings of a CFC could be repatriated without further U.S. tax. Thus under the proposal, all CFC earnings would be subject to U.S. tax either immediately or not at all.

Foreign source royalty and interest payments paid to U.S. persons would be taxed at the U.S. statutory rate, but certain income attributable to a foreign branch or to the performance of services abroad would be eligible for taxation at the minimum tax rate. Interest expense allocated and apportioned to earnings for which the minimum tax is paid would be deductible at the U.S. minimum tax rate on those earnings. No deduction would be permitted for interest expense allocated and apportioned to foreign earnings for which no U.S. income tax is paid. While subpart F generally would continue in effect as under current law, the rules regarding CFC investments in U.S. property and previously taxed earnings would be repealed, and the subpart F high-tax exception would be made mandatory. In addition, the look-through exception, excluding from subpart F income interest, dividends, rents and royalties received or accrued from a related CFC (to the extent attributable or properly allocable to income of the CFC that is neither subpart F income nor income treated as effectively connected with the conduct of a trade or business in the United States), currently applicable to taxable years of foreign corporations beginning after December 31, 2005 and before January 1, 2020, would be permanently extended, and income qualifying for the look-through exception would be subject to the minimum tax. The proposal would be effective for taxable years beginning after December 31, 2016.

Impose a 14-percent one-time tax on previously untaxed foreign income.—Under current law, U.S. multinational companies do not pay U.S. tax on the profits earned by their CFCs until those profits are repatriated, subject to a limited exception under subpart F for passive and other highly mobile income. Under the Administration's proposal for companies to pay a minimum tax on foreign income, no U.S. tax would be imposed on a CFC's payment of a dividend to a U.S. shareholder. Therefore, the Administration proposes to impose a one-time 14-percent tax on the accumulated earnings of CFCs that were not previously subject to U.S. tax. A credit would be allowed for the amount of foreign income taxes associated with such earnings, multiplied by the ratio of the one-time tax rate to the otherwise applicable U.S. corporate tax rate. The earnings subject to the one-time tax could then be repatriated without any further U.S. tax.

Limit shifting of income through intangible property transfers.—Under current law, there is a lack of clarity regarding the scope of the definition of intangible property under section 936(h)(3)(B) of the Internal Revenue Code. This definition of intangible property applies for purposes of the special rules under section 367 of the Internal Revenue Code relating to transfers of intangible property by a U.S. person to a foreign corporation and the allocation of income and deductions among taxpayers under section 482 of the Internal Revenue Code to prevent inappropriate shifting of income outside the United States. The Administration's proposal would provide that the definition of intangible property under section 936(h)(3)(B) (and therefore for purposes of sections 367 and 482) also includes workforce in place, goodwill and going concern value, and any other item owned or controlled by a taxpayer that is not a tangible or financial asset and that has substantial value independent of the services of any individual. The proposal would be effective for taxable years beginning after December 31, 2016.

Disallow the deduction for excess non-taxed reinsurance premiums paid to affiliates.—U.S affiliates of foreign insurance companies can avoid U.S. taxation of their profits from their U.S. insurance business by reinsuring that business with affiliated foreign insurance companies. Under the Administration's proposal, a U.S. insurance company would be denied a deduction for certain non-taxed reinsurance premiums paid to foreign affiliates, offset by an income exclusion for return premiums, ceding commissions, reinsurance recovered, or other amounts received from such affiliates. A foreign corporation that is paid premiums that would be affected by this provision could instead elect to treat those premiums and the associated investment income as income effectively connected with the conduct of a trade or business in the United States and attributable to a permanent establishment for tax treaty purposes. For foreign tax credit purposes, such effectively connected income would be treated as foreign source income and would be placed into a separate category for purposes of applying the credit limitation rules. The proposal would be effective for policies issued in taxable years beginning after December 31, 2016.

Modify tax rules for dual capacity taxpayers.—The Administration proposes to tighten the foreign tax credit rules that apply to taxpayers that are subject to a foreign levy and that also receive (directly or indirectly) a specific economic benefit from the levying country (so-called "dual capacity" taxpayers). The proposal would be effective for taxable years beginning after December 31, 2016.

Tax gain from the sale of a partnership interest on look-through basis.—Under the Administration's proposal, gain or loss from the sale of a partnership interest would be treated as effectively connected with the conduct of a trade or business in the United States and subject to U.S. income taxation to the extent attributable to the partner's share of the partnership's unrealized gain or loss from property used in a trade or business in the United States. The proposal would also require the purchaser of a partnership interest to withhold 10 percent of the purchase price to ensure the seller's compliance. The proposal would be effective for sales and exchanges after December 31, 2016.

Modify sections 338(h)(16) and 902 to limit credits when non-double taxation exists.—The Administration proposes to modify the foreign tax credit rules to reduce the availability of foreign tax credits in circumstances where no double taxation would otherwise exist. Under section 338 of the Internal Revenue Code, taxpayers can elect to treat certain acquisitions of the stock of a corporation as an acquisition of the corporation's assets for U.S. tax purposes. Because this election does not alter the foreign tax consequences of the transaction, section 338(h)(16) limits the ability of taxpayers to claim additional foreign tax credits by generally requiring the seller to continue to treat the gain recognized on the transaction as gain from the sale of stock for foreign tax credit purposes. The Administration proposes to extend these rules to other similar transactions that are treated as asset acquisitions for U.S. tax purposes but as acquisitions of an equity interest in an entity for foreign tax purposes. In addition, under the Administration's proposal, foreign income taxes paid by a foreign corporation would be reduced for U.S. tax purposes if a redemption transaction results in the elimination of earnings and profits of the foreign corporation. The foreign income taxes reduced under the proposal would be the foreign income taxes that are associated with the eliminated earnings and profits. The proposals would be effective for transactions occurring after December 31, 2016.

Close loopholes under subpart F.—Certain rules under subpart F rely on technical distinctions that may be manipulated or circumvented contrary to subpart F's policy of requiring current U.S. taxation of passive and other highly mobile income earned by CFCs. In order to close these loopholes, the Administration proposes to: (1) create a new category of subpart F income, foreign base company digital income, which generally would include income of a CFC from the lease or sale of a digital copyrighted article or from the provision of a digital service in cases where the CFC uses intangible property developed by a related party (including property developed under a cost sharing arrangement) to produce the income and the CFC does not, through its own employees, make a substantial contribution to the development of the property or services that give rise to the income; (2) expand the category of foreign base company sales income to include income of a CFC from the sale of property manufactured on behalf of the CFC by a related person, regardless of whether the CFC is characterized as obtaining the property through a purchase transaction or through a manufacturing service contract; (3) amend the ownership attribution rules of section 958(b) of the Internal Revenue Code so that certain stock directly owned by a foreign person is attributed to a related U.S. person for purposes of determining whether a foreign corporation is a CFC or a U.S. person is a U.S. shareholder; and (4) eliminate the requirement that a foreign corporation must be a CFC for an uninterrupted period of at least 30 days in order for a U.S. shareholder

to have a subpart F income inclusion with respect to the corporation. The proposal would be effective for taxable years beginning after December 31, 2016.

Restrict the use of hybrid arrangements that create stateless income.—Taxpayers currently use a variety of cross-border hybrid arrangements to claim deductions without corresponding inclusions in any jurisdiction or to claim multiple deductions for the same payment in different jurisdictions. The Administration proposes to deny deductions for interest and royalty payments paid to related parties when either: (1) as a result of a hybrid arrangement there is no corresponding inclusion to the recipient in the foreign jurisdiction; or (2) a hybrid arrangement would permit the taxpayer to claim an additional deduction for the same payment in more than one jurisdiction. Additionally, sections 954(c)(3) and 954(c)(6) of the Internal Revenue Code would not apply to payments made to a foreign reverse hybrid held directly by a U.S. owner when such amounts are treated as deductible payments by a foreign related person. Regulatory authority would be granted to the Department of the Treasury to issue any regulations necessary to carry out the purposes of this proposal, including regulations that would deny all or a portion of the deduction claimed with respect to an interest or royalty payment that, as a result of the hybrid arrangement, is subject to inclusion in the recipient's jurisdiction pursuant to a preferential regime that has the effect of reducing the generally applicable statutory rate by at least 25 percent. The proposal would be effective for taxable years beginning after December 31, 2016.

Limit the ability of domestic entities to expatriate.—Section 7874 of the Internal Revenue Code applies to certain transactions (known as "inversion transactions") in which a U.S. corporation is replaced by a foreign corporation as the parent company of a worldwide affiliated group. Under current law, if an inversion transaction occurs, certain adverse tax consequences apply depending upon whether the continuing ownership of historical shareholders of the U.S. corporation in the foreign acquiring corporation is either 80 percent or more (in which case the foreign acquiring corporation is treated as a domestic corporation for all U.S. tax purposes) or at least 60 percent but less than 80 percent (in which case the foreign status of the acquiring corporation is respected but other penalties apply). The Administration proposes to broaden the definition of an inversion transaction by reducing the 80-percent shareholder continuity threshold to a greater-than-50-percent threshold, and by eliminating the 60-percent threshold. The Administration also proposes to provide that, regardless of the level of shareholder continuity, an inversion transaction will occur if the fair market value of the stock of the U.S. corporation is greater than the fair market value of the stock of the foreign acquiring corporation, and the affiliated group is primarily managed and controlled in the United States and does not conduct substantial business activities in the relevant foreign country. In addition, the proposal would provide the IRS with authority to share with authorized employees of other Federal agencies, upon request, information collected with respect to the identity of companies that are the subject of an inversion transaction. The proposal generally would be effective for transactions that are completed after December 31, 2016, except that, effective January 1, 2017, the proposal would provide the IRS with the authority to share with other Federal agencies the specified information without regard to when the inversion transaction occurred.

Simplification and Tax Relief for Small Business

Expand expensing for small business.—Business taxpayers are allowed to expense up to $500,000 in annual investment expenditures for qualifying property. However, only $25,000 of the cost of any sport utility vehicle (SUV) may be taken into account. The maximum amount that can be expensed is reduced by the amount by which the taxpayer's cost of qualifying property exceeds $2 million. The maximum expensing limit and the phase-out threshold amount are indexed for inflation for taxable years beginning after December 31, 2015. The Administration proposes to increase the maximum expensing limit to $1 million, indexed for inflation, effective for qualifying property placed in service in taxable years beginning after December 31, 2016. The $25,000 expensing limit for SUVs would also be indexed for inflation for taxable years beginning after December 31, 2016.

Expand simplified accounting for small business and establish a uniform definition of small business for accounting methods.—Current law contains several small business exceptions from various accounting requirements based on a taxpayer's average annual gross receipts. Exception thresholds vary between $1 million and $25 million of gross receipts, depending on the specific accounting rule, and the legal status and business activity of the taxpayer. The Administration proposes to create a uniform small business threshold at $25 million in average annual gross receipts for allowing exceptions from certain accounting rules, effective for taxable years beginning after December 31, 2016. This threshold would be indexed for inflation with respect to taxable years beginning after December 31, 2017. Satisfaction of the gross receipts test would allow an entity to elect one or more of the following items: (1) use of the cash method of accounting in lieu of an accrual method (regardless of whether the entity holds inventories); (2) the non-application of the uniform capitalization (UNICAP) rules; and (3) the use of an inventory method of accounting that either conforms to the taxpayer's financial accounting method or is otherwise properly reflective of income. These rules would supersede the special cash method exceptions that apply to farm corporations, but current exceptions allowing the cash method by personal service corporations and by business entities that are not C corporations (other than partnerships with a C corporation partner) would continue. The exceptions from UNICAP not based on a gross receipts test would also continue.

Increase the limitations for deductible new business expenditures and consolidate provisions for start-up and organizational expenditures.—A taxpayer generally is allowed to elect to deduct up to $5,000

of start-up expenditures in the taxable year in which an active trade or business begins. Similarly, a taxpayer may also elect to deduct up to $5,000 of organizational expenditures in the taxable year in which a corporation or partnership begins business. In each case, the $5,000 amount is reduced (but not below zero), by the amount by which such expenditures exceed $50,000. To lower the tax cost of investigating new business opportunities and investing in new business activities, as well as tax administration and business compliance costs, the Administration proposes to consolidate the Internal Revenue Code provisions relating to start-up expenditures and organizational expenditures and to double permanently, from $10,000 to $20,000, the combined amount of new business expenditures that a taxpayer may elect to deduct, effective for taxable years beginning after December 31, 2016. That amount would be reduced (but not below zero) by the amount by which the combined new business expenditures exceed $120,000. Start-up and organizational expenditures that are not deducted under these provisions would continue to be amortized over a 180-month period, beginning with the month in which the active trade or business begins.

Expand and simplify the tax credit provided to qualified small employers for non-elective contributions to employee health insurance.—The ACA provides a tax credit to help small employers provide health insurance for employees and their families. To claim the credit, a qualified employer must have fewer than 25 full-time equivalent employees during the taxable year, pay annual full-time equivalent employee wages that average less than $50,000 and make non-elective uniform contributions of at least 50 percent of the premium. The credit is generally available only for health insurance purchased through an Affordable Insurance Exchange and only for a maximum coverage period of two consecutive taxable years. The maximum credit, which is a specified percentage of premiums the employer pays during the taxable year, is reduced on a sliding scale between 10 and 25 full-time equivalent employees as well as between average annual wages of $25,000 and $50,000. Because the reductions are additive, an employer with fewer than 25 full-time equivalent employees paying average wages of less than $50,000 might not be eligible for any tax credit. The qualified amount of the employer contribution on which the credit is based is reduced if the premium for the coverage purchased exceeds the average premium for the small group market in the rating areas in which the employee enrolls for coverage.

The Administration proposes to expand the credit to employers with up to 50 (rather than 25) full-time equivalent employees and to begin the phaseout of the maximum credit at 20 full-time equivalent employees (the credit would be reduced on a sliding scale between 20 and 50, rather than between 10 and 25, full-time equivalent employees). In addition, there would be a change to the coordination of the phaseouts of the credit that apply as the number of employees and average wages increase (using a formula that is multiplicative rather than additive) so as to provide a more gradual combined phaseout and to ensure that employers with fewer than 50 employees and an average wage less than $50,000 may be eligible for the credit, even if they are nearing the end of both phaseouts. The Administration also proposes to reduce taxpayer complexity by eliminating the requirement that an employer make a uniform contribution on behalf of each employee (although applicable non-discrimination laws will still apply), and eliminating the reduction in the qualifying contribution for premiums that exceed the average premium in the rating area. The proposal would be effective for taxable years beginning after December 31, 2015.

Incentives for Job Creation, Manufacturing, Research, and Clean Energy

Enhance and simplify research incentives.—The R&E tax credit calculated according to the "traditional" method is 20 percent of qualified research and experimentation expenditures above an historic base amount. An alternative simplified credit (ASC) of 14 percent is also provided. The Administration proposes to repeal the traditional method, which would not apply for expenditures paid or incurred after December 31, 2016. In addition, for expenditures paid or incurred after December 31, 2016, the following changes would apply: (1) the rate of the ASC would be increased to 18 percent; (2) the reduced ASC rate of 6 percent for businesses without qualified research expenses in the prior three years would be eliminated; (3) the credit would be allowed to offset AMT liability for all taxpayers; (4) contract research expenses would include 75 percent of payments to qualified non-profit organizations (such as educational institutions) for qualified research; and (5) the special rule for owners of a pass-through entity, which limits the amount of credit to the amount of tax attributable to that portion of a person's taxable income that is allocable or apportionable to the person's interest in such trade, business or entity would be repealed.

In addition, the proposal would repeal the requirement that research and experimentation costs be amortized over 10 years when calculating individual AMT. This would apply to expenditures paid or incurred after December 31, 2016.

Extend and modify certain employment tax credits, including incentives for hiring veterans.—The WOTC provides incentives to employers for hiring individuals from one or more of nine targeted groups and the Indian employment tax credit provides incentives to employers for hiring individuals who are members of an Indian tribe. The Indian employment tax credit applies to increases in qualified wages and health insurance costs over qualified wages and health insurance costs incurred in calendar year 1993 (the base year). The Administration proposes to permanently extend both credits, which include the Returning Heroes and Wounded Warrior credits enacted in 2011. In addition, beginning in 2017, the Administration proposes to: (1) expand the definition of disabled veterans eligible for the WOTC to include disabled veterans who use the GI bill to receive education or

training starting within one year after discharge and who are hired within six months of leaving the program; and (2) modify the Indian employment tax credit by changing the base year wages and health insurance costs to the average of those costs in the two years prior to the year for which the credit is being claimed.

Provide new Manufacturing Communities tax credit.—The Administration proposes to provide new tax credit authority to support qualified investments in communities affected by military base closures or mass layoffs, such as those arising from plant closures. This would provide about $2 billion in credits for qualified investments approved in each of the three years, 2017 through 2019.

Provide Community College Partnership tax credit.—The Administration proposes a new tax credit authority to support collaboration between employers and community or technical colleges to encourage employer engagement and investment in these education and training pathways, and to facilitate the hiring of graduates of such colleges. This would provide $500 million in credit authority for each of the five years, 2017 through 2021. The credit authority would be allocated annually to States on a per capita basis. Credits would be available to qualifying employers that hire qualifying community college graduates. The designated State agency would competitively award credit authority to qualifying community college consortia and certify employers' participation and eligibility to claim the credit.

Designate Promise Zones.—The Administration proposes to provide two tax incentives to the 20 designated Promise Zones. First, an employment credit would be provided to businesses that employ zone residents that would apply to the first $15,000 of qualifying wages annually. The credit rate would be 20 percent for zone residents who are employed within the zone and 10 percent for zone residents employed outside of the zone. Second, qualifying property placed in service within the zone would be eligible for additional first-year depreciation of 100 percent of the adjusted basis of the property. Qualifying property would generally consist of depreciable property with a recovery period of 20 years or less. Zone designations for the purpose of the tax incentives would be in effect from January 1, 2017, through December 31, 2026.

Modify and permanently extend renewable electricity production tax credit and investment tax credit.—Current law provides production tax credits for renewable energy facilities. Qualified energy resources include wind, closed-loop biomass, open-loop biomass, geothermal energy, small irrigation power, municipal solid waste, qualified hydropower production, and marine and hydrokinetic renewable energy. Current law also provides an investment tax credit for renewable energy property. The investment tax credit is 30 percent of eligible basis for solar, fuel cell, and small wind property, and 10 percent for microturbine, combined heat and power system property, and geothermal property. Under current law, the production tax credit expires for wind facilities on which construction begins after December 31, 2019 and for eligible renewable sources other than wind, December

31, 2016. The Administration proposes to permanently extend the production tax credit at current credit rates (adjusted annually for inflation), make it refundable, and make it available to otherwise eligible renewable electricity consumed directly by the producer rather than sold to an unrelated third party, to the extent that its production can be independently verified. The production tax credit would also be available to individuals who install qualified solar electric and solar water heating property on a dwelling unit. Individuals would not be permitted to claim both the residential energy efficient property credit and the production tax credit. In addition, the proposal would permanently extend the investment tax credit under the terms available in 2016. Specifically, the proposal would permanently extend the 30-percent investment tax credit for solar (including solar process heat), fuel cell, and small wind property and the 10-percent credit for geothermal, microturbine, and combined heat and power property. The proposal would also make permanent the election to claim the proposed investment tax credit in lieu of the production tax credit for qualified facilities eligible for the production tax credit.

Modify and permanently extend the deduction for energy-efficient commercial building property.—Under current law, taxpayers are allowed to deduct expenditures for energy efficient commercial building property placed in service on or before December 31, 2016. For energy-efficient commercial building property placed in service after calendar year 2016, the Administration proposes to offer fixed deductions for the installation of energy-efficient commercial building property that reach an energy savings target. The proposal would also update the standard against which energy savings are measured in the definition of energy efficient commercial building property. In addition, the proposal would modify the baseline against which the required energy savings are measured for buildings with at least 10 years of occupancy. The new deductions would be permanent.

Provide a carbon dioxide investment and sequestration tax credit.—The Administration proposes to authorize $2 billion in refundable investment tax credits for property installed at a new or retrofitted electric generating unit that captures and permanently "sequesters" carbon dioxide. Projects must capture and store at least one million metric tons of carbon dioxide per year. Projects that treat the entire flue gas stream from an electric generating unit or set of units must sequester at least 50 percent of the carbon dioxide in the stream. Projects that treat only a portion of the flue gas stream must capture at least 80 percent of the carbon dioxide in the stream. The investment tax credit would be available for 30 percent of the installed cost of eligible property. Eligible property includes only property that is part of a new project or retrofit placed in service after December 31, 2015. No more than $800 million of the credits would be allowed to flow to projects that capture and store less than 80 percent of their carbon dioxide emissions. A minimum of 70 percent of the credits must flow to projects fueled by greater than 75 percent coal. The Administration also proposes to provide a 20-year, refundable sequestration tax credit for facilities qualifying for the investment credit at a rate of $50 per metric ton for carbon dioxide permanently sequestered and not beneficially reused and $10 per metric ton for carbon dioxide that is permanently sequestered and beneficially reused. The sequestration credit would be indexed for inflation.

Provide additional tax credits for investment in qualified property used in a qualifying advanced energy manufacturing project.—A 30-percent credit for investment in eligible property used in a qualifying advanced energy manufacturing project was provided under ARRA. A qualifying advanced energy manufacturing project re-equips, expands, or establishes a manufacturing facility for the production of: (1) property designed to be used to produce energy from the sun, wind, geothermal deposits, or other renewable resources; (2) fuel cells, microturbines, or an energy storage system for use with electric or hybrid-electric motor vehicles; (3) electric grids to support the transmission of intermittent sources of renewable energy, including the storage of such energy; (4) property designed to capture and sequester carbon dioxide; (5) property designed to refine or blend renewable fuels (excluding fossil fuels) or to produce energy conservation technologies; (6) new qualified plug-in electric drive motor vehicles or components that are designed specifically for use with such vehicles; or (7) other advanced energy property designed to reduce greenhouse gas emissions as may be determined by the Department of the Treasury. Eligible property must be depreciable (or amortizable) property used in a qualifying advanced energy project and does not include property designed to manufacture equipment for use in the refining or blending of any transportation fuel other than renewable fuels. The credit is available only for projects certified by the Department of the Treasury (in consultation with the Department of Energy). The Administration proposes to provide an additional $2.5 billion in credits, thereby increasing the amount of credits to $4.8 billion. In addition, the Administration proposes to allow up to $200 million of these credits to be allocated to the construction of infrastructure that contributes to networks of refueling stations that serve alternative fuel vehicles.

Extend the tax credit for second generation biofuel production.—The nonrefundable tax credit of $1.01 per gallon for blending cellulosic fuel expires on December 31, 2016. The Administration proposes to extend the tax credit at the expired level through December 31, 2022. The amount of the credit would then be reduced by 20.2 cents per gallon in each subsequent year, so that the credit would expire after December 31, 2026.

Provide a tax credit for the production of advanced technology vehicles.—Current law provides a tax credit for plug-in electric drive motor vehicles. The Administration proposes to replace this credit with a credit for advanced technology vehicles. The credit would be available for a vehicle that meets the following criteria: (1) the vehicle operates primarily on an alternative to petroleum; (2) as of January 1, 2015, there are few vehicles in operation in the United States using the same technology as such vehicle; and (3) the technology used by the vehicle substantially exceeds the footprint-based target miles per gallon. In general, the credit would be scalable based on the vehicle's miles per gallon gasoline equivalent, but would be capped at $10,000 ($7,500 for vehicles with a manufacturer's suggested retail price above $45,000). The credit for a battery-powered vehicle would be determined under current law rules for the credit for plug-in electric drive motor vehicles if that computation results in a greater credit. The credit would be allowed for vehicles placed in service after December 31, 2016, and before January 1, 2024. The credit would be limited to 75 percent of the otherwise allowable amount for vehicles placed in service in 2021, to 50 percent of such amount for vehicles placed in service in 2022, and to 25 percent of such amount for vehicles placed in service in 2023. The credit would be allowed to the vehicle manufacturer and would be transferable.

Provide a tax credit for medium- and heavy-duty alternative-fuel commercial vehicles.—Current law provides no tax incentive for alternative-fuel vehicles (other than fuel-cell vehicles) weighing more than 14,000 pounds. The Administration proposes to provide a tax credit for dedicated alternative-fuel commercial vehicles weighing more than 14,000 pounds. The credit would be $25,000 for vehicles weighing between 14,000 and 26,000 pounds and $40,000 for vehicles weighing more than 26,000 pounds. The credit would be allowed for vehicles placed in service after December 31, 2016, and before January 1, 2023. For vehicles placed in service in calendar year 2022, the credit would be limited to 50 percent of the otherwise allowable amount. The credit would be allowed to the manufacturer of the vehicle and would be transferable. If the credit is transferred to an end-use business purchaser, the purchaser would not be required to reduce the basis of depreciable property by the amount of the credit.

Modify and extend the tax credit for the construction of energy-efficient new homes.—Under the Administration's proposal, the tax credit for energy-efficient new homes, which expires on December 31, 2016, would be replaced with a two-tier credit starting in 2017. The first tier would provide a $1,000 tax credit to homebuilders for the construction of each qualified ENERGY STAR certified new home that meets guidelines for energy efficiency and construction set by the Environmental Protection Agency. The second tier would provide a $4,000 tax credit for the construction of each qualified Department of Energy (DOE) Zero Energy Ready Home certified to meet substantially higher standards for energy savings and construction set by the DOE. To ensure that a new home meets the ENERGY STAR or DOE Zero Energy Ready Home guidelines, verification by a qualified third party would be required. The new credits would apply to qualified new homes acquired from the homebuilder for use as a residence after December 31, 2016, and before January 1, 2027.

Incentives to Promote Regional Growth

Modify and permanently extend the NMTC.—The NMTC is a 39-percent credit for qualified equity investments made in qualified community development entities that are held for a period of seven years. The NMTC provision expires at the end of 2019. The Administration proposes to permanently extend the NMTC. Up to $5 billion in qualifying investment would be allowed in each year beginning in 2020. The proposal would also permit the NMTC to permanently offset AMT liability for qualified equity investments made after December 31, 2019.

Reform and expand the LIHTC.—The LIHTC provides a tax incentive for affordable rental housing developments. The Administration proposes to make several changes to the rules governing LIHTCs. First, States would be empowered to convert some private-activity-bond volume cap into authority to allocate additional LIHTCs. Also, a building would be able to qualify for 30-percent-present-value LIHTCs without issuing bonds if the building receives an adequate allocation of tax-exempt volume cap. This proposal would provide States greater flexibility to address their affordable housing priorities, and would reduce transaction and financing costs. These changes would be effective for new volume cap received by States for calendar years beginning after the date of enactment, or for volume cap that is allocated to a building after that date.

Second, to provide incentives for creating mixed-income housing, projects would be allowed to comply with an income-average rule for LIHTC eligibility. Under this new rule, the average income for at least 40 percent of the units in a project could not exceed 60 percent of area median income (AMI). None of these units could be occupied by households with income greater than 80 percent of AMI. Buildings must meet this new average income threshold calculated both: (1) with all low-income units weighted equally; and (2) with each low-income unit weighted according to imputed LIHTC occupancy rules. For rehabilitation projects containing units that receive ongoing subsidies administered by the Department of Housing and Urban Development or the Department of Agriculture (e.g., rental assistance, operating subsidies, or interest subsidies), a special rule would permit certain non-income qualified tenants to remain in residence without impairing the LIHTCs earned by the project. This provision adds to the two income criteria currently available for LIHTC developments, and would apply to LIHTC elections that are made after the date of enactment.

Third, preservation of federally-assisted affordable housing would be added to the selection criteria for LIHTC allocation. This factor would join the 10 criteria that State housing agencies must include in the qualified action plans that they consider when awarding LIHTCs. This change would apply to allocations made in calendar years beginning after the date of enactment.

Fourth, to remove any doubt, affirmatively furthering fair housing would be made an explicit fourth allocation preference in qualified allocation plans. This change would also apply to allocations made in calendar years beginning after the date of enactment.

Fifth, the Administration proposes to allow the Department of Housing and Urban Development (HUD) to designate as a qualified census tract (QCT) any census tract that meets certain criteria for the prevalence of poverty or low-income households. A building in a QCT earns 30 percent more LIHTCs than it would in another location. The proposal would remove a current limit under which the aggregate population in census tracts designated as QCTs cannot exceed 20 percent of the metropolitan area's population. As a result of this limit, some census tracts with qualifying levels of poverty or low-income households may currently fail to be designated as QCTs because neighboring tracts also qualify. This change would apply to allocations made after the date of enactment.

Sixth, the proposal adds protection for victims of domestic violence as a mandatory provision of the long-term-use agreement required by the Internal Revenue Code between each LIHTC taxpayer and the State. To make the protection meaningful, victims of domestic violence would be given a right to enforce the agreement in State courts.

Incentives for Investment in Infrastructure

Provide America Fast Forward Bonds and expand eligible uses.—ARRA created the Build America Bond program as an optional new lower cost borrowing incentive for State and local governments on taxable bonds issued in 2009 and 2010 to finance new investments in governmental capital projects. Under the original program applicable to Build America Bonds issued in 2009 and 2010, the Department of the Treasury makes direct subsidy payments (called "refundable tax credits") to State and local governmental issuers in a subsidy amount equal to 35 percent of the coupon interest on the bonds. The Administration proposes to create a new permanent America Fast Forward Bond program, which would be an optional alternative to traditional tax-exempt bonds. Like Build America Bonds, America Fast Forward Bonds would be conventional taxable bonds issued by State and local governments in which the Federal Government makes direct payments to State and local governmental issuers (refundable tax credits). The subsidy rate would be 28 percent, which is approximately revenue neutral in comparison to the Federal tax losses from traditional tax-exempt bonds. The Administration proposes to expand the eligible uses for America Fast Forward Bonds beyond those for the Build America Bond program to include financing for governmental capital projects, current refundings of prior public capital project financings, short-term governmental working capital financings for governmental operating expenses subject to a 13-month maturity limitation, financing for section 501(c)(3) nonprofit entities, and financing for the types of projects and programs that can be financed with qualified private activity bonds subject to applicable State bond volume caps for the qualified private activity bond category. Further,

eligible uses would include projects that can be financed with a new category of qualified private activity bond, known as "Qualified Public Infrastructure bonds," under a separate budget proposal described below. The proposal, which would be effective for bonds issued beginning in 2017, recommends exempting direct payments to State and local government issuers under the American Fast Forward Bond program from sequestration under the Balanced Budget and Emergency Deficit Control Act (BBEDCA).

Allow current refundings of State and local governmental bonds.—Current law provides Federal tax subsidies to lower borrowing costs on debt obligations issued by State and local governments for eligible purposes under various programs. These programs include traditional tax-exempt bonds and other temporary or targeted qualified tax credit bond programs (e.g., qualified school construction bonds) and direct borrowing subsidy payment programs (e.g., Build America Bonds). State and local bond programs have varied in the extent to which they expressly allow or treat refinancings (as distinguished from original financings to fund eligible program purposes). In a "current refunding" of State and local bonds, the refunded bonds are retired promptly within 90 days after issuance of the refinancing bonds. These refundings generally reduce borrowing costs for State and local governmental issuers, and they also reduce Federal revenue losses due to the Federal borrowing subsidies for State and local bonds. A general authorization for current refundings of State and local bonds not currently covered by specific refunding authority would promote greater uniformity, tax certainty, and borrowing cost savings. The Administration proposes to allow current refundings of these State and local bonds if: (1) the principal amount of the current refunding bonds is no greater than the outstanding principal amount of the refunded bonds, and (2) the weighted average maturity of the current refunding bonds is no longer than the remaining weighted average maturity of the refunded bonds. This proposal would be effective as of the date of enactment.

Repeal the $150 million non-hospital bond limitation on qualified 501(c)(3) bonds.—The Tax Reform Act of 1986 established a $150 million limit on the volume of outstanding non-hospital, tax-exempt bonds used for the benefit of a section 501(c)(3) organization. The provision was repealed in 1997 with respect to bonds issued after August 5, 1997, at least 95 percent of the net proceeds of which are used to finance capital expenditures incurred after that date. The limitation continues to apply to bonds more than five percent of the net proceeds of which finance or refinance: (1) working capital expenditures, or (2) capital expenditures incurred on or before August 5, 1997. The Administration proposes to repeal in its entirety the $150 million limit on the volume of outstanding, non-hospital, tax-exempt bonds for the benefit of a section 501(c)(3) organization, effective for bonds issued after the date of enactment.

Increase national limitation amount for qualified highway or surface freight transfer facility bonds.—Tax-exempt private activity bonds may be used to finance qualified highway or surface freight transfer facilities. A qualified highway or surface freight transfer facility is any surface transportation, international bridge, or tunnel project that receives Federal assistance under title 23 of the United States Code, or any facility for the transfer of freight from truck to rail or rail to truck that receives Federal assistance under title 23 or title 49 of the United States Code. Tax-exempt bonds issued to finance qualified highway or surface freight transfer facilities are not subject to State volume cap limitations. Instead, the Secretary of Transportation is authorized to allocate a total of $15 billion of issuance authority to qualified highway or surface freight transfer facilities in such manner as the Secretary determines appropriate. The Administration proposes to increase the $15 billion aggregate amount permitted to be allocated by the Secretary of Transportation to $19 billion with the elimination of this category of bond and conversion to qualified public infrastructure bonds once these funds are allocated.

Provide a new category of qualified private activity bonds for infrastructure projects referred to as "qualified public infrastructure bonds" (QPIBs).— Under the proposal, QPIBs, a new category of tax-exempt private activity bonds, would be available for the financing of newly constructed or substantially rehabilitated infrastructure facilities owned by governmental entities and available for general public use. Infrastructure facilities eligible for QPIB financing would include airports, docks and wharves, mass commuting facilities, facilities for the furnishing of water, sewage facilities, solid waste disposal facilities, qualified highway or surface freight transfer facilities, and broadband telecommunications assets for high-speed internet access. Existing overlapping categories of qualified private activity bonds that can be financed with QPIBs generally would be eliminated. The existing category for qualified highway or surface freight transfer facilities would continue to be available for the existing $15 billion bond volume authorization and the proposed additional $4 billion authorization under the preceding proposal. QPIBs would not be subject to volume cap and the interest would not be a preference that is subject to tax under the AMT. The proposal also expands the safe harbor rule for ownership by a governmental unit where such facilities are leased or subject to concession agreements or management contracts to QPIBs, which would open up use of tax-exempt financing for public-private partnerships. The proposal would be effective for bonds issued beginning in 2017.

Modify qualified private activity bonds for public education facilities.—Current law permits tax-exempt private activity bond financing for different specified types of eligible exempt facilities and programs, including, among others, "qualified public educational facilities" that are part of public elementary or secondary schools. The current eligibility rules require that a private "corporation" own the public school facilities under a public-private partnership agreement with a public State or local educational agency and that the private corporation transfer the ownership of the school facilities to the public agency at the end of the term of the bonds for no addi-

tional consideration. The proposal would eliminate the private corporation ownership requirement and instead would allow any private person, including private entities organized in ways other than as corporations, either to own the public school facilities or to operate those school facilities through lease, concession, or other operating arrangements. Further, since private ownership would no longer be an eligibility condition, the proposal would remove the requirement to transfer the school facilities to a public agency at the end of the term of the bonds for no additional consideration. In addition, the proposal would remove the separate volume cap for qualified public educational facilities and instead would include these facilities under the unified annual State bond volume cap. The proposal would be effective for bonds issued after the date of enactment.

Modify treatment of banks investing in tax-exempt bonds.—Under current law, financial institutions' interest deductions are generally reduced by 100 percent of the interest expense allocable to assets that produce tax-exempt interest income. Financial institutions, however, can generally deduct 80 percent of interest expense allocated to qualified small issuer bonds. Qualified small issuer bonds are certain tax-exempt bonds issued by States and localities that annually issue no more than $10 million of such bonds. The proposal would increase the size limit for the qualified small issuer bond exception from $10 million to $30 million. Moreover, under current law, if a bank has made the election to be taxed under subchapter S or if the bank is a qualified subchapter S subsidiary, the bank is exempt even from the 20-percent disallowance of interest expense allocable to qualified small issuer bonds. The proposal would make these banks subject to the 20-percent disallowance and thus would equalize the treatment of financial institutions. Finally, the proposal also would allow financial institutions to deduct up to 80 percent of interest expense allocable to any tax-exempt obligations (whether or not a qualified small issuer bond) subject to a cap that would limit the benefit of this rule to interest expense allocable to bonds representing no more than two percent of the basis of the institution's assets. This two-percent cap, however, would not apply to the qualified small issuer bond exception. The proposal would apply to bonds issued in calendar years beginning on or after January 1, 2017.

Repeal tax-exempt bond financing of professional sports facilities.—Current law permits the use of tax-exempt governmental bond proceeds for private activities unless both of the following apply: (1) more than 10 percent of the payment of the debt service is from a private business source, and (2) more than 10 percent of the use of the facility is for a private business use. Thus, even if use by a professional sports team of a bond-financed stadium exceeds 10 percent of the total use of the facility, the financing will be tax-exempt if the debt service is paid from sources other than sports facility revenues or other private payments. The proposal would eliminate the private payment test for professional sports facilities such that bonds to finance professional sports facilities would be taxable private activity bonds if more than 10 percent of the use of the facility is for a private business purpose. By removing the private payment test, tax-exempt governmental bond financing of sports facilities for professional sports teams would be eliminated. The proposal would be effective for bonds issued after December 31, 2016.

Allow more flexible research arrangements for purposes of private business use limits.—Under current law, the IRS provides safe harbors that allow certain basic research arrangements with private businesses at tax-exempt bond financed research facilities. The existing safe harbors impose certain constraints on setting the terms of use of patents or other products resulting from the research, based on specific legislative history. In particular, the terms of use of resulting products for both research sponsors and other users alike must be set only after the products become available for use even though research arrangements typically are made prior to discoveries. The Administration proposes to provide additional flexibility for bona fide arm's length arrangements relating to basic research that would allow setting the terms of use of resulting products in advance of when the products become available for use. The proposal would be effective for research arrangements entered into after the date of enactment.

Modify tax-exempt bonds for Indian tribal governments (ITGs).—In general, current law limits ITGs in their use of tax-exempt bonds to the financing of certain "essential governmental function" activities that are customarily performed by State and local governments. ARRA provided a limited $2 billion authorization of "Tribal Economic Development Bonds," which gives ITGs more flexibility to use tax-exempt bonds under standards that are more comparable to those applied to State and local governments in their use of tax-exempt bonds (subject to certain express targeting restrictions that require financed projects to be located on Indian reservations and that prohibit the financing of certain gaming facilities). In December 2011, the Department of the Treasury submitted a required report to the Congress regarding its study of the Tribal Economic Development Bond provision and its recommendations for ITG tax-exempt bond financing. The Administration proposes to modify the standards for ITG tax-exempt bond financing to reflect the recommendations in this report. In particular, the Administration's proposal generally would adopt the State or local government standard for tax-exempt governmental bonds without a bond volume cap on such governmental bonds for purposes of ITG eligibility to issue tax-exempt governmental bonds. The proposal would repeal the existing essential governmental function standard for ITG tax-exempt bond financing. In addition, the proposal would allow ITGs to issue tax-exempt private activity bonds for the same types of projects and activities as are allowed for State and local governments, under a modified national bond volume cap to be administered by the Department of the Treasury. Further, the proposal generally would continue an existing targeting restriction that would require projects financed with ITG bonds to be located on Indian reservations, with some additional flexibility to finance projects that have a requisite nexus to Indian res-

ervations and that serve resident populations of Indian reservations. Finally, the proposal would continue an existing targeting restriction that prohibits financing of certain gaming projects. This proposal would be effective as of the date of enactment.

Eliminate Fossil Fuel Tax Preferences

Eliminate fossil fuel tax preferences.—Current law provides a number of credits and deductions that are targeted towards certain oil, natural gas, and coal activities. In accordance with the President's agreement at the G-20 Summit in Pittsburgh to phase out inefficient subsidies for fossil fuels so that the Nation can transition to a 21st century energy economy, the Administration proposes to repeal a number of tax preferences available for fossil fuels. The following tax preferences available for oil and natural gas activities are proposed to be repealed beginning in 2017: (1) the enhanced oil recovery credit for eligible costs attributable to a qualified enhanced oil recovery project; (2) the credit for oil and natural gas produced from marginal wells; (3) the expensing of intangible drilling costs; (4) the deduction for costs paid or incurred for any tertiary injectant used as part of a tertiary recovery method; (5) the exception to passive loss limitations provided to working interests in oil and natural gas properties; (6) the use of percentage depletion with respect to oil and natural gas wells; (7) the ability to claim the domestic manufacturing deduction against income derived from the production of oil and natural gas; and (8) two-year amortization of independent producers' geological and geophysical expenditures, instead allowing amortization over the same seven-year period as for integrated oil and natural gas producers. The following tax preferences available for coal activities are proposed to be repealed beginning in 2017: (1) expensing of exploration and development costs; (2) percentage depletion for hard mineral fossil fuels; (3) capital gains treatment for royalties; and (4) the ability to claim the domestic manufacturing deduction against income derived from the production of coal and other hard mineral fossil fuels. In addition, under the proposal, publicly traded partnerships with qualifying income and gains from activities relating to fossil fuels would be taxed as C corporations beginning in 2022.

Reform the Treatment of Financial and Insurance Industry Products

Require that derivative contracts be marked to market with resulting gain or loss treated as ordinary.—Under current law, derivative contracts are subject to various rules on timing and character. The Administration's proposal would require that gain or loss from a derivative contract be reported on an annual basis as if the contract were sold for its fair market value no later than the last business day of the taxpayer's taxable year. Gain or loss resulting from the contract would be treated as ordinary and as attributable to a trade or business of the taxpayer. A derivative contract would be broadly defined to include any contract the value of which is determined, directly or indirectly, in whole or in part, by actively traded property. A derivative contract that is embedded in another financial instrument or contract is subject to mark to market if the derivative by itself would be marked. In addition, a taxpayer that enters into a derivative contract that substantially diminishes the risk of loss on actively traded stock that is not otherwise marked to market would be required to mark the stock to market with preexisting gain recognized at that time and loss recognized when the financial instrument would have been recognized in the absence of the straddle. An exception from mark-to-market treatment would be provided for business hedging transactions. The proposal would apply to contracts entered into after December 31, 2016.

Modify rules that apply to sales of life insurance contracts.—The seller of an interest in a life insurance contract generally must report as taxable income the difference between the amount received from the buyer and the adjusted basis of the contract. The recipient of a death benefit under a life insurance contract that had been transferred for a valuable consideration is generally subject to tax on the excess of those benefits over the amounts paid for the contract, plus any subsequent premiums paid, unless an exception to this "transfer-for-value" rule applies. Among the exceptions are transfers to the insured, to a partner of the insured, to a partnership in which the insured is a partner, or to a corporation in which the insured is a shareholder or officer. The Administration proposes to replace these excepted transfers with exceptions for transfers to the insured, or to a partnership or a corporation of which the insured owns at least 20 percent of the partnership or corporation. Furthermore, in response to the growth in the number and size of life settlement transactions, the Administration proposes to expand information reporting on the sale of life insurance contracts and the payment of death benefits on contracts that were sold. The proposal would apply to sales or assignments of interests in life insurance policies occurring after December 31, 2016.

Modify proration rules for life insurance company general and separate accounts.—Under current law, a life insurance company is required to "prorate" its net investment income between a company's share and the policyholders' share. The result of this proration calculation is used to limit the funding of tax-deductible reserve increases with tax-preferred income. However, the complexity of this proration regime has generated significant controversy between life insurance companies and the IRS. The Administration proposes to replace the current regime with one that is simpler and less controversial. Under the proposal, a company's share would be calculated for a life insurance company's general account and individually for each of its separate accounts. The company's share would equal one less the ratio of an account's mean reserves to its mean assets. The company's share would determine the portion of the non-affiliated corporate dividends received by the company that would be eligible for a dividends-received deduction. It would also determine the portion of interest earned on State and local bonds and the portion of increases for the taxable year in certain policy cash values of life insurance and annuity policies that would be exempt from tax. The proposal would be effective for taxable years beginning after December 31, 2016.

Expand pro rata interest expense disallowance for corporate-owned life insurance.—The interest deductions of a business other than an insurance company are reduced to the extent the interest paid or accrued is allocable to unborrowed policy cash values on life insurance and annuity contracts. The purpose of this pro rata disallowance is to prevent the deduction of interest expense that is allocable to the inside buildup of insurance and annuity contracts that is either tax-deferred or not taxed at all. An exception to this rule applies under current law to contracts covering the lives of officers, directors, employees, and 20-percent owners of the taxpayer. The Administration proposes to repeal the exception for officers, directors, and employees unless those individuals are also 20-percent owners of the business that is the owner or beneficiary of the contracts. Thus, purchases of life insurance by small businesses and other taxpayers that depend heavily on the services of a 20-percent owner would be unaffected, but the funding of deductible interest expenses with tax-exempt or tax-deferred inside buildup would be curtailed. The proposal would apply to contracts issued after December 31, 2016, in taxable years ending after that date.

Conform net operating loss (NOL) rules of life insurance companies to those of other corporations.—Current law generally allows businesses to carry back an NOL up to two taxable years preceding the taxable year of loss (loss year) and to carry forward an NOL up to 20 taxable years following the loss year. Life insurance companies, however, may carry a "loss from operations" (a life insurance company's NOL equivalent) back three taxable years preceding the loss year and forward 15 taxable years following the loss year. The proposal would establish operating loss conformity for life insurance companies by allowing a loss from operations to be carried back up to two taxable years prior to the loss year, and carried forward 20 taxable years following the loss year. The proposal would be effective for taxable years beginning after December 31, 2016.

Other Business Revenue Changes and Loophole Closers

Repeal last-in, first-out (LIFO) method of accounting for inventories.—Under the LIFO method of accounting for inventories, it is assumed that the cost of the items of inventory that are sold is equal to the cost of the items of inventory that were most recently purchased or produced. The Administration proposes to repeal the use of the LIFO accounting method for Federal tax purposes, effective for taxable years beginning after December 31, 2016. Taxpayers required to change from the LIFO method would be required to change their method of accounting for inventory and report their beginning-of-year inventory at its first-in, first-out (FIFO) value in the year of change. Taxpayers would recognize any income resulting from the change in accounting ratably over 10 years.

Repeal lower-of-cost-or-market inventory accounting method.—The Administration proposes to prohibit the use of the lower-of-cost-or-market and subnormal goods methods of inventory accounting, which currently allow certain taxpayers to take cost-of-goods-sold deductions on certain merchandise before the merchandise is sold. The proposed prohibition would be effective for taxable years beginning after December 31, 2016. Taxpayers would recognize any income resulting from the change in accounting method ratably over four years.

Modify like-kind exchange rules.—Under section 1031 of the Internal Revenue Code, no gain or loss is recognized when business or investment property is exchanged for "like-kind" business or investment property. The Administration proposes to limit the amount of capital gain deferred under section 1031 to $1 million (indexed for inflation) per taxpayer per taxable year. In addition, art and collectibles would no longer be eligible for like-kind exchanges. The proposal would be effective for like-kind exchanges completed after December 31, 2016.

Modify depreciation rules for purchases of general aviation passenger aircraft.—Under current law, airplanes used in commercial and contract carrying of passengers and freight generally are depreciated over seven years. Airplanes not used in commercial or contract carrying of passengers or freight, such as corporate jets, generally are depreciated over five years. The Administration proposes to increase the depreciation recovery period for general aviation airplanes that carry passengers to seven years, effective for such airplanes placed in service after December 31, 2016.

Expand the definition of substantial built-in loss for purposes of partnership loss transfers.—Upon a sale or exchange of a partnership interest, certain partnerships, including partnerships that have a substantial built-in loss in their assets, must adjust the basis of those assets. A substantial built-in loss is defined by reference to the partnership's adjusted basis – that is, there is a substantial built-in loss if the partnership's adjusted basis in its assets exceeds by more than $250,000 the fair market value of such property. Although the provision prevents the duplication of losses where the partnership has a substantial built-in loss in its assets, it does not prevent the duplication of losses where the transferee partner would be allocated a loss in excess of $250,000 if the partnership sold all of its assets, but the partnership itself does not have a substantial built-in loss in its assets. Accordingly, the Administration proposes to measure a substantial built-in loss also by reference to whether the transferee would be allocated a loss in excess of $250,000 if the partnership sold all of its assets immediately after the sale or exchange. The proposal would apply to sales or exchanges after the date of enactment.

Extend partnership basis limitation rules to non-deductible expenditures.—A partner's distributive share of loss is allowed as a deduction only to the extent of the partner's adjusted basis in its partnership interest at the end of the partnership year in which such loss occurred. Any excess is allowed as a deduction at the end of the partnership year in which the partner has sufficient basis in its partnership interest to take the deductions. This basis limitation does not apply to partnership expenditures that are not deductible in computing its taxable income and not properly chargeable to capital account. Thus, even though a partner's distributive share of nondeductible expenditures reduces the partner's basis in its partnership interest, such items are not subject to the basis limitation and the partner may deduct or credit them currently even if the partner's basis in its partnership interest is zero. The Administration proposes to allow a partner's distributive share of expenditures not deductible in computing the partnership's taxable income and not properly chargeable to capital account only to the extent of the partner's adjusted basis in its partnership interest at the end of the partnership year in which such expenditure occurred. The proposal would apply to a partnership's taxable year beginning on or after the date of enactment.

Deny deduction for punitive damages.—The Administration proposes to deny tax deductions for punitive damages paid or incurred by a taxpayer, whether upon a judgment or in settlement of a claim. Where the liability for punitive damages is covered by insurance, such damages paid or incurred by the insurer would be included in the gross income of the insured person. This proposal would apply to damages paid or incurred after December 31, 2016.

Conform corporate ownership standards.—Tax-free treatment of corporate reorganizations, distributions, and incorporations generally turns on whether shareholders acquire or retain "control" of the relevant corporation. For this purpose, control is defined as the ownership of 80 percent of the corporation's voting stock and 80 percent of the number of shares of all other classes of stock of the corporation. In contrast, the ownership standard for corporate affiliation (required for filing consolidated returns, tax-free parent-subsidiary liquidations, and treating certain stock dispositions as asset sales) is the direct or indirect ownership by a parent corporation of at least 80 percent of the total voting power of another corporation's stock and at least 80 percent of the total value of that other corporation's stock. The control test for tax-free reorganizations, distributions, and incorporations is easily manipulated by allocating voting power among the shares of a corporation, and the absence of a value component allows shareholders to retain voting control of a corporation but to economically "sell" a significant amount of the value of the corporation. In addition, the existence of two ownership standards in the corporate tax area causes unnecessary complexity and traps for the unwary. The Administration proposes to substitute the ownership test for affiliation for the control test used in connection with tax-free incorporations, distributions, and reorganizations. The proposal would be effective for transactions occurring after December 31, 2016.

Tax corporate distributions as dividends.—The Administration proposes to amend the Internal Revenue Code to ensure that a transfer of property by a corporation to its shareholder better reflects the corporation's dividend paying capacity. First, the Administration proposes to tax non-dividend "leveraged distributions" from a distributing corporation as a dividend distribution made by a related corporation directly to the distributing corporation's shareholder to the extent the related corporation funded the distribution with a principal purpose of not treating the distribution from the distributing corporation to its shareholder as a dividend. Second, the Administration proposes to repeal the "boot-within-gain" limitation under section 356(a) of the Internal Revenue Code in reorganization transactions in which the shareholder's exchange has the effect of the distribution of a dividend. For this purpose, the Administration also proposes to align the available pool of earnings and profits for such distributions with that for ordinary distributions. Third, the Administration proposes amending section 312(a)(3) of the Internal Revenue Code so that earnings and profits are reduced only by the distributing corporation's basis in any high-basis distributed stock, determined without regard to basis adjustments resulting from actual or deemed dividend equivalent redemptions, or any series of distributions or transactions undertaken with a view to create and distribute high-basis stock of any corporation. Fourth, the Administration proposes disregarding a subsidiary's purchase of "hook stock" issued by a controlling corporation in exchange for property so that the property used to purchase the hook stock gives rise to a deemed distribution from the purchasing subsidiary (through any intervening entities) to the issuing corporation. The hook stock would be treated as being contributed by the issuer (through any intervening entities) to the subsidiary. The proposal would grant the Secretary of the Treasury authority to prescribe regulations necessary to achieve the purposes of this proposal, including regulations to: (1) treat transactions as leveraged distributions; (2) treat purchases of interests in shareholder entities other than corporations as hook stock and provide rules related to hook stock within a consolidated group; and (3) treat a transaction as undertaken with a view to create and distribute high-basis stock of any corporation. The first, second and fourth proposals would be effective for transactions occurring after December 31, 2016. The third proposal would be effective upon enactment.

Repeal Federal Insurance Contribution Act (FICA) tip credit.—Certain employers in food and beverage service industries may receive an income tax credit for FICA taxes they pay on employee tip income. The credit applies to Social Security and Medicare taxes paid on the portion of an employee's tip income that, when added to the employee's non-tip wages, exceeds $5.15 per hour. The Administration proposes to repeal the income tax credit for the FICA taxes an employer pays on tips, effective for taxable years beginning after December 31, 2016.

Repeal the excise tax credit for distilled spirits with flavor and wine additives.—Distilled spirits are taxed at a rate of $13.50 per proof gallon. Some distilled spirits are flavored with wine or other additives. Current law allows a credit against the $13.50 per proof gallon excise tax on distilled spirits for flavor and wine additives. As a result of the credit, flavorings of up to 2.5 percent of the distilled spirit mixture are tax exempt, and wine in a distilled spirits mixture is taxed at the lower rate on wine. Thus, the credit reduces the effective excise tax rate paid on distilled spirits with such content. The proposal would repeal this credit effective for all spirits produced in or imported into the United States after December 31, 2016.

TRANSITION TO A REFORMED BUSINESS TAX SYSTEM

The Administration's proposal to impose a 14-percent one-time tax on previously untaxed foreign income generates one-time transition revenue in the short run. This proposal is described above as part of the business tax reform discussion, because it should be enacted in the context of comprehensive business tax reform.

MIDDLE CLASS AND PRO-WORK TAX REFORMS

Reform child care tax incentives.—Taxpayers with child or dependent care expenses who are working or looking for work are eligible for a nonrefundable tax credit that partially offsets these expenses. To qualify for this benefit, the child and dependent care expenses must be for either a child under age 13 when the care was provided or a disabled dependent of any age with the same place of abode as the taxpayer. Any allowable expense is reduced by the aggregate amount excluded from income under a dependent care assistance program. Eligible taxpayers may claim the credit of up to 35 percent of up to $3,000 in eligible expenses for one child or dependent and up to $6,000 in eligible expenses for more than one child or dependent. The percentage of expenses for which a credit may be taken decreases by one percentage point for every $2,000 of adjusted gross income (AGI) over $15,000 until the percentage of expenses reaches 20 percent (at incomes above $43,000). The income phasedown and the credit are not indexed for inflation. The proposal would repeal dependent care flexible spending accounts, increase the start of income phasedown of the child and dependent care credit from $15,000 to $120,000, and create a larger credit for taxpayers with children under age five. Taxpayers with young children could claim a child care credit of up to 50 percent of up to $6,000 ($12,000 for two children) of eligible expenses. The credit rate for the young child credit would phase down at a rate of one percentage point for every $2,000 (or part thereof) of AGI over $120,000 until the rate reaches 20 percent for taxpayers with incomes above $178,000. The expense limits and incomes at which the credit rates begin to phase down would be indexed for inflation for both young children and other dependents. The proposal would be effective for taxable years beginning after December 31, 2016.

Simplify and better target tax benefits for education.—Because there are multiple tax benefits for the same higher education expenses, incomplete information reporting, and a lack of coordination between Federal grant and tax benefits, many middle- and lower-income families do not claim all the education-related tax benefits to which they are entitled. To simplify and better target these benefits, the Administration proposes to consolidate the lifetime learning credit and AOTC into an expanded AOTC, which would be available for five years instead of four. As under current law, the AOTC for students attending school at least half time would be 100 percent of the first $2,000 of expenses and 25 percent of the next $2,000 of expenses for a maximum annual credit of $2,500. In addition, less than half-time undergraduate students would be eligible for a part-time AOTC equal to 50 percent of the first $2,000 of eligible expenses plus 12.5 percent of the next $2,000 of eligible expenses for a maximum credit of $1,250. The Administration also proposes to increase the refundable portion of the AOTC from 40 percent of the otherwise allowable credit to the first $1,500 of AOTC (first $750 for students enrolled less than half time). The expense limits and the amount that is refundable would be indexed for inflation.

To further simplify education benefits for low-income students, the proposal would exclude all Pell Grants from gross income to allow low-income students to claim an AOTC without reducing eligible expenses by the amount of their Pell Grant. In addition, the Administration proposes to require any entity issuing a scholarship or grant in excess of $500 (indexed for inflation) that is not processed or administered by an institution of higher education to report the scholarship or grant on Form 1098-T.

In addition, the Administration proposes to repeal the deduction for student loan interest for new students. Not only would new students be able to reduce their borrowing due to the expanded AOTC, but all new student borrowers would have access to Pay-As-You-Earn, a generous income-driven repayment option that limits payments to affordable levels and forgives remaining balances after a limited repayment period. The Administration further proposes to exclude from gross income the forgiven portion of Federal student loans in cases where the loan was forgiven or discharged as part of a program administered by the Department of Education, and debt forgiven and certain scholarship amounts for participants in the Indian Health Service Health Professions Programs. The Administration would also allow the Department of Education to obtain from the IRS the addresses of borrowers who are delinquent in repaying their loans (in addition to allowing access to addresses of defaulted borrowers as under current law).

The proposal would generally be effective for taxable years beginning after December 31, 2016.

Expand the EITC for workers without qualifying children.—Low and moderate income workers may be eligible for a refundable EITC. The EITC generally equals a specified percentage of earned income, up to a maximum dollar amount, and is gradually phased out once income exceeds a specified threshold. Different credit schedules apply for taxpayers based on the number of qualifying children the taxpayer claims. Taxpayers with

low wages who do not have a qualifying child and are at least 25 years old and less than 65 years old (or for whom, if filing jointly, the age of at least one spouse is within these limits) may be eligible to claim the small EITC for workers without qualifying children. The Administration proposes to increase the credit for workers without qualifying children. The phasein rate and the phaseout rate would be increased from 7.65 percent to 15.30 percent, which would double the size of the maximum credit from about $500 to about $1,000 in 2017. The income at which the credit would begin to phase out would be increased to $11,500 ($17,100 for joint filers) in 2017 and indexed thereafter. The Administration also proposes to expand eligibility to workers at least 21 years old and less than 67 years old. As under current law, taxpayers who may be claimed as a dependent or as the qualifying child of another taxpayer (e.g., taxpayers who are dependent students age 19 to age 23) may not claim the EITC for workers without children. This proposal would be effective for taxable years beginning after December 31, 2016.

Simplify the rules for claiming the EITC for workers without qualifying children.—The EITC generally equals a specified percentage of earned income, up to a maximum dollar amount, that is reduced by the product of a specified phaseout rate and the amount of earned income or AGI, if greater, in excess of a specified income threshold. Different credit schedules apply for taxpayers based on the number of qualifying children the taxpayer claims. In general, taxpayers with low wages who do not have a qualifying child may be eligible to claim the small EITC for workers without qualifying children. However, if the taxpayer resides with a qualifying child whom the taxpayer does not claim (perhaps because that child is claimed by another individual within the household), the taxpayer is not eligible for any EITC. The Administration proposes to allow otherwise eligible taxpayers residing with qualifying children to claim the EITC for workers without qualifying children. This proposal would be effective for taxable years beginning after December 31, 2016.

Provide a second-earner tax credit.—Married couples generally file jointly on their Federal individual income tax returns and cannot choose single or head of household filing status. Because tax rates rise with taxable income under a progressive tax system, the lower earner in a married couple may be discouraged to work when these second earners make their labor supply decisions conditional on the primary earners' decisions, effectively treating their earnings as taxed at the couples' highest marginal rates. In addition, low- and moderate-income married couples can face a high marginal tax rate due to the phaseout of tax credits and other benefits. To provide tax relief for working families and promote employment among second earners, the Administration proposes a second-earner tax credit. Two-earner married couples who file a joint Federal income tax return would be eligible for a nonrefundable tax credit equal to a percentage of the lower earner's earned income up to $10,000. The credit rate would be 5 percent and would phase down at a rate of one-half of one percentage point for every $10,000 of AGI over $120,000. Therefore, the credit would be fully phased out at AGI above $210,000. The maximum creditable earned income ($10,000) and the AGI at which the credit rate starts to phase down ($120,000) would be indexed for inflation. The proposal would be effective for taxable years beginning after December 31, 2016.

Extend exclusion from income for cancellation of certain home mortgage debt.—Under current law, amounts that are realized from discharges of qualified principal residence indebtedness may be excluded from gross incomes for amounts that are discharged before January 1, 2017. The Administration proposes to extend this provision for one year, to apply to amounts that are discharged after December 31, 2016, and before January 1, 2018, or that are discharged pursuant to an arrangement entered into before January 1, 2018.

REFORMS TO RETIREMENT AND HEALTH BENEFIT PLANS

Provide for automatic enrollment in IRAs, including a small employer tax credit, increase the tax credit for small employer plan start-up costs, and provide an additional tax credit for small employer plans newly offering auto-enrollment.—The Administration proposes to encourage saving and increase participation in retirement savings arrangements by requiring employers that do not currently offer a retirement plan to their employees to provide automatic enrollment in an IRA. Employers with 10 or fewer employees and employers in existence for less than two years would be exempt. An employee not providing a written participation election would be enrolled at a default rate of three percent of the employee's compensation in a Roth IRA. Employees would always have the option of opting out, opting for a lower or higher contribution within the IRA limits, or opting for a traditional IRA. Contributions by employees to automatic payroll-deposit IRAs would qualify for the saver's credit (to the extent the contributor and the contributions otherwise qualified).

Small employers (those that have no more than 100 employees) that offer an automatic IRA arrangement (including those that are not required to do so) would be entitled to a temporary business tax credit for the employer's expenses associated with the arrangement up to $1,000 per year for three years. Furthermore, these employers would be entitled to an additional credit of $25 per participating employee up to a total of $250 per year for six years.

Under current law, small employers (those that have no more than 100 employees) that adopt a new qualified retirement plan, Simplified Employee Plan (SEP), or Savings Incentive Match Plan for Employees (SIMPLE plan) are entitled to a temporary business tax credit equal to 50 percent of the employer's expenses of establishing or administering the plan, including expenses of retirement-related employee education with respect to the plan and any employer contributions. The credit is limited to a maximum of $500 per year for three years. In conjunction with the automatic IRA proposal, the Administration proposes to encourage small employers not currently sponsoring a qualified retirement plan, SEP, or SIMPLE plan to do so by tripling this tax credit to a maximum of $1,500 per year for three years and extending it to four years (rather than three) for any small employer that adopts a new qualified retirement plan, SEP, or SIMPLE plan during the three years beginning when it first offers or first is required to offer an automatic IRA arrangement. In addition, small employers would be allowed a credit of $500 per year for up to three years, for new or existing defined contribution plans that add auto-enrollment. The proposal would be effective for taxable years beginning after December 31, 2017.

Expand penalty-free withdrawals for long-term unemployed.—Under current law, a 10-percent additional tax applies to early withdrawals from a tax-qualified retirement plan or IRA, unless an exception applies. IRA account holders who have been unemployed for 12 weeks can withdraw funds during a two-year period to pay for health insurance without paying the 10-percent additional tax, but the unemployment exception does not extend to withdrawals used for any other purpose. There is no exception to the 10-percent additional tax for early withdrawals from a qualified plan due to unemployment. The Administration proposes to expand the exception from the 10-percent additional tax to withdrawals by long-term unemployed individuals from IRAs, 401(k) plans, or other tax-qualified defined contribution plans for any use. For this purpose, long-term unemployed individuals would be individuals who have been unemployed for at least 27 weeks (or, if less, the maximum period of unemployment benefits available under applicable state law). Under the proposal, the exception would not apply to IRA distributions that exceed 50 percent of the fair market value of all the individual's IRAs or a distribution from a retirement plan that exceeds 50 percent of the individual's vested accrued benefit in all tax-qualified retirement plans, and would be subject to an aggregate annual maximum of $50,000. The first $10,000 of distributions would not be subject to the 50-percent of the IRA or plan limitation. The proposal would be effective for distributions occurring after December 31, 2016.

Require retirement plans to allow long-term part-time workers to participate.—Under current law, a qualified retirement plan sponsor generally is not required to extend eligibility for coverage to employees who are credited with fewer than 1,000 hours in a year (about half time). Similar to the 1,000-hour threshold for coverage eligibility, employees also are not required to be credited with a year of service for purposes of vesting in employer contributions unless they earn 1,000 hours of service in a year. To increase coverage and vesting for long-term part-time employees, the Administration proposes to require that employees be permitted to make contributions in lieu of salary if they have had at least 500 hours of service per year with the employer for at least three consecutive years. These plans would also be required to credit, for each year in which employees have at least 500 hours of service, a year of service for purposes of vesting in any employer contributions. With respect to employees newly covered under the proposed change, employers would receive nondiscrimination testing relief (similar to current-law relief for plans covering otherwise excludable employees), including permission to exclude these employees from top-heavy benefit requirements. The proposal would be effective for plan years beginning after December 31, 2016.

Facilitate annuity portability.—Under current law, 401(k) and other defined contribution retirement plans may not permit distributions absent a distributable event. Distributable events for 401(k) plans include severance from employment and attainment of age 59½. Sponsors of defined contribution plans that want to offer annuities (for example, qualified longevity annuity contracts (QLACs) and deferred annuities inside target date funds) may be discouraged from doing so if the sponsor has no clear way to allow employees to continue existing annuities if the annuity product is no longer supported by the plan at some point in the future (for example, because of a change in trustee or recordkeeper or a reassessment of the value of an annuity option in light of take-up or because the annuity product is no longer available on favorable terms). To facilitate the offering of annuities, the Administration proposes to allow defined contribution plans to let participants take a distribution – through a direct rollover to an IRA or other retirement plan – of an annuity in the event the annuity is no longer authorized to be held as an investment under the plan, without regard to whether a distributable event (such as severance from employment) has occurred. The proposal would be effective for plan years beginning after December 31, 2016.

Simplify minimum required distribution (MRD) rules.—The MRD rules generally require that owners of IRAs and participants in tax-favored retirement plans commence distributions shortly after attaining age 70½ and that these retirement assets be distributed to them (or their spouses or other beneficiaries) over a period based on the joint life expectancy of the owner or plan participant and the designated beneficiary. The penalty for failure to take a minimum required distribution by the applicable deadline is 50 percent of the amount not withdrawn. The Administration proposes to simplify tax compliance for retirees of modest means by exempting an individual from the MRD requirements if the aggregate value of the individual's IRA and tax-favored retirement plan accumulations does not exceed $100,000 on a measurement date. The MRD requirements would phase in for individuals with aggregate retirement balances between $100,000 and $110,000. The initial measurement date for the dollar threshold would be the beginning of the year in which the individual turns 70½ or dies, with additional measurement dates only if the individual is subsequently credited with amounts (other than earnings) that were not previously taken into account. The Administration also proposes to harmonize the application of the MRD requirements for holders of designated Roth accounts and of Roth IRAs by generally treating Roth IRAs in the same manner as all other tax-favored

retirement accounts, i.e., requiring distributions to begin shortly after age 70½, without regard to whether amounts are held in designated Roth accounts or in Roth IRAs. Consistent with this change to the MRD rules for Roth IRAs, individuals also would not be permitted to make additional contributions to Roth IRAs after they reach age 70½. The proposal would be effective for taxpayers attaining age 70½ and taxpayers who die before age 70½ after December 31, 2016.

Allow all inherited plan and IRA balances to be rolled over within 60 days.—Generally, most amounts distributed from qualified plans or IRAs may be rolled over into another IRA or into an eligible retirement plan. However, the movement of assets from a plan or IRA account inherited by a non-spouse beneficiary cannot be accomplished by means of a 60-day rollover. This difference in treatment between plan and IRA accounts inherited by a non-spouse beneficiary and accounts of living participants serves little if any purpose, generates confusion among plan and IRA administrators, and creates a trap for unwary beneficiaries. The Administration proposes to permit rollovers of distributions to all designated beneficiaries of inherited IRA and plan accounts, subject to inherited IRA treatment, under the same rules that apply to other IRA accounts, beginning January 1, 2017.

Permit unaffiliated employers to maintain a single multiple-employer defined contribution plan.—Although the Internal Revenue Code imposes no constraints on the ability of unrelated or otherwise unaffiliated employers to participate in a multiple-employer plan (MEP) that is considered a single plan, under the Employee Retirement Income Security Act (ERISA), each unaffiliated employer participating in a MEP is generally considered to have established a separate plan that must separately meet the reporting, disclosure, fiduciary and other requirements of ERISA. MEPs are seen as a means of expanding defined contribution plan coverage for unaffiliated small employers through a plan offering economies of scale and a professional administrator willing to assume many responsibilities for compliance. However, those economies of scale and simplification of administration cannot be realized if each employer's arrangement must separately meet the requirements of ERISA. The proposal would permit unaffiliated employers to adopt a defined contribution MEP that would be treated as a single plan for purposes of ERISA, provided that the entity promoting and administering the plan (the provider), the participating employers, and the plan meet certain conditions designed to provide protections for the employees. Most significantly, the provider would be required to be a regulated financial institution that agrees to be a named fiduciary and the ERISA plan administrator and that registers with the Secretary of Labor. The proposal would be effective for years beginning after December 31, 2016.

Enact changes to the military retirement reform enacted in the FY 2016 National Defense Authorization Act.—This proposal more closely aligns the enacted retirement reform with the Administration's

FY 2016 proposal. Specifically, the Administration proposes to allow flexibility in timing and amount of continuation pay, increasing government contributions up to 6 percent (1 percent automatic plus up to 5 percent matching), starting TSP matching in the 5th year of service, and providing TSP matching for the entire military career.

Improve the excise tax on high cost employer-sponsored health coverage.—Under current law for 2020 and later, the cost of employer-sponsored health coverage in excess of a threshold is subject to a 40-percent excise tax. The threshold is $10,200 for self-only coverage and $27,500 for other coverage in 2018 dollars, indexed to the CPI plus one percentage point for 2019 and to the CPI thereafter. The threshold is increased for plan participants in firms likely to face higher health coverage costs due to the age and gender of their workforces or the occupations of plan participants, and for qualified retirees. The cost of coverage includes premiums (whether paid by the employer or the employee) plus certain contributions to flexible spending arrangements (FSAs), health savings accounts and Archer Medical Savings Accounts. To ensure that the tax is only applied to higher-cost plans, the proposal would increase the tax threshold to the greater of the current law threshold or a "gold plan average premium" that would be calculated for each State. The proposal would also define the cost of coverage with respect to salary reduction contributions to an FSA as the average amount elected for the year by similarly-situated employees (rather than amounts actually contributed on an employee-by-employee basis). Finally, building off of a required study of the methodology used to adjust the tax threshold for differences in age and gender mix across employers, the proposal would require a study of the potential effects of the tax on firms with unusually sick employees, conducted by the Government Accountability Office in consultation with the Department of the Treasury and other experts. The proposal would be effective for taxable years after December 31, 2016 (with the tax first levied in 2020, as under current law).

Extend CHIP through 2019.—The Administration proposes to extend CHIP funding for two years, through fiscal year 2019. As a result, more children will be enrolled in CHIP and fewer children will be enrolled in Marketplace qualified health plans and employment-based health insurance. This will increase tax revenues and reduce outlays associated with the premium tax credit.

Create State option to provide 12-month continuous Medicaid eligibility for adults.—The Administration proposes to create a new continuous eligibility State plan option that would allow all adult Medicaid beneficiaries, or at State option, only those who qualify on the basis of modified adjusted gross income (MAGI), to maintain Medicaid eligibility during a 12-month continuous coverage period, regardless of changes to income or other eligibility criteria. The expanded Medicaid eligibility will result in fewer individuals being enrolled in Marketplace qualified health plans, which will increase tax revenues and reduce outlays associated with the pre-

mium tax credit. The proposal would be effective January 1, 2017.

Standardize definition of American Indian and Alaska Native in the ACA.—The Administration proposes to revise the definitions of "Indian" in the ACA to align with eligibility requirements used for delivery of other federally supported health services to American Indians and Alaska Natives under Medicaid, CHIP, and the Indian Health Service (IHS). As a result, more American Indians and Alaska Natives will meet eligibility requirements for certain ACA provisions, including enrollment in qualified health plans without cost-sharing requirements. This will increase outlays associated with the Refundable Premium Tax Credit and Cost Sharing Reductions account.

REFORMS TO CAPITAL GAINS TAXATION, UPPER-INCOME TAX BENEFITS, AND THE TAXATION OF FINANCIAL INSTITUTIONS

Reduce the value of certain tax expenditures.—The Administration proposes to limit the tax rate at which upper-income taxpayers can use itemized deductions and other tax preferences to reduce tax liability to a maximum of 28 percent. This limitation would reduce the value of the specified exclusions and deductions that would otherwise reduce taxable income in the top three individual income tax rate brackets of 33, 35, and 39.6 percent to 28 percent. The limit would apply to all itemized deductions, interest on tax-exempt bonds, employer-sponsored health insurance, deductions and income exclusions for employee retirement contributions, and certain above-the-line deductions. If a deduction or exclusion for contributions to retirement plans or individual retirement arrangements is limited by this proposal, the taxpayer's basis would be increased to reflect the additional tax paid. The limit would be effective for taxable years beginning after December 31, 2016.

Reform the taxation of capital income.—Capital gains are taxable only upon the sale or other disposition of an appreciated asset. Under current law, most capital gains are taxed at graduated rates, with 20 percent generally being the highest rate. In addition, higher-income taxpayers are subject to a tax of 3.8 percent of the lesser of net investment income, including capital gains, or modified AGI in excess of a threshold. When a donor gives an appreciated asset to a donee during life, the donee takes the donor's basis in the asset and there is no recognition of capital gains until the donee later disposes of that asset. When an appreciated asset is held by a decedent at death, the decedent's heir receives a basis in that asset equal to its fair market value at the date of decedent's death. As a result, the appreciation accruing during the decedent's life on assets that are still held by the decedent at death is never subjected to the capital gains tax.

Under this proposal, the 20-percent capital gains tax rate would be increased to 24.2 percent (for a total of 28 percent for gains also subject to the net investment income tax). This would also increase the tax rate on qualified dividends, which would be taxed at the same rate as capital gains. In addition, transfers at death or by gift would result in recognition of gain. In the case of a gift, the gain would be taxable on the donor's income tax return for the year in which the gift was made. In the case of death, the tax would be reported either on the decedent's final income tax return or on a new income tax return created for this purpose. The proposal would exempt gain on household furnishings and personal effects (excluding collectibles) and allow a $100,000 exclusion of other gains recognized at death (which would be indexed for inflation and would be portable to a surviving spouse resulting in a $200,000 per couple exclusion). In addition, the current law ($250,000 per person) exclusion of capital gains from a principal residence would apply to all residences at death. If any share of a personal residence is bequeathed to a spouse, the spouse would be allowed the use of the first spouse's exclusion of gain (that is, the $250,000 personal residence exclusion would be portable). The unlimited use of capital losses and carryforwards would be allowed against ordinary income on the decedent's final income tax return, and the capital gains tax imposed at death would be deductible on the decedent's estate tax return. Appreciated property given to charity would be exempt from the capital gains tax. Gifts or bequests to a spouse would carry the basis of the donor or decedent, and capital gain would not be realized until the spouse disposes of the asset or dies. The proposal would provide for the deferral of tax payment (with interest) on the appreciation of certain small family-owned businesses, until the business is sold or transferred to owners outside the family. The proposal would further allow a 15-year fixed-rate payment plan for the capital gains tax on assets other than liquid assets such as publicly traded financial assets transferred at death. This proposal would be effective for gifts, deaths, qualified dividends received, and other capital gains realizations in taxable years beginning after December 31, 2016.

Implement the Buffett Rule by imposing a new "Fair Share Tax".—The Administration proposes a new minimum tax, called the Fair Share Tax (FST), for high-income taxpayers. The tentative FST equals 30 percent of AGI less a charitable credit. The charitable credit equals 28 percent of itemized charitable contributions allowed after the overall limitation on itemized deductions (Pease). The final FST is the excess, if any, of the tentative FST over the sum of the taxpayer's: (1) regular income tax (after certain credits) including the 3.8 percent net investment income tax, (2) the AMT, and (3) the employee portion of payroll taxes. The set of certain credits subtracted from regular income tax excludes the foreign tax credit, the credit for tax withheld on wages, and the credit for certain uses of gasoline and special fuels. The tax is phased in linearly starting at $1 million of AGI ($500,000 in the case of a married individual filing a separate return). The tax is fully phased in at $2 million of AGI ($1 million in the case of a married individual filing a separate return). The threshold is indexed for inflation beginning after 2017. The proposal would be effective for taxable years beginning after December 31, 2016.

Impose a financial fee.—The Administration proposes to impose a fee on banks, both U.S. and foreign, and would also apply to bank holding companies and "nonbanks," such as insurance companies, savings and loan holding companies, exchanges, asset managers, broker-dealers, specialty finance corporations, and financial affiliates with assets in excess of $50 billion. Firms with worldwide consolidated assets of less than $50 billion would not be subject to the fee for the period when their assets are below this threshold. U.S. subsidiaries of international firms that fall into these categories with assets in excess of $50 billion would also be covered. The fee base is assets less equity (also known as liabilities) for banks and nonbanks based on audited financial statements with a deduction for separate account (primarily for insurance companies). The fee rate would be seven basis points and would be effective on January 1, 2017. The fee is intended to discourage excessive risk-taking by financial firms, who were key contributors to the recent financial crisis. The fee would also satisfy the statutory requirement for the President to propose a means to recoup the net costs of assistance provided through the Troubled Asset Relief Program.

LOOPHOLE CLOSERS

Require current inclusion in income of accrued market discount and limit the accrual amount for distressed debt.—Just as original issue discount (OID) is part of the yield of a debt instrument purchased at original issuance, market discount generally enhances the yield to a purchaser of debt in the secondary market. Unlike OID, however, recognition of market discount is generally deferred under current law until a debt instrument matures or is otherwise sold or transferred. The Administration's proposal would require taxpayers to accrue market discount into income currently, in the same manner as original issue discount. To prevent over-accrual of market discount on distressed debt, the accrual would be limited to the greater of (1) an amount equal to the bond's yield to maturity at issuance plus five percentage points, or (2) an amount equal to the Applicable Federal Rate plus 10 percentage points. The proposal would apply to debt securities acquired after December 31, 2016.

Require that the cost basis of stock that is a covered security must be determined using an average cost basis method.—Current regulations permit taxpayers to use "specific identification" when they sell or otherwise dispose of stock. Specific identification allows taxpayers who hold identical shares of stock that have different tax basis to select the amount of gain or loss to recognize on the disposition. The Administration's proposal would require the use of average cost basis for all identical shares of portfolio stock held by a taxpayer that have a long-term holding period. The proposal would apply to covered securities acquired after December 31, 2016.

Tax carried (profits) interests as ordinary income.—A partnership does not pay Federal income tax; instead, an item of income or loss of the partnership and associated character flows through to the partners who must include such items on their income tax returns. Certain partners receive partnership interests, typically interests in future profits, in exchange for services (commonly referred to as "profits interests" or "carried interests"). Because the partners, including partners who provide services, reflect their share of partnership items on their tax return in accordance with the character of the income at the partnership level, long-term capital gains and qualifying dividends attributable to carried interests may be taxed at a maximum 20-percent rate (the maximum tax rate on capital gains) rather than at ordinary income tax rates. The Administration proposes to designate a carried interest in an investment partnership as an "investment services partnership interest" (ISPI) and to tax a partner's share of income from an ISPI that is not attributable to invested capital as ordinary income, regardless of the character of the income at the partnership level. In addition, the partner would be required to pay self-employment taxes on such income, and the gain recognized on the sale of an ISPI that is not attributable to invested capital would generally be taxed as ordinary income, not as capital gain. However, any allocation of income or gain attributable to invested capital on the part of the partner would be taxed as ordinary income or capital gain based on its character to the partnership and any gain realized on a sale of the interest attributable to such partner's invested capital would be treated as capital gain or ordinary income as provided under current law. The proposal would be effective for taxable years ending after December 31, 2016.

Require non-spouse beneficiaries of deceased IRA owners and retirement plan participants to take inherited distributions over no more than five years.—Under current law, owners of IRAs and employees with tax-favored retirement plans generally must take distributions from those retirement accounts beginning at age 70½. The minimum amount required to be distributed is based on the joint life expectancy of the owner or plan participant and the designated beneficiary, calculated at the end of each year. Minimum distribution rules also apply to balances remaining after a participant or IRA owner has died. Heirs who are designated as beneficiaries under IRAs and qualified retirement plans may receive distributions over their lifetimes, no matter what the age difference between the deceased IRA owner or plan participant and the beneficiary. The Administration proposes to require non-spouse beneficiaries of IRA owners and retirement plan participants to take inherited distributions over no more than five years. Exceptions would be provided for disabled beneficiaries and beneficiaries within 10 years of age of the deceased IRA owner or plan participant. Minor children would be allowed to receive payments up to five years after they attain the age of majority. This proposal would be effective for distributions with respect to participants or IRA owners who die after December 31, 2016.

Limit the total accrual of tax-favored retirement benefits.—The Administration proposes to limit the deduction or exclusion for contributions to defined contribution plans, defined benefit plans, or IRAs for an individual who has total balances or accrued benefits under those plans that are sufficient to provide an annuity equal to the maximum allowable defined benefit plan benefit. This maximum, currently an annual benefit of $210,000 payable in the form of a joint and survivor benefit commencing at age 62, is indexed for inflation. The proposal would be effective for taxable years beginning after December 31, 2016.

Rationalize Net Investment Income and Self-Employment Contributions Act (SECA) taxes.—A gap between the definitions of "net investment income" and "net earnings from self-employment" may create uncertainty in the treatment of limited partners and limited liability company (LLC) members who materially participate in the business, for purposes of net investment income and SECA taxes. Furthermore, the distributive shares of S corporation owner-employees, in many cases, are subject to neither tax. This gap exists even though the net investment income tax (NIIT) was specifically designed to tax the investment income of high-income taxpayers in the same way that earned income is taxed for Medicare purposes. The proposal would ensure that all trade or business income of high-income taxpayers is subject to a 3.8 percent tax, either through NIIT or SECA taxes, that investment income of high-income taxpayers continues to be subject to the NIIT, and that labor income derived from professional service pass-throughs is subject to self-employment tax. It would do so in two ways: (1) It would amend the definition of net investment income to include gross income and gain of individuals from trades or businesses not otherwise subject to employment taxes. This would include active income of S corporation shareholders, partners, and LLC members, and would include income from the sale of business property. Proceeds from the NIIT would be directed to the Medicare trust fund, as are Medicare taxes on employment earnings. (2) The proposal would treat all individual owners of professional service businesses (as defined in the proposal) as subject to SECA in the same manner and to the same degree, regardless of the legal form of the organization. Partners and S corporation shareholders who provide services and materially participate in a business that provides professional services would be subject to self-employment tax on their distributive shares of income, as currently applied to general partners and sole proprietors. Owners who do not materially participate would be subject to self-employment tax only on an amount equal to reasonable compensation for services provided and would continue to be subject to the NIIT on the remainder of their distributive shares of income. The proposal would be effective for taxable years beginning after December 31, 2016.

Limit Roth conversions to pre-tax dollars.—Subject to certain restrictions, taxpayers can convert traditional IRA/401(k) balances to Roth IRA/Roth 401(k) balances by paying tax at ordinary rates on the amount of the conversion in excess of basis. No tax is paid on the portion of the conversion that is a return of basis. The limits on after-tax contributions to plans and nondeductible contributions to IRAs (which generate basis) are weaker than those on pre-tax and Roth contributions. Taxpayers may exploit those weaker limits by performing a Roth conversion immediately after making such a contribution and thereby obtain—at no additional cost—the full benefits of Roth treatment on a less-advantaged after-tax or non-deductible contribution. The proposal would limit Roth conversions to pre-tax dollars, which would reduce the scope for strategies of this nature by precluding Roth conversions of after tax or nondeductible contributions. The proposal would be effective for taxable years beginning after December 31, 2016.

Eliminate deduction for dividends on stock of publicly-traded corporations held in employee stock ownership plans (ESOPs).—Generally, corporations do not receive a corporate income tax deduction for dividends paid to their shareholders. However, a deduction for dividends paid on employer securities is allowed under a special rule for ESOPs, including, for example, dividends paid on employer stock held in an "ESOP account" that is one of the investment options available to employees under a typical 401(k) plan. This special rule has been justified as encouraging employee ownership, which has been viewed as having a productivity incentive effect. However, ownership of stock of a publicly-traded corporation generally does not result in employees owning a significant percentage of the corporation and can result in an excessive concentration of assets intended for retirement security in a single investment. The Administration's proposal would repeal the deduction for dividends paid with respect to employer stock held by an ESOP that is sponsored by a publicly-traded corporation. This proposal would be effective with respect to dividends paid after the date of enactment.

Repeal exclusion of net unrealized appreciation (NUA) in employer securities.—In general, distributions from retirement plans are taxed as ordinary income. However, for employer securities received as part of a lump-sum distribution, more favorable tax treatment generally is available under which the excess of the market value of the employer stock at the time of the distribution over the cost or other basis of that stock to the plan (the net unrealized appreciation) is excluded from gross income at the time of distribution. The net unrealized appreciation generally is taxed as a capital gain at the time the employer stock is sold by the recipient. The Administration proposes to repeal this special exclusion for employer stock for retirement plan participants who have not attained age 50 on or before December 31, 2016. The proposal would be effective for distributions occurring after December 31, 2016.

Disallow the deduction for charitable contributions that are a prerequisite for purchasing tickets to college sporting events.—Under current law, donors who receive benefits in exchange for a charitable contribution must reduce the value of their charitable contribution deduction by the fair market value of the benefits they receive. Many colleges and universities give exclusive or priority purchasing privileges for sports ticket sales to donors, with the priority often dependent on the size of the gift. In contrast to the general rule for valuing donations in exchange for benefits, donors to colleges and universities who receive the right to purchase tickets for seating at an athletic event may deduct 80 percent of the contribution even when the value of the ability to purchase the tickets is far in excess of 20 percent of the contributed amount. The proposal would deny the deduction for contributions that entitle donors to a right to purchase tickets to sporting events. The proposal would be effective for contributions made in taxable years beginning after December 31, 2016.

MODIFY ESTATE AND GIFT TAX PROVISIONS

Restore the estate, gift, and generation-skipping transfer (GST) tax parameters in effect in 2009.—Under current law, estates, gifts, and GSTs are taxed at a maximum tax rate of 40 percent with a lifetime exclusion of $5 million, indexed for inflation after 2011. The Administration proposes to restore and permanently extend estate, gift, and GST tax parameters as they applied for calendar year 2009. Under those parameters, estates and GSTs would be taxed at a maximum tax rate of 45 percent with a life-time exclusion of $3.5 million. Gifts would be taxed at a maximum tax rate of 45 percent with a lifetime exclusion of $1 million. These parameters would be effective for the estates of decedents dying and transfers made after December 31, 2016, and would not be indexed for inflation.

Expand requirement of consistency in value for transfer and income tax purposes.—Current law provides generally that the basis of property inherited from a decedent is the property's fair market value at the decedent's death, and that the basis of property received by gift is the donor's basis (but limited to the fair market value of the gift for purposes of determining the donee's loss on a sale, if the donor's basis exceeds that value at the time of the transfer). Elsewhere in this Budget the Administration proposes to tax accrued capital gains (that is, fair market value in excess of the basis) when assets are transferred by death or gift. Generally, the same standards apply to determine the value subject to estate and gift taxes as apply to computing the beneficiary's basis or to computing gain under the Administration's proposal. However, prior to the enactment on July 31, 2015, of the Surface Transportation and Veterans Health Care Choice Improvement Act of 2015, there was no explicit consistency rule that would have required the recipient of the property to use for income tax purposes the value used for estate tax purposes as the recipient's basis in that property when the basis is determined by reference to the fair market value on the date of death. Similarly, there was no explicit consistency rule that would have required the recipient to use the same value of the gifted property for determining loss as the value used for gift tax purposes. That Act amended the basis rules to provide that a beneficiary's initial basis in property inherited from a decedent that increased the estate's Federal estate tax liability may not exceed the final value of the property for Federal estate tax purposes. The Administration proposes to require that, for property with respect to which a required estate tax return is filed after enactment, the property subject to the consistency requirement be expanded to also include property qualifying for the estate tax marital deduction, even though that property does not increase the estate's Federal estate tax liability. In addition, the Administration proposes to require that the value used to determine the donee's loss, if the donor's basis exceeded that value on the date of the gift, cannot exceed the value of the property for gift tax purposes.

Modify transfer tax rules for grantor retained annuity trusts (GRATs) and other grantor trusts.— Current law provides that the value of the remainder interest in a GRAT for gift tax purposes is determined by deducting the present value of the annuity to be paid during the GRAT term from the fair market value of the property contributed to the GRAT. If the grantor of the GRAT dies during that term, the portion of the trust assets needed to produce the annuity is included in the grantor's gross estate for estate tax purposes. In practice, grantors commonly use brief GRAT terms (often of less than two years) and significant annuities to minimize both the risk of estate tax inclusion and the value of the remainder for gift tax purposes. The Administration proposes to add the following requirements for GRATs: (1) the GRAT must have a minimum term of 10 years and a maximum term of 10 years more than the annuitant's life expectancy, (2) the remainder interest must have a minimum value at the creation of the GRAT equal to the greater of 25 percent of the value of the property contributed to the GRAT or $500,000 (but not more than the value of the assets contributed), (3) no decrease in the annuity during the GRAT term is permitted, and (4) no tax-free exchange of any GRAT asset with the grantor is permitted.

This proposal also would address the sale of an asset to a grantor trust, specifically, a trust of which the seller is the deemed owner for income tax purposes. A grantor trust is ignored for income tax purposes, even though the trust may be irrevocable and the deemed owner may have no beneficial interest in the trust or its assets. The lack of coordination between the income tax and transfer tax rules applicable to a grantor trust creates opportunities to structure transactions between the trust and its deemed owner that are ignored for income tax purposes and can result in the transfer of significant wealth by the deemed owner without transfer tax consequences. The proposal would provide that, if a person who is a deemed owner of all or a portion of a trust engages in a transaction with that trust that constitutes a sale, exchange, or comparable transaction that is disregarded for income tax purposes by reason of the person's treatment as a deemed owner of the trust under the grantor trust rules, then the portion of the trust attributable to the property received by the trust in that transaction, net of the consideration received by the person in the transaction, will be: (1) subject to estate tax as part of the deemed owner's gross estate, (2) subject to gift tax at any time during the deemed owner's life when his or her treatment as a deemed owner of the trust is terminated, and (3) treated as a gift by the deemed owner to the extent any distribution is made to another (except in discharge of the deemed owner's obligation to the distributee) during the deemed owner's life. The transfer taxes would be payable from the trust. The proposal would be effective with regard to GRATs created after the date of enactment, and to other grantor trusts that engage in a described transaction on or after the date of enactment.

Limit duration of GST tax exemption.—Current law provides that each person has a lifetime GST tax exemption ($5,450,000 in 2016) that may be allocated to the person's transfers to or for the benefit of transferees who are two or more generations younger than the transferor ("skip persons"). The allocation of a person's GST exemption to such a transfer made in trust exempts from the GST tax not only the amount of the transfer (up to the amount of exemption allocated), but also all future appreciation and income from that amount during the existence of the trust. At the time of the enactment of the GST tax provisions, the law of almost all States included a Rule Against Perpetuities (RAP) that required the termination of every trust after a certain period of time. Because many States now either have repealed or limited the application of their RAP laws, trusts subject to the laws of those States may continue in perpetuity. As a result of this change in State laws, the transfer tax shield provided by the GST exemption effectively has been expanded from trusts funded with $1 million and a maximum duration limited by the RAP, to trusts funded with $5,450,000 and continuing (and growing) in perpetuity. The Administration proposes to limit the duration of the benefit of the GST tax exemption by imposing a bright-line test, more clearly administrable than the common law RAP, which, in effect, would terminate the GST tax exclusion on the 90th anniversary of the creation of the trust. An exception would be made for trusts that are distributed to another trust for the sole benefit of one individual if the distributee trust will be includable in the individual's gross estate for Federal estate tax purposes to the extent it is not distributed to that individual during his or her life. The proposal would apply to trusts created after enactment, and to the portion of a pre-existing trust attributable to additions to such a trust made after that date.

Extend the lien on estate tax deferrals where estate consists largely of interest in closely held business.—There is a lien on nearly all estate assets for the 10-year period immediately following a decedent's death to secure the full payment of the Federal estate tax. However, the estate tax payments on interests in certain closely held businesses are deferred for 14 years after the due date of the return (or nearly 15 years after the date of death). Thus, this lien expires approximately five years before the due date of the final payment of the deferred tax. Existing methods of protecting the Federal Government's interest in collecting the amounts due are expensive and may be harmful to businesses. The Administration proposes to extend the existing estate tax lien throughout the deferral period to eliminate the need for any additional security in most cases in a manner that is economical and efficient for both taxpayers and the Federal Government.

The proposal would be effective for the estates of all decedents dying on or after the date of enactment, as well as for all estates of decedents dying before the date of enactment as to which the lien has not then expired.

Modify GST tax treatment of Health and Education Exclusion Trusts (HEETs).—Payments made by a donor directly to the provider of medical care for another or directly to a school for another's tuition are exempt from gift tax. These direct transfers also are exempt from the GST tax. However, payments made to a trust, to be expended by the trust for the same purposes, are not exempt from the gift tax. Some contributors to HEETs interpret the GST tax exclusion to apply also to distributions made from the HEET in payment of medical expenses or tuition, and claim that those distributions are exempt from the GST tax. The Administration proposes to provide that the GST tax exclusion for transfers exempt from the gift tax is limited to outright transfers by the donor to the provider of the medical care or education and does not apply to distributions for those same purposes from a trust. The proposal would apply to trusts created after the introduction of the bill enacting this change and to transfers after that date made to pre-existing trusts.

Simplify gift tax exclusion for annual gifts.—The annual per-donee gift tax exclusion (currently $14,000) is available only for gifts of "present interests," but generally a transfer can be converted into a present interest by granting the donee an immediate right to withdraw the property ("Crummey power"). In an effort to simplify tax compliance and administration, and to prevent the possible abuse of such withdrawal powers, the Administration proposes to eliminate the present interest requirement, define a new category of transfers that will not be affected by withdrawal or put rights, and impose an annual per-donor cap of $50,000 (indexed for inflation) on the total amount of gifts in that new category that can be exempted from gift tax by the annual per-donee exclusion. The new category would include transfers in trust (other than to a trust described in section 2642(c)(2) of the Internal Revenue Code), transfers of interests in pass-through entities, transfers of interests subject to a prohibition on sale, and other transfers of property that, without regard to withdrawal, put, or other such rights in the donee, cannot be immediately liquidated by the donee. The proposal would be effective for gifts made after the year of enactment.

Expand applicability of definition of executor.—Under current law, the statutory definition of executor applies only for purposes of the estate tax; therefore, an executor of an estate does not have the authority to extend a statute of limitations, claim a refund, agree to a compromise or assessment, or pursue judicial relief for a tax liability that arose prior to the decedent's death. To empower an authorized party to act on behalf of the decedent in such matters (whether arising before, upon, or after death), the Administration proposes to make the statutory definition of executor applicable for all tax purposes, and to authorize such executor to do anything on behalf of the decedent in connection with the decedent's pre-death tax liabilities or obligations that the decedent could have done if still living. In addition, because this definition frequently results in multiple parties being an executor, the proposal would grant regulatory authority to adopt rules to resolve conflicts among multiple executors authorized by that definition. The proposal would be effective upon enactment, regardless of the decedent's date of death.

OTHER REVENUE RAISERS

Impose an Oil Fee.—The Administration proposes to impose an oil fee, which would be the equivalent of $10.25 per barrel of crude oil, to support critical infrastructure and climate resiliency needs. The fee would be collected on domestically produced as well as imported petroleum products. Exported petroleum products would not be subject to the fee and home heating oil would be temporarily exempted. Revenue from the fee would fund the 21st Century Clean Transportation Plan to upgrade the Nation's transportation system, improve resilience, and reduce emissions. In addition, 15 percent of the revenues from the fee would be dedicated for assistance for households with particularly burdensome energy costs. Other fuel-related trust funds would be held harmless. The fee would be phased in over a five-year period beginning October 1, 2016. The fee would be fully phased in for petroleum produced or imported beginning October 1, 2021.

Increase and modify Oil Spill Liability Trust Fund financing.—An excise tax is imposed on: (1) crude oil received at a U.S. refinery; (2) imported petroleum products entered into the United States for consumption, use, or warehousing; and (3) any domestically produced crude oil that is used in (other than on the premises where produced for extracting oil or natural gas) or exported from the United States if, before such use or exportation, no taxes were imposed on the crude oil. Under current law, the tax does not apply to some types of crudes such as those produced from bituminous deposits as well as kerogen-rich rock. The tax is deposited in the Oil Spill Liability Trust Fund. Amounts in the trust fund are used for several purposes, including the payment of costs associated with responding to and removing oil spills. The tax imposed on crude oil and imported petroleum products is eight cents per barrel, effective for periods after December 31, 2008, and before January 1, 2017, and nine cents per barrel, effective for periods after December 31, 2016. The Administration proposes to increase these taxes by one cent per barrel to 10 cents per barrel for periods after December 31, 2016. In addition, the Administration proposes to update the law to include other sources of crudes such as those produced from bituminous deposits as well as kerogen-rich rock. The tax would cover, at the applicable rate, other sources of crudes received at a U.S. refinery, entered into the United State, or used or exported as described above after December 31, 2016. Finally, the proposal would place a prohibition on the drawback (refunding) of the tax. The prohibition would be effective for periods after December 31, 2016.

Reinstate Superfund taxes.—The Administration proposes to reinstate the taxes that were deposited in the

Hazardous Substance Superfund prior to their expiration on December 31, 1995. These taxes, which contributed to financing the cleanup of the Nation's highest risk hazardous waste sites, are proposed to be reinstated for periods (excise taxes) or taxable years (income tax) beginning after 2016, with expiration for periods and taxable years after 2026. The proposed taxes include the following: (1) an excise tax of 9.7 cents per barrel on crude oil and imported petroleum products; (2) an excise tax on specified hazardous chemicals at rates that vary from 22 cents to $4.87 per ton; (3) an excise tax on imported substances that use the specified hazardous chemicals as a feedstock (in an amount equivalent to the tax that would have been imposed on domestic production of the chemicals); and (4) a corporate environmental income tax imposed at a rate of 0.12 percent on the amount by which the modified AMT income of a corporation exceeds $2 million. Consistent with the Administration's proposal regarding taxes deposited in the Oil Spill Liability Trust Fund, the Superfund excise tax on crude oil and petroleum products would cover other sources of crudes such as those produced from bituminous deposits as well as kerogen-rich rock.

Increase tobacco taxes and index for inflation.— Under current law, cigarettes are taxed at a rate of $50.33 per 1,000 cigarettes. This is equivalent to just under $1.01 per pack, or approximately $22.88 per pound of tobacco. Taxes on other tobacco products range from $0.5033 per pound for chewing tobacco to $24.78 per pound of roll-your-own tobacco. The Administration proposes to raise tobacco taxes and create parity in tax rates among similar tobacco products. Cigarettes and small cigars would be taxed at $97.50 per 1,000 units, or about $1.95 per pack of cigarettes. Large cigars would be taxed at an approximately equivalent rate (using five per-unit rates that vary according to the cigar's weight). Chewing tobacco, pipe tobacco, roll-your-own tobacco, and snuff would be taxed at $44.23 per-pound, also roughly equivalent to the implied per-pound tax for cigarettes and cigars. The Administration also proposes to clarify that roll-your-own tobacco includes any processed tobacco that is removed for delivery to anyone other than a manufacturer of tobacco products or exporter. The new tax rates would be effective for articles held for sale or removed after December 31, 2016, and indexed for inflation after 2017.

Make unemployment insurance (UI) surtax permanent.—The net Federal UI tax on employers dropped from 0.8 percent to 0.6 percent with respect to wages paid after June 30, 2011. The Administration proposes to permanently reinstate the 0.8 percent rate, effective with respect to wages paid on or after January 1, 2017.

Expand FUTA base and reform FUTA credit reduction rules.—Many States' UI systems are chronically underfunded and required Federal borrowing to cover benefits during the most recent downturn. The Administration proposes to improve system solvency by helping States rebuild their trust fund balances to repay their loans, cover current benefits, and create reserves so they are better prepared for the next downturn. Under this proposal, the FUTA taxable wage base would increase in 2018 to $40,000 (approximately average insured wages) and would be indexed thereafter. This wage base increase would be accompanied by a decrease in the tax rate to avoid a Federal tax increase in the first year. In addition, currently, States that must borrow from the Federal Government for extended periods of time to cover benefits are assessed a reduction in their FUTA tax credits. The Administration proposes to change the rules governing credit reductions so they apply for any State with an average high cost multiple (AHCM) of less than 0.5 percent. An AHCM of 1.0 means a State has approximately enough funds to cover benefits during one year of an average recession, a commonly used solvency measure. Any revenues earned through the credit reduction would first be applied to repaying any State borrowing and would then be applied to the State trust fund to help it build up balances to prepare for the next downturn.

Modernize the UI program.—The Administration proposes to modernize the UI system by improving its connection to jobs and making sure benefits are available to more workers who need them. To do this, the Budget includes a UI modernization fund that will provide incentive payments to States that adopt measures to expand both program eligibility and work-based learning opportunities and training for unemployed workers. A State can receive incentive payments if it adopts one measure that expands eligibility and two measures that improve connections to training and employment. States that maintain these changes for at least four years will also receive a bonus payment. In addition, all States—whether or not they apply for incentive funds—will be required to have an alternative base period, provide coverage for workers seeking part-time work, provide coverage for workers that quit their jobs for compelling family reasons, and provide at least 26 weeks of benefits. States will need to raise additional revenue to cover the proposed benefit expansions.

Create a mandatory reemployment services and eligibility assessment (RESEA) program.—The Administration proposes to require States to provide RESEAs to the one-third of claimants identified as most likely to exhaust benefits. This proposal would provide grants to States for these services through mandatory funding beginning in 2018. In general, reduced outlays allow States to keep UI taxes lower, reducing overall receipts to the UI trust funds.

Levy a fee on the production of hardrock minerals to restore abandoned mines.—Until 1977, there were no Federal requirements to restore land after mining for coal, leaving nearly $4 billion worth of abandoned coal mine hazards remaining today. The Department of the Interior collects a fee on every ton of coal produced in the United States to finance the reclamation of these abandoned coal mines. Historic mining of hardrock minerals, such as gold and copper, also left numerous abandoned mine lands; however, there is no similar source of Federal funding to reclaim these sites. Just as the coal industry is held responsible for past mining practices, the Administration proposes to hold the hardrock mining industry responsible for abandoned hardrock mines. The proposed fee on the production of hardrock minerals would be charged per volume of material displaced after December 31, 2017, and the receipts would be distributed through a set allocation between Federal and non-Federal lands. Funds would be used to restore the most hazardous hardrock abandoned mine sites, on both public and private lands. The receipts allocated to restoration of non-Federal lands would be distributed to States and Tribes based on need, with each State and Tribe selecting its own priority projects within certain national criteria.

Return fees on the production of coal to pre-2006 levels to restore abandoned mines.—Since October 1, 1977, the Department of the Interior has collected fees on every ton of coal produced in the United States to finance the reclamation of abandoned coal mines. The fees levied on mine operators were originally $0.35 per ton for surfaced mined coal and $0.15 per ton for underground mined coal. The 2006 amendments to the Surface Mining Control and Reclamation Act instituted a phased reduction in these fees beginning in 2006. However, nearly $4 billion worth of abandoned coal mine hazards remain today. The Administration proposes to restore the fees to their original level, effective for coal mined after September 30, 2016, to provide additional resources to continue addressing the legacy of abandoned coal mines.

REDUCE THE TAX GAP AND MAKE REFORMS

Expand Information Reporting

Improve information reporting for certain businesses and contractors.—The Administration proposes to require a contractor receiving payments of $600 or more in a calendar year from a particular business to furnish to the business (on Form W-9) the contractor's certified TIN. A business would be required to verify the contractor's TIN with the IRS, which would be authorized to disclose, solely for this purpose, whether the certified TIN-name combination matches IRS records. If a contractor failed to furnish an accurate certified TIN, the business would be required to withhold a flat-rate percentage of gross payments. Contractors receiving payments of $600 or more in a calendar year from a particular business could require the business to withhold a flat-rate percentage of their gross payments, with the flat-rate percentage of 15, 25, 30, or 35 percent being selected by the contractor.

In addition, the Administration proposes to require life insurance companies to report to the IRS, for each contract whose cash value is partially or wholly invested in a private separate account for any portion of the taxable year and represents at least 10 percent of the value of the account, the policyholder's TIN, the policy number, the amount of accumulated untaxed income, the total contract account value, and the portion of that value that was invested in one or more private separate accounts. For this purpose, a private separate account would be defined as any account with respect to which a related group of persons owns policies whose cash values, in the aggregate, represent at least 10 percent of the value of the separate account. Whether a related group of persons owns policies whose cash values represent at least 10 percent of the value of the account would be determined quarterly, based on information reasonably within the issuer's possession.

The proposal would be effective for payments made to contractors after December 31, 2016, or private separate accounts maintained on or after December 31, 2016.

Provide an exception to the limitation on disclosing tax return information to expand TIN matching beyond forms where payments are subject to backup withholding.—The IRS is prohibited from disclosing Federal tax returns and return information (FTI). There are certain very narrow exceptions. Even where disclosure is permitted, recipients of FTI must safeguard the information and cannot redisclose it unless permitted. The Secretary of the Treasury is required to notify information return filers in certain circumstances where backup withholding is required if the recipient's TIN is not correct. Filers are required to keep this information confidential and are prohibited from using the information for purposes other than backup withholding. The IRS has broad regulatory authority to implement backup withholding. Under this authority, the IRS has established a TIN matching program that allows the IRS to verify the TINs of payees submitted by filers in the case of payments subject to backup withholding. The proposal would provide an exception to the limitation on disclosing FTI to permit the IRS to do TIN matching even in cases where the filer is not making a payment that is subject to backup withholding. The proposal would be effective on the date of enactment.

Provide for reciprocal reporting of information in connection with the implementation of the Foreign Account Tax Compliance Act (FATCA).—In many cases, foreign law would prevent foreign financial institutions from complying with the FATCA provisions of the Hiring Incentives to Restore Employment Act of 2010 by reporting to the IRS information about U.S. accounts. Such legal impediments can be addressed through intergovernmental agreements under which the foreign government agrees to provide the information required by FATCA to the IRS. Requiring U.S. financial institutions to report similar information to the IRS with respect to non-resident accounts would facilitate such intergovernmental cooperation by enabling the IRS to reciprocate in appropriate circumstances by exchanging similar information with cooperative foreign governments to support their efforts to address tax evasion by their residents. The proposal would require certain financial institutions to report the account balance for U.S. financial accounts held by foreign persons, expand the current reporting required with respect to U.S. source income paid to accounts held by foreign persons to include similar non-U.S. source payments, and provide the Secretary of the Treasury with authority to prescribe regulations that would require reporting of such other information that is necessary to enable the IRS to facilitate FATCA implementation by exchanging similar information with cooperative foreign governments in appropriate circumstances. The proposal would also require that this information, as well as information reported by foreign financial institutions to the IRS, be furnished to the account holders in order to encourage voluntary tax compliance. The proposal would be effective for returns required to be filed after December 31, 2017.

Require Form W-2 reporting for employer contributions to defined contribution plans.—Employers are currently required to report on Form W-2 an employee's elective deferrals under a cash or deferred arrangement, such as a 401(k) plan. Employers, however, are not required to report amounts that they contribute to an employee's retirement plan accounts. The proposal would require employer contributions to a defined contribution plan to be reported on Form W-2, thus providing employees with a convenient annual statement of the amounts that are contributed on their behalf by their employers under defined contribution plans and facilitating compliance with overall contribution limits.

Improve Compliance by Businesses

Increase certainty with respect to worker classification.—Under current law, worker classification as an employee or as a self-employed person (independent contractor) is generally based on a common-law test for determining whether an employment relationship exists. Under a special provision (section 530 of the Revenue Act of 1978), a service recipient may treat a worker who may actually be an employee as an independent contractor for Federal employment tax purposes if, among other things, the service recipient has a reasonable basis for treating the worker as an independent contractor. If a service recipient meets the requirements of this special provision with respect to a class of workers, the IRS is prohibited from reclassifying the workers as employees, even prospectively. The special provision also prohibits the IRS from issuing generally applicable guidance about the proper classification of workers. The Administration proposes to permit the IRS to issue generally applicable guidance about the proper classification of workers and to permit the IRS to require prospective reclassification of workers who are currently misclassified and whose reclassification is prohibited under the special provision. Penalties would be waived for service recipients with only a small number of employees and a small number of misclassified workers, if the service recipient had consistently filed all required information returns reporting all payments to all misclassified workers and the service recipient agreed to prospective reclassification of misclassified workers. It is anticipated that after enactment, new enforcement activity would focus mainly on obtaining the proper worker classification prospectively, since in many cases the proper classification of workers may not be clear.

Increase information sharing to administer excise taxes.—Current law allows the IRS and the Alcohol and Tobacco Tax and Trade Bureau to disclose specific items of tax return information to permit the effective administration of excise taxes. This disclosure provision is too narrow and prevents effective administration and enforcement of the excise tax rules. The Administration proposes to facilitate excise tax administration and increase collections by amending current law to permit disclosure of tax return information to Department of Homeland Security employees (customs officials) whose job responsibilities include tax administration. The proposal would be effective upon enactment.

Provide authority to readily share information about beneficial ownership information of U.S. companies with law enforcement.—Illicit actors may abuse legal entities to commit financial crimes, including laundering criminal proceeds and financing terrorism through the international banking system. Knowledge of beneficial owners of an entity can help law enforcement officials identify and investigate criminals engaged in these activities.

For anti-money laundering and counter-terrorism financing (AML/CTF) purposes, the beneficial owner of a foreign private banking account is currently defined in Treasury regulations under Title 31 of the U.S. Code to mean an individual who has a level of control over, or entitlement to, the funds or assets in the account that, as a practical matter, enables the individual(s), directly or indirectly, to control, manage, or direct the account. For Federal tax purposes, most U.S. entities are required to obtain an EIN. A company applying for an EIN must provide the IRS with the name of a responsible party who will be the IRS contact for the company. Generally, for a company that is not publicly traded, the responsible party is the person who has a level of control over, or entitlement to, the funds or assets in the entity that, as a practical matter, enables the individual to directly or indirectly control, manage, or direct the entity and the disposition of its funds or assets. Because this definition is similar to the AML/CTF definition of beneficial owner, the responsible party of an entity for Federal tax purposes will generally be considered a beneficial owner of an account nominally owned by the entity for AML/CTF purposes. Although this responsible party information may be useful to law enforcement when investigating financial crimes, under current law it cannot be shared with law enforcement officials without a court order.

The proposal would allow the Secretary of the Treasury or his delegate to share responsible party information with law enforcement without a court order to combat money laundering, terrorist financing, and other financial crimes. Such sharing would advance criminal investigations and successful prosecution, and assist in identifying criminal proceeds and assets. In addition, the proposal would require all companies formed in the United States to obtain an EIN, which would provide a universal identifier for these companies and ensure that responsible party information is provided for every U.S. entity. Further, the proposal would provide the Secretary of the Treasury with the authority to impose AML/CTF obligations on persons in the business of forming companies. Finally, the proposal would establish standards that States would be encouraged to adopt to improve their regulation and oversight of the incorporation process.

Strengthen Tax Administration

Modify the conservation easement deduction and pilot a conservation credit.—A deduction is generally available for charitable contributions of cash and property. In general, no charitable deduction is allowed for a contribution of a partial interest in property. An exception to this rule allows a donor to deduct the value of a conservation easement (a partial interest) that is donated to a qualified charitable organization exclusively for conservation purposes, including the preservation of recreational outdoor spaces and certain certified historical structures. The value of the deduction for any contribution that produces a return benefit to the donor must be reduced by the value of the benefit received. Special rules raise the usual contribution base limitations for gifts of conservation easements, allowing individuals to deduct up to 50 percent of their contribution base (generally, adjusted gross income computed without regard to the net operating loss carryback) and allowing qualified farmers and ranchers to deduct up to 100 percent of their contribution base. Certain corporate farmers and ranchers can deduct the value of contributions of property used in agriculture or livestock production (and restricted so as to remain available for such production) up to 100 percent of taxable income. Additionally, these donors can deduct any remaining value of the donated easement over the succeeding 15 years.

The Administration proposes the following modifications to the conservation easement deduction, effective for contributions made after the date of enactment, unless otherwise stated. First, to address concerns regarding abusive uses of this deduction and to promote effective, high-value conservation efforts, the Administration proposes to strengthen standards for organizations to qualify to receive deductible contributions of conservation easements; modify the definition of eligible conservation purpose and require that, prior to taking a deduction, donors of conservation easements establish that the easement furthers a clearly delineated Federal conservation policy or an authorized State or tribal government policy and will yield a significant public benefit; require that organizations receiving deductible contributions of easements acknowledge the Federal conservation purposes served and public benefits yielded by the easement and attest that the fair market value of the easement reported by the donor to the IRS is not inaccurate; penalize organizations that attest to values that they know (or should know) are substantially overstated or for receiving contributions that do not serve a conservation purpose; and require additional reporting by organizations receiving deductible contributions of conservation easements, including information about the contributed easements and their fair market values.

Second, contributions of easements on golf courses have raised concerns that the deduction amounts claimed for such easements are excessive and that the conservation easement deduction is not narrowly tailored to promote only bona fide conservation activities, as opposed to the private interests of donors. The Administration proposes to amend the charitable contribution deduction provision to prohibit a deduction for any contribution of a partial interest in property that is, or is intended to be, used as a golf course.

Third, concerns have been raised that the deduction amounts claimed for contributions of conservation easements for historic preservation are excessive and may not appropriately take into account existing limitations on the property. The Administration proposes to disallow a deduction for any value associated with forgone upward development above an historic building. The Administration also proposes to require contributions of conservation easements on all historic buildings, including those listed in the National Register of Historic Places, to comply with a 2006 amendment that requires contributions of historic preservation easements on buildings in registered historic districts to comply with special rules relating to the preservation of the entire exterior of the building and the documentation of the easement contribution.

Fourth, the Administration proposes to pilot a non-refundable credit of $100 million per year for conservation easement contributions as an alternative to the current deduction. (This credit amount is for the pilot program only. If successful, a full replacement of the deduction with a conservation easement credit of $475 million per year, indexed for inflation, is estimated to be revenue neutral.) The credits would be allocated by a Federal board to qualified charitable organizations and govern-mental entities that hold and enforce conservation easements. These conservation organizations would in turn allocate the credits to donors of conservation easements. Donors would receive up to a maximum of 50 percent of the fair market value of the contributed easement in credits and could use the credits to offset up to 100 percent of their income tax liability. Any unused credit amounts could be carried forward for up to 15 years. Under the proposal, donors would have enhanced incentives to contribute because the value of the credits is not limited to the donor's tax rate, and there would be fewer regulatory requirements and restrictions on taking the credit. Qualified conservation organizations would have flexibility to direct the credits toward easements with greatest conservation value and to utilize their credit allocation to maximize the conservation achieved in exchange for the tax benefits. Finally, the costs of tax administration could be reduced because conservation organizations, rather than donors, would determine the value of easements and be responsible for allocating the tax benefits to donors of valuable easements, eliminating much of the need for IRS enforcement activity to challenge overvalued easements deductions. Verification of donor compliance would be simplified as well, as regulatory requirements on donors necessary to support significant IRS examination activity of deductions would no longer be needed for the credit. The proposal also calls for a report to the Congress from the Department of the Treasury in collaboration with the Department of Agriculture and the Department of the Interior on the relative merits of the conservation credit and the deduction for conservation contributions, including an assessment of the conservation benefits and costs of conservation of both tax benefits.

Impose liability on shareholders to collect unpaid income taxes of applicable corporations.—Certain shareholders, corporate officers and directors, and their advisors have engaged in "Intermediary Transaction Tax Shelters." In a typical case, an intermediary entity purportedly purchases the shareholders' stock, either after or shortly before the corporation sells its assets. The cash from the asset sale effectively finances the purchase of the shareholders' stock and no assets are left to pay the corporate tax liability. Existing law does not adequately protect the Federal Government's interest in collecting the amounts due from selling shareholders as a result of these transactions. The Administration therefore proposes to add a new section to the Internal Revenue Code that would impose on the shareholders who sell stock of an "applicable C corporation" secondary liability (without resort to any State law) for payment of such corporation's unpaid corporate taxes. Shareholders would be liable to the extent they received proceeds, directly or indirectly, for their shares in an applicable C corporation. This proposal would be effective for sales of stock of applicable C corporations occurring on or after April 10, 2013.

Implement a program integrity statutory cap adjustment for tax administration.—The Administration proposes an adjustment to the discretionary spending limits, as established in the BBEDCA, as amended, for IRS tax enforcement, compliance, and related activities, including tax administration activities at the Alcohol and Tobacco Tax and Trade Bureau (TTB). In general, such cap adjustments help protect increases above a base level for activities that generate benefits that exceed programmatic costs. The proposed fiscal year 2017 cap adjustment for the IRS and TTB will fund $515 million in enforcement and compliance initiatives and investments above current levels of enforcement and compliance activity. Beyond 2017, the Administration proposes further increases in additional new tax enforcement initiatives each fiscal year from 2018 through 2021 and to sustain all of the new initiatives plus inflationary costs via adjustments through fiscal year 2026. The total cost of starting and sustaining the new initiatives above current levels of enforcement and compliance activity would be $18 billion over the 10-year budget window, and is estimated to generate an additional $64 billion in revenue over that same period for a net savings of $46 billion. These resources will help the IRS and TTB continue to work on closing the tax gap, defined as the difference between taxes owed and those paid on time and estimated at $450 billion in 2006. Enforcement funds provided through the 2017 cap adjustment will continue to target international tax compliance and restore previously reduced enforcement levels.

Revise offer-in-compromise application rules.—Current law provides that the IRS may compromise with a taxpayer to settle any civil or criminal case arising under the Internal Revenue Code prior to a referral to the Department of Justice for prosecution or defense.

In 2006, a provision was enacted to require taxpayers to make certain nonrefundable payments with any initial offer-in-compromise of a tax case. Requiring nonrefundable payments with an offer-in-compromise may substantially reduce access to the offer-in-compromise program. Reducing access to the offer-in-compromise program makes it more difficult and costly for the IRS to obtain the collectable portion of existing tax liabilities. Accordingly, the Administration proposes eliminating the requirement that an initial offer-in-compromise include a nonrefundable payment of any portion of the taxpayer's offer. The proposal would be effective for offers-in-compromise submitted after the date of enactment.

Make repeated willful failure to file a tax return a felony.—Current law provides that willful failure to file a tax return is a misdemeanor punishable by a term of imprisonment for not more than one year, a fine of not more than $25,000 ($100,000 in the case of a corporation), or both. The Administration would modify this rule such that any person who willfully fails to file tax returns in any three years within any period of five consecutive years, if the aggregate tax liability for such period is at least $50,000, would be subject to a new aggravated failure to file criminal penalty. The proposal would classify such failure as a felony and, upon conviction, impose a term of imprisonment for not more than five years, a fine of not more than $250,000 ($500,000 in the case of a corporation), or both. The proposal would be effective for returns required to be filed after December 31, 2016.

Facilitate tax compliance with local jurisdictions.—Although Federal tax returns and return information (FTI) generally are confidential, the IRS and Department of the Treasury may share FTI with States as well as certain local government entities that are treated as States for this purpose. IRS and Department of the Treasury compliance activity, especially with respect to alcohol, tobacco, and fuel excise taxes, may necessitate information sharing with Indian Tribal Governments (ITGs). The Administration's proposal would specify that ITGs that impose alcohol, tobacco, or fuel excise taxes, or income or wage taxes, would be treated as States for purposes of information sharing to the extent necessary for ITG tax administration. The ITG that receives FTI would be required to safeguard it according to prescribed protocols. The proposal would be effective for disclosures made after enactment.

Improve investigative disclosure statute.—Generally, tax return information is confidential, unless a specific exception in the Internal Revenue Code applies. In the case of tax administration, the Internal Revenue Code permits the Department of the Treasury and IRS officers and employees to disclose return information to the extent necessary to obtain information not otherwise reasonably available, in the course of an audit or investigation, as prescribed by regulation. Department of the Treasury regulations effective since 2003 state that the term "necessary" in this context does not mean essential or indispensable, but rather appropriate and helpful in obtaining the information sought. Determining if an investigative disclosure is "necessary" is inherently factual, leading to inconsistent opinions by the courts. Eliminating this uncertainty from the statute would facilitate investigations by IRS officers and employees, while setting forth clear guidance for taxpayers, thus enhancing compliance with the Internal Revenue Code. The Administration proposes to clarify the taxpayer privacy law by stating that it does not prohibit Department of the Treasury and IRS officers and employees from identifying themselves, their organizational affiliation, and the nature and subject of an investigation, when contacting third parties in connection with a civil or criminal tax investigation. The proposal would be effective for disclosures made after enactment.

Allow the IRS to absorb credit and debit card processing fees for certain tax payments.—Taxpayers may make credit or debit card payments by phone through IRS-designated third-party service providers, who charge taxpayers a convenience fee for processing the payment over and above the taxes due. Under current law, if the IRS were to accept credit or debit card payments directly from taxpayers, the IRS would be prohibited from absorbing credit and debit card processing fees. The Administration recognizes that it is inefficient for both the IRS and taxpayers to require credit and debit card payments to be made through a third-party service provider, and that charging an additional convenience fee increases taxpayers' costs. The proposal would permit the IRS to accept credit and debit card payments directly from taxpayers and to absorb the credit and debit card processing fees, but only in situations authorized by regulations. The proposal would be effective for payments made after the date of enactment.

Provide the IRS with greater flexibility to address correctable errors.—The IRS may correct certain mathematical or clerical errors made on tax returns to reflect the taxpayer's correct tax liability without following the regular deficiency procedures (this authority is generally referred to as "math error authority"). The Internal Revenue Code specifically identifies a list of circumstances where the IRS has math error authority. The Administration proposes to remove the existing specific grants of math error authority, and provide that "math error authority" will refer only to computational errors and the incorrect use of any table provided by the IRS. In addition, the proposal will add a new category of "correctable errors." Under this new category, the Department of the Treasury would have regulatory authority to permit the IRS to correct errors in cases where: (1) the information provided by the taxpayer does not match the information contained in government databases; (2) the taxpayer has exceeded the lifetime limit for claiming a deduction or credit; or (3) the taxpayer has failed to include with his or her return documentation that is required by statute. The proposal would increase efficiency by eliminating the need to enact legislation specifically extending math error authority to the IRS on a case-by-case basis, and would promote the efficient use of IRS and taxpayer resources. The proposal would be effective on the date of enactment. However, the IRS' current grant of math error authority would continue to apply until the Department of the

Treasury and the IRS issue final regulations addressing correctable errors.

Enhance electronic filing of returns.—Generally, regulations may require businesses and tax-exempt organizations that file at least 250 returns and information returns during the calendar year to file electronically (e-File). Partnerships with more than 100 partners are required to e-File, regardless of how many returns they file. A tax return preparer that expects to file more than 10 individual income tax returns (Forms 1040 and 1041) is generally required to e-File these tax returns. Certain pension plans are required to electronically file certain information with the Department of Labor, which shares the information with the IRS. However, certain tax-only information is not required to be e-filed to the IRS. The proposal would strengthen the requirements for entities to e-File, expand the preparer e-File mandate for individual returns to apply to entity returns, require scannable codes on paper returns prepared using software, expand regulatory authority related to information returns, and add a specific penalty for failure to e-File when required to do so. Regulatory authority would be expanded to allow reduction of the 250-return threshold for certain other information returns and disclosure of returns electronically filed by tax-exempt organizations would be required to be in a machine readable format. The proposal would generally be effective for taxable years beginning after the date of enactment, with transition relief available for certain taxpayers.

Improve the whistleblower program.—Under current law, the Internal Revenue Code does not protect whistleblowers from retaliatory actions; therefore, potential whistleblowers may be discouraged from filing claims with the IRS. The Administration proposes to amend the Internal Revenue Code to protect whistleblowers from retaliation, which should incentivize potential whistleblowers to file claims and increase the tax administration benefit of the whistleblower program. The IRS Whistleblower Office may disclose tax return information, which is generally confidential, to whistleblowers and their legal representatives as part of a whistleblower administrative proceeding. Although whistleblowers and their legal representatives must sign a confidentiality agreement before tax return information is shared, the statutory prohibitions on redisclosure of tax return information and safeguarding requirements do not apply. The Administration proposes to amend the whistleblower rules to explicitly protect whistleblowers from retaliatory actions, consistent with the protections currently available to whistleblowers under the False Claims Act. In addition, the Administration proposes to amend the taxpayer information protections to extend the safeguarding requirements and prohibition on redisclosure of tax return information to whistleblowers and their legal representatives. In addition, the Administration proposes to extend penalties for unauthorized redisclosure of tax return information to whistleblowers and their legal representatives. This proposal will improve the efficiency of the whistleblower award determination proceedings, while increasing the protection available to taxpayers. The proposal would be effective upon enactment.

Index all civil tax penalties for inflation.— Currently, the amount of a tax penalty that is a set dollar amount is established when the penalty is added to the Internal Revenue Code and is only increased by amendments to the Internal Revenue Code. As a result, under current practices, the amount of the penalty is often not increased until significant time has passed and the penalty amount is too low to continue serving as an effective deterrent. The Administration proposes to index all penalties for inflation and round the indexed amount to the next hundred dollars. This proposal would increase the penalty regime's effectiveness in deterring negative behavior and would increase efficiency by eliminating the need to enact increases to individual penalties. While recent amendments to the Internal Revenue Code index select penalty provisions to inflation and resolve these issues for those few penalties, a more comprehensive approach is needed to achieve increased effectiveness and efficiency of tax penalties. The proposal would be effective upon enactment.

Combat tax-related identity theft.—Tax refund-related identity theft has expanded exponentially in recent years. The Aggravated Identity Theft Statute contains a list of felony violations that constitute predicate offenses for aggravated identity theft but the list does not currently include any tax offenses. The Administration proposes to add tax-related offenses to the list of predicate offenses contained in the Aggravated Identity Theft Statute. The Administration also proposes to impose a $5,000 civil penalty (indexed) in tax identity theft cases. The proposal would be effective upon enactment.

Allow States to send notices of intent to offset Federal tax refunds to collect State tax obligations by regular first-class mail instead of certified mail.— Under current law, the Department of the Treasury, Bureau of Fiscal Service, may offset Federal tax refunds to collect delinquent State income tax obligations only after the State sends the delinquent debtor a notice by certified mail. With respect to all other types of debts, including Federal nontax, child support, and State unemployment insurance compensation debts, the statute is silent as to the notice delivery method. However, the regulations require that for all debts other than State income tax obligations, Federal and State creditor agencies send notices by regular first class mail. Similarly, notice requirements for other debt collection actions, including administrative wage garnishment, do not require delivery by certified mail. The Administration's proposal would remove the statutory requirement to use certified mail, thereby allowing States to send notices for delinquent State income tax obligations by first class mail, saving States certified mail costs and standardizing notice procedures across debt types. The proposal would be effective upon enactment.

Accelerate information return filing due dates.— Under current law, many information returns are required to be filed with the IRS by February 28 of the year following the year for which the information is being reported, and the due date for filing information returns with IRS is generally extended until March 31 if the returns are filed electronically. Recent legislation accelerated the filing due date for Forms W-2, W-3, and returns and statements reporting nonemployee compensation to January 31 and eliminated the March 31 electronic filing due date for these forms. The IRS uses third-party information to determine a taxpayer's compliance with Federal tax obligations and therefore accelerating the IRS' receipt of third-party information will facilitate detection of non-compliance earlier in the filing season. The Administration proposes to accelerate the date for filing most information returns (other than Forms W-2, W-3, and returns reporting nonemployee compensation) with the IRS to January 31 and eliminate the extended due date for electronically filed returns for these forms. The proposal would be effective for returns required to be filed after December 31, 2016.

Increase oversight of paid tax return preparers.— Paid tax return preparers have an important role in tax administration because they assist taxpayers in complying with their obligations under the tax laws. Incompetent and dishonest tax return preparers increase collection costs, reduce revenues, disadvantage taxpayers by potentially subjecting them to penalties and interest as a result of incorrect returns, and undermine confidence in the tax system. To promote high quality services from paid tax return preparers, the proposal would explicitly provide that the Secretary of the Treasury has the authority to regulate all paid tax return preparers. This proposal would be effective on or after the date of enactment.

Enhance administrability of the appraiser penalty.—Current law imposes a penalty on preparers of appraisals that result in a substantial or gross valuation misstatement. There is an exception to the penalty if the value in the appraisal is "more likely than not" the proper value. Valuations of property are generally provided as a specific value or a range of values that are applicable, not as a value that is "more likely than not" the proper value. Further, there is no coordination between this penalty and the preparer understatement penalty in cases where the person providing the appraisal is also treated as a paid tax return preparer with respect to the position on the return or claim for refund relying on the valuation in the appraisal. The proposal would increase administrability of the appraiser penalty by replacing the existing "more likely than not" exception with a reasonable cause exception. In addition, under the proposal, an appraiser would not be subject to both penalties for the same conduct. The proposal would be effective for returns required to be filed after December 31, 2016.

Enhance UI program integrity.—The Administration proposes a broad package of proposals aimed at improving the integrity of the UI program. Included in this package are proposals to: allow for data disclosure to contractors for the Treasury Offset Program; expand State use of the Separation Information Data Exchange System (SIDES), which already improves program integrity by allowing States and employers to exchange information on reasons for a claimant's separation from employment and thereby helping States to determine UI eligibility; mandate the use of the National Directory of New Hires to conduct cross-matches for program integrity purposes; allow the Secretary to set corrective action measures for poor State performance; require States to cross-match claimants against the Prisoner Update Processing System (PUPS), which is currently used by some States; and allow States to retain five percent of overpayment and tax investigation recoveries to fund program integrity activities. In general, these proposals will reduce UI benefit payments, thereby reducing State UI taxes.

Request a program integrity cap adjustment for the RESEA program.—The Administration proposes a program integrity cap adjustment for 2017 to fund RESEAs for approximately one-third of claimants identified as most likely to exhaust benefits. These assessments and supplemental services help ensure that benefits go only to eligible claimants and that they get the services they need to return to work. In general, reduced outlays allow States to keep UI taxes lower, reducing overall receipts to the UI trust funds.

SIMPLIFY THE TAX SYSTEM

Modify adoption credit to allow tribal determination of special needs.—Current law allows a more generous credit for the adoption of children with special needs. To claim this credit, a State must have made a determination that the child has special needs. Like States, many ITGs facilitate adoptions involving special needs children; however, currently, a tribe is not permitted to make the determination of special needs. The Administration proposes to allow ITGs to make this determination, effective for taxable years beginning after December 31, 2016.

Repeal non-qualified preferred stock designation.—In 1997, a provision was added to the Internal Revenue Code that treats as taxable "boot" the receipt of certain types of preferred stock known as non-qualified preferred stock (NQPS), where NQPS is issued in a corporate organization or reorganization exchange. Since enactment, taxpayers have often exploited the hybrid nature of NQPS, issuing NQPS in transactions that are inconsistent with the purpose of the 1997 provision. The Administration proposes to repeal the NQPS designation, and no longer treat the receipt of such stock as taxable boot. The proposal would be effective for stock issued after December 31, 2016.

Reform excise tax based on investment income of private foundations.—Under current law, private foundations that are exempt from Federal income tax are subject to a two-percent excise tax on their net investment income (one-percent if certain requirements are met). The excise tax on private foundations that are not exempt from Federal income tax, such as certain charitable trusts, is equal to the excess of the sum of the excise tax that would have been imposed if the foundation were tax exempt and the amount of the unrelated business income tax that would have been imposed if the foundation were tax exempt, over the income tax imposed on the foundation. To simplify the tax laws and encourage increased charitable activity, the Administration proposes to replace the two rates of tax on the net investment income of private foundations that are exempt from Federal income tax with a single tax rate of 1.35 percent. The excise tax on private foundations not exempt from Federal income tax would be equal to the excess of the sum of the 1.35-percent excise tax that would have been imposed if the foundation were tax exempt and the amount of the unrelated business income tax that would have been imposed if the foundation were tax exempt, over the income tax imposed on the foundation. The proposed change would be effective for taxable years beginning after the date of enactment.

Simplify arbitrage investment restrictions.—Current law arbitrage investment restrictions imposed on investments of tax-exempt bond proceeds create unnecessary complexity and compliance burdens for State and local governments. These restrictions generally limit investment returns that exceed the effective interest rate on the tax-exempt bonds. One type of restriction, called "yield restriction," limits arbitrage earnings in the first instance, and the second type of restriction, called "rebate," requires repayment of arbitrage earnings to the Federal Government at periodic intervals. The two types of arbitrage restrictions are duplicative and overlapping and they address the same tax policy goal to limit arbitrage profit incentives for excess use of tax-exempt bonds. The Administration proposes to simplify the arbitrage investment restrictions on tax-exempt bonds in several respects. First, the Administration proposes to unify the arbitrage restrictions to rely primarily on the rebate requirement and to repeal yield restriction in most circumstances. Second, recognizing that limited arbitrage potential exists if issuers spend bond proceeds fairly promptly, the Administration proposes a streamlined broad three-year prompt spending exception to the arbitrage rebate requirement on tax-exempt bonds. Finally, recognizing the particular compliance burdens for small issuers, the Administration proposes to increase the small issuer exception to the arbitrage rebate requirement from $5 million to $10 million, index the size limit for inflation, and remove the general taxing power constraint on small issuer eligibility. The proposal would be effective for bonds issued after the date of enactment.

Simplify single-family housing mortgage bond targeting requirements.—Current law allows use of tax-exempt private activity bonds to finance qualified mortgages for single-family residences, subject to a number of targeting requirements, including, among others: (1) a mortgagor income limitation (generally not more than 115 percent of applicable median family income, increased to 140 percent of such income for certain targeted areas, and also increased for certain high-cost areas); (2) a purchase price limitation (generally not more than 90 percent of average area purchase prices, increased to 110 percent in targeted areas); (3) a refinancing limitation (generally permitting only new mortgages for first-time homebuyers); and (4) a targeted area availability requirement. The Administration proposes to simplify the targeting requirements for tax-exempt qualified mortgage bonds by repealing the purchase price limitation and the refinancing limitation. This proposal would be effective for bonds issued after the date of enactment.

Streamline private activity limits on governmental bonds.—Tax-exempt bonds issued by State and local governments are treated as governmental bonds if the issuer limits private business use and other private involvement sufficiently to avoid treatment as "private activity bonds." Bonds generally are classified as private activity bonds under a two-part test if more than 10 percent of the bond proceeds are both: (1) used for private business use; and (2) payable or secured from property or payments derived from private business use. Additional restrictions further reduce permitted private involvement for governmental bonds in several ways, including the following: a five percent unrelated or disproportionate private business limit; a $15 million cap on private business involvement for governmental output facilities (e.g., electric and gas facilities); and a separate private loan limit for the lesser of five percent or $5 million of bond proceeds. These additional restrictions are unduly complex and increase compliance burdens for State and local governments. The general 10-percent private involvement limit and the bond volume cap requirement for larger governmental bond issues transactions with over $15 million in private involvement represent sufficient and workable boundaries for private involvement for governmental bonds. The Administration proposes to streamline these limits on governmental bonds by repealing the five-percent unrelated or disproportionate private business limit and the $15 million private business cap on output facilities. As an overall constraint, the Administration proposes to modify the bond volume cap requirement for private involvement over $15 million in larger governmental bond issues and apply the modified cap to both private business use and private loans. This proposal would be effective for bonds issued after the date of enactment.

Repeal technical terminations of partnerships.— A partnership will terminate when 50 percent or more of the total interest in partnership capital and profits is sold or exchanged within a 12-month period. This is referred to as a "technical termination." This provision is a holdover that addressed the notion common under prior State laws that tied the identity of a partnership to its partners. As this view of partnerships has evolved, the utility of the provision has essentially been eliminated, and it is now primarily a trap for unwary taxpayers. The Administration proposes eliminating technical terminations effective for transfers after December 31, 2016.

Repeal anti-churning rules of section 197.— Section 197 of the Internal Revenue Code was enacted in 1993 to allow amortization of certain intangibles (such as goodwill and going concern value) that had not been amortizable under prior law. Anti-churning rules were enacted at that time to prevent taxpayers from engaging in transactions with related parties soon after the enactment of section 197 solely to generate amortizable basis. Because it has been 20 years since the enactment of section 197, the anti-churning rules are no longer necessary, and the complexity of the provision outweighs the potential application. The Administration proposes eliminating the anti-churning rules effective for acquisitions after December 31, 2016.

Repeal special estimated tax payment provision for certain insurance companies.—The deductible unpaid loss reserves of insurance companies are required to be computed on a discounted basis to reflect the time value of money. However, a taxpayer may elect to deduct an additional amount equal to the difference between discounted and undiscounted reserves, if it also makes a "special estimated tax payment" equal to the tax benefit attributable to the extra deduction. The special estimated tax payments are applied against the company's tax liability in future years as reserves are released. This provision requires complex record keeping yet, by design, is approximately revenue neutral. The Administration proposes to repeal the provision effective for taxable years beginning after December 31, 2016.

Repeal the telephone excise tax.—Current law imposes a three-percent excise tax on amounts paid for taxable communications services, which include local telephone service and toll telephone service. Local telephone service is defined as access to a local telephone system and the privilege of telephonic communication with substantially all persons having telephones in the local system. Taxpayers are no longer required to pay tax on similar services, such as plans that provide bundled local and long distance service for either a flat monthly fee or a charge that varies with the elapsed transmission time for which the service is used. As a result, the only communications services that remain subject to the tax are purely local telephone services, of which the poor and the elderly are the primary users. The Administration proposes to repeal the tax on these services. The proposal would be effective for amounts paid pursuant to bills first rendered more than 90 days after the date of enactment.

Increase the standard mileage rate for automobile use by volunteers.—Under current law, volunteers may take a charitable contribution deduction for the use of their car in the service of charitable organizations at a standard mileage rate of 14 cents per mile driven. This rate is set by statute and is not indexed for inflation; it was last increased in 1997. The Administration proposes to harmonize the standard mileage rate for the charitable contribution deduction with the rate for miles driven for purposes of the medical and moving expense deductions, which are set annually by the IRS to cover the estimated variable costs of operating an automobile. The proposal would be effective for contributions made in taxable years beginning after December 31, 2016.

Consolidate contribution limitations for charitable deductions and extend the carryforward period for excess charitable contribution deduction amounts.—The income tax system limits the amount of charitable contribution deductions a donor may claim to a share of the donor's contribution base (the taxpayer's adjusted gross income computed without regard to any net operating loss carryback for the taxable year). An individual taxpayer may generally deduct up to 50 percent of his contribution base for contributions of cash to public charities, and up to 30 percent for cash contributions to most private foundations. An individual taxpayer may generally deduct up to 30 percent of his contribution base for contributions of appreciated capital gain property to public charities, and up to 20 percent to most private foundations. Finally, an individual taxpayer may deduct up to 20 percent of his contribution base for contributions of capital gain property for the use of a charitable organization. Charitable contributions made to an organization exceeding these limits may generally be carried forward to be deducted in the subsequent five years. Special rules apply for contributions of conservation easements. The proposal would simplify this complicated set of rules regarding deductions of charitable contributions by individual taxpayers. Under the proposal, the general contribution base limit would remain at 50 percent for contributions of cash to public charities. For all other contributions (except contributions of conservation easements), a single deduction limit of 30 percent of the taxpayer's contribution base would apply, irrespective of the type of property donated, the type of organization receiving the donation, and whether the contribution is to or for the use of the organization. In addition, the proposal would extend the carry-forward period for contributions in excess of these limitations from 5 to 15 years. The proposal would be effective for contributions made in taxable years beginning after December 31, 2016.

Exclude from gross income subsidies from public utilities for purchase of water runoff management.— Under current law, subsidies for water conservation and stormwater management must be included by individuals in reported income. The Administration proposes to exclude from gross income for individuals the value of any subsidy provided by a public utility for the purchase of any water conservation measure or stormwater management measure. The term "water conservation measure" means any installation, modification, or water-use evaluation primarily designed to reduce consumption of water or to improve the management of water demand with respect to a dwelling unit. The term "stormwater management measure" means any installation or modification of property to offset or safely manage the amounts of stormwater runoff associated with a dwelling unit. The term "public utility" means an entity engaged in the sale of water to customers and includes the Federal government or a state or local government.

Provide relief for certain accidental dual citizens.—Individuals who became at birth both a citizen of the United States and a citizen of another country may not have learned until recently that they are U.S. citizens subject to U.S. Federal income tax on their worldwide income, even though they may have had minimal contacts with the United States. Some of these individuals would like to relinquish their U.S. citizenship (i.e., "expatriate"), but doing so would require them to pay significant U.S. tax under current law. The Administration's proposal would provide relief from these U.S. tax obligations for certain individuals who relinquish their U.S. citizenship within two years after the later of January 1, 2017, the effective date of the proposal, or the date on which the individual learns that he or she is a U.S. citizen.

USER FEES

Reform inland waterways funding.—The Administration proposes legislation to reform the laws governing the Inland Waterways Trust Fund, including establishing an annual per vessel fee to increase the amount paid by commercial navigation users of the inland waterways. In 1986, the Congress provided that commercial traffic on the inland waterways would be responsible for 50 percent of the capital costs of the locks, dams, and other features that make barge transportation possible on the inland waterways. The additional revenue would help finance future capital investments in these waterways, as well as 25 percent of the operation and maintenance costs, to support economic growth. The current excise tax on diesel fuel used in inland waterways commerce, which was recently increased to 29 cents per gallon, will not produce the revenue needed to cover these costs.

Reauthorize special assessment on domestic nuclear utilities.— Established in 1992, the Uranium Enrichment Decontamination and Decommissioning Fund pays, subject to appropriation, the decontamination and decommissioning costs of the Department of Energy's gaseous diffusion plants in Tennessee, Ohio, and Kentucky. The Administration proposes to reauthorize the special assessment on domestic nuclear utilities, for deposit in the Uranium Enrichment Decontamination and Decommissioning Fund due to higher-than-expected cleanup costs. In addition, the Administration proposes to authorize the use of balances in the United States Enrichment Corporation Fund for the same purpose as the Uranium Enrichment Decontamination and Decommissioning Fund. The reauthorization of the special assessment on domestic nuclear utilities will also offset the cost of the United States Enrichment Corporation Fund proposal.

Establish user fee for the Electronic Visa Update System (EVUS).—The Administration proposes to establish a user fee for EVUS, a new U.S. Customs and Border Protection (CBP) program to collect biographic and travel-related information from certain non-immigrant visa holders prior to traveling to the United States. This process will complement existing visa application process and enhance CBP's ability to make pre-travel admissibility and risk determinations. CBP proposes to establish a user fee to fund the costs of establishing, providing, and administering the system.

TRADE INITIATIVES

Enact the Trans-Pacific Partnership (TPP) Trade Agreement.—TPP, negotiated between the United States and 11 countries in the Asia-Pacific region, levels the playing field for U.S. workers, farmers, ranchers, small business owners, and manufacturers by eliminating more than 18,000 taxes and other trade barriers on American goods. The Agreement also includes groundbreaking, enforceable labor and environmental provisions. Overall, TPP will strengthen strategic relationships with the Nation's partners and allies in a region that will be vital to the 21st century while creating higher-paying jobs for middle-class families at home.

OTHER INITIATIVES

Allow offset of Federal income tax refunds to collect delinquent State income taxes for out-of-state residents.—Under current law, Federal tax refunds may be offset to collect delinquent State income tax obligations, but only if the delinquent taxpayer resides in the State collecting the tax. The Administration proposes to allow Federal tax refunds to be offset to collect delinquent State tax obligations regardless of where the debtor resides. The proposal would be effective on the date of enactment.

Improve disclosure for child support enforcement.—Current law permitting disclosure of tax return information with respect to child support enforcement is complex and diffused and often crosses jurisdictional lines, resulting in items of tax return information that may not be shared with parties that are integral to child support enforcement. The inability to disclose tax return information to these parties and in these circumstances presents challenges to the effective operation of child support enforcement activities. The proposal would amend section 6103(l) to: (1) consolidate the child support enforcement disclosure rules into a single provision; (2) define key terms, (3) permit disclosure to parties integral to child support enforcement; and (4) update and streamline the items of tax return information that may be disclosed. The proposal clarifies the use of tax data for child support purposes and the safeguarding responsibilities of agency and agent recipients.

Authorize the limited sharing of business tax return information to improve the accuracy of important measures of the economy.—Synchronization of business lists among the Bureau of Economic Analysis (BEA), the Bureau of Labor Statistics (BLS), and the Bureau of the Census (Census Bureau) would significantly improve the consistency and quality of sensitive economic statistics including productivity, payroll, employment, and average hourly earnings. The availability of accurate economic statistics is crucial to policy makers. Current law authorizes IRS disclosure of certain Federal tax information (FTI) for governmental statistical use. Business FTI may be disclosed to officers and employees of the Census Bureau for all businesses. Similarly, business FTI may be disclosed to BEA officers and employees, but only for corporate businesses. Currently, BLS is not authorized to receive FTI. The Census Bureau's Business Register is constructed using both FTI and non-tax business data derived from the Economic Census and current economic surveys, so that under current law it is not possible for the Census Bureau to share data with BEA and BLS in any meaningful way, making synchronizing of their business lists impossible. In addition, given the growth of non-corporate businesses, especially in the service sector, the current limitation on BEA's access to corporate FTI impedes the measurement of income and international transactions in the National Accounts. The Administration proposes to give officers and employees of BEA and BLS access to certain FTI of corporate and non-corporate businesses. Additionally, for the purpose of synchronizing BLS and Census Bureau business lists, the proposal would permit employees of State agencies to receive certain business FTI from BLS. No BEA, BLS, or State agency contractor would have access to FTI. Additionally, the Census Bureau, BEA, BLS, and the State agencies would be subject to the confidentiality safeguard procedures in the Confidential Information Protection and Statistical Efficiency Act, as well as taxpayer privacy law and related safeguards and penalties. The proposal would be effective upon enactment.

Eliminate certain reviews conducted by the U.S. Treasury Inspector General for Tax Administration (TIGTA).—Under current law, TIGTA conducts reviews to comply with reporting requirements. The Administration proposes to eliminate TIGTA's obligation to report information regarding any administrative or civil actions related to Fair Tax Collection Practices violations in one of TIGTA's Semiannual Reports, review and certify annually that the IRS is complying with the requirements of section 6103(e)(8) of the Internal Revenue Code regarding information on joint filers, and annually report on the IRS's compliance with requirements that IRS employees stop a taxpayer interview whenever a taxpayer requests to consult with a representative and to obtain their immediate supervisor's approval to contact the taxpayer instead of the representative if the representative has unreasonably delayed the completion of an examination or investigation. The proposal would revise the annual reporting requirement for all remaining provisions in the IRS Restructuring and Reform Act of 1998 to a biennial reporting requirement. The proposal would be effective after December 31, 2016.

Modify indexing to prevent deflationary adjustments.—Many parameters of the tax system— including the size of personal exemptions and standard deductions, the width of income tax rate brackets, the amount of other deductions and credits, and the maximum amount of various saving and retirement deductions—may be adjusted annually for the effects of inflation, based on annual changes in the CPI. Under current law, if price levels decline, most (but not all) of the inflation adjustment provisions would permit tax parameters to become smaller, so long as they do not decline to less than their base period values. The Administration proposes to modify inflation adjustment provisions to prevent the size of any indexed tax parameters from decreasing from the previous year's levels if the underlying price index falls. Subsequent inflation-related increases in the price index relevant for adjusting the particular tax parameter would be taken into account only to the extent that the index exceeds its highest previous level. The proposal would be effective as of the date of enactment.

IMMIGRATION REFORM

Enact comprehensive immigration reform.—The Administration proposes to enact comprehensive immigration reform that strengthens the Nation's border security, cracks down on employers who hire undocumented workers, and provides a pathway to earned citizenship for individuals who pay a penalty and taxes, learn English, pass a background check, and go to the back of the line. Comprehensive immigration reform will contribute to a safer and more just society, boost economic growth, reduce

deficits, and improve the solvency of Social Security. The Administration supports the approach to immigration reform in S. 744, which passed the Senate in 2013 with bipartisan support. The Congressional Budget Office (CBO) has estimated that comprehensive immigration reform along the lines of the Senate-passed bill would reduce the deficit by about $170 billion in the first decade and by nearly $1 trillion over 20 years. The 2017 Budget includes an allowance for the budget effects of immigration reform based on the CBO cost estimate for this bill.

Table 12–2.   EFFECT OF BUDGET PROPOSALS
(In millions of dollars)

	2016	2017	2018	2019	2020	2021	2022	2023	2024	2025	2026	2017-2021	2017-2026
Elements of business tax reform:													
Reform the U.S. international tax system:													
Restrict deductions for excessive interest of members of financial reporting groups	....	2,822	4,986	5,485	6,033	6,637	7,300	8,030	8,833	9,717	10,688	25,963	70,531
Provide tax incentives for locating jobs and business activity in the United States and remove tax deductions for shipping jobs overseas	....	−11	−18	−20	−20	−21	−22	−23	−24	−26	−26	−90	−211
Repeal delay in the implementation of worldwide interest allocation	....	−1,406	−2,400	−2,496	−2,596	−1,055	....	....	....	....	....	−9,953	−9,953
Impose a 19-percent minimum tax on foreign income ..	....	24,201	38,418	35,969	33,192	32,831	34,211	35,651	37,117	38,635	40,166	164,611	350,391
Impose a 14-percent one-time tax on previously untaxed foreign income [1]	....	....	....	....	....	....	....	....	....	....	....	....	....
Limit shifting of income through intangible property transfers	....	88	167	201	237	275	315	361	413	473	542	968	3,072
Disallow the deduction for excess non-taxed reinsurance premiums paid to affiliates	....	411	657	697	731	771	815	848	882	918	958	3,267	7,688
Modify tax rules for dual capacity taxpayers	....	465	814	878	930	970	992	1,032	1,074	1,121	1,359	4,057	9,635
Tax gain from the sale of a partnership interest on look-through basis	....	146	251	264	277	291	305	321	337	354	371	1,229	2,917
Modify sections 338(h)(16) and 902 to limit credits when non-double taxation exists	....	59	102	105	105	105	105	105	106	106	107	476	1,005
Close loopholes under subpart F	....	1,517	2,635	2,821	3,019	3,230	3,453	3,692	3,945	4,215	4,501	13,222	33,028
Restrict the use of hybrid arrangements that create stateless income	....	115	201	215	230	247	264	283	304	326	350	1,008	2,535
Limit the ability of domestic entities to expatriate	....	118	327	556	807	1,083	1,383	1,711	2,068	2,457	2,880	2,891	13,390
Total, reform the U.S. international tax system	....	28,525	46,140	44,675	42,945	45,364	49,121	52,011	55,055	58,296	61,896	207,649	484,028
Simplification and tax relief for small business:													
Expand expensing for small business	....	−2,101	−2,863	−2,072	−1,625	−1,335	−1,132	−1,009	−961	−971	−997	−9,996	−15,066
Expand simplified accounting for small business and establish a uniform definition of small business for accounting methods	....	−6,248	−4,874	−2,819	−1,975	−1,814	−1,745	−1,724	−1,819	−1,839	−1,845	−17,730	−26,702
Increase the limitations for deductible new business expenditures and consolidate provisions for start-up and organizational expenditures	....	−490	−484	−477	−473	−471	−469	−465	−461	−456	−452	−2,395	−4,698
Expand and simplify the tax credit provided to qualified small employers for non-elective contributions to employee health insurance [2]	−10	−170	−163	−146	−131	−100	−118	−80	−60	−27	−14	−710	−1,009
Total, simplification and tax relief for small business	−10	−9,009	−8,384	−5,514	−4,204	−3,720	−3,464	−3,278	−3,301	−3,293	−3,308	−30,831	−47,475
Incentives for job creation, manufacturing, research, and clean energy:													
Enhance and simplify research incentives	....	−959	−1,896	−2,154	−2,409	−2,660	−2,913	−3,166	−3,426	−3,690	−3,964	−10,078	−27,237
Extend and modify certain employment tax credits, including incentives for hiring veterans	....	−2	−7	−9	−511	−1,062	−1,194	−1,308	−1,406	−1,492	−1,573	−1,591	−8,564
Provide new Manufacturing Communities tax credit	....	−97	−277	−483	−619	−693	−751	−788	−677	−417	−107	−2,169	−4,909
Provide Community College Partnership tax credit	....	−109	−277	−380	−406	−405	−273	−124	−96	−79	−64	−1,577	−2,213
Designate Promise Zones [2]	....	−301	−610	−681	−829	−902	−836	−786	−752	−730	−723	−3,323	−7,150
Modify and permanently extend renewable electricity production tax credit and investment tax credit [2]	....	−122	−230	−345	−587	−1,041	−1,359	−1,633	−3,990	−6,549	−8,287	−2,325	−24,143

Table 12–2. EFFECT OF BUDGET PROPOSALS—Continued

(In millions of dollars)

	2016	2017	2018	2019	2020	2021	2022	2023	2024	2025	2026	2017-2021	2017-2026
Modify and permanently extend the deduction for energy-efficient commercial building property	....	−159	−268	−281	−285	−283	−279	−277	−273	−270	−272	−1,276	−2,647
Provide a carbon dioxide investment and sequestration tax credit [2]	....	−9	−34	−47	−48	−388	−709	−409	−791	−677	−338	−526	−3,450
Provide additional tax credits for investment in qualified property used in a qualifying advanced energy manufacturing project	....	−74	−194	−1,118	−787	−111	−4	34	28	14	3	−2,284	−2,209
Extend the tax credit for second generation biofuel production	....	−87	−157	−172	−175	−175	−175	−153	−118	−83	−48	−766	−1,343
Provide a tax credit for the production of advanced technology vehicles	....	−505	−503	−497	−469	−386	−220	−83	161	296	267	−2,360	−1,939
Provide a tax credit for medium- and heavy-duty alternative-fuel commercial vehicles	....	−44	−78	−85	−89	−93	−61	−15	....	....	....	−389	−465
Modify and extend the tax credit for the construction of energy-efficient new homes	....	−82	−182	−238	−268	−288	−306	−323	−351	−382	−405	−1,058	−2,825
Total, incentives for job creation, manufacturing, research, and clean energy	....	−2,550	−4,713	−6,490	−7,482	−8,487	−9,080	−9,031	−11,691	−14,059	−15,511	−29,722	−89,094
Incentives to promote regional growth:													
Modify and permanently extend the New Markets tax credit	....	....	....	....	−97	−278	−483	−716	−970	−1,235	−1,505	−375	−5,284
Reform and expand the Low-Income Housing tax credit	−1	−19	−99	−272	−512	−769	−1,031	−1,300	−1,576	−1,860	−2,152	−1,671	−9,590
Total, incentives to promote regional growth	−1	−19	−99	−272	−609	−1,047	−1,514	−2,016	−2,546	−3,095	−3,657	−2,046	−14,874
Incentives for investment in infrastructure:													
Provide America Fast Forward Bonds and expand eligible uses [2]	....	−1	−4	−10	−14	−21	−26	−32	−37	−44	−48	−50	−237
Allow current refundings of State and local governmental bonds	....	−1	−5	−5	−5	−5	−5	−5	−5	−5	−5	−21	−46
Repeal the $150 million non-hospital bond limitation on all qualified 501(c)(3) bonds	....	....	−1	−3	−5	−7	−9	−11	−13	−16	−17	−16	−82
Increase national limitation amount for qualified highway or surface freight transfer facility bonds	−6	−28	−60	−93	−125	−153	−167	−163	−136	−96	−55	−459	−1,076
Provide a new category of qualified private activity bonds for infrastructure projects referred to as "qualified public infrastructure bonds"	....	−27	−121	−258	−397	−534	−646	−698	−714	−728	−741	−1,337	−4,864
Modify qualified private activity bonds for public education facilities	....	....	....	....	....	....	....	....	....	....	....	....	....
Modify treatment of banks investing in tax-exempt bonds	....	−5	−38	−131	−225	−317	−405	−493	−574	−630	−616	−716	−3,434
Repeal tax-exempt bond financing of professional sports facilities	....	3	11	23	35	47	60	72	85	97	109	119	542
Allow more flexible research arrangements for purposes of private business use limits	....	....	....	....	−1	−1	−1	−3	−3	−3	−4	−2	−16
Modify tax-exempt bonds for Indian tribal governments	....	−4	−12	−12	−12	−12	−12	−12	−12	−12	−12	−52	−112
Total, incentives for investment in infrastructure	−6	−63	−230	−489	−749	−1,003	−1,211	−1,345	−1,409	−1,437	−1,389	−2,534	−9,325
Eliminate fossil fuel tax preferences:													
Treat publicly-traded partnerships for fossil fuels as C corporations	....	....	....	....	....	....	201	280	295	309	323	....	1,408
Eliminate oil and natural gas preferences:													
Repeal enhanced oil recovery credit	....	235	559	792	979	1,070	1,049	1,011	1,010	1,038	1,060	3,635	8,803
Repeal credit for oil and natural gas produced from marginal wells [3]	....	....	....	....	....	....	....	....	....	....	....	....	....
Repeal expensing of intangible drilling costs	....	966	1,541	1,439	1,645	1,526	1,100	733	472	340	288	7,117	10,050
Repeal deduction for tertiary injectants	....	5	8	8	8	8	8	8	8	8	8	37	77
Repeal exception to passive loss limitations for working interests in oil and natural gas properties	....	9	12	12	12	11	10	10	9	9	9	56	103
Repeal percentage depletion for oil and natural gas wells	....	483	770	725	666	589	509	429	350	270	199	3,233	4,990
Repeal domestic manufacturing deduction for oil and natural gas production	....	470	836	869	901	932	962	993	1,026	1,062	1,098	4,008	9,149
Increase geological and geophysical amortization period for independent producers to seven years	....	54	197	307	296	235	170	103	58	47	48	1,089	1,515

Table 12–2. EFFECT OF BUDGET PROPOSALS—Continued

(In millions of dollars)

	2016	2017	2018	2019	2020	2021	2022	2023	2024	2025	2026	2017-2021	2017-2026
Subtotal, eliminate oil and natural gas preferences	....	2,222	3,923	4,152	4,507	4,371	3,808	3,287	2,933	2,774	2,710	19,175	34,687
Eliminate coal preferences:													
Repeal expensing of exploration and development costs	....	20	35	35	33	32	30	27	25	24	24	155	285
Repeal percentage depletion for hard mineral fossil fuels	....	113	183	177	145	114	99	87	75	66	62	732	1,121
Repeal capital gains treatment for royalties	....	26	52	52	52	52	52	52	52	52	52	234	494
Repeal domestic manufacturing deduction for the production of coal and other hard mineral fossil fuels	....	11	20	21	22	23	24	25	26	27	28	97	227
Subtotal, eliminate coal preferences	....	170	290	285	252	221	205	191	178	169	166	1,218	2,127
Total, eliminate fossil fuel tax preferences	....	2,392	4,213	4,437	4,759	4,592	4,214	3,758	3,406	3,252	3,199	20,393	38,222
Reform the treatment of financial and insurance industry products:													
Require that derivative contracts be marked to market with resulting gain or loss treated as ordinary	....	3,674	5,415	4,347	2,743	1,665	1,124	679	466	434	405	17,844	20,952
Modify rules that apply to sales of life insurance contracts	....	26	44	46	48	50	54	56	58	61	63	214	506
Modify proration rules for life insurance company general and separate accounts	....	345	527	534	551	579	609	628	642	658	681	2,536	5,754
Expand pro rata interest expense disallowance for corporate-owned life insurance	....	116	232	337	457	597	753	910	1,075	1,245	1,422	1,739	7,144
Conform net operating loss (NOL) rules of life insurance companies to those of other corporations	....	18	28	30	31	33	35	36	38	39	41	140	329
Total, reform the treatment of financial and insurance industry products	....	4,179	6,246	5,294	3,830	2,924	2,575	2,309	2,279	2,437	2,612	22,473	34,685
Other business revenue changes and loophole closers:													
Repeal LIFO method of accounting for inventories	....	5,369	7,647	8,307	8,394	8,611	8,082	8,032	8,455	9,475	8,963	38,328	81,335
Repeal lower-of-cost-or-market inventory accounting method		878	1,321	1,381	1,390	521	240	250	260	271	283	5,491	6,795
Modify like-kind exchange rules		2,684	7,828	6,889	5,903	4,870	3,986	3,668	3,748	3,831	3,916	28,174	47,323
Modify depreciation rules for purchases of general aviation passenger aircraft	....	48	159	260	345	460	511	434	346	286	208	1,272	3,057
Expand the definition of substantial built-in loss for purposes of partnership loss transfers		7	8	8	8	9	9	10	10	10	10	40	89
Extend partnership basis limitation rules to nondeductible expenditures		89	122	126	129	132	134	136	139	141	144	598	1,292
Deny deduction for punitive damages		48	70	72	73	76	77	79	80	82	84	339	741
Conform corporate ownership standards		1	16	31	32	33	34	35	36	38	40	113	296
Tax corporate distributions as dividends		48	82	87	91	95	99	104	109	114	119	403	948
Repeal FICA tip credit		729	883	921	961	1,004	1,047	1,092	1,140	1,189	1,241	4,498	10,207
Repeal the excise tax credit for distilled spirits with flavor and wine additives [4]		82	109	109	109	109	109	109	109	109	109	518	1,063
Total, other business revenue changes and loophole closers	....	9,983	18,245	18,191	17,435	15,920	14,328	13,949	14,432	15,546	15,117	79,774	153,146
Total, elements of business tax reform	−17	33,438	61,418	59,832	55,925	54,543	54,969	56,357	56,225	57,647	58,959	265,156	549,313
Transition to a reformed business tax system:													
Impose a 14-percent one-time tax on previously untaxed foreign income [1]	....	35,930	59,883	59,883	59,883	59,883	23,953	....	....	....	....	275,462	299,415
Middle-class and pro-work tax reforms:													
Reform child care tax incentives [2]	....	−684	−3,539	−3,720	−3,909	−4,081	−4,277	−4,459	−4,652	−5,009	−5,492	−15,933	−39,822
Simplify and better target tax benefits for education [2]	....	−19	−4,518	−4,622	−4,561	−5,089	−5,375	−5,778	−6,090	−6,465	−6,272	−18,809	−48,789
Expand the EITC for workers without qualifying children [2]	....	−468	−6,255	−6,387	−6,495	−6,628	−6,756	−6,894	−7,028	−7,176	−7,322	−26,233	−61,409
Simplify the rules for claiming the EITC for workers without qualifying children [2]	....	−41	−550	−540	−547	−560	−572	−587	−601	−615	−629	−2,238	−5,242
Provide a second-earner tax credit [2]	....	−2,037	−8,926	−9,065	−9,160	−9,281	−9,429	−9,563	−9,703	−9,841	−10,016	−38,469	−87,021

Table 12–2. EFFECT OF BUDGET PROPOSALS—Continued
(In millions of dollars)

	2016	2017	2018	2019	2020	2021	2022	2023	2024	2025	2026	2017-2021	2017-2026
Extend exclusion from income for cancellation of certain home mortgage debt	....	-2,467	-822	....	....	....	....	....	....	....	....	-3,289	-3,289
Total, middle-class and pro-work tax reforms		-5,716	-24,610	-24,334	-24,672	-25,639	-26,409	-27,281	-28,074	-29,106	-29,731	-104,971	-245,572
Reforms to retirement and health benefit plans:													
Provide for automatic enrollment in IRAs, including a small employer tax credit, increase the tax credit for small employer plan start-up costs, and provide an additional tax credit for small employer plans newly offering auto-enrollment [2]			-959	-1,556	-1,672	-1,722	-1,779	-1,885	-1,989	-2,119	-2,221	-5,909	-15,902
Expand penalty-free withdrawals for long-term unemployed		-226	-231	-235	-240	-245	-250	-255	-260	-265	-270	-1,177	-2,477
Require retirement plans to allow long-term part-time workers to participate		-46	-47	-49	-50	-51	-52	-53	-55	-56	-57	-243	-516
Facilitate annuity portability		....	....	....	....	....	....	....	....	....	....	....	....
Simplify minimum required distribution rules		-5	-6	-2	4	19	37	61	91	127	172	10	498
Allow all inherited plan and IRA balances to be rolled over within 60 days		....	....	....	....	....	....	....	....	....	....	....	....
Permit unaffiliated employers to maintain a single multi-employer defined contribution plan		-97	-137	-147	-155	-169	-181	-196	-209	-230	-246	-705	-1,767
Enact changes to the military retirement reform enacted in the FY 2016 National Defense Authorization Act			-53	-85	-94	-110	-126	-144	-154	-169	-180	-342	-1,115
Improve the excise tax on high cost employer-sponsored health coverage					-66	-112	-138	-172	-209	-254	-314	-178	-1,265
Extend CHIP through 2019 [2]			846	4,622	1,002	....	....	....	....	....	....	6,470	6,470
Create State option to provide 12-month continuous Medicaid eligibility for adults [2]		333	949	2,000	2,427	2,560	2,803	2,944	3,095	3,249	3,405	8,269	23,765
Standardize definition of American Indian and Alaska Native in the ACA [2]		-30	-40	-50	-50	-50	-50	-60	-60	-60	-70	-220	-520
Subtotal, reforms to retirement and health benefit plans		-71	322	4,498	1,106	120	264	240	250	223	219	5,975	7,171
Reforms to capital gains taxation, upper-income tax benefits, and the taxation of financial institutions:													
Reduce the value of certain tax expenditures		31,092	50,403	54,946	59,515	63,910	68,322	72,776	77,183	81,525	85,866	259,866	645,538
Reform the taxation of capital income		14,757	24,669	20,639	22,015	23,211	23,426	24,696	25,976	27,254	28,565	105,291	235,208
Implement the Buffett Rule by imposing a new "Fair Share Tax"		7,848	-62	1,317	3,102	4,035	4,136	4,170	4,240	4,334	4,388	16,240	37,508
Impose a financial fee		5,653	11,084	10,949	11,163	11,420	11,683	11,952	12,226	12,508	12,795	50,269	111,433
Total, reforms to capital gains taxation, upper-income tax benefits, and the taxation of financial institutions		59,350	86,094	87,851	95,795	102,576	107,567	113,594	119,625	125,621	131,614	431,666	1,029,687
Loophole closers:													
Require current inclusion in income of accrued market discount and limit the accrual amount for distressed debt		4	12	20	28	34	42	50	58	69	79	98	396
Require that the cost basis of stock that is a covered security must be determined using an average cost basis method			74	223	377	539	634	657	684	713	744	1,213	4,645
Tax carried (profits) interests as ordinary income		2,619	2,633	2,520	2,420	2,351	1,932	1,472	1,213	1,121	1,029	12,543	19,310
Require non-spouse beneficiaries of deceased IRA owners and retirement plan participants to take inherited distributions over no more than five years		111	285	471	660	853	891	841	780	718	654	2,380	6,264
Limit the total accrual of tax-favored retirement benefits		1,616	2,302	2,406	2,639	2,947	3,084	3,465	3,606	3,828	4,085	11,910	29,978
Rationalize net investment income and SECA taxes		16,660	23,276	24,773	25,913	26,943	28,124	29,421	30,816	32,163	33,570	117,565	271,659
Limit Roth conversions to pre-tax dollars		....	5	10	16	20	20	21	28	32	99	51	251
Eliminate deduction for dividends on stock of publicly-traded corporations held in ESOPs		702	945	962	978	995	1,011	1,028	1,044	1,062	1,079	4,582	9,806
Repeal exclusion of net unrealized appreciation in employer securities		16	27	28	13	4	4	-12	-23	-23	-24	88	10
Disallow the deduction for charitable contributions that are a prerequisite for purchasing tickets to college sporting events		150	237	255	272	290	308	327	348	369	391	1,204	2,947
Total, loophole closers		21,878	29,796	31,668	33,316	34,976	36,050	37,270	38,554	40,052	41,706	151,634	345,266
Modify estate and gift tax provisions:													

Table 12–2. EFFECT OF BUDGET PROPOSALS—Continued

(In millions of dollars)

	2016	2017	2018	2019	2020	2021	2022	2023	2024	2025	2026	2017-2021	2017-2026
Restore the estate, gift, and GST tax parameters in effect in 2009	....	....	15,717	17,102	18,415	20,027	21,695	23,660	25,815	28,303	31,020	71,261	201,754
Expand requirement of consistency in value for transfer and income tax purposes	....	....	142	143	169	174	185	198	211	228	243	628	1,693
Modify transfer tax rules for grantor retained annuity trusts (GRATs) and other grantor trusts	....	....	1,123	1,241	1,478	1,622	1,969	2,374	2,743	3,194	3,405	5,464	19,149
Limit duration of generation-skipping transfer (GST) tax exemption	....	....	....	....	....	....	....	....	....	....	....	....	....
Extend the lien on estate tax deferrals where estate consists largely of interest in closely held business	....	....	24	25	26	27	28	29	31	34	36	102	260
Modify GST tax treatment of Health and Education Exclusion Trusts	....	....	−35	−33	−30	−29	−27	−26	−24	−23	−20	−127	−247
Simplify gift tax exclusion for annual gifts	....	....	84	160	259	336	413	453	548	657	770	839	3,680
Expand applicability of definition of executor	....	....	....	....	....	....	....	....	....	....	....	....	....
Total, modify estate and gift tax provisions	....	....	17,055	18,638	20,317	22,157	24,263	26,688	29,324	32,393	35,454	78,167	226,289
Other revenue raisers:													
Impose an oil fee [4]	....	7,221	14,439	21,505	28,450	35,135	41,377	41,989	42,521	42,977	43,456	106,750	319,070
Increase and modify Oil Spill Liability Trust Fund financing [4]	....	94	133	135	138	138	139	141	143	144	147	638	1,352
Reinstate Superfund taxes [4]	....	1,596	2,087	2,163	2,202	2,276	2,300	2,359	2,399	2,445	2,492	10,324	22,319
Increase tobacco taxes and index for inflation [4]	....	9,982	12,910	12,715	12,719	12,329	11,880	11,436	10,877	10,399	9,902	60,655	115,149
Make unemployment insurance surtax permanent [4]	....	1,172	1,604	1,624	1,645	1,667	1,690	1,712	1,737	1,762	1,789	7,712	16,402
Expand Federal Unemployment Tax Act (FUTA) base and reform FUTA credit reduction rules [4]	....	....	3,128	3,185	3,923	4,303	5,424	6,802	6,068	6,346	7,113	14,539	46,292
Modernize the unemployment insurance program [4]	....	....	....	514	468	415	429	410	560	585	604	1,397	3,985
Create a mandatory RESEA program [4]	....	....	....	−4	−24	−65	−168	−195	−216	−267	−293	−93	−1,232
Levy a fee on the production of hardrock minerals to restore abandoned mines	....	....	200	200	200	200	200	200	200	200	200	800	1,800
Return fees on the production of coal to pre–2006 levels to restore abandoned mines	....	49	50	52	53	54	....	....	....	....	....	258	258
Total, other revenue raisers	....	20,114	34,551	42,089	49,774	56,452	63,271	64,854	64,289	64,591	65,410	202,980	525,395
Reduce the tax gap and make reforms:													
Expand information reporting:													
Improve information reporting for certain businesses and contractors	....	15	36	60	82	85	89	93	97	102	106	278	765
Provide an exception to the limitation on disclosing tax return information to expand TIN matching beyond forms where payments are subject to backup withholding	....	....	....	....	....	....	....	....	....	....	....	....	....
Provide for reciprocal reporting of information in connection with the implementation of FATCA	....	....	....	....	....	....	....	....	....	....	....	....	....
Require Form W–2 reporting for employer contributions to defined contribution plans	....	....	....	....	....	....	....	....	....	....	....	....	....
Subtotal, expand information reporting	....	15	36	60	82	85	89	93	97	102	106	278	765
Improve compliance by businesses:													
Increase certainty with respect to worker classification	5	93	451	871	1,038	1,127	1,220	1,321	1,428	1,544	1,668	3,580	10,761
Increase information sharing to administer excise taxes [4]	....	4	9	13	14	16	17	17	18	18	19	56	145
Provide authority to readily share information about beneficial ownership information of U.S. companies with law enforcement	....	....	1	2	9	6	4	3	3	3	3	18	34
Subtotal, improve compliance by businesses	5	97	461	886	1,061	1,149	1,241	1,341	1,449	1,565	1,690	3,654	10,940
Strengthen tax administration:													
Modify the conservation easement deduction and pilot a conservation credit	....	6	22	46	63	72	79	83	89	94	101	209	655
Impose liability on shareholders to collect unpaid income taxes of applicable corporations	....	395	423	442	461	481	502	524	546	570	595	2,202	4,939
Implement a program integrity statutory cap adjustment for tax administration	....	278	1,585	3,263	5,008	6,763	8,327	9,264	9,590	9,737	9,814	16,897	63,629
Revise offer-in-compromise application rules	....	1	2	2	2	2	2	2	2	2	2	9	19
Make repeated willful failure to file a tax return a felony	....	....	....	....	1	1	1	1	2	2	2	2	10

Table 12–2. EFFECT OF BUDGET PROPOSALS—Continued
(In millions of dollars)

	2016	2017	2018	2019	2020	2021	2022	2023	2024	2025	2026	2017-2021	2017-2026
Facilitate tax compliance with local jurisdictions	....	1	1	1	2	2	2	2	2	2	2	7	17
Improve investigative disclosure statute	....	....	....	....	1	1	1	1	2	2	2	2	10
Allow the IRS to absorb credit and debit card processing fees for certain tax payments	....	2	2	2	2	2	2	2	2	2	2	10	20
Provide the IRS with greater flexibility to address correctable errors [2]	....	31	62	62	63	65	66	68	70	72	74	283	633
Enhance electronic filing of returns	....	....	....	....	1	1	1	1	2	2	2	2	10
Improve the whistleblower program	....	....	....	....	....	....	....	....	....	....	....	....	....
Index all civil tax penalties for inflation	....	....	....	....	....	....	....	....	....	....	....	....	....
Combat tax-related identity theft	....	....	....	....	....	....	....	....	....	....	....	....	....
Allow States to send notices of intent to offset Federal tax refunds to collect State tax obligations by regular first-class mail instead of certified mail	....	....	....	....	....	....	....	....	....	....	....	....	....
Accelerate information return filing due dates [2]	....	3	5	11	12	12	13	13	13	13	14	43	109
Increase oversight of paid tax return preparers [2]	....	14	31	34	37	41	45	49	54	57	62	157	424
Enhance administrability of the appraiser penalty	....	....	....	....	....	....	....	....	....	....	....	....	....
Enhance UI program integrity [4]	....	....	–1	–7	–16	–29	–43	–60	–96	–61	–99	–53	–412
Request a program integrity cap adjustment for the RESEA program [4]			–2	–7	–10	–11	–10	–9	–9	–7	–5	–30	–70
Subtotal, strengthen tax administration		731	2,130	3,849	5,627	7,403	8,988	9,941	10,269	10,487	10,568	19,740	69,993
Total, reduce the tax gap and make reforms	5	843	2,627	4,795	6,770	8,637	10,318	11,375	11,815	12,154	12,364	23,672	81,698
Simplify the tax system:													
Modify adoption credit to allow tribal determination of special needs	....	....	....	....	–1	–1	–1	–1	–1	–1	–1	–2	–7
Repeal non-qualified preferred stock designation	....	33	55	55	53	50	46	41	36	32	29	246	430
Reform excise tax based on investment income of private foundations	....	–5	–5	–6	–6	–6	–6	–6	–7	–7	–7	–28	–61
Simplify arbitrage investment restrictions	....	....	–2	–10	–18	–28	–38	–46	–58	–68	–76	–58	–344
Simplify single-family housing mortgage bond targeting requirements	....	....	–1	–3	–5	–7	–10	–12	–17	–20	–22	–16	–97
Streamline private activity limits on governmental bonds	....	....	–1	–3	–5	–7	–9	–11	–13	–15	–17	–16	–81
Repeal technical terminations of partnerships	....	13	19	21	23	25	27	29	30	32	33	101	252
Repeal anti-churning rules of section 197	....	–24	–99	–198	–281	–338	–370	–378	–378	–378	–378	–940	–2,822
Repeal special estimated tax payment provision for certain insurance companies	....	....	....	....	....	....	....	....	....	....	....	....	....
Repeal the telephone excise tax [4]	....	–368	–327	–287	–248	–209	–170	–132	–94	–57	–44	–1,439	–1,936
Increase the standard mileage rate for automobile use by volunteers	....	–20	–62	–65	–68	–69	–71	–72	–74	–76	–79	–284	–656
Consolidate contribution limitations for charitable deductions and extend the carryforward period for excess charitable contribution deduction amounts	....	....	–93	–51	–6	–6	–6	–491	–1,188	–1,830	–2,416	–156	–6,087
Exclude from gross income subsidies from public utilities for purchase of water runoff management	....	....	....	....	....	....	....	....	....	....	....	....	....
Provide relief for certain accidental dual citizens	....	–63	–108	–58	–23	–25	–26	–28	–29	–30	–32	–277	–422
Total, simplify the tax system	....	–434	–624	–605	–585	–621	–634	–1,107	–1,793	–2,418	–3,010	–2,869	–11,831
User fees:													
Reform inland waterways funding [4]	....	3	78	118	156	156	156	156	156	155	155	511	1,289
Reauthorize special assessment on domestic nuclear utilities	....	208	212	217	222	227	232	237	243	248	254	1,086	2,300
Establish user fee for Electronic Visa Update System	....	31	25	27	31	27	31	29	34	24	28	141	287
Total, user fees	....	242	315	362	409	410	419	422	433	427	437	1,738	3,876
Trade initiatives:													
Enact the Trans-Pacific Partnership Trade Agreement [4]	....	....	–1,690	–2,343	–2,586	–2,858	–3,147	–3,445	–3,724	–4,003	–4,318	–9,477	–28,114
Other initiatives:													
Allow offset of Federal income tax refunds to collect delinquent State income taxes for out-of-state residents	....	....	....	....	....	....	....	....	....	....	....	....	....
Improve disclosure for child support enforcement	....	....	....	....	....	....	....	....	....	....	....	....	....

Table 12–2. EFFECT OF BUDGET PROPOSALS—Continued
(In millions of dollars)

	2016	2017	2018	2019	2020	2021	2022	2023	2024	2025	2026	2017-2021	2017-2026
Authorize the limited sharing of business tax return information to improve the accuracy of important measures of the economy	....	....	....	....	....	....	....	....	....	....	....	....	....
Eliminate certain reviews conducted by the U.S. Treasury Inspector General for Tax Administration (TIGTA)	....	....	....	....	....	....	....	....	....	....	....	....	....
Modify indexing to prevent deflationary adjustments	....	....	....	....	....	....	....	....	....	....	....	....	....
Total, other initiatives	....	....	....	....	....	....	....	....	....	....	....	....	....
Enact comprehensive immigration reform	....	1,000	7,000	20,000	30,000	40,000	45,000	55,000	64,000	74,000	84,000	98,000	420,000
Total, effect of budget proposals	−12	166,574	272,137	302,334	325,452	350,636	335,884	333,967	350,924	371,581	393,104	1,417,133	3,202,593

[1] The Administration believes that this proposal should be enacted in the context of comprehensive business tax reform. However, the proposal generates one-time transition revenue in the short run, which is shown in the "Transition to a reformed business tax system" category.

[2] This proposal affects both receipts and outlays for refundable tax credits. Both effects are shown above. The outlay effects included in these estimates are listed:

	2016	2017	2018	2019	2020	2021	2022	2023	2024	2025	2026	2017-2021	2017-2026
Expand and simplify the tax credit provided to qualified small employers for non-elective contributions to employee health insurance	....	21	23	19	17	12	14	10	7	4	2	92	129
Designate Promise Zones	....	27	29	29	31	31	33	35	37	37	39	147	328
Modify and permanently extend renewable electricity production tax credit and investment tax credit	....	58	155	281	453	695	973	1,300	1,695	2,117	2,629	1,642	10,356
Provide a carbon dioxide investment and sequestration tax credit	....	....	....	....	....	142	280	123	338	226	....	142	1,109
Provide America Fast Forward Bonds and expand eligible uses	....	288	1,306	2,803	4,377	6,022	7,714	9,435	11,176	12,935	14,709	14,796	70,765
Reform child care tax incentives	....	....	962	1,009	1,051	1,091	1,147	1,182	1,227	1,264	1,268	4,113	10,201
Simplify and better target tax benefits for education	....	....	4,377	4,521	4,479	4,663	5,079	5,255	5,679	5,870	5,833	18,040	45,756
Expand the EITC for workers without qualifying children	....	273	5,468	5,577	5,677	5,796	5,906	6,020	6,134	6,262	6,383	22,791	53,496
Simplify the rules for claiming the EITC for workers without qualifying children	....	24	484	475	481	492	503	516	528	541	553	1,956	4,597
Provide a second-earner tax credit	....	....	739	735	735	740	754	758	760	759	754	2,949	6,734
Provide for automatic enrollment in IRAs, including a small employer tax credit, increase the tax credit for small employer plan start-up costs, and provide an additional tax credit for small employer plans newly offering auto-enrollment	....	....	126	198	203	207	215	222	228	230	236	734	1,865
Extend CHIP through 2019	....	....	−780	−4,168	−474	....	....	....	....	....	....	−5,422	−5,422
Create State option to provide 12-month continuous Medicaid eligibility for adults	....	−333	−912	−1,923	−2,269	−2,395	−2,629	−2,763	−2,904	−3,049	−3,196	−7,832	−22,373
Standardize definition of American Indian and Alaska Native in the ACA	....	30	40	50	50	50	50	60	60	60	70	220	520
Provide the IRS with greater flexibility to address correctable errors	....	−26	−53	−52	−53	−54	−55	−56	−58	−59	−61	−238	−527
Accelerate information return filing due dates	....	−1	−3	−6	−7	−7	−8	−8	−8	−8	−8	−24	−64
Increase oversight of tax return preparers	....	−2	−14	−15	−16	−18	−19	−21	−23	−24	−26	−65	−178
Total, outlay effects of budget proposals	....	359	11,947	9,533	14,735	17,467	19,957	22,068	24,876	27,165	29,185	54,041	177,292

[3] This provision is estimated to have zero receipt effect under the Administration's current economic projections.

[4] Net of income offsets.

Table 12–3. RECEIPTS BY SOURCE
(In millions of dollars)

Source	2015 Actual	2016	2017	2018	2019	2020	2021	2022	2023	2024	2025	2026
Individual income taxes:												
Federal funds	1,540,802	1,627,824	1,724,055	1,793,016	1,878,054	1,987,644	2,094,996	2,205,155	2,318,828	2,436,572	2,559,406	2,688,326
Legislative proposal, not subject to PAYGO	....	....	278	1,585	3,263	5,011	6,770	8,341	9,279	9,608	9,756	9,836
Legislative proposal, subject to PAYGO	....	10	63,640	96,693	103,650	113,598	120,161	125,627	132,585	139,744	147,212	155,195
Total, Individual income taxes	**1,540,802**	**1,627,834**	**1,787,973**	**1,891,294**	**1,984,967**	**2,106,253**	**2,221,927**	**2,339,123**	**2,460,692**	**2,585,924**	**2,716,374**	**2,853,357**
Corporation income taxes:												
Federal funds:												
Federal funds	343,797	292,593	342,676	364,027	400,701	453,989	461,255	466,836	470,900	478,017	485,759	494,534
Legislative proposal, subject to PAYGO	....	–32	75,138	127,581	123,288	119,465	119,780	85,935	64,689	66,453	69,165	71,791
Total, Federal funds	343,797	292,561	417,814	491,608	523,989	573,454	581,035	552,771	535,589	544,470	554,924	566,325
Trust funds:												
Legislative proposal, subject to PAYGO	....	....	920	1,175	1,242	1,273	1,340	1,354	1,402	1,436	1,473	1,507
Total, Corporation income taxes	**343,797**	**292,561**	**418,734**	**492,783**	**525,231**	**574,727**	**582,375**	**554,125**	**536,991**	**545,906**	**556,397**	**567,832**
Social insurance and retirement receipts (trust funds):												
Employment and general retirement:												
Old-age survivors insurance (off-budget)	658,543	655,143	668,748	698,776	757,783	798,229	840,156	881,186	919,264	963,058	1,005,667	1,056,426
Legislative proposal, not subject to PAYGO	....	....	....	....	3	7	14	29	33	41	42	50
Legislative proposal, subject to PAYGO	....	2	86	–529	–926	–1,651	–2,244	–2,836	–2,896	–2,678	–2,722	–2,968
Disability insurance (off-budget)	111,829	142,512	158,019	165,114	141,506	135,548	142,668	149,635	156,101	163,538	170,774	179,393
Legislative proposal, not subject to PAYGO	....	....	....	....	....	1	2	5	6	7	7	9
Legislative proposal, subject to PAYGO	....	....	15	–90	–157	–280	–380	–481	–491	–454	–462	–504
Hospital Insurance	234,189	243,538	253,293	264,355	275,936	287,008	302,270	317,204	331,173	347,008	362,486	380,932
Legislative proposal, not subject to PAYGO	....	....	....	....	....	1	3	7	8	11	12	14
Legislative proposal, subject to PAYGO	....	8	506	1,048	1,578	1,613	1,561	1,507	1,611	1,796	1,932	2,056
Railroad retirement:												
Social security equivalent account	2,530	2,523	2,558	2,625	2,694	2,769	2,846	2,926	3,008	3,092	3,170	3,253
Rail pension & supplemental annuity	3,336	3,380	3,416	3,500	3,587	3,683	3,782	3,884	3,989	4,098	4,201	4,502
Total, Employment and general retirement	1,010,427	1,047,106	1,086,641	1,134,799	1,182,004	1,226,928	1,290,678	1,353,066	1,411,806	1,479,517	1,545,107	1,623,163
On-budget	(240,055)	(249,449)	(259,773)	(271,528)	(283,795)	(295,074)	(310,462)	(325,528)	(339,789)	(356,005)	(371,801)	(390,757)
Off-budget	(770,372)	(797,657)	(826,868)	(863,271)	(898,209)	(931,854)	(980,216)	(1,027,538)	(1,072,017)	(1,123,512)	(1,173,306)	(1,232,406)
Unemployment insurance:												
Deposits by States [1]	42,177	41,354	40,570	39,690	39,881	40,494	41,266	41,732	42,837	43,149	44,139	45,301
Legislative proposal, not subject to PAYGO	....	....	....	–3	–19	–59	–126	–269	–316	–382	–405	–475
Legislative proposal, subject to PAYGO	....	....	7	3,940	4,546	4,101	4,437	4,645	4,868	5,139	4,912	5,364
Federal unemployment receipts [1]	8,926	8,399	8,113	6,020	6,096	6,176	6,259	6,343	6,431	6,523	6,618	6,716
Legislative proposal, subject to PAYGO	....	....	1,466	2,010	2,170	3,513	3,614	4,855	6,358	5,382	6,030	6,588
Railroad unemployment receipts [1]	75	121	134	149	157	139	111	112	137	153	145	132
Total, Unemployment insurance	51,178	49,874	50,290	51,806	52,831	54,364	55,561	57,418	60,315	59,964	61,439	63,626
Other retirement:												
Federal employees retirement-employee share	3,629	3,794	4,254	4,510	4,822	5,171	5,556	5,977	6,426	6,904	7,405	7,889

Table 12–3. RECEIPTS BY SOURCE—Continued

(In millions of dollars)

Source	2015 Actual	2016	2017	2018	2019	2020	2021	2022	2023	2024	2025	2026
Non-Federal employees retirement[2]	23	22	21	20	19	18	16	15	15	14	13	12
Total, Other retirement	3,652	3,816	4,275	4,530	4,841	5,189	5,572	5,992	6,441	6,918	7,418	7,901
Total, Social insurance and retirement receipts (trust funds)	**1,065,257**	**1,100,796**	**1,141,206**	**1,191,135**	**1,239,676**	**1,286,481**	**1,351,811**	**1,416,476**	**1,478,562**	**1,546,399**	**1,613,964**	**1,694,690**
On-budget	(294,885)	(303,139)	(314,338)	(327,864)	(341,467)	(354,627)	(371,595)	(388,938)	(406,545)	(422,887)	(440,658)	(462,284)
Off-budget	(770,372)	(797,657)	(826,868)	(863,271)	(898,209)	(931,854)	(980,216)	(1,027,538)	(1,072,017)	(1,123,512)	(1,173,306)	(1,232,406)
Excise taxes:												
Federal funds:												
Alcohol	9,639	9,583	9,707	9,783	9,875	9,951	10,035	10,112	10,186	10,258	10,322	10,380
Legislative proposal, subject to PAYGO	....	....	109	146	146	146	146	146	146	146	146	146
Tobacco	14,453	14,368	14,252	14,136	14,019	13,903	13,787	13,671	13,554	13,438	13,322	13,205
Legislative proposal, subject to PAYGO	....	....	13,309	17,212	16,955	16,959	16,438	15,839	15,249	14,505	13,865	13,203
Transportation fuels	−3,394	−3,462	−3,383	−958	−957	−955	−956	−959	−962	−966	−966	−969
Telephone and teletype services	607	545	490	436	383	330	278	227	176	126	76	59
Legislative proposal, subject to PAYGO	....	....	−490	−436	−383	−330	−278	−227	−176	−126	−76	−59
High-cost health insurance coverage	....	....	....	....	....	1,349	4,955	6,585	8,524	10,715	13,362	16,613
Legislative proposal, subject to PAYGO	....	....	....	....	....	−27	−48	−60	−75	−91	−113	−143
Health insurance providers	11,261	11,295	7	14,281	15,065	15,861	16,700	17,573	18,491	19,461	20,479	21,551
Indoor tanning services	85	85	86	86	87	88	88	88	89	90	90	90
Medical devices	1,987	610	−10	1,601	2,371	2,537	2,704	2,886	3,060	3,243	3,432	3,629
Other Federal fund excise taxes	3,121	2,605	2,577	2,539	2,581	2,637	2,710	2,792	2,875	2,965	3,050	3,144
Legislative proposal, subject to PAYGO	....	....	3,175	4,493	5,961	7,238	8,396	9,305	9,218	8,577	7,769	7,569
Total, Federal funds	37,759	35,629	39,829	63,319	66,103	69,687	74,955	77,978	80,355	82,341	84,758	88,418
Trust funds:												
Transportation	40,813	41,323	41,068	40,988	40,868	40,773	40,755	40,814	40,805	40,824	40,861	40,966
Legislative proposal, subject to PAYGO	....	....	6,454	14,767	22,723	30,713	38,470	45,884	46,787	48,137	49,554	50,392
Airport and airway	14,268	14,351	15,063	15,639	16,123	16,779	17,319	17,620	18,001	18,347	18,907	19,392
Sport fish restoration and boating safety	574	542	545	548	551	554	558	562	565	569	572	576
Tobacco assessments	49	....	....	....	....	....	....	....	....	....	....	....
Black lung disability insurance	552	525	530	539	340	227	213	208	202	194	194	199
Inland waterway	98	107	106	105	104	103	102	101	100	100	99	98
Legislative proposal, subject to PAYGO	....	....	3	3	3	3	3	3	3	3	2	2
Hazardous substance superfund (Legislative proposal subject to PAYGO)	....	....	902	1,216	1,227	1,239	1,249	1,261	1,275	1,285	1,297	1,312
Oil spill liability	496	530	585	607	611	616	617	618	622	623	621	624
Legislative proposal, subject to PAYGO	....	....	127	178	180	183	183	187	189	191	192	195
Vaccine injury compensation	275	311	318	325	334	343	349	357	366	376	385	396
Leaking underground storage tank	179	212	211	209	208	205	206	205	204	201	201	199
Supplementary medical insurance	2,991	2,969	3,980	4,098	2,826	2,800	2,800	2,800	2,800	2,800	2,800	2,800
Patient-centered outcomes research	225	322	339	356	377	399	423	447	471	496	523	552
Total, Trust funds	60,520	61,192	70,231	79,578	86,475	94,937	103,247	111,067	112,390	114,146	116,208	117,703
Total, Excise taxes	**98,279**	**96,821**	**110,060**	**142,897**	**152,578**	**164,624**	**178,202**	**189,045**	**192,745**	**196,487**	**200,966**	**206,121**
Estate and gift taxes:												
Federal funds	19,232	21,094	22,399	23,730	25,073	26,421	28,079	29,686	31,493	33,492	35,613	37,869

Table 12–3. RECEIPTS BY SOURCE—Continued

(In millions of dollars)

Source	2015 Actual	2016	2017	2018	2019	2020	2021	2022	2023	2024	2025	2026
Legislative proposal, subject to PAYGO	....	....	....	7,787	8,941	10,258	11,756	13,360	15,254	17,403	19,867	22,329
Total, Estate and gift taxes	**19,232**	**21,094**	**22,399**	**31,517**	**34,014**	**36,679**	**39,835**	**43,046**	**46,747**	**50,895**	**55,480**	**60,198**
Customs duties and fees:												
Federal funds:												
Federal funds	33,527	35,083	37,779	40,310	42,180	43,781	45,541	47,217	48,871	50,361	51,829	53,588
Legislative proposal, subject to PAYGO	....	....	....	–2,253	–3,124	–3,448	–3,811	–4,196	–4,593	–4,966	–5,337	–5,758
Total, Federal funds	33,527	35,083	37,779	38,057	39,056	40,333	41,730	43,021	44,278	45,395	46,492	47,830
Trust funds:												
Trust funds	1,514	1,638	1,758	1,853	1,935	2,019	2,108	2,187	2,270	2,343	2,422	2,518
Total, Customs duties and fees	**35,041**	**36,721**	**39,537**	**39,910**	**40,991**	**42,352**	**43,838**	**45,208**	**46,548**	**47,738**	**48,914**	**50,348**
Miscellaneous receipts:												
Federal funds:												
Miscellaneous taxes	528	536	535	526	526	526	525	525	525	525	525	525
Deposit of earnings, Federal Reserve System	96,468	116,445	64,818	44,492	37,878	41,598	47,924	54,717	60,314	64,870	69,366	74,423
Transfers from the Federal Reserve	485	565	636	649	663	677	691	706	720	736	751	767
Fees for permits and regulatory and judicial services	25,349	24,446	23,957	21,602	23,588	24,739	26,309	28,120	28,571	29,991	29,677	30,376
Legislative proposal, subject to PAYGO	....	....	288	487	496	506	508	463	466	477	472	482
Fines, penalties, and forfeitures	23,236	16,190	30,766	32,348	32,389	34,392	35,850	37,454	39,093	40,674	42,364	44,199
Legislative proposal, subject to PAYGO	....	....	....	–1	–11	1	6	4	3	3	3	3
Refunds and recoveries	–34	–35	–35	–35	–35	–35	–35	–35	–35	–35	–35	–35
Total, Federal funds	146,032	158,147	120,965	100,068	95,494	102,404	111,778	121,954	129,657	137,241	143,123	150,740
Trust funds:												
United Mine Workers of America, combined benefit fund	25	23	21	19	18	16	15	11	10	9	8	7
Defense cooperation	330	249	353	531	534	536	539	140	142	145	148	151
Inland waterways (Legislative proposal, subject to PAYGO)	....	....	....	75	115	153	153	153	153	153	153	153
Fines, penalties, and forfeitures	1,091	1,256	1,494	1,396	1,436	1,476	1,517	1,567	1,606	1,622	1,661	1,702
Total, Trust funds	1,446	1,528	1,868	2,021	2,103	2,181	2,224	1,871	1,911	1,929	1,970	2,013
Total, Miscellaneous receipts	**147,478**	**159,675**	**122,833**	**102,089**	**97,597**	**104,585**	**114,002**	**123,825**	**131,568**	**139,170**	**145,093**	**152,753**
Allowance for immigration reform	....	....	**1,000**	**7,000**	**20,000**	**30,000**	**40,000**	**45,000**	**55,000**	**64,000**	**74,000**	**84,000**
Total, budget receipts	**3,249,886**	**3,335,502**	**3,643,742**	**3,898,625**	**4,095,054**	**4,345,701**	**4,571,990**	**4,755,848**	**4,948,853**	**5,176,519**	**5,411,188**	**5,669,299**
On-budget	(2,479,514)	(2,537,845)	(2,816,874)	(3,035,354)	(3,196,845)	(3,413,847)	(3,591,774)	(3,728,310)	(3,876,836)	(4,053,007)	(4,237,882)	(4,436,893)
Off-budget	(770,372)	(797,657)	(826,868)	(863,271)	(898,209)	(931,854)	(980,216)	(1,027,538)	(1,072,017)	(1,123,512)	(1,173,306)	(1,232,406)

[1] Deposits by States cover the benefit part of the program. Federal unemployment receipts cover administrative costs at both the Federal and State levels. Railroad unemployment receipts cover both the benefits and administrative costs of the program for the railroads.

[2] Represents employer and employee contributions to the civil service retirement and disability fund for covered employees of Government-sponsored, privately owned enterprises and the District of Columbia municipal government.

13. OFFSETTING COLLECTIONS AND OFFSETTING RECEIPTS

I. INTRODUCTION AND BACKGROUND

The Government records money collected in one of two ways. It is either recorded as a governmental receipt and included in the amount reported on the receipts side of the budget or it is recorded as an offsetting collection or offsetting receipt, which reduces (or "offsets") the amount reported on the outlay side of the budget. Governmental receipts are discussed in the previous chapter, "Governmental Receipts." The first section of this chapter broadly discusses offsetting collections and offsetting receipts. The second section discusses user charges, which consist of a subset of offsetting collections and offsetting receipts and a small share of governmental receipts. The third and final section of this chapter describes the Administration's user charge proposals.

As discussed below, offsetting collections and offsetting receipts are cash inflows to a budget account that are usually used to finance Government activities. The spending associated with these activities is included in total or "gross outlays." For 2015, gross outlays to the public were $4,204 billion,[1] or 23.6 percent of gross domestic product (GDP). Offsetting collections and offsetting receipts from the public are subtracted from gross outlays to the public to yield "net outlays," which is the most common measure of outlays cited and generally referred to as simply "outlays." For 2015, net outlays were $3,688 billion or 20.7 percent of GDP. Government-wide net outlays reflect the Government's net disbursements to the public and are subtracted from governmental receipts to derive the Government's deficit or surplus. For 2015, governmental receipts were $3,250 billion, or 18.3 percent of GDP, and the deficit was $438 billion, or 2.5 percent of GDP.

There are two sources of offsetting receipts and offsetting collections: from the public and from other budget accounts. In 2015, offsetting receipts and offsetting collections from the public were $516.0 billion, while intragovernmental offsetting receipts and offsetting collections were $1,034 billion. Regardless of how it is recorded (as governmental receipts, offsetting receipts, or offsetting collections), money collected from the public reduces the deficit or increases the surplus. In contrast, intragovernmental collections from other budget accounts exactly offset the payments made by these accounts, with no net impact on the deficit or surplus.[2]

When measured by the magnitude of the dollars collected, most offsetting collections and offsetting receipts from the public arise from business-like transactions with the public. Unlike governmental receipts, which are derived from the Government's exercise of its sovereign power, these offsetting collections and offsetting receipts arise primarily from voluntary payments from the public for goods or services provided by the Government. They are classified as offsets to outlays for the cost of producing the goods or services for sale, rather than as governmental receipts on the receipts side of the budget. Treating offsetting collections and offsetting receipts as offsets to outlays produces budget totals for receipts and (net) outlays that reflect the amount of resources allocated by the Government through collective political choice, rather than through the marketplace.[3] These activities include the sale of postage stamps, land, timber, and electricity; charging fees for services provided to the public (e.g., admission to national parks); and collecting premiums for health care benefits (e.g., Medicare Parts B and D).

A relatively small portion ($34.7 billion in 2015) of offsetting collections and offsetting receipts from the public is derived from the Government's exercise of its sovereign power. From a conceptual standpoint, these should be classified as governmental receipts. However, they are classified as offsetting rather than governmental receipts either because this classification has been specified in law or because these collections have traditionally been classified as offsets to outlays. Most of the offsetting collections and offsetting receipts in this category derive from fees from Government regulatory services or Government licenses, and include, for example, charges for regulating the nuclear energy industry, bankruptcy filing fees, immigration fees, food inspection fees, passport fees, and patent and trademark fees.[4]

A third source of offsetting collections and offsetting receipts is intragovernmental transfers. Examples of intragovernmental transfers include interest payments to funds that hold Government securities (such as the Social

---

[1] Gross outlays to the public are derived by subtracting intragovernmental outlays from gross outlays. For 2015, gross outlays were $5,238 billion. Intragovernmental outlays are payments from one Government account to another Government account. For 2015, intragovernmental outlays totaled $1,034 billion.

[2] For the purposes of this discussion, "collections from the public" include collections from non-budgetary Government accounts, such as credit financing accounts and deposit funds. For more information on these non-budgetary accounts, see Chapter 10, "Coverage of the Budget."

[3] Showing collections from business-type transactions as offsets on the spending side of the budget follows the concept recommended by the Report of the President's Commission on Budget Concepts in 1967 and is discussed in Chapter 9 of this volume, "Budget Concepts."

[4] This category of receipts is known as "offsetting governmental receipts." Some argue that regulatory or licensing fees should be viewed as payments for a particular service or for the right to engage in a particular type of business. However, these fees are conceptually much more similar to taxes because they are compulsory, and they fund activities that are intended to provide broadly dispersed benefits, such as protecting the health of the public. Reclassifying these fees as governmental receipts could require a change in law, and because of conventions for scoring appropriations bills, would make it impossible for fees that are controlled through annual appropriations acts to be scored as offsets to discretionary spending.

Table 13–1.   OFFSETTING COLLECTIONS AND OFFSETTING RECEIPTS FROM THE PUBLIC
(In billions of dollars)

		Estimate	
	Actual 2015	2016	2017
Offsetting collections (credited to expenditure accounts):			
User charges:			
Postal Service stamps and other USPS fees (off-budget)	73.5	74.8	75.3
Defense Commissary Agency	5.5	6.0	5.7
Employee contributions for employees and retired employees health benefits funds	13.9	15.1	16.1
Sale of energy:			
Tennessee Valley Authority	43.2	40.9	41.5
Bonneville Power Administration	3.3	4.0	4.2
All other user charges	68.7	65.2	71.8
Subtotal, user charges	208.1	206.0	214.6
Other collections credited to expenditure accounts:			
Commodity Credit Corporation fund	5.5	6.8	7.0
Supplemental Security Income (collections from the States)	2.6	2.7	2.7
Other collections	17.6	8.2	7.5
Subtotal, other collections	25.7	17.7	17.2
Subtotal, offsetting collections	233.9	223.7	231.8
Offsetting receipts (deposited in receipt accounts):			
User charges:			
Medicare premiums	67.1	72.1	79.1
Spectrum auction, relocation, and licenses	30.1	12.9	13.9
Outer Continental Shelf rents, bonuses, and royalties	3.5	2.8	3.2
All other user charges	34.2	35.7	40.1
Subtotal, user charges deposited in receipt accounts	134.9	123.5	136.3
Other collections deposited in receipt accounts:			
Military assistance program sales	32.4	36.0	37.4
Interest received from credit financing accounts	38.7	60.0	65.3
Proceeds, GSE equity related transactions	20.7	16.0	18.7
All other collections deposited in receipt accounts	55.5	51.1	44.4
Subtotal, other collections deposited in receipt accounts	147.3	163.1	165.8
Subtotal, offsetting receipts	282.2	286.6	302.2
Total, offsetting collections and offsetting receipts from the public	**516.0**	**510.3**	**534.0**
Total, offsetting collections and offsetting receipts excluding off-budget	442.4	435.4	458.6
ADDENDUM:			
User charges that are offsetting collections and offsetting receipts[1]	343.0	329.5	350.9
Other offsetting collections and offsetting receipts from the public	173.0	180.8	183.1

[1] Excludes user charges that are classified on the receipts side of the budget. For total user charges, see Table 13-3.

Security trust funds), general fund transfers to civilian and military retirement pension and health benefits funds, and agency payments to funds for employee health insurance and retirement benefits. Although these intragovernmental collections exactly offset the payments themselves, with no effect on the deficit or surplus, it is important to record these transactions in the budget to show how much the Government is allocating to fund various programs. For example, in the case of civilian retirement pensions, Government agencies make accrual payments to the Civil Service Retirement and Disability Fund on behalf of current employees to fund their future retirement benefits; the receipt of these payments to the Fund is shown in a single receipt account. Recording the receipt of these payments is important because it demonstrates the total cost to the Government today of providing this future benefit.

The final source of offsetting collections and offsetting receipts is gifts. Gifts are voluntary contributions to the Government to support particular purposes or reduce the amount of Government debt held by the public.

Although both offsetting collections and offsetting receipts are subtracted from gross outlays to derive net outlays, they are treated differently when it comes to accounting for specific programs and agencies. Offsetting collections are usually authorized to be spent for the purposes of an expenditure account and are generally available for use when collected, without further action by the Congress. Therefore, offsetting collections are recorded as offsets to spending within expenditure accounts, so that the account total highlights the net flow of funds.

Like governmental receipts, offsetting receipts are credited to receipt accounts, and any spending of the re-

Table 13–2. OFFSETTING RECEIPTS BY TYPE SUMMARY

(In millions of dollars)

Receipt Type	Actual 2015	Estimate					
		2016	2017	2018	2019	2020	2021
Intragovernmental	686,493	823,097	770,912	820,655	888,642	922,187	966,150
Receipts from non-Federal sources:							
Proprietary	252,655	262,143	273,983	272,422	289,209	306,332	321,718
Offsetting governmental	29,535	24,445	28,181	21,277	14,468	15,033	15,315
Total, receipts from non-Federal sources	282,190	286,588	302,164	293,699	303,677	321,365	337,033
Total, offsetting receipts	968,683	1,109,685	1,073,076	1,114,354	1,192,319	1,243,552	1,303,183

ceipts is recorded in separate expenditure accounts. As a result, the budget separately displays the flow of funds into and out of the Government. Offsetting receipts may or may not be designated for a specific purpose, depending on the legislation that authorizes their collection. If designated for a particular purpose, the offsetting receipts may, in some cases, be spent without further action by the Congress. When not designated for a particular purpose, offsetting receipts are credited to the general fund, which contains all funds not otherwise allocated and which is used to finance Government spending that is not financed out of dedicated funds. In some cases where the receipts are designated for a particular purpose, offsetting receipts are reported in a particular agency and reduce or offset the outlays reported for that agency. In other cases, the offsetting receipts are "undistributed," which means they reduce total Government outlays, but not the outlays of any particular agency.

Table 13–1 summarizes offsetting collections and offsetting receipts from the public. Note that this table does not include intragovernmental transactions. The amounts shown in the table are not evident in the commonly cited budget measure of (net) outlays. For 2017, the table shows that total offsetting collections and offsetting receipts from the public are estimated to be $534.0 billion or 2.8 percent of GDP. Of these, an estimated $231.8 billion are offsetting collections and an estimated $302.2 billion are offsetting receipts. Table 13–1 also identifies those offsetting collections and offsetting receipts that are considered user charges, as defined and discussed below.

As shown in the table, major offsetting collections from the public include proceeds from Postal Service sales,

electrical power sales, loan repayments to the Commodity Credit Corporation for loans made prior to enactment of the Federal Credit Reform Act, and Federal employee payments for health insurance. As also shown in the table, major offsetting receipts from the public include premiums for Medicare Parts B and D, proceeds from military assistance program sales, rents and royalties from Outer Continental Shelf oil extraction, proceeds from auctions of the electromagnetic spectrum, dividends on holdings of preferred stock of the Government-sponsored enterprises, and interest income.

Tables 13–2 and 13–5 provide further detail about offsetting receipts, including both offsetting receipts from the public (as summarized in Table 13–1) and intragovernmental transactions. Table 13–5, formerly printed in this chapter, is available on the Internet at *www.budget. gov/budget/Analytical_Perspectives* and on the Budget CD-ROM. In total, offsetting receipts are estimated to be $1,073.1 billion in 2017; $770.9 billion are from intragovernmental transactions and $302.2 billion are from the public. The offsetting receipts from the public consist of proprietary receipts ($274.0 billion) and those classified as offsetting receipts by law or long-standing practice ($28.2 billion) and shown as offsetting governmental receipts in the table. Proprietary receipts from the public result from business-like transactions such as the sale of goods or services, or the rental or use of Government land. Offsetting governmental receipts are composed of fees from Government regulatory services or Government licenses that, absent a specification in law or a long-standing practice, would be classified on the receipts side of the budget.

II. USER CHARGES

User charges or user fees[5] refer generally to those monies that the Government receives from the public for market-oriented activities and regulatory activities. In combination with budget concepts, laws that authorize

user charges determine whether a user charge is classified as an offsetting collection, an offsetting receipt, or a governmental receipt. Almost all user charges, as defined below, are classified as offsetting collections or offsetting receipts; for 2017, only an estimated 1.5 percent of user charges are classified as governmental receipts. As summarized in Table 13–3, total user charges for 2017 are estimated to be $356.2 billion with $350.9 billion being offsetting collections or offsetting receipts, and accounting for more than half of all offsetting collections and offsetting receipts from the public.

---

[5] In this chapter, the term "user charge" is generally used and has the same meaning as the term "user fee." The term "user charge" is the one used in OMB Circular No. A–11, "Preparation, Submission, and Execution of the Budget"; OMB Circular No. A–25, "User Charges"; and Chapter 9 of this volume, "Budget Concepts." In common usage, the terms "user charge" and "user fee" are often used interchangeably, and in *A Glossary of Terms Used in the Federal Budget Process*, GAO provides the same definition for both terms.

Table 13–3. GROSS OUTLAYS, USER CHARGES, OTHER OFFSETTING COLLECTIONS AND OFFSETTING RECEIPTS FROM THE PUBLIC, AND NET OUTLAYS

(In billions of dollars)

	Actual 2015	Estimate	
		2016	2017
Gross outlays to the public	4,204.3	4,461.6	4,681.2
Offsetting collections and offsetting receipts from the public:			
User charges[1]	343.0	329.5	350.9
Other	173.0	180.8	183.1
Subtotal, offsetting collections and offsetting receipts from the public	516.0	510.3	534.0
Net outlays	3,688.3	3,951.3	4,147.2

[1] $4.8 billion of the total user charges for 2015 were classified as governmental receipts, and the remainder were classified as offsetting collections and offsetting receipts. $4.6 billion and $5.3 billion of the total user charges for 2016 and 2017 are classified as governmental receipts, respectively.

Definition. In this chapter, user charges refer to fees, charges, and assessments levied on individuals or organizations directly benefiting from or subject to regulation by a Government program or activity, where the payers do not represent a broad segment of the public such as those who pay income taxes.

Examples of business-type or market-oriented user charges and regulatory and licensing user charges include those charges listed in Table 13–1 for offsetting collections and offsetting receipts. User charges exclude certain offsetting collections and offsetting receipts from the public, such as payments received from credit programs, interest, and dividends, and also exclude payments from one part of the Federal Government to another. In addition, user charges do not include dedicated taxes (such as taxes paid to social insurance programs or excise taxes on gasoline) or customs duties, fines, penalties, or forfeitures.

Alternative definitions. The definition for user charges used in this chapter follows the definition used in OMB Circular No. A–25, "User Charges," which provides policy guidance to Executive Branch agencies on setting the amount for user charges. Alternative definitions may be used for other purposes. Much of the discussion of user charges below—their purpose, when they should be levied, and how the amount should be set—applies to these alternative definitions as well.

A narrower definition of user charges could be limited to proceeds from the sale of goods and services, excluding the proceeds from the sale of assets, and to proceeds that are dedicated to financing the goods and services being provided. This definition is similar to one the House of Representatives uses as a guide for purposes of committee jurisdiction. (See the Congressional Record, January 3, 1991, p. H31, item 8.) The definition of user charges could be even narrower by excluding regulatory fees and focusing solely on business-type transactions. Alternatively, the user charge definition could be broader than the one used in this chapter by including beneficiary- or liability-based excise taxes.[6]

_____

[6] Beneficiary- and liability-based taxes are terms taken from the Congressional Budget Office, _The Growth of Federal User Charges_, August 1993, and updated in October 1995. Gasoline taxes are an example of beneficiary-based taxes. An example of a liability-based tax is the excise tax that formerly helped fund the hazardous substance superfund

What is the purpose of user charges? User charges are intended to improve the efficiency and equity of financing certain Government activities. Charging users for activities that benefit a relatively limited number of people reduces the burden on the general taxpayer, as does charging regulated parties for regulatory activities in a particular sector.

User charges that are set to cover the costs of production of goods and services can result in more efficient resource allocation within the economy. When buyers are charged the cost of providing goods and services, they make better cost-benefit calculations regarding the size of their purchase, which in turn signals to the Government how much of the goods or services it should provide. Prices in private, competitive markets serve the same purposes. User charges for goods and services that do not have special social or distributional benefits may also improve equity or fairness by requiring those who benefit from an activity to pay for it and by not requiring those who do not benefit from an activity to pay for it.

When should the Government impose a charge? Discussions of whether to finance spending with a tax or a fee often focus on whether the benefits of the activity accrue to the public in general or to a limited group of people. In general, if the benefits of spending accrue broadly to the public or include special social or distributional benefits, then the program should be financed by taxes paid by the public. In contrast, if the benefits accrue to a limited number of private individuals or organizations and do not include special social or distributional benefits, then the program should be financed by charges paid by the private beneficiaries. For Federal programs where the benefits are entirely public or entirely private, applying this principle can be relatively easy. For example, the benefits from national defense accrue to the public in general, and according to this principle should be (and are) financed by taxes. In contrast, the benefits of electricity sold by the Tennessee Valley Authority accrue primarily to those using the electricity, and should be (and are) financed by user charges.

_____

in the Environmental Protection Agency. This tax was paid by industry groups to finance environmental cleanup activities related to the industry activity but not necessarily caused by the payer of the fee.

In many cases, however, an activity has benefits that accrue to both public and private groups, and it may be difficult to identify how much of the benefits accrue to each. Because of this, it can be difficult to know how much of the program should be financed by taxes and how much by fees. For example, the benefits from recreation areas are mixed. Fees for visitors to these areas are appropriate because the visitors benefit directly from their visit, but the public in general also benefits because these areas protect the Nation's natural and historic heritage now and for posterity. For this reason, visitor recreation fees generally cover only part of the cost to the Government of maintaining the recreation property. Where a fee may be appropriate to finance all or part of an activity, the extent to which a fee can be easily administered must be considered. For example, if fees are charged for entering or using Government-owned land then there must be clear points of entry onto the land and attendants patrolling and monitoring the land's use.

What amount should be charged? When the Government is acting in its capacity as sovereign and where user charges are appropriate, such as for some regulatory activities, current policy supports setting fees equal to the full cost to the Government, including both direct and indirect costs. When the Government is not acting in its capacity as sovereign and engages in a purely business-type transaction (such as leasing or selling goods, services, or resources), market price is generally the basis for establishing the fee.[7] If the Government is engaged in a purely business-type transaction and economic resources are allocated efficiently, then this market price should be equal to or greater than the Government's full cost of production.

Classification of user charges in the budget. As shown in the note to Table 13–3, most user charges are classified as offsets to outlays on the spending side of the budget, but a few are classified on the receipts side of the budget. An estimated $5.3 billion in 2017 of user charges are classified on the receipts side and are included in the governmental receipts totals described in the previous chapter, "Governmental Receipts." They are classified as receipts because they are regulatory charges collected by the Federal Government by the exercise of its sovereign powers. Examples include filing fees in the United States courts and agricultural quarantine inspection fees.

The remaining user charges, an estimated $350.9 billion in 2017, are classified as offsetting collections and offsetting receipts on the spending side of the budget. As discussed above in the context of all offsetting collections and offsetting receipts, some of these user charges are collected by the Federal Government by the exercise of its sovereign powers and conceptually should appear on the receipts side of the budget, but they are required by law or a long-standing practice to be classified on the spending side.

---

[7] Policies for setting user charges are promulgated in OMB Circular No. A–25: "User Charges" (July 8, 1993).

III. USER CHARGE PROPOSALS

As shown in Table 13–1, an estimated $231.8 billion of user charges for 2017 will be credited directly to expenditure accounts and will generally be available for expenditure when they are collected, without further action by the Congress. An estimated $302.2 billion of user charges for 2017 will be deposited in offsetting receipt accounts and will be available to be spent only according to the legislation that established the charges.

As shown in Table 13–4, the Administration is proposing new or increased user charges that would, in the aggregate, increase collections by an estimated $4.2 billion in 2017 and an average of $11.1 billion per year from 2018 through 2026. These estimates reflect only the amounts to be collected; they do not include related spending. Each proposal is classified as either discretionary or mandatory, as those terms are defined in the Balanced Budget and Emergency Deficit Control Act of 1985, as amended. "Discretionary" refers to user charges controlled through annual appropriations acts and generally under the jurisdiction of the appropriations committees in the Congress. "Mandatory" refers to user charges controlled by permanent laws and under the jurisdiction of the authorizing committees. These and other terms are discussed further in this volume in Chapter 9, "Budget Concepts."

A. Discretionary User Charge Proposals

1. Offsetting collections

Department of Agriculture

Forest Service: Grazing administrative processing fee. The Budget proposes, beginning on March 1, 2017, and in each subsequent year through February 28, 2020, to recover some of the costs of issuing grazing permits and leases on Forest Service lands. The Forest Service would charge a fee of $2.50 per head month for cattle and its equivalent for other livestock, which would be collected along with current grazing fees. The fee would allow the Forest Service to more expeditiously address pending applications for grazing permit renewals and perform other necessary grazing activities.

Department of Commerce

National Oceanic and Atmospheric Administration (NOAA): Infrastructure permitting fee. The Budget includes a proposal to allow NOAA to collect user fees from private entities for activities related to regulatory permitting. This authority would allow NOAA to expedite studies and data collection supporting decision-making in collaboration with private entities seeking regulatory permits. Annual collections are estimated to be $100,000.

Department of Health and Human Services

Food and Drug Administration (FDA): Food facilities registration, inspection, and import fees. The Budget includes a proposed fee to finance activities that support the safety and security of America's food supply and help meet the requirements of the FDA Food Safety Modernization Act.

FDA: International courier fees. The volume of imports, predominantly medical products, being brought into the United States by international couriers is growing substantially. To ensure the safety of these FDA-regulated products through increased surveillance efforts, the Budget includes a new charge to international couriers.

FDA: Cosmetic facility registration fees. FDA promotes the safety of cosmetics and other health and beauty products. The Budget includes a new facility registration fee for cosmetic and other health and beauty product facilities that will improve FDA's capacity to promote greater safety and understanding of these products.

FDA: Food contact substances notification fee. Food contact substances include components of food packaging and food processing equipment that come in contact with food. This new fee will allow FDA to promote greater safety and understanding of the products that come into contact with food when used.

FDA: Export certification user fee cap increase. Firms exporting products from the United States are often asked by foreign customers or foreign governments to supply a "certificate" for products regulated by the FDA to document the product's regulatory or marketing status. The proposal increases the maximum user fee cap from $175 per export certification to $600 to meet FDA's true cost of issuing export certificates and to ensure better and faster service for American companies that request the service.

Health Resources and Services Administration: 340B Pharmacy Affairs fee. To improve the administration and oversight of the 340B Drug Discount Program, the Budget includes a new charge to those entities participating in the program.

Centers for Medicare and Medicaid Services (CMS): Survey and certification revisit fee. The Budget proposes a revisit user fee to provide CMS with a greater ability to revisit poor performing health care facilities to build greater accountability by creating an incentive for facilities to correct deficiencies and ensure quality of care.

Department of Homeland Security

Transportation Security Administration (TSA): Aviation passenger security fee increase. Since 2001 the aviation passenger security fee had been limited to $2.50 per passenger enplanement with a maximum fee of $5.00 per one-way trip pursuant to the Aviation and Transportation Security Act. Pursuant to the Bipartisan Budget Act (BBA) of 2013, starting in July 2014, this fee was restructured into a single per-trip charge and increased to $5.60 per one-way trip. Over the next 10 years, this restructured fee is projected to provide $40 billion in additional discretionary offsetting collections and $13 billion for deficit reduction.

The 2017 Budget proposes to increase the $5.60 fee established by the BBA of 2013 to $6.60 for 2017 and by an additional 40 cents in 2018, and by an additional 25 cents in 2019 and 2020, resulting in a fee of $7.50 in 2020 that will capture 69 percent of the costs of aviation security in 2020 and 70 percent by 2026. Under this proposal, starting in 2018, a portion of the collections would be allocated between general fund deposits and discretionary offsetting collections. In total, this proposal will increase receipts by an estimated $12.3 billion from 2017 through 2026. Of that amount, $6.9 billion will be categorized as discretionary offsetting collections to pay for the costs of aviation security while the remaining $5.4 billion will be deposited in the general fund for deficit reduction.

TSA: Aviation security infrastructure fee. The aviation security infrastructure fee was authorized in 2001 by the Aviation and Transportation Security Act, requiring air carriers to pay a fee reflecting the aviation industry's share of the costs for screening passengers and property as well as providing other aviation security services. The BBA of 2013 repealed the Aviation Security Infrastructure Fee, effective October 1, 2014, causing offsetting collections to decrease by $4.2 billion over ten years. The 2017 Budget proposes that TSA continue to collect the aviation security infrastructure fee, starting in 2017. The Budget also proposes to reinstate the Aviation Security Infrastructure Fee permanently in the future while providing a mechanism for the agency to more equitably apportion the collection of $420 million among air carriers on the basis of current market share. This proposal increases collections by an estimated $4.2 billion from 2017 through 2026.

Department of Housing and Urban Development

Federal Housing Administration (FHA): Administrative support fee. The Budget requests authority to charge lenders using FHA mortgage insurance an administrative support fee, which would generate an estimated $30 million annually in offsetting collections. These additional collections will offset the cost of enhancements to administrative contract support and FHA staffing, including increasing the number of loans reviewed annually for quality assurance.

Department of the Interior (DOI)

Bureau of Land Management (BLM): Public lands oil and gas lease inspection fees. The Budget proposes new inspection fees for oil and gas facilities that are subject to inspection by BLM. The fees would be based on the number of oil and gas wells per facility, providing for costs to be shared equitably across the industry. In 2017, BLM will spend $48 million on managing the compliance inspection program. Inspection costs include, among other things, the salaries and travel expenses of inspectors. The proposed fees will generate approximately $48 million in 2017, thereby fully offsetting the Bureau's cost of compliance inspections and requiring energy developers on Federal lands to fund the majority of inspection-related compliance costs incurred by BLM.

BLM: Grazing administrative processing fee. The Budget proposes a three-year pilot project to allow BLM to recover some of the costs of issuing grazing permits and leases on BLM lands. BLM would charge a fee of $2.50 per animal unit month, which would be collected along with current grazing fees. The fee would allow BLM to address pending applications for grazing permit renewals more expeditiously. BLM would promulgate regulations for the continuation of the grazing administrative fee as a cost recovery fee after the pilot expires.

Bureau of Safety and Environmental Enforcement: Inspection fees. The Budget proposes to update the existing inspection fee structure for offshore oil and gas production facilities to allow fees to be collected for each inspection that is conducted when a facility is subject to multiple inspections during a given year. This will reduce the need for taxpayer funds to support the program, while more equitably distributing costs among operators based on risk factors such as an operator's history of compliance with safety regulations. The proposed fees are estimated to generate $65 million in 2017, an increase of approximately $11 million over the amount that would be collected under the current fee structure.

Department of Justice

Antitrust Division: Increase Hart-Scott-Rodino fees. The Federal Trade Commission and the Department of Justice Antitrust Division are responsible for reviewing corporate mergers to ensure they do not promote anticompetitive practices. Revenues collected from pre-merger filing fees, known as Hart-Scott-Rodino (HSR) fees, are split evenly between the two agencies. The Budget proposes to increase the HSR fees and index them to the annual change in the gross national product. The fee proposal would also create a new merger fee category for mergers valued at over $1 billion. Under the proposal, the fee increase would take effect in 2018, and it is estimated that in 2018 HSR fees would total $378 million ($189 million for each of Federal Trade Commission and DOJ Antitrust Division), an increase of $118 million per year ($59 million for each of Federal Trade Commission and DOJ Antitrust Division).

Commodity Futures Trading Commission (CFTC)

CFTC fee. The Budget proposes an amendment to the Commodity Exchange Act, effective in 2017, authorizing the CFTC to collect fees, like other Federal financial and banking regulators, from its regulated community equal to the agency's annual appropriation. Fee rates would be designed in a way that supports market access, market liquidity, and the efficiency of the Nation's futures, options, and swaps markets. Fee funding would shift the costs of regulatory services provided by the CFTC from the general taxpayer to the primary beneficiaries of the CFTC's oversight. Subject to enactment of authorizing legislation permitting the CFTC to collect user fees, the Administration proposes that collections begin with the fiscal year 2018 appropriation.

Consumer Product Safety Commission (CPSC)

Import surveillance user fee. The fee, effective in 2018, will expand a CPSC initiative to keep dangerous products out of the hands of U.S. consumers. CPSC proactively detects and stops hazardous products that do not meet safety standards from entering U.S. ports, while expediting compliant trade. The program uses a risk-based methodology as a cost-efficient means to target and inspect high risk imports.

Federal Trade Commission

Increase Hart-Scott-Rodino fees. See description under Department of Justice.

2. Offsetting receipts

Department of Justice

U.S. Trustee Program (USTP): Chapter 11 quarterly filing fee increase. The USTP is responsible for promoting the integrity and efficiency of the Nation's bankruptcy system for the benefit of all stakeholders – debtors, creditors, and the public. Since 1989, the Program has been fully funded through bankruptcy fees paid primarily by those who use the bankruptcy system. Bankruptcy filings have fallen for the last five years, and have not in recent years followed traditional historical patterns. Unlike other bankruptcy fees that are set administratively by the Judicial Conference of the United States, USTP quarterly fees are set in statute. The Budget proposes to adjust the current quarterly fee structure only for those larger chapter 11 debtors in which quarterly disbursements total $1 million or more, excluding 98% of all debtors. The quarterly fees for these large cases would be assessed at 1% of the disbursements with a $250,000 per quarter cap.

Department of State

Western Hemisphere Travel Initiative surcharge extension. The Administration proposes to extend the authority for the Department of State to collect the Western Hemisphere Travel Initiative surcharge for one year, through September 30, 2017. The surcharge was initially enacted by the Passport Services Enhancement Act of 2005 (P.L. 109–167) to cover the Department's costs of meeting increased demand for passports, which resulted from the implementation of the Western Hemisphere Travel Initiative.

Border Crossing Card (BCC) fee increase. The Budget includes a proposal to allow the fee charged for BCC minor applicants to be set administratively, rather than statutorily, at one-half the fee charged for processing an adult border crossing card. Administrative fee setting will allow the fee to better reflect the associated cost of service, consistent with other fees charged for consular services. As a result of this change, annual BCC fee collections beginning in 2017 are projected to increase by $1.8 million (from $0.4 million to $2.2 million).

Department of Transportation

Pipeline and Hazardous Materials Safety Administration: Pipeline design review fees. The Pipeline Safety, Regulatory Certainty, and Job Creation Act of 2011 (P.L. 112-90) established a new fee for companies engaged in the design, permitting, and construction of new pipeline projects. The legislation allowed for the collection of the fee as a mandatory receipt with the spending subject to appropriations. No fees have been collected to date pursuant to this authority. The Consolidated Appropriations Act of 2014 and the Consolidated and Further Continuing Appropriations Act of 2015 provided the authority to retain fees collected in 2014 pursuant to P.L. 112-90. However, since the Administration would like to use these fees as an offset for discretionary spending and does not wish to collect them as a mandatory receipt in exactly the manner prescribed in P.L. 112-90, the Administration proposes collection of this fee pursuant to appropriations language.

B. Mandatory User Charge Proposals

1. *Offsetting collections*

Department of Agriculture (USDA)

Biobased labeling fee. Biobased products are industrial products (other than food or feed) that are composed, in whole or in part, of biological products, including renewable domestic agricultural materials and forestry materials or an intermediate ingredient or feedstock. USDA issues labels for biobased products through the BioPreferred® program that producers can use in advertising their products. To ensure the integrity of the label, the Budget requests authority for USDA to: 1) impose civil penalties on companies who misuse the label, and 2) assess each producer who applies for the label a $500 fee to fund a program audit. This fee, which will begin to be collected once authorizing legislation is enacted, was broadly supported by potential users who commented on the label's proposed rule, which was issued in May 2010.

Rural Housing Service: Guaranteed Underwriting System (GUS) fee. The 2017 Budget includes a proposal that would allow up to a $50 per loan guaranteed underwriting fee for lenders who participate in the section 502 single family housing loan guarantee program, which would become a dedicated funding source to offset the cost of systems upgrades and maintenance for the GUS. Estimates assume the collections will begin in 2019 with a charge of $25 per loan generating $4 million per year for the GUS system.

Department of Labor (DOL)

Pension Benefit Guaranty Corporation (PBGC): Premium increases. PBGC acts as a backstop to protect pension payments for workers whose companies have failed. Currently, PBGC's pension insurance programs are underfunded, and its liabilities far exceed its assets. PBGC receives no taxpayer funds and its premiums are currently much lower than what a private financial institution would charge for insuring the same risk. The Budget proposes to give the PBGC Board the authority to adjust premiums and directs PBGC to take into account the risks that different sponsors pose to their retirees and to PBGC. This reform will both encourage companies to fully fund their pension benefits and ensure the continued

financial soundness of PBGC. The PBGC Board would use this authority to increase premiums in the multiemployer program by adding a variable rate premium based on plan underfunding as well as an exit premium, which would be assessed to employers that leave the system. This proposal is estimated to save $15 billion over the next decade.

Foreign Labor Certification fees. The Budget proposes legislation to allow DOL to charge fees for new applications filed under the Permanent and H-2B foreign labor certification programs, to improve the speed and quality of certification processing. The Budget also proposes legislation to allow DOL to retain fees for certified applications filed under the H-2A temporary labor certification program and modify the fee to cover full program costs. The fees would partially offset Federal costs for administering these programs and, once fully implemented, would eliminate the need for appropriations for this purpose.

Environmental Protection Agency (EPA)

Confidential business information (CBI) management fee. EPA receives filings under the Toxic Substances Control Act that may contain information claimed as CBI. The Budget proposes to expand EPA's existing authority to collect fees to recover approximately 40 percent annually of the costs of reviewing and maintaining the CBI. These costs relate to the management and maintenance of headquarters and regional CBI repositories, a standalone secure CBI database and communications system, physical security, and CBI reviews and sanitizations.

2. *Offsetting receipts*

Department of Agriculture

Food Safety and Inspection Service: Performance and other charges. This fee would be charged to those meat processing plants that have sample failures that result in retesting, have recalls, or are linked to an outbreak. This arrangement will offset the Federal Government's costs for resampling and retesting, while encouraging better food safety practice for processing plants. This fee is expected to generate $4 million in 2017.

Grain Inspection, Packers, and Stockyards Administration: Standardization and licensing activities. These fees would recover the full cost for the development, review, and maintenance of official U.S. grain standards and also for licensing fees to livestock market agencies, dealers, stockyards, packers, and swine contractors. The fees are expected to generate $30 million in 2017.

Animal and Plant Health Inspection Service: Inspection and licensing charges. The Administration proposes to establish charges for: 1) animal welfare inspections for animal research facilities, carriers, and in-transit handlers of animals, 2) licenses for individuals or companies who seek to market a veterinary biologic, and 3) reviews and inspections related to authorized activities to ensure that the regulated entities provide sufficient safeguards for regulated products of biotechnology.

Natural Resources Conservation Service (NRCS) Conservation user fee: The BBA of 2013 provided NRCS with the authority to establish a modest fee to partially offset the agency's cost to develop conservation plans. While this authority included provisions that would exempt beginning, limited resource, and socially disadvantaged farmers, it did not provide NRCS with the authority to retain and spend any fees collected. To more closely associate the fee with the service being provided, the Budget includes language that would allow NRCS to retain and spend any fees collected for the development of conservation plans.

Department of Health and Human Services

CMS: Income-related premium increase under Medicare Parts B and D. The Budget contains a proposal to increase income-related premiums under Medicare Parts B and D. Beginning in 2020, this proposal would increase premiums for certain high-income beneficiaries and maintains the income thresholds associated with these income-related premiums until 25 percent of beneficiaries under Parts B and D are subject to these premiums. This will help improve the financial stability of the Medicare program by reducing the Federal subsidy of Medicare costs for those who need the subsidy the least.

CMS: Medicare Provider Enrollment Application Fee. The Budget proposes an enrollment application fee for all individuals and groups enrolling as Medicare providers, to be adjusted by inflation annually. Providers may request hardship exemptions where applicable. Amounts collected would cover the costs of conducting required provider screening and related program integrity efforts.

CMS: Medicare Billing Agent Enrollment Application Fee. The Budget proposes to establish an enrollment and registration process for clearinghouses and billing agents who act on behalf of Medicare providers and suppliers, introducing an application fee to be consistent with program integrity safeguards in place for institutional and individual providers.

CMS: Medicare Provider Fee for Ordering Services or Supplies without Proper Documentation. Improperly documented items and services account for the majority of Medicare fee-for-service improper payments. The Budget proposes a fee for physicians and practitioners when items or services ordered are not supported by sufficient documentation. Amounts collected would cover the costs of conducting medical claim reviews.

CMS: Refundable Filing Fee for Medicare Parts A & B Appeals. The Budget proposes a refundable filing fee on providers, suppliers, and State Medicaid Agencies to pay a per-claim filing fee beginning at the first level of appeals. The fee will be assessed at each level of appeal and is estimated to reflect 30 percent of the applicable administrative costs associated with adjudicating claims. If an appellant's appeal receives a favorable determination, the fee will be refunded. The fee will not apply to beneficiary appeals and will be phased in over a three-year period.

Department of Homeland Security

Customs and Border Protection (CBP): COBRA and Express Consignment Courier Facilities fees. The Budget proposes to increase COBRA fees (statutorily set under the Consolidated Omnibus Budget Reconciliation Act of 1985) and the Express Consignment Courier Facilities (ECCF) fee created under the Trade Act of 2002. COBRA created a series of user fees for air and sea passengers, commercial trucks, railroad cars, private aircraft and vessels, commercial vessels, dutiable mail packages, broker permits, barges and bulk carriers from Canada and Mexico, cruise vessel passengers, and ferry vessel passengers. This proposal would increase the customs inspection fee by $2 and increase other COBRA fees by a proportional amount.

The ECCF fee was created to reimburse CBP for inspection costs related to express consignment and the proposal would increase the fee by $0.36. The additional revenue raised from increasing the COBRA and ECCF user fees will allow CBP to recover more costs associated with customs related inspections, and reduce waiting times by helping to support the hiring of 840 new CBP officers.

CBP: Increase immigration inspection user fee (IUF) and lift IUF fee limitation. The Budget proposes to increase the immigration inspection user fee by $2. The current fees are $7 for air and commercial vessel passengers and $3 for partially exempted commercial vessel passengers whose trips originate in Canada, Mexico, U.S. territories, and adjacent islands. This fee is paid by passengers and is used to recover some of the costs related to determining the admissibility of passengers entering the U.S. Specifically, the fees collected support immigration inspections, personnel, the maintenance and updating of systems to track criminal and illegal aliens in areas with high apprehensions, asylum hearings, and the repair and maintenance of equipment. CBP has also identified several automation and technology development initiatives to improve its business processes related to cruise ship processing, should this fee increase be realized, including mobile devices for passenger processing; automated passport control and Global Entry Kiosks; and Entry/Exit Biometric technology development, all for the cruise environment.

The Budget also proposes to lift the exemption for passengers traveling from those partially-exempt regions so that the same fee will be applied to all sea passengers. As noted, each sea passenger arriving in the United States is currently charged a $7 fee if his or her journey originated from a place outside of the United States except for certain regions. Lifting this fee limitation will bring collections more in line with the cost of conducting sea passenger inspections as well as help modernize and create more efficient and effective business processes and systems in the cruise environment. Together, the additional receipts collected from these increases would fund 1,230 new CBP officers, which will reduce wait times at air and sea ports of entry, especially as cruise volumes continue to grow as projected in future years.

TSA: Aviation passenger security fee increase. As discussed above in the section on discretionary user charge proposals, the Budget includes a proposal to increase the aviation passenger security fee incrementally over 2017-2020. The fee would be $7.50 per one-way trip beginning in 2020 and would generate $5.4 billion in mandatory receipts over the 10-year budget window, which would be deposited in the general fund for deficit reduction.

Department of the Interior

Federal oil and gas management reforms. The Budget includes a package of legislative reforms to bolster and backstop administrative actions being taken to reform the management of DOI's onshore and offshore oil and gas programs, with a key focus on improving the return to taxpayers from the sale of these Federal resources. Proposed statutory and administrative changes fall into three general categories: 1) advancing royalty reforms, 2) encouraging diligent development of oil and gas leases, and 3) improving revenue collection processes. Royalty reforms include: establishing minimum royalty rates for oil, gas, and similar products; increasing the standard onshore oil and gas royalty rate; piloting a price-based sliding scale royalty rate; and repealing legislatively-mandated royalty relief for "deep gas" wells. Diligent development requirements include shorter primary lease terms, stricter enforcement of lease terms, and monetary incentives to move leases into production (e.g., a new statutory per-acre fee on nonproducing leases). Revenue collection improvements include simplification of the royalty valuation process and permanent repeal of DOI's authority to accept in-kind royalty payments. Collectively, these reforms will generate roughly $1.7 billion in net receipts to the Treasury over 10 years, of which about $1.2 billion would result from statutory changes. Many States will also benefit from higher Federal revenue sharing payments.

BLM: Reform of hardrock mineral production on Federal lands. The Administration proposes to institute a leasing process under the Mineral Leasing Act of 1920 for certain minerals (gold, silver, lead, zinc, copper, uranium, and molybdenum) currently covered by the General Mining Law of 1872. After enactment, mining for these metals on Federal lands would be governed by the new leasing process and subject to annual rental payments and a royalty of not less than 5 percent of gross proceeds. Half of the receipts would be distributed to the States in which the leases are located and the remaining half would be retained by the Treasury. Existing mining claims would be exempt from the change to the leasing system, but would be subject to increases in the annual maintenance fees under the General Mining Law of 1872.

BLM: Reauthorize the Federal Land Transaction Facilitation Act (FLTFA). The Budget proposes to reauthorize the FLTFA, which expired in July 2011, and allow lands identified as suitable for disposal in recent land use plans to be sold using the FLTFA authority. The FLTFA sales revenues would continue to be used to fund the acquisition of environmentally sensitive lands and to cover BLM's administrative costs associated with conducting sales.

Environmental Protection Agency (EPA)

Pre-manufacture notice fee. EPA currently collects fees from chemical manufacturers seeking to market new chemicals. These fees are authorized by the Toxic Substances Control Act and are subject to a statutory cap.

The Budget proposes to lift the cap so that EPA can recover a greater portion of the program cost.

Federal Communications Commission (FCC)

Spectrum license fee authority. To promote efficient use of the electromagnetic spectrum, the Administration proposes to provide the FCC with new authority to use other economic mechanisms, such as fees, as a spectrum management tool. The FCC would be authorized to set charges for unauctioned spectrum licenses based on spectrum-management principles. Fees would be phased in over time as part of an ongoing rulemaking process to determine the appropriate application and level for fees.

Auction domestic satellite service spectrum licenses. The FCC would be allowed to assign licenses for certain satellite services that are predominantly domestic through competitive bidding, as had been done before a 2005 court decision called the practice into question on technical grounds. The proposal is expected to raise $50 million from 2017–2026. These receipts would be deposited in the general fund for deficit reduction.

Auction or assign via fee 1675-1680 megahertz. The Budget proposes that the FCC either auction or use fee authority to assign spectrum frequencies between 1675-1680 megahertz for flexible use by 2020, subject to sharing arrangements with Federal weather satellites. Currently, the spectrum is being used for radiosondes (weather balloons), weather satellite downlinks, and data broadcasts, and the band will also support future weather satellite operations. NOAA began transitioning radiosondes operations out of the band in 2016 as part of the Advanced Wireless Services 3 (AWS-3) relocation process. If this proposal is enacted, NOAA would establish limited protection zones for the remaining weather satellite downlinks and develop alternative data broadcast systems for users of its data products. Without this proposal, these frequencies are unlikely to be auctioned and repurposed to commercial use. The proposal is expected to raise $300 million in receipts over 10 years.

C. User Charge Proposals that are Governmental Receipts

Department of Energy

Reauthorize special assessment on domestic nuclear facilities. The Administration proposes to authorize the use of balances in the United States Enrichment Corporation Fund for the same purpose as the Uranium Enrichment Decontamination and Decommissioning Fund, in order to fund higher-than-expected cleanup costs. Established in 1992, the Uranium Enrichment Decontamination and Decommissioning Fund pays, subject to appropriation, the decontamination and decommissioning costs of the Department of Energy's gaseous diffusion plants in Tennessee, Ohio, and Kentucky. To offset the PAYGO cost of the United States Enrichment Corporation Fund proposal, the

Budget proposes to reauthorize the special assessment on domestic nuclear utilities.

Department of Homeland Security

CBP: Establish user fee for Electronic Visa Update System. The Budget proposes to establish a user fee for the Electronic Visa Update System (EVUS), a new CBP program to collect biographic and travel-related information from certain non-immigrant visa holders prior to traveling to the United States. This process will complement existing visa application process and enhance CBP's ability to make pre-travel admissibility and risk determinations. CBP proposes to establish a user fee to fund the costs of establishing, providing, and administering the system.

Corps of Engineers—Civil Works

Reform inland waterways funding. The Administration proposes legislation to reform the laws governing the Inland Waterways Trust Fund, including establishing an annual per vessel fee to increase the amount paid by commercial navigation users of the inland waterways. In 1986, the Congress provided that commercial traffic on the inland waterways would be responsible for 50 percent of the capital costs of the locks and dams, and other features that make barge transportation possible on the inland waterways. The additional revenue would help finance future capital investments in these waterways, as well as 25 percent of the operation and maintenance costs, to support economic growth. The current excise tax on diesel fuel used in inland waterways commerce, which was recently increased to 29 cents per gallon, will not produce the revenue needed to cover these costs.

Table 13–4. USER CHARGE PROPOSALS IN THE FY 2017 BUDGET
(Estimated collections in millions of dollars)

	2016	2017	2018	2019	2020	2021	2022	2023	2024	2025	2026	2017-2021	2017-2026
OFFSETTING COLLECTIONS AND OFFSETTING RECEIPTS													
DISCRETIONARY:													
Offsetting collections													
Department of Agriculture													
Forest Service: Grazing administrative processing fee	....	15	15	15	15	....	....	....	....	....	....	60	60
Department of Commerce													
National Oceanic and Atmospheric Administration: Infrastructure permitting fee	*	*	*	*	*	*	*	*	*	*	*	*	–1
Department of Health and Human Services													
Food and Drug Administration (FDA): Food facilities registration, inspection, and import fees import fees	....	166	169	172	176	180	183	187	191	194	198	863	1,816
FDA: International courier fees	....	6	6	6	6	6	7	7	7	7	7	30	65
FDA: Cosmetic facility registration fees	....	20	20	21	21	22	22	23	23	23	24	104	219
FDA: Food contact substances notification fee	....	5	5	5	6	6	6	6	6	6	6	27	57
FDA: Export certification user fee cap increase	....	4	4	4	4	4	4	5	5	5	5	20	44
Health Resources and Services Administration: 340B Pharmacy Affairs fee	....	9	9	9	9	9	9	9	9	9	9	45	90
Centers for Medicare and Medicaid Services (CMS): Survey and certification revisit fee	....	*	5	10	10	20	25	25	25	25	25	45	170
Department of Homeland Security													
Transportation Security Administration (TSA): Aviation passenger security fee increase	....	489	521	629	764	930	967	1,005	1,043	1,081	–520	3,333	6,909
TSA: Aviation security infrastructure fee	....	420	420	420	420	420	420	420	420	420	420	2,100	4,200
Department of Housing and Urban Development													
Federal Housing Administration: Administrative support fee	....	30	30	30	30	30	30	30	30	30	30	150	300
Department of the Interior													
Bureau of Land Management (BLM): Public lands oil and gas lease inspection fees	....	48	48	48	48	48	48	48	48	48	48	240	480
BLM: Grazing administrative processing fee	....	17	17	17	....	....	....	....	....	....	....	51	51
Bureau of Safety and Environmental Enforcement: Inspection fee	....	11	11	11	12	12	12	12	13	13	13	57	120
Department of Justice													
Antitrust Division: Increase Hart-Scott-Rodino fees	....	....	59	61	62	64	66	67	69	72	74	246	594
Commodity Futures Trading Commission (CFTC)													
CFTC fee	....	....	337	343	350	357	364	372	379	387	394	1,387	3,283
Consumer Product Safety Commission													
Import surveillance user fee	....	....	36	36	36	36	36	36	36	36	36	144	324
Federal Trade Commission													
Increase Hart-Scott-Rodino fees	....	....	59	61	62	64	66	67	69	72	74	246	594
Offsetting receipts													
Department of Justice													
U.S. Trustee Program: Chapter 11 quarterly filing fee increase	....	125	128	130	133	135	138	141	144	146	149	651	1,369
Department of State													
Western Hemisphere Travel Initiative surcharge extension	....	461	....	....	....	....	....	....	....	....	....	461	461
Border Crossing Card fee increase	....	2	2	2	2	2	2	2	2	2	2	10	20
Department of Transportation													
Pipeline and Hazardous Materials Safety Administration: Pipeline design review fees	....	2	2	2	2	2	2	2	2	2	2	10	20
Subtotal, discretionary user charge proposals	....	1,830	1,903	2,032	2,168	2,347	2,407	2,464	2,521	2,578	996	10,280	21,246
MANDATORY:													
Offsetting collections													
Department of Agriculture													
Biobased labeling fee	....	1	1	1	1	1	1	1	1	1	1	5	10

Table 13–4. USER CHARGE PROPOSALS IN THE FY 2017 BUDGET—Continued

(Estimated collections in millions of dollars)

	2016	2017	2018	2019	2020	2021	2022	2023	2024	2025	2026	2017-2021	2017-2026
Rural Housing Service: Guaranteed Underwriting System fee	....	....	....	4	4	4	4	4	4	4	4	12	32
Department of Labor													
Pension Benefit Guaranty Corporation: Premium increases		1,220	1,265	1,310	1,401	1,446	1,536	1,581	1,672	2,991	578	6,642	15,000
Foreign Labor Certification fees		38	78	81	85	88	92	96	100	104	109	370	871
Environmental Protection Agency													
Confidential Business Information management fee		....	2	8	8	8	8	8	8	8	8	26	66
Offsetting receipts													
Department of Agriculture													
Food Safety and Inspection Service: Performance and other charges	....	4	4	4	5	5	5	5	5	5	5	22	47
Grain, Inspection, Packers, and Stockyards Administration: Standardization and licensing activities	....	30	30	30	30	30	30	30	30	30	30	150	300
Animal and Plant Health Inspection Service: Inspection and licensing charges	....	20	27	27	28	29	30	31	32	33	34	131	291
Natural Resource Conservation Service: Conservation user fee	....	....	4	4	4	4	4	4	4	4	4	16	36
Department of Health and Human Services													
CMS: Income-related premium increase under Medicare Parts B and D		....	....	....	1,870	3,370	4,620	6,170	7,950	7,740	9,080	5,240	40,800
CMS: Allow collection of application fees from individual providers	....	9	9	9	10	10	10	10	10	10	11	47	98
CMS: Establish registration process for clearinghouses and billing agents		15	16	17	18	19	20	21	22	23	24	85	195
CMS: Medicare provider fee for ordering services or supplies without proper documentation		....	....	....	....	....	....	....	....	....	....	....	....
CMS: Medicare appeals refundable filing fee		9	86	131	131	131	136	141	146	146	151	488	1,208
Department of Homeland Security													
Customs and Border Protection (CBP): COBRA fee		264	276	292	308	328	344	361	380	400	....	1,468	2,953
CBP: Express Consignment Courier Facilities fee		12	12	14	14	16	16	18	18	18	....	68	138
CBP: Increase immigration inspection user fee (IUF) and lift IUF limitation		270	279	316	327	396	408	484	500	550	602	1,588	4,132
TSA: Aviation passenger security fee increase		....	410	490	550	410	400	390	380	370	2,000	1,860	5,400
Department of the Interior													
Federal oil and gas management reforms		20	70	90	110	120	140	150	170	180	190	410	1,240
BLM: Reform of hardrock mineral production on Federal lands		....	2	4	5	5	6	6	11	17	24	16	80
BLM: Reauthorize the Federal Land Transaction Facilitation Act		5	10	20	30	30	30	30	30	30	30	95	245
Environmental Protection Agency													
Pre-manufacture notice fee		4	8	8	8	8	8	8	8	8	8	36	76
Federal Communications Commission													
Spectrum license fee authority		200	300	425	550	550	550	550	550	550	550	2,025	4,775
Auction domestic satellite service spectrum licenses		25	25	....	....	....	....	....	....	....	....	50	50
Auction or assign via fee 1675–1680 megahertz		....	....	150	150	....	....	....	....	....	....	300	300
Subtotal, mandatory user charge proposals		2,146	2,914	3,435	5,647	7,028	8,438	10,169	12,121	13,322	13,553	21,169	78,772
Subtotal, user charge proposals that are offsetting collections and offsetting receipts		3,976	4,817	5,467	7,815	9,375	10,845	12,633	14,642	15,900	14,549	31,449	100,018
GOVERNMENTAL RECEIPTS													
Department of Energy													
Reauthorize special assessment on domestic nuclear facilities		208	212	217	222	227	232	237	243	248	254	1,086	2,300
Department of Homeland Security													
CBP: Establish user fee for Electronic Visa Update System		31	25	27	31	27	31	29	34	24	28	141	287
Corps of Engineers - Civil Works													
Reform inland waterways funding		3	78	118	156	156	156	156	156	155	155	511	1,289
Subtotal, governmental receipts user charge proposals		242	315	362	409	410	419	422	433	427	437	1,738	3,876
Total, user charge proposals	....	**4,218**	**5,132**	**5,829**	**8,224**	**9,785**	**11,264**	**13,055**	**15,075**	**16,327**	**14,986**	**33,187**	**103,894**

* $500,000 or less.

14. TAX EXPENDITURES

The Congressional Budget Act of 1974 (Public Law 93–344) requires that a list of "tax expenditures" be included in the budget. Tax expenditures are defined in the law as "revenue losses attributable to provisions of the Federal tax laws which allow a special exclusion, exemption, or deduction from gross income or which provide a special credit, a preferential rate of tax, or a deferral of tax liability." These exceptions may be viewed as alternatives to other policy instruments, such as spending or regulatory programs.

Identification and measurement of tax expenditures depends crucially on the baseline tax system against which the actual tax system is compared. The tax expenditure estimates presented in this document are patterned on a comprehensive income tax, which defines income as the sum of consumption and the change in net wealth in a given period of time.

An important assumption underlying each tax expenditure estimate reported below is that other parts of the Tax Code remain unchanged. The estimates would be different if tax expenditures were changed simultaneously because of potential interactions among provisions. For that reason, this document does not present a grand total for the estimated tax expenditures.

Tax expenditures relating to the individual and corporate income taxes are estimated for fiscal years 2015–2025 using two methods of accounting: current revenue effects and present value effects. The present value approach provides estimates of the revenue effects for tax expenditures that generally involve deferrals of tax payments into the future.

A discussion of performance measures and economic effects related to the assessment of the effect of tax expenditures on the achievement of program performance goals is presented in the Appendix. This section is a complement to the Government-wide performance plan required by the Government Performance and Results Act of 1992.

TAX EXPENDITURES IN THE INCOME TAX

Tax Expenditure Estimates

All tax expenditure estimates and their descriptions presented here are based upon current tax law enacted as of July 1, 2015 and reflect the economic assumptions from the Mid-Session Review of the 2016 Budget. In some cases, expired or repealed provisions are listed if their revenue effects occur in fiscal year 2015 or later. The estimates and their descriptions do not include the effects of the Protecting Americans from Tax Hikes Act of 2015 (PATH) which was enacted on December 17, 2015. Revised estimates reflecting the enacted legislation will be included in the tax expenditure tables in the 2018 Budget. In particular, PATH extended and modified expiring provisions in the tax code. In some instances the extensions were temporary in nature and are set to expire in a year or more, while in other instances the provisions were made permanent. Examples of permanent extensions include the research credit, the American Opportunity tax credit, the deduction for state and local general sales taxes, the expansion in the earned income tax credit, the increase in the limitation on expensing of real property, and the reduction in the earnings threshold for the refundable portion of the child tax credit. Temporary extensions include bonus depreciation, the work opportunity tax credit, the deduction for mortgage insurance premiums, and the exclusion for discharge of indebtedness on principal residence, among others. Expanded descriptions are available in the Receipts Chapter.

The total revenue effects for tax expenditures for fiscal years 2015–2025 are displayed according to the Budget's functional categories in Table 1. Descriptions of the specific tax expenditure provisions follow the discussion of general features of the tax expenditure concept.

Two baseline concepts—the normal tax baseline and the reference tax law baseline—are used to identify and estimate tax expenditures.[1] For the most part, the two concepts coincide. However, items treated as tax expenditures under the normal tax baseline, but not the reference tax law baseline, are indicated by the designation "normal tax method" in the tables. The revenue effects for these items are zero using the reference tax rules. The alternative baseline concepts are discussed in detail below.

Tables 2A and 2B report separately the respective portions of the total revenue effects that arise under the individual and corporate income taxes. The location of the estimates under the individual and corporate headings does not imply that these categories of filers benefit from the special tax provisions in proportion to the respective tax expenditure amounts shown. Rather, these breakdowns show the form of tax liability that the various provisions affect. The ultimate beneficiaries of corporate tax expenditures could be shareholders, employees, customers, or other providers of capital, depending on economic forces.

---

[1] These baseline concepts are thoroughly discussed in Special Analysis G of the 1985 Budget, where the former is referred to as the pre-1983 method and the latter the post-1982 method.

Table 3 ranks the major tax expenditures by the size of their 2016–2025 revenue effect. The first column provides the number of the provision in order to cross reference this table to Tables 1, 2A, and 2B, as well as to the descriptions below.

Interpreting Tax Expenditure Estimates

The estimates shown for individual tax expenditures in Tables 1 through 3 do not necessarily equal the increase in Federal revenues (or the change in the budget balance) that would result from repealing these special provisions, for the following reasons.

First, eliminating a tax expenditure may have incentive effects that alter economic behavior. These incentives can affect the resulting magnitudes of the activity or of other tax provisions or Government programs. For example, if capital gains were taxed at ordinary rates, capital gain realizations would be expected to decline, resulting in lower tax receipts. Such behavioral effects are not reflected in the estimates.

Second, tax expenditures are interdependent even without incentive effects. Repeal of a tax expenditure provision can increase or decrease the tax revenues associated with other provisions. For example, even if behavior does not change, repeal of an itemized deduction could increase the revenue costs from other deductions because some taxpayers would be moved into higher tax brackets. Alternatively, repeal of an itemized deduction could lower the revenue cost from other deductions if taxpayers are led to claim the standard deduction instead of itemizing. Similarly, if two provisions were repealed simultaneously, the increase in tax liability could be greater or less than the sum of the two separate tax expenditures, because each is estimated assuming that the other remains in force. In addition, the estimates reported in Table 1 are the totals of individual and corporate income tax revenue effects reported in Tables 2A and 2B, and do not reflect any possible interactions between individual and corporate income tax receipts. For this reason, the estimates in Table 1 should be regarded as approximations.

Present-Value Estimates

The annual value of tax expenditures for tax deferrals is reported on a cash basis in all tables except Table 4. Cash-based estimates reflect the difference between taxes deferred in the current year and incoming revenues that are received due to deferrals of taxes from prior years. Although such estimates are useful as a measure of cash flows into the Government, they do not accurately reflect the true economic cost of these provisions. For example, for a provision where activity levels have changed over time, so that incoming tax receipts from past deferrals are greater than deferred receipts from new activity, the cash-basis tax expenditure estimate can be negative, despite the fact that in present-value terms current deferrals have a real cost to the Government. Alternatively, in the case of a newly enacted deferral provision, a cash-based estimate can overstate the real effect on receipts to the Government because the newly deferred taxes will ultimately be received.

Discounted present-value estimates of revenue effects are presented in Table 4 for certain provisions that involve tax deferrals or other long-term revenue effects. These estimates complement the cash-based tax expenditure estimates presented in the other tables.

The present-value estimates represent the revenue effects, net of future tax payments, that follow from activities undertaken during calendar year 2015 which cause the deferrals or other long-term revenue effects. For instance, a pension contribution in 2015 would cause a deferral of tax payments on wages in 2015 and on pension fund earnings on this contribution (e.g., interest) in later years. In some future year, however, the 2015 pension contribution and accrued earnings will be paid out and taxes will be due; these receipts are included in the present-value estimate. In general, this conceptual approach is similar to the one used for reporting the budgetary effects of credit programs, where direct loans and guarantees in a given year affect future cash flows.

Tax Expenditure Baselines

A tax expenditure is an exception to baseline provisions of the tax structure that usually results in a reduction in the amount of tax owed. The 1974 Congressional Budget Act, which mandated the tax expenditure budget, did not specify the baseline provisions of the tax law. As noted previously, deciding whether provisions are exceptions, therefore, is a matter of judgment. As in prior years, most of this year's tax expenditure estimates are presented using two baselines: the normal tax baseline and the reference tax law baseline. Tax expenditures may take the form of credits, deductions, special exceptions and allowances.

The normal tax baseline is patterned on a practical variant of a comprehensive income tax, which defines income as the sum of consumption and the change in net wealth in a given period of time. The normal tax baseline allows personal exemptions, a standard deduction, and deduction of expenses incurred in earning income. It is not limited to a particular structure of tax rates, or by a specific definition of the taxpaying unit.

The reference tax law baseline is also patterned on a comprehensive income tax, but it is closer to existing law. Reference law tax expenditures are limited to special exceptions from a generally provided tax rule that serve programmatic functions in a way that is analogous to spending programs. Provisions under the reference law baseline are generally tax expenditures under the normal tax baseline, but the reverse is not always true.

Both the normal and reference tax baselines allow several major departures from a pure comprehensive income tax. For example, under the normal and reference tax baselines:

- Income is taxable only when it is realized in exchange. Thus, the deferral of tax on unrealized capital gains is not regarded as a tax expenditure. Accrued income would be taxed under a comprehensive income tax.

- There is a separate corporate income tax.
- Tax rates on noncorporate business income vary by level of income.
- Individual tax rates, including brackets, standard deduction, and personal exemptions, are allowed to vary with marital status.
- Values of assets and debt are not generally adjusted for inflation. A comprehensive income tax would adjust the cost basis of capital assets and debt for changes in the general price level. Thus, under a comprehensive income tax baseline, the failure to take account of inflation in measuring depreciation, capital gains, and interest income would be regarded as a negative tax expenditure (i.e., a tax penalty), and failure to take account of inflation in measuring interest costs would be regarded as a positive tax expenditure (i.e., a tax subsidy).

Although the reference law and normal tax baselines are generally similar, areas of difference include:

Tax rates. The separate schedules applying to the various taxpaying units are included in the reference law baseline. Thus, corporate tax rates below the maximum statutory rate do not give rise to a tax expenditure. The normal tax baseline is similar, except that, by convention, it specifies the current maximum rate as the baseline for the corporate income tax. The lower tax rates applied to the first $10 million of corporate income are thus regarded as a tax expenditure under the normal tax. By convention, the Alternative Minimum Tax is treated as part of the baseline rate structure under both the reference and normal tax methods.

Income subject to the tax. Income subject to tax is defined as gross income less the costs of earning that income. Under the reference tax rules, gross income does not include gifts defined as receipts of money or property that are not consideration in an exchange nor does gross income include most transfer payments from the Government.[2] The normal tax baseline also excludes gifts between individuals from gross income. Under the normal tax baseline, however, all cash transfer payments from the Government to private individuals are counted in gross income, and exemptions of such transfers from tax are identified as tax expenditures. The costs of earning income are generally deductible in determining taxable income under both the reference and normal tax baselines.[3]

---

[2] Gross income does, however, include transfer payments associated with past employment, such as Social Security benefits.

[3] In the case of individuals who hold "passive" equity interests in businesses, the pro-rata shares of sales and expense deductions reportable in a year are limited. A passive business activity is defined generally to be one in which the holder of the interest, usually a partnership interest, does not actively perform managerial or other participatory functions. The taxpayer may generally report no larger deductions for a year than will reduce taxable income from such activities to zero. Deductions in excess of the limitation may be taken in subsequent years, or when the interest is liquidated. In addition, costs of earning income may

Capital recovery. Under the reference tax law baseline no tax expenditures arise from accelerated depreciation. Under the normal tax baseline, the depreciation allowance for property is computed using estimates of economic depreciation.

Treatment of foreign income. Both the normal and reference tax baselines allow a tax credit for foreign income taxes paid (up to the amount of U.S. income taxes that would otherwise be due), which prevents double taxation of income earned abroad. Under the normal tax method, however, controlled foreign corporations (CFCs) are not regarded as entities separate from their controlling U.S. shareholders. Thus, the deferral of tax on income received by CFCs is regarded as a tax expenditure under this method. In contrast, except for tax haven activities, the reference law baseline follows current law in treating CFCs as separate taxable entities whose income is not subject to U.S. tax until distributed to U.S. taxpayers. Under this baseline, deferral of tax on CFC income is not a tax expenditure because U.S. taxpayers generally are not taxed on accrued, but unrealized, income.

Descriptions of Income Tax Provisions

Descriptions of the individual and corporate income tax expenditures reported on in this document follow. These descriptions relate to current law as of July 1, 2015.

National Defense

1. ***Exclusion of benefits and allowances to armed forces personnel.***—Under the baseline tax system, all compensation, including dedicated payments and in-kind benefits, should be included in taxable income because they represent accretions to wealth that do not materially differ from cash wages. As an example, a rental voucher of $100 is (approximately) equal in value to $100 of cash income. In contrast to this treatment, certain housing and meals, in addition to other benefits provided military personnel, either in cash or in kind, as well as certain amounts of pay related to combat service, are excluded from income subject to tax.

International Affairs

2. ***Exclusion of income earned abroad by U.S. citizens.***—Under the baseline tax system, all compensation received by U.S. citizens and residents is properly included in their taxable income. It makes no difference whether the compensation is a result of working abroad or whether it is labeled as a housing allowance. In contrast to this treatment, U.S. tax law allows U.S. citizens and residents who live abroad, work in the private sector, and satisfy a foreign residency requirement to exclude up to $80,000, plus adjustments for inflation since 2004, in foreign earned income from U.S. taxes. In addition, if these taxpayers are provided housing by their employers, then they may also exclude the cost of such housing from their income to the extent that it exceeds 16 percent of the

---

be limited under the Alternative Minimum Tax.

Table 14–1. ESTIMATES OF TOTAL INCOME TAX EXPENDITURES FOR FISCAL YEARS 2015–2025

(In millions of dollars)

	Total from corporations and individuals											
	2015	2016	2017	2018	2019	2020	2021	2022	2023	2024	2025	2016–25
National Defense												
1 Exclusion of benefits and allowances to armed forces personnel	13,680	14,220	13,170	13,310	13,780	14,340	14,970	15,640	16,360	17,130	17,950	150,870
International affairs:												
2 Exclusion of income earned abroad by U.S. citizens	5,990	6,280	6,600	6,930	7,280	7,640	8,020	8,420	8,840	9,290	9,750	79,050
3 Exclusion of certain allowances for Federal employees abroad	1,240	1,300	1,370	1,430	1,510	1,580	1,660	1,740	1,830	1,920	2,020	16,360
4 Inventory property sales source rules exception	3,890	4,210	4,560	4,940	5,350	5,790	6,270	6,790	7,350	7,960	8,620	61,840
5 Deferral of income from controlled foreign corporations (normal tax method)	64,560	67,780	71,170	74,730	78,470	82,390	86,510	90,840	95,380	100,150	105,160	852,580
6 Deferred taxes for financial firms on certain income earned overseas	4,470	0	0	0	0	0	0	0	0	0	0	0
General science, space, and technology:												
7 Expensing of research and experimentation expenditures (normal tax method)	7,900	6,350	5,820	6,270	6,830	7,310	7,600	7,840	8,120	8,450	8,820	73,410
8 Credit for increasing research activities	5,710	3,320	2,980	2,670	2,370	2,090	1,840	1,620	1,420	1,240	1,080	20,630
Energy:												
9 Expensing of exploration and development costs, fuels	660	470	460	510	560	600	580	570	600	620	580	5,550
10 Excess of percentage over cost depletion, fuels	650	710	860	1,010	1,150	1,240	1,290	1,400	1,540	1,690	1,810	12,700
11 Exception from passive loss limitation for working interests in oil and gas properties	40	40	40	40	40	30	30	30	30	30	30	340
12 Capital gains treatment of royalties on coal	110	120	130	130	130	140	140	150	150	160	170	1,420
13 Exclusion of interest on energy facility bonds	20	20	30	30	30	30	40	40	40	40	50	350
14 Energy production credit [1]	1,550	1,950	2,250	2,310	2,230	2,120	2,050	1,970	1,840	1,590	1,160	19,470
15 Energy investment credit [1]	1,010	1,470	970	250	40	130	320	440	510	530	400	5,060
16 Alcohol fuel credits [2]	20	0	0	0	0	0	0	0	0	0	0	0
17 Bio-Diesel and small agri-biodiesel producer tax credits [3]	70	30	20	10	0	0	0	0	0	0	0	60
18 Tax credits for clean-fuel burning vehicles and refueling property	540	550	670	820	810	700	500	290	140	130	160	4,770
19 Exclusion of utility conservation subsidies	430	450	470	490	520	540	570	590	620	650	680	5,580
20 Credit for holding clean renewable energy bonds [4]	70	70	70	70	70	70	70	70	70	70	70	700
21 Deferral of gain from dispositions of transmission property to implement FERC restructuring	−120	−220	−180	−150	−130	−110	−70	−20	0	0	0	−880
22 Credit for investment in clean coal facilities	40	160	400	440	230	30	−20	−20	−20	−10	−10	1,180
23 Temporary 50% expensing for equipment used in the refining of liquid fuels	−2,250	−2,050	−1,820	−1,500	−1,220	−970	−680	−420	−200	−40	0	−8,900
24 Natural gas distribution pipelines treated as 15-year property	160	160	160	170	170	170	150	80	−20	−120	−230	690
25 Amortize all geological and geophysical expenditures over 2 years	90	100	100	90	90	90	90	100	100	100	100	960
26 Allowance of deduction for certain energy efficient commercial building property	30	−10	−30	−30	−30	−30	−30	−30	−30	−30	−30	−280
27 Credit for construction of new energy efficient homes	60	20	0	0	0	0	0	0	0	0	0	20
28 Credit for energy efficiency improvements to existing homes	270	0	0	0	0	0	0	0	0	0	0	0
29 Credit for residential energy efficient property	850	770	460	180	40	0	0	0	0	0	0	1,450
30 Qualified energy conservation bonds [5]	30	30	30	30	30	30	30	30	30	30	30	300
31 Advanced energy property credit	60	10	−30	−30	−30	−10	0	0	0	0	0	−90
32 Advanced nuclear power production credit	0	140	140	140	340	620	690	690	690	580	550	4,580
33 Reduced tax rate for nuclear decommissioning funds	160	170	200	220	240	250	270	280	290	300	320	2,540
Natural resources and environment:												
34 Expensing of exploration and development costs, nonfuel minerals	10	0	10	30	50	60	60	70	70	50	50	450
35 Excess of percentage over cost depletion, nonfuel minerals	520	530	540	540	550	520	470	470	460	450	440	4,970
36 Exclusion of interest on bonds for water, sewage, and hazardous waste facilities	450	490	550	620	690	730	780	860	920	980	1,060	7,680
37 Capital gains treatment of certain timber income	110	120	130	130	130	140	140	150	150	160	170	1,420
38 Expensing of multiperiod timber growing costs	320	330	350	370	380	400	420	420	430	430	450	3,980
39 Tax incentives for preservation of historic structures	450	460	470	470	480	490	510	520	530	540	540	5,010
40 Industrial CO_2 capture and sequestration tax credit	80	110	150	190	80	0	0	0	0	0	0	530
41 Deduction for endangered species recovery expenditures	20	30	30	30	30	40	50	50	50	50	70	430

Table 14–1. ESTIMATES OF TOTAL INCOME TAX EXPENDITURES FOR FISCAL YEARS 2015–2025—Continued

(In millions of dollars)

	Total from corporations and individuals											
	2015	2016	2017	2018	2019	2020	2021	2022	2023	2024	2025	2016–25
Agriculture:												
42 Expensing of certain capital outlays	220	210	230	240	250	270	280	290	310	330	350	2,760
43 Expensing of certain multiperiod production costs	350	370	390	410	440	460	490	520	550	590	630	4,850
44 Treatment of loans forgiven for solvent farmers	40	40	40	40	40	40	40	40	40	40	40	400
45 Capital gains treatment of certain income	1,150	1,240	1,280	1,300	1,320	1,360	1,410	1,470	1,530	1,590	1,670	14,170
46 Income averaging for farmers	130	140	140	140	140	140	140	140	140	140	140	1,400
47 Deferral of gain on sale of farm refiners	20	20	20	20	20	20	30	30	30	30	30	250
48 Expensing of reforestation expenditures	50	50	60	60	60	70	70	80	80	80	80	690
Commerce and housing:												
Financial institutions and insurance:												
49 Exemption of credit union income	1,690	2,300	2,200	2,200	2,350	2,440	2,700	2,890	2,980	3,120	3,570	26,750
50 Exclusion of interest on life insurance savings	17,450	18,870	23,380	28,950	33,790	37,820	41,010	43,550	45,750	47,820	49,900	370,840
51 Special alternative tax on small property and casualty insurance companies	30	30	40	40	40	40	50	50	50	50	60	450
52 Tax exemption of certain insurance companies owned by tax-exempt organizations	670	700	730	760	800	850	890	910	940	960	980	8,520
53 Small life insurance company deduction	30	30	30	40	40	40	40	40	40	50	50	400
54 Exclusion of interest spread of financial institutions	380	420	450	470	480	500	510	530	540	550	560	5,010
Housing:												
55 Exclusion of interest on owner-occupied mortgage subsidy bonds	1,250	1,350	1,530	1,700	1,900	2,020	2,190	2,380	2,550	2,730	2,940	21,290
56 Exclusion of interest on rental housing bonds	1,050	1,120	1,270	1,420	1,590	1,690	1,820	1,990	2,140	2,280	2,450	17,770
57 Deductibility of mortgage interest on owner-occupied homes	58,850	62,440	68,610	75,980	83,760	91,380	98,930	106,150	113,320	120,560	127,360	948,490
58 Deductibility of State and local property tax on owner-occupied homes	31,120	33,080	35,580	38,330	41,150	43,850	46,580	49,280	52,060	55,010	57,890	452,810
59 Deferral of income from installment sales	1,570	1,620	1,640	1,650	1,670	1,720	1,770	1,840	1,920	2,000	2,090	17,920
60 Capital gains exclusion on home sales	37,220	40,580	43,460	46,560	49,870	53,420	57,230	61,300	65,670	70,340	75,350	563,780
61 Exclusion of net imputed rental income	97,920	101,100	104,950	108,460	111,480	114,070	118,400	122,900	127,570	132,420	137,450	1,178,800
62 Exception from passive loss rules for $25,000 of rental loss	6,810	7,210	7,540	7,870	8,240	8,600	8,880	9,170	9,490	9,850	10,160	87,010
63 Credit for low-income housing investments	7,990	7,880	8,130	8,350	8,520	8,660	8,800	8,960	9,160	9,420	9,690	87,570
64 Accelerated depreciation on rental housing (normal tax method)	1,230	1,650	2,270	3,000	3,770	4,570	5,510	6,480	7,350	8,160	8,930	51,690
65 Discharge of mortgage indebtedness	1,100	0	0	0	0	0	0	0	0	0	0	0
Commerce:												
66 Discharge of business indebtedness	−160	−120	−50	−10	0	10	30	40	50	50	50	50
67 Exceptions from imputed interest rules	40	50	60	60	60	70	70	80	80	80	90	700
68 Treatment of qualified dividends	25,650	25,530	26,470	27,490	28,590	29,760	31,030	32,380	33,810	35,310	36,880	307,250
69 Capital gains (except agriculture, timber, iron ore, and coal)	85,710	92,820	95,870	96,790	98,660	101,520	105,170	109,410	114,070	119,080	124,380	1,057,770
70 Capital gains exclusion of small corporation stock	220	380	620	800	780	680	580	490	430	390	360	5,510
71 Step-up basis of capital gains at death	54,850	58,270	61,910	65,770	69,870	74,220	78,850	83,770	88,990	94,540	100,440	776,630
72 Carryover basis of capital gains on gifts	2,490	2,740	3,010	3,300	3,620	3,970	4,340	4,750	5,170	5,530	5,820	42,250
73 Ordinary income treatment of loss from small business corporation stock sale	50	50	50	50	50	50	50	50	50	50	50	500
74 Deferral of gains from like-kind exchanges	6,980	7,320	7,700	8,090	8,480	8,920	9,360	9,830	10,320	10,830	11,380	92,230
75 Accelerated depreciation of buildings other than rental housing (normal tax method)	−9,300	−9,170	−9,390	−9,790	−10,440	−11,200	−11,930	−12,630	−13,350	−14,160	−14,690	−116,750
76 Accelerated depreciation of machinery and equipment (normal tax method)	−7,510	−8,870	12,180	26,230	35,920	42,260	45,710	47,770	48,950	51,610	54,570	356,330
77 Expensing of certain small investments (normal tax method)	−1,180	−2,290	−790	90	720	1,120	1,530	1,850	2,020	2,160	2,280	8,690
78 Graduated corporation income tax rate (normal tax method)	3,860	3,770	3,670	3,540	3,610	3,570	3,660	3,780	3,940	3,800	3,740	37,080
79 Exclusion of interest on small issue bonds	170	170	200	220	250	260	280	310	330	350	380	2,750
80 Deduction for US production activities	15,230	15,680	16,440	17,220	17,980	18,770	19,580	20,440	21,320	22,250	23,210	192,890
81 Special rules for certain film and TV production	190	110	60	30	10	0	0	0	0	0	0	210
Transportation:												
82 Tonnage tax	70	70	80	80	90	90	90	100	100	100	110	910
83 Deferral of tax on shipping companies	20	20	20	20	20	20	20	20	20	20	20	200
84 Exclusion of reimbursed employee parking expenses	2,790	2,900	3,000	3,100	3,220	3,340	3,440	3,550	3,670	3,790	3,870	33,880

Table 14–1. ESTIMATES OF TOTAL INCOME TAX EXPENDITURES FOR FISCAL YEARS 2015–2025—Continued

(In millions of dollars)

		Total from corporations and individuals										
		2015	2016	2017	2018	2019	2020	2021	2022	2023	2024	2025	2016–25
85	Exclusion for employer-provided transit passes	730	770	820	860	920	980	1,030	1,100	1,170	1,220	1,290	10,160
86	Tax credit for certain expenditures for maintaining railroad tracks	100	0	0	0	0	0	0	0	0	0	0	0
87	Exclusion of interest on bonds for Highway Projects and rail-truck transfer facilities	220	210	200	190	170	170	160	160	140	140	130	1,670
	Community and regional development:												
88	Investment credit for rehabilitation of structures (other than historic)	20	20	20	20	20	20	20	20	20	20	20	200
89	Exclusion of interest for airport, dock, and	740	800	900	1,010	1,130	1,200	1,300	1,410	1,510	1,610	1,730	12,600
90	Exemption of certain mutuals' and cooperatives'	140	140	150	150	150	160	160	160	170	170	170	1,580
91	Empowerment zones	100	40	30	30	30	20	10	10	10	10	10	200
92	New markets tax credit	1,200	1,230	1,130	910	640	420	230	20	−110	−160	−180	4,130
93	Credit to holders of Gulf Tax Credit Bonds.	240	250	290	310	360	370	410	440	480	510	550	3,970
94	Recovery Zone Bonds [6]	130	140	150	180	190	210	220	240	250	280	290	2,150
95	Tribal Economic Development Bonds	40	40	50	60	60	70	70	80	80	80	90	680
	Education, training, employment, and social services:												
	Education:												
96	Exclusion of scholarship and fellowship income (normal tax method)	3,130	3,250	3,360	3,450	3,510	3,640	3,770	3,900	4,040	4,190	4,340	37,450
97	HOPE tax credit	0	0	0	670	6,740	6,880	7,290	7,380	7,500	7,880	7,960	52,300
98	Lifetime Learning tax credit	2,270	2,450	2,460	2,660	4,340	4,410	4,500	4,530	4,590	4,660	4,690	39,290
99	American Opportunity Tax Credit [7]	13,470	13,430	13,500	12,190	0	0	0	0	0	0	0	39,120
100	Education Individual Retirement Accounts	30	30	40	40	40	40	40	40	50	50	50	420
101	Deductibility of student-loan interest	1,800	1,800	1,780	1,780	1,790	1,820	1,820	1,810	1,840	1,830	1,820	18,090
102	Deduction for higher education expenses	390	0	0	0	0	0	0	0	0	0	0	0
103	Qualified tuition programs	1,680	1,870	2,080	2,290	2,510	2,760	3,020	3,310	3,610	3,960	4,330	29,740
104	Exclusion of interest on student-loan bonds	490	530	600	670	750	800	860	940	1,000	1,080	1,150	8,380
105	Exclusion of interest on bonds for private nonprofit educational facilities	2,270	2,440	2,760	3,090	3,450	3,660	3,960	4,320	4,630	4,940	5,310	38,560
106	Credit for holders of zone academy bonds [8]	160	130	120	110	100	100	90	90	80	80	80	980
107	Exclusion of interest on savings bonds redeemed to finance educational expenses	30	30	30	30	30	30	40	40	40	40	40	350
108	Parental personal exemption for students age 19 or over	4,400	4,400	4,420	4,460	4,590	4,710	4,840	4,950	5,050	5,140	5,250	47,810
109	Deductibility of charitable contributions (education)	4,820	5,180	5,560	5,970	6,400	6,790	7,170	7,550	7,930	8,300	8,680	69,530
110	Exclusion of employer-provided educational assistance	800	850	890	940	980	1,030	1,080	1,130	1,190	1,240	1,300	10,630
111	Special deduction for teacher expenses	210	0	0	0	0	0	0	0	0	0	0	0
112	Discharge of student loan indebtedness	90	90	90	90	90	90	90	90	90	90	90	900
113	Qualified school construction bonds [9]	650	650	650	650	650	650	650	650	650	650	650	6,500
	Training, employment, and social services:												
114	Work opportunity tax credit	720	420	240	180	140	100	70	60	40	30	30	1,310
115	Employer provided child care exclusion	900	930	980	1,050	1,120	1,180	1,250	1,330	1,410	1,500	1,590	12,340
116	Employer-provided child care credit	10	10	10	10	20	20	20	20	20	20	20	170
117	Assistance for adopted foster children	560	540	560	580	610	630	650	680	710	740	770	6,470
118	Adoption credit and exclusion [10]	270	250	260	290	270	320	310	320	320	320	330	2,990
119	Exclusion of employee meals and lodging (other than military)	4,410	4,500	4,600	4,710	4,840	4,970	5,100	5,230	5,360	5,490	5,620	50,420
120	Credit for child and dependent care expenses	4,500	4,520	4,560	4,650	4,760	4,900	5,000	5,120	5,220	5,330	5,440	49,500
121	Credit for disabled access expenditures	10	10	10	10	20	20	20	20	20	20	20	170
122	Deductibility of charitable contributions, other than education and health	40,910	44,240	47,630	51,380	55,250	58,830	62,180	65,530	68,810	72,130	75,410	601,390
123	Exclusion of certain foster care payments	430	460	480	500	510	520	530	550	560	570	580	5,260
124	Exclusion of parsonage allowances	690	730	770	810	850	900	940	990	1,050	1,100	1,160	9,300
125	Indian employment credit	40	30	30	20	10	10	10	10	10	10	0	140
	Health:												
126	Exclusion of employer contributions for medical insurance premiums and medical care [11]	201,450	210,980	220,550	229,620	243,160	259,520	275,600	293,420	313,810	336,070	359,590	2,742,320
127	Self-employed medical insurance premiums	6,690	7,060	7,440	7,680	7,980	8,400	8,820	9,240	9,690	10,210	10,770	87,290
128	Medical Savings Accounts / Health Savings Accounts	4,810	5,730	6,830	8,060	9,560	11,390	13,550	16,130	19,190	22,830	27,150	140,420

Table 14–1. ESTIMATES OF TOTAL INCOME TAX EXPENDITURES FOR FISCAL YEARS 2015–2025—Continued

(In millions of dollars)

	Total from corporations and individuals											
	2015	2016	2017	2018	2019	2020	2021	2022	2023	2024	2025	2016–25
129 Deductibility of medical expenses	7,660	8,260	8,700	9,530	10,980	12,850	14,810	16,840	19,380	22,350	25,460	149,160
130 Exclusion of interest on hospital construction bonds	3,570	3,840	4,350	4,870	5,420	5,760	6,230	6,810	7,290	7,780	8,360	60,710
131 Refundable Premium Assistance Tax Credit [12]	1,960	2,340	3,870	4,880	6,880	7,580	7,810	8,140	8,430	8,730	9,090	67,750
132 Credit for employee health insurance expenses of small business [13]	513	544	543	517	453	395	301	358	242	181	78	3,612
133 Deductibility of charitable contributions (health)	4,620	4,990	5,390	5,810	6,240	6,640	7,030	7,400	7,770	8,150	8,520	67,940
134 Tax credit for orphan drug research	1,460	1,760	2,120	2,570	3,090	3,730	4,490	5,430	6,540	7,890	9,520	47,140
135 Special Blue Cross/Blue Shield deduction	250	250	260	270	280	290	300	320	330	340	350	2,990
136 Tax credit for health insurance purchased by certain displaced and retired individuals [14]	0	30	30	20	10	0	0	0	0	0	0	90
137 Distributions from retirement plans for premiums for health and long-term care insurance	400	440	460	480	500	520	540	560	580	600	620	5,300
Income security:												
138 Child credit [15]	23,980	24,000	24,290	24,700	25,190	25,080	24,770	24,440	24,040	23,600	23,180	243,290
139 Exclusion of railroad retirement system benefits	300	300	300	290	280	270	250	240	220	190	170	2,510
140 Exclusion of workers' compensation benefits	9,720	9,820	9,920	10,010	10,110	10,220	10,320	10,420	10,530	10,630	10,730	102,710
141 Exclusion of public assistance benefits (normal tax method)	560	570	590	600	630	650	670	680	710	730	680	6,510
142 Exclusion of special benefits for disabled coal miners	30	30	20	20	20	10	10	10	10	10	0	140
143 Exclusion of military disability pensions	220	220	240	250	260	270	290	300	310	330	340	2,810
Net exclusion of pension contributions and earnings:												
144 Defined benefit employer plans	66,620	66,600	66,760	67,020	66,180	64,820	63,190	60,910	58,470	55,930	52,650	622,530
145 Defined contribution employer plans	62,070	64,710	65,620	68,120	73,930	78,960	98,370	107,980	114,420	121,240	128,130	921,480
146 Individual Retirement Accounts	16,400	16,850	16,970	17,240	18,080	19,270	19,680	20,630	21,780	22,840	24,080	197,420
147 Low and moderate income savers credit	1,280	1,280	1,270	1,270	1,300	1,310	1,310	1,330	1,340	1,350	1,360	13,120
148 Self-Employed plans	25,490	28,030	30,800	33,760	37,030	40,480	44,020	47,870	52,060	56,610	61,560	432,220
Exclusion of other employee benefits:												
149 Premiums on group term life insurance	2,340	2,450	2,560	2,610	2,700	2,800	2,900	3,000	3,110	3,240	3,350	28,720
150 Premiums on accident and disability insurance	310	320	320	330	330	330	340	340	340	350	350	3,350
151 Income of trusts to finance supplementary unemployment benefits	20	20	30	40	40	50	50	60	60	60	60	470
152 Special ESOP rules	1,890	2,000	2,100	2,210	2,320	2,450	2,580	2,710	2,860	3,010	3,160	25,400
153 Additional deduction for the blind	40	40	40	40	40	50	50	50	60	60	60	490
154 Additional deduction for the elderly	2,890	3,080	3,310	3,560	3,760	4,010	4,210	4,500	4,870	5,170	5,530	42,000
155 Tax credit for the elderly and disabled	10	10	10	10	10	10	10	0	0	0	0	60
156 Deductibility of casualty losses	350	370	390	410	430	450	460	470	490	500	520	4,490
157 Earned income tax credit [16]	2,120	2,820	2,340	3,040	1,820	1,910	1,980	2,080	2,180	2,280	2,380	22,830
Social Security:												
Exclusion of social security benefits:												
158 Social Security benefits for retired workers	25,780	26,900	28,280	29,490	30,730	31,760	32,510	33,130	33,690	34,340	34,590	315,420
159 Social Security benefits for disabled workers	8,280	8,490	8,580	8,730	8,970	9,210	9,500	9,840	10,190	10,540	10,870	94,920
160 Social Security benefits for spouses, dependents and survivors	4,060	4,160	4,310	4,440	4,610	4,750	4,870	5,000	5,140	5,310	5,420	48,010
161 Credit for certain employer contributions to social security	980	1,010	1,060	1,110	1,160	1,210	1,260	1,320	1,370	1,440	1,500	12,440
Veterans benefits and services:												
162 Exclusion of veterans death benefits and disability compensation	6,150	6,760	7,250	7,590	7,870	8,170	8,460	8,770	9,080	9,400	9,740	83,090
163 Exclusion of veterans pensions	420	450	490	510	530	560	580	600	630	650	680	5,680
164 Exclusion of GI bill benefits	1,530	1,690	1,830	1,960	2,070	2,190	2,310	2,440	2,580	2,720	2,880	22,670
165 Exclusion of interest on veterans housing bonds	10	10	10	10	10	10	10	10	10	10	30	120
General purpose fiscal assistance:												
166 Exclusion of interest on public purpose State and local bonds	29,430	31,700	35,900	40,180	44,810	47,550	51,430	56,190	60,140	64,220	69,030	501,150
167 Build America Bonds [17]	0	0	0	0	0	0	0	0	0	0	0	0
168 Deductibility of nonbusiness State and local taxes other than on owner-occupied homes	48,430	51,380	55,130	59,030	62,870	66,730	70,830	75,060	79,410	83,920	88,280	692,640
Interest:												
169 Deferral of interest on U.S. savings bonds	1,020	1,010	1,000	990	980	970	960	950	940	930	920	9,650

Table 14–1. ESTIMATES OF TOTAL INCOME TAX EXPENDITURES FOR FISCAL YEARS 2015–2025—Continued

(In millions of dollars)

	Total from corporations and individuals											
	2015	2016	2017	2018	2019	2020	2021	2022	2023	2024	2025	2016–25
Addendum: Aid to State and local governments:												
Deductibility of:												
Property taxes on owner-occupied homes	31,120	33,080	35,580	38,330	41,150	43,850	46,580	49,280	52,060	55,010	57,890	452,810
Nonbusiness State and local taxes other than on owner-occupied homes	48,430	51,380	55,130	59,030	62,870	66,730	70,830	75,060	79,410	83,920	88,280	692,640
Exclusion of interest on State and local bonds for:												
Public purposes	29,430	31,700	35,900	40,180	44,810	47,550	51,430	56,190	60,140	64,220	69,030	501,150
Energy facilities	20	20	30	30	30	30	40	40	40	40	50	350
Water, sewage, and hazardous waste disposal facilities	450	490	550	620	690	730	780	860	920	980	1,060	7,680
Small-issues	170	170	200	220	250	260	280	310	330	350	380	2,750
Owner-occupied mortgage subsidies	1,250	1,350	1,530	1,700	1,900	2,020	2,190	2,380	2,550	2,730	2,940	21,290
Rental housing	1,050	1,120	1,270	1,420	1,590	1,690	1,820	1,990	2,140	2,280	2,450	17,770
Airports, docks, and similar facilities	740	800	900	1,010	1,130	1,200	1,300	1,410	1,510	1,610	1,730	12,600
Student loans	490	530	600	670	750	800	860	940	1,000	1,080	1,150	8,380
Private nonprofit educational facilities	2,270	2,440	2,760	3,090	3,450	3,660	3,960	4,320	4,630	4,940	5,310	38,560
Hospital construction	3,570	3,840	4,350	4,870	5,420	5,760	6,230	6,810	7,290	7,780	8,360	60,710
Veterans' housing	10	10	10	10	10	10	10	10	10	10	30	120

[1] Firms can take an energy grant in lieu of the energy production credit or the energy investment credit for facilities placed in service in 2009 and 2010 or whose construction commenced in 2009 and 2010. The effect of the grant on outlays (in millions of dollars) is as follows: 2015 $2,300; 2016 $1,200; 2017 $650; and $0 thereafter.

[2] The alternative fuel mixture credit results in a reduction in excise tax receipts (in millions of dollars) as follows: 2015 $630; and $0 thereafter.

[3] In addition, the biodiesel producer tax credit results in a reduction in excise tax receipts (in millions of dollars) as follows: 2015 $1,870; and $0 thereafter.

[4] In addition, the inventory property sales source rules exception has outlay effects of (in millions of dollars):
2015 $30; 2016 $30; 2017 $30; 2018 $30; 2019 $30; 2020 $30; 2021 $30; 2022 $30; 2023 $30; 2024 $30; and 2025 $30.

[5] In addition, the deferral of income from controlled foreign corporations (normal tax method) has outlay effects of (in millions of dollars):
2015 $30; 2016 $30; 2017 $30; 2018 $30; 2019 $30; 2020 $30; 2021 $30; 2022 $30; 2023 $30; 2024 $30; 2025 $30.

[6] In addition, recovery zone bonds have outlay effects (in millions of dollars) as follows:
2015 $220; 2016 $220; 2017 $220; 2018 $220; 2019 $220; 2020 $220; 2021 $220; 2022 $220; 2023 $220; 2024 $220; and 2025 $220.

[7] In addition, the expensing of research and experimentation expenditures has outlay effects of (in millions of dollars):
2015 $4,200; 2016 $4,360; 2017 $4,490; 2018 $4,630; and 2019 $2,620.

[8] In addition, the credit for holders of zone academy bonds has outlay effects of (in millions of dollars):
2015 $50; 2016 $50; 2017 $50; 2018 $50; 2019 $50; 2020 $50; 2021 $50; 2022 $50; 2023 $50; 2024 $50; and 2025 $50.

[9] In addition, the provision for school construction bonds has outlay effects of (in millions of dollars):
2015 $740; 2016 $740; 2017 $740; 2018 $740; 2019 $740; 2020 $740; 2021 $740; 2022 $740; 2023 $740; 2024 $740; and 2025 $740.

[10] In addition, the adoption tax credit has outlay effects of (in millions of dollars): 2015 $30 and $0 thereafter.

[11] In addition, the employer contributions for health have effects on payroll tax receipts (in millions of dollars) as follows: 2015 $127,500; 2016 $131,380; 2017 $135,470;
2018 $140,080; 2019 $147,360; 2020 $156,090; 2021 $164,510; 2022 $172,600; 2023 $181,400; 2024 $190,900; and 2025 $200,930.

[12] In addition, the premium assistance credit provision has outlay effects (in millions of dollars) as follows:
2015 $20,730; 2016 $38,030; 2017 $53,030; 2018 $75,400; 2019 $88,990; 2020 $95,320; 2021 $100,580; 2022 $106,400; 2023 $110,970; 2024 $115,910; and 2025 $121,040.

[13] In addition, the small business credit provision has outlay effects (in millions of dollars) as follows:
2015 $70; 2016 $80; 2017 $70; 2018 $70; 2019 $60; 2020 $50; 2021 $30; 2022 $30; 2023 $20; 2024 $20; and 2025 $10.

[14] In addition, the effect of the health coverage tax credit on receipts has outlay effects of (in millions of dollars)
2015 $0; 2016 $10; 2017 $20; 2018 $30; 2019 $30; 2020 $10; and $0 thereafter.

[15] In addition, the effect of the child tax credit on receipts has outlay effects of (in millions of dollars):
2015 $26,990; 2016 $27,060; 2017 $27,050; 2018 $26,890; 2019 $15,330; 2020 $15,240; 2021 $15,340; 2022 $15,340; 2023 $15,390; 2024 $15,430; and 2025 $15,400.

[16] In addition, the earned income tax credit on receipts has outlay effects of (in millions of dollars):
2015 $61,880; 2016 $63,370; 2017 $63,100; 2018 $63,380; 2019 $61,620; 2020 $63,670; 2021 $63,040; 2022 $64,520; 2023 $66,090; 2024 $67,700; and 2025 $69,120.

[17] In addition, the Build America Bonds have outlay effects of (in millions of dollars):
2015 $3,800; 2016 $3,800; 2017 $3,800; 2018 $3,800; 2019 $3,800; 2020 $3,800; 2021 $3,800; 2022 $3,800; 2023 $3,800; 2024 $3,800; and 2025 $3,800.

Note: Provisions with estimates denoted normal tax method have no revenue loss under the reference tax law method. All estimates have been rounded to the nearest $10 million. Provisions with estimates that rounded to zero in each year are not included in the table.

Table 14–2A. ESTIMATES OF TOTAL CORPORATE INCOME TAX EXPENDITURES FOR FISCAL YEARS 2015–2025
(In millions of dollars)

	Total from corporations											
	2015	2016	2017	2018	2019	2020	2021	2022	2023	2024	2025	2016–25
National Defense												
1 Exclusion of benefits and allowances to armed forces personnel	0	0	0	0	0	0	0	0	0	0	0	0
International affairs:												
2 Exclusion of income earned abroad by U.S. citizens	0	0	0	0	0	0	0	0	0	0	0	0
3 Exclusion of certain allowances for Federal employees abroad .	0	0	0	0	0	0	0	0	0	0	0	0
4 Inventory property sales source rules exception	3,890	4,210	4,560	4,940	5,350	5,790	6,270	6,790	7,350	7,960	8,620	61,840
5 Deferral of income from controlled foreign corporations (normal tax method)	64,560	67,780	71,170	74,730	78,470	82,390	86,510	90,840	95,380	100,150	105,160	852,580
6 Deferred taxes for financial firms on certain income earned overseas	4,470	0	0	0	0	0	0	0	0	0	0	0
General science, space, and technology:												
7 Expensing of research and experimentation expenditures (normal tax method)	7,130	5,730	5,410	5,840	6,360	6,810	7,070	7,300	7,560	7,870	8,210	68,160
8 Credit for increasing research activities	5,420	3,160	2,840	2,540	2,250	1,990	1,750	1,540	1,350	1,180	1,020	19,620
Energy:												
9 Expensing of exploration and development costs, fuels	500	360	350	390	430	460	430	420	440	450	420	4,150
10 Excess of percentage over cost depletion, fuels	520	570	690	810	920	990	1,030	1,120	1,230	1,350	1,450	10,160
11 Exception from passive loss limitation for working interests in oil and gas properties	0	0	0	0	0	0	0	0	0	0	0	0
12 Capital gains treatment of royalties on coal	0	0	0	0	0	0	0	0	0	0	0	0
13 Exclusion of interest on energy facility bonds	10	10	10	10	10	10	10	10	10	10	10	100
14 Energy production credit [1]	1,160	1,460	1,690	1,730	1,670	1,590	1,540	1,480	1,380	1,190	870	14,600
15 Energy investment credit [1]	810	1,180	780	200	30	100	260	350	410	420	320	4,050
16 Alcohol fuel credits [2]	10	0	0	0	0	0	0	0	0	0	0	0
17 Bio-Diesel and small agri-biodiesel producer tax credits [3]	40	20	10	10	0	0	0	0	0	0	0	40
18 Tax credits for clean-fuel burning vehicles and refueling property	210	220	280	310	280	220	130	50	20	30	50	1,590
19 Exclusion of utility conservation subsidies	30	30	30	30	30	30	30	30	30	30	30	300
20 Credit for holding clean renewable energy bonds [4]	20	20	20	20	20	20	20	20	20	20	20	200
21 Deferral of gain from dispositions of transmission property to implement FERC restructuring policy	–120	–220	–180	–150	–130	–110	–70	–20	0	0	0	–880
22 Credit for investment in clean coal facilities	40	140	360	400	210	30	–20	–20	–20	–10	–10	1,060
23 Temporary 50% expensing for equipment used in the refining of liquid fuels	–2,250	–2,050	–1,820	–1,500	–1,220	–970	–680	–420	–200	–40	0	–8,900
24 Natural gas distribution pipelines treated as 15-year property ...	160	160	160	170	170	170	150	80	–20	–120	–230	690
25 Amortize all geological and geophysical expenditures over 2 years	70	80	80	70	70	70	70	80	80	80	80	760
26 Allowance of deduction for certain energy efficient commercial building property	10	0	–10	–10	–10	–10	–10	–10	–10	–10	–10	–90
27 Credit for construction of new energy efficient homes	20	10	0	0	0	0	0	0	0	0	0	10
28 Credit for energy efficiency improvements to existing homes	0	0	0	0	0	0	0	0	0	0	0	0
29 Credit for residential energy efficient property	0	0	0	0	0	0	0	0	0	0	0	0
30 Qualified energy conservation bonds [5]	10	10	10	10	10	10	10	10	10	10	10	100
31 Advanced energy property credit	50	10	–20	–20	–20	–10	0	0	0	0	0	–60
32 Advanced nuclear power production credit	0	140	140	140	340	620	690	690	690	580	550	4,580
33 Reduced tax rate for nuclear decommissioning funds	160	170	200	220	240	250	270	280	290	300	320	2,540
Natural resources and environment:												
34 Expensing of exploration and development costs, nonfuel minerals	10	0	10	30	50	60	60	60	60	50	50	430
35 Excess of percentage over cost depletion, nonfuel minerals	490	500	510	510	520	490	450	450	440	430	420	4,720
36 Exclusion of interest on bonds for water, sewage, and hazardous waste facilities	130	170	190	200	210	200	200	220	230	240	270	2,130
37 Capital gains treatment of certain timber income	0	0	0	0	0	0	0	0	0	0	0	0
38 Expensing of multiperiod timber growing costs	190	200	210	230	240	250	260	260	270	270	280	2,470
39 Tax incentives for preservation of historic structures	380	390	400	400	410	420	430	440	450	460	460	4,260
40 Industrial CO_2 capture and sequestration tax credit	80	110	150	190	80	0	0	0	0	0	0	530
41 Deduction for endangered species recovery expenditures	10	10	10	10	10	20	20	20	20	20	30	170

Table 14–2A. ESTIMATES OF TOTAL CORPORATE INCOME TAX EXPENDITURES FOR FISCAL YEARS 2015–2025—Continued

(In millions of dollars)

	Total from corporations											
	2015	2016	2017	2018	2019	2020	2021	2022	2023	2024	2025	2016–25
Agriculture:												
42 Expensing of certain capital outlays	10	10	20	20	20	20	20	20	20	30	30	210
43 Expensing of certain multiperiod production costs	20	20	30	30	30	30	40	40	40	50	50	360
44 Treatment of loans forgiven for solvent farmers	0	0	0	0	0	0	0	0	0	0	0	0
45 Capital gains treatment of certain income	0	0	0	0	0	0	0	0	0	0	0	0
46 Income averaging for farmers	0	0	0	0	0	0	0	0	0	0	0	0
47 Deferral of gain on sale of farm refiners	20	20	20	20	20	20	30	30	30	30	30	250
48 Expensing of reforestation expenditures	20	20	20	20	20	30	30	30	30	30	30	260
Commerce and housing:												
Financial institutions and insurance:												
49 Exemption of credit union income	1,690	2,300	2,200	2,200	2,350	2,440	2,700	2,890	2,980	3,120	3,570	26,750
50 Exclusion of interest on life insurance savings	1,630	1,740	2,020	2,350	2,630	2,860	3,040	3,210	3,360	3,520	3,680	28,410
51 Special alternative tax on small property and casualty insurance companies	30	30	40	40	40	40	50	50	50	50	60	450
52 Tax exemption of certain insurance companies owned by tax-exempt organizations	670	700	730	760	800	850	890	910	940	960	980	8,520
53 Small life insurance company deduction	30	30	30	40	40	40	40	40	40	50	50	400
54 Exclusion of interest spread of financial institutions	0	0	0	0	0	0	0	0	0	0	0	0
Housing:												
55 Exclusion of interest on owner-occupied mortgage subsidy bonds	360	460	530	550	580	550	570	610	640	680	750	5,920
56 Exclusion of interest on rental housing bonds	300	380	440	460	490	460	470	510	540	570	620	4,940
57 Deductibility of mortgage interest on owner-occupied homes	0	0	0	0	0	0	0	0	0	0	0	0
58 Deductibility of State and local property tax on owner-occupied homes	0	0	0	0	0	0	0	0	0	0	0	0
59 Deferral of income from installment sales	0	0	0	0	0	0	0	0	0	0	0	0
60 Capital gains exclusion on home sales	0	0	0	0	0	0	0	0	0	0	0	0
61 Exclusion of net imputed rental income	0	0	0	0	0	0	0	0	0	0	0	0
62 Exception from passive loss rules for $25,000 of rental loss	0	0	0	0	0	0	0	0	0	0	0	0
63 Credit for low-income housing investments	7,590	7,490	7,720	7,930	8,090	8,230	8,360	8,510	8,700	8,950	9,210	83,190
64 Accelerated depreciation on rental housing (normal tax method)	190	260	370	500	630	770	920	1,080	1,220	1,350	1,470	8,570
65 Discharge of mortgage indebtedness	0	0	0	0	0	0	0	0	0	0	0	0
Commerce:												
66 Discharge of business indebtedness	0	0	0	0	0	0	0	0	0	0	0	0
67 Exceptions from imputed interest rules	0	0	0	0	0	0	0	0	0	0	0	0
68 Treatment of qualified dividends	0	0	0	0	0	0	0	0	0	0	0	0
69 Capital gains (except agriculture, timber, iron ore, and coal)	0	0	0	0	0	0	0	0	0	0	0	0
70 Capital gains exclusion of small corporation stock	0	0	0	0	0	0	0	0	0	0	0	0
71 Step-up basis of capital gains at death	0	0	0	0	0	0	0	0	0	0	0	0
72 Carryover basis of capital gains on gifts	0	0	0	0	0	0	0	0	0	0	0	0
73 Ordinary income treatment of loss from small business corporation stock sale	0	0	0	0	0	0	0	0	0	0	0	0
74 Deferral of gains from like-kind exchanges	5,450	5,720	6,010	6,310	6,620	6,960	7,300	7,670	8,050	8,450	8,880	71,970
75 Accelerated depreciation of buildings other than rental housing (normal tax method)	–3,890	–3,850	–4,020	–4,280	–4,620	–5,000	–5,330	–5,630	–5,940	–6,290	–6,520	–51,480
76 Accelerated depreciation of machinery and equipment (normal tax method)	–5,850	–7,250	6,410	15,890	22,610	27,120	29,640	31,210	32,150	34,040	36,130	227,950
77 Expensing of certain small investments (normal tax method)	–230	–380	–200	–80	10	70	130	180	200	220	230	380
78 Graduated corporation income tax rate (normal tax method)	3,860	3,770	3,670	3,540	3,610	3,570	3,660	3,780	3,940	3,800	3,740	37,080
79 Exclusion of interest on small issue bonds	50	60	70	70	80	70	70	80	80	90	100	770
80 Deduction for US production activities	11,540	11,850	12,440	13,040	13,610	14,210	14,820	15,470	16,140	16,840	17,570	145,990
81 Special rules for certain film and TV production	150	90	50	20	10	0	0	0	0	0	0	170
Transportation:												
82 Tonnage tax	70	70	80	80	90	90	90	100	100	100	110	910
83 Deferral of tax on shipping companies	20	20	20	20	20	20	20	20	20	20	20	200

Table 14–2A. ESTIMATES OF TOTAL CORPORATE INCOME TAX EXPENDITURES FOR FISCAL YEARS 2015–2025—Continued

(In millions of dollars)

		Total from corporations											
		2015	2016	2017	2018	2019	2020	2021	2022	2023	2024	2025	2016–25
84	Exclusion of reimbursed employee parking expenses	0	0	0	0	0	0	0	0	0	0	0	0
85	Exclusion for employer-provided transit passes	0	0	0	0	0	0	0	0	0	0	0	0
86	Tax credit for certain expenditures for maintaining railroad tracks	90	0	0	0	0	0	0	0	0	0	0	0
87	Exclusion of interest on bonds for Highway Projects and rail-truck transfer facilities	50	50	50	50	40	40	40	40	30	30	30	400
Community and regional development:													
88	Investment credit for rehabilitation of structures (other than historic)	10	10	10	10	10	10	10	10	10	10	10	100
89	Exclusion of interest for airport, dock, and similar bonds	210	270	310	330	350	330	340	360	380	400	440	3,510
90	Exemption of certain mutuals' and cooperatives' income	140	140	150	150	150	160	160	160	170	170	170	1,580
91	Empowerment zones	40	20	10	10	10	10	0	0	0	0	0	60
92	New markets tax credit	1,170	1,200	1,110	890	620	410	220	20	–110	–160	–180	4,020
93	Credit to holders of Gulf Tax Credit Bonds.	70	80	100	100	110	100	110	110	120	130	140	1,100
94	Recovery Zone Bonds [6]	40	50	50	60	60	60	60	60	60	70	70	600
95	Tribal Economic Development Bonds	10	10	20	20	20	20	20	20	20	20	20	190
Education, training, employment, and social services:													
	Education:												
96	Exclusion of scholarship and fellowship income (normal tax method)	0	0	0	0	0	0	0	0	0	0	0	0
97	HOPE tax credit	0	0	0	0	0	0	0	0	0	0	0	0
98	Lifetime Learning tax credit	0	0	0	0	0	0	0	0	0	0	0	0
99	American Opportunity Tax Credit [7]	0	0	0	0	0	0	0	0	0	0	0	0
100	Education Individual Retirement Accounts	0	0	0	0	0	0	0	0	0	0	0	0
101	Deductibility of student-loan interest	0	0	0	0	0	0	0	0	0	0	0	0
102	Deduction for higher education expenses	0	0	0	0	0	0	0	0	0	0	0	0
103	Qualified tuition programs	0	0	0	0	0	0	0	0	0	0	0	0
104	Exclusion of interest on student-loan bonds	140	180	210	220	230	220	220	240	250	270	290	2,330
105	Exclusion of interest on bonds for private nonprofit educational facilities	650	830	960	1,000	1,060	1,000	1,030	1,110	1,160	1,230	1,350	10,730
106	Credit for holders of zone academy bonds [8]	160	130	120	110	100	100	90	90	80	80	80	980
107	Exclusion of interest on savings bonds redeemed to finance educational expenses	0	0	0	0	0	0	0	0	0	0	0	0
108	Parental personal exemption for students age 19 or over	0	0	0	0	0	0	0	0	0	0	0	0
109	Deductibility of charitable contributions (education)	860	900	940	980	1,030	1,070	1,120	1,170	1,220	1,270	1,320	11,020
110	Exclusion of employer-provided educational assistance	0	0	0	0	0	0	0	0	0	0	0	0
111	Special deduction for teacher expenses	0	0	0	0	0	0	0	0	0	0	0	0
112	Discharge of student loan indebtedness	0	0	0	0	0	0	0	0	0	0	0	0
113	Qualified school construction bonds [9]	160	160	160	160	160	160	160	160	160	160	160	1,600
	Training, employment, and social services:												
114	Work opportunity tax credit	540	300	170	130	100	70	50	40	30	20	20	930
115	Employer provided child care exclusion	0	0	0	0	0	0	0	0	0	0	0	0
116	Employer-provided child care credit	10	10	10	10	20	20	20	20	20	20	20	170
117	Assistance for adopted foster children	0	0	0	0	0	0	0	0	0	0	0	0
118	Adoption credit and exclusion [10]	0	0	0	0	0	0	0	0	0	0	0	0
119	Exclusion of employee meals and lodging (other than military)	0	0	0	0	0	0	0	0	0	0	0	0
120	Credit for child and dependent care expenses	0	0	0	0	0	0	0	0	0	0	0	0
121	Credit for disabled access expenditures	0	0	0	0	0	0	0	0	0	0	0	0
122	Deductibility of charitable contributions, other than education and health	1,800	1,890	1,970	2,060	2,150	2,250	2,340	2,450	2,550	2,650	2,750	23,060
123	Exclusion of certain foster care payments	0	0	0	0	0	0	0	0	0	0	0	0
124	Exclusion of parsonage allowances	0	0	0	0	0	0	0	0	0	0	0	0
125	Indian employment credit	20	10	10	10	0	0	0	0	0	0	0	30
Health:													
126	Exclusion of employer contributions for medical insurance premiums and medical care [11]	0	0	0	0	0	0	0	0	0	0	0	0

Table 14–2A. ESTIMATES OF TOTAL CORPORATE INCOME TAX EXPENDITURES FOR FISCAL YEARS 2015–2025—Continued

(In millions of dollars)

		Total from corporations										
		2015	2016	2017	2018	2019	2020	2021	2022	2023	2024	2025	2016–25
127	Self-employed medical insurance premiums	0	0	0	0	0	0	0	0	0	0	0	0
128	Medical Savings Accounts / Health Savings Accounts	0	0	0	0	0	0	0	0	0	0	0	0
129	Deductibility of medical expenses	0	0	0	0	0	0	0	0	0	0	0	0
130	Exclusion of interest on hospital construction bonds	1,020	1,300	1,510	1,580	1,660	1,580	1,620	1,750	1,830	1,930	2,130	16,890
131	Refundable Premium Assistance Tax Credit [12]	0	0	0	0	0	0	0	0	0	0	0	0
132	Credit for employee health insurance expenses of small business [13]	137	154	162	160	149	129	113	118	82	56	25	1,148
133	Deductibility of charitable contributions (health)	240	250	270	280	290	300	320	330	340	360	380	3,120
134	Tax credit for orphan drug research	1,450	1,750	2,110	2,550	3,070	3,710	4,470	5,400	6,510	7,850	9,480	46,900
135	Special Blue Cross/Blue Shield deduction	250	250	260	270	280	290	300	320	330	340	350	2,990
136	Tax credit for health insurance purchased by certain displaced and retired individuals [14]	0	0	0	0	0	0	0	0	0	0	0	0
137	Distributions from retirement plans for premiums for health and long-term care insurance	0	0	0	0	0	0	0	0	0	0	0	0
	Income security:												
138	Child credit [15]	0	0	0	0	0	0	0	0	0	0	0	0
139	Exclusion of railroad retirement system benefits	0	0	0	0	0	0	0	0	0	0	0	0
140	Exclusion of workers' compensation benefits	0	0	0	0	0	0	0	0	0	0	0	0
141	Exclusion of public assistance benefits (normal tax method)	0	0	0	0	0	0	0	0	0	0	0	0
142	Exclusion of special benefits for disabled coal miners	0	0	0	0	0	0	0	0	0	0	0	0
143	Exclusion of military disability pensions	0	0	0	0	0	0	0	0	0	0	0	0
	Net exclusion of pension contributions and earnings:												
144	Defined benefit employer plans	0	0	0	0	0	0	0	0	0	0	0	0
145	Defined contribution employer plans	0	0	0	0	0	0	0	0	0	0	0	0
146	Individual Retirement Accounts	0	0	0	0	0	0	0	0	0	0	0	0
147	Low and moderate income savers credit	0	0	0	0	0	0	0	0	0	0	0	0
148	Self-Employed plans	0	0	0	0	0	0	0	0	0	0	0	0
	Exclusion of other employee benefits:												
149	Premiums on group term life insurance	0	0	0	0	0	0	0	0	0	0	0	0
150	Premiums on accident and disability insurance	0	0	0	0	0	0	0	0	0	0	0	0
151	Income of trusts to finance supplementary unemployment benefits	0	0	0	0	0	0	0	0	0	0	0	0
152	Special ESOP rules	1,780	1,880	1,980	2,090	2,200	2,320	2,450	2,580	2,720	2,870	3,020	24,110
153	Additional deduction for the blind	0	0	0	0	0	0	0	0	0	0	0	0
154	Additional deduction for the elderly	0	0	0	0	0	0	0	0	0	0	0	0
155	Tax credit for the elderly and disabled	0	0	0	0	0	0	0	0	0	0	0	0
156	Deductibility of casualty losses	0	0	0	0	0	0	0	0	0	0	0	0
157	Earned income tax credit [16]	0	0	0	0	0	0	0	0	0	0	0	0
	Social Security:												
	Exclusion of social security benefits:												
158	Social Security benefits for retired workers	0	0	0	0	0	0	0	0	0	0	0	0
159	Social Security benefits for disabled workers	0	0	0	0	0	0	0	0	0	0	0	0
160	Social Security benefits for spouses, dependents and survivors	0	0	0	0	0	0	0	0	0	0	0	0
161	Credit for certain employer contributions to social security	430	440	460	490	510	530	550	580	600	630	660	5,450
	Veterans benefits and services:												
162	Exclusion of veterans death benefits and disability compensation	0	0	0	0	0	0	0	0	0	0	0	0
163	Exclusion of veterans pensions	0	0	0	0	0	0	0	0	0	0	0	0
164	Exclusion of GI bill benefits	0	0	0	0	0	0	0	0	0	0	0	0
165	Exclusion of interest on veterans housing bonds	0	0	0	0	0	0	0	0	0	0	10	10
	General purpose fiscal assistance:												
166	Exclusion of interest on public purpose State and local bonds	8,410	10,750	12,450	13,030	13,750	13,020	13,350	14,430	15,070	15,940	17,560	139,350
167	Build America Bonds [17]	0	0	0	0	0	0	0	0	0	0	0	0

Table 14–2A. ESTIMATES OF TOTAL CORPORATE INCOME TAX EXPENDITURES FOR FISCAL YEARS 2015–2025—Continued

(In millions of dollars)

		Total from corporations											
		2015	2016	2017	2018	2019	2020	2021	2022	2023	2024	2025	2016–25
168	Deductibility of nonbusiness State and local taxes other than on owner-occupied homes	0	0	0	0	0	0	0	0	0	0	0	0
Interest:													
169	Deferral of interest on U.S. savings bonds	0	0	0	0	0	0	0	0	0	0	0	0
Addendum: Aid to State and local governments:													
	Deductibility of:													
	Property taxes on owner-occupied homes	0	0	0	0	0	0	0	0	0	0	0	0
	Nonbusiness State and local taxes other than on owner-occupied homes	0	0	0	0	0	0	0	0	0	0	0	0
	Exclusion of interest on State and local bonds for:													
	Public purposes	8,410	10,750	12,450	13,030	13,750	13,020	13,350	14,430	15,070	15,940	17,560	139,350
	Energy facilities	10	10	10	10	10	10	10	10	10	10	10	100
	Water, sewage, and hazardous waste disposal facilities	130	170	190	200	210	200	200	220	230	240	270	2,130
	Small-issues	50	60	70	70	80	70	70	80	80	90	100	770
	Owner-occupied mortgage subsidies	360	460	530	550	580	550	570	610	640	680	750	5,920
	Rental housing	300	380	440	460	490	460	470	510	540	570	620	4,940
	Airports, docks, and similar facilities	210	270	310	330	350	330	340	360	380	400	440	3,510
	Student loans	140	180	210	220	230	220	220	240	250	270	290	2,330
	Private nonprofit educational facilities	650	830	960	1,000	1,060	1,000	1,030	1,110	1,160	1,230	1,350	10,730
	Hospital construction	1,020	1,300	1,510	1,580	1,660	1,580	1,620	1,750	1,830	1,930	2,130	16,890
	Veterans' housing	0	0	0	0	0	0	0	0	0	0	10	10

See Table 1 footnotes for specific table information

Table 14–2B. ESTIMATES OF TOTAL INDIVIDUAL INCOME TAX EXPENDITURES FOR FISCAL YEARS 2015–2025

(In millions of dollars)

	Total from individuals											
	2015	2016	2017	2018	2019	2020	2021	2022	2023	2024	2025	2016–2025
National Defense												
1 Exclusion of benefits and allowances to armed forces personnel	13,680	14,220	13,170	13,310	13,780	14,340	14,970	15,640	16,360	17,130	17,950	150,870
International affairs:												
2 Exclusion of income earned abroad by U.S. citizens	5,990	6,280	6,600	6,930	7,280	7,640	8,020	8,420	8,840	9,290	9,750	79,050
3 Exclusion of certain allowances for Federal employees abroad	1,240	1,300	1,370	1,430	1,510	1,580	1,660	1,740	1,830	1,920	2,020	16,360
4 Inventory property sales source rules exception	0	0	0	0	0	0	0	0	0	0	0	0
5 Deferral of income from controlled foreign corporations (normal tax method)	0	0	0	0	0	0	0	0	0	0	0	0
6 Deferred taxes for financial firms on certain income earned overseas	0	0	0	0	0	0	0	0	0	0	0	0
General science, space, and technology:												
7 Expensing of research and experimentation expenditures (normal tax method)	770	620	410	430	470	500	530	540	560	580	610	5,250
8 Credit for increasing research activities	290	160	140	130	120	100	90	80	70	60	60	1,010
Energy:												
9 Expensing of exploration and development costs, fuels	160	110	110	120	130	140	150	150	160	170	160	1,400
10 Excess of percentage over cost depletion, fuels	130	140	170	200	230	250	260	280	310	340	360	2,540
11 Exception from passive loss limitation for working interests in oil and gas properties	40	40	40	40	40	30	30	30	30	30	30	340
12 Capital gains treatment of royalties on coal	110	120	130	130	130	140	140	150	150	160	170	1,420
13 Exclusion of interest on energy facility bonds	10	10	20	20	20	20	30	30	30	30	40	250
14 Energy production credit [1]	390	490	560	580	560	530	510	490	460	400	290	4,870
15 Energy investment credit [1]	200	290	190	50	10	30	60	90	100	110	80	1,010
16 Alcohol fuel credits [2]	10	0	0	0	0	0	0	0	0	0	0	0
17 Bio-Diesel and small agri-biodiesel producer tax credits [3]	30	10	10	0	0	0	0	0	0	0	0	20
18 Tax credits for clean-fuel burning vehicles and refueling property	330	330	390	510	530	480	370	240	120	100	110	3,180
19 Exclusion of utility conservation subsidies	400	420	440	460	490	510	540	560	590	620	650	5,280
20 Credit for holding clean renewable energy bonds [4]	50	50	50	50	50	50	50	50	50	50	50	500
21 Deferral of gain from dispositions of transmission property to implement FERC restructuring policy	0	0	0	0	0	0	0	0	0	0	0	0
22 Credit for investment in clean coal facilities	0	20	40	40	20	0	0	0	0	0	0	120
23 Temporary 50% expensing for equipment used in the refining of liquid fuels	0	0	0	0	0	0	0	0	0	0	0	0
24 Natural gas distribution pipelines treated as 15-year property	0	0	0	0	0	0	0	0	0	0	0	0
25 Amortize all geological and geophysical expenditures over 2 years	20	20	20	20	20	20	20	20	20	20	20	200
26 Allowance of deduction for certain energy efficient commercial building property	20	−10	−20	−20	−20	−20	−20	−20	−20	−20	−20	−190
27 Credit for construction of new energy efficient homes	40	10	0	0	0	0	0	0	0	0	0	10
28 Credit for energy efficiency improvements to existing homes	270	0	0	0	0	0	0	0	0	0	0	0
29 Credit for residential energy efficient property	850	770	460	180	40	0	0	0	0	0	0	1,450
30 Qualified energy conservation bonds [5]	20	20	20	20	20	20	20	20	20	20	20	200
31 Advanced energy property credit	10	0	−10	−10	−10	0	0	0	0	0	0	−30
32 Advanced nuclear power production credit	0	0	0	0	0	0	0	0	0	0	0	0
33 Reduced tax rate for nuclear decommissioning funds	0	0	0	0	0	0	0	0	0	0	0	0
Natural resources and environment:												
34 Expensing of exploration and development costs, nonfuel minerals	0	0	0	0	0	0	0	10	10	0	0	20
35 Excess of percentage over cost depletion, nonfuel minerals	30	30	30	30	30	30	20	20	20	20	20	250
36 Exclusion of interest on bonds for water, sewage, and hazardous waste facilities	320	320	360	420	480	530	580	640	690	740	790	5,550
37 Capital gains treatment of certain timber income	110	120	130	130	130	140	140	150	150	160	170	1,420
38 Expensing of multiperiod timber growing costs	130	130	140	140	140	150	160	160	160	160	170	1,510
39 Tax incentives for preservation of historic structures	70	70	70	70	70	70	80	80	80	80	80	750
40 Industrial CO2 capture and sequestration tax credit	0	0	0	0	0	0	0	0	0	0	0	0

Table 14–2B. ESTIMATES OF TOTAL INDIVIDUAL INCOME TAX EXPENDITURES FOR FISCAL YEARS 2015–2025—Continued

(In millions of dollars)

	Total from individuals											
	2015	2016	2017	2018	2019	2020	2021	2022	2023	2024	2025	2016–2025
41 Deduction for endangered species recovery expenditures	10	20	20	20	20	20	30	30	30	30	40	260
Agriculture:												
42 Expensing of certain capital outlays	210	200	210	220	230	250	260	270	290	300	320	2,550
43 Expensing of certain multiperiod production costs	330	350	360	380	410	430	450	480	510	540	580	4,490
44 Treatment of loans forgiven for solvent farmers	40	40	40	40	40	40	40	40	40	40	40	400
45 Capital gains treatment of certain income	1,150	1,240	1,280	1,300	1,320	1,360	1,410	1,470	1,530	1,590	1,670	14,170
46 Income averaging for farmers	130	140	140	140	140	140	140	140	140	140	140	1,400
47 Deferral of gain on sale of farm refiners	0	0	0	0	0	0	0	0	0	0	0	0
48 Expensing of reforestation expenditures	30	30	40	40	40	40	40	50	50	50	50	430
Commerce and housing:												
Financial institutions and insurance:												
49 Exemption of credit union income	0	0	0	0	0	0	0	0	0	0	0	0
50 Exclusion of interest on life insurance savings	15,820	17,130	21,360	26,600	31,160	34,960	37,970	40,340	42,390	44,300	46,220	342,430
51 Special alternative tax on small property and casualty insurance companies	0	0	0	0	0	0	0	0	0	0	0	0
52 Tax exemption of certain insurance companies owned by tax-exempt organizations	0	0	0	0	0	0	0	0	0	0	0	0
53 Small life insurance company deduction	0	0	0	0	0	0	0	0	0	0	0	0
54 Exclusion of interest spread of financial institutions	380	420	450	470	480	500	510	530	540	550	560	5,010
Housing:												
55 Exclusion of interest on owner-occupied mortgage subsidy bonds	890	890	1,000	1,150	1,320	1,470	1,620	1,770	1,910	2,050	2,190	15,370
56 Exclusion of interest on rental housing bonds	750	740	830	960	1,100	1,230	1,350	1,480	1,600	1,710	1,830	12,830
57 Deductibility of mortgage interest on owner-occupied homes	58,850	62,440	68,610	75,980	83,760	91,380	98,930	106,150	113,320	120,560	127,360	948,490
58 Deductibility of State and local property tax on owner-occupied homes	31,120	33,080	35,580	38,330	41,150	43,850	46,580	49,280	52,060	55,010	57,890	452,810
59 Deferral of income from installment sales	1,570	1,620	1,640	1,650	1,670	1,720	1,770	1,840	1,920	2,000	2,090	17,920
60 Capital gains exclusion on home sales	37,220	40,580	43,460	46,560	49,870	53,420	57,230	61,300	65,670	70,340	75,350	563,780
61 Exclusion of net imputed rental income	97,920	101,100	104,950	108,460	111,480	114,070	118,400	122,900	127,570	132,420	137,450	1,178,800
62 Exception from passive loss rules for $25,000 of rental loss	6,810	7,210	7,540	7,870	8,240	8,600	8,880	9,170	9,490	9,850	10,160	87,010
63 Credit for low-income housing investments	400	390	410	420	430	430	440	450	460	470	480	4,380
64 Accelerated depreciation on rental housing (normal tax method)	1,040	1,390	1,900	2,500	3,140	3,800	4,590	5,400	6,130	6,810	7,460	43,120
65 Discharge of mortgage indebtedness	1,100	0	0	0	0	0	0	0	0	0	0	0
Commerce:												
66 Discharge of business indebtedness	−160	−120	−50	−10	0	10	30	40	50	50	50	50
67 Exceptions from imputed interest rules	40	50	60	60	60	70	70	80	80	80	90	700
68 Treatment of qualified dividends	25,650	25,530	26,470	27,490	28,590	29,760	31,030	32,380	33,810	35,310	36,880	307,250
69 Capital gains (except agriculture, timber, iron ore, and coal)	85,710	92,820	95,870	96,790	98,660	101,520	105,170	109,410	114,070	119,080	124,380	1,057,770
70 Capital gains exclusion of small corporation stock	220	380	620	800	780	680	580	490	430	390	360	5,510
71 Step-up basis of capital gains at death	54,850	58,270	61,910	65,770	69,870	74,220	78,850	83,770	88,990	94,540	100,440	776,630
72 Carryover basis of capital gains on gifts	2,490	2,740	3,010	3,300	3,620	3,970	4,340	4,750	5,170	5,530	5,820	42,250
73 Ordinary income treatment of loss from small business corporation stock sale	50	50	50	50	50	50	50	50	50	50	50	500
74 Deferral of gains from like-kind exchanges	1,530	1,600	1,690	1,780	1,860	1,960	2,060	2,160	2,270	2,380	2,500	20,260
75 Accelerated depreciation of buildings other than rental housing (normal tax method)	−5,410	−5,320	−5,370	−5,510	−5,820	−6,200	−6,600	−7,000	−7,410	−7,870	−8,170	−65,270
76 Accelerated depreciation of machinery and equipment (normal tax method)	−1,660	−1,620	5,770	10,340	13,310	15,140	16,070	16,560	16,800	17,570	18,440	128,380
77 Expensing of certain small investments (normal tax method)	−950	−1,910	−590	170	710	1,050	1,400	1,670	1,820	1,940	2,050	8,310
78 Graduated corporation income tax rate (normal tax method)	0	0	0	0	0	0	0	0	0	0	0	0
79 Exclusion of interest on small issue bonds	120	110	130	150	170	190	210	230	250	260	280	1,980
80 Deduction for US production activities	3,690	3,830	4,000	4,180	4,370	4,560	4,760	4,970	5,180	5,410	5,640	46,900
81 Special rules for certain film and TV production	40	20	10	10	0	0	0	0	0	0	0	40
Transportation:												
82 Tonnage tax	0	0	0	0	0	0	0	0	0	0	0	0

Table 14–2B.   ESTIMATES OF TOTAL INDIVIDUAL INCOME TAX EXPENDITURES FOR FISCAL YEARS 2015–2025—Continued

(In millions of dollars)

		Total from individuals											
		2015	2016	2017	2018	2019	2020	2021	2022	2023	2024	2025	2016–2025
83	Deferral of tax on shipping companies	0	0	0	0	0	0	0	0	0	0	0	0
84	Exclusion of reimbursed employee parking expenses	2,790	2,900	3,000	3,100	3,220	3,340	3,440	3,550	3,670	3,790	3,870	33,880
85	Exclusion for employer-provided transit passes	730	770	820	860	920	980	1,030	1,100	1,170	1,220	1,290	10,160
86	Tax credit for certain expenditures for maintaining railroad tracks	10	0	0	0	0	0	0	0	0	0	0	0
87	Exclusion of interest on bonds for Highway Projects and rail-truck transfer facilities	170	160	150	140	130	130	120	120	110	110	100	1,270
Community and regional development:													
88	Investment credit for rehabilitation of structures (other than historic)	10	10	10	10	10	10	10	10	10	10	10	100
89	Exclusion of interest for airport, dock, and similar bonds	530	530	590	680	780	870	960	1,050	1,130	1,210	1,290	9,090
90	Exemption of certain mutuals' and cooperatives' income	0	0	0	0	0	0	0	0	0	0	0	0
91	Empowerment zones	60	20	20	20	20	10	10	10	10	10	10	140
92	New markets tax credit	30	30	20	20	20	10	10	0	0	0	0	110
93	Credit to holders of Gulf Tax Credit Bonds.	170	170	190	210	250	270	300	330	360	380	410	2,870
94	Recovery Zone Bonds [6]	90	90	100	120	130	150	160	180	190	210	220	1,550
95	Tribal Economic Development Bonds	30	30	30	40	40	50	50	60	60	60	70	490
Education, training, employment, and social services:													
	Education:												
96	Exclusion of scholarship and fellowship income (normal tax method)	3,130	3,250	3,360	3,450	3,510	3,640	3,770	3,900	4,040	4,190	4,340	37,450
97	HOPE tax credit	0	0	0	670	6,740	6,880	7,290	7,380	7,500	7,880	7,960	52,300
98	Lifetime Learning tax credit	2,270	2,450	2,460	2,660	4,340	4,410	4,500	4,530	4,590	4,660	4,690	39,290
99	American Opportunity Tax Credit [7]	13,470	13,430	13,500	12,190	0	0	0	0	0	0	0	39,120
100	Education Individual Retirement Accounts	30	30	40	40	40	40	40	40	50	50	50	420
101	Deductibility of student-loan interest	1,800	1,800	1,780	1,780	1,790	1,820	1,820	1,810	1,840	1,830	1,820	18,090
102	Deduction for higher education expenses	390	0	0	0	0	0	0	0	0	0	0	0
103	Qualified tuition programs	1,680	1,870	2,080	2,290	2,510	2,760	3,020	3,310	3,610	3,960	4,330	29,740
104	Exclusion of interest on student-loan bonds	350	350	390	450	520	580	640	700	750	810	860	6,050
105	Exclusion of interest on bonds for private nonprofit educational facilities	1,620	1,610	1,800	2,090	2,390	2,660	2,930	3,210	3,470	3,710	3,960	27,830
106	Credit for holders of zone academy bonds [8]	0	0	0	0	0	0	0	0	0	0	0	0
107	Exclusion of interest on savings bonds redeemed to finance educational expenses	30	30	30	30	30	30	40	40	40	40	40	350
108	Parental personal exemption for students age 19 or over	4,400	4,400	4,420	4,460	4,590	4,710	4,840	4,950	5,050	5,140	5,250	47,810
109	Deductibility of charitable contributions (education)	3,960	4,280	4,620	4,990	5,370	5,720	6,050	6,380	6,710	7,030	7,360	58,510
110	Exclusion of employer-provided educational assistance	800	850	890	940	980	1,030	1,080	1,130	1,190	1,240	1,300	10,630
111	Special deduction for teacher expenses	210	0	0	0	0	0	0	0	0	0	0	0
112	Discharge of student loan indebtedness	90	90	90	90	90	90	90	90	90	90	90	900
113	Qualified school construction bonds [9]	490	490	490	490	490	490	490	490	490	490	490	4,900
	Training, employment, and social services:												
114	Work opportunity tax credit	180	120	70	50	40	30	20	20	10	10	10	380
115	Employer provided child care exclusion	900	930	980	1,050	1,120	1,180	1,250	1,330	1,410	1,500	1,590	12,340
116	Employer-provided child care credit	0	0	0	0	0	0	0	0	0	0	0	0
117	Assistance for adopted foster children	560	540	560	580	610	630	650	680	710	740	770	6,470
118	Adoption credit and exclusion [10]	270	250	260	290	270	320	310	320	320	320	330	2,990
119	Exclusion of employee meals and lodging (other than military)	4,410	4,500	4,600	4,710	4,840	4,970	5,100	5,230	5,360	5,490	5,620	50,420
120	Credit for child and dependent care expenses	4,500	4,520	4,560	4,650	4,760	4,900	5,000	5,120	5,220	5,330	5,440	49,500
121	Credit for disabled access expenditures	10	10	10	10	20	20	20	20	20	20	20	170
122	Deductibility of charitable contributions, other than education and health	39,110	42,350	45,660	49,320	53,100	56,580	59,840	63,080	66,260	69,480	72,660	578,330
123	Exclusion of certain foster care payments	430	460	480	500	510	520	530	550	560	570	580	5,260
124	Exclusion of parsonage allowances	690	730	770	810	850	900	940	990	1,050	1,100	1,160	9,300
125	Indian employment credit	20	20	20	10	10	10	10	10	10	10	0	110

Health:

Table 14–2B.   ESTIMATES OF TOTAL INDIVIDUAL INCOME TAX EXPENDITURES FOR FISCAL YEARS 2015–2025—Continued

(In millions of dollars)

		Total from individuals										
		2015	2016	2017	2018	2019	2020	2021	2022	2023	2024	2025	2016–2025
126	Exclusion of employer contributions for medical insurance premiums and medical care [11]	201,450	210,980	220,550	229,620	243,160	259,520	275,600	293,420	313,810	336,070	359,590	2,742,320
127	Self-employed medical insurance premiums	6,690	7,060	7,440	7,680	7,980	8,400	8,820	9,240	9,690	10,210	10,770	87,290
128	Medical Savings Accounts / Health Savings Accounts	4,810	5,730	6,830	8,060	9,560	11,390	13,550	16,130	19,190	22,830	27,150	140,420
129	Deductibility of medical expenses	7,660	8,260	8,700	9,530	10,980	12,850	14,810	16,840	19,380	22,350	25,460	149,160
130	Exclusion of interest on hospital construction bonds	2,550	2,540	2,840	3,290	3,760	4,180	4,610	5,060	5,460	5,850	6,230	43,820
131	Refundable Premium Assistance Tax Credit [12]	1,960	2,340	3,870	4,880	6,880	7,580	7,810	8,140	8,430	8,730	9,090	67,750
132	Credit for employee health insurance expenses of small business [13]	376	390	381	357	304	266	188	240	160	125	53	2,464
133	Deductibility of charitable contributions (health)	4,380	4,740	5,120	5,530	5,950	6,340	6,710	7,070	7,430	7,790	8,140	64,820
134	Tax credit for orphan drug research	10	10	10	20	20	20	20	30	30	40	40	240
135	Special Blue Cross/Blue Shield deduction	0	0	0	0	0	0	0	0	0	0	0	0
136	Tax credit for health insurance purchased by certain displaced and retired individuals [14]	0	30	30	20	10	0	0	0	0	0	0	90
137	Distributions from retirement plans for premiums for health and long-term care insurance	400	440	460	480	500	520	540	560	580	600	620	5,300
Income security:													
138	Child credit [15]	23,980	24,000	24,290	24,700	25,190	25,080	24,770	24,440	24,040	23,600	23,180	243,290
139	Exclusion of railroad retirement system benefits	300	300	300	290	280	270	250	240	220	190	170	2,510
140	Exclusion of workers' compensation benefits	9,720	9,820	9,920	10,010	10,110	10,220	10,320	10,420	10,530	10,630	10,730	102,710
141	Exclusion of public assistance benefits (normal tax method)	560	570	590	600	630	650	670	680	710	730	680	6,510
142	Exclusion of special benefits for disabled coal miners	30	30	20	20	20	10	10	10	10	10	0	140
143	Exclusion of military disability pensions	220	220	240	250	260	270	290	300	310	330	340	2,810
	Net exclusion of pension contributions and earnings:												
144	Defined benefit employer plans	66,620	66,600	66,760	67,020	66,180	64,820	63,190	60,910	58,470	55,930	52,650	622,530
145	Defined contribution employer plans	62,070	64,710	65,620	68,120	73,930	78,960	98,370	107,980	114,420	121,240	128,130	921,480
146	Individual Retirement Accounts	16,400	16,850	16,970	17,240	18,080	19,270	19,680	20,630	21,780	22,840	24,080	197,420
147	Low and moderate income savers credit	1,280	1,280	1,270	1,270	1,300	1,310	1,310	1,330	1,340	1,350	1,360	13,120
148	Self-Employed plans	25,490	28,030	30,800	33,760	37,030	40,480	44,020	47,870	52,060	56,610	61,560	432,220
	Exclusion of other employee benefits:												
149	Premiums on group term life insurance	2,340	2,450	2,560	2,610	2,700	2,800	2,900	3,000	3,110	3,240	3,350	28,720
150	Premiums on accident and disability insurance	310	320	320	330	330	330	340	340	340	350	350	3,350
151	Income of trusts to finance supplementary unemployment benefits	20	20	30	40	40	50	50	60	60	60	60	470
152	Special ESOP rules	110	120	120	120	120	130	130	130	140	140	140	1,290
153	Additional deduction for the blind	40	40	40	40	40	50	50	50	60	60	60	490
154	Additional deduction for the elderly	2,890	3,080	3,310	3,560	3,760	4,010	4,210	4,500	4,870	5,170	5,530	42,000
155	Tax credit for the elderly and disabled	10	10	10	10	10	10	10	0	0	0	0	60
156	Deductibility of casualty losses	350	370	390	410	430	450	460	470	490	500	520	4,490
157	Earned income tax credit [16]	2,120	2,820	2,340	3,040	1,820	1,910	1,980	2,080	2,180	2,280	2,380	22,830
Social Security:													
	Exclusion of social security benefits:												
158	Social Security benefits for retired workers	25,780	26,900	28,280	29,490	30,730	31,760	32,510	33,130	33,690	34,340	34,590	315,420
159	Social Security benefits for disabled workers	8,280	8,490	8,580	8,730	8,970	9,210	9,500	9,840	10,190	10,540	10,870	94,920
160	Social Security benefits for spouses, dependents and survivors	4,060	4,160	4,310	4,440	4,610	4,750	4,870	5,000	5,140	5,310	5,420	48,010
161	Credit for certain employer contributions to social security	550	570	600	620	650	680	710	740	770	810	840	6,990
Veterans benefits and services:													
162	Exclusion of veterans death benefits and disability compensation	6,150	6,760	7,250	7,590	7,870	8,170	8,460	8,770	9,080	9,400	9,740	83,090
163	Exclusion of veterans pensions	420	450	490	510	530	560	580	600	630	650	680	5,680
164	Exclusion of GI bill benefits	1,530	1,690	1,830	1,960	2,070	2,190	2,310	2,440	2,580	2,720	2,880	22,670
165	Exclusion of interest on veterans housing bonds	10	10	10	10	10	10	10	10	10	10	20	110
General purpose fiscal assistance:													
166	Exclusion of interest on public purpose State and local bonds	21,020	20,950	23,450	27,150	31,060	34,530	38,080	41,760	45,070	48,280	51,470	361,800
167	Build America Bonds [17]	0	0	0	0	0	0	0	0	0	0	0	0

Table 14–2B.   ESTIMATES OF TOTAL INDIVIDUAL INCOME TAX EXPENDITURES FOR FISCAL YEARS 2015–2025—Continued

(In millions of dollars)

	Total from individuals											
	2015	2016	2017	2018	2019	2020	2021	2022	2023	2024	2025	2016–2025
168 Deductibility of nonbusiness State and local taxes other than on owner-occupied homes	48,430	51,380	55,130	59,030	62,870	66,730	70,830	75,060	79,410	83,920	88,280	692,640
Interest:												
169 Deferral of interest on U.S. savings bonds	1,020	1,010	1,000	990	980	970	960	950	940	930	920	9,650
Addendum: Aid to State and local governments:												
Deductibility of:												
Property taxes on owner-occupied homes	31,120	33,080	35,580	38,330	41,150	43,850	46,580	49,280	52,060	55,010	57,890	452,810
Nonbusiness State and local taxes other than on owner-occupied homes	48,430	51,380	55,130	59,030	62,870	66,730	70,830	75,060	79,410	83,920	88,280	692,640
Exclusion of interest on State and local bonds for:												
Public purposes	21,020	20,950	23,450	27,150	31,060	34,530	38,080	41,760	45,070	48,280	51,470	361,800
Energy facilities	10	10	20	20	20	20	30	30	30	30	40	250
Water, sewage, and hazardous waste disposal facilities	320	320	360	420	480	530	580	640	690	740	790	5,550
Small-issues	120	110	130	150	170	190	210	230	250	260	280	1,980
Owner-occupied mortgage subsidies	890	890	1,000	1,150	1,320	1,470	1,620	1,770	1,910	2,050	2,190	15,370
Rental housing	750	740	830	960	1,100	1,230	1,350	1,480	1,600	1,710	1,830	12,830
Airports, docks, and similar facilities	530	530	590	680	780	870	960	1,050	1,130	1,210	1,290	9,090
Student loans	350	350	390	450	520	580	640	700	750	810	860	6,050
Private nonprofit educational facilities	1,620	1,610	1,800	2,090	2,390	2,660	2,930	3,210	3,470	3,710	3,960	27,830
Hospital construction	2,550	2,540	2,840	3,290	3,760	4,180	4,610	5,060	5,460	5,850	6,230	43,820
Veterans' housing	10	10	10	10	10	10	10	10	10	10	20	110

See Table 1 footnotes for specific table information

Table 14–3.   INCOME TAX EXPENDITURES RANKED BY TOTAL FISCAL YEAR 2016-2025 PROJECTED REVENUE EFFECT
(In millions of dollars)

	Provision	2016	2017	2016-2025
126	Exclusion of employer contributions for medical insurance premiums and medical care	210,980	220,550	2,742,320
61	Exclusion of net imputed rental income	101,100	104,950	1,178,800
69	Capital gains (except agriculture, timber, iron ore, and coal)	92,820	95,870	1,057,770
57	Deductibility of mortgage interest on owner-occupied homes	62,440	68,610	948,490
145	Defined contribution employer plans	64,710	65,620	921,480
5	Deferral of income from controlled foreign corporations (normal tax method)	67,780	71,170	852,580
71	Step-up basis of capital gains at death	58,270	61,910	776,630
168	Deductibility of nonbusiness State and local taxes other than on owner-occupied homes	51,380	55,130	692,640
144	Defined benefit employer plans	66,600	66,760	622,530
122	Deductibility of charitable contributions, other than education and health	44,240	47,630	601,390
60	Capital gains exclusion on home sales	40,580	43,460	563,780
166	Exclusion of interest on public purpose State and local bonds	31,700	35,900	501,150
58	Deductibility of State and local property tax on owner-occupied homes	33,080	35,580	452,810
148	Self-Employed plans	28,030	30,800	432,220
50	Exclusion of interest on life insurance savings	18,870	23,380	370,840
76	Accelerated depreciation of machinery and equipment (normal tax method)	-8,870	12,180	356,330
158	Social Security benefits for retired workers	26,900	28,280	315,420
68	Treatment of qualified dividends	25,530	26,470	307,250
136	Child credit	24,000	24,290	243,290
146	Individual Retirement Accounts	16,850	16,970	197,420
80	Deduction for US production activities	15,680	16,440	192,890
1	Exclusion of benefits and allowances to armed forces personnel	14,220	13,170	150,870
129	Deductibility of medical expenses	8,260	8,700	149,160
128	Medical Savings Accounts / Health Savings Accounts	5,730	6,830	140,420
140	Exclusion of workers' compensation benefits	9,820	9,920	102,710
159	Social Security benefits for disabled workers	8,490	8,580	94,920
74	Deferral of gains from like-kind exchanges	7,320	7,700	92,230
63	Credit for low-income housing investments	7,880	8,130	87,570
127	Self-employed medical insurance premiums	7,060	7,440	87,290
62	Exception from passive loss rules for $25,000 of rental loss	7,210	7,540	87,010
162	Exclusion of veterans death benefits and disability compensation	6,760	7,250	83,090
2	Exclusion of income earned abroad by U.S. citizens	6,280	6,600	79,050
7	Expensing of research and experimentation expenditures (normal tax method)	6,350	5,820	73,410
109	Deductibility of charitable contributions (education)	5,180	5,560	69,530
133	Deductibility of charitable contributions (health)	4,990	5,390	67,940
131	Refundable Premium Assistance Tax Credit	2,340	3,870	67,750
4	Inventory property sales source rules exception	4,210	4,560	61,840
130	Exclusion of interest on hospital construction bonds	3,840	4,350	60,710
97	HOPE tax credit	0	0	52,300
64	Accelerated depreciation on rental housing (normal tax method)	1,650	2,270	51,690
119	Exclusion of employee meals and lodging (other than military)	4,500	4,600	50,420
120	Credit for child and dependent care expenses	4,520	4,560	49,500
160	Social Security benefits for spouses, dependents and survivors	4,160	4,310	48,010
108	Parental personal exemption for students age 19 or over	4,400	4,420	47,810
134	Tax credit for orphan drug research	1,760	2,120	47,140
72	Carryover basis of capital gains on gifts	2,740	3,010	42,250
154	Additional deduction for the elderly	3,080	3,310	42,000
98	Lifetime Learning tax credit	2,450	2,460	39,290
99	Lifetime Learning tax credit	13,430	13,500	39,120
105	Exclusion of interest on bonds for private nonprofit educational facilities	2,440	2,760	38,560
96	Exclusion of scholarship and fellowship income (normal tax method)	3,250	3,360	37,450
78	Graduated corporation income tax rate (normal tax method)	3,770	3,670	37,080
84	Exclusion of reimbursed employee parking expenses	2,900	3,000	33,880
103	Qualified Tuition Programs	1,870	2,080	29,740
149	Premiums on group term life insurance	2,450	2,560	28,720

Table 14–3. INCOME TAX EXPENDITURES RANKED BY TOTAL FISCAL YEAR 2016-2025 PROJECTED REVENUE EFFECT—Continued

(In millions of dollars)

	Provision	2016	2017	2016-2025
49	Exemption of credit union income	2,300	2,200	26,750
152	Special ESOP rules	2,000	2,100	25,400
157	Earned income tax credit	2,820	2,340	22,830
164	Exclusion of GI bill benefits	1,690	1,830	22,670
55	Exclusion of interest on owner-occupied mortgage subsidy bonds	1,350	1,530	21,290
8	Credit for increasing research activities	3,320	2,980	20,630
14	New technology credit	1,950	2,250	19,470
101	Deductibility of student-loan interest	1,800	1,780	18,090
59	Deferral of income from installment sales	1,620	1,640	17,920
56	Exclusion of interest on rental housing bonds	1,120	1,270	17,770
3	Exclusion of certain allowances for Federal employees abroad	1,300	1,370	16,360
45	Capital gains treatment of certain income	1,240	1,280	14,170
147	Low and moderate income savers credit	1,280	1,270	13,120
10	Excess of percentage over cost depletion, fuels	710	860	12,700
89	Exclusion of interest for airport, dock, and similar bonds	800	900	12,600
161	Credit for certain employer contributions to social security	1,010	1,060	12,440
115	Employer provided child care exclusion	930	980	12,340
110	Exclusion of employer-provided educational assistance	850	890	10,630
85	Exclusion for employer-provided transit passes	770	820	10,160
169	Deferral of interest on U.S. savings bonds	1,010	1,000	9,650
124	Exclusion of parsonage allowances	730	770	9,300
77	Expensing of certain small investments (normal tax method)	-2,290	-790	8,690
52	Tax exemption of certain insurance companies owned by tax-exempt organizations	700	730	8,520
104	Exclusion of interest on student-loan bonds	530	600	8,380
36	Exclusion of interest on bonds for water, sewage, and hazardous waste facilities	490	550	7,680
141	Exclusion of public assistance benefits (normal tax method)	570	590	6,510
113	Qualified school construction bonds	650	650	6,500
117	Assistance for adopted foster children	540	560	6,470
163	Exclusion of veterans pensions	450	490	5,680
19	Exclusion of utility conservation subsidies	450	470	5,580
9	Expensing of exploration and development costs, fuels	470	460	5,550
70	Capital gains exclusion of small corporation stock	380	620	5,510
138	Distributions from retirement plans for premiums for health and long-term care insurance	440	460	5,300
123	Exclusion of certain foster care payments	460	480	5,260
15	Energy investment credit	1,470	970	5,060
39	Tax incentives for preservation of historic structures	460	470	5,010
54	Exclusion of interest spread of financial institutions	420	450	5,010
35	Excess of percentage over cost depletion, nonfuel minerals	530	540	4,970
43	Expensing of certain multiperiod production costs	370	390	4,850
18	Tax credits for clean-fuel burning vehicles	550	670	4,770
32	Advanced nuclear power production credit	140	140	4,580
156	Deductibility of casualty losses	370	390	4,490
92	New markets tax credit	1,230	1,130	4,130
38	Expensing of multiperiod timber growing costs	330	350	3,980
93	Credit to holders of Gulf Tax Credit Bonds.	250	290	3,970
132	Credit for employee health insurance expenses of small business.	544	543	3,612
150	Premiums on accident and disability insurance	320	320	3,350
118	Adoption credit and exclusion	250	260	2,990
135	Special Blue Cross/Blue Shield deduction	250	260	2,990
143	Exclusion of military disability pensions	220	240	2,810
42	Expensing of certain capital outlays	210	230	2,760
79	Exclusion of interest on small issue bonds	170	200	2,750
33	Advanced nuclear power production credit	170	200	2,540
139	Exclusion of railroad retirement system benefits	300	300	2,510
94	Recovery Zone Bonds	140	150	2,150

Table 14–3. INCOME TAX EXPENDITURES RANKED BY TOTAL FISCAL YEAR 2016-2025 PROJECTED REVENUE EFFECT—Continued

(In millions of dollars)

Provision	2016	2017	2016-2025
87 Exclusion of interest on bonds for Financing of Highway Projects and rail-truck transfer facilities	210	200	1,670
90 Exemption of certain mutuals' and cooperatives' income	140	150	1,580
29 30% credit for residential purchases/installations of solar and fuel cells	770	460	1,450
12 Capital gains treatment of royalties on coal	120	130	1,420
37 Capital gains treatment of certain timber income	120	130	1,420
46 Income averaging for farmers	140	140	1,400
114 Work opportunity tax credit	420	240	1,310
22 Credit for investment in clean coal facilities	160	400	1,180
106 Credit for holders of zone academy bonds	130	120	980
25 Amortize all geological and geophysical expenditures over 2 years	100	100	960
82 Tonnage tax	70	80	910
112 Discharge of student loan indebtedness	90	90	900
20 Credit for holding clean renewable energy bonds	70	70	700
67 Exceptions from imputed interest rules	50	60	700
24 Natural gas distribution pipelines treated as 15-year property	160	160	690
48 Expensing of reforestation expenditures	50	60	690
95 Tribal Economic Development Bonds	40	50	680
40 Industrial CO2 capture and sequestration tax credit	110	150	530
73 Ordinary income treatment of loss from small business corporation stock sale	50	50	500
153 Additional deduction for the blind	40	40	490
151 Income of trusts to finance supplementary unemployment benefits	20	30	470
34 Expensing of exploration and development costs, nonfuel minerals	0	10	450
51 Special alternative tax on small property and casualty insurance companies	30	40	450
41 Deduction for endangered species recovery expenditures	30	30	430
100 Education Individual Retirement Accounts	30	40	420
44 Treatment of loans forgiven for solvent farmers	40	40	400
53 Small life insurance company deduction	30	30	400
13 Exclusion of interest on energy facility bonds	20	30	350
107 Exclusion of interest on savings bonds redeemed to finance educational expenses	30	30	350
11 Exception from passive loss limitation for working interests in oil and gas properties	40	40	340
30 Qualified energy conservation bonds	30	30	300
47 Deferral of gain on sale of farm refiners	20	20	250
81 Special rules for certain film and TV production	110	60	210
83 Deferral of tax on shipping companies	20	20	200
88 Investment credit for rehabilitation of structures (other than historic)	20	20	200
91 Empowerment zones	40	30	200
116 Employer-provided child care credit	10	10	170
121 Credit for disabled access expenditures	10	10	170
125 Indian employment credi	30	30	140
142 Exclusion of special benefits for disabled coal miners	30	20	140
165 Exclusion of interest on veterans housing bonds	10	10	120
137 Tax credit for health insurance purchased by certain displaced and retired individuals	30	30	90
17 Bio-Diesel and small agri-biodiesel producer tax credits	30	20	60
155 Tax credit for the elderly and disabled	10	10	60
66 Discharge of business indebtedness	-120	-50	50
27 Credit for construction of new energy efficient homes	20	0	20
6 Deferred taxes for financial firms on certain income earned overseas	0	0	0
16 Alcohol fuel credits	0	0	0
28 Credit for energy efficiency improvements to existing homes	0	0	0
65 Discharge of mortgage indebtedness	0	0	0
86 Tax credit for certain expenditures for maintaining railroad tracks	0	0	0
102 Deduction for higher education expenses	0	0	0
111 Special deduction for teacher expenses	0	0	0
167 Build America Bonds	0	0	0
31 Advanced Energy Property Credit	10	-30	-90

Table 14–3.   INCOME TAX EXPENDITURES RANKED BY TOTAL FISCAL YEAR 2016-2025 PROJECTED REVENUE EFFECT—Continued

(In millions of dollars)

Provision		2016	2017	2016-2025
26	Allowance of deduction for certain energy efficient commercial building property	-10	-30	-280
21	Deferral of gain from dispositions of transmission property to implement FERC restructuring policy	-220	-180	-880
23	Temporary 50% expensing for equipment used in the refining of liquid fuels	-2,050	-1,820	-8,900
75	Accelerated depreciation of buildings other than rental housing (normal tax method)	-9,170	-9,390	-116,750

earned income exclusion limit. This housing exclusion is capped at 30 percent of the earned income exclusion limit, with geographical adjustments. If taxpayers do not receive a specific allowance for housing expenses, they may deduct housing expenses up to the amount by which foreign earned income exceeds their foreign earned income exclusion.

3. *Exclusion of certain allowances for Federal employees abroad.*—In general, all compensation received by U.S. citizens and residents is properly included in their taxable income. It makes no difference whether the compensation is a result of working abroad or whether it is labeled as an allowance for the high cost of living abroad. In contrast to this treatment, U.S. Federal civilian employees and Peace Corps members who work outside the continental United States are allowed to exclude from U.S. taxable income certain special allowances they receive to compensate them for the relatively high costs associated with living overseas. The allowances supplement wage income and cover expenses such as rent, education, and the cost of travel to and from the United States.

4. *Inventory property sales source rules exception.*—The United States generally taxes the worldwide income of U.S. persons and business entities. Under the baseline tax system, taxpayers receive a credit for foreign taxes paid which is limited to the pre-credit U.S. tax on the foreign source income. In contrast, the sales source rules for inventory property under current law allow U.S. exporters to use more foreign tax credits by allowing the exporters to attribute a larger portion of their earnings to foreign sources than would be the case if the allocation of earnings was based on actual economic activity.

5. *Deferral of income from controlled foreign corporations (normal tax method).*—Under the baseline tax system, the United States generally taxes the worldwide income of U.S. persons and business entities. In contrast, certain active income of foreign corporations controlled by U.S. shareholders is not subject to U.S. taxation when it is earned. The income becomes taxable only when the controlling U.S. shareholders receive dividends or other distributions from their foreign stockholding. The reference law tax baseline reflects this tax treatment where only realized income is taxed. Under the normal tax method, however, the currently attributable foreign source pre-tax income from such a controlling interest is considered to be subject to U.S. taxation, whether or not distributed. Thus, the normal tax method considers the amount of controlled foreign corporation income not yet distributed to a U.S. shareholder as tax-deferred income.

6. *Deferred taxes for financial firms on certain income earned overseas.*—The United States generally taxes the worldwide income of U.S. persons and business entities. The baseline tax system would not allow the deferral of tax or other relief targeted at particular industries or activities. In contrast, the Tax Code allowed financial firms to defer taxes on income earned overseas in an active business. This provision expired at the end of 2014.

General Science, Space, and Technology

7. *Expensing of research and experimentation expenditures (normal tax method).*—The baseline tax system allows a deduction for the cost of producing income. It requires taxpayers to capitalize the costs associated with investments over time to better match the streams of income and associated costs. Research and experimentation (R&E) projects can be viewed as investments because, if successful, their benefits accrue for several years. It is often difficult, however, to identify whether a specific R&E project is successful and, if successful, what its expected life will be. Because of this ambiguity, the reference law baseline tax system would allow expensing of R&E expenditures. In contrast, under the normal tax method, the expensing of R&E expenditures is viewed as a tax expenditure. The baseline assumed for the normal tax method is that all R&E expenditures are successful and have an expected life of five years.

8. *Credit for increasing research activities.*—The baseline tax system would uniformly tax all returns to investments and not allow credits for particular activities, investments, or industries. In contrast, the Tax Code allowed an R&E credit of up to 20 percent of qualified research expenditures in excess of a base amount. The base amount of the credit was generally determined by multiplying a "fixed-base percentage" by the average amount of the company's gross receipts for the prior four years. The taxpayer's fixed base percentage generally was the ratio of its research expenses to gross receipts for 1984 through 1988. Taxpayers could elect the alternative simplified credit regime, which equaled 14 percent of qualified research expenses that exceeded 50 percent of the average qualified research expenses for the three preceding taxable years. The credit does not apply to expenses paid or incurred after December 31, 2014.

Table 14–4. PRESENT VALUE OF SELECTED TAX EXPENDITURES FOR ACTIVITY IN CALENDAR YEAR 2015

(In millions of dollars)

	Provision	2015 Present Value of Revenue Loss
5	Deferral of income from controlled foreign corporations (normal tax method)	44,630
7	Expensing of research and experimentation expenditures (normal tax method)	3,030
20	Credit for holding clean renewable energy bonds	0
9	Expensing of exploration and development costs - fuels	338
35	Expensing of exploration and development costs - nonfuels	63
39	Expensing of multiperiod timber growing costs	110
44	Expensing of certain multiperiod production costs - agriculture	-80
43	Expensing of certain capital outlays - agriculture	-30
49	Expensing of reforestation expenditures	20
51	Deferral of income on life insurance and annuity contracts 1/	13,920
65	Accelerated depreciation on rental housing	14,780
76	Accelerated depreciation of buildings other than rental	−11,280
77	Accelerated depreciation of machinery and equipment	12,130
78	Expensing of certain small investments (normal tax method)	550
107	Credit for holders of zone academy bonds	160
64	Credit for low-income housing investments	5,760
104	Deferral for state prepaid tuition plans	3,790
145	Defined benefit employer plans	24,960
146	Defined contribution employer plans	67,150
147	Exclusion of IRA contributions and earnings	1,350
147	Exclusion of Roth earnings and distributions	4,720
147	Exclusion of non-deductible IRA earnings	420
149	Exclusion of contributions and earnings for Self-Employed plans	4,960
167	Exclusion of interest on public-purpose bonds	12,420
	Exclusion of interest on non-public purpose bonds	4,170
170	Deferral of interest on U.S. savings bonds	250

[1] Estimate is for annuities only. Life insurance earnings are mostly excluded from taxable income.

Energy

9. *Expensing of exploration and development costs.*—Under the baseline tax system, the costs of exploring and developing oil and gas wells would be capitalized and then amortized (or depreciated) over an estimate of the economic life of the well. This insures that the net income from the well is measured appropriately each year. In contrast to this treatment, current law allows intangible drilling costs for successful investments in domestic oil and gas wells (such as wages, the cost of using machinery for grading and drilling, and the cost of unsalvageable materials used in constructing wells) to be deducted immediately, i.e., expensed. Because it allows recovery of costs sooner, expensing is more generous for the taxpayer than would be amortization. Integrated oil companies may deduct only 70 percent of such costs and must amortize the remaining 30 percent over five years. Non-integrated oil companies may expense all such costs. The same rule applies to the exploration and development costs of surface stripping and the construction of shafts and tunnels for other fuel minerals.

10. *Excess of percentage over cost depletion.*— The baseline tax system would allow recovery of the costs of developing certain oil and mineral properties using cost depletion. Cost depletion is similar in concept to depreciation, in that the costs of developing or acquiring the asset are capitalized and then gradually reduced over an estimate of the asset's economic life, as is appropriate for measuring net income. In contrast, the Tax Code generally allows independent fuel and mineral producers and royalty owners to take percentage depletion deductions rather than cost depletion on limited quantities of output. Under percentage depletion, taxpayers deduct a percentage of gross income from mineral production. In certain cases the deduction is limited to a fraction of the asset's net income. Over the life of an investment, percentage depletion deductions can exceed the cost of the investment. Consequently, percentage depletion offers more generous tax treatment than would cost depletion, which would limit deductions to an investment's cost.

11. *Exception from passive loss limitation for working interests in oil and gas properties.*—The baseline tax system accepts current law's general rule limiting taxpayers' ability to deduct losses from passive activities against nonpassive income (e.g., wages, interest, and dividends). Passive activities generally are defined as those in which the taxpayer does not materially participate, and there are numerous additional considerations brought to bear on the determination of which activities

are passive for a given taxpayer. Losses are limited in an attempt to limit tax sheltering activities. Passive losses that are unused may be carried forward and applied against future passive income. An exception from the passive loss limitation is provided for a working interest in an oil or gas property that the taxpayer holds directly or through an entity that does not limit the liability of the taxpayer with respect to the interest. Thus, taxpayers can deduct losses from such working interests against nonpassive income without regard to whether they materially participate in the activity.

12. **Capital gains treatment of royalties on coal.**—The baseline tax system generally would tax all income under the regular tax rate schedule. It would not allow preferentially low tax rates to apply to certain types or sources of income. For individuals, tax rates on regular income vary from 10 percent to 39.6 percent (plus a 3.8-percent surtax on high income taxpayers), depending on the taxpayer's income. In contrast, current law allows capital gains realized by individuals to be taxed at a preferentially low rate that is no higher than 20 percent (plus the 3.8-percent surtax). Certain sales of coal under royalty contracts qualify for taxation as capital gains rather than ordinary income, and so benefit from the preferentially low 20 percent maximum tax rate on capital gains.

13. **Exclusion of interest on energy facility bonds.**—The baseline tax system generally would tax all income under the regular tax rate schedule. It would not allow preferentially low (or zero) tax rates to apply to certain types or sources of income. In contrast, the Tax Code allows interest earned on State and local bonds used to finance construction of certain energy facilities to be exempt from tax. These bonds are generally subject to the State private-activity-bond annual volume cap.

14. **Energy production credit.**—The baseline tax system would not allow credits for particular activities, investments, or industries. Instead, it generally would seek to tax uniformly all returns from investment-like activities. In contrast, the Tax Code provides a credit for certain electricity produced from wind energy, biomass, geothermal energy, solar energy, small irrigation power, municipal solid waste, or qualified hydropower and sold to an unrelated party. Qualified facilities must have begun construction before January 1, 2015. In addition to the electricity production credit, an income tax credit is allowed for the production of refined coal for facilities placed in service before January 1, 2012. The Tax Code also provided an income tax credit for Indian coal facilities placed in service before January 1, 2009. The Indian coal facilities credit expired on December 31, 2014.

15. **Energy investment credit.**—The baseline tax system would not allow credits for particular activities, investments, or industries. Instead, it generally would seek to tax uniformly all returns from investment-like activities. However, the Tax Code provides credits for investments in solar and geothermal energy property, qualified fuel cell power plants, stationary microturbine power plants, geothermal heat pumps, small wind property and combined heat and power property. A temporary credit of up to 30 percent is available for qualified proper-

ty placed in service before January 1, 2017. A permanent 10 percent credit is available for qualified solar and geothermal property placed in service after this date. Owners of renewable power facilities that qualify for the energy production credit may instead elect to take an energy investment credit.

16. **Alcohol fuel credits.**—The baseline tax system would not allow credits for particular activities, investments, or industries. Instead, it generally would seek to tax uniformly all returns from investment-like activities. In contrast, the Tax Code provided an income tax credit for qualified cellulosic biofuel production which was renamed the Second generation biofuel producer credit. This provision expired on December 31, 2014.

17. **Bio-diesel and small agri-biodiesel producer tax credits.**—The baseline tax system would not allow credits for particular activities, investments, or industries. Instead, it generally would seek to tax uniformly all returns from investment-like activities. However, the Tax Code allowed an income tax credit for Bio-diesel and for Bio-diesel derived from virgin sources. In lieu of the Bio-diesel credit, the taxpayer could claim a refundable excise tax credit. In addition, small agri-biodiesel producers were eligible for a separate income tax credit for biodiesel production and a separate credit was available for qualified renewable diesel fuel mixtures. This provision expired on December 31, 2014.

18. **Tax credits for clean-fuel burning vehicles and refueling property.**—The baseline tax system would not allow credits for particular activities, investments, or industries. Instead, it generally would seek to tax uniformly all returns from investment-like activities. In contrast, the Tax Code allows a credit for plug-in electric-drive motor vehicles. Credits for alternative fuel vehicle refueling property and fuel cell vehicles expired on December 31, 2014.

19. **Exclusion of utility conservation subsidies.**—The baseline tax system generally takes a comprehensive view of taxable income that includes a wide variety of (measurable) accretions to wealth. In certain circumstances, public utilities offer rate subsidies to non-business customers who invest in energy conservation measures. These rate subsidies are equivalent to payments from the utility to its customer, and so represent accretions to wealth, income that would be taxable to the customer under the baseline tax system. In contrast, the Tax Code exempts these subsidies from the non-business customer's gross income.

20. **Credit for holding clean renewable energy bonds.**—The baseline tax system would uniformly tax all returns to investments and not allow credits for particular activities, investments, or industries. In contrast, the Tax Code provides for the issuance of Clean Renewable Energy Bonds which entitles the bond holder to a Federal income tax credit in lieu of interest. As of March 2010, issuers of the unused authorization of such bonds could opt to receive direct payment with the yield becoming fully taxable.

21. **Deferral of gain from dispositions of transmission property to implement FERC restructuring**

policy.—The baseline tax system generally would tax gains from sale of property when realized. It would not allow an exception for particular activities or individuals. However, the Tax Code allowed electric utilities to defer gains from the sale of their transmission assets to a FERC-approved independent transmission company. The sale of property must have been made prior to January 1, 2015.

22. ***Credit for investment in clean coal facilities.***—The baseline tax system would uniformly tax all returns to investments and not allow credits for particular activities, investments, or industries. In contrast, the Tax Code provides investment tax credits for clean coal facilities producing electricity and for industrial gasification combined cycle projects.

23. ***Temporary 50 percent expensing for equipment used in the refining of liquid fuels.***—The baseline tax system allows the taxpayer to deduct the decline in the economic value of an investment over its economic life. However, the Tax Code provided for an accelerated recovery of the cost of certain investments in refineries by allowing partial expensing of the cost, thereby giving such investments a tax advantage. Qualified refinery property must have been placed in service before January 1, 2014.

24. ***Natural gas distribution pipelines treated as 15-year property.***—The baseline tax system allows taxpayers to deduct the decline in the economic value of an investment over its economic life. However, the Tax Code allows depreciation of natural gas distribution pipelines (placed in service between 2005 and 2011) over a 15 year period. These deductions are accelerated relative to deductions based on economic depreciation.

25. ***Amortize all geological and geophysical expenditures over two years.***—The baseline tax system allows taxpayers to deduct the decline in the economic value of an investment over its economic life. However, the Tax Code allows geological and geophysical expenditures incurred in connection with oil and gas exploration in the United States to be amortized over two years for non-integrated oil companies, a span of time that is generally shorter than the economic life of the assets.

26. ***Allowance of deduction for certain energy efficient commercial building property.***—The baseline tax system would not allow deductions in addition to normal depreciation allowances for particular investments in particular industries. Instead, it generally would seek to tax uniformly all returns from investment-like activities. In contrast, the Tax Code allowed a deduction, per square foot, for certain energy efficient commercial buildings. This provision expired on December 31, 2014.

27. ***Credit for construction of new energy efficient homes.***—The baseline tax system would not allow credits for particular activities, investments, or industries. Instead, it generally would seek to tax uniformly all returns from investment-like activities. However, the Tax Code allowed contractors a tax credit of $2,000 for the construction of a qualified new energy-efficient home that had an annual level of heating and cooling energy consumption at least 50 percent below the annual consumption under the 2006 International Energy Conservation Code. The credit equaled $1,000 in the case of a new manufactured home that met a 30 percent standard or requirements for EPA's Energy Star homes. This provision expired on December 31, 2014.

28. ***Credit for energy efficiency improvements to existing homes.***—The baseline tax system would not allow credits for particular activities, investments, or industries. However, the Tax Code provided an investment tax credit for expenditures made on insulation, exterior windows, and doors that improved the energy efficiency of homes and met certain standards. The Tax Code also provided a credit for purchases of advanced main air circulating fans, natural gas, propane, or oil furnaces or hot water boilers, and other qualified energy efficient property. This provision expired on December 31, 2014.

29. ***Credit for residential energy efficient property.***—The baseline tax system would uniformly tax all returns to investments and not allow credits for particular activities, investments, or industries. However, the Tax Code provides a credit for the purchase of a qualified photovoltaic property and solar water heating property, as well as for fuel cell power plants, geothermal heat pumps and small wind property.

30. ***Credit for qualified energy conservation bonds.***—The baseline tax system would uniformly tax all returns to investments and not allow credits for particular activities, investments, or industries. However, the Tax Code provides for the issuance of energy conservation bonds which entitle the bond holder to a Federal income tax credit in lieu of interest. As of March 2010, issuers of the unused authorization of such bonds could opt to receive direct payment with the yield becoming fully taxable.

31. ***Advanced energy property credit.***—The baseline tax system would not allow credits for particular activities, investments, or industries. However, the Tax Code provides a 30 percent investment credit for property used in a qualified advanced energy manufacturing project. The Treasury Department may award up to $2.3 billion in tax credits for qualified investments.

32. ***Advanced nuclear power facilities production credit.***—The baseline tax system would not allow credits or deductions for particular activities, investments, or industries. Instead, it generally would seek to tax uniformly all returns from investment-like activities. In contrast, the Tax Code allows a tax credit equal to 1.8 cents times the number of kilowatt hours of electricity produced at a qualifying advanced nuclear power facility. A taxpayer may claim no more than $125 million per 1,000 megawatts of capacity. The Treasury Department may allocate up to 6,000 megawatts of credit-eligible capacity.

33. ***Reduced tax rate for nuclear decommissioning funds.***—The baseline tax system would uniformly tax all returns to investments and not allow special rates for particular activities, investments, or industries. In contrast, the Tax Code provides a special 20% tax rate for investments made by Nuclear Decommissioning Reserve Funds.

Natural Resources and Environment

34. *Expensing of exploration and development costs.*—The baseline tax system allows the taxpayer to deduct the depreciation of an asset according to the decline in its economic value over time. However, certain capital outlays associated with exploration and development of nonfuel minerals may be expensed rather than depreciated over the life of the asset.

35. *Excess of percentage over cost depletion.*— The baseline tax system allows the taxpayer to deduct the decline in the economic value of an investment over time. Under current law, however, most nonfuel mineral extractors may use percentage depletion (whereby the deduction is fixed as a percentage of revenue) rather than cost depletion, with percentage depletion rates ranging from 22 percent for sulfur to 5 percent for sand and gravel. Over the life of an investment, percentage depletion deductions can exceed the cost of the investment. Consequently, percentage depletion offers more generous tax treatment than would cost depletion, which would limit deductions to an investment's cost.

36. *Exclusion of interest on bonds for water, sewage, and hazardous waste facilities.*—The baseline tax system generally would tax all income under the regular tax rate schedule. It would not allow preferentially low (or zero) tax rates to apply to certain types or sources of income. In contrast, the Tax Code allows interest earned on State and local bonds used to finance construction of sewage, water, or hazardous waste facilities to be exempt from tax. These bonds are generally subject to the State private-activity-bond annual volume cap.

37. *Capital gains treatment of certain timber.*— The baseline tax system generally would tax all income under the regular tax rate schedule. It would not allow preferentially low tax rates to apply to certain types or sources of income. However, under current law certain timber sales can be treated as a capital gain rather than ordinary income and therefore subject to the lower capital-gains tax rate. For individuals, tax rates on regular income vary from 10 percent to 39.6 percent (plus a 3.8-percent surtax on high income taxpayers), depending on the taxpayer's income. In contrast, current law allows capital gains to be taxed at a preferentially low rate that is no higher than 20 percent (plus the 3.8-percent surtax).

38. *Expensing of multi-period timber growing costs.*—The baseline tax system requires the taxpayer to capitalize costs associated with investment property. However, most of the production costs of growing timber may be expensed under current law rather than capitalized and deducted when the timber is sold, thereby accelerating cost recovery.

39. *Tax incentives for preservation of historic structures.*—The baseline tax system would not allow credits for particular activities, investments, or industries. However, expenditures to preserve and restore certified historic structures qualify for an investment tax credit of 20 percent under current law for certified rehabilitation activities. The taxpayer's recoverable basis must be reduced by the amount of the credit.

40. *Industrial CO_2 capture and sequestration tax credit.*—The baseline tax system would uniformly tax all returns to investments and not allow credits for particular activities, investments, or industries. In contrast, the Tax Code allows a credit for qualified carbon dioxide captured at a qualified facility and disposed of in secure geological storage. In addition, the provision allows a credit for qualified carbon dioxide that is captured at a qualified facility and used as a tertiary injectant in a qualified enhanced oil or natural gas recovery project.

41. *Deduction for endangered species recovery expenditures.*—The baseline tax system would not allow deductions in addition to normal depreciation allowances for particular investments in particular industries. Instead, it generally would seek to tax uniformly all returns from investment-like activities. In contrast, under current law farmers can deduct up to 25 percent of their gross income for expenses incurred as a result of site and habitat improvement activities that will benefit endangered species on their farm land, in accordance with site specific management actions included in species recovery plans approved pursuant to the Endangered Species Act of 1973.

Agriculture

42. *Expensing of certain capital outlays.*—The baseline tax system requires the taxpayer to capitalize costs associated with investment property. However, farmers may expense certain expenditures for feed and fertilizer, for soil and water conservation measures and certain other capital improvements under current law.

43. *Expensing of certain multiperiod production costs.*—The baseline tax system requires the taxpayer to capitalize costs associated with an investment over time. However, the production of livestock and crops with a production period greater than two years (e.g., establishing orchards or constructing barns) is exempt from the uniform cost capitalization rules, thereby accelerating cost recovery.

44. *Treatment of loans forgiven for solvent farmers.*—Because loan forgiveness increases a debtors net worth the baseline tax system requires debtors to include the amount of loan forgiveness as income or else reduce their recoverable basis in the property related to the loan. If the amount of forgiveness exceeds the basis, the excess forgiveness is taxable if the taxpayer is not insolvent. For bankrupt debtors, the amount of loan forgiveness reduces carryover losses, unused credits, and then basis, with the remainder of the forgiven debt excluded from taxation. Qualified farm debt that is forgiven, however, is excluded from income even when the taxpayer is solvent.

45. *Capital gains treatment of certain income.*— For individuals, tax rates on regular income vary from 10 percent to 39.6 percent (plus a 3.8-percent surtax on high income taxpayers), depending on the taxpayer's income. The baseline tax system generally would tax all income under the regular tax rate schedule. It would not allow preferentially low tax rates to apply to certain types or sources of income. In contrast, current law allows capi-

tal gains to be taxed at a preferentially low rate that is no higher than 20 percent (plus the 3.8-percent surtax). Certain agricultural income, such as unharvested crops, qualify for taxation as capital gains rather than ordinary income, and so benefit from the preferentially low 20 percent maximum tax rate on capital gains.

46. *Income averaging for farmers.*—The baseline tax system generally taxes all earned income each year at the rate determined by the income tax. However, taxpayers may average their taxable income from farming and fishing over the previous three years.

47. *Deferral of gain on sales of farm refiners.*—The baseline tax system generally subjects capital gains to taxes the year that they are realized. However, the Tax Code allows a taxpayer who sells stock in a farm refiner to a farmers' cooperative to defer recognition of the gain if the proceeds are re-invested in a qualified replacement property.

48. *Expensing of reforestation expenditures.*—The baseline tax system requires the taxpayer to capitalize costs associated with an investment over time. In contrast, the Tax Code provides for the expensing of the first $10,000 in reforestation expenditures with 7-year amortization of the remaining expenses.

Commerce and Housing

This category includes a number of tax expenditure provisions that also affect economic activity in other functional categories. For example, provisions related to investment, such as accelerated depreciation, could be classified under the energy, natural resources and environment, agriculture, or transportation categories.

49. *Exemption of credit union income.*—Under the baseline tax system, corporations pay taxes on their profits under the regular tax rate schedule. However, in the Tax Code the earnings of credit unions not distributed to members as interest or dividends are exempt from the income tax.

50. *Exclusion of interest on life insurance savings.*—Under the baseline tax system, individuals and corporations generally pay taxes on their income when it is (actually or constructively) received or accrued, depending on their method of accounting. Nevertheless, the Tax Code provides favorable tax treatment for investment income earned within qualified life insurance and annuity contracts. In general, investment income earned on qualified life insurance contracts held until death is permanently exempt from income tax. Investment income distributed prior to the death of the insured is tax-exempt to the extent that investment in the contract is overstated (because premiums paid for the cost of life insurance protection are credited to investment in the contract).The remaining distributed amounts are tax-deferred because income is not taxed on a current basis, but is recognized only when distributed from the contract. Investment income earned on annuities benefits from tax deferral.

51. *Special alternative tax on small property and casualty insurance companies.*—Under the baseline tax system, corporations pay taxes on their profits

under the regular tax rate schedule. The baseline tax system would not allow preferentially low (or zero) tax rates to apply to certain types or sources of income. Under current law, however, stock non-life insurance companies are generally exempt from tax if their gross receipts for the taxable year do not exceed $600,000 and more than 50 percent of such gross receipts consist of premiums. Mutual non-life insurance companies are generally tax-exempt if their annual gross receipts do not exceed $150,000 and more than 35 percent of gross receipts consist of premiums. Also, non-life insurance companies with no more than $1.2 million of annual net premiums may elect to pay tax only on their taxable investment income.

52. *Tax exemption of certain insurance companies owned by tax-exempt organizations.*—Under the baseline tax system, corporations pay taxes on their profits under the regular tax rate schedule. The baseline tax system would not allow preferentially low (or zero) tax rates to apply to certain types or sources of income. Generally the income generated by life and property and casualty insurance companies is subject to tax, albeit by special rules. Insurance operations conducted by such exempt organizations as fraternal societies, voluntary employee benefit associations, and others, however, are exempt from tax.

53. *Small life insurance company deduction.*—Under the baseline tax system, corporations pay taxes on their profits under the regular tax rate schedule. The baseline tax system would not allow preferentially low (or zero) tax rates to apply to certain types or sources of income. However, under current law, small life insurance companies (with gross assets of less than $500 million) can deduct 60 percent of the first $3 million of otherwise taxable income. The deduction phases out for otherwise taxable income between $3 million and $15 million.

54. *Exclusion of interest spread of financial institutions.*—The baseline tax system generally would tax all income under the regular tax rate schedule. It would not allow preferentially low (or zero) tax rates to apply to certain types or sources of income. Consumers and nonprofit organizations pay for some deposit-linked services, such as check cashing, by accepting a below-market interest rate on their demand deposits. If they received a market rate of interest on those deposits and paid explicit fees for the associated services, they would pay taxes on the full market rate and (unlike businesses) could not deduct the fees. The Government thus foregoes tax on the difference between the risk-free market interest rate and below-market interest rates on demand deposits, which under competitive conditions should equal the value added of deposit services.

55. *Exclusion of interest on owner-occupied mortgage subsidy bonds.*—The baseline tax system generally would tax all income under the regular tax rate schedule. It would not allow preferentially low (or zero) tax rates to apply to certain types or sources of income. In contrast, the Tax Code allows interest earned on State and local bonds used to finance homes purchased by first-time, low-to-moderate-income buyers to be exempt from

tax. These bonds are generally subject to the State private-activity-bond annual volume cap.

56. Exclusion of interest on rental housing bonds.—The baseline tax system generally would tax all income under the regular tax rate schedule. It would not allow preferentially low (or zero) tax rates to apply to certain types or sources of income. In contrast, the Tax Code allows interest earned on State and local government bonds used to finance multifamily rental housing projects to be tax-exempt.

57. Mortgage interest expense on owner-occupied residences.—Under the baseline tax system, expenses incurred in earning income would be deductible. However, such expenses would not be deductible when the income or the return on an investment is not taxed. In contrast, the Tax Code allows an exclusion from a taxpayer's taxable income for the value of owner-occupied housing services and also allows the owner-occupant to deduct mortgage interest paid on his or her primary residence and one secondary residence as an itemized non-business deduction. In general, the mortgage interest deduction is limited to interest on debt no greater than the owner's basis in the residence, and is also limited to interest on debt of no more than $1 million. Interest on up to $100,000 of other debt secured by a lien on a principal or second residence is also deductible, irrespective of the purpose of borrowing, provided the total debt does not exceed the fair market value of the residence. As an alternative to the deduction, holders of qualified Mortgage Credit Certificates issued by State or local governmental units or agencies may claim a tax credit equal to a proportion of their interest expense.

58. Deduction for property taxes on real property.—Under the baseline tax system, expenses incurred in earning income would be deductible. However, such expenses would not be deductible when the income or the return on an investment is not taxed. In contrast, the Tax Code allows an exclusion from a taxpayer's taxable income for the value of owner-occupied housing services and also allows the owner-occupant to deduct property taxes paid on real property.

59. Deferral of income from installment sales.—The baseline tax system generally would tax all income under the regular tax rate schedule. It would not allow preferentially low (or zero) tax rates, or deferral of tax, to apply to certain types or sources of income. Dealers in real and personal property (i.e., sellers who regularly hold property for sale or resale) cannot defer taxable income from installment sales until the receipt of the loan repayment. Nondealers (i.e., sellers of real property used in their business) are required to pay interest on deferred taxes attributable to their total installment obligations in excess of $5 million. Only properties with sales prices exceeding $150,000 are includable in the total. The payment of a market rate of interest eliminates the benefit of the tax deferral. The tax exemption for nondealers with total installment obligations of less than $5 million is, therefore, a tax expenditure.

60. Capital gains exclusion on home sales.—The baseline tax system would not allow deductions and ex-

emptions for certain types of income. In contrast, the Tax Code allows homeowners to exclude from gross income up to $250,000 ($500,000 in the case of a married couple filing a joint return) of the capital gains from the sale of a principal residence. To qualify, the taxpayer must have owned and used the property as the taxpayer's principal residence for a total of at least two of the five years preceding the date of sale. In addition, the exclusion may not be used more than once every two years.

61. Exclusion of net imputed rental income.—Under the baseline tax system, the taxable income of a taxpayer who is an owner-occupant would include the implicit value of gross rental income on housing services earned on the investment in owner-occupied housing and would allow a deduction for expenses, such as interest, depreciation, property taxes, and other costs, associated with earning such rental income. In contrast, the Tax Code allows an exclusion from taxable income for the implicit gross rental income on housing services, while in certain circumstances allows a deduction for some costs associated with such income, such as for mortgage interest and property taxes.

62. Exception from passive loss rules for $25,000 of rental loss.—The baseline tax system accepts current law's general rule limiting taxpayers' ability to deduct losses from passive activities against nonpassive income (e.g., wages, interest, and dividends). Passive activities generally are defined as those in which the taxpayer does not materially participate and there are numerous additional considerations brought to bear on the determination of which activities are passive for a given taxpayer. Losses are limited in an attempt to limit tax sheltering activities. Passive losses that are unused may be carried forward and applied against future passive income. In contrast to the general restrictions on passive losses, the Tax Code exempts certain owners of rental real estate activities from "passive income" limitations. The exemption is limited to $25,000 in losses and phases out for taxpayers with income between $100,000 and $150,000.

63. Credit for low-income housing investments.—The baseline tax system would uniformly tax all returns to investments and not allow credits for particular activities, investments, or industries. However, under current law taxpayers who invest in certain low-income housing are eligible for a tax credit. The credit rate is set so that the present value of the credit is equal to 70 percent for new construction and 30 percent for (1) housing receiving other Federal benefits (such as tax-exempt bond financing), or (2) substantially rehabilitated existing housing. The credit can exceed these levels in certain statutorily defined and State designated areas where project development costs are higher. The credit is allowed in equal amounts over 10 years and is generally subject to a volume cap.

64. Accelerated depreciation on rental housing.—Under an economic income tax, the costs of acquiring a building are capitalized and depreciated over time in accordance with the decline in the property's economic value due to wear and tear or obsolescence. This insures that the net income from the rental property is measured appropriately each year. Current law allows depreciation that is accelerated relative to economic depreciation. However, the depreciation provisions of the Tax Code are part of the reference law rules, and thus do not give rise to tax expenditures under reference law. Under normal law, in contrast, depreciation allowances reflect estimates of economic depreciation.

65. *Discharge of mortgage indebtedness.*—Under the baseline tax system, all income would generally be taxed under the regular tax rate schedule. The baseline tax system would not allow preferentially low (or zero) tax rates to apply to certain types or sources of income. In contrast, the Tax Code allowed an exclusion from a taxpayer's taxable income for any discharge of indebtedness of up to $2 million ($1 million in the case of a married individual filing a separate return) from a qualified principal residence. The provision applied to debt discharged after January 1, 2007, and before January 1, 2015.

66. *Discharge of business indebtedness.*—Under the baseline tax system, all income would generally be taxed under the regular tax rate schedule. The baseline tax system would not allow preferentially low (or zero) tax rates to apply to certain types or sources of income. In contrast, the Tax Code allows an exclusion from a taxpayer's taxable income for any discharge of qualified real property business indebtedness by taxpayers other than a C corporation. If the canceled debt is not reported as current income, however, the basis of the underlying property must be reduced by the amount canceled.

67. *Exceptions from imputed interest rules.*—Under the baseline tax system, holders (issuers) of debt instruments are generally required to report interest earned (paid) in the period it accrues, not when received. In addition, the amount of interest accrued is determined by the actual price paid, not by the stated principal and interest stipulated in the instrument. But under current law, any debt associated with the sale of property worth less than $250,000 is exempted from the general interest accounting rules. This general $250,000 exception is not a tax expenditure under reference law but is under normal law. Current law also includes exceptions for certain property worth more than $250,000. These are tax expenditure under reference law and normal law. These exceptions include, sales of personal residences worth more than $250,000, and sales of farms and small businesses worth between $250,000 and $1 million.

68. *Treatment of qualified dividends.*—The baseline tax system generally would tax all income under the regular tax rate schedule. It would not allow preferentially low tax rates to apply to certain types or sources of income. For individuals, tax rates on regular income vary from 10 percent to 39.6 percent (plus a 3.8-percent surtax on high income taxpayers), depending on the taxpayer's income. In contrast, under current law, qualified dividends are taxed at a preferentially low rate that is no higher than 20 percent (plus the 3.8-percent surtax).

69. *Capital gains (except agriculture, timber, iron ore, and coal).*—The baseline tax system generally would tax all income under the regular tax rate schedule. It would not allow preferentially low tax rates to apply to certain types or sources of income. For individuals, tax rates on regular income vary from 10 percent to 39.6 percent (plus a 3.8-percent surtax on high income taxpayers), depending on the taxpayer's income. In contrast, under current law, capital gains on assets held for more than one year are taxed at a preferentially low rate that is no higher than 20 percent (plus the 3.8-percent surtax).

70. *Capital gains exclusion of small corporation stock.*—The baseline tax system would not allow deductions and exemptions, or provide preferential treatment of certain sources of income or types of activities. In contrast, the Tax Code provided an exclusion of 50 percent, applied to ordinary rates with a maximum of a 28 percent tax rate, for capital gains from qualified small business stock held by individuals for more than 5 years; 75 percent for stock issued after February 17, 2009 and before September 28, 2010; and 100 percent for stock issued after September 27, 2010 and before January 1, 2015. A qualified small business is a corporation whose gross assets do not exceed $50 million as of the date of issuance of the stock.

71. *Step-up basis of capital gains at death.*—Under the baseline tax system, unrealized capital gains would be taxed when assets are transferred at death. It would not allow for exempting gains upon transfer of the underlying assets to the heirs. In contrast, capital gains on assets held at the owner's death are not subject to capital gains tax under current law. The cost basis of the appreciated assets is adjusted to the market value at the owner's date of death which becomes the basis for the heirs.

72. *Carryover basis of capital gains on gifts.*—Under the baseline tax system, unrealized capital gains would be taxed when assets are transferred by gift. In contrast, when a gift of appreciated asset is made under current law, the donor's basis in the transferred property (the cost that was incurred when the transferred property was first acquired) carries over to the donee. The carryover of the donor's basis allows a continued deferral of unrealized capital gains.

73. *Deferral of capital gains from like-kind exchanges.*—The baseline tax system generally would tax all income under the regular tax rate schedule. It would not allow preferentially low (or zero) tax rates, or deferral of tax, to apply to certain types or sources of income. In contrast, current law allows the deferral of accrued gains on assets transferred in qualified like-kind exchanges.

74. *Ordinary income treatment of loss from small business corporation stock sale.*—The baseline tax system limits to $3,000 the write-off of losses from capital assets, with carryover of the excess to future years. In contrast, the Tax Code allows up to $100,000 in losses from the sale of small business corporate stock (capitalization less than $1 million) to be treated as ordinary losses and fully deducted.

75. *Accelerated depreciation of buildings other than rental housing.*—Under an economic income tax, the costs of acquiring a building are capitalized and depreciated over time in accordance with the decline in the property's economic value due to wear and tear or obsolescence. This insures that the net income from the property

is measured appropriately each year. Current law allows depreciation deductions that are accelerated relative to economic depreciation. However, the depreciation provisions of the Tax Code are part of the reference law rules, and thus do not give rise to tax expenditures under reference law. Under normal law, in contrast, depreciation allowances reflect estimates of economic depreciation.

76. *Accelerated depreciation of machinery and equipment.*—Under an economic income tax, the costs of acquiring machinery and equipment are capitalized and depreciated over time in accordance with the decline in the property's economic value due to wear and tear or obsolescence. This insures that the net income from the property is measured appropriately each year. Current law allows depreciation deductions that are accelerated relative to economic depreciation. However, the depreciation provisions of the Tax Code are part of the reference law rules, and thus do not give rise to tax expenditures under reference law. Under normal law, in contrast depreciation allowances reflect estimates of economic depreciation.

77. *Expensing of certain small investments.*— Under the reference law baseline, the costs of acquiring tangible property and computer software would be depreciated using the Tax Code's depreciation provisions. Under the normal tax baseline, depreciation allowances are estimates of economic depreciation. However, the Tax Code allows qualifying investments by small businesses in tangible property and certain computer software to be expensed rather than depreciated over time.

78. *Graduated corporation income tax rate.*— Because the corporate rate schedule is part of reference tax law, it is not considered a tax expenditure under the reference method. A flat corporation income tax rate is taken as the baseline under the normal tax method; therefore the lower rate is considered a tax expenditure under this concept.

79. *Exclusion of interest on small issue bonds.*— The baseline tax system generally would tax all income under the regular tax rate schedule. It would not allow preferentially low (or zero) tax rates to apply to certain types or sources of income. In contrast, the Tax Code allows interest earned on small issue industrial development bonds (IDBs) issued by State and local governments to finance manufacturing facilities to be tax exempt. Depreciable property financed with small issue IDBs must be depreciated, however, using the straight-line method. The annual volume of small issue IDBs is subject to the unified volume cap discussed in the mortgage housing bond section above.

80. *Deduction for U.S. production activities.*— The baseline tax system generally would tax all income under the regular tax rate schedule. It would not allow preferentially low (or zero) tax rates to apply to certain types or sources of income. In contrast, the Tax Code allows for a deduction equal to a portion of taxable income attributable to domestic production.

81. *Special rules for certain film and TV production.*—The baseline tax system generally would tax all income under the regular tax rate schedule. It would not allow deductions and exemptions or preferentially low

(or zero) tax rates to apply to certain types or sources of income. In contrast, the Tax Code allowed taxpayers to deduct up to $15 million per production ($20 million in certain distressed areas) in non-capital expenditures incurred during the year. This provision expired at the end of 2014.

Transportation

82. *Tonnage tax.*—The baseline tax system generally would tax all profits and income under the regular tax rate schedule. U.S. shipping companies may choose to be subject to a tonnage tax based on gross shipping weight in lieu of an income tax, in which case profits would not be subject to tax under the regular tax rate schedule.

83. *Deferral of tax on shipping companies.*—The baseline tax system generally would tax all profits and income under the regular tax rate schedule. It would not allow preferentially low (or zero) tax rates to apply to certain types or sources of income. In contrast, the Tax Code allows certain companies that operate U.S. flag vessels to defer income taxes on that portion of their income used for shipping purposes (e.g., primarily construction, modernization and major repairs to ships, and repayment of loans to finance these investments).

84. *Exclusion of reimbursed employee parking expenses.*—Under the baseline tax system, all compensation, including dedicated payments and in-kind benefits, would be included in taxable income. Dedicated payments and in-kind benefits represent accretions to wealth that do not differ materially from cash wages. In contrast, the Tax Code allows an exclusion from taxable income for employee parking expenses that are paid for by the employer or that are received by the employee in lieu of wages. In 2015, the maximum amount of the parking exclusion is $250 per month. The tax expenditure estimate does not include any subsidy provided through employer-owned parking facilities.

85. *Exclusion for employer-provided transit passes.*—Under the baseline tax system, all compensation, including dedicated payments and in-kind benefits, would be included in taxable income. Dedicated payments and in-kind benefits represent accretions to wealth that do not differ materially from cash wages. In contrast, the Tax Code allows an exclusion from a taxpayer's taxable income for passes, tokens, fare cards, and vanpool expenses that are paid for by an employer or that are received by the employee in lieu of wages to defray an employee's commuting costs. The maximum amount of the transit exclusion is $130 per month in 2015. (There had been a parity provision that had temporary resulted in a higher maximum equal to those for parking passes for several years, but it expired on December 31, 2014).

86. *Tax credit for certain expenditures for maintaining railroad tracks.*—The baseline tax system would not allow credits for particular activities, investments, or industries. However, the Tax Code allowed eligible taxpayers to claim a credit equal to the lesser of 50 percent of maintenance expenditures and the product of $3,500 and the number of miles of track owned or leased. This provision expired at the end of 2014.

87. *Exclusion of interest on bonds for Highway Projects and rail-truck transfer facilities.*—The baseline tax system generally would tax all income under the regular tax rate schedule. It would not allow preferentially low (or zero) tax rates to apply to certain types or sources of income. In contrast, the Tax Code provides for $15 billion of tax-exempt bond authority to finance qualified highway or surface freight transfer facilities.

Community and Regional Development

88. *Investment credit for rehabilitation of structures.*—The baseline tax system would uniformly tax all returns to investments and not allow credits for particular activities, investments, or industries. However, the Tax Code allows a 10-percent investment tax credit for the rehabilitation of buildings that are used for business or productive activities and that were erected before 1936 for other than residential purposes. The taxpayer's recoverable basis must be reduced by the amount of the credit.

89. *Exclusion of interest for airport, dock, and similar bonds.*—The baseline tax system generally would tax all income under the regular tax rate schedule. It would not allow preferentially low (or zero) tax rates to apply to certain types or sources of income. In contrast, the Tax Code allows interest earned on State and local bonds issued to finance high-speed rail facilities and Government-owned airports, docks, wharves, and sport and convention facilities to be tax-exempt. These bonds are not subject to a volume cap.

90. *Exemption of certain mutuals' and cooperatives' income.*—Under the baseline tax system, corporations pay taxes on their profits under the regular tax rate schedule. In contrast, the Tax Code provides for the incomes of mutual and cooperative telephone and electric companies to be exempt from tax if at least 85 percent of their revenues are derived from patron service charges.

91. *Empowerment zones.*—The baseline tax system generally would tax all income under the regular tax rate schedule. It would not allow preferentially low tax rates to apply to certain types or sources of income, tax credits, and write-offs faster than economic depreciation. In contrast, the Tax Code allowed qualifying businesses in designated economically depressed areas to receive tax benefits such as an employment credit, increased expensing of investment in equipment, special tax-exempt financing, and certain capital gains incentives. A taxpayer's ability to accrue new tax benefits for empowerment zones expired on December 31, 2014.

92. *New markets tax credit.*—The baseline tax system would not allow credits for particular activities, investments, or industries. However, the Tax Code allowed taxpayers who made qualified equity investments in a community development entity (CDE), which then made qualified investments in low-income communities, to be eligible for a tax credit that is received over 7 years. The total equity investment available for the credit across

all CDEs was $3.5 billion for 2014, the last year for which credit allocations could be made.

93. *Credit to holders of Gulf and Midwest Tax Credit Bonds.*—The baseline tax system would not allow credits for particular activities, investments, or industries. Instead, under current law taxpayers that own Gulf and Midwest Tax Credit bonds receive a non-refundable tax credit rather than interest. The credit is included in gross income.

94. *Recovery Zone Bonds.*—The baseline tax system would not allow credits for particular activities, investments, or industries. In addition, it would tax all income under the regular tax rate schedule. It would not allow preferentially low (or zero) tax rates to apply to certain types or sources of income. In contrast, the Tax Code allowed local governments to issue up $10 billion in taxable Recovery Zone Economic Development Bonds in 2009 and 2010 and receive a direct payment from Treasury equal to 45 percent of interest expenses. In addition, local governments could issue up to $15 billion in tax exempt Recovery Zone Facility Bonds. These bonds financed certain kinds of business development in areas of economic distress.

95. *Tribal Economic Development Bonds.*—The baseline tax system generally would tax all income under the regular tax rate schedule. It would not allow preferentially low (or zero) tax rates to apply to certain types or sources of income. In contrast, the Tax Code was modified in 2009 to allow Indian tribal governments to issue tax exempt "tribal economic development bonds." There is a national bond limitation of $2 billion on such bonds.

Education, Training, Employment, and Social Services

96. *Exclusion of scholarship and fellowship income.*—Scholarships and fellowships are excluded from taxable income to the extent they pay for tuition and course-related expenses of the grantee. Similarly, tuition reductions for employees of educational institutions and their families are not included in taxable income. From an economic point of view, scholarships and fellowships are either gifts not conditioned on the performance of services, or they are rebates of educational costs. Thus, under the baseline tax system of the reference law method, this exclusion is not a tax expenditure because this method does not include either gifts or price reductions in a taxpayer's gross income. The exclusion, however, is considered a tax expenditure under the normal tax method, which includes gift-like transfers of Government funds in gross income (many scholarships are derived directly or indirectly from Government funding).

97. *HOPE tax credit.*—The baseline tax system would not allow credits for particular activities, investments, or industries. Under current law, however, the non-refundable HOPE tax credit allows a credit for 100 percent of an eligible student's first $1,300 of tuition and fees and 50 percent of the next $1,300 of tuition and fees (2015 levels, indexed). The credit only covers tuition and fees paid during the first two years of a student's post-sec-

ondary education. In 2015, the credit is phased out ratably for taxpayers with modified AGI between $110,000 and $130,000 if married filing jointly ($55,000 and $65,000 for other taxpayers), indexed. This credit is replaced by the American Opportunity Tax Credit for 2009 through 2017. See provision number 99, American Opportunity Tax Credit.

98. *Lifetime Learning tax credit.*—The baseline tax system would not allow credits for particular activities, investments, or industries. Under current law, however, the non-refundable Lifetime Learning tax credit allows a credit for 20 percent of an eligible student's tuition and fees, up to a maximum credit per return of $2,000. In 2015, the credit is phased out ratably for taxpayers with modified AGI between $110,000 and $130,000 if married filing jointly ($55,000 and $65,000 for other taxpayers), indexed. The credit applies to both undergraduate and graduate students.

99. *American Opportunity Tax Credit.*—The baseline tax system would not allow credits for particular activities, investments, or industries. Under current law in 2015, however, the American Opportunity Tax Credit allows a partially refundable credit of up to $2,500 per eligible student for qualified tuition and related expenses paid during each of the first four years of the student's post-secondary education. The credit is phased out for taxpayers with modified adjusted gross income between $80,000 and $90,000 ($160,000 and $180,000 for married taxpayers filing a joint return). The credit expires at the end of 2017.

100. *Education Individual Retirement Accounts (IRA).*—The baseline tax system generally would tax all income under the regular tax rate schedule. It would not allow preferentially low (or zero) tax rates to apply to certain types or sources of income. While contributions to an education IRA are not tax-deductible under current law, investment income earned by education IRAs is not taxed when earned, and investment income from an education IRA is tax-exempt when withdrawn to pay for a student's education expenses. The maximum contribution to an education IRA in 2015 is $2,000 per beneficiary. In 2015, the maximum contribution is phased down ratably for taxpayers with modified AGI between $190,000 and $220,000 if married filing jointly ($95,000 and $110,000 for other taxpayers).

101. *Deductibility of student loan interest.*— The baseline tax system accepts current law's general rule limiting taxpayers' ability to deduct non-business interest expenses. In contrast, taxpayers may claim an above-the-line deduction of up to $2,500 on interest paid on an education loan. In 2015, the maximum deduction is phased down ratably for taxpayers with modified AGI between $130,000 and $160,000 if married filing jointly ($65,000 and $80,000 for other taxpayers).

102. *Deduction for higher education expenses.*— The baseline tax system would not allow a deduction for personal expenditures. In contrast, the Tax Code provided a maximum annual deduction of $4,000 for qualified higher education expenses for taxpayers with adjusted gross income up to $130,000 on a joint return ($65,000 for

other taxpayers). Taxpayers with adjusted gross income up to $160,000 on a joint return ($80,000 for other taxpayers) could deduct up to $2,000. This provision expired on December 31, 2014.

103. *Qualified tuition programs.*—The baseline tax system generally would tax all income under the regular tax rate schedule. It would not allow preferentially low (or zero) tax rates to apply to certain types or sources of income. Some States have adopted prepaid tuition plans, prepaid room and board plans, and college savings plans, which allow persons to pay in advance or save for college expenses for designated beneficiaries. Under current law, investment income, or the return on prepayments, is not taxed when earned, and is tax-exempt when withdrawn to pay for qualified expenses.

104. *Exclusion of interest on student-loan bonds.*—The baseline tax system generally would tax all income under the regular tax rate schedule. It would not allow preferentially low (or zero) tax rates to apply to certain types or sources of income. In contrast, interest earned on State and local bonds issued to finance student loans is tax-exempt under current law. The volume of all such private activity bonds that each State may issue annually is limited.

105. *Exclusion of interest on bonds for private nonprofit educational facilities.*—The baseline tax system generally would tax all income under the regular tax rate schedule. It would not allow preferentially low (or zero) tax rates to apply to certain types or sources of income. In contrast, under current law interest earned on State and local Government bonds issued to finance the construction of facilities used by private nonprofit educational institutions is not taxed.

106. *Credit for holders of zone academy bonds.*— The baseline tax system would not allow credits for particular activities, investments, or industries. Under current law, however, financial institutions that own zone academy bonds receive a non-refundable tax credit rather than interest. The credit is included in gross income. Proceeds from zone academy bonds may only be used to renovate, but not construct, qualifying schools and for certain other school purposes. The total amount of zone academy bonds that may be issued was limited to $1.4 billion in 2009 and 2010. As of March 2010, issuers of the unused authorization of such bonds could opt to receive direct payment with the yield becoming fully taxable. An additional $0.4 billion of these bonds with a tax credit was authorized to be issued before January 1, 2015.

107. *Exclusion of interest on savings bonds redeemed to finance educational expenses.*—The baseline tax system generally would tax all income under the regular tax rate schedule. It would not allow preferentially low (or zero) tax rates to apply to certain types or sources of income. Under current law, however, interest earned on U.S. savings bonds issued after December 31, 1989 is tax-exempt if the bonds are transferred to an educational institution to pay for educational expenses. The tax exemption is phased out for taxpayers with AGI between $115,751 and $145,749 if married filing jointly ($77,200 and $92,199 for other taxpayers) in 2015.

108. *Parental personal exemption for students age 19 or over.*—Under the baseline tax system, a personal exemption would be allowed for the taxpayer, as well as for the taxpayer's spouse and dependents who do not claim a personal exemption on their own tax returns. To be considered a dependent, a child would have to be under age 19. In contrast, the Tax Code allows taxpayers to claim personal exemptions for children aged 19 to 23, as long as the children are full-time students and reside with the taxpayer for over half the year (with exceptions for temporary absences from home, such as for school attendance).

109. *Charitable contributions to educational institutions.*—The baseline tax system would not allow a deduction for personal expenditures. In contrast, the Tax Code provides taxpayers a deduction for contributions to nonprofit educational institutions that are similar to personal expenditures. Moreover, taxpayers who donate capital assets to educational institutions can deduct the asset's current value without being taxed on any appreciation in value. An individual's total charitable contribution generally may not exceed 50 percent of adjusted gross income; a corporation's total charitable contributions generally may not exceed 10 percent of pre-tax income.

110. *Exclusion of employer-provided educational assistance.*—Under the baseline tax system, all compensation, including dedicated payments and in-kind benefits, should be included in taxable income because they represent accretions to wealth that do not materially differ from cash wages. Under current law, however, employer-provided educational assistance is excluded from an employee's gross income, even though the employer's costs for this assistance are a deductible business expense. The maximum exclusion is $5,250 per taxpayer.

111. *Special deduction for teacher expenses.*—The baseline tax system would not allow a deduction for personal expenditures. In contrast, the Tax Code allowed educators in both public and private elementary and secondary schools, who worked at least 900 hours during a school year as a teacher, instructor, counselor, principal or aide, to subtract up to $250 of qualified expenses when determining their adjusted gross income (AGI). This provision expired on December 31, 2014.

112. *Discharge of student loan indebtedness.*—Under the baseline tax system, all compensation, including dedicated payments and in-kind benefits, should be included in taxable income. In contrast, the Tax Code allows certain professionals who perform in underserved areas or specific fields, and as a consequence have their student loans discharged, not to recognize such discharge as income.

113. *Qualified school construction bonds.*—The baseline tax system would not allow credits for particular activities, investments, or industries. Instead, it generally would seek to tax uniformly all returns from investment-like activities. In contrast, the Tax Code was modified in 2009 to provide a tax credit in lieu of interest to holders of qualified school construction bonds. The national volume limit is $22.4 billion over 2009 and 2010. As of March 2010, issuers of such bonds could opt to receive direct payment with the yield becoming fully taxable.

114. *Work opportunity tax credit.*—The baseline tax system would not allow credits for particular activities, investments, or industries. Instead, it generally would seek to tax uniformly all returns from investment-like activities. In contrast, the Tax Code provides employers with a tax credit for qualified wages paid to individuals. The credit applies to employees who began work on or before December 31, 2014 and who are certified as members of various targeted groups. The amount of the credit that can be claimed is 25 percent of qualified wages for employment less than 400 hours and 40 percent for employment of 400 hours or more. Generally, the maximum credit per employee is $2,400 and can only be claimed on the first year of wages an individual earns from an employer. However, the credit for long-term welfare recipients can be claimed on second year wages as well and has a $9,000 maximum. Also, certain categories of veterans are eligible for a higher maximum credit of up to $9,600. Employers must reduce their deduction for wages paid by the amount of the credit claimed.

115. *Employer-provided child care exclusion.*—Under the baseline tax system, all compensation, including dedicated payments and in-kind benefits, should be included in taxable income. In contrast, under current law up to $5,000 of employer-provided child care is excluded from an employee's gross income even though the employer's costs for the child care are a deductible business expense.

116. *Employer-provided child care credit.*—The baseline tax system would not allow credits for particular activities, investments, or industries. In contrast, current law provides a credit equal to 25 percent of qualified expenses for employee child care and 10 percent of qualified expenses for child care resource and referral services. Employer deductions for such expenses are reduced by the amount of the credit. The maximum total credit is limited to $150,000 per taxable year.

117. *Assistance for adopted foster children.*—Under the baseline tax system, all compensation, including dedicated payments and in-kind benefits, should be included in taxable income. Taxpayers who adopt eligible children from the public foster care system can receive monthly payments for the children's significant and varied needs and a reimbursement of up to $2,000 for nonrecurring adoption expenses; special needs adoptions receive the maximum benefit even if that amount is not spent. These payments are excluded from gross income under current law.

118. *Adoption credit and exclusion.*—The baseline tax system would not allow credits for particular activities. In contrast, taxpayers can receive a tax credit for qualified adoption expenses under current law. Taxpayers may also exclude qualified adoption expenses provided or reimbursed by an employer from income, subject to the same maximum amounts and phase-out as the credit. The same expenses cannot qualify for tax benefits under both programs; however, a taxpayer may use the

benefits of the exclusion and the tax credit for different expenses.

119. **Exclusion of employee meals and lodging.**—Under the baseline tax system, all compensation, including dedicated payments and in-kind benefits, should be included in taxable income. In contrast, under current law employer-provided meals and lodging are excluded from an employee's gross income even though the employer's costs for these items are a deductible business expense.

120. **Credit for child and dependent care expenses.**—The baseline tax system would not allow credits for particular activities or targeted at specific groups. In contrast, the Tax Code provides parents who work or attend school and who have child and dependent care expenses a tax credit. Expenditures up to a maximum $3,000 for one dependent and $6,000 for two or more dependents are eligible for the credit. The credit is equal to 35 percent of qualified expenditures for taxpayers with incomes of up to $15,000. The credit is reduced to a minimum of 20 percent by one percentage point for each $2,000 of income in excess of $15,000.

121. **Credit for disabled access expenditures.**—The baseline tax system would not allow credits for particular activities, investments, or industries. In contrast, the Tax Code provides small businesses (less than $1 million in gross receipts or fewer than 31 full-time employees) a 50-percent credit for expenditures in excess of $250 to remove access barriers for disabled persons. The credit is limited to $5,000.

122. **Deductibility of charitable contributions, other than education and health.**—The baseline tax system would not allow a deduction for personal expenditures including charitable contributions. In contrast, the Tax Code provides taxpayers a deduction for contributions to charitable, religious, and certain other nonprofit organizations. Taxpayers who donate capital assets to charitable organizations can deduct the assets' current value without being taxed on any appreciation in value. An individual's total charitable contribution generally may not exceed 50 percent of adjusted gross income; a corporation's total charitable contributions generally may not exceed 10 percent of pre-tax income.

123. **Exclusion of certain foster care payments.**—The baseline tax system generally would tax all income under the regular tax rate schedule. It would not allow preferentially low (or zero) tax rates to apply to certain types or sources of income. Foster parents provide a home and care for children who are wards of the State, under contract with the State. Under current law, compensation received for this service is excluded from the gross incomes of foster parents; the expenses they incur are nondeductible.

124. **Exclusion of parsonage allowances.**—Under the baseline tax system, all compensation, including dedicated payments and in-kind benefits, would be included in taxable income. Dedicated payments and in-kind benefits represent accretions to wealth that do not differ materially from cash wages. In contrast, the Tax Code allows an exclusion from a clergyman's taxable income for the value of the clergyman's housing allowance or the rental value of the clergyman's parsonage.

125. **Indian employment credit.**—The baseline tax system would not allow credits for particular activities, investments, or industries. Instead, it generally would seek to tax uniformly all returns from investment-like activities. In contrast, the Tax Code provided employers with a tax credit for qualified wages paid to employees who were enrolled members of Indian tribes. The amount of the credit that could be claimed was 20 percent of the excess of qualified wages and health insurance costs paid by the employer in the current tax year over the amount of such wages and costs paid by the employer in 1993. Qualified wages and health insurance costs with respect to any employee for the taxable year could not exceed $20,000. Employees had to live on or near the reservation where he or she worked to be eligible for the credit. Employers had to reduce their deduction for wages paid by the amount of the credit claimed. The credit does not apply to taxable years beginning after December 31, 2014.

Health

126. **Exclusion of employer contributions for medical insurance premiums and medical care.**—Under the baseline tax system, all compensation, including dedicated payments and in-kind benefits, should be included in taxable income. In contrast, under current law, employer-paid health insurance premiums and other medical expenses (including long-term care) are not included in employee gross income even though they are deducted as a business expense by the employee.

127. **Self-employed medical insurance premiums.**—Under the baseline tax system, all compensation and remuneration, including dedicated payments and in-kind benefits, should be included in taxable income. In contrast, under current law self-employed taxpayers may deduct their family health insurance premiums. Taxpayers without self-employment income are not eligible for this special deduction. The deduction is not available for any month in which the self-employed individual is eligible to participate in an employer-subsidized health plan and the deduction may not exceed the self-employed individual's earned income from self-employment.

128. **Medical Savings Accounts and Health Savings Accounts.**—Under the baseline tax system, all compensation, including dedicated payments and in-kind benefits, should be included in taxable income. Also, the baseline tax system would not allow a deduction for personal expenditures and generally would tax investment earnings. In contrast, individual contributions to Archer Medical Savings Accounts (Archer MSAs) and Health Savings Accounts (HSAs) are allowed as a deduction in determining adjusted gross income whether or not the individual itemizes deductions. Employer contributions to Archer MSAs and HSAs are excluded from income and employment taxes. Archer MSAs and HSAs require that the individual have coverage by a qualifying high deductible health plan. Earnings from the accounts are excluded from taxable income. Distributions from the accounts

used for medical expenses are not taxable. The rules for HSAs are generally more flexible than for Archer MSAs and the deductible contribution amounts are greater (in 2015, $3,350 for taxpayers with individual coverage and $6,650 for taxpayers with family coverage). Thus, HSAs have largely replaced MSAs.

129. **Deductibility of medical expenses.**—The baseline tax system would not allow a deduction for personal expenditures. In contrast, under current law personal expenditures for medical care (including the costs of prescription drugs) exceeding 7.5 percent of the taxpayer's adjusted gross income are deductible. For tax years beginning after 2012, only medical expenditures exceeding 10 percent of the taxpayer's adjusted gross income are deductible. However, for the years 2013, 2014, 2015 and 2016, if either the taxpayer or the taxpayer's spouse turns 65 before the end of the taxable year, the threshold remains at 7.5 percent of adjusted income. Beginning in 2017, the 10-percent threshold will apply to all taxpayers, including those over 65.

130. **Exclusion of interest on hospital construction bonds.**—The baseline tax system generally would tax all income under the regular tax rate schedule. It would not allow preferentially low (or zero) tax rates to apply to certain types or sources of income. In contrast, under current law interest earned on State and local government debt issued to finance hospital construction is excluded from income subject to tax.

131. **Refundable Premium Assistance Tax Credit.**—The baseline tax system would not allow credits for particular activities or targeted at specific groups. In contrast, for taxable years ending after 2013, the Tax Code provides a premium assistance credit to any eligible taxpayer for any qualified health insurance purchased through a Health Insurance Exchange. In general, an eligible taxpayer is a taxpayer with annual household income between 100% and 400% of the federal poverty level for a family of the taxpayer's size and that does not have access to affordable minimum essential health care coverage. The amount of the credit equals the lesser of (1) the actual premiums paid by the taxpayer for such coverage or (2) the difference between the cost of a statutorily-identified benchmark plan offered on the exchange and a required payment by the taxpayer that increases with income.

132. **Credit for employee health insurance expenses of small business.**—The baseline tax system would not allow credits for particular activities or targeted at specific groups. In contrast, the Tax Code provides a tax credit to qualified small employers that make a certain level of non-elective contributions towards the purchase of certain health insurance coverage for its employees. To receive a credit, an employer must have fewer than 25 full-time-equivalent employees whose average annual full-time-equivalent wages from the employer are less than $50,000 (indexed for taxable years after 2013). However, to receive a full credit, an employer must have no more than 10 full-time employees, and the average wage paid to these employees must be no more than $25,000 (indexed for taxable years after 2013). A

qualifying employer may claim the credit for any taxable year beginning in 2010, 2011, 2012, and 2013 and for up to two years for insurance purchased through a Health Insurance Exchange thereafter. For taxable years beginning in 2010, 2011, 2012, and 2013, the maximum credit is 35 percent of premiums paid by qualified taxable employers and 25 percent of premiums paid by qualified tax-exempt organizations. For taxable years beginning in 2014 and later years, the maximum tax credit increases to 50 percent of premiums paid by qualified taxable employers and 35 percent of premiums paid by qualified tax-exempt organizations.

133. **Deductibility of charitable contributions to health institutions.**—The baseline tax system would not allow a deduction for personal expenditures including charitable contributions. In contrast, the Tax Code provides individuals and corporations a deduction for contributions to nonprofit health institutions. Tax expenditures resulting from the deductibility of contributions to other charitable institutions are listed under the education, training, employment, and social services function.

134. **Tax credit for orphan drug research.**—The baseline tax system would not allow credits for particular activities, investments, or industries. In contrast, under current law drug firms can claim a tax credit of 50 percent of the costs for clinical testing required by the Food and Drug Administration for drugs that treat rare physical conditions or rare diseases.

135. **Special Blue Cross/Blue Shield deduction.**—The baseline tax system generally would tax all profits under the regular tax rate schedule using broadly applicable measures of baseline income. It would not allow preferentially low tax rates to apply to certain types or sources of income. In contrast, Blue Cross and Blue Shield health insurance providers in existence on August 16, 1986 and certain other nonprofit health insurers are provided exceptions from otherwise applicable insurance company income tax accounting rules that substantially reduce their tax liabilities, provided that their percentage of total premium revenue expended on reimbursement for clinical services provided to enrollees or for activities that improve health care quality is not less than 85 percent for the taxable year.

136. **Tax credit for health insurance purchased by certain displaced and retired individuals.**—The baseline tax system would not allow credits for particular activities, investments, or industries. In contrast, the Tax Code provides a refundable tax credit of 72.5 percent for the purchase of health insurance coverage by individuals eligible for Trade Adjustment Assistance and certain Pension Benefit Guarantee Corporation pension recipients. This provision will expire on December 31, 2019.

137. **Distributions from retirement plans for premiums for health and long-term care insurance.**—Under the baseline tax system, all compensation, including dedicated and deferred payments, should be included in taxable income. In contrast, the Tax Code provides for tax-free distributions of up to $3,000 from governmental retirement plans for premiums for health and long term care premiums of public safety officers.

Income Security

138. ***Child credit.***—The baseline tax system would not allow credits for particular activities or targeted at specific groups. Under current law, however, taxpayers with children under age 17 can qualify for a $1,000 partially refundable per child credit. Any unclaimed credit due to insufficient tax liability may be refundable – taxpayers may claim a refund for 15 percent of earnings in excess of a $3,000 floor, up to the amount of unused credit. Alternatively, taxpayers with three or more children may claim a refund of the amount of payroll taxes paid in excess of *the Earned Income Tax Credit received (up to the amount of unused credit) if this results in a larger refund.* The credit is phased out for taxpayers at the rate of $50 per $1,000 of modified AGI above $110,000 ($75,000 for single or head of household filers and $55,000 for married taxpayers filing separately). After 2017 refundability is based on earnings in excess of $10,000 indexed from 2001, rather than from $3,000 (unindexed); taxpayers with three or more children may continue to use the alternative calculation.

139. ***Exclusion of railroad Social Security equivalent benefits.***—Under the baseline tax system, all compensation, including dedicated and deferred payments, should be included in taxable income. In contrast, the Social Security Equivalent Benefit paid to railroad retirees is not generally subject to the income tax unless the recipient's gross income reaches a certain threshold under current law. See provision number 158, Social Security benefits for retired workers, for discussion of the threshold.

140. ***Exclusion of workers' compensation benefits.***—Under the baseline tax system, all compensation, including dedicated payments and in-kind benefits, should be included in taxable income. However, workers compensation is not subject to the income tax under current law.

141. ***Exclusion of public assistance benefits.***— Under the reference law baseline tax system, gifts and transfers are not treated as income to the recipients. In contrast, the normal tax method considers cash transfers from the Government as part of the recipients' income, and thus, treats the exclusion for public assistance benefits under current law as a tax expenditure.

142. ***Exclusion of special benefits for disabled coal miners.***—Under the baseline tax system, all compensation, including dedicated payments and in-kind benefits, should be included in taxable income. However, disability payments to former coal miners out of the Black Lung Trust Fund, although income to the recipient, are not subject to the income tax.

143. ***Exclusion of military disability pensions.***—Under the baseline tax system, all compensation, including dedicated payments and in-kind benefits, should be included in taxable income. In contrast, most of the military disability pension income received by current disabled military retirees is excluded from their income subject to tax.

144. ***Defined benefit employer plans.***—Under the baseline tax system, all compensation, including deferred and dedicated payments, should be included in taxable income. In addition, investment income would be taxed as earned. In contrast, under current law certain contributions to defined benefit pension plans are excluded from an employee's gross income even though employers can deduct their contributions. In addition, the tax on the investment income earned by defined benefit pension plans is deferred until the money is withdrawn.

145. ***Defined contribution employer plans.***— Under the baseline tax system, all compensation, including deferred and dedicated payments, should be included in taxable income. In addition, investment income would be taxed as earned. In contrast, under current law individual taxpayers and employers can make tax-preferred contributions to employer-provided 401(k) and similar plans (e.g. 403(b) plans and the Federal Government's Thrift Savings Plan). In 2015, an employee could exclude up to $18,000 of wages from AGI under a qualified arrangement with an employer's 401(k) plan. Employees age 50 or over could exclude up to $24,000 in contributions. The defined contribution plan limit, including both employee and employer contributions, is $53,000 in 2015. The tax on contributions made by both employees and employers and the investment income earned by these plans is deferred until withdrawn.

146. ***Individual Retirement Accounts (IRAs).***— Under the baseline tax system, all compensation, including deferred and dedicated payments, should be included in taxable income. In addition, investment income would be taxed as earned. In contrast, under current law individual taxpayers can take advantage of traditional and Roth IRAs to defer or otherwise reduce the tax on the return to their retirement savings. The IRA contribution limit is $5,500 in 2015; taxpayers age 50 or over are allowed to make additional "catch-up" contributions of $1,000. Contributions to a traditional IRA are generally deductible but the deduction is phased out for workers with incomes above certain levels who, or whose spouses, are active participants in an employer-provided retirement plan. Contributions and account earnings are includible in income when withdrawn from traditional IRAs. Roth IRA contributions are not deductible, but earnings and withdrawals are exempt from taxation. Income limits also apply to Roth IRA contributions.

147. ***Low and moderate-income savers' credit.***—The baseline tax system would not allow credits for particular activities or targeted at specific groups. In contrast, the Tax Code provides an additional incentive for lower-income taxpayers to save through a nonrefundable credit of up to 50 percent on IRA and other retirement contributions of up to $2,000. This credit is in addition to any deduction or exclusion. The credit is completely phased out by $61,000 for joint filers, $45,750 for head of household filers, and $30,500 for other filers in 2015.

148. ***Self-employed plans.***—Under the baseline tax system, all compensation, including deferred and dedicated payments, should be included in taxable income. In addition, investment income would be taxed as earned. In contrast, under current law self-employed individuals can make deductible contributions to their own retire-

ment plans equal to 25 percent of their income, up to a maximum of $53,000 in 2015. Total plan contributions are limited to 25 percent of a firm's total wages. The tax on the investment income earned by self-employed SEP, SIMPLE, and qualified plans is deferred until withdrawn.

149. ***Premiums on group term life insurance.***— Under the baseline tax system, all compensation, including deferred and dedicated payments, should be included in taxable income. In contrast, under current law employer-provided life insurance benefits are excluded from an employee's gross income (to the extent that the employer's share of the total costs does not exceed the cost of $50,000 of such insurance) even though the employer's costs for the insurance are a deductible business expense.

150. ***Premiums on accident and disability insurance.***—Under the baseline tax system, all compensation, including dedicated payments and in-kind benefits, should be included in taxable income. In contrast, under current law employer-provided accident and disability benefits are excluded from an employee's gross income even though the employer's costs for the benefits are a deductible business expense.

151. ***Income of trusts to finance supplementary unemployment benefits.***—Under the baseline tax system, all compensation, including dedicated payments and in-kind benefits, should be included in taxable income. In addition, investment income would be taxed as earned. Under current law, employers may establish trusts to pay supplemental unemployment benefits to employees separated from employment. Investment income earned by such trusts is exempt from taxation.

152. ***Special ESOP rules.***—ESOPs are a special type of tax-exempt employee benefit plan. Under the baseline tax system, all compensation, including dedicated payments and in-kind benefits, should be included in taxable income. In addition, investment income would be taxed as earned. In contrast, employer-paid contributions (the value of stock issued to the ESOP) are deductible by the employer as part of employee compensation costs. They are not included in the employees' gross income for tax purposes, however, until they are paid out as benefits. In addition, the following special income tax provisions for ESOPs are intended to increase ownership of corporations by their employees: (1) annual employer contributions are subject to less restrictive limitations than other qualified retirement plans; (2) ESOPs may borrow to purchase employer stock, guaranteed by their agreement with the employer that the debt will be serviced by his payment (deductible by him) of a portion of wages (excludable by the employees) to service the loan; (3) employees who sell appreciated company stock to the ESOP may defer any taxes due until they withdraw benefits; (4) dividends paid to ESOP-held stock are deductible by the employer; and (5) earnings are not taxed as they accrue.

153. ***Additional deduction for the blind.***—Under the baseline tax system, the standard deduction is allowed. An additional standard deduction for a targeted group within a given filing status would not be allowed. In contrast, the Tax Code allows taxpayers who are blind to claim an additional $1,550 standard deduction if single, or $1,250 if married in 2015.

154. ***Additional deduction for the elderly.***— Under the baseline tax system, the standard deduction is allowed. An additional standard deduction for a targeted group within a given filing status would not be allowed. In contrast, the Tax Code allows taxpayers who are 65 years or older to claim an additional $1,550 standard deduction if single, or $1,250 if married in 2015.

155. ***Tax credit for the elderly and disabled.***— Under the baseline tax system, a credit targeted at a specific group within a given filing status or for particular activities would not be allowed. In contrast, the Tax Code allows taxpayers who are 65 years of age or older, or who are permanently disabled, to claim a non-refundable tax credit equal to 15 percent of the sum of their earned and retirement income. The amount to which the 15-percent rate is applied is limited to no more than $5,000 for single individuals or married couples filing a joint return where only one spouse is 65 years of age or older or disabled, and up to $7,500 for joint returns where both spouses are 65 years of age or older or disabled. These limits are reduced by one-half of the taxpayer's adjusted gross income over $7,500 for single individuals and $10,000 for married couples filing a joint return.

156. ***Deductibility of casualty losses.***—Under the baseline tax system, neither the purchase of property nor insurance premiums to protect the property's value are deductible as costs of earning income. Therefore, reimbursement for insured loss of such property is not included as a part of gross income, and uninsured losses are not deductible. In contrast, the Tax Code provides a deduction for uninsured casualty and theft losses of more than $100 each, to the extent that total losses during the year exceed 10 percent of the taxpayer's adjusted gross income.

157. ***Earned income tax credit (EITC).***—The baseline tax system would not allow credits for particular activities or targeted at specific groups. In contrast, the Tax Code provides an EITC to low-income workers at a maximum rate of 45 percent of income. For a family with one qualifying child, the credit is 34 percent of the first $9,880 of earned income in 2015. The credit is 40 percent of the first $13,870 of income for a family with two qualifying children, and it is 45 percent of the first $13,870 of income for a family with three or more qualifying children. Low-income workers with no qualifying children are eligible for a 7.65-percent credit on the first $6,580 of earned income. The credit is phased out at income levels and rates which depend upon how many qualifying children are eligible and marital status. In 2015, the phasedown for married filers begins at incomes $5,520 greater than for otherwise similar unmarried filers. Earned income tax credits in excess of tax liabilities owed through the individual income tax system are refundable to individuals. After 2017, the additional benefit for families with three or more children will be eliminated and the marriage penalty relief will be reduced to $3,000 (indexed from 2008).

Social Security

158. *Social Security benefits for retired workers.*—The baseline tax system would tax Social Security benefits to the extent that contributions to Social Security were not previously taxed. Thus, the portion of Social Security benefits that is attributable to employer contributions and earnings on employer and employee contributions (and not attributable to employee contributions) would be subject to tax. In contrast, the Tax Code may not tax all of the Social Security benefits that exceed the beneficiary's contributions from previously taxed income. Actuarially, previously taxed contributions generally do not exceed 15 percent of benefits, even for retirees receiving the highest levels of benefits. Up to 85 percent of recipients' Social Security and Railroad Social Security Equivalent retirement benefits are included in (phased into) the income tax base if the recipient's provisional income exceeds certain base amounts. (Provisional income is equal to other items included in adjusted gross income plus foreign or U.S. possession income, tax-exempt interest, and one half of Social Security and Railroad Social Security Equivalent retirement benefits.) The untaxed portion of the benefits received by taxpayers who are below the income amounts at which 85 percent of the benefits are taxable is counted as a tax expenditure. See also provision number 139, Exclusion of railroad Social Security equivalent benefits.

159. *Social Security benefits for disabled workers.*—Under the baseline tax system, insurance benefits would be taxed to the extent that premiums were paid out of pre-tax income. Under current law, however, benefit payments from the Social Security Trust Fund for disability are fully or partially excluded from a beneficiary's gross income in excess of any exclusion justified by contributions made from pre-tax income.

160. *Social Security benefits for spouses, dependents and survivors.*—Under the baseline tax system, Social Security benefits would be taxed to the extent they exceed contributions out of after-tax income. Under current law, however, benefit payments from the Social Security Trust Fund for spouses, dependents and survivors are fully or partially excluded from a beneficiary's gross income.

161. *Credit for certain employer social security contributions.*—Under the baseline tax system, employer contributions to Social Security represent labor cost and are deductible expenses. Under current law, however, certain employers are allowed a tax credit, instead of a deduction, against taxes paid on tips received from customers in connection with the providing, delivering, or serving of food or beverages for consumption, The tip credit equals the full amount of the employer's share of FICA taxes paid on the portion of tips, when added to the employee's non-tip wages, in excess of $5.15 per hour. The credit is available only with respect to FICA taxes paid on tips.

Veterans Benefits and Services

162. *Exclusion of veterans death benefits and disability compensation.*—Under the baseline tax system, all compensation, including dedicated payments and in-kind benefits, should be included in taxable income because they represent accretions to wealth that do not materially differ from cash wages. In contrast, all compensation due to death or disability paid by the Veterans Administration is excluded from taxable income under current law.

163. *Exclusion of veterans pensions.*—Under the baseline tax system, all compensation, including dedicated payments and in-kind benefits, should be included in taxable income because they represent accretions to wealth that do not materially differ from cash wages. Under current law, however, pension payments made by the Veterans Administration are excluded from gross income.

164. *Exclusion of G.I. Bill benefits.*—Under the baseline tax system, all compensation, including dedicated payments and in-kind benefits, should be included in taxable income because they represent accretions to wealth that do not materially differ from cash wages. Under current law, however, G.I. Bill benefits paid by the Veterans Administration are excluded from gross income.

165. *Exclusion of interest on veterans housing bonds.*—The baseline tax system generally would tax all income under the regular tax rate schedule. It would not allow preferentially low (or zero) tax rates to apply to certain types or sources of income. In contrast, under current law, interest earned on general obligation bonds issued by State and local governments to finance housing for veterans is excluded from taxable income.

General Government

166. *Exclusion of interest on public purpose State and local bonds.*—The baseline tax system generally would tax all income under the regular tax rate schedule. It would not allow preferentially low (or zero) tax rates to apply to certain types or sources of income. In contrast, under current law interest earned on State and local government bonds issued to finance public-purpose construction (e.g., schools, roads, sewers), equipment acquisition, and other public purposes is tax-exempt. Interest on bonds issued by Indian tribal governments for essential governmental purposes is also tax-exempt.

167. *Build America Bonds.*—The baseline tax system would not allow credits for particular activities or targeted at specific group. In contrast, the Tax Code in 2009 allowed State and local governments to issue taxable bonds through 2010 and receive a direct payment from Treasury equal to 35 percent of interest expenses. Alternatively, State and local governments could issue taxable bonds and the private lenders receive the 35-percent credit which is included in taxable income.

168. *Deductibility of nonbusiness State and local taxes other than on owner-occupied homes.*—Under the baseline tax system, a deduction for personal

consumption expenditures would not be allowed. In contrast, the Tax Code allows taxpayers who itemize their deductions to claim a deduction for State and local income taxes (or, at the taxpayer's election, State and local sales taxes) and property taxes, even though these taxes primarily pay for services that, if purchased directly by taxpayers, would not be deductible. The ability for taxpayers to elect to deduct State and local sales taxes in lieu of State and local income taxes applied to taxable years beginning after December 31, 2003 and before January 1, 2015. (The estimates for this tax expenditure do not include the estimates for the deductibility of State and local property tax on owner-occupied homes. See item 58.)

Interest

169. *Deferral of interest on U.S. savings bonds.*— The baseline tax system would uniformly tax all returns to investments and not allow an exemption or deferral for particular activities, investments, or industries. In contrast, taxpayers may defer paying tax on interest earned on U.S. savings bonds until the bonds are redeemed.

APPENDIX

Performance Measures and the Economic Effects of Tax Expenditures

The Government Performance and Results Act of 1993 (GPRA) directs Federal agencies to develop annual and strategic plans for their programs and activities. These plans set out performance objectives to be achieved over a specific time period. Most of these objectives are achieved through direct expenditure programs. Tax expenditures – spending programs implemented through the tax code by reducing tax obligations for certain activities -- contribute to achieving these goals in a manner similar to direct expenditure programs.

Tax expenditures by definition work through the tax system and, particularly, the income tax. Thus, they may be relatively advantageous policy approaches when the benefit or incentive is related to income and is intended to be widely available. Because there is an existing public administrative and private compliance structure for the tax system, income-based programs that require little oversight might be efficiently run through the tax system. In addition, some tax expenditures actually simplify the operation of the tax system (for example, the exclusion for up to $500,000 of capital gains on home sales). Tax expenditures also implicitly subsidize certain activities in a manner similar to direct expenditures. For example, exempting employer-sponsored health insurance from income taxation is equivalent to a direct spending subsidy equal to the forgone tax obligations for this type of compensation. Spending, regulatory or tax-disincentive policies can also modify behavior, but may have different economic effects. Finally, a variety of tax expenditure tools can be used, e.g., deductions; credits; exemptions; deferrals; floors; ceilings; phase-ins; phase-outs; and these can be dependent on income, expenses, or demographic characteristics (age, number of family members, etc.). This wide range of policy instruments means that tax expenditures can be flexible and can have very different economic effects.

Tax expenditures also have limitations. In many cases they add to the complexity of the tax system, which raises both administrative and compliance costs. For example, personal exemptions, deductions, credits, and phase-outs can complicate filing and decision-making. The income tax system may have little or no contact with persons who have no or very low incomes, and does not require information on certain characteristics of individuals used in some spending programs, such as wealth or duration of employment. These features may reduce the effectiveness of tax expenditures for addressing socioeconomic disparities. Tax expenditures also generally do not enable the same degree of agency discretion as an outlay program. For example, grant or direct Federal service delivery programs can prioritize activities to be addressed with specific resources in a way that is difficult to emulate with tax expenditures.

Outlay programs have advantages where the direct provision of government services is particularly warranted, such as equipping and maintaining the armed forces or administering the system of justice. Outlay programs may also be specifically designed to meet the needs of low-income families who would not otherwise be subject to income taxes or need to file a tax return. Outlay programs may also receive more year-to-year oversight and fine tuning through the legislative and executive budget process. In addition, many different types of spending programs include direct Government provision; credit programs; and payments to State and local governments, the private sector, or individuals in the form of grants or contracts provide flexibility for policy design. On the other hand, certain outlay programs may rely less directly on economic incentives and private-market provision than tax incentives, thereby reducing the relative efficiency of spending programs for some goals. Finally, spending programs, particularly on the discretionary side, may respond less rapidly to changing activity levels and economic conditions than tax expenditures.

Regulations may have more direct and immediate effects than outlay and tax-expenditure programs because regulations apply directly and immediately to the regulated party (i.e., the intended actor), generally in the private sector. Regulations can also be fine-tuned more quickly than tax expenditures because they can often be changed as needed by the Executive Branch without legislation. Like tax expenditures, regulations often rely largely on voluntary compliance, rather than detailed inspections and policing. As such, the public administrative costs tend to be modest relative to the private resource costs associated with modifying activities. Historically, regulations have tended to rely on proscriptive measures, as opposed to economic incentives. This reliance can diminish their economic efficiency, although this feature can also promote full compliance where (as in certain safety-related cases) policymakers believe that trade-offs with economic considerations are not of paramount importance. Also, regulations generally do not directly affect Federal outlays or receipts. Thus, like tax expenditures, they may escape the degree of scrutiny that outlay programs receive. Some policy objectives are achieved using multiple approaches. For example, minimum wage legislation, the earned income tax credit, and the food stamp program (SNAP) are regulatory, tax expenditure, and direct outlay programs, respectively, all having the objective of improving the economic welfare of low-wage workers and families.

A Framework for Evaluating the Effectiveness of Tax Expenditures

Across all major budgetary categories - from housing and health to space, technology, agriculture, and national defense - tax expenditures make up a significant portion of Federal activity and affect every area of the economy. For these reasons, a comprehensive evaluation framework that examines incentives, direct results, and spillover effects will benefit the budgetary process by informing decisions on tax expenditure policy.

As described above, tax expenditures, like spending and regulatory programs, have a variety of objectives and economic effects. These include: encouraging certain types of activities (e.g., saving for retirement or investing in certain sectors); increasing certain types of after-tax income (e.g., favorable tax treatment of Social Security income); and reducing private compliance costs and Government administrative costs (e.g., the exclusion for up to $500,000 of capital gains on home sales). Some of these objectives are well suited to quantitative measurement and evaluation, while others are less well suited.

Performance measurement is generally concerned with inputs, outputs, and outcomes. In the case of tax expenditures, the principal input is usually the revenue effect. Outputs are quantitative or qualitative measures of goods and services, or changes in income and investment, directly produced by these inputs. Outcomes, in turn, represent the changes in the economy, society, or environment that are the ultimate goals of programs. Evaluations assess whether programs are meeting intended goals, but may also encompass analyzing whether initiatives are superior to other policy alternatives.

The Administration is working towards examining the objectives and effects of the wide range of tax expenditures in our budget, despite challenges related to data availability, measurement, and analysis. Evaluations include an assessment of whether tax expenditures are achieving intended policy results in an efficient manner, with minimal burdens on individual taxpayers, consumers, and firms; and an examination of possible unintended effects and their consequences.

As an illustration of how evaluations can inform budgetary decisions, consider education, and research investment credits.

Education. There are millions of individuals taking advantage of tax credits designed to help pay for educational expenses. There are a number of different credits available as well as other important forms of Federal support for higher education such as subsidized loans and grants. An evaluation would explore the possible relationships between use of the credits and the use of loans and grants, seeking to answer, for example, whether the use of credits reduce or increase the likelihood of the students applying for loans. Such an evaluation would allow stakeholders to determine the most effective program – whether it is a tax credit, a subsidized loan, or a grant.

Investment. A series of tax expenditures reduce the cost of investment, both in specific activities such as research and experimentation, extractive industries, and certain financial activities and more generally throughout the economy, through accelerated depreciation for plant and equipment. These provisions can be evaluated along a number of dimensions. For example, it is useful to consider the strength of the incentives by measuring their effects on the cost of capital (the return which investments must yield to cover their costs) and effective tax rates. The impact of these provisions on the amounts of corresponding forms of investment (e.g., research spending, exploration activity, equipment) might also be estimated. In some cases, such as research, there is evidence that the investment can provide significant positive externalities—that is, economic benefits that are not reflected in the market transactions between private parties. It could be useful to quantify these externalities and compare them with the size of tax expenditures. Measures could also indicate the effects on production from these investments such as numbers or values of patents, energy production and reserves, and industrial production. Issues to be considered include the extent to which the preferences increase production (as opposed to benefiting existing output) and their cost-effectiveness relative to other policies. Analysis could also consider objectives that are more difficult to measure but still are ultimate goals, such as promoting the Nation's technological base, energy security, environmental quality, or economic growth. Such an assessment is likely to involve tax analysis as well as consideration of non-tax matters such as market structure, scientific, and other information (such as the effects of increased domestic fuel production on imports from various regions, or the effects of various energy sources on the environment).

The tax proposals subject to these analyses include items that indirectly affect the estimated value of tax expenditures (such as changes in income tax rates), proposals that make reforms to improve tax compliance and administration, as well as proposals which would change, add, or delete tax expenditures.

Barriers to Evaluation. Developing a framework that is sufficiently comprehensive, accurate, and flexible is a significant challenge. Evaluations are constrained by the availability of appropriate data and challenges in economic modeling:

- Data availability. Data may not exist, or may not exist in an analytically appropriate form, to conduct rigorous evaluations of certain types of expenditures. For example, measuring the effects of tax expenditures designed to achieve tax neutrality for individuals and firms earning income abroad, and foreign firms could require data from foreign governments or firms which are not readily available.

- Analytical constraints. Evaluations of tax expenditures face analytical constraints even when data are available. For example, individuals might have access to several tax expenditures and programs aimed at improving the same outcome. Isolating the effect of a single tax credit is challenging absent a well-specified research design.

- Resources. Tax expenditure analyses are seriously constrained by staffing considerations. Evaluations typically require expert analysts who are often engaged in other more competing areas of work related to the budget.

The Executive Branch is focused on addressing these challenges to lay the foundation for the analysis of tax expenditures comprehensively, alongside evaluations of the effectiveness of direct spending initiatives.

Current Administration Proposals on Tax Expenditures

The Administration considers performance measurement, evaluations, and the economic effects of tax expenditures each year in its deliberation for the Budget, and proposals are informed by these analyses. The President's National Commission on Fiscal Responsibility and Reform submitted a report in 2010 in which they said that the income tax system is unduly complicated and that the government should "sharply reduce rates, broaden the base, simplify the tax code, and reduce the many 'tax expenditures' —another name for spending through the tax code."

The current Budget includes many proposals that would change existing tax expenditures to raise revenue, eliminate ineffective or counterproductive tax expenditures, and enhance effective tax expenditures. The tax expenditure proposals in the budget further the Administration's goals of clean and secure energy, a world-class education for all Americans, and fairness in the tax code. Some of these proposals are highlighted below.

Reduce the value of certain tax expenditures. The Administration proposes to limit the tax rate at which

upper-income taxpayers can use itemized deductions and other tax preferences to reduce tax liability to a maximum of 28 percent, a limitation that would affect only the highest-income households. The limit would apply to all itemized deductions, interest on tax-exempt bonds, employer-sponsored health insurance, deductions and income exclusions for employee retirement contributions, and certain above-the-line deductions, effective for taxable years beginning after December 31, 2016. These are among the largest tax expenditures. This proposal would make the tax code more equitable because the value of the tax expenditure as a percentage of the deduction is proportional to one's tax bracket, so it is less valuable to those in lower brackets.

Enhance and simplify the Research and Experimentation (R&E) credit and modify and make permanent the Renewable Energy Production Tax Credit. The Budget proposes to simplify the R&E credit by creating a single formula for calculating the credit and increasing the rate. For similar reasons, the Budget also proposes to permanently extend and enhance the production tax credit for renewable energy property.

Simplify and better target benefits for education. A significant portion of federal spending on higher education occurs through the tax code, but current higher education tax benefits are complicated and do not provide enough help for low and middle income families that struggle to afford college. Building on bipartisan Congressional proposals, the Budget proposes to simplify, consolidate, and better target higher education tax benefits. It would repeal or let expire duplicative and less effective provisions, including the Lifetime Learning Credit and the student loan interest deduction (for new borrowers). Meanwhile, it would enhance the $2,500 American Opportunity Tax Credit by indexing the maximum credit for inflation, making the credit available for a fifth year, providing a partial credit to part-time students, and increasing the amount of the credit available to low-income students without income tax liability.

Eliminate a range of tax expenditures in the context of business tax reform. The President's framework for business tax reform calls for eliminating dozens of tax loopholes and subsidies and reinvesting the revenue to lower the corporate tax rate. Consistent with the framework, the Budget includes a number of proposals to eliminate inefficient business tax expenditures. For example, current law provides a number of credits and deductions that are targeted towards certain oil, gas, and coal activities. In accordance with the President's agreement at the G-20 Summit in Pittsburgh to phase out inefficient subsidies for fossil fuels so that the Nation can transition to a 21st century energy economy, the Administration proposes to repeal a number of tax preferences available for fossil fuels.

SPECIAL TOPICS

15. AID TO STATE AND LOCAL GOVERNMENTS

State and local governments serve a vital role in providing services to their residents. The Federal Government contributes to that role by aiding State and local governments through grants, loans, and the tax system. This chapter focuses on Federal grants-in-aid and highlights some of the Administration initiatives in this area in the 2017 Budget. Information on Federal credit programs may be found in Chapter 20, "Credit and Insurance," in this volume. Chapter 14, "Tax Expenditures," in this volume, includes a display of tax expenditures that particularly aid State and local governments at the end of Tables 14-1 and 14-2.

Federal grants-in-aid are assistance provided to State and local governments, U.S. territories, and American Indian Tribal governments to support government operations or provision of services to the public. Most often grants are awarded as direct cash assistance, but Federal grants-in-aid can also include payments for grants-in-kind—non-monetary aid, such as commodities purchased for the National School Lunch Program. Federal revenues shared with State and local governments are also considered grants-in-aid.

Federal grants generally fall into one of two broad categories—categorical grants or block grants—depending on the requirements of the grant program. In addition, grants may be characterized by how the funding is awarded such as by formula, by project, or by matching State and local funds.

Categorical grants have a narrowly defined purpose and may be awarded on a formula basis or as a project grant. An example of a categorical grant is the Special Supplemental Nutrition Program for Women, Infants, and Children, also known as WIC, administered by the Department of Agriculture. WIC targets the nutrition needs of low-income pregnant and postpartum women, infants, and children up to age five. Applicants to this program must meet defined categorical, residential, income, and nutrition risk eligibility requirements.

In contrast to categorical grants, block grants provide the recipient with more latitude to define the use of the funding and are awarded on a formula basis specified in law. The Department of Health and Human Services' Temporary Assistance for Needy Families (TANF) program is an example of a block grant. States may use TANF funds in a variety of ways to meet any of four purposes set out in law. Each State also has broad discretion to determine eligibility requirements for TANF benefits. In addition, TANF has a matching requirement known as "maintenance of effort" which specifies a minimum amount that States must spend to assist low-income families in order to receive the full Federal grant.

Project grants can be awarded competitively and are typified by a predetermined end product or duration.

They can include grants for research, training, evaluation, planning, technical assistance, survey work, and construction.

The Government Accountability Office describes the various types of grants as each striking "a different balance between the interests of the Federal grant-making agency that funds be used efficiently and effectively to meet national objectives, and the interests of the recipient to use the funds to meet local priorities and to minimize the administrative burdens associated with accepting the grant." [1] As recipients of Federal grant funding, State and local governments may provide services directly to beneficiaries or States may act as a pass-through, disbursing grant funding to localities using a formula or a competitive process. This pass-through structure allows States to set priorities and determine the allocation methodology within the rules of the Federal grant guidance.[2]

In balancing interests across levels of government, the Administration has led efforts to transform how the Federal Government partners with State and local governments to achieve positive outcomes. The Administration has cultivated a place-based approach, customizing support for communities based on their specific assets and challenges. This new approach seeks out communities' plans or vision for addressing a set of challenges and then works across agency and program silos to support those communities in implementing their plans. In addition, the Federal Government and its partners focus on what works, using data to measure success and monitor progress, fostering communities of practice to share and build on innovations. The Federal Government's use of a place-based approach helps to maximize the effectiveness of resources through greater coordination and collaboration with other levels of government. For more detail on the place-based approach and specific Administration initiatives, see "Partnering with Communities to Expand Opportunity" and "Reshaping the Way Government Engages with Citizens and Communities" in the main Budget volume.

Across all States, in State fiscal year 2014 (the most recent year for which final data are available), 25.6 percent of total State spending was for Medicaid; 19.8 percent for elementary and secondary education; 10.5 percent for higher education; 7.9 percent for transportation; 3.2 percent for corrections; 1.5 percent for public assistance; and 31.4 percent for all other expenditures. The share of spending dedicated to Medicaid is estimated to have increased to 27.4 percent in State fiscal year 2015, while

---

[1] United States Government Accountability Office. "Grants to State and Local Governments, An Overview of Federal Funding Levels and Selected Challenges." September 2012. p. 3.

[2] Keegan, Natalie. "Federal Grants-in-Aid Administration: A Primer." Congressional Research Service. October 3, 2012. p. 6-7.

all other categories are estimated to have slightly smaller shares.[3]

The impact of Medicaid is again evident when State spending is examined by source. Although most State spending comes from general fund revenues, Federal funds are also a significant part of States' overall budgets. In State fiscal year 2014, 41.1 percent of total State spending came from general funds,[4] 30.1 percent from Federal funds, 26.9 percent from other State funds, and 1.9 percent from bonds.[5] In State fiscal year 2015, it is estimated that the percentage of total State spending that came from Federal funds increased to 31.3 percent because it was the first full year of Medicaid expansion under the Affordable Care Act, while spending from general funds decreased to 40.0 percent.[6]

In its Fiscal Survey of States, the National Association of State Budget Officers (NASBO) looks at enacted State budgets to make projections for the coming year and at general fund spending as an indication of State financial health. According to the most recent report, State fiscal conditions have been improving gradually over the last several years, however, progress has been slow and somewhat uneven. In addition, States face long-term financial challenges such as infrastructure needs, and pension and health care costs. State general fund spending is expected to increase by 4.1 percent in State fiscal year 2016, according to enacted budgets. This would be the sixth straight year of annual increases to general fund spending.[7] Total State spending increased by 3.8 percent in 2014 to $1.7 billion, and is expected to increase by another 7.3 percent in 2015 to $1.9 billion.[8]

NASBO's Fiscal Survey of States does not include the territory of Puerto Rico, which has been experiencing an economic downturn since 2006. Puerto Rico is experiencing expanding deficits, high levels of unemployment, the highest poverty rate of any State or territory, and, as a result, outmigration and the loss of investment and jobs. Puerto Rico has not had access to the traditional bond market since its rating was downgraded below investment status in 2013. The measures Puerto Rico has taken to pay its debts, such as increasing taxes and delaying pension contributions, are creating other strains. The Budget includes a package of reforms to allow Puerto Rico to navigate through the crisis. The proposal includes four key elements: first, provide tools for Puerto Rico to comprehensively restructure its financial liabilities; second, enact strong fiscal oversight and help strengthen Puerto Rico's fiscal governance; third, strengthen Medicaid in Puerto Rico and other U.S. territories; and finally, to re-ward work and support growth including an Earned Income Tax Credit for Puerto Rico.

As a share of the total Federal budget, outlays for Federal grants-in-aid accounted for 16.9 percent of total outlays in 2015 and totaled $624.4 billion, a 7.6 percent increase over 2014. Federal grant spending in 2016 is estimated to be $666.7 billion, an increase of 6.3 percent from 2015. The Budget provides $694.2 billion in outlays for aid to State and local governments in 2017, an increase of 4.0 percent from 2016. Medicaid, by itself, accounts for over 50 percent of total grant spending. Excluding Medicaid, spending is estimated to increase from $274.6 billion in 2015, to $299.4 billion in 2016, and to increase to $308.7 billion in 2017.

Federal grants help State and local governments finance programs covering most areas of domestic public spending including infrastructure, education, health care, social services, and public safety. Of the total proposed grant spending in 2017, 59.4 percent is for health programs, with most of the funding going to Medicaid. Beyond health programs, 16.6 percent of Federal aid is estimated to go to income security programs; 9.9 percent to transportation; 9.1 percent to education, training, and social services; and 5.0 for all other functions. Section A of Table 15-1, Trends in Federal Grants to State and Local Governments, shows actual spending at the start of each decade since 1960, actual spending for 2015, and estimates for 2016 and 2017 by budget function.

The Federal budget also classifies grant spending by BEA category—mandatory and discretionary.[9] Funding for discretionary grant programs is determined annually through appropriations acts. Funding for mandatory programs is provided directly in authorizing legislation that establishes eligibility criteria or benefit formulas; funding for mandatory programs usually is not limited by the annual appropriations process. Section B of Table 15-1 shows the distribution of grants between mandatory and discretionary spending.

Outlays for mandatory grant programs were $438.5 billion in 2015 and are estimated to increase by 6.5 percent in 2016 to $467.1 billion. In 2017, outlays for mandatory grant programs are estimated to be $496.6 billion, a 6.3 percent increase over 2016. Medicaid is by far the largest mandatory grant program with estimated outlays of $385.6 million in 2017. After Medicaid, the three largest mandatory grant programs by outlays in 2017 are estimated to be Child Nutrition programs, which include the School Breakfast Program, the National School Lunch Program and others, $23.1 billion; the Temporary Assistance for Needy Families program, $17.0 billion; and the Children's Health Insurance program, $15.2 billion.[10]

Outlays for discretionary grant programs were $185.9 billion in 2015 and are estimated to increase by 7.3 percent to $199.5 billion in 2016. In 2017, grants-in-aid with discretionary funding are estimated to have outlays of

---

[3] "State Expenditure Report, Examining Fiscal 2013-2015 State Spending." National Association of State Budget Officers (2015). p. 6.

[4] State general funds are raised from States' own taxes and fees.

[5] "State Expenditure Report, Examining Fiscal 2013-2015 State Spending." National Association of State Budget Officers (2015). p. 5.

[6] Ibid. p. 1.

[7] "The Fiscal Survey of States." National Association of State Budget Officers. Fall 2015. p. vii.

[8] "State Expenditure Report, Examining Fiscal 2013-2015 State Spending." National Association of State Budget Officers (2015). p. 8.

[9] For more information on these categories, see Chapter 9, "Budget Concepts," in this volume.

[10] Obligation data by State for programs in each of these budget accounts may be found in the State-by-State tables included with other budget materials on the OMB web site and Budget CD-ROM.

Table 15–1. TRENDS IN FEDERAL GRANTS TO STATE AND LOCAL GOVERNMENTS
(Outlays in billions of dollars)

	Actual								Estimate	
	1960	1970	1980	1990	2000	2005	2010	2015	2016	2017
A. Distribution of grants by function:										
Natural resources and environment	0.1	0.4	5.4	3.7	4.6	5.9	9.1	7.0	6.6	6.6
Agriculture	0.2	0.6	0.6	1.3	0.7	0.9	0.8	0.7	1.1	1.1
Transportation	3.0	4.6	13.0	19.2	32.2	43.4	61.0	60.8	62.2	69.0
Community and regional development	0.1	1.8	6.5	5.0	8.7	20.2	18.8	14.4	17.4	13.4
Education, training, employment, and social services	0.5	6.4	21.9	21.8	36.7	57.2	97.6	60.5	64.5	63.1
Health	0.2	3.8	15.8	43.9	124.8	197.8	290.2	368.0	392.7	412.2
Income security	2.6	5.8	18.5	36.8	68.7	90.9	115.2	101.1	106.9	114.9
Administration of justice	....	0.0	0.5	0.6	5.3	4.8	5.1	3.7	7.2	6.1
General government	0.2	0.5	8.6	2.3	2.1	4.4	5.2	3.8	3.1	3.4
Other	0.0	0.1	0.7	0.8	2.1	2.6	5.4	4.3	5.0	4.5
Total	**7.0**	**24.1**	**91.4**	**135.3**	**285.9**	**428.0**	**608.4**	**624.4**	**666.7**	**694.2**
B. Distribution of grants by BEA category:										
Discretionary	N/A	10.2	53.3	63.3	116.7	181.7	207.7	185.9	199.5	197.6
Mandatory	N/A	13.9	38.1	72.0	169.2	246.3	400.7	438.5	467.1	496.6
Total	**7.0**	**24.1**	**91.4**	**135.3**	**285.9**	**428.0**	**608.4**	**624.4**	**666.7**	**694.2**
C. Composition:										
Current dollars:										
Payments for individuals [1]	2.5	8.7	32.6	77.3	182.6	273.9	384.5	463.4	493.3	518.9
Physical capital [1]	3.3	7.1	22.6	27.2	48.7	60.8	93.3	77.2	78.0	85.3
Other grants	1.2	8.3	36.2	30.9	54.6	93.3	130.6	83.7	95.3	90.1
Total	**7.0**	**24.1**	**91.4**	**135.3**	**285.9**	**428.0**	**608.4**	**624.4**	**666.7**	**694.2**
Percentage of total grants:										
Payments for individuals [1]	35.3%	36.2%	35.7%	57.1%	63.9%	64.0%	63.2%	74.2%	74.0%	74.7%
Physical capital [1]	47.3%	29.3%	24.7%	20.1%	17.0%	14.2%	15.3%	12.4%	11.7%	12.3%
Other grants	17.4%	34.5%	39.6%	22.8%	19.1%	21.8%	21.5%	13.4%	14.3%	13.0%
Total	**100.0%**	**100.0%**	**100.0%**	**100.0%**	**100.0%**	**100.0%**	**100.0%**	**100.0%**	**100.0%**	**100.0%**
Constant (FY 2009) dollars:										
Payments for individuals [1]	14.2	39.8	75.8	115.9	221.2	304.1	385.3	419.1	437.9	451.1
Physical capital [1]	23.8	38.2	54.7	45.7	68.6	74.2	93.7	69.1	67.9	72.1
Other grants	14.4	64.7	134.1	62.8	77.1	101.8	123.9	72.3	80.2	73.5
Total	**52.4**	**142.7**	**264.7**	**224.3**	**366.9**	**480.1**	**602.9**	**560.6**	**585.9**	**596.7**
D. Total grants as a percent of:										
Federal outlays:										
Total	7.6%	12.3%	15.5%	10.8%	16.0%	17.3%	17.6%	16.9%	16.9%	16.7%
Domestic programs [2]	18.0%	23.2%	22.2%	17.1%	22.0%	23.5%	23.4%	22.1%	21.8%	21.9%
State and local expenditures	14.3%	19.6%	27.3%	18.7%	21.8%	23.5%	26.4%	25.1%	N/A	N/A
Gross domestic product	1.3%	2.3%	3.3%	2.3%	2.8%	3.3%	4.1%	3.5%	3.6%	3.6%
E. As a share of total State and local gross investments:										
Federal capital grants	24.6%	25.4%	35.4%	21.9%	22.0%	22.0%	27.5%	22.3%	N/A	N/A
State and local own-source financing	75.4%	74.6%	64.6%	78.1%	78.0%	78.0%	72.5%	77.7%	N/A	N/A
Total	**100.0%**	**100.0%**	**100.0%**	**100.0%**	**100.0%**	**100.0%**	**100.0%**	**100.0%**		

N/A: Not available at publishing.

[1] Grants that are both payments for individuals and capital investment are shown under capital investment.

[2] Excludes national defense, international affairs, net interest, and undistributed offsetting receipts.

$197.6 billion, a decrease of less than one percent from 2016. The three largest discretionary programs in 2017 are estimated to be Federal-aid Highways programs, with outlays of $41.9 billion; Tenant Based Rental Assistance, with outlays of $20.8 billion; and Education for the Disadvantaged, with outlays of $15.9 billion.[11]

---

[11] Obligation data by State for programs in each of these budget ac-

Over time the number of grants has grown in an incremental fashion creating a wide variety of types of grants, purposes, and requirements. Currently, there are 16 Executive Branch agencies and 14 independent agencies that provide grants to State and local governments. The

counts may be found in the State-by-State tables included with other budget materials on the OMB web site and Budget CD-ROM.

growing number and variety of grants created complexity for grantees and has made it difficult to compare program performance and conduct oversight.[12] To reduce this complexity, the Office of Management and Budget, working with 28 Federal agencies and public stakeholders, implemented new Uniform Guidance in 2014 that streamlined the financial management regulations for Federal grants and other assistance. These reforms reduced the number of financial management regulations for Federal grants and other assistance by 75 percent, and co-located the streamlined regulations in Title 2 of the Code of Federal Regulations part 200 with the goal of reducing administrative burdens and the risk of waste, fraud, and abuse for

_____
[12] Keegan, Natalie. "Federal Grants-in-Aid Administration: A Primer." Congressional Research Service. October 3, 2012. p. 2.

all of the Federal grant dollars expended annually. Also in 2014, President Obama signed into law the Digital Accountability and Transparency Act of 2014 (DATA Act), Public Law 113-101. The DATA Act will help improve the transparency of Federal grants oversight and spending by setting data standards and by improving the way the data can be accessed.

Below is a summary of grants initiatives in the budget. The funding level for grants in every budget account can be found in Table 15-2, organized by functional category, and by Federal agency. Table 15-2, Federal Grants to State and Local Governments, Budget Authority and Outlays, formerly printed in this chapter, is available on the OMB web site at *www.budget.gov / budget / Analytical_ Perspectives* and on the Budget CD-ROM.

HIGHLIGHTS OF FEDERAL AID PROPOSALS

Natural Resources and the Environment

Coastal Resilience. First, the Budget proposes a $2 billion Coastal Climate Resilience program, which will provide resources over 10 years for at-risk coastal States, local governments, and their communities to prepare for and adapt to climate change. This program would be paid for by redirecting roughly half of the savings that result from repealing unnecessary and costly offshore oil and gas revenue sharing payments that are set to be paid to a handful of States under current law. A portion of these program funds would be set aside to cover the unique circumstances that climate change forces some Alaskan communities to confront, such as relocation expenses for Alaska native villages threatened by rising seas, coastal erosion, and storm surges. The Budget also provides the Denali Commission—an independent Federal agency created to facilitate technical assistance and economic development in Alaska—with an additional $4 million above the 2016 enacted level to coordinate Federal, State, and Tribal assistance to communities to develop and implement solutions to address the impacts of climate change. Second, the Budget invests $20 million to help coastal regions plan for and implement activities related to mitigating extreme weather, changing ocean conditions and uses, and climate hazards through NOAA's Regional Coastal Resilience grants program. These competitive grants to State, local, Tribal, private, and non-governmental organization partners will support activities such as vulnerability assessments, regional ocean partnerships, and development and implementation of adaptation strategies.

Multi-Hazard Resilience. The Budget invests $54 million in mitigation projects—including mitigation planning, facilities hardening, and buyouts and elevation of structures—through the Federal Emergency Management Agency's Pre-disaster Mitigation Grant Program. Studies on mitigation activities conclude that Americans save approximately $4 for every dollar invested in pre-disaster mitigation.

Transportation

Investments in America's Transportation Infrastructure. The Budget proposes a 21st Century Clean Transportation System investment initiative to lay the foundation today for the American transportation system of tomorrow. The proposal refocuses Federal investment by providing more than $10 billion on average per year for the Federal Transit Administration (FTA) New Starts, Small Starts, and Transit Formula Grants programs to invest in the safety, performance, and efficiency of existing, new, and expanded transit systems. It also creates a new Rapid Growth Area Transit program for fast growing communities to implement multi-modal solutions to challenges caused by rapid growth. It reaffirms the Administration's commitment to high-speed rail by investing on average almost $7 billion per year on a competitive basis, with an emphasis on incorporating advanced rail technologies. The proposal also provides an average of $1 billion per year for a multi-modal freight program through grants for innovative rail, highway, and port projects that seek to reduce both emissions and particulate matter that harm local community health. It nearly doubles the amount of grant funding available through the Transportation Investment Generating Economic Recovery (also known as TIGER) competitive grant program to support innovative, multi-modal investments in our nation's infrastructure to make communities more livable and sustainable. The Budget rewards State and local governments for innovations that lead to smarter, cleaner, regional transportation system by proposing over $6 billion per year on average for a 21st Century Regions grant program to empower metropolitan and regional planners to implement regional-scale transportation and land-use strategies that achieve significant reductions in per capita greenhouse gas (GHG) emissions and vehicles miles traveled (VMT), while improving climate resilience. The budget provides nearly $1.5 billion per year on average in Clean Communities competitive grants to support transit oriented development, reconnect downtowns, clean up brownfields, implement complete streets policies, and pursue other policies that make our cities and towns greener and better places to live. It also provides nearly $1.7 billion per year on average for Climate-Smart Performance Formula Funds that are designed to reorient transportation formula funding by rewarding states that make investments to mitigate transportation impacts like air pollution. The budget provides $750 million on average per year for Resilient Transportation competitive grants to spur investments that bolster resilience to climate impacts. Cutting-edge projects will incorporate resilience strategies, such as adaptive materials, risk-sensitive design, and next generation transportation and logistics technology.

Education, Training, and Employment

Preschool for All. The Budget provides $350 million for Preschool Development Grants, an increase of $100 million above the 2016 enacted level. Preschool Development Grants are jointly administered by the Departments of Health and Human Services (HHS) and Education under the Every Student Succeeds Act (ESSA), Public Law 114-95, signed into law in December 2015, with funding residing at HHS. The Budget also provides $907 million for the Department of Education's early intervention and preschool services for children with disabilities, an increase of $80 million from the 2016 enacted level. This proposal includes up to $15 million for competitive grants for early identification of and intervention for developmental delays and disabilities, with a potential focus on autism, intended to help identify, develop, and scale up evidence-based practices.

Investments in Head Start. The Budget provides $434 million in additional funding over the 2016 enacted level for the Head Start program within HHS, which delivers comprehensive early childhood services to support the learning and development of America's neediest children.

Expanding Access to Quality Child Care for Working Families. The Budget invests $82 billion in additional mandatory funding over 10 years to ensure that all low- and moderate-income working families with children ages three and under have access to quality, affordable child care. The Budget also provides $200 million in discretionary funding to help States implement the policies required by the bipartisan Child Care and Development Block Grant Act of 2014, Public Law 113-186, designed to improve the safety and quality of care while giving parents the information they need to make good choices about their child care providers. The new funding will help States improve quality while preserving access to care. The additional funding in the Budget will also go toward new pilot grants to States and local communities to help build a supply of high-quality child care in rural areas and during non-traditional hours. These grants will focus on what low-income working families need most—high-quality, affordable care that is close to home and available during the hours they work and on short notice.

Home Visiting. The Budget invests $15 billion in new funding over the next 10 years to extend and expand evidence-based, voluntary home visiting programs, which enable nurses, social workers, and other professionals to work with new and expecting parents to help families track their children's healthy development and learning,

connect them to services to address any issues, and utilize good parenting practices that foster healthy development and later school success. The program builds on research showing that home visiting programs can significantly improve maternal and child health, child development, learning, and success.

Title I Education Grants. The Budget proposes a $450 million increase for Title I, which ESSA maintained as the Department's largest K-12 grant program and the cornerstone of its commitment to supporting schools in low-income communities with the funding necessary to provide high-need students access to an excellent education. Title I supports local solutions in States and school districts, while ensuring that students make progress toward high academic standards. The Budget also calls for dedicating additional funds within Title I to address the urgent need to improve our Nation's lowest performing schools. This dedicated funding, which will be distributed based on the Title I formulas, will ensure States and school districts have the support necessary to successfully turn around these schools.

STEM and Computer Science for All. Under the Computer Science for All proposal, the Budget includes $4 billion in mandatory funding over three years for States to increase access to K-12 computer science and other rigorous STEM coursework by training more than 250,000 teachers, providing infrastructure upgrades, offering online courses and building effective partnerships. Complementing the mandatory proposal, the Budget also dedicates $100 million in discretionary funding for Computer Science for All Development Grants to help school districts, alone or in consortia, execute ambitious computer science expansion efforts, particularly for traditionally under-represented students. Both the mandatory and discretionary proposal would also encourage States and districts to expand overall access to rigorous STEM coursework.

Student Support and Academic Enrichment Grant. The Budget provides $500 million for Student Support and Academic Enrichment Grants, newly authorized in ESSA, which provides funds for States and school districts to support student achievement and promote academic enrichment opportunities. This flexible funding can support expanding STEM opportunities and the arts, improving supports for student learning, and enhancing the use of technology for instruction.

Stronger Together Initiative. The Budget supports the Stronger Together initiative, which would make $120 million in voluntary competitive grants available to school districts or consortia of school districts that are interested in exploring ways to foster socioeconomic diversity through a robust process of parental, educator and community engagement, and data analysis; and to school districts and consortia of school districts that already have set goals and developed strategies and are ready to begin implementation. The funding would be available for five-year projects.

Support for Teachers. The Budget invests nearly $2.8 billion in discretionary funding for programs to provide broad support for educators at every phase of their careers, from ensuring they have strong preparation before entering the classroom, to pioneering new approaches to help teachers succeed in the classroom and equipping them with tools and training they need to implement college- and career-ready standards. The Budget provides $250 million for the Teacher and School Leader Incentive Program to drive improvements in school districts' human capital management systems through innovative strategies for recruiting, developing, evaluating, and retaining excellent educators. A new $125 million Teacher and Principals Pathways program, to be proposed in the next Higher Education Act reauthorization, will support teacher and principal preparation programs and nonprofits partnering with school districts to create or expand high quality pathways into teaching and school leadership, particularly into high-need schools and high-need subjects such as STEM. Finally, the Budget includes RESPECT: Best Job in the World, a $1 billion mandatory initiative that will support a nationwide effort to attract and retain effective teachers in high-need schools by increasing compensation and paths for advancement, implementing teacher-led development opportunities to improve instruction, and creating working conditions and school climates conducive to student success. This proposal is a key strategy in the Department's efforts to ensure all students' equitable access to effective teachers.

Education and Training in High Demand Fields. The Budget includes $75 million for a tuition-free investment in the American Technical Training Fund (ATTF). ATTF will provide competitive grants to support the development, operation, and expansion of innovative, evidence-based, tuition-free job training programs in high-demand fields such as manufacturing, healthcare, and IT.

Supporting WIOA Implementation. The Budget builds on prior progress by funding the core Department of Labor (DOL) Workforce Innovation and Opportunity Act (WIOA), Public Law 113-128, formula grants at their full authorized level for the first time since the law's enactment—a $138 million (5 percent) increase. The Budget also gives DOL and States the funding they need to oversee and implement the extensive changes envisioned in the law. The Budget includes a $40 million investment to build State and local capacity to track the employment and educational outcomes of WIOA program participants, and give those seeking training meaningful information—including past participants' success in finding jobs—so they can make good choices about which program will best prepare them for the labor market.

Building a System of Apprenticeships. The Budget invests in the proven learn-and-earn strategy of apprenticeship by sustaining the $90 million in grants provided in 2016— a landmark investment—and adding a $2 billion mandatory Apprenticeship Training Fund. These investments would help meet the President's goal to double the number of apprentices across the United States, giving more workers the opportunity to develop job-relevant skills while they are earning a paycheck.

Reconnecting Workers to Jobs. The Administration makes significant investments to reach those who have been left on the sidelines of the economic recovery. The Budget provides $1.5 billion in mandatory funding to States to fund Career Navigators in American Job Centers who will proactively reach out to all people who have been unemployed for approximately six months or more, those who have dropped out of the labor force altogether and people who are only able to find part time work. These Career Navigators would help workers look for a job, identify training options, and access additional supportive services. The Budget also includes almost $190 million in discretionary funding to provide in-person reemployment services to the one-third of Unemployment Insurance (UI) beneficiaries most at risk of exhausting their benefits, as well as all returning veterans who are receiving UI. Evidence suggests these services are a cost-effective strategy that gets workers back into jobs faster with higher wages.

Income Security

Encouraging State Paid Leave Initiatives. The Budget includes $2.2 billion for the Paid Leave Partnership Initiative to assist up to five States that wish to launch paid leave programs, following the example of California, New Jersey, and Rhode Island. States that participate in the Paid Leave Partnership Initiative would be eligible to receive funds for the initial set up and three years of benefits. The Budget also includes funding to help States and localities conduct analysis to inform the development of paid family and medical leave programs. These grants have helped recipients obtain the information they needed to understand how a paid family leave policy could work in their communities.

Strengthen TANF. The Budget (1) increases resources for TANF and ensures that States are also meeting their State funding requirements without using funding gimmicks; (2) requires States to spend a majority of their funds on core purposes of TANF including welfare-to-work efforts, child care, and basic assistance, and ensures all TANF funds are spent on low-income families; (3) calls on Congress to provide States more flexibility to design effective work programs in exchange for holding States accountable for the outcome that really matters—helping parents find jobs; (4) proposes authority to publish a measure or measures related to child poverty in States; and (5) creates a workable countercyclical measure modeled after the effective TANF Emergency Fund created during the Great Recession and utilized by governors of both parties. The Budget also continues a prior proposal to redirect funds in the contingency fund to finance two important innovative approaches to reducing poverty and promoting self-sufficiency—subsidized jobs programs, and two-generation initiatives that seek to improve employment outcomes of parents and developmental and educational outcomes of children.

The Upward Mobility Project. The Budget continues to support the Upward Mobility Project, a place-based initiative that will allow up to 10 communities, States, or a consortium of States and communities more flexibility to use funding from up to four Federal programs for efforts designed to implement and rigorously evaluate promising approaches to helping families achieve self-sufficiency, improving children's education and health outcomes, and revitalizing communities. Projects will have to rely on evidence-based approaches or be designed to test new ideas, and will have a significant evaluation component that will determine whether they meet a set of robust outcomes. The funding streams that States and communities can use in these projects are currently block grants—the Social Services Block Grant, the Community Development Block Grant, the Community Services Block Grant, and the HOME Investment Partnerships Program—that share a common goal of promoting opportunity and reducing poverty, but do not facilitate cross-sector planning and implementation as effectively as they could. The Budget also provides $1.5 billion in additional funding over five years that States and communities can apply for to help support their Upward Mobility Projects.

Promise Zone Initiative. The Budget supports all 20 Promise Zones through intensive, tailored Federal assistance at the local level. The Budget further supports efforts to transform distressed communities by expanding the Department of Education's Promise Neighborhoods program and the Department of Housing and Urban Development (HUD)'s Choice Neighborhoods program. These programs have already provided critical funding for comprehensive and community-driven approaches to improving the educational and life outcomes of residents in over 100 distressed communities. The Budget provides $128 million for Promise Neighborhoods and $200 million for Choice Neighborhoods, an overall increase of $130 million over 2016 enacted levels for the two programs. This additional funding would support implementation grants for approximately 15 new Promise Neighborhoods and six new Choice Neighborhoods, and numerous other planning grants for communities to engage with stakeholders to create plans for future revitalization.

Improving Emergency Aid and Family Connections Grants. The Budget provides $2 billion for robust pilots to test new approaches to providing emergency aid for families facing financial crisis. Building on the promising rapid rehousing approach—a strategy that helps stabilize families' housing and then assists them to become more self-sufficient—these pilots will seek to both prevent families from financial collapse when emergency help is needed, and connect families to services and supports, such as TANF, employment assistance, SNAP, child care, or Medicaid, that can help them find jobs, stabilize their families, and become more financially secure. The pilots will be rigorously evaluated to inform future policy and program decisions at the local, State, and Federal levels.

Improving Mobility with Housing Choice Vouchers. The President proposes $20.9 billion for the Housing Choice Vouchers program in 2017, an increase of $1.2 billion over 2016 enacted, to expand opportunities for very low-income families. This includes $2.1 billion for Public Housing Authorities (PHAs) to ensure they have sufficient resources to promote mobility and greater access to opportunity, as well as cover fundamental functions, such as housing quality inspections and tenant income certifi-

cations. In addition, the Budget proposes $15 million for a mobility counseling grant and evaluation designed to help HUD-assisted families move and stay in higher quality neighborhoods.

Ending Homelessness. The Budget sustains funding to support programs dedicated to ending veteran homelessness, while also providing $11 billion in housing vouchers and rapid rehousing over the next ten years to reach and maintain the goal of ending homelessness among all of America's families in 2020. This significant investment is based on recent rigorous research that found that families who were offered vouchers—compared to alternative forms of homeless assistance—had fewer incidents of homelessness, child separations, intimate partner violence and school moves, less food insecurity, and generally less economic stress. Complementing this mandatory proposal, the Budget provides targeted discretionary increases to address homelessness, including 25,500 new units of permanent, supportive housing to end chronic homelessness, 10,000 new Housing Choice Vouchers targeted to homeless families with children, $25 million to test innovative projects that support homeless youth, and 8,000 new units of rapid re-housing, which provides tailored assistance to help homeless families stabilize in housing and then assists them to become more self-sufficient.

Ensuring Adequate Food for Children Throughout the Year. Rigorous evaluations of Dept of Agriculture pilots have found that providing additional nutrition benefits on debit cards to low-income families with school-aged children during summer months can significantly reduce food insecurity. The Budget invests $12 billion over ten years to create a permanent Summer Electronic Benefits Transfer for Children (SEBTC) program that will provide all families with children eligible for free and reduced price school meals access to supplemental food benefits during the summer months.

Health Care

Medicaid and the Children's Health Insurance Program (CHIP). The Budget gives States the option to streamline eligibility determinations for children in Medicaid and CHIP and to maintain Medicaid coverage for adults by providing one-year of continuous eligibility. The Budget proposes to extend funding for CHIP through 2019, ensuring continued, comprehensive, affordable coverage for these children. The Budget also extends full Medicaid coverage to pregnant and post-partum Medicaid beneficiaries, expands access to preventive benefits and tobacco cessation for adults in Medicaid, streamlines appeals processes, and ensures children in inpatient psychiatric treatment facilities have access to comprehensive benefits. Finally, the Budget fully covers the costs of the Urban Indian Health Program (UIHP) clinics for Medicaid services provided to eligible American Indians and Alaska Natives, supporting the expansion of UIHP service offerings and improving beneficiary care.

Supporting Medicaid Expansion. The Budget provides a further incentive for States to expand Medicaid to serve individuals earning up to 133 percent of the Federal poverty level by covering the full cost of expansion for the first three years a State expands, ensuring equity between States that already expanded and those that do so in the future.

Strengthening Medicaid in Puerto Rico and other U.S. Territories. The Medicaid programs in Puerto Rico and the other U.S. territories of American Samoa, Guam, Northern Mariana Islands, and the U.S. Virgin Islands are fundamentally different from the Medicaid program in the States, leading to a lower standard of care than may be otherwise experienced on the mainland. Medicaid funding in Puerto Rico and the other territories is capped; beneficiaries are offered fewer benefits; and the Federal Government contributes less on a per-capita basis than it does to the rest of the Nation. The ACA increased the Federal match rate and provided $7.3 billion above the territory funding caps between July 1, 2011 and the end of 2019. To avoid a loss in coverage when the supplemental funds provided in the ACA run out and to better align Puerto Rico and other territory Medicaid programs with the mainland, the Budget would remove the cap on Medicaid funding in Puerto Rico and the other territories. It also would gradually increase the Federal support territories receive through the Federal Medicaid match by transitioning them to the same level of Federal support as is received on the mainland, and expand eligibility to 100 percent of the Federal poverty level in territories currently below this level. To be eligible for maximum Federal financial support, territories would have to meet financial management and program integrity requirements and achieve milestones related to providing full Medicaid benefits.

Combating Prescription Drug Abuse and Heroin Use. The Budget takes a two-pronged approach to address this epidemic. First, it includes approximately $500 million to continue and expand current efforts across HHS and the Department of Justice to expand State-level prescription drug overdose prevention strategies, increase the availability of medication-assisted treatment programs, and improve access to the overdose-reversal drug naloxone. A portion of this funding is targeted specifically to rural areas, where rates of overdose and opioid use are particularly high. Second, the Budget includes $1 billion in new mandatory funding over the next two years to boost State efforts to help individuals seek treatment, successfully complete treatment, and sustain recovery. States will receive funds based on the severity of the epidemic and on the strength of their strategy to respond to it. States can use these funds to expand treatment capacity and make services more affordable to those who cannot afford it. This funding will also help expand the addiction treatment workforce through the National Health Service Corps and support the evaluation of treatment services.

Criminal Justice

Community Policing Initiative. The President's Community Policing Initiative aims to build and sustain trust between law enforcement and the people they serve. The Budget provides $97 million to expand training and oversight for local law enforcement, increase the use of body-worn cameras, provide additional opportunities for police department reform, and facilitate community and law enforcement engagement in 10 pilot sites, with additional technical assistance and training for dozens of communities and police departments across the Nation.

Incentivizing Justice Reform. The Administration continues to support criminal justice reform that simultaneously enhances public safety, avoids excessive punishment and unnecessary incarceration, and builds trust between the justice system and the community. The Budget provides $500 million per year over 10 years— a $5 billion investment—for a new 21st Century Justice Initiative. The program will focus on achieving three objectives: reducing violent crime, reversing practices that have led to unnecessarily long sentences and unnecessary incarceration, and building community trust. Specifically, States would focus on one or more opportunities for reform in both the adult and juvenile systems, including: examining and changing State laws and policies that contribute to unnecessarily long sentences and unnecessary incarceration, without sacrificing public safety; promoting critical advancements in community-oriented policing; and providing comprehensive front-end and re-entry services.

OTHER SOURCES OF INFORMATION ON FEDERAL GRANTS-IN-AID

A number of other sources provide State-by-State spending data and other information on Federal grants, but may use a broader definition of grants beyond what is included in this chapter.

The website *Grants.gov* is a primary source of information for communities wishing to apply for grants and other domestic assistance. *Grants.gov* hosts all open notices of opportunities to apply for Federal grants.

The *Catalog of Federal Domestic Assistance* hosted by the General Services Administration contains detailed listings of grant and other assistance programs; discussions of eligibility criteria, application procedures, and estimated obligations; and related information. The *Catalog* is available on the Internet at *www.cfda.gov*.

Current and updated grant receipt information by State and local governments and other non-Federal entities can be found on *USASpending.gov*. This public website also contains contract and loan information and is updated twice per month. Additionally, information about grants provided specifically by the Recovery Act can be found on *Recovery.gov*.

The Federal Audit Clearinghouse maintains an on-line database *(harvester.census.gov/sac)* that provides access to summary information about audits conducted under OMB Circular A–133, "Audits to States, Local Governments, and Non-Profit Organizations." Information is available for each audited entity, including the amount of Federal money expended by program and whether there were audit findings.

The Bureau of Economic Analysis, in the Department of Commerce, produces the monthly *Survey of Current Business*, which provides data on the national income and product accounts (NIPA), a broad statistical concept encompassing the entire economy. These accounts, which are available at *bea.gov / national*, include data on Federal grants to State and local governments.

In addition, information on grants and awards can be found through individual Federal agencies web sites:

- USDA Current Research Information System, http://cris.csrees.usda.gov/

- DOD Medical Research Programs, http://cdmrp.army.mil/search.aspx

- DOD Small Business Innovation Research (SBIR) and Small Business Technology Transfer (STTR) programs, http://www.dodsbir.net/awards/Default.asp

- Department of Education, Institute of Education Sciences, Funded Research Grants and Contracts, http://ies.ed.gov/funding/grantsearch/index.asp

- HHS Tracking Accountability in Government Grants System (TAGGS), http://taggs.hhs.gov/AdvancedSearch.cfm

- National Institutes of Health (NIH) Research Portfolio Online Reporting Tools RePORTER, http://projectreporter.nih.gov/reporter.cfm

- DOJ Office of Justice Programs (OJP), OJP Grant Awards and OJP Award Data by Location, http://grants.ojp.usdoj.gov:85/selector/main and http://ojp.gov/funding/Explore/OJPAwardData.htm

- Department of Labor Employment and Training Administration (ETA), Grants Awarded, http://www.doleta.gov/grants/grants_awarded.cfm

- Environmental Protection Agency (EPA), Integrated Grants Management System (IGMS), http://www.epa.gov/enviro/facts/igms/index.html

- Institute of Museum and Library Services (IMLS), http://www.imls.gov/recipients/grantsearch.aspx

- National Endowment for the Arts (NEA), Grant Search, https://apps.nea.gov/grantsearch/

- National Endowment for the Humanities (NEH) Funded Projects, https://securegrants.neh.gov/publicquery/main.aspx

- National Library of Medicine (NLM), Health Services Research Projects in Progress (HSRProj), http://wwwcf.nlm.nih.gov/hsr_project/home_proj.cfm

- National Science Foundation (NSF) Awards, http://www.nsf.gov/awardsearch/

- Small Business Innovation Research (SBIR) and Small Business Technology Transfer (STTR) Awards, https://www.sbir.gov/sbirsearch/award/all

APPENDIX: SELECTED GRANT DATA BY STATE

The Appendix includes two tables that summarize State-by-State spending for select grant programs to State and local governments. The first summary table, "Summary of Programs by Agency, Bureau, and Program," shows obligations for each program by agency and bureau. The second summary table, "Summary of Grant Programs by State," shows total obligations across all programs for each State. The programs selected here cover more than 90 percent of total grant spending.

Individual program tables with State-by-State obligation data may be found on the OMB web site at *www.budget.gov / budget / Analytical_Perspectives* and on the Budget CD-ROM. The individual program tables display obligations for each program on a State-by-State basis, consistent with the estimates in this Budget. Each table reports the following information:

- The Federal agency that administers the program.

- The program title and number as contained in the

Catalog of Federal Domestic Assistance.

- The Treasury budget account number from which the program is funded.

- Actual 2015 obligations for States, Federal territories, or Indian Tribes in thousands of dollars. Undistributed obligations are generally project funds that are not distributed by formula, or programs for which State-by-State data are not available.

- Obligations in 2016 from balances of previous budget authority and obligations in 2016 from new budget authority distributed by State.

- Estimates of 2017 obligations by State, which are based on the 2017 Budget request, unless otherwise noted.

- The percentage share of 2017 estimated program funds distributed to each State.

Table 15–3. SUMMARY OF PROGRAMS BY AGENCY, BUREAU, AND PROGRAM

(Obligations in millions of dollars)

Agency, Bureau, and Program	FY 2015 (actual)	Estimated FY2016 obligations from:			FY 2017 (estimated)
		Previous authority	New authority	Total	
Department of Agriculture, Food and Nutrition Service					
School Breakfast Program (10.553)	4,057	....	4,339	4,339	4,486
National School Lunch Program (10.555)	11,929	374	12,155	12,528	13,032
Special Supplemental Nutrition Program for Women, Infants, and Children (WIC) (10.557)	6,676	851	6,260	7,111	6,801
Child and Adult Care Food Program (10.558)	3,350	....	3,340	3,340	3,446
State Administrative Matching Grants for the Supplemental Nutrition Assistance Program (Food Stamps) (10.561)	4,730	9	5,076	5,085	5,228
Department of Education, Office of Elementary and Secondary Education					
Title I Grants to Local Educational Agencies (84.010)	14,410	....	14,910	14,910	15,360
Supporting Effective Instruction State Grants (formerly Improving Teacher Quality State Grants) (84.367)	2,350	....	2,350	2,350	2,250
Department of Education, Office of Special Education and Rehabilitative Services					
Special Education-Grants to States (84.027)	11,498	....	11,913	11,913	11,913
Vocational Rehabilitation Grants (84.126)	3,092	....	3,161	3,161	3,399
Department of Health and Human Services, Centers for Medicare and Medicaid Services					
Affordable Insurance Exchange Grants (93.525)	449	....	....	....	....
Children's Health Insurance Program (93.767)	11,286	....	13,499	13,499	15,901
Grants to States for Medicaid (93.778)	378,897	....	369,621	369,621	378,553
Department of Health and Human Services, Administration for Children and Families					
Temporary Assistance for Needy Families (TANF)-Family Assistance Grants (93.558)	16,562	....	16,562	16,562	17,312
Child Support Enforcement-Federal Share of State and Local Administrative Costs and Incentives (93.563)	4,288	....	4,260	4,260	4,511
Low Income Home Energy Assistance Program (93.568)	3,395	....	3,390	3,390	3,000
Child Care and Development Block Grant (93.575)	2,435	....	2,761	2,761	2,962
Child Care and Development Fund-Mandatory (93.596A)	1,236	....	1,254	1,254	1,348
Child Care and Development Fund-Matching (93.596B)	1,681	....	1,663	1,663	5,234
Head Start (93.600)	8,098	....	8,533	8,533	8,957
Foster Care-Title IV-E (93.658)	4,669	....	4,800	4,800	5,293
Adoption Assistance (93.659)	2,473	....	2,674	2,674	2,780
Social Services Block Grant (93.667)	1,576	....	1,584	1,584	2,000
Department of Health and Human Services, Health Resources and Services Administration					
Ryan White HIV/AIDS Treatment Modernization Act-Part B HIV Care Grants (93.917)	1,288	....	1,315	1,315	1,315
Department of Homeland Security, Federal Emergency Management Agency					
FEMA State and Local Programs (97.067 et al)	2,287	....	2,307	2,307	1,877
Department of Housing and Urban Development, Public and Indian Housing Programs					
Public Housing Operating Fund (14.850)	4,398	....	4,500	4,500	4,569
Section 8 Housing Choice Vouchers (14.871)	19,333	251	19,665	19,916	20,955
Public Housing Capital Fund (14.872)	1,870	96	1,808	1,904	1,860
Department of Housing and Urban Development, Community Planning and Development					
Community Development Block Grant (14.218; 14.225; 14.228; 14.862)	2,675	915	2,723	3,638	2,890
Community Development Block Grant - Disaster Recovery (14.218; 14.228; 14.269)	3,529	4,592	299	4,891	3,529
Department of Labor, Employment and Training Administration					
Unemployment Insurance (17.225)	2,771	....	2,746	2,746	2,778
Department of Transportation, Federal Transit Administration					
Transit Formula Grants Programs (20.507)	9,241	6,219	4,767	10,987	15,176
Department of Transportation, Federal Aviation Administration					
Airport Improvement Program (20.106)	3,071	....	3,192	3,192	2,739
Department of Transportation, Federal Highway Administration					
Highway Planning and Construction (20.205)	38,616	....	43,421	43,421	51,645
Environmental Protection Agency, Office of Water					
Capitalization Grants for Clean Water State Revolving Fund (66.458)	1,438	42	1,352	1,394	980
Capitalization Grants for Drinking Water State Revolving Fund (66.468)	907	26	837	863	1,021
Federal Communications Commission					
Universal Service Fund E-Rate	1,675	....	2,518	2,518	3,076
Total	592,234	13,376	585,555	598,931	628,174

Table 15–4. SUMMARY OF PROGRAMS BY STATE

(Obligations in millions of dollars)

State or Territory	FY 2015 (actual)	Estimated FY 2016 obligations from: Previous authority	New authority	Total	FY 2017 (estimated)	FY 2017 Percentage of distributed total
Alabama	6,902	93	7,389	7,482	7,653	1.26
Alaska	1,968	47	2,315	2,362	2,357	0.39
Arizona	11,617	84	12,444	12,528	13,237	2.18
Arkansas	6,583	31	7,331	7,362	7,433	1.22
California	84,267	1,211	82,866	84,077	82,674	13.61
Colorado	7,356	208	7,884	8,092	8,391	1.38
Connecticut	6,963	139	6,994	7,133	7,353	1.21
Delaware	1,889	17	2,024	2,041	2,135	0.35
District of Columbia	3,790	629	3,516	4,144	4,332	0.71
Florida	22,861	497	23,472	23,969	25,302	4.16
Georgia	12,910	196	12,804	13,000	13,259	2.18
Hawaii	2,292	46	2,523	2,568	2,622	0.43
Idaho	2,251	24	2,312	2,336	2,477	0.41
Illinois	19,330	479	17,081	17,560	18,867	3.11
Indiana	10,404	103	13,032	13,135	12,838	2.11
Iowa	4,831	40	5,085	5,125	5,402	0.89
Kansas	3,378	34	3,671	3,705	3,795	0.62
Kentucky	10,655	66	11,493	11,559	11,902	1.96
Louisiana	8,561	175	8,990	9,166	9,368	1.54
Maine	2,553	20	2,612	2,633	2,704	0.45
Maryland	9,487	179	9,677	9,856	10,453	1.72
Massachusetts	14,107	248	15,073	15,321	14,994	2.47
Michigan	17,977	181	19,589	19,770	19,339	3.18
Minnesota	9,678	110	10,002	10,112	10,546	1.74
Mississippi	6,249	40	6,526	6,565	6,747	1.11
Missouri	9,873	155	10,281	10,437	10,678	1.76
Montana	1,812	23	1,792	1,815	1,876	0.31
Nebraska	2,190	34	2,184	2,218	2,286	0.38
Nevada	3,913	55	4,110	4,165	4,130	0.68
New Hampshire	1,781	17	1,987	2,004	2,058	0.34
New Jersey	16,387	1,165	15,120	16,285	16,732	2.75
New Mexico	5,486	47	6,189	6,235	6,340	1.04
New York	52,413	3,866	55,239	59,105	59,061	9.72
North Carolina	14,373	190	14,899	15,089	16,175	2.66
North Dakota	1,039	17	1,702	1,719	1,717	0.28
Ohio	22,643	188	23,376	23,565	24,971	4.11
Oklahoma	5,626	110	5,840	5,950	5,973	0.98
Oregon	9,123	114	10,341	10,455	10,817	1.78
Pennsylvania	21,586	406	25,966	26,372	26,025	4.28
Rhode Island	2,595	47	2,748	2,795	2,851	0.47
South Carolina	6,868	46	7,232	7,278	7,706	1.27
South Dakota	1,223	16	1,237	1,253	1,337	0.22
Tennessee	9,868	92	10,795	10,887	11,287	1.86
Texas	36,918	501	39,143	39,645	40,239	6.62
Utah	3,064	59	3,350	3,409	3,583	0.59
Vermont	1,669	22	1,877	1,899	1,860	0.31
Virginia	8,473	175	8,788	8,963	9,341	1.54
Washington	11,277	192	13,359	13,551	14,091	2.32
West Virginia	4,374	23	4,680	4,703	4,475	0.74
Wisconsin	8,078	62	8,459	8,521	8,731	1.44
Wyoming	875	10	893	903	913	0.15
American Samoa	75	3	72	75	82	0.01
Guam	231	6	251	257	267	0.04
Northern Mariana Islands	100	2	123	125	139	0.02
Puerto Rico	4,105	85	4,133	4,218	4,186	0.69
Freely Associated States	46	....	38	38	37	0.01

Table 15–4. SUMMARY OF PROGRAMS BY STATE—Continued

(Obligations in millions of dollars)

State or Territory	All programs distributed in all years by state					FY 2017 Percentage of distributed total
	FY 2015 (actual)	Estimated FY 2016 obligations from:			FY 2017 (estimated)	
		Previous authority	New authority	Total		
Virgin Islands	172	4	185	189	182	0.03
Indian Tribes	960	78	1,068	1,146	1,237	0.20
Total, programs distributed by State in all years	**558,071**	**12,708**	**584,156**	**596,864**	**607,506**	**100.00**
MEMORANDUM:						
Not distributed by State in all years [1]	34,163	688	1,399	2,066	20,667	N/A
Total, including undistributed	592,234	13,376	585,555	598,931	628,174	N/A

[1] The sum of programs not distributed by State in all years.

16. STRENGTHENING FEDERAL STATISTICS

The ability of governments, businesses, and the general public to make informed choices about budgets, employment, investments, taxes, and a host of other important matters depends critically on the ready and equitable availability of relevant, accurate, timely, and objective Federal statistics. Taken together, the data produced by the decentralized Federal statistical system form a robust evidence base to support both public and private decision-making.

Federal statistical programs have been a cornerstone of this evidence base for many decades, producing fundamental information to illuminate public and private decisions on a range of topics, including the economy, the population, the environment, agriculture, crime, education, energy, health, science, and transportation. These statistics are used in part to describe and increase understanding of the basic condition and performance of our economy and society, as discussed in Chapter 5, "Social Indicators."

The share of budget resources devoted to supporting Federal statistics is relatively modest—about 0.04 percent of GDP in non-decennial census years and roughly double that in decennial census years. This funding is leveraged to inform crucial decisions in a wide variety of spheres. The Administration is committed to continuing cost-effective investment in Federal statistical programs in order to build and support agencies' capacity to incorporate evidence and evaluation analyses into budget, management, and policy decisions. For example, this budget proposes strategic investments to strengthen the Federal statistical infrastructure for acquiring, linking, and curating administrative and other alternative datasets, and to make those datasets available to additional Federal and academic researchers through the Federal Statistical Research Data Center program. It also highlights emerging efforts to harness and inform sound statistical practice for "big data" and "big data" analytics.

The Federal statistical community has leveraged a number of other opportunities to improve these measures of our Nation's performance and strengthen our Federal evidence base. For example, during 2015 and 2016, Federal statistical agencies:

- published, for the first time, information on changes in the prices of treating different diseases, laying the groundwork to improve the measurement of health care spending in the U.S. economy *(Bureau of Economic Analysis);*

- issued newly developed crime victimization rates for the 50 States and select large counties covering 1999 to 2013 that required almost no additional data collection, but instead were derived from statistical

models that used national survey and other auxiliary data for violent and property crimes as well as for intimate partner and domestic violence incidents *(Bureau of Justice Statistics);*

- introduced experimental disease-based price indexes to provide alternative estimates of inflation for medical output and consumption using price data from both the Producer Price Index and the Consumer Price Index programs along with quantity data from the Department of Health and Human Services' Medical Expenditure Panel Survey in order to provide data users additional ongoing insight into the evolution of the Nation's healthcare system *(Bureau of Labor Statistics);*

- initiated development of a port performance freight statistics program of the Nation's ports to provide timely and nationally consistent measures of performance in terms of capacity and throughput for the Nation's top 25 ports by tonnage, intermodal container volume, and dry bulk *(Bureau of Transportation Statistics);*

- identified, researched, and tested four major cost saving innovations (i.e., reengineering address canvassing, optimizing self-response, utilizing administrative records and third-party data, and reengineering field operations) that have the potential to save approximately $5.2 billion in the 2020 Census compared with repeating the 2010 Census design *(Census Bureau);*

- began the regular release of quarterly Gross Domestic Product by State data, presenting businesses and policy-makers with a more detailed and timely picture of economic activity at the State level *(Bureau of Economic Analysis);*

- expanded the use of billions of observations of proprietary household and retail scanner data to provide unique detailed insights into consumer food purchase behaviors and nutrition-related policy, program, and regulatory impacts and combined them with other multifaceted data products to enhance the depth of nutrition data offerings, facilitating research into the food choices, nutrition, and health of Americans *(Economic Research Service);*

- initiated monthly State-level estimates of small-scale distributed solar photovoltaic (PV) arrays, including rooftop generation, based on a blend of survey, administrative, and third-party data sources to provide the public, government, and industry with the ability to track where and by how much small-scale distributed PV generation contributes to the

Nation's electricity supply (*Energy Information Administration*);

- released a comprehensive set of statistics on land tenure for the first time in 15 years, including information on whether land owners either operate the land they own or rent it out to others as well as projected the future outlook of land transition to help estimate new or expanding farming operations (*National Agricultural Statistics Service*);

- released more than 1,500 data products from the 2012 Economic Census covering the economic activity of more than 1,000 industries and providing detailed industry statistics by geographic area and enhanced the Longitudinal Business Database to provide more information about business innovation and entrepreneurship to the public (Census Bureau);

- administered the first nationally representative large-scale high school senior assessment in advanced mathematics and physics in two decades, TIMSS Advanced (TIMSS is the Trends in International Mathematics and Science Study), to measure the college and career-readiness of our "top" students compared with their peers in other countries (*National Center for Education Statistics*);

- redesigned Science and Engineering Indicators 2016, a primary source of evidence supporting the National Science Board and other decision-makers, into a fully digital document supporting interactive graphics, enhanced navigation, and increased accessibility to its data sources (*National Center for Science and Engineering Statistics*);

- implemented methodological improvements for existing geographic administrative population-based data that expand the population of included tax returns and provide an enhanced year-to-year matching process (*Statistics of Income Division, Internal Revenue Service*); and

- published data from a new survey on how much foreign investors are spending to acquire, establish, or expand U.S. businesses, providing additional insight into the impact of foreign direct investment in the United States (*Bureau of Economic Analysis*).

In order for Federal statistical products to be beneficial to their wide range of users, the underlying data systems that produce them must be credible. To foster this credibility, Federal statistical programs seek to adhere to high quality standards and to maintain integrity, transparency, and efficiency in the production and curation of data. As the collectors and providers of these basic statistics, the responsible Federal statistical agencies act as data stewards—balancing public information demands and decision-makers' needs for information with legal and ethical obligations to minimize reporting burden, respect respondents' privacy, and protect the confidentiality of the data provided to the Government. To reinforce the fundamental responsibilities that Federal statistical agencies

have related to the collection, analysis, and dissemination of data, the Office of Management and Budget (OMB) has affirmed and codified them by issuing OMB Statistical Policy Directive No. 1, *Fundamental Responsibilities of Federal Statistical Agencies and Recognized Statistical Units*.[1] The Administration remains committed to these principles, as agencies work to codify them within their own policies and practices. By unlocking the power of Government data to improve the quality of information available to the American people, the Federal statistical system fosters the Nation's long-term global competitiveness while maximizing the cost-effective use of resources for the provision of Federal statistics within a constrained fiscal environment. The remainder of this chapter presents highlights of principal statistical agencies' 2017 program budget proposals.

Highlights of 2017 Program Budget Proposals

The programs that provide essential statistical information for use by governments, businesses, researchers, and the public are carried out by agencies spread across every department and several independent agencies. Excluding cyclical funding for the decennial census, approximately 40 percent of the total budget for these programs provides resources for 13 agencies or units that have statistical activities as their principal mission (see Table 16–1). The remaining funding supports work in approximately 115 agencies or units that carry out statistical activities in conjunction with other missions such as providing services, conducting research, or implementing regulations. More comprehensive budget and program information about the Federal statistical system, including its core programs, will be available in OMB's annual report, *Statistical Programs of the United States Government, Fiscal Year 2017*, when it is published later this year. The following highlights the Administration's proposals for the programs of the principal Federal statistical agencies, giving particular attention to new initiatives and to other program changes.

Bureau of Economic Analysis (BEA), Department of Commerce: Funding is requested to provide support for ongoing BEA programs and to: (1) expand the scope of geographic information available from BEA's economic accounts, including developing new statistics on gross domestic product (GDP) by county and creating a Regional Economic Dashboard that will allow users to quickly access, manipulate, and extract information on the performance of local economies across the United States; and (2) improve the measures of GDP and other key BEA statistics by incorporating expanded and accelerated economic indicators to foster economic growth by providing users with more timely and accurate information to drive decisions on investment and job creation.

Bureau of Justice Statistics (BJS), Department of Justice: Funding is requested to provide support for ongoing BJS programs and to: (1) continue to improve BJS'

---

[1] OMB Statistical Policy Directive No. 1: Fundamental Responsibilities of Federal Statistical Agencies and Recognized Statistical Units. *http://www.gpo.gov/fdsys/pkg/FR-2014-12-02/pdf/2014-28326.pdf*.

criminal victimization statistics derived from the National Crime Victimization Survey with special emphasis on generating sub-national estimates and enhancing data on rape and sexual assault; (2) increase the use of administrative records data in police and correctional agencies to provide new statistics on topics such as recidivism, arrests, and offenses known to the police; (3) expand the use of "open source" information to foster the production of statistics on police use of force; (4) expand surveys of inmates of prisons and jails to inform the process of re-entry and support the linking of survey data with criminal history administrative records; (5) improve the availability of justice statistics for Indian country; and (6) continue to support the enhancement of criminal justice statistics available through State statistical analysis centers.

Bureau of Labor Statistics (BLS), Department of Labor: Funding is requested to provide support for ongoing BLS programs and to: (1) add an annual supplement to the Current Population Survey, capturing data on contingent work and alternative work arrangements biennially, with data on other topics collected in the intervening years; (2) fund the first year of activities for a survey of employer-provided training; and (3) support the Census Bureau in the development of a statistical supplemental poverty measure using Consumer Expenditure Survey data.

Bureau of Transportation Statistics (BTS), Department of Transportation: Funding is requested to support ongoing BTS programs and to: (1) estimate the inventory and use of motor vehicles; (2) improve methods and data for calculating the value of transportation infrastructure and services; and (3) implement a port performance freight statistics program.

Census Bureau, Department of Commerce: Funding is requested to provide continued support for ongoing Census Bureau programs and to: (1) build operations and systems for a reengineered 2020 Census that has the potential to save over $5 billion, including field-testing a suite of integrated operations and systems to collect and process data for over 120 million housing units, finalize methodologies for key design areas and most census operations, and complete the development of interoperable production systems for an end-to-end test in 2018; (2) move to 100 percent Internet response to increase the efficiency of the 2017 Economic Census; (3) continue research into in-office geographic imagery to inform decisions about areas of the country where in-field address canvassing operations are required; (4) support the third year of the Census Enterprise Data Collection and Processing Initiative and deliver scheduled systems into production in support of the 2017 Economic Census and the Company Organization Survey/Annual Survey of Manufactures; and (5) collaborate in a joint venture with BEA to accelerate and improve the quality of economic indicators by integrating multifaceted approaches to increase the accuracy and timeliness of a substantial number of key economic indicators.

Economic Research Service (ERS), Department of Agriculture: Funding is requested to provide support for ongoing ERS programs and to: (1) conduct a second round of USDA's National Household Food Purchase and Acquisition Survey, including representative populations of participants in Women, Infant and Children (WIC) and school meal programs; (2) analyze barriers to entry for beginning farmers and ranchers that will examine differences in demographic characteristics of new farmers and ranchers, including the socially disadvantaged, women, and veterans; and (3) analyze drought resilience issues in the agricultural sector.

Energy Information Administration (EIA), Department of Energy: Funding is requested to enable EIA to continue its core programs and to: (1) revamp petroleum data and analysis to provide more regional detail; (2) improve renewable generation information; (3) provide timely international analyses, including petroleum trade estimates related to Canada-Mexico collaboration; (4) collect transportation energy consumption data; and (5) enhance commercial building energy efficiency data.

National Agricultural Statistics Service (NASS), Department of Agriculture: Funding is requested to provide support for ongoing NASS programs and to: (1) collect data on new and beginning farmers in order to gauge the effectiveness of programs implemented by USDA; (2) conduct new surveys on hogs, cattle and poultry to support the President's National Strategy for Combating Antimicrobial Resistant Bacteria (CARB); (3) expand geospatial research to augment current satellite-based agriculture statistics monitoring, extend current monitoring capabilities of CropScape and VegScape, and enrich the evaluation of climate change effects at the local level on crop production; (4) conduct a special study on farm structure to better reflect the changing face of agriculture, especially including women, new farmers, and veterans; (5) continue preparations for the 2017 Census of Agriculture; and (6) maintain the annual Census of Agriculture Current Agriculture Industrial Reports.

National Center for Education Statistics (NCES), Department of Education: Funding is requested to provide support for NCES ongoing activities and to: (1) support the conduct of a new round of the Early Childhood Longitudinal Study -- Birth cohort, and U.S. participation in the International Early Learning Assessment, which will allow policymakers to better understand the range of outcomes for children in early childhood education; (2) collect selected National Postsecondary Student Aid Survey data every two years instead of every four years to provide more timely data on educational costs, financial aid, enrollment, and student progress and fresh information on student loan borrower behavior and choices through a new study on college loan performance; (3) support full U.S. participation in the next Teaching and Learning International Survey (TALIS), including the TALIS video study to provide the only internationally comparable data on the behavior of teachers in the classroom since 1999; (4) support NCES contributions to the My Brother's Keeper initiative; and (5) support new awards to States under the Statewide Longitudinal Data Systems program to advance their use of data to improve education and information policy and enhance data coordination, quality, and use at the national, State, and local levels.

National Center for Health Statistics (NCHS), Department of Health and Human Services: Funding is requested to provide support for ongoing NCHS programs and to: 1) continue the expansion and upgrading of electronic death reporting to provide faster access to data on prescription drug overdose deaths and other deaths significant for public health, such as the Vital Statistics Rapid Release program initiated in 2015; 2) further reduce the turnaround time associated with research access to NCHS-compiled birth and death data, including for tracking priority initiatives in prevention and teenage pregnancy, such as the NCHS Data Visualization Gallery with national and State trends on teen births; 3) enhance the quality and usability of health data through improved access and presentation methods; 4) test and implement modules to the National Health and Nutrition Examination Survey to address the growing need for information on infectious diseases and chronic health conditions; 5) incorporate electronic health record information into the family of health care provider surveys following the inclusion of NCHS in the Final Rule for Stage 3 of the Electronic Health Record Incentive Programs (Meaningful Use); 6) launch a new, more efficient sample for the National Health Interview Survey that incorporates information on changing population demographics from the Decennial Census; and 7) update the content and structure of the National Health Interview Survey to harmonize with other Federal health surveys, improve measurement of covered health topics, and incorporate advances in survey methodology and measurement.

National Center for Science and Engineering Statistics (NCSES), National Science Foundation: Funding is requested to provide support for ongoing NCSES programs and to: (1) continue the development of enhanced data access tools, techniques, and visualizations, including integration of the Scientists and Engineers Data System (SESTAT) with the Integrated Science and Engineering Resources Data System (WebCASPAR) and the NSF Survey of Earned Doctorates Tabulation Engine databases; (2) improve survey instruments and data collection techniques to enhance measures of innovation and address data gaps related to educational and career pathways of scientists and engineers, and research activities in non-profit organizations; and (3) provide support for research and education grants under the NCSES Research on Science and Technology Enterprise: Statistics and Surveys program.

Office of Research, Evaluation, and Statistics (ORES), Social Security Administration: Funding is requested to provide support for ongoing ORES programs and to continue to: (1) support outside survey and linkage of SSA administrative data to surveys; (2) complete data collection, produce data files, and provide SSA with data from the redesigned Survey of Income and Program Participation to address Social Security's data needs for microsimulation models, program evaluation, and analysis; (3) provide enhanced statistical and analytical support for initiatives to improve Social Security and other government agency programs; (4) fund the three centers of SSA's Retirement Research Consortium; and (5) fund the two centers of SSA's Disability/Research Consortium.

Statistics of Income Division (SOI), Internal Revenue Service, Department of the Treasury: Funding is requested to provide support for ongoing SOI programs and to: (1) provide opportunities to study the impacts of tax law and economic changes on tax administration by further integrating existing administrative data with edited data to allow for improved data linkages across sectors, while reducing cost and improving timeliness by streamlining data processing, thus reducing the number of, or eliminating the need for, fields to be transcribed; (2) implement recommended sample improvements to expand population coverage and improve estimation; (3) complete statistical tables and analysis on complex corporations and new data provided in compliance with the Foreign Account Tax Compliance Act and the Affordable Care Act; (4) support innovative research with the potential to improve tax administration by working with experts within and outside Government; (5) complete an extensive reprogramming of all SOI studies using modernized software and continue to upgrade SOI's information technology infrastructure and deploy virtualization throughout the agency to improve security and reduce costs; and (6) continue to modernize data dissemination practices, developing more web-based products and data visualizations and conducting social media outreach to increase the public's awareness and understanding of the tax system.

Table 16–1.   2015-2017 BUDGET AUTHORITY FOR PRINCIPAL STATISTICAL AGENCIES[1]

(In millions of dollars)

	Actual	Estimate	
	2015	2016	2017
Bureau of Economic Analysis	96	105	111
Bureau of Justice Statistics[2]	66	52	67
Bureau of Labor Statistics	592	609	641
Bureau of Transportation Statistics	26	26	26
Census Bureau[3]	1113	1397	1660
Salaries and Expenses/Current Surveys and Programs[3]	295	299	314
Periodic Censuses and Programs	818	1098	1346
Economic Research Service	85	85	91
Energy Information Administration	117	122	131
National Agricultural Statistics Service[4]	172	168	177
National Center for Education Statistics[5]	256	282	296
Statistics[5]	116	125	139
Assessment	132	149	149
National Assessment Governing Board	8	8	8
National Center for Health Statistics	155[6]	160	160
National Center for Science and Engineering Statistics, NSF[7]	58	58	60
Office of Research, Evaluation, and Statistics, SSA	29	26	27
Statistics of Income Division, IRS	37	38	38

[1]Reflects any rescissions and sequestration.

[2]Includes directly appropriated funds as well as funds transferred to BJS for research and statistical services; minus assessments for management and administrative (M&A) costs, and known rescissions.

[3]Salaries and Expenses/Current Surveys and Programs funds include discretionary and mandatory funds. FY15 Actuals are displayed in the prior FY15 budget structure; FY16 is the start of the new FY16 budget structure.

[4]Includes funds for the periodic Census of Agriculture of $48, $42, and $42 million in 2015, 2016, and 2017, respectively.

[5]Includes funds for salaries and expenses of $13, $13, and $14 million in 2015, 2016, and 2017, respectively, that are displayed in the Budget *Appendix* under the Institute of Education Sciences (IES). In addition, NCES manages the IES grant program for the State Longitudinal Data System which is funded at $35 million, $35 million, and $81 million in 2015, 2016, and 2017, respectively, and the EDFacts Initiativewhich is funded at $11 million in 2015, 2016, and 2017.

[6] All funds from Budget Authority. Amounts include funds to implement the CDC Working Capital Fund.

[7]Includes funds for salaries and expenses of $7.6, $7.7, and $7.8 million in 2015, 2016, and 2017, respectively.

17. INFORMATION TECHNOLOGY

With the radical evolution of technology, the Federal Government has an unprecedented opportunity to accelerate the quality, timeliness, and security of services delivered to the public. In recent years, agency adoption of emerging technologies has had a dramatic impact in efficiency. For example, the United States Digital Service (USDS) supported the United States Citizenship and Immigration Services (USCIS) transition to electronic filings to renew or replace green cards and pay certain immigration fees. Closing down the legacy Electronic Immigration System (ELIS) will save the Department of Homeland Security $33 million a year in ongoing operations, maintenance, and licensing costs. The newly launched myUSCIS makes it easier for users to access information about the immigration process and services. In addition, over the past year major policy milestones were accomplished with the release of government-wide Federal Information Technology Acquisition Reform Act (FITARA) implementation guidance and the launch of the Cybersecurity Strategy Implementation Plan (CSIP) – a sweeping series of actions to continue enhancing the management of information technology (IT) resources and strengthening Federal civilian cybersecurity. The Administration will continue to integrate modern solutions to enhance mission and service delivery by prioritizing four core objectives across the Federal IT portfolio: (1) driving value in Federal IT investments, (2) delivering world-class digital services, to include opening Government data to fuel innovation, (3) protecting Federal IT assets and information, and (4) developing the next generation IT workforce. Highlights of activities and initiatives undertaken to advance these objectives are provided in the Government of the Future chapter in the Budget volume, and in additional detail below.

DRIVING VALUE IN FEDERAL IT INVESTMENTS

Federal Spending on IT—Through a combination of policy guidance and oversight, this Administration has optimized IT spending to save taxpayers money by driving value and cost savings in Federal IT investments, and by delivering better services to American citizens. As shown in Table 17-1, the Budget's total planned spending on IT

Table 17–1.   FEDERAL IT SPENDING
(Millions of dollars)

	2015	2016	2017
Department of Defense	36,727	37,987	38,551
Non-Defense	49,965	50,726	51,300
Total	86,692	88,712	89,850

Note: Defense IT spending includes estimates for IT investments for which details are classified and not reflected on the IT Dashboard. All spending estimates reflect data available as of January 19, 2016.

in 2017 is estimated to be $89.9 billion.[1] Chart 17-1 depicts how 7.1 percent annual growth in IT spending over 2001-2009 has been slowed to 1.8 percent annually for 2009-2017, due in part to the Administration's achievements in improving the efficiency of how funds are spent on IT.

Focusing Agency IT Oversight on Comprehensive IT Portfolio Reviews—In 2016 and 2017, the Administration will continue to manage Federal IT through the application of PortfolioStat—data driven reviews of agency IT portfolios led by the Office of Management and Budget's (OMB) Office of E-Government and Information Technology (E-Gov). These reviews have evolved each year to ensure Federal IT policy goals are aligned with agency IT portfolios. In addition to assisting agencies with financial savings through reform efforts, PortfolioStat analyzes agency IT investments by using a variety of performance metrics, including whether agencies are delivering their IT investments on budget and on schedule, the use of innovation to meet customer needs, and the protection of Federal data and systems. As part of its ongoing commitment to transparency, the Administration has updated PortfolioStat performance metrics publicly on the IT Dashboard throughout FY 2015, and for the first time will publish continuously updated agency-specific cost savings information.

OMB requires that agency Chief Information Officers (CIOs) rate all major IT investments reflected on the IT Dashboard on a continuous basis and assess how risks for major development efforts are being addressed and mitigated. The IT Dashboard shows continued improvements in the general health of IT investments across government, as denoted by the increased proportion of CIO-rated "Green" investments on the IT Dashboard, which comprised 77 percent of all rated investments in January 2016 compared to 69 percent in 2012 (assessments based on total life cycle of investments).

Implementing FITARA—On December 19, 2014, the President signed FITARA[2], the most comprehensive IT reform law in almost two decades. To aid in government-wide implementation, the Administration released the policy M-15-14: *Management and Oversight of Information Technology*[3] in June. This guidance took major steps toward ensuring agency CIOs have significant involvement in procurement, workforce, and technology-related budget matters. The guidance provides direction on the CIOs' and other Senior Agency Officials' roles and responsibili-

---

[1] Based on agencies represented on the IT Dashboard, located at: *http://itdashboard.gov*.

[2] See *http://www.gpo.gov/fdsys/pkg/CPRT-113HPRT91496/pdf/CPRT-113HPRT91496.pdf*, page 355.

[3] See *https://www.whitehouse.gov/sites/default/files/omb/memoranda/2015/m-15-14.pdf*

ties for the management of IT and creates a foundation for lasting partnerships among agency leadership including CIOs, CFOs, CAOs[4] and program leaders to make technology decisions that best support agency missions. It also positions CIOs so that they can be held accountable for how effectively agencies manage the full lifecycle of IT products and services and use modern digital approaches, including agile development, to achieve the objectives of efficient, effective, and secure programs and operations. Over the last year, the Administration has made significant progress in facilitating agency implementation of FITARA and our Common Baseline by requiring agencies to thoroughly review agency implementation plans and integrating FITARA implementation oversight into quarterly PortfolioStat sessions. For example, OMB recently launched a central location for tools and resources to support agencies in implementation, and a dashboard to publicly track agencies' progress.[5] Ensuring full implementation of FITARA remains a top priority in FY 2016 and 2017.

Buying as One—In 2015, the Administration announced the launch of the government-wide Category Management initiative[6] to move the Federal Government toward the goal of buying as one customer. This approach, used extensively by private industry, enables the Federal Government to act more like a single enterprise for a variety of "categories[7]," and the IT category is leader of this new initiative. The Federal Government is the single largest buyer of IT in the world with annual IT contract spending in excess of $50 billion for hardware, software, telecommunications, security, and professional services. Category management has already begun to make significant improvements in IT acquisitions. For example, the first IT Category Management memorandum, M-16-02[8], established policies to prohibit new contracts for laptops and desktops, mandated use of standard configurations, and implemented demand management strategies. The Federal Government has already seen workstation prices from some vendors drop as much as 50 percent. In FY 2017 the Administration will continue to expand Category Management in the areas of hardware, software, telecommunications and services.

Software Reuse and Open Source—In 2016, the Administration will take important steps to improve value to taxpayers when Federal agencies procure software code that has been custom-developed for Federal use. This will enable the brightest minds from around the country to review, improve, and collaborate on Federal Government code, thereby helping to ensure that the code is safe, reliable, and effective in furthering our national objectives.

Government-Wide Successes—The Administration's continued focus on driving value in Federal IT invest-

---

[4] CFOs are Chief Financial Officers and CAOs are Chief Acquisition Officers.

[5] See *https://management.cio.gov*

[6] See *https://www.whitehouse.gov/sites/default/files/omb/procurement/memo/simplifying-federal-procurement-to-improve-performance-drive-innovation-increase-savings.pdf*

[7] Government-wide Category Management includes ten super categories: IT, Professional Services, Security and Protection, Facilities and Construction, Industrial Products and Services, Office Management, Transportation and Logistics Services, Travel and Lodging, Human Capital and Medical. See *https://www.whitehouse.gov/blog/2015/10/14/update-drive-category-management-government-wide* for more detail.

[8] See *https://www.whitehouse.gov/sites/default/files/omb/memoranda/2016/m-16-02.pdf*

Chart 17-1. Trends in Federal IT Spending

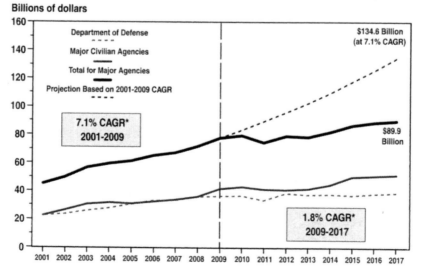

*Compound Annual Growth Rate.

Source: Total IT spending for agencies reporting to the IT Dashboard. Department of Defense has provided estimates for classified IT investments not shown on the IT Dashboard. Chart reflects data available as of January 19, 2016.

ments has led to key successes across the Federal IT portfolio. Specific examples include:

- Government-wide cost savings—Since 2012, the Federal Government has saved over $3.5 billion[9] as a result of the Administration's IT reform efforts, including initiatives such as PortfolioStat, the Federal Cloud Computing Strategy,[10] commodity IT consolidation, migration to shared services, increased use of modern development practices, and data center consolidation and optimization efforts.[11]

- Shifting to more efficient computing services—The Federal Government now spends approximately 8.2 percent of its IT budget on provisioned services such as cloud, on par with leading private sector companies.

- Increased use of modern, agile development practices[12]—Agencies have increased their use of agile

development practices and are delivering value 23 days (12 percent) faster since May 2013. Evidence in the IT portfolio shows that these agile projects have been nearly twice as likely to deliver on time as those using "waterfall" development techniques,[13] and have been 33 percent more likely to deliver planned capabilities on budget.[14]

- Data center efforts—As part of the Administration's data center consolidation and optimization efforts, agencies have closed 3,179 data centers as of November 2015, reversing the previous unsustainable data center growth trends, reducing energy consumption and the Federal real estate footprint, and enhancing the Federal IT security posture. The General Services Administration (GSA) leads the Government in data center closures, having closed 88 of its 124 (71 percent) total data centers.

---

[9] As reported by agencies. Savings described in this chapter can be recognized in two different ways, as defined in OMB Circular A-131: (a) Cost-Savings: A reduction in actual expenditures below the projected level of costs to achieve a specific objective; and, (b) Cost-Avoidance: An action taken in the immediate timeframe that will decrease costs in the future. For example, an engineering improvement that increases the mean time between failures and thereby decreases operation and maintenance costs is a cost-avoidance action.

[10] See *http://www.whitehouse.gov/sites/default/files/omb/assets/egov_docs/federal-cloud-computing-strategy.pdf*

[11] See *http://www.whitehouse.gov/sites/default/files/omb/assets/egov_docs/fdcci-update-memo-07202011.pdf*

[12] Agile development is an incremental, fast-paced style of software

development to reduce the risk of failure by getting working software into users' hands quickly by releasing bundles of features in frequent sprints based on evolving user needs. For additional information on the benefits of agile development, see *http://www.whitehouse.gov/sites/default/files/omb/procurement/guidance/modular-approaches-for-information-technology.pdf*.

[13] Waterfall development typically proceeds in sequential phases of consistent, fixed duration to produce a complete system. Such full system development efforts can take several years, potentially resulting in a product that is either outdated by the time it is released or contains features that are not aligned with user needs.

[14] Projects which are "on time" and "on budget" have schedule and cost variance of less than 10 percent and are depicted as "green" on the IT Dashboard.

DELIVERING WORLD CLASS DIGITAL SERVICES

Smarter IT Delivery—The Administration has embarked on a comprehensive approach to fundamentally improve the way that the Government delivers technology services to the public. This agenda for the Smarter IT Delivery Cross-Agency Priority (CAP)[15] goal focuses on ensuring that all agencies have access to the best partners, people, and digital practices. As part of this work, top technologists are being recruited to work within agencies on the highest priority projects.

U.S. Digital Service and agency digital service teams—Recruiting the best technologists to work inside of government is a key component of our Smarter IT delivery strategy. The Budget will support the continued recruitment of private sector innovators, entrepreneurs, and engineers to government service. Since 2014, Digital Service Experts recruited into the United States Digital Services (USDS)[16] have worked in collaboration with Federal agencies to implement cutting-edge digital practices on the Nation's highest impact programs, including the continued success and stability of *Healthcare.gov*, the Veterans Benefits Management System, myUSCIS, and

the College Scorecard at the Department of Education[17], as well as partnering with the Internal Revenue Service to deliver better online taxpayer services to citizens. The College Scorecard was redesigned with direct input from students, families, and their advisers to provide the clearest, most accessible, and reliable national data on college cost, graduation, debt, and post-college earnings. For the first time the public can access the most reliable and comprehensive data on students' outcomes at specific colleges, including former students' earnings, graduates' student debt, and borrowers' repayment rates. Various organizations are already using this data to provide tools to consumers to help them make better informed financial decisions for themselves and their families[18].

USDS also created a new Rapid Response team. This team's work included supporting *Healthcare.gov* during the 2015 open enrollment season and restoring service for the State Department's Consolidated Consular Database, after an outage led to a two-week suspension of visa issuances worldwide.

Digital Acquisition Efforts—In addition to its delivery efforts, USDS is promoting innovation within government contracting and working to build a more ag-

---

[15] The mission of the Smarter IT CAP goal is to improve outcomes and customer satisfaction with Federal services through smarter IT delivery and stronger agency accountability for success. For more information on CAP goals, see *http://www.performance.gov*.

[16] See *https://whitehouse.gov/digital/united-states-digital-service*

[17] *https://collegescorecard.ed.gov*

[18] See *https://www.whitehouse.gov/blog/2015/09/12/under-hood-building-new-college-scorecard-students*

ile procurement process. In partnership with the Office of Federal Procurement Policy (OFPP), USDS created and launched the Digital Service Contracting Professional Training and Development Program, which seeks to spur innovation in the training of Contracting Officers. This program challenged companies to develop a program that will teach best practices in the procurement of digital services and the important role Contracting Officers can play in building meaningful, successful services. USDS and OFPP identified the winning training program, and the first class of Contracting Officers enrolled in October of 2015.

Information as an Asset—Government Open Data—Open government data enables private sector innovation, facilitates use, and maximizes the nation's return on its investment in data. Since releasing Executive Order 13642[19] and OMB Memorandum M-13-13[20] in 2013, this Administration has continued to make progress to-

wards its open data commitment. *Data.gov* now features over 200,000 datasets on topics such as education, public safety, health care, energy, and agriculture. To further this progress and to support the federal open data ecosystem, additional resources have been provided and expanded such as Project Open Data[21] which provides tools that enable agencies to make their data publicly available, and the Project Open Data Dashboard[22] which provides the public and relevant stakeholders a quarterly evaluation of agencies' open data progress. To facilitate the usage of open data and to increase public dialogue around open data, eight Federal agencies co-hosted Open Data Roundtables to conduct action-oriented dialogues that connect agencies with the organizations that use their data to help identify high value datasets and establish open data priorities. Going forward, this Administration will continue to increase agency data inventories, improve the discoverability of existing data, and work to reduce open data barriers within agencies.

---

[19] See *https://www.whitehouse.gov/the-press-office/2013/05/09/executive-order-making-open-and-machine-readable-new-default-government-*

[20] See *https://www.whitehouse.gov/sites/default/files/omb/memoranda/2013/m-13-13.pdf*

[21] See *https://project-open-data.cio.gov*

[22] See *http://labs.data.gov/dashboard/offices*

CYBERSECURITY: PROTECTING FEDERAL IT ASSETS AND INFORMATION

Strengthening the cybersecurity of Federal networks, systems, and data is one of the most important challenges we face as a Nation. As cyber risks have grown in severity over recent years, the Administration has executed a comprehensive strategy to address cybersecurity across the Nation, as outlined in the National Security Chapter. Building upon the Administration's broader efforts for 21st Century Cybersecurity, in 2015 the Office of Management and Budget, in coordination with the National Security Council (NSC), the Department of Homeland Security (DHS), the Department of Commerce, as well as other departments and agencies, executed a series of actions to bolster Federal cybersecurity and secure Federal information systems through the Cybersecurity Strategy and Implementation Plan (CSIP).

In 2015, these actions and others led to areas of significant progress across the Federal Government. Federal civilian agencies took action to patch critical vulnerabilities, identify high-value assets, tightly limit the number of privileged users with access to authorized systems, and dramatically accelerate the use of Personal Identity Verification (PIV) cards or alternative forms of strong authentication for accessing networks and systems. Indeed, since the Cybersecurity Sprint, an intensive effort conducted in July 2015 to assess and improve the health of all Federal assets and networks, both civilian and military, Federal Civilian agencies have nearly doubled their use of strong authentication for all users from 42 percent to 81 percent.

Still, as outlined in the CSIP, challenges remain. The Federal Government has identified three primary challenges:

- Outdated Technology – The Federal Government relies significantly on hard-to-defend legacy hardware, software, applications, and infrastructure, which make it particularly vulnerable to malicious cyber

activity, as well as costly to defend and protect.

- Fragmented Governance – Governance and management structures are unable to consistently provide effective, well-coordinated cybersecurity across the Federal Government.

- Workforce Gaps—Workforce shortages and skill gaps, including training, education, and recruitment and retention of cybersecurity and privacy professionals, are significant.

To address these challenges and continue moving the needle on cybersecurity for the Federal Government, the President's 2017 Budget invests over $19 billion, or a 35 percent increase from FY 2016, in overall Federal resources for cybersecurity.

Enhancing Federal IT to Secure Federal Information and Assets

The technology, architectures, and processes underpinning Federal Government operations need to be modernized to improve cybersecurity. Of the $51 billion in Federal civilian IT spending planned for FY 2017, approximately 71 percent ($36 billion) is dedicated to maintaining legacy IT investments. Improving Federal cybersecurity will require an accelerated push to strengthen the Government's highest value IT and information assets and to retire, replace, or upgrade hard-to-defend legacy IT. This will require not just modernizing hardware and software, but also improving how we manage the lifecycle of IT investments so that security gains can be sustained over time. This approach will improve the government's risk management capability, improve the cyber-defense landscape, and enhance our ability to respond to changing threats. Therefore, the Administration is proposing a revolving fund at GSA, seeded with an initial capital injection of $3.1 billion, to retire, replace or upgrade hard-to-secure legacy IT systems and transition to new, more secure, efficient, modern IT systems, while also establishing long-term mechanisms for Federal agencies to regularly refresh their networks and systems based on up-to-date technologies and best practices.

A project review board, comprised of experts in IT acquisition, cybersecurity, and agile development, will review agency business cases and select projects for funding to ensure prioritization of projects with the highest risk profile, government-wide impact, and probability of success. The board will identify opportunities to replace multiple legacy systems with a smaller number of common platforms – something that is difficult for agencies to do when acting on their own with limited insight into other agencies' operations. As a result, the central fund will achieve a far greater and more rapid impact than if the funds were allocated directly to agencies. In addition, a team of systems architects and developers will provide additional oversight and development capabilities to make these major changes. The revolving fund will be self-sustaining by requiring agencies to repay the initial investments through efficiencies gained from modernization, ensuring the fund can continue to support projects well beyond the initial infusion of capital. Seed funding of $3.1 billion would address an estimated $12 billion worth of modernization projects over 10 years.

Finally, the Budget includes $275 million in funding to accelerate implementation of the DHS continuous diagnostics and monitoring (CDM) program. CDM enables agencies to invest in a centralized continuous monitoring program that will allow them to quickly and efficiently identify cybersecurity vulnerabilities and mitigate risk.

Streamlining Governance and Ensuring Effective Oversight

Over the long term, the Federal Government will need to move away from a model of IT and cybersecurity governance where individual departments and agencies build, provision, and manage nearly all aspects of their IT and cybersecurity, from infrastructure to platforms to applications. Instead, IT systems and cybersecurity capabilities will need to be built, acquired, and managed in a more holistic way, one that treats the Federal Government as an enterprise and that relies more on shared platforms and common services. This Budget lays the foundation for shifting to this more effective approach to Federal cybersecurity by supporting investments in common IT solutions for small agencies, more secure, enterprise-wide email systems, and common cybersecurity tools and services. Further, the Federal Government needs to improve not only its hardware and software, but how it acquires technology, so that it can keep up to date with industry best practices and emerging technologies in the future.

Today's sophisticated cyber incidents have also demonstrated the need for more coordinated and nimble Government efforts when they occur. In such instances, the Government may need to play an important coordi-

nating role. Moving forward, the Budget supports Federal Government efforts to continue developing policy and plans that establish a foundation for a scalable, flexible, and cooperative approach to significant cyber incident coordination involving both public and private sector stakeholders, and anchors it within the broader National Preparedness System.

In 2016 and 2017, the Administration, including OMB and NSC staff, will also coordinate with DHS to continue working with agencies to identify and remediate weaknesses in cybersecurity programs while ensuring agency progress towards the Cybersecurity Cross-Agency Priority (CAP) Goal through CyberStat reviews. These reviews provide the opportunity for agencies to identify the cybersecurity areas where they may be facing implementation and organizational challenges.

Strengthening the Cybersecurity Workforce

There is a shortage of skilled cybersecurity experts and privacy professionals throughout the IT industry as a whole, and that shortage is more acute within the Federal Government. The Budget includes $62 million for three initiatives to address this recruitment challenge by:

1. Expanding the National Science Foundation's (NSF) CyberCorps®: Scholarship for Service (SFS) program to establish a sustainable cadre of cyber reservists and enhance opportunities for career cybersecurity experts across departments and agencies that can serve the Federal Government to help rapidly respond to cybersecurity challenges;

2. Developing a foundational cybersecurity curriculum for academic institutions to consult and adopt; and

3. Providing grants to academic institutions to develop or expand cyber education programs as part of the National Centers of Academic Excellence in Cybersecurity Program.

In addition to funding these foundational workforce initiatives, this Budget also invests over $37 million to expand standing teams of cybersecurity experts within DHS to provide readily-available cybersecurity capabilities to departments and agencies.

As malicious cyber activity becomes increasingly sophisticated and persistent in the digital age, so must our actions to tackle it. Cyber threats cannot be eliminated entirely, but they can be managed much more effectively. Through these investments, the Administration continues to lead a broad, strategic effort to combat cyber threats, update and modernize Federal cybersecurity policies and procedures, and strengthen the Federal Government's overall cybersecurity infrastructure through modernization efforts.

To complement these steps and focus on long-term challenges in cybersecurity, the Budget also supports the creation of the first Federal Chief Information Security Officer, and the establishment of a blue ribbon commission consisting of leaders in the fields of cybersecurity, technology, privacy, national security, and government.

This commission will identify recommendations for the President, future Administrations, and the Nation to enhance cybersecurity awareness and protections inside and outside of government and to empower Americans to take better control of their digital security.

DEVELOPING THE NEXT GENERATION IT WORKFORCE

Having a high-caliber IT workforce is key to lasting success in each of the Administration's technology initiatives. For example, the Administration has set an aggressive goal of hiring and placing 500 top technology and design experts to serve in the U.S. Government by January 2017 to dramatically improve customer satisfaction with federal technology services. To aid in this, USDS worked with OPM to create a term-appointment hiring authority for Digital Services Experts to more quickly get talent into government, which is now being used by USDS and Agency Digital Service teams. Individuals hired under this authority may serve up to two years once appointed, meaning staff appointed at the end of 2017 could extend into 2019. Working with OPM to expand flexible hiring options and spread proven hiring practices will remain a focus area in FY 2017.

Additionally, in FY 2017 OMB will continue to build off of existing training opportunities being offered to current Federal IT professionals to scale modern development practices across the workforce. For example, this past year the CIO Council, CAO Council and OMB launched the IT Solutions Challenge. Over several months, more than 40 IT and Acquisition professionals in the GS-9 through GS-13 range worked in teams to develop innovative solutions for some of the biggest challenges in IT and acquisitions. These types of training programs work in tandem with expanding the Government's digital acquisition expertise. In the past year, 30 Federal acquisition professionals piloted an innovative approach to training to improve digital IT acquisition capabilities.

CONCLUSION

Ensuring the efficiency, effectiveness, and security of Federal IT has never been more central to how Americans are served by their Government. Over the past seven years, this Administration has focused on driving efficiencies in the way the Government buys, builds, and delivers IT solutions to provide improved services to citizens, and these efforts will be strengthened in 2016 and further scaled across Government in 2017. The 21st Century digital service delivery standards being set by this Administration represent an important commitment to future generations. The 2017 Budget includes funding that will launch the Nation on a path to hire the leading digital experts, institutionalize modern digital delivery practices, and establish more effective partnerships both within Government and with the private sector that will provide services to our citizens at a historical level of quality and timeliness.

18. FEDERAL INVESTMENT

Federal investment is the portion of Federal spending intended to yield long-term benefits for the economy and the country. It promotes improved efficiency within Federal agencies, as well as growth in the national economy by increasing the overall stock of capital. Investment spending can take the form of direct Federal spending or of grants to State and local governments.[1] It can be designated for physical capital, which creates a tangible asset that yields a stream of services over a period of years. It also can be for research and development, education, or training, all of which are intangible but still increase income in the future or provide other long-term benefits.

Most presentations in this volume combine investment spending with spending intended for current use. This chapter focuses solely on Federal and federally financed investment. It provides a comprehensive picture of Federal investment spending for physical capital, research and development, and education and training, but because it disregards spending for non-investment activities, it provides only a partial picture of Federal support for specific national needs, such as defense, transportation, or environmental protection.

---

[1] For more information on Federal grants to State and local governments see Chapter 15, "Aid to State and Local Governments," in this volume.

DESCRIPTION OF FEDERAL INVESTMENT

The distinction between investment spending and current outlays is a matter of judgment. The budget has historically employed a relatively broad classification of investment, encompassing physical investment, research, development, education, and training. The budget further classifies investments into those that are grants to State and local governments, such as grants for highways, and all other investments, or "direct Federal programs." This "direct Federal" category consists primarily of spending for assets owned by the Federal Government, such as weapons systems and buildings, but also includes grants to private organizations and individuals for investment, such as capital grants to Amtrak or higher education loans directly to individuals.

The definition of investment in a particular presentation can vary depending on specific considerations:

- Taking the approach of a traditional balance sheet would limit investment to only those physical assets owned by the Federal Government, excluding capital financed through grants and intangible assets such as research and education.

- Focusing on the role of investment in improving national productivity and enhancing economic growth would exclude items such as national defense assets, the direct benefits of which enhance national security rather than economic growth.

- Examining the efficiency of Federal operations would confine the coverage to investments that reduce costs or improve the effectiveness of internal Federal agency operations, such as computer systems.

- Considering a "social investment" perspective would broaden the coverage of investment beyond what is included in this chapter to include programs such as maternal health, certain nutrition programs, and substance abuse treatment, which are designed in part to prevent more costly health problems in future years.

This analysis takes the relatively broad approach of including all investment in physical assets, research and development, and education and training, regardless of ultimate ownership of the resulting asset or the purpose it serves. It does not include "social investment" items like health care or social services where it is difficult to separate out the degree to which the spending provides current versus future benefits. The definition of investment used in this section provides consistency over time (historical figures on investment outlays back to 1940 can be found in the Budget's historical tables).[2] Table 18–2 at the end of this section allows disaggregation of the data to focus on those investment outlays that best suit a particular purpose.

In addition to this basic issue of definition, there are two technical problems in the classification of investment data: the treatment of grants to State and local governments, and the classification of spending that could be shown in multiple categories.

First, for some grants to State and local governments it is the recipient jurisdiction, not the Federal Government, that ultimately determines whether the money is used to finance investment or current purposes. This analysis classifies all of the outlays into the category in which the recipient jurisdictions are expected to spend a majority of the money. Hence, the Community Development Block Grants are classified as physical investment, although some may be spent for current purposes. General purpose fiscal assistance is classified as current spending, although some may be spent by recipient jurisdictions on investment.

---

[2] The historical tables are available at http://www.budget.gov/budget/Historicals and on the Budget CD-ROM.

Second, some spending could be classified in more than one category of investment. For example, outlays for construction of research facilities finance the acquisition of physical assets, but they also contribute to research and development. To avoid double counting, the outlays are classified hierarchically in the category that is most commonly recognized as investment: physical assets, followed by research and development, followed by education and training. Consequently, outlays for the conduct of research and development do not include outlays for the construction of research facilities, because these outlays are included in the category for investment in physical assets.

When direct loans and loan guarantees are used to fund investment, the subsidy value is included as investment. The subsidies are classified according to their program purpose, such as construction or education and training. For more information about the treatment of Federal credit programs, refer to the section on Federal credit in Chapter 9, "Budget Concepts," in this volume.

This discussion presents spending for gross investment, without adjusting for depreciation.

Composition of Federal Investment Outlays

Major Federal Investment

The composition of major Federal investment outlays is summarized in Table 18–1. They include major public physical investment, the conduct of research and development, and the conduct of education and training. Total Federal investment outlays were $489.2 billion in 2015. Federal investment outlays are estimated to increase to $491.0 billion, less than one percent, in 2016, and increase by 1.0 percent to $495.6 billion in 2017. In 2017, defense investment outlays are estimated to increase by $6.1 billion, while nondefense investment outlays are expected to decrease by $1.4 billion. The major factors contributing to these changes are described below.

Major Federal investment outlays will comprise an estimated 12.0 percent of total Federal outlays in 2017 and 2.6 percent of the Nation's gross domestic product. Greater detail on Federal investment is available in Table 18–2 at the end of this section. That table includes both budget authority and outlays.

Physical investment. Outlays for major public physical capital investment (hereafter referred to as "physical in-

Table 18–1. COMPOSITION OF FEDERAL INVESTMENT OUTLAYS
(In billions of dollars)

Federal Investment	Actual 2015	Estimate 2016	Estimate 2017
Major public physical capital investment:			
Direct Federal:			
National defense	108.9	110.8	109.7
Nondefense	40.3	42.5	39.4
Subtotal, direct major public physical capital investment	149.2	153.3	149.1
Grants to State and local governments	77.2	78.0	85.3
Subtotal, major public physical capital investment	226.4	231.3	234.4
Conduct of research and development:			
National defense	70.7	71.7	78.9
Nondefense	61.3	63.8	67.8
Subtotal, conduct of research and development	132.1	135.5	146.7
Conduct of education and training:			
Grants to State and local governments	55.9	60.3	59.3
Direct Federal	74.7	63.9	55.3
Subtotal, conduct of education and training	130.7	124.2	114.6
Total, major Federal investment outlays	**489.2**	**491.0**	**495.6**
MEMORANDUM			
Major Federal investment outlays:			
National defense	179.6	182.5	188.6
Nondefense	309.5	308.5	307.1
Total, major Federal investment outlays	489.2	491.0	495.6
Miscellaneous physical investment:			
Commodity inventories	–*	–0.2	–0.0
Other physical investment (direct)	2.4	2.4	4.1
Total, miscellaneous physical investment	2.4	2.2	4.0
Total, Federal investment outlays, including miscellaneous physical investment	491.5	493.2	499.7

vestment outlays") are estimated to grow by one percent in 2017 to $234.4 billion. Physical investment outlays are for construction and rehabilitation, the purchase of major equipment, and the purchase or sale of land and structures. Just under two-thirds of these outlays are for direct physical investment by the Federal Government, with the remainder being grants to State and local governments for physical investment.

Direct physical investment outlays by the Federal Government are primarily for national defense. Defense outlays for physical investment are estimated to be $109.7 billion in 2017, $1.1 billion lower than in 2016. Approximately 93 percent of defense physical investment outlays, or an estimated $102.0 billion, are for the procurement of weapons and other defense equipment, and the remainder is primarily for construction on military bases, family housing for military personnel, and Department of Energy defense facilities.

Outlays for direct physical investment for nondefense purposes are estimated to be $39.4 billion in 2017. Outlays for 2017 include $21.0 billion for construction and rehabilitation. This amount includes funds for water, power, and natural resources projects of the Corps of Engineers, the Bureau of Reclamation within the Department of the Interior, the Power Marketing Administrations within the Department of Energy, and the Tennessee Valley Authority; construction and rehabilitation of veterans' hospitals and Indian Health Service hospitals and clinics; facilities for space and science programs; Postal Service facilities; construction for the administration of justice programs (largely in Customs and Border Protection within the Department of Homeland Security); construction of office buildings by the General Services Administration; and construction for embassy security. Outlays for this category are estimated to decrease by $3.8 billion in 2017 primarily because outlays for 2016 include upward reestimates of the cost of past guaranteed loans for the construction and repair of apartment buildings, hospitals, and other health care facilities.

Outlays for grants to State and local governments for physical investment are estimated to be $85.3 billion in 2017, a 10.1 percent increase from the 2016 estimate of $78.0 billion. Most of the increase is for the 21st Century Clean Transportation System proposal, which includes a number of grants and programs within the Department of Transportation. For more information on this proposal see Chapter 11, "Budget Process," in this volume. Other major grants for physical investment fund sewage treatment plants and other State and tribal assistance grants, community and regional development, and public housing.

Conduct of research and development. Outlays for the conduct of research and development are estimated to be $146.7 billion in 2017, an $11.2 billion or 8.3 percent increase over 2016. These outlays are devoted to increasing basic scientific knowledge and promoting research and development. They increase the Nation's security, improve the productivity of capital and labor for both public and private purposes, and enhance the quality of life. With an increase of $7.3 billion over 2016, more than half

of research and development outlays, an estimated $78.9 billion, are for national defense. Physical investment for research and development facilities and equipment is included in the physical investment category.

Non-defense outlays for the conduct of research and development are estimated to be $67.8 billion in 2017, a $4.0 billion or 6.2 percent increase over 2016. Most investments in this area are funded through programs in the National Institutes of Health (which accounts for half of the increase in 2017), the National Aeronautics and Space Administration, the Department of Energy, and the National Science Foundation.

A more detailed discussion of research and development funding can be found in Chapter 19, "Research and Development," in this volume.

Conduct of education and training. Outlays for the conduct of education and training were $130.7 billion in 2015. Outlays are estimated to decrease to $124.2 billion in 2016, and decrease again in 2017 to $114.6 billion. Investments in this category add to the stock of human capital by developing a more skilled and productive labor force. Grants to State and local governments for this category are estimated to be $59.3 billion in 2017, 52 percent of the total. They include education programs for the disadvantaged and individuals with disabilities, training programs in the Department of Labor, Head Start, and other education programs. Direct Federal education and training outlays in 2017 are estimated to be $55.3 billion, which is a decrease of $8.6 billion, or 13.4 percent, from 2016. Programs in this category primarily consist of aid for higher education through student financial assistance, loan subsidies, and veterans' education, training, and rehabilitation. The decrease in outlays for the conduct of education and training from 2015 to 2017 is more than accounted for by revisions in the cost of past student loan activity. Adjusting for these reestimates of past activity, this category of outlays would increase from year to year.

This category does not include outlays for education and training of Federal civilian and military employees. Outlays for education and training that are for physical investment and for research and development are in the categories for physical investment and the conduct of research and development.

Miscellaneous Physical Investment

In addition to the categories of major Federal investment, several miscellaneous categories of investment outlays are shown at the bottom of Table 18–1. These items, all for physical investment, are generally unrelated to improving Government operations or enhancing economic activity.

Outlays for commodity inventories are for the purchase or sale of agricultural products pursuant to farm price support programs and other commodities. Sales are estimated to exceed purchases by $36 million in 2017.

Outlays for other miscellaneous physical investment are estimated to be $4.1 billion in 2017. This category consists entirely of direct Federal outlays and includes primarily conservation programs.

Detailed Table on Investment Spending

The following table provides data on budget authority as well as outlays for major Federal investment divided according to grants to State and local governments and direct Federal spending. Miscellaneous investment is not included because it is generally unrelated to improving Government operations or enhancing economic activity.

Table 18–2.   FEDERAL INVESTMENT BUDGET AUTHORITY AND OUTLAYS: GRANT AND DIRECT FEDERAL PROGRAMS

(In millions of dollars)

Description	Budget Authority			Outlays		
	2015 Actual	2016 Estimate	2017 Estimate	2015 Actual	2016 Estimate	2017 Estimate
GRANTS TO STATE AND LOCAL GOVERNMENTS						
Major public physical investment:						
Construction and rehabilitation:						
Transportation:						
Highways	39,018	41,382	39,658	42,002	42,030	42,863
Mass transportation	12,190	12,950	14,684	11,784	11,669	12,859
Rail transportation	1,394	1,452	2,269	2,415	3,342	4,778
Air and other transportation	3,548	3,677	18,327	3,454	3,779	7,125
Subtotal, transportation	56,150	59,461	74,938	59,655	60,820	67,625
Other construction and rehabilitation:						
Pollution control and abatement	2,651	2,880	2,721	3,310	3,281	3,324
Community and regional development	3,964	4,322	3,810	7,766	8,467	7,886
Housing assistance	3,498	3,601	3,631	4,036	3,131	3,849
Other	387	514	1,140	360	431	663
Subtotal, other construction and rehabilitation	10,500	11,317	11,302	15,472	15,310	15,722
Subtotal, construction and rehabilitation	66,650	70,778	86,240	75,127	76,130	83,347
Other physical assets	1,912	2,021	2,389	2,117	1,869	1,937
Subtotal, major public physical investment	68,562	72,799	88,629	77,244	77,999	85,284
Conduct of research and development:						
Agriculture	334	339	335	247	478	388
Other	221	214	221	164	168	167
Subtotal, conduct of research and development	555	553	556	411	646	555
Conduct of education and training:						
Elementary, secondary, and vocational education	37,063	38,167	42,842	38,021	39,792	38,195
Higher education	328	363	363	373	392	381
Research and general education aids	736	781	837	741	783	804
Training and employment	3,073	3,375	3,529	3,309	3,600	3,676
Social services	11,764	12,678	13,411	11,099	12,588	12,649
Agriculture	416	418	456	402	586	611
Other	2,232	2,265	2,294	1,994	2,579	2,982
Subtotal, conduct of education and training	55,612	58,047	63,732	55,939	60,320	59,298
Subtotal, grants for investment	**124,729**	**131,399**	**152,917**	**133,594**	**138,965**	**145,137**
DIRECT FEDERAL PROGRAMS						
Major public physical investment:						
Construction and rehabilitation:						
National defense:						
Military construction and family housing	5,156	6,672	6,274	7,524	7,671	7,702
Atomic energy defense activities and other	138	145	190	3	6	186
Subtotal, national defense	5,294	6,817	6,464	7,527	7,677	7,888
Nondefense:						
International affairs	1,731	1,602	1,752	956	1,007	1,270
General science, space, and technology	1,173	1,219	1,254	1,373	1,279	1,254
Water resources projects	2,935	2,990	2,010	3,326	3,468	3,448
Other natural resources and environment	1,093	1,161	1,518	1,169	1,219	1,267
Energy	5,986	5,593	4,596	6,142	5,075	4,567
Postal service	429	402	402	385	402	524

Table 18–2. FEDERAL INVESTMENT BUDGET AUTHORITY AND OUTLAYS: GRANT AND DIRECT FEDERAL PROGRAMS—Continued

(In millions of dollars)

Description	Budget Authority			Outlays		
	2015 Actual	2016 Estimate	2017 Estimate	2015 Actual	2016 Estimate	2017 Estimate
Transportation	291	385	274	294	236	413
Veterans hospitals and other health facilities	3,385	3,635	3,005	3,278	3,482	3,248
Administration of justice	1,959	2,561	1,456	1,645	2,206	1,543
GSA real property activities	1,361	2,343	2,172	995	1,166	1,644
Other construction	3,292	5,171	11,894	3,902	5,271	1,835
Subtotal, nondefense	23,635	27,062	30,333	23,465	24,811	21,013
Subtotal, construction and rehabilitation	28,929	33,879	36,797	30,992	32,488	28,901
Acquisition of major equipment:						
National defense:						
Department of Defense	101,956	115,961	109,057	101,237	102,802	101,382
Atomic energy defense activities	474	450	490	184	353	439
Subtotal, national defense	102,430	116,411	109,547	101,421	103,155	101,821
Nondefense:						
General science and basic research	328	394	420	321	379	419
Postal service	1,325	1,388	1,388	850	1,392	1,389
Air transportation	3,309	3,393	3,906	3,459	3,382	3,696
Water transportation (Coast Guard)	918	1,581	945	1,258	1,196	1,280
Hospital and medical care for veterans	1,838	1,550	2,313	1,760	1,512	1,987
Federal law enforcement activities	1,649	1,580	2,323	1,272	1,379	996
Department of the Treasury (fiscal operations)	292	292	345	231	266	281
National Oceanic and Atmospheric Administration	2,098	2,313	2,152	1,932	2,126	1,979
Other	4,728	4,941	5,127	5,120	5,523	5,704
Subtotal, nondefense	16,485	17,432	18,919	16,203	17,155	17,731
Subtotal, acquisition of major equipment	118,915	133,843	128,466	117,624	120,310	119,552
Purchase or sale of land and structures:						
National defense	−40	−36	−38	−48	−28	−34
Natural resources and environment	223	328	557	201	271	406
General government	....	....	....	....	7	....
Other	−72	−37	−37	431	252	250
Subtotal, purchase or sale of land and structures	111	255	482	584	502	622
Subtotal, major public physical investment	147,955	167,977	165,745	149,200	153,300	149,075
Conduct of research and development:						
National defense:						
Defense military	65,431	70,839	72,630	65,666	66,754	71,959
Atomic energy and other	6,038	5,567	6,970	5,062	4,915	6,958
Subtotal, national defense	71,469	76,406	79,600	70,728	71,669	78,917
Nondefense:						
International affairs	290	315	327	290	315	327
General science, space, and technology:						
NASA	11,565	11,773	11,225	11,170	10,872	11,096
National Science Foundation	5,569	5,693	6,070	5,059	5,231	5,218
Department of Energy	4,399	4,502	4,827	4,159	4,520	5,060
Subtotal, general science, space, and technology	21,533	21,968	22,122	20,388	20,623	21,374
Energy	3,019	3,331	4,347	2,785	2,966	3,615
Transportation:						
Department of Transportation	696	742	881	645	790	868
NASA	516	500	681	555	555	644
Other transportation	17	18	23	24	17	24
Subtotal, transportation	1,229	1,260	1,585	1,224	1,362	1,536
Health:						
National Institutes of Health	28,880	30,490	31,204	28,358	29,222	31,220
Other health	1,745	1,689	1,786	1,314	1,273	1,734
Subtotal, health	30,625	32,179	32,990	29,672	30,495	32,954

Table 18–2. FEDERAL INVESTMENT BUDGET AUTHORITY AND OUTLAYS: GRANT AND DIRECT FEDERAL PROGRAMS—Continued

(In millions of dollars)

Description	Budget Authority			Outlays		
	2015 Actual	2016 Estimate	2017 Estimate	2015 Actual	2016 Estimate	2017 Estimate
Agriculture	1,655	1,669	2,077	1,623	1,818	1,907
Natural resources and environment	2,124	2,320	2,457	2,050	2,279	2,490
National Institute of Standards and Technology	589	624	681	482	639	681
Hospital and medical care for veterans	1,178	1,220	1,252	1,224	1,222	1,255
All other research and development	1,485	1,570	1,556	1,181	1,420	1,067
Subtotal, nondefense	63,727	66,456	69,394	60,919	63,139	67,206
Subtotal, conduct of research and development	135,196	142,862	148,994	131,647	134,808	146,123
Conduct of education and training:						
Elementary, secondary, and vocational education	1,410	1,472	1,709	1,271	1,230	1,369
Higher education	49,235	39,102	35,114	51,335	38,715	29,459
Research and general education aids	2,119	2,239	2,429	2,172	2,179	2,260
Training and employment	2,184	2,263	2,385	2,111	2,368	2,605
Health	1,595	1,776	1,857	1,677	1,802	1,866
Veterans education, training, and rehabilitation	15,369	14,647	16,668	13,605	15,129	15,296
General science and basic research	927	864	915	805	784	790
International affairs	612	608	657	642	763	668
Other	1,051	816	1,103	1,097	918	1,001
Subtotal, conduct of education and training	74,502	63,787	62,837	74,715	63,888	55,314
Subtotal, direct Federal investment	**357,653**	**374,626**	**377,576**	**355,562**	**351,996**	**350,512**
Total, Federal investment	**482,382**	**506,025**	**530,493**	**489,156**	**490,961**	**495,649**

19. RESEARCH AND DEVELOPMENT

The President is committed to making investments in research and development (R&D) that will grow our economy and enable America to remain the world leader in innovation. The Nation depends on science, technology, and innovation to promote sustainable economic growth and job creation, maintain a safe and sufficient food supply, improve the health of all Americans, move toward a clean energy future, address global climate change, manage competing demands on environmental resources, and ensure the Nation's security. Investing in science and technology-based innovation will produce vaccines that stay ahead of drug-resistant bacteria, find new answers in the fight against Alzheimer's and other diseases, devise new clean energy technologies, and promote new advanced manufacturing opportunities in areas such as robotics.

The President's 2017 Budget provides $152 billion for Federal research and development (R&D), including the conduct of R&D and investments in R&D facilities and equipment (see Table 19-1). Detailed definitions and discussion are available in Section II below. The Administration continues to prioritize R&D, providing a

4 percent funding increase over 2016 enacted levels[1] for R&D. Reflecting the high priority of R&D in a time of limited discretionary funding, the FY 2017 Budget includes $4 billion in R&D supported by new mandatory funding proposals across a range of topics from health to clean energy technologies. In conjunction with this investment, the 2017 Budget proposes to build on recently-enacted legislation expanding and making permanent the Research and Experimentation tax credit by proposing to simplify and further expand the credit, spurring increased private investment in R&D.

The 2017 Budget continues to strengthen U.S. international leadership by investing in the high-tech knowledge-based economy and innovation-fueled growth industries. The investments proposed in the 2017 Budget align with the recent update to the Strategy for American Innovation to help ensure that the United States continues its long-standing and robust leadership in public and private sector R&D and maintains the high quality of our R&D institutions and the entrepreneurial nature of our R&D enterprise.

---

[1] R&D spending figures for FY 2016 are preliminary and may change as agency operating plans are finalized.

I. PRIORITIES FOR FEDERAL RESEARCH AND DEVELOPMENT

The Budget provides support for a broad spectrum of research and development, including multidisciplinary research and exploratory, potentially transformative, high-risk research proposals that could fundamentally improve our understanding of nature, revolutionize fields of science, and lead to the development of radically new technologies. Federal Government funding for R&D is essential to address societal needs in areas in which the private sector does not have sufficient economic incentive to make the required investments. Key among these is the fundamental, curiosity-driven inquiry that has been a hallmark of the American research enterprise and a powerful driver of surprising, new technology. The Budget provides $73 billion for basic and applied research, an increase of $4 billion (6%) from 2016 enacted because research is a reliable source of the new knowledge that drives job creation and lasting economic growth.

Many research investments into the most promising areas for future industry, scientific discovery, and job creation are being addressed through multi-agency research activities coordinated through the National Science and Technology Council (NSTC) and other interagency forums. Most of these challenges simply cannot be addressed effectively by a single agency. Moreover, innovation often arises from combining the tools, techniques, and insights from multiple agencies.

The 2017 Budget proposes both discretionary and new mandatory funding to continue increasing the total Federal investment in the combined budgets of three key basic research agencies: the National Science Foundation (NSF), the Department of Energy (DOE) Office of Science, and the laboratories of the Department of Commerce (DOC) National Institute of Standards and Technology (NIST). The Budget proposes $14.6 billion in 2017 for these three agencies, an increase of $0.9 billion over the 2016 enacted level.

Moving Toward Cleaner American Energy

The President's Climate Action Plan outlines several key objectives for the United States to lead the world in clean energy. The Administration is committed to a future where the United States leads the world in research, development, demonstration, and deployment of clean-energy technologies to reduce air pollution, greenhouse-gas emissions, and dependence on oil, while creating high-wage, highly-skilled clean energy jobs and new businesses.

The 2017 Budget supports the United States' participation in Mission Innovation, the landmark 20-nation commitment to dramatically accelerate public and private global clean energy innovation that was launched at the start of the Paris climate change conference in November 2015. As part of its participation in Mission Innovation, the U.S. Government will seek to double its current level of Federal fiscal year investment in clean energy R&D over five years, from $6.4 billion in 2016 to $12.8 billion in 2021. New funding will initially be strategically allocated to early stage research and development, which offers some of the greatest opportunities for breakthroughs and transformative change. However, this investment portfolio spans the full range of research and development – from basic research to demonstration activities. The 2017 Budget provides $7.7 billion in discretionary funding for clean energy R&D, demonstrating a strong U.S. commitment to the Mission Innovation doubling pledge.

Funding for clean energy R&D is part of a broader portfolio of clean energy technology programs that includes investments in deployment and other related activities. In total, the 2017 Budget provides approximately $9 billion in discretionary funding government-wide for clean energy technology programs.

In DOE, the 2017 Budget provides about $6.8 billion in discretionary funding for clean energy technology programs, including $5.9 billion for research, development, and demonstration activities that contribute to Mission Innovation. Specifically, it provides $2.9 billion for the Office of Energy Efficiency and Renewable Energy, of which $2.1 billion is part of Mission Innovation. This $2.9 billion supports efforts to accelerate research and development, build on ongoing successes, increase the use of critical clean energy technologies, and further reduce costs and reflects increases above 2016 enacted levels of 37 percent for sustainable vehicle and fuel technologies, 28 percent for energy efficiency and advanced manufacturing activities, and 34 percent for innovative renewable power projects. The 2017 Budget also provides over $1.8 billion for basic clean energy research in the Office of Science and supports investments in a modernized electric grid with $177 million for clean energy R&D in the Office of Electricity Delivery and Energy Reliability. The Budget supports clean energy R&D through the Office of Nuclear Energy and Office of Fossil Energy, including funding for advanced reactors R&D, quantification and mitigation of methane emissions from natural gas infrastructure, and activities primarily dedicated to further lowering the costs of carbon capture and storage. In addition, the Budget includes $500 million through a mix of discretionary and mandatory funding for the Advanced Research Projects Agency–Energy (ARPA-E).

The Budget also supports the Administration's 21st Century Clean Transportation Plan, a new mandatory proposal, which includes a number of R&D programs, as well as support for clean transportation system deployment. Through this Plan the Budget provides $500 million in FY 2017 to scale-up clean transportation R&D through initiatives to accelerate cutting the cost of battery technology; advance the next generation of low carbon biofuels, in particular for intermodal freight and fleets; and establish a smart mobility research center to investigate systems level energy implications of vehicle connectivity and automation. Also as part of the Plan, the Budget provides $100 million at NASA to support a new era of low carbon emission aircraft by initiating a series of experimental aircraft in partnership with indus-

try and universities, and $200 million in Department of Transportation funding for safety research to accelerate the development of autonomous vehicles.

The Budget invests in breakthrough R&D that reduces the price, energy input, and carbon emissions levels of new water supply technology, which can provide communities in water-stressed regions with new and more effective options to meet their increasing water supply needs. Examples include $45 million for the Department of Energy to launch a new Energy-Water Desalination Hub and conduct complementary R&D; $98.6 million for the Department of the Interior's WaterSMART program, which promotes water conservation initiatives, improved water data, and technological breakthroughs; $15 million in additional funding for Department of Agriculture's (USDA) research on water supplies and conservation practices such as building healthy soils that retain water; and $88 million for the National Science Foundation (NSF) to support basic water research to enhance the scientific and engineering knowledge base.

Understanding and Responding to Global Climate Change and Its Impacts

While investing in clean energy, the President's Climate Action Plan also provides a blueprint for responsible national and international action to slow the effects of climate change. 2015, on the heels of record-warm 2014, was the warmest year on record, and by a record margin. One of the key activities supported in the Climate Action Plan is actionable climate science, which is critical in helping government officials, communities, and businesses better understand and manage the risks associated with climate change. In support of this goal, the Administration has continued, through the U.S. Global Change Research Program (USGCRP), to advance actionable climate science to improve our understanding of climate change and its impacts, requesting approximately $2.8 billion for these programs. The USGCRP coordinates and integrates Federal research and applications to assist the Nation and the world in understanding, assessing, predicting, and responding to the human-induced and natural processes of climate change and their related impacts and effects. Within coordinated USGCRP interagency investments, the 2017 Budget supports the goals set forth in the program's 2012-2021 strategic plan, which include: advancing scientific knowledge of the integrated natural and human components of the Earth; providing the scientific basis to inform and enable timely decisions on adaptation and mitigation; building sustained assessment capacity that improves the United States' ability to document changes on the regional, landscape, and local level to understand, anticipate, and respond to climate change impacts and vulnerabilities; and advancing communications and education to broaden public understanding of climate change. The 2017 Budget also supports an integrated suite of climate change observations, process-based research, modeling and assessment, and adaptation science activities that serve as a foundation for providing timely and responsive information, including but not limited to technical reports, impact and vulnerability assessments, and adaptation response strategies to a broad array of stakeholders. The Budget prioritizes the development and use of actionable data, information, and related tools needed to prepare for and reduce climate-related risks and prioritizes investments that support technical assistance for community climate-preparedness efforts. This includes $20 million to continue expanding and improving the online Climate Resilience Toolkit, which provides scientific tools and information to help tribes, communities, citizens, businesses, planners, and others manage their climate-related risks and opportunities, and improve their resilience to extreme events.

Observing our Planet

Earth-observation data are instrumental to services that protect human life, property, the economy, and national security, and advance understanding of the Earth as a system. The Budget supports investments in Earth observations, such as Earth-observing satellites and monitoring of water, air, wildlife, invasive species, and ecosystems, consistent with the 2014 National Plan for Civil Earth Observations. Within the National Aeronautics and Space Administration (NASA), the Budget provides $2.0 billion to sustain progress toward satellite missions and research that will improve our understanding of Earth, its atmosphere, and oceans. The Budget provides $2.1 billion for the National Oceanic and Atmospheric Administration's (NOAA) satellite programs, including the next generation of polar-orbiting and geostationary satellite systems that are critical to weather forecasting. Satellite observations contribute directly to the National Weather Service's ability to issue public warnings to protect life and property. The Budget also supports space weather science and preparedness according to the 2015 National Space Weather Strategy and Action Plan; space weather observations and R&D are essential to address the growing societal needs for accurate and timely space weather information. The Budget begins planning for the next generation of NOAA space-weather satellites, increases funding for space weather-related research at NASA, and provides $1.7 million at the U.S. Geological Survey for improved geomagnetic monitoring to support space weather alerts and warnings.

Promoting Advanced Manufacturing and Industries of the Future

The Administration is committed to the continued strengthening of America's manufacturing sector. The Budget continues to support the National Strategic Plan for Advanced Manufacturing, a blueprint for Federal efforts in partnership with industry and universities to develop and commercialize the emerging technologies that will create high-quality manufacturing jobs and sustain a renaissance in American manufacturing. The 2017 Budget provides $2.0 billion for Federal R&D directly supporting advanced manufacturing at NSF, the Department of Defense (DOD), DOE, DOC, and other agencies, consistent with the goals and recommendations of the Strategic Plan. The Budget funds a national network of 45 manufacturing innovation institutes that will position the United States as a global leader in advanced manufacturing technology. Specifically, the Budget builds on the 13 institutes already funded through 2016 with more than $250 million in additional discretionary funds to support these and 5 new manufacturing innovation institutes in DOC, DOD, and DOE, which will solicit proposals on a wide-range of focus areas across the manufacturing sector. The Budget also includes a mandatory spending proposal of $1.9 billion to fund the remaining 27 institutes in the network.

Improving Americans' Health through Innovation in Life Sciences, Biology, and Neuroscience

The Administration is committed to Federal R&D investments in fundamental biological discovery research that could generate unexpected, high-impact scientific and technological advances in health. The 2017 Budget strongly supports research that has the potential to foster innovations in health and to accelerate the pace of discovery in the life sciences, especially cancer, neuroscience, and Precision Medicine. These discoveries will help improve the prevention and treatment of diseases and support the bioeconomy of the future.

The 2017 Budget proposes $33.1 billion for the National Institutes of Health (NIH), through a mix of discretionary, enacted mandatory, and new mandatory funding to support high-quality, innovative biomedical research both on-campus and at research institutions across the country. The Budget supports basic and translational research to increase understanding of the causes of disease and spur development of diagnostic tests, treatments, and cures. As a part of the cancer "moonshot," an effort that will be led by the Vice President, the Budget provides an increase of $680 million to accelerate progress in preventing, diagnosing, and treating cancer. The Budget's multi-year cancer initiative, which begins in FY 2016, provides resources to improve health and outcomes for patients through investments in research and infrastructure, and brings together researchers across sectors and scientific disciplines. The Budget also increases NIH investments in the multi-agency BRAIN initiative and includes $300 million for NIH's contribution to the Precision Medicine Initiative aimed at tailoring medical care to the individual patient.

The Budget includes $530 million in mandatory R&D funding for the independent Patient-Centered Outcomes Research Institute to conduct clinical comparative effectiveness research, as authorized by the Affordable Care Act.

The Budget also proposes $1.3 billion for medical and prosthetic research across the Department of Veterans Affairs (VA). VA supports a robust program of basic and clinical research with a focus on ensuring continuous lifecycle care for veterans with an emphasis on Precision Medicine.

Strengthening Our National and Homeland Security through Science and Technology

Federal R&D investments in security aim to meet the threats of the future and to develop new innovative security capabilities. DOD R&D investments in the 2017 Budget focus on areas deemed to have the greatest impact on our nation and future military requirements. To this end, the 2017 Budget provides $72.8 billion for DOD R&D, an increase of 2.8 percent from the 2016 enacted level. The 2017 Budget proposes $12.5 billion for DOD's Science & Technology program, a subset of DOD R&D which consists of basic research, applied research and advanced technology development.

The 2017 Budget also maintains DOD's critical role in fostering breakthrough approaches for promising technologies with $3.0 billion for the Defense Advanced Research Projects Agency (DARPA), which promotes advanced research to create breakthrough technologies for tomorrow's military systems. Investing in DARPA's high-risk and high-reward science is an Administration priority and critical to maintaining the technological superiority of the U.S. military.

For DOE's National Nuclear Security Administration, the Budget proposes $7.1 billion for investments in R&D to help effectively manage the Nation's nuclear stockpile, advance naval nuclear propulsion, and achieve our non-proliferation goals.

The Budget supports investments in state-of-the-art technologies and solutions for Federal, State, and local homeland security operators, including $583 million in funding for the Department of Homeland Security R&D programs that protect the Nation's people and critical infrastructure from chemical, biological, radiological, nuclear, and cyber-attacks as well as other hazards.

Innovating in Information Technology and High-Performance Computing

High-performance computing (HPC) systems, through a combination of processing capability and storage capacity, can solve computational problems that are beyond the capability of small- to medium-scale systems. They are vital to the Nation's interests in science, medicine, engineering, technology, and industry. In July 2015, the Administration launched the National Strategic Computing Initiative (NSCI) as a whole-of-government effort to create a cohesive, multi-agency strategic vision and Federal investment strategy in HPC. This strategy will be executed in collaboration with industry and academia, maximizing the benefits of HPC for the United States. The NSCI will spur the creation and deployment of computing technology at the leading edge, helping to advance Administration priorities for economic competitiveness, scientific discovery, and national security. The 2017 Budget supports NSCI investments through many agencies, with major investments within DOE ($285 million) and NSF ($33 million).

Federal IT R&D, which launched and fueled the digital revolution, continues to drive innovation in scientific research, national security, communication, and commerce to sustain U.S. technological leadership. The multi-agency Networking and Information Technology Research and Development (NITRD) Program provides strategic planning for and coordination of agency research efforts in big data, cyber-physical systems, cybersecurity, health IT

high-confidence systems, high-end computing systems, human computer interaction, IT workforce development, large-scale networking, software design, wireless spectrum sharing, and other research relevant to advanced information technologies.

The 2017 Budget includes a focus on research to address the challenges and opportunities afforded by big data while providing appropriate privacy protections for personal data. The Budget continues to prioritize cybersecurity research to develop novel approaches and technologies that can protect U.S. systems from cyberattacks, consistent with the Federal Cybersecurity Research and Development Strategic Plan, to be released concurrently with the Budget.

Informing Better Stewardship of the Ocean and the Arctic

Sustainable stewardship of the ocean and the Arctic requires strong investments in research and development in the natural sciences to strengthen the scientific basis for decision-making. The 2017 Budget provides robust R&D funding to support responsible ocean stewardship, including observations, modeling, and data accessibility needed to support ecosystem-based management, as well as to advance understanding and inform responses to current and future climate impacts on oceans, Great Lakes, and surrounding communities. The Budget provides $520 million for NOAA's oceanic and atmospheric research programs and $63 million for NSF's arctic research programs. The 2017 Budget also advances the objectives of the Interagency Arctic Research Policy Committee Arctic Research Plan and the newly-created Arctic Executive Steering Committee, which coordinates efforts on Arctic science, resource management, conservation, indigenous peoples, and international engagement through the 2015-17 U.S. Chairmanship of the eight-nation Arctic Council.

Growing Agriculture Research for Future Generations

Agriculture has a significant impact on the economy and well-being of the United States. The Budget recognizes the importance of science and technology to meet the challenges and opportunities in agriculture, and provides significant investment increases, through a mix of discretionary, enacted mandatory, and new mandatory funding. There are three major agricultural R&D programs. They are (1) competitive research grants through the Department of Agriculture's flagship Agriculture and Food Research Initiative, which are funded at the authorized level of $700 million, double the funding provided in FY 2016; (2) the Department's in-house research programs, which are funded at $1.16 billion, and include increases for key initiatives: anti-microbial resistance, climate change, foreign animal diseases and Highly Pathogenic Avian Influenza, and water resources to support agricultural production; and (3) key infrastructure investments , which are funded at $95 million, which would continue the Department's program to prepare its facilities for the 21st Century.

Expanding Our Capabilities in Space

The Budget provides $19.0 billion for NASA to support the President's vision for innovation and scientific discovery on Earth and beyond, through a mix of discretionary and new mandatory funding proposals. NASA drives innovation in the aerospace sector and enhances the Nation's capabilities in space in areas such as communications, space-based observations, space transportation, and scientific discovery. The Budget provides $1.2 billion for the Commercial Crew program, continuing the development of safe and affordable systems to transport astronauts to orbit and working to eliminate our sole reliance on Russia for crew transport to the International Space Station. The Budget also provides $827 million for Space Technology and $324 million for Advanced Exploration Systems to develop technologies that will reduce the cost and increase the capabilities of NASA, other government, and commercial space activities. Within this funding the Budget supports early-stage public-private partnerships leading to the development of habitation modules that will play an important part in human space exploration and may have spinoff benefits to the commercial space economy closer to Earth.

Nanotechnology R&D

Working cooperatively through the National Nanotechnology Initiative (NNI), Federal agencies continue to support R&D aimed at creating a future in which the ability to understand and control matter at the nanoscale leads to a revolution in technology and industry that benefits society. Agencies participating in the NNI conduct R&D on materials, devices, and systems that exploit the unique physical, chemical, and biological properties that emerge in materials at the nanoscale (approximately 1 to 100 nanometers). Participating agencies continue to support fundamental research for nanotechnology-based innovation, technology transfer, and nanomanufacturing through individual investigator awards; multidisciplinary centers of excellence; education and training; and infrastructure and standards development, including openly-accessible user facilities and networks. NNI agencies will also continue their strong support for R&D on the environmental, health, and safety aspects of nanotechnology needed to ensure responsible development. NNI agencies and the National Nanotechnology Coordination Office (NNCO) will work with the business community, state and local governments, and the private sector to explore new approaches and leverage existing programs to foster broader commercialization of nanotechnology-enabled products. In addition, NNI agencies and the NNCO will continue to expand stakeholder engagement to advance nanotechnology-based STEM education, training, and outreach. Budget information is available at *www.nano.gov*.

Bridging the Barriers from Lab-to-Market

After the work of research and technology development is completed, additional work is necessary to translate the results into new capabilities and products that can spur economic growth and other societal benefits. The Federal R&D enterprise will continue to support fundamental research that is motivated primarily by our interest in expanding the frontiers of human knowledge, and will continue to diffuse this knowledge through open data and publications. At the same time, there remains significant potential to increase the public's return on this investment through effective partnerships with academia, industry, and regional innovation networks. For example, NASA has partnered with companies to make experimentation on the International Space Station more accessible to researchers – an approach that has played a significant role in jump-starting a new industry in very small satellites. In the case of the Department of Energy, industry partnerships can help broadly develop and deploy important next generation energy technologies and high-performance computers.

The Budget reflects the Administration's commitment to accelerating the transfer of the results of Federally funded research to the commercial marketplace by prioritizing funding for Lab-to-Market programs at the National Institute of Standards and Technology (NIST) ($8 million) and for the National Science Foundation's (NSF) Innovation Corps (I-Corps) program ($30 million). Both of these efforts are developing tools and best practices to commercialize the results of Federally-funded R&D. For example, the I-Corps program at NSF has 10 agreements with other Federal agencies that are using its experiential entrepreneurial curriculum to train research scientists, graduate students, and other entrepreneurs in how to identify and mature discoveries ripe for commercialization. In addition, I-Corps has a growing number of partnerships with non-Federal entities such as the State of Ohio. The Budget also provides $50 million in mandatory funding for a new competitive grant program, building on the success of prior Economic Development Administration led activities, to incentivize partnerships between Federal Labs, academia and regional economic development organizations enabling the transfer of knowledge and technologies from Labs to private industry for commercialization. In addition, the Department of Energy (DOE) is making the technologies and tools developed by its national labs more available to small businesses and entrepreneurs through innovative approaches designed to unlock new business or productive opportunities. (For additional details on this Cross Agency Priority goal see *performance.gov*)

Preparing Our Students with Skills through Science, Technology, Engineering, and Mathematics (STEM) Education

Our Nation's competitiveness depends on our ability to improve and expand STEM learning in the United States. Over the past several years, the Administration has made considerable progress towards creating a more cohesive framework for delivering STEM education. Guided by the Federal STEM Education Five-Year Strategic Plan, agencies are increasing coordination, strengthening partnerships, and identifying ways to leverage existing resources to improve the reach of agency assets. The

2017 Budget builds on these efforts, ensuring that investments are aligned with the Strategic Plan and support effective programs with strategic approaches to evaluation. The Budget invests $3.0 billion in STEM education programs, maintaining the level supported in 2016 enacted, including $100 million for a new Computer Science for All program within the Department of Education; as well as $332 million for graduate fellowships, $59 million for graduate traineeships, and $109 million for improving undergraduate education at NSF.

II. FEDERAL R&D DATA

R&D is defined as the collection of efforts directed toward gaining greater knowledge or understanding and applying knowledge toward the production of useful materials, devices, and methods. R&D investments can be characterized as basic research, applied research, development, R&D equipment, or R&D facilities. The Office of Management and Budget has used those or similar categories in its collection of R&D data since 1949.

Background on Federal R&D Funding

More than 20 Federal agencies fund R&D in the United States. The character of the R&D that these agencies fund depends on the mission of each agency and on the role of R&D in accomplishing it. Table 19–1 shows agency-by-agency spending on basic research, applied research, development, and R&D equipment and facilities.

Basic research is systematic study directed toward a fuller knowledge or understanding of the fundamental aspects of phenomena and of observable facts without specific applications towards processes or products in mind. Basic research, however, may include activities with broad applications in mind.

Applied research is systematic study to gain knowledge or understanding necessary to determine the means by which a recognized and specific need may be met.

Development is systematic application of knowledge or understanding, directed toward the production of useful materials, devices, and systems or methods, including design, development, and improvement of prototypes and new processes to meet specific requirements.

Research and development equipment includes acquisition or design and production of movable equipment, such as spectrometers, research satellites, detectors, and other instruments. At a minimum, this category includes programs devoted to the purchase or construction of R&D equipment.

Research and development facilities include the acquisition, design, and construction of, or major repairs or alterations to, all physical facilities for use in R&D activities. Facilities include land, buildings, and fixed capital equipment, regardless of whether the facilities are to be used by the Government or by a private organization, and regardless of where title to the property may rest. This category includes such fixed facilities as reactors, wind tunnels, and particle accelerators.

While the definitions for R&D activities have been stable for decades, interpretations of which programs are conducting R&D can vary with time. During the past year, DOE has been working to improve the consistency of their reporting of administrative activities that support R&D, consistent with the international standards. Because of these efforts, the DOE R&D amounts have increased in comparison to previous years. This effort is an example of more comprehensive Government-wide efforts currently underway to increase the accuracy and consistency of the R&D budget. The Federal executive agencies are working collaboratively, under a NSTC working group, to identify best practices and standards for the most accurate classification and reporting of R&D activities.

Table 19–1. FEDERAL RESEARCH AND DEVELOPMENT SPENDING
(Mandatory and discretionary budget authority [1], dollar amounts in millions)

	2015 Actual	2016 Enacted	2017 Proposed	Dollar Change: 2016 to 2017	Percent Change: 2016 to 2017
By Agency [2]					
Defense	65,547	70,872	72,825	1,953	3%
Health and Human Services	30,453	31,942	32,714	772	2%
Energy [3]	14,354	14,405	17,160	2,755	19%
NASA	12,145	12,410	12,043	−367	−3%
National Science Foundation	5,944	6,117	6,529	412	7%
Agriculture	2,452	2,674	2,923	249	9%
Commerce	1,524	1,913	1,888	−25	−1%
Veterans Affairs	1,178	1,220	1,252	32	3%
Interior	863	981	1,082	101	10%
Transportation	885	924	1,065	141	15%
Homeland Security	919	579	585	6	1%
Environmental Protection Agency	523	516	530	14	3%
Patient-Centered Outcomes Research Trust Fund	396	472	530	58	12%
U.S. Agency for International Development	250	275	287	12	4%
Smithsonian Institution	246	250	270	20	8%
Education	279	242	248	6	2%
Other	320	346	402	56	16%
TOTAL	**138,278**	**146,138**	**152,333**	**6,195**	**4%**
Basic Research					
Defense	2,225	2,320	2,115	−205	−9%
Health and Human Services	15,055	15,972	16,323	351	2%
Energy	4,477	4,609	4,932	323	7%
NASA	3,198	3,562	3,537	−25	−1%
National Science Foundation	4,878	4,941	5,257	316	6%
Agriculture	993	1,028	1,162	134	13%
Commerce	214	223	239	16	7%
Veterans Affairs	484	505	542	37	7%
Interior	53	54	63	9	17%
Transportation	....	....	....	....	....
Homeland Security	41	41	40	−1	−2%
Environmental Protection Agency	....	....	....	....	....
Patient-Centered Outcomes Research Trust Fund	....	....	....	....	....
U.S. Agency for International Development	1	1	4	3	300%
Smithsonian Institution	210	218	237	19	9%
Education	7	18	16	−2	−11%
Other	18	18	18	0	0%
SUBTOTAL	**31,854**	**33,510**	**34,485**	**975**	**3%**
Applied Research					
Defense	4,653	5,056	4,884	−172	−3%
Health and Human Services	15,199	15,760	16,138	378	2%
Energy	5,624	5,346	7,108	1,762	33%
NASA	2,402	2,757	3,012	255	9%
National Science Foundation	691	752	813	61	8%
Agriculture	1,114	1,113	1,357	244	22%
Commerce	891	942	1,015	73	8%
Veterans Affairs	618	639	634	−5	−1%
Interior	685	790	886	96	12%
Transportation	688	612	758	146	24%
Homeland Security	207	176	168	−8	−5%
Environmental Protection Agency	442	430	446	16	4%
Patient-Centered Outcomes Research Trust Fund	396	472	530	58	12%
U.S. Agency for International Development	202	223	211	−12	−5%

Table 19–1. FEDERAL RESEARCH AND DEVELOPMENT SPENDING—Continued
(Mandatory and discretionary budget authority[1], dollar amounts in millions)

	2015 Actual	2016 Enacted	2017 Proposed	Dollar Change: 2016 to 2017	Percent Change: 2016 to 2017
Smithsonian Institution	....	....	....	....	....
Education	159	135	132	–3	–2%
Other	207	236	269	33	14%
SUBTOTAL	**34,178**	**35,439**	**38,361**	**2,922**	**8%**
Development					
Defense	58,553	63,463	65,631	2,168	3%
Health and Human Services	26	30	30	0	0%
Energy	3,263	3,338	3,982	644	19%
NASA	6,481	5,954	5,357	–597	–10%
National Science Foundation	....	....	....	....	....
Agriculture	177	176	179	3	2%
Commerce	188	348	303	–45	–13%
Veterans Affairs	76	76	76	0	0%
Interior	89	135	131	–4	–3%
Transportation	172	277	272	–5	–2%
Homeland Security	356	354	377	23	6%
Environmental Protection Agency	76	81	79	–2	–2%
Patient-Centered Outcomes Research Trust Fund	....	....	....	....	....
U.S. Agency for International Development	47	51	72	21	41%
Smithsonian Institution	....	....	....	....	....
Education	113	89	100	11	12%
Other	102	94	115	21	22%
SUBTOTAL	**69,719**	**74,466**	**76,704**	**2,238**	**3%**
Facilities and Equipment					
Defense	116	33	195	162	491%
Health and Human Services	173	180	223	43	24%
Energy	990	1,112	1,138	26	2%
NASA	64	137	137	0	0%
National Science Foundation	375	424	459	35	8%
Agriculture	168	357	225	–132	–37%
Commerce	231	400	331	–69	–17%
Veterans Affairs	....	....	....	....	....
Interior	36	2	2	0	0%
Transportation	25	35	35	0	0%
Homeland Security	315	8	0	–8	–1
Environmental Protection Agency	5	5	5	0	0%
Patient-Centered Outcomes Research Trust Fund	....	....	....	....	....
U.S. Agency for International Development	....	....	....	....	....
Smithsonian Institution	36	32	33	1	3%
Education	....	....	....	....	....
Other	–7	–2	0	2	100%
SUBTOTAL	**2,527**	**2,723**	**2,783**	**60**	**2%**

[1] This table shows funding levels for Departments or Independent agencies with more than $200 million in R&D activities in 2017.

[2] Some numbers in the chapter text include non-R&D activities and thus will be different from the R&D numbers in this table.

[3] In this Budget, Department of Energy began reporting additional administrative expenses, consistent with international and government-wide standards. This led to an increase in reporting of R&D investments on the order of $2 to $3 billion a year.

20. CREDIT AND INSURANCE

The Federal Government offers direct loans and loan guarantees to support a wide range of activities including home ownership, education, small business, farming, energy efficiency, infrastructure investment, and exports. Also, Government-sponsored enterprises (GSEs) operate under Federal charters for the purpose of enhancing credit availability for targeted sectors. Through its insurance programs, the Federal Government insures deposits at depository institutions, guarantees private defined-benefit pensions, and insures against some other risks such as flood and terrorism.

This chapter discusses the roles of these diverse programs:

- The first section emphasizes the roles of Federal credit and insurance programs in addressing market imperfections that may prevent the private market from efficiently providing credit and insurance.

- The second section discusses individual credit programs and the GSEs. Credit programs are broadly classified into five categories: housing, education, small business and farming, energy and infrastructure, and international lending.

- The third section reviews Federal deposit insurance, pension guarantees, disaster insurance, and insurance against terrorism and other security-related risks.

I. THE FEDERAL ROLE

Credit and insurance markets sometimes fail to function smoothly due to market imperfections. Relevant market imperfections include information failures, monitoring problems, limited ability to secure resources, insufficient competition, externalities, and financial market instability. Federal credit and insurance programs may improve economic efficiency if they effectively fill the gaps created by market imperfections. Addressing market imperfections, however, is a subtle task. To be effective, a credit or insurance program should be carefully designed to reduce inefficiencies in the targeted area without disturbing efficiently functioning areas. In addition to correcting market failures, Federal credit and insurance programs may provide subsidies to serve other policy purposes, such as reducing inequalities and extending opportunities to disadvantaged regions or segments of the population. The effectiveness of credit assistance in serving these purposes should be carefully compared with that of more direct policy tools, such as grants and tax credits.

Information Failures. When lenders have insufficient information about borrowers, they may fail to evaluate the creditworthiness of borrowers accurately. As a result, some creditworthy borrowers may fail to obtain credit at a reasonable interest rate, while some high-risk borrowers obtain credit at an attractive interest rate. The problem becomes more serious when borrowers are much better informed about their own creditworthiness than lenders (asymmetric information). With asymmetric information, raising the interest rate can disproportionately draw high-risk borrowers who care less about the interest rate (adverse selection). Thus, lenders may limit the amount of credit to a group of borrowers with highly uncertain creditworthiness, or even exclude the group all

together, instead of charging a high interest rate. In this situation, many creditworthy borrowers may fail to obtain credit even at a high interest rate. Ways to deal with this problem in the private sector include equity financing and pledging collateral. Federal credit programs play a crucial role for those populations that are vulnerable to this information failure and do not have effective means to deal with it. Start-up businesses lacking a credit history, for example, are vulnerable to the information failure, but most of them are unable to raise equity publicly and do not have sufficient collateral. Another example is students who have little income, little credit experience, and no collateral to pledge. Without Federal credit assistance, many in these groups may be unable to pursue their entrepreneurial or academic goals. In addition, a moderate subsidy provided by the Government can alleviate adverse selection by attracting more low-risk borrowers, although an excessive subsidy can cause economic inefficiency by attracting many borrowers with unworthy or highly risky projects.

Monitoring Needs. Monitoring is a critical part of credit and insurance businesses. Once the price (the interest rate or the insurance premium) is set, borrowers and policyholders may have incentives to engage in risky activities. Insured banks, for example, might take more risk to earn a higher return. Although private lenders and insurers can deter risk-taking through covenants, re-pricing, and cancellation, Government regulation and supervision can be more effective in some cases, especially where covering a large portion of the target population is important. For a complex business like banking, close examination may be necessary to deter risk-taking. Without legal authority, close examination may be impractical. When it is difficult to prevent risk-taking, private insurers may turn down many applicants and often cancel policies, which is socially undesirable in some cases, such as deposit insurance and pension guarantees. It is important to protect bank deposits to prevent disruption to the financial market. Without pension guarantees, many retirees could experience financial hardships and strain other social safety nets.

Limited Ability to Secure Resources. The ability of private entities to absorb losses is often more limited than that of the Federal Government. For some events potentially involving a very large loss concentrated in a short time period, therefore, Government insurance can be more reliable. Such events include massive bank failures and some natural and man-made disasters that can threaten the solvency of private insurers. In addition, some lenders may have limited funding sources. Small local banks, for example, may have to rely largely on local deposits.

Insufficient Competition. Competition can be insufficient in some markets because of barriers to entry or economies of scale. Insufficient competition may result in unduly high prices of credit and insurance in those markets.

Externalities. Decisions at the individual level are not socially optimal when individuals do not capture the full benefit (positive externalities) or bear the full cost (negative externalities) of their activities. Education, for example, generates positive externalities because the general public benefits from the high productivity and good citizenship of a well-educated person. Pollution, in contrast, is a negative externality, from which other people suffer. Without Government intervention, people may engage less than the socially optimal level in activities that generate positive externalities and more in activities that generate negative externalities.

Financial Market Instability. Another rationale for Federal intervention is to prevent instability in the financial market. Without deposit insurance, for example, the financial market would be much less stable. When an economic shock impairs the financial structure of many banks, depositors may find it difficult to distinguish between solvent banks and insolvent ones. In this situation, failures of some banks might prompt depositors to withdraw deposits from all banks (bank runs), making bank failures contagious. Deposit insurance is critical in preventing bank runs, which harm the entire economy.

II. CREDIT IN VARIOUS SECTORS

Housing Credit Programs and GSEs

Through housing credit programs, the Federal Government promotes homeownership among various target groups, including low- and moderate-income people, veterans, and rural residents. Recently, the target market expanded dramatically due to the financial crisis.

The consequences of inflated house prices and loose mortgage underwriting during the housing bubble that peaked in 2007 created perilous conditions for many American homeowners. Millions of families were foreclosed upon and millions more found themselves owing more on their homes than their homes were worth. Private capital all but disappeared from the market. Without the Federal support provided to the housing market since 2008, the situation would have been more problematic.

Federal Housing Administration

The Federal Housing Administration (FHA) guarantees mortgage loans to provide access to homeownership for people who may have difficulty obtaining a conventional mortgage. FHA has been a primary facilitator of mortgage credit for first-time and minority buyers, a pioneer of products such as the 30-year self-amortizing mortgage, and a vehicle to enhance credit for many moderate and low-income households.

FHA and the Mortgage Market

In the early 2000s, FHA's market presence diminished greatly as low interest rates increased the affordability of mortgage financing and more borrowers used emerging non-prime mortgage products, including subprime and Alt-A mortgages. Many of these products had risky and hard-to-understand features such as low "teaser rates" offered for periods as short as the first two years of the mortgage, high loan-to-value ratios (with some mortgages exceeding the value of the house), and interest-only loans with balloon payments that require full payoff at a set future date. The Alt-A mortgage made credit easily available by waiving documentation of income or assets. This competition eroded the market share of FHA's single-family loans, reducing it from 9 percent in 2000 to less than 2 percent in 2005.

Starting at the end of 2007, the availability of FHA and Government National Mortgage Association (which supports the secondary market for federally-insured housing loans by guaranteeing securities backed by mortgages guaranteed by FHA, VA, and USDA) credit guarantees has been an important factor countering the tightening of private-sector credit. The annual volume of FHA's single-family mortgages soared from $52 billion in 2006 to $330 billion in 2009.

FHA's presence has supported the home purchase market and enabled many existing homeowners to re-finance at today's lower rates. If not for such re-financing options, many homeowners would remain stuck in high-interest mortgages and face higher risk of foreclosure given the economic challenges resulting from the Great Recession and decreased house prices.

The return of conventional financing to the mortgage market—with appropriate safeguards for consumers and investors including prudent underwriting and disclosure of risk—will broaden both the options available to borrowers and the sources of capital to fund those options. The Administration supports a greater role for non-federally assisted mortgage credit, while recognizing that FHA will continue to play an important role in the mortgage market going forward.

Although loan volume declined since its 2009 peak, FHA enjoyed strong demand in 2015 as mortgage rates remained low and the improving economy brought new home buyers into the market. Also contributing was a reduction in FHA premiums, as discussed in detail below. FHA's new origination loan volume in 2015 was $213 billion and FHA's market share of home purchase financing was 21 percent. For 2017, the Budget projects FHA volume will be $204 billion.

FHA's Budget Costs

FHA's budget estimates can be volatile and prone to forecast error because default claim rates are sensitive to a variety of dynamics. FHA insurance premium revenues are spread thinly but universally over pools of policyholders. Mortgage insurance costs for FHA, however, are concentrated in only those borrowers who default and whose lender files a claim, with the average per claim cost being much larger than the average premium income. Therefore, if claims change by even a small fraction of borrowers (e.g., one percentage point), net FHA insurance costs will move by a multiple of that change. For other forms of insurance, such as life and health, these changes tend to gradually occur over time, allowing actuaries to anticipate the effects and modify risk and pricing models accordingly. The history of FHA, however, has been spotted with rapid, unanticipated changes in claim costs and recoveries. FHA is vulnerable to "Black Swans," outlier events that are difficult to predict and have deep effect. For FHA, these include the collapse of house prices after market bubbles burst and the effects of lending practices with very high claim rates, such as the now illegal seller-financed down-payment mortgage.

One of the major benefits of an FHA-insured mortgage is that it provides a homeownership option for borrowers who can make only a modest down-payment, but show that they are creditworthy and have sufficient income to afford the house they want to buy. In 2015, over 72 percent of new FHA loans were financed with less than five percent down. The disadvantage to low down-payment mortgages is that they have little in the way of an equity cushion should house prices decline or events such as income loss or unexpected medical expenses make it difficult for households to remain current on their mortgage payment. When these occur, the net sales proceeds from home sales may not be sufficient to support exit strategies that allow borrowers to completely pay off the debt and relocate to more affordable housing.

According to its annual actuarial analysis, in 2015 FHA achieved its statutory minimum capital reserve ratio of 2 percent for the first time since 2008. As the housing market has recovered and FHA has improved its risk management, the actuarial review found that FHA's capital reserve increased by $41 billion over the last three years. Even a low capital ratio as existed from 2009 to 2014 does not threaten FHA's operations, however, either for its existing portfolio or for new books of business.

FHA accounts contain sufficient funds to pay anticipated claims and unlike private lenders, the guarantee on FHA and other Federal loans is backed by the full faith and credit of the Federal Government and is not dependent on capital reserves to honor its commitments.

In 2009, the FHA capital reserve was broadened to include Home Equity Conversion Mortgages (HECMs) in addition to single-family purchase and re-finance (forward) mortgages. This change has increased the volatility of FHA's capital reserves. The financial performance of HECMs is highly sensitive to changes in house prices and interest rates. While the trend in capital reserves of forward mortgages has been consistently upward over the last three years, HECM capital reserves experienced a downward spike in 2014 followed by a large upward swing in 2015. For 2015, the capital reserve ratio was 6.4 percent for HECMs and 1.6 percent for forward mortgages.

FHA increased insurance premiums to bolster its capital resources five times starting in 2008. For a typical borrower, the cumulative increases were 0.25 percentage points in the upfront premium and 0.85 percentage points in annual premiums. Given the improvement in FHA's financial position, it makes sense to partially reverse these premium increases to promote access to housing credit. A 0.50 percentage point reduction of annual premiums, from 1.35 percent to .85 percent, was rolled out in January 2015. Even with this reduction, FHA will collect premiums on new mortgages that are well above the estimated costs of guaranteeing those mortgages against default. As a result, FHA will stay on a strong trajectory with its capital reserve ratio. This reduction also provides pricing to new FHA borrowers more in line with the stronger underwriting requirements they have to meet in order to qualify and will make homeownership more likely for many borrowers, including those who have sufficient credit quality but would lack the income to support mortgage payments at the higher premium levels.

In addition to the single-family mortgage insurance provided through the MMI program, FHA's General Insurance and Special Risk Insurance (GISRI) loan programs continue to facilitate the construction, rehabilitation, and refinancing of multifamily housing, hospitals and other health care facilities. GISRI's new origination loan volume in 2015 was $13.4 billion and the Budget projects $13.8 billion for 2017, including $10.6 billion in multifamily loans and $3.1 billion in healthcare loans.

In 2016, FHA will reduce upfront and annual premiums for affordable and energy efficient rental housing. For loans insured under FHA's three signature new construction/substantial rehabilitation and refinance programs, the annual premium will be reduced by a range of 10 to 40 basis points. These targeted reductions will: (1) support the production and preservation of affordable rental housing; (2) incent energy efficiency improvements in both affordable and market rate housing; and (3) improve housing choice for low-income families by tying certain premium reductions to landlord acceptance of Federal rental vouchers.

VA Housing Program

The Department of Veterans Affairs (VA) assists veterans, members of the Selected Reserve, and active duty personnel in purchasing homes in recognition of their service to the Nation. The housing program effectively substitutes the Federal guarantee for the borrower's down payment, making the lending terms more favorable than loans without a VA guarantee. VA does not guarantee the entire mortgage loan to veterans, but provides a 100 percent guarantee on the first 25 percent of losses upon default. The number of loans that VA guaranteed reached a new record level in 2015, as the tightened credit markets continued to make the VA housing program more attractive to eligible homebuyers. VA provided 264,057 zero down payment loans. The continued historically low interest rate environment of 2015 allowed 309,027 Veteran borrowers to lower interest rates on their home mortgages through refinancing. VA provided over $38 billion in guarantees to assist 631,142 borrowers in 2015, of which 238,013 were fee-exempt loans to Veterans with service-connected disabilities. This followed $25 billion and 438,398 borrowers in 2014.

VA, in cooperation with VA-guaranteed loan servicers, also assists borrowers through home retention options and alternatives to foreclosure. VA intervenes when needed to help veterans and service members avoid foreclosure through loan modifications, special forbearances, repayment plans, and acquired loans; as well as assistance to complete compromise sales or deeds-in-lieu of foreclosure. These joint efforts helped resolve over 83 percent of defaulted VA-guaranteed loans in 2015.

Rural Housing Service

The Rural Housing Service (RHS) at the U.S. Department of Agriculture (USDA) offers direct and guaranteed loans to help very-low- to moderate-income rural residents buy and maintain adequate, affordable housing. RHS housing loans and loan guarantees differ from other Federal housing loan programs in that they are means-tested, making them more accessible to low-income, rural residents. For the direct loan program, approximately 40 percent of borrowers earn less than 50 percent of their area's median income; the remainder earn between 50 percent and 80 percent (maximum for the program) of area median income. The single family housing guaranteed loan program is designed to provide home loan guarantees for moderate-income rural residents whose incomes are between 80 percent and 115 percent (maximum for the program) of area median income.

The 2017 Budget continues USDA single family housing assistance programs. Within its $24 billion guarantee loan level, the Budget expects RHS to potentially provide over $3.0 billion in loan guarantees for low-income rural borrowers, which could provide 20,800 new homeownership opportunities to that income group. Overall, the program could potentially provide approximately 160,000 new homeownership or refinancing opportunities to low- to moderate-income rural residents in 2017. The Budget assumes this level will only be reached in the event of increased market demand for mortgage credit in rural areas, a possibility for which this funding level is accommodative. Typical program funding utilization will be within 80 percent of the funding level.

This funding level includes the continuation of an annual and up-front fee structure. These fees reduce the overall subsidy cost of the loans without adding significant burden to the borrowers. The Budget also proposes to make USDA's guaranteed home loan program a delegated underwriting program, allowing approved lenders with a strong track record with the program to make the loans on behalf of the government and no longer requiring USDA to sign-off in conjunction with each loan. This change will make RHS more efficient and allow the single family housing staff to refocus on other important needs.

For USDA's single family housing direct loan program, the 2017 Budget provides a loan level of $900 million, which is expected to allow approximately 6,500 low to very-low income rural residents an opportunity to realize the dream of home-ownership.

For USDA's multifamily housing portfolio, the Budget focuses primarily on portfolio management. Management includes the retention of its existing portfolio of affordable rental housing as well as the rehabilitation of that housing to continue to provide safe and decent housing for residents. USDA is working with OMB and other Federal housing partners, as well as program participants, to develop solutions that will continue to provide rental subsidies for the low and very-low income residents in those properties with maturing mortgages at the lowest cost to the government. The Budget fully funds this rehabilitation effort by providing $66.5 million for the multifamily housing revitalization activities, which include loan modifications, grants, zero percent loans, and soft second loans as well as some funding for traditional multifamily housing direct loans to allow USDA to better address its inventory property. These activities allow borrowers to restructure their debt so that they can effectively rehabilitate properties within the portfolio in order for them to continue to supply decent, safe, affordable rental housing to the low- and very-low-income population in rural America. The Budget also proposes to codify these activities into permanent law.

In addition, rental assistance grants, which supplement tenant rental payments to the property owners and are vital to the proper underwriting of the multifamily housing direct loan portfolio, are funded at $1.405 billion, which is sufficient to renew outstanding agreements. The Budget also provides $230 million in guaranteed multifamily housing loans and $15.4 million in budget authority for the Farm Labor Housing grants and loans. Collectively, the 2017 Budget request in the rural development multifamily housing portfolio reflects the Administration's support for the poorest rural tenant population base.

Government-Sponsored Enterprises in the Housing Market

The Federal National Mortgage Association, or Fannie Mae, created in 1938, and the Federal Home Loan Mortgage Corporation, or Freddie Mac, created in 1970, were established to support the stability and liquidity of a secondary market for residential mortgage loans. Fannie Mae's and Freddie Mac's public missions were later broadened to promote affordable housing.

Growing stress and losses in the mortgage markets in 2007 and 2008 seriously eroded the capital of Fannie Mae and Freddie Mac, and responsive legislation enacted in July 2008 strengthened regulation of the housing GSEs and provided the Treasury Department with authorities to purchase GSE securities. In September 2008, reacting to growing GSE losses and uncertainty that threatened to paralyze the mortgage markets, the GSEs' independent regulator, the Federal Housing Finance Agency (FHFA), placed Fannie Mae and Freddie Mac under Federal conservatorship, and Treasury began to exercise its purchase authorities to provide support to the GSEs. The Budget continues to reflect the GSEs as non-budgetary entities in keeping with their temporary status in conservatorship. However, all of the current Federal assistance being provided to Fannie Mae and Freddie Mac, including capital provided by Treasury through the Senior Preferred Stock Purchase Agreements (PSPA), is shown on-budget, and discussed below.

The Federal Home Loan Bank (FHLB) System, created in 1932, is comprised of eleven individual banks with shared liabilities. Together they lend money to financial institutions—mainly banks and thrifts—that are involved in mortgage financing to varying degrees, and they also finance some mortgages using their own funds.

Mission

The mission of the housing GSEs is to support certain aspects of the U.S. mortgage market. Fannie Mae and Freddie Mac's mission is to provide liquidity and stability to the secondary mortgage market and to promote affordable housing. Currently, they engage in two major lines of business.

1. Credit Guarantee Business—Fannie Mae and Freddie Mac guarantee the timely payment of principal and interest on mortgage-backed securities (MBS). They create MBS by pooling mortgages acquired through either purchase from or swap arrangements with mortgage originators. Over time these MBS held by the public have averaged nearly 40 percent of the U.S. mortgage market, and as of November 30, 2015, they totaled $4.3 trillion.

2. Mortgage Investment Business—Fannie Mae and Freddie Mac manage retained mortgage portfolios composed of their own MBS, MBS issued by others, and individual mortgages. The GSEs finance the purchase of these portfolio assets through debt issued in the credit markets. As of November 30, 2015, these retained mortgages, financed largely by GSE debt, totaled $698 billion. As a term of their PSPA contracts with Treasury, the combined investment portfolios of Fannie Mae and Freddie Mac were limited to no more than $1.8 trillion as of December 31, 2009, and this limitation was directed to decline by 10 percent each year. To accelerate the wind-down of the GSEs' retained mortgage portfolios, Treasury revised the PSPA terms in August 2012, setting the effective portfolio limitation at $1.1 trillion as of December 31, 2013, and accelerating the reduction in this limitation to 15 percent each year until December 31, 2018, when the combined limitation will be fixed at $500 billion ($250 billion for each company).

As of November 30, 2015, the combined debt and guaranteed MBS of Fannie Mae and Freddie Mac totaled $5.1 trillion.

The mission of the FHLB System is broadly defined as promoting housing finance, and the System also has specific requirements to support affordable housing. Its principal business remains lending (secured by mortgages and financed by System debt issuances) to regulated depository institutions and insurance companies engaged in residential mortgage finance. Historically, investors in GSE debt have included thousands of banks, institutional investors such as insurance companies, pension funds, foreign governments and millions of individuals through mutual funds and 401k investments.

Together these three GSEs currently are involved, in one form or another, with approximately half of the $11 trillion residential mortgages outstanding in the U.S. today.

Regulatory Reform

The 2008 Housing and Economic Recovery Act (HERA) reformed and strengthened the GSEs' safety and soundness regulator by creating the Federal Housing Finance Agency (FHFA), a new independent regulator for Fannie Mae, Freddie Mac, and the Federal Home Loan Banks. The FHFA authorities consolidate and expand upon the regulatory and supervisory roles of what were previously three distinct regulatory bodies: the Federal Housing Finance Board as the FHLB's overseer; the Office of Federal Housing Enterprise Oversight as the safety and soundness regulator of the other GSEs; and HUD as their public mission overseer. FHFA was given substantial authority and discretion to influence the size and composition of Fannie Mae and Freddie Mac investment portfolios through the establishment of housing goals, monitoring GSE compliance with those goals, and capital requirements.

FHFA is required to issue housing goals, such as for purchases of single-family mortgages provided to low-income families, for each of the regulated enterprises, including the FHLBs, with respect to single family and multi-family mortgages and has the authority to require a corrective "housing plan" if an enterprise does not meet its goals and statutory reporting requirements, and in some instances impose civil money penalties. The housing goals for 2012 through 2014, promulgated on November 13, 2012, established revised benchmarks for Fannie Mae and Freddie Mac, comprising four goals and one subgoal for single-family, and one goal and one subgoal for multi-family housing. FHFA determined that both Fannie Mae and Freddie Mac exceeded the 2012 benchmark levels on all of the single-family and multifamily goals, while in 2013 Fannie Mae fell short on one goal and Freddie Mac fell short on three goals. FHFA's evaluation of the GSEs' performance in reaching the 2014 goals indicates that Fannie Mae achieved all its goals and that Freddie Mac fell short on two goals. Freddie Mac will be required to submit a housing plan to address their plans to achieve those goals. On August 19, 2015, FHFA published a final rule that establishes new affordable housing goals for years 2015-2017, including for the first time a goal for low-income rental units in small multifamily properties.

The expanded authorities of FHFA also include the ability to place any of the regulated enterprises into conservatorship or receivership based on a finding of under-capitalization or a number of other factors.

Conservatorship

On September 6, 2008, FHFA placed Fannie Mae and Freddie Mac under Federal conservatorship. This action was taken in response to the GSEs' declining capital adequacy and to support the safety and soundness of the GSEs, given the role they played in the secondary mortgage market and the potential impact of their failure on broader financial markets. HERA provides that as conservator FHFA may take any action that is necessary to put Fannie Mae and Freddie Mac in a sound and solvent condition and to preserve and conserve the assets of each firm. As conservator, FHFA has assumed by operation of law the powers of the Board and shareholders at Fannie Mae and Freddie Mac. FHFA has appointed Directors and CEOs who are responsible for the day-to-day operations of the two firms. While in conservatorship, FHFA expects Fannie Mae and Freddie Mac to continue to fulfill their core statutory purposes, including their support for affordable housing discussed above. In its Strategic Plan for the Conservatorships of Fannie Mae and Freddie Mac, released in 2014, FHFA outlined three key goals for conservatorship: 1) maintain, in a safe and sound manner, foreclosure prevention activities and credit availability for new and refinanced mortgages to foster liquid, efficient, competitive and resilient national housing finance markets; 2) reduce taxpayer risk through increasing the role of private capital in the mortgage market; and 3) build a new single-family securitization infrastructure for use by the GSEs and adaptable for use by other participants in the secondary market in the future.

Department of Treasury GSE Support Programs under HERA

On September 7, 2008, the U.S. Treasury launched three programs to provide temporary financial support to the GSEs under the temporary authority provided in HERA to purchase GSE securities. These purchase authorities expired on December 31, 2009.

1. PSPAs with Fannie Mae and Freddie Mac

Treasury entered into agreements with Fannie Mae and Freddie Mac to make investments in senior preferred stock in each GSE in order to ensure that each company maintains a positive net worth. In exchange for the substantial funding commitment, the Treasury received $1 billion in senior preferred stock for each GSE and warrants to purchase up to a 79.9 percent share of common stock at a nominal price. The initial agreements established funding commitments for up to $100 billion in each of these GSEs. On February 18, 2009, Treasury announced that the funding commitments for these agreements would be increased to $200 billion for each GSE. On December 24, 2009, Treasury announced that the funding commitments in the purchase agreements would be modified to the greater of $200 billion or $200 billion plus cumulative net worth deficits experienced during 2010-2012, less any positive net worth remaining as of December 31, 2012. Based on the financial results reported by each company as of December 31, 2012, the cumulative funding commitment for Fannie Mae and Freddie Mac was set at $445.5 billion. In total, as of December 31, 2015, $187.5 billion has been invested in the GSEs, and the initial liquidation preference of the senior preferred stock held by Treasury has increased accordingly. The PSPAs also require that Fannie Mae and Freddie Mac pay quarterly dividends to Treasury. Prior to calendar year 2013, the quarterly dividend amount was based on an annual rate of 10 percent of the liquidation preference of Treasury's senior preferred stock. Amendments to the PSPAs effected on August 17th, 2012, replaced the 10 percent dividend with an amount equivalent to the GSE's positive net worth above a capital reserve amount. The capital reserve amount for each company was set at $3.0 billion for calendar year 2013, and declines by $600 million at the beginning of each calendar year thereafter until it reaches zero. Through December 31, 2015, the GSEs have paid a total of $241.2 billion in dividends payments to Treasury on the senior preferred stock. The Budget estimates additional dividend receipts of $151.5 billion from January 1, 2016, through FY 2026. The cumulative budgetary impact of the PSPAs from the establishment of the PSPAs through FY 2026 is estimated to be a net return to taxpayers of $205.2 billion. The Temporary Payroll Tax Cut Continuation Act of 2011 signed into law on December 23, 2011, required that the GSEs increase their fees on security guarantees issued through FY 2021 by an average of at least 0.10 percentage points above the average guarantee fee imposed in 2011. Revenues generated by this fee increase are remitted directly to the Treasury for deficit reduction and are not included in the PSPA amounts. The Budget estimates resulting deficit reductions from this fee of $40.5 billion from FY 2012 through FY 2026.

2. GSE MBS Purchase Programs

Treasury initiated a temporary program during the financial crisis to purchase MBS issued by Fannie Mae and Freddie Mac, which carry the GSEs' standard guarantee against default. The purpose of the program was to promote liquidity in the mortgage market and, thereby, affordable homeownership by stabilizing the interest rate spreads between mortgage rates and corresponding rates on Treasury securities. Treasury purchased $226 billion in MBS from September 2008 to December 31, 2009, when the statutory purchase authority that Treasury used for this program expired, and sold the last of its MBS holdings in March 2012. The MBS purchase program generated $11.9 billion in net budgetary savings, calculated on a net present value basis as required by the Federal Credit Reform Act.

3. *GSE Credit Facility*

Treasury promulgated the terms of a temporary secured credit facility available to Fannie Mae, Freddie Mac, and the Federal Home Loan Banks. The facility was intended to serve as an ultimate liquidity backstop to the GSEs if necessary. No loans were needed or issued through December 31, 2009, when Treasury's HERA purchase authority expired.

4. *State Housing Finance Agency Programs*

In December 2009, Treasury used its purchase authorities under HERA to initiate two programs to support state and local Housing Financing Agencies (HFAs). Under the New Issue Bond Program (NIBP), Treasury purchased $15.3 billion in securities of Fannie Mae and Freddie Mac backed by new HFA housing bond issuances. As of December 31 2015, NIBP balances had decreased to approximately $7.5 billion. The Temporary Credit and Liquidity Program (TCLP) provided HFAs with credit and liquidity facilities supporting up to $8.2 billion in existing HFA bonds. The TCLP ended in July 2015 after the last participating HFAs received alternative liquidity facilities from private sector banks.

Recent GSE Role in Administration Initiatives to Relieve the Foreclosure Crisis and Support Access to Affordable Housing

While under Federal conservatorship, Fannie Mae and Freddie Mac have continued to play a leading role in Government and private market initiatives to prevent homeowners who are having difficulty making their mortgage payments from losing their homes. In March 2009, the Administration announced its Making Home Affordable (MHA) initiative, which includes the Home Affordable Modification Program (HAMP) and the Home Affordable Refinance Program (HARP).

Fannie Mae and Freddie Mac are participating in HAMP both for mortgages they own or guarantee and as the Treasury Department's contractual financial agents. Under HAMP, investors, servicers, and borrowers receive incentive payments to reduce eligible homeowners' monthly payments to affordable levels. The incentive payments for the modification of loans not held by the GSEs are paid by Treasury's Troubled Asset Relief Program (TARP) fund, while the incentive payments for the modification of loans held by the GSEs are generally paid by the GSEs, with a small portion paid through TARP. As of December 31, 2015, nearly 2.4 million trial modi-

fications have been initiated, resulting in more than 1.6 million homeowners entering permanent mortgage modifications. HAMP has also encouraged the mortgage industry to adopt similar programs that have helped millions more at no cost to the taxpayer. In December 2015, the Consolidated Appropriations Act, 2016 set December 31, 2016 as the termination date for new applications under MHA. However, through HAMP and other TARP housing programs, the Administration continues to support homeowners who are facing foreclosure, those who are struggling with increasing interest rates on their mortgages, and those whose homes are underwater. For more information on HAMP and other TARP housing programs, see the Budgetary Effects of the Troubled Asset Relief Program chapter of this volume.

Fannie Mae and Freddie Mac also facilitate underwater refinancing through HARP. Under the program, borrowers with a mortgage that is owned by Fannie Mae or Freddie Mac and who are current on their loan payments may be eligible to refinance their mortgage to take advantage of the current low interest rate environment regardless of their current loan-to-value (LTV) ratio. Prior to HARP, the LTV limit of 80 percent for conforming purchase mortgages without a credit enhancement such as private mortgage insurance applied to refinancing of mortgages owned by the GSEs. Thus, borrowers whose home values had dropped such that their LTVs had increased above 80 percent could not take advantage of the refinance opportunity. With the introduction of HARP in 2009, eligible borrowers with LTVs up to 105 percent (later extended to 125 percent) could qualify. On October 24, 2011, FHFA announced that HARP would be enhanced by lowering the fees charged by Fannie Mae and Freddie Mac on these refinancings, streamlining the application process, and removing the previous LTV cap of 125 percent. In May of 2015, FHFA announced that it would extend HARP through December 31, 2016. From the inception of the program through October 2015, nearly 3.4 million refinancings have been completed through HARP.

As the housing market strengthens, the Administration has worked to expand responsible lending to creditworthy borrowers and to increase access to affordable rental housing for families not ready or wanting to buy a home. Under the direction of FHFA, the GSEs continue to play a role in these efforts. In 2014, Fannie Mae and Freddie Mac announced a revised framework that clarifies the circumstances under which lenders may be required to repurchase a loan when the GSEs determine that the purchased loan does not meet their underwriting guidelines. In 2015, they continued these efforts by publishing guidance that for the first time defines severity levels for loan origination defects and establishes a process for remedying them, and by releasing updated guidance on servicing remedies. These steps are expected to help alleviate lender uncertainty that has contributed to increased credit overlays that drive up lending costs and reduce access to credit. In December 2015, FHFA issued a proposed rule that establishes a framework for evaluating the GSEs' progress toward serving three underserved markets, as required by HERA: manufactured housing, affordable housing preservation, and rural markets. Finally, FHFA has directed the GSEs to begin setting aside 4.2 basis points for each dollar of unpaid principal balance of new business purchases (such as mortgages purchased for securitization) in each year to fund several federal affordable housing programs created by HERA: the Housing Trust Fund, the Capital Magnet Fund, and the HOPE Reserve Fund. These set-asides, initially authorized by HERA, were suspended by FHFA in November 2008 and were reinstated effective January 1, 2015. The first set-aside of approximately $373 million is projected to be transferred to the affordable housing funds in early 2016, subject to terms and conditions as prescribed by FHFA.

Future of the GSEs

To finish addressing the weaknesses exposed by the financial crisis, the housing finance system must be reformed, and Fannie Mae and Freddie Mac should be wound down. The bipartisan progress in the Senate in the previous session was a meaningful step towards securing a system that aligns with many of the Administration's principles for reform, including ensuring that private capital is at the center of the housing finance system so that taxpayer assistance is never again required, and that the new system supports broad access to credit and affordable rental housing through programs like the Housing Trust and Capital Magnet Funds. Further, the Consolidated Appropriations Act, 2016, included a provision that prohibits Treasury from selling or otherwise disposing of the preferred stock it holds in Fannie Mae or Freddie Mac until January 1, 2018, unless legislation instructing Treasury on how to do so is enacted into law. Further, this provision recommends that legislation regarding the future of Fannie Mae and Freddie Mac be enacted and, notwithstanding the previous limitation, suggests that Treasury should not sell or dispose of its stock until such legislation is enacted. The Administration will continue to work with Congress to pass comprehensive reform, centered on several core principles: require more private capital in the system; end the Fannie Mae/Freddie Mac duopoly business model in order to improve system stability and better protect taxpayers; ensure broad access for all creditworthy families to sustainable products like the 30-year fixed rate mortgage in good times and bad; and help ensure sustainable rental options are widely available.

In the absence of comprehensive housing finance reform legislation, the Administration continues to take actions that balance the desire to reduce taxpayer risk with the need to support the continued flow of mortgage credit in a recovering housing market. Starting in 2013, Fannie Mae and Freddie Mac began to initiate a series of credit risk-sharing transactions with private market participants that add an additional layer of private loss coverage, further limiting taxpayer exposure to credit losses from the GSEs and potentially providing a model for future reforms. As of October 2015, the GSEs have transferred a significant portion of credit risk on single-family mortgages with a total unpaid principal balance over $700 billion. The GSEs and FHFA also plan to continue building a new single-family securitization platform for the GSEs that can be adapted for use by non-GSE users in order to increase liquidity in the secondary mortgage market.

Education Credit Programs

Historically, the Department of Education financed student loans through two programs: the Federal Family Education Loan (FFEL) program and the William D. Ford Federal Direct Student Loan (Direct Loan) program. In March 2010, President Obama signed the Student Aid and Fiscal Responsibility Act (SAFRA) which ended the FFEL program. On July 1, 2010, ED became the sole originator of Federal student loans through the Direct Loan program, and despite significant technical challenges, ED made all loans on time and without disruption.

The Direct Loan program was authorized by the Student Loan Reform Act of 1993. Under the program, the Federal Government provides loan capital directly to over 6,000 domestic and foreign schools, which then disburse loan funds to students. Loans are available to students and parents of students regardless of income, but the terms of the loans differ. There are three types of Direct Loans: Federal Direct Subsidized Stafford Loans, Federal Direct Unsubsidized Stafford Loans, and Federal Direct PLUS Loans. For Direct Subsidized Stafford loans, which are available to undergraduate borrowers from low and moderate income families, the Federal Government provides more benefits, including not charging interest while the borrowers are in school and during certain deferment periods.

In 2013 President Obama signed the Bipartisan Student Loan Certainty Act which established interest rates for all types of new Direct Loans made on or after July 1, 2013. Interest rates on Direct Loans are set annually based on Treasury rates but once the rate is set, the rate is fixed for the life of the loan. Interest rates are set by: (1) indexing the interest rate to the rate of ten-year Treasury notes; and (2) adding the indexed rate to a specific base percent for each loan type with specific caps for each loan type. For Federal Direct Subsidized Stafford Loans and Federal Direct Unsubsidized Stafford Loans issued to undergraduate students, the rate is 2.05 percentage points above the Treasury 10-year note rate and capped at 8.25 percent. For Federal Direct Unsubsidized Stafford Loans issued to graduate and professional students, the rate is 3.6 percentage points above the Treasury rate and capped at 9.5 percent. For Federal Direct PLUS Loans issued to parents and graduate and professional students, the rate is 4.6 percentage points above the Treasury rate and capped at 10.5 percent.

The Direct Loan program offers a variety of flexible repayment plans including income-driven ones for all student borrowers, regardless of the type of loan. In October 2011, the Administration announced a "Pay As You Earn" (PAYE) initiative for certain eligible student borrowers that set monthly loan payments at no more than 10 percent of the borrowers' discretionary incomes and with their remaining balances forgiven after 20 years. In

December 2015, similar benefits were extended to all student borrowers, regardless of when they borrowed. The 2017 Budget would continue to allow all borrowers access to PAYE, but proposes reforms to ensure that the program's benefits are better targeted.

In addition, the Federal Perkins Loan Program has provided low interest loans to help students finance the costs of postsecondary education. Students at approximately 1,500 participating postsecondary institutions could obtain Perkins loans from the school. In 2016, Congress extended the authority to make loans under the existing program through September 30, 2017. The 2017 Budget proposes to create an expanded, modernized Perkins Loan program providing $8.5 billion in loan volume annually, beginning in the 2017-2018 school year, so that students will continue to have access to credit after the scheduled program termination.

The Department of Education offers two types of loan forgiveness to incentivize student borrowers to enter teaching careers in high-needs schools. The 2017 Budget consolidates into one new program these forgiveness programs and the TEACH Grant program. TEACH currently offers annual grants to undergraduate and graduate students who agree to teach in high-needs subjects and schools, which convert to loans for participants who do not fulfill their service requirements. Beginning in 2021, the proposed streamlined teacher loan forgiveness program increases the maximum benefit available to teachers graduating from effective teacher preparation programs, seeks to incentivize retention by staggering forgiveness over five years, and maintains the requirement to teach in a high-need school.

Small Business and Farm Credit Programs and GSEs

The Government offers direct loans and loan guarantees to small businesses and farmers, who may have difficulty obtaining credit elsewhere. It also provides guarantees of debt issued by certain investment funds that invest in small businesses. Two GSEs, the Farm Credit System and the Federal Agricultural Mortgage Corporation, increase liquidity in the agricultural lending market.

Loans to Small Businesses

The Small Business Administration (SBA) helps entrepreneurs start, sustain, and grow small businesses. As a "gap lender," SBA works to supplement market lending and provide access to credit where private lenders are reluctant to do so at a reasonable price without a Government guarantee. SBA also helps home- and business-owners, as well as renters, cover the uninsured costs of recovery from disasters through its direct loan program. At the end of 2015 SBA's outstanding balance of direct and guaranteed loans totaled approximately $119 billion. Due to the improved economy, past fee waivers, and SBA improvements in streamlining lender documentation requirements, demand for SBA guaranteed loans has significantly increased in the last two years. For this reason, the 2016 limitation on SBA's 7(a) loan guarantees

was increased to $26.5 billion following nearly $22 billion in lending net of cancellations in 2015, and the Budget increases it to $27 billion to accommodate expected demand as the economy and opportunities for small businesses grow. The 2017 Budget appropriations language also includes a provision that would provide the Administrator of SBA flexibility to further increase the program level if needed.

The 2017 Budget supports $42 billion in financing for small businesses with no subsidy costs through the 7(a) General Business Loan program and the 504 Certified Development Company (CDC) program. As noted, the 7(a) program will support $27 billion in guaranteed loans that will help small businesses operate and expand. The 504 program will support $7.5 billion in guaranteed loans for fixed-asset financing, and $7.5 billion in 504 guarantees to allow small businesses to refinance to take advantage of current interest rates and free up resources for expansion. In addition, SBA will supplement the capital of Small Business Investment Corporations (SBICs) with up to $4 billion in long-term, guaranteed loans to support SBICs' venture capital investments in small businesses. SBA is able to continue all borrower fee waivers on 7(a) loans less than $150 thousand as well as partial waivers on 7(a) loans less than $500 thousand to veteran-owned businesses in the 2017 Budget.

The Budget also supports SBA's disaster direct loan program at its 10-year average volume of $1.1 billion in loans, and includes $187 million to administer the program. Of this amount, $159 million is provided through the Budget Control Act's disaster relief cap adjustment for costs related to Stafford Act (Presidentially-declared) disasters.

For the 2017 Budget, SBA recorded a net downward reestimate of $1.3 billion in the expected costs of its outstanding loan portfolio, reflecting an improved loan performance forecast, which will decrease the 2016 budget deficit.

The Budget also requests subsidy to support $44 million in direct loans, and $31 million in technical assistance grant funds for the Microloan program. The Microloan program provides low-interest loan funds to non-profit intermediaries who in turn provide loans of up to $50,000 to new entrepreneurs.

The 2017 Budget also includes a mandatory proposal to create the Scale-Up Manufacturing Investment Companies (SUMIC) program within SBA that would support young, innovative manufacturing technologies by financing their scale-up from prototypes to commercial-scale facilities in the United States. The SUMIC program is designed to generate $10 billion in investment activity over five years, using $5 billion in Federal financing and a matching amount of private funds to bridge a significant portion of the financing gap for small advanced manufacturing startups. The program would support private funds in a similar way to how SBA operates its SBIC debt guarantee program, but of a much larger fund and project size necessary to support the needs of manufacturing scale-up efforts. The estimated subsidy costs associated with each application for a Federal contribution to a fund would be determined on a fund-by-fund basis using actual fund financial information. For purposes of the 2017 Budget, a subsidy rate of 25 percent is assumed, based on conservative cash flow assumptions and an annual fee to offset some expected default costs.

To help small businesses drive economic recovery and create jobs, the Small Business Jobs Act of 2010 created two new mandatory programs that provide financing assistance to small businesses: State Small Business Credit Initiative (SSBCI) and Small Business Lending Fund. The Department of the Treasury administers those programs, and SSBCI remains highly active. SSBCI is designed to support state programs that make new loans or investments to small businesses and small manufacturers. SSBCI has offered states and territories (and in certain circumstances, municipalities) the opportunity to apply for Federal funds to finance programs that partner with private lenders to extend new credit to small businesses to create jobs. These funds have allowed States to create or improve various small business programs, including collateral support programs, capital access programs, revolving loan and loan guarantee programs, loan participation programs, and State venture capital programs. SSBCI guidelines state that all approved programs must demonstrate a reasonable expectation of minimum overall leverage of $10 in new private lending for every $1 in Federal funding. Treasury is providing approximately $1.5 billion for SSBCI, which translates into $15 billion in new lending to small businesses at the 10-to-1 leverage ratio. As of September 14, 2015, SSBCI had approved funding for 47 states, 5 territories, 4 municipalities, and the District of Columbia for a total of nearly $1.5 billion in obligations, of which $1.35 billion had already been disbursed. Through December 31st, 2014, SSBCI has supported more than 12,400 loans or investments, which helped create 87 new businesses and are estimated to create or save 140,000 American jobs.

The Budget proposes a new authorization of $1.5 billion for a second round of the SSBCI to build on the momentum of the program's first round, strengthen the Federal government's relationship with state economic development agencies, and provide capital to America's diverse community of entrepreneurs. The proposal requires $1 billion of the funding to be competitively awarded to States best able to target local market needs, promote inclusion, attract private capital for start-up and scale-up businesses, strengthen regional entrepreneurial ecosystems, and evaluate results. The remaining $500 million will be allocated to States according to a need-based formula reflecting economic factors such as job losses and pace of economic recovery.

Treasury's Community Development Financial Institutions (CDFI) Fund Bond Guarantee program, also authorized in the Small Business Jobs Act of 2010, provides CDFIs access to long term capital to fund large economic development projects such as multi-family rental properties, charter schools, and health care centers in low-income communities. Treasury is authorized to guarantee up to 10 bond issuances per year with a $100 million minimum individual bond size. Program authority initial-

ly expired on September 30, 2014, but has been extended twice in annual appropriations bills and now expires in 2016. The Bond Guarantee program does not require discretionary budget authority for credit subsidy but annual loan guarantee limitations must be appropriated. Through September 30, 2015, Treasury had issued $852 million in bond guarantee commitments to 16 CDFIs, supporting investments in low-income and underserved communities. The Consolidated Appropriations Act, 2016, provides $750 million in additional commitment authority, and the Budget proposes to extend the Bond Guarantee program through 2017 with an annual commitment limitation of $1 billion and introduce reforms that will increase participation and ensure credit-worthy CDFIs have access to this important source of capital while continuing to maintain strong protections against credit risk.

Loans to Farmers

The Farm Service Agency (FSA) assists low-income family farmers in starting and maintaining viable farming operations. Emphasis is placed on aiding beginning and socially disadvantaged farmers. FSA offers operating loans and ownership loans, both of which may be either direct or guaranteed loans. Operating loans provide credit to farmers and ranchers for annual production expenses and purchases of livestock, machinery, and equipment, while farm ownership loans assist producers in acquiring and developing their farming or ranching operations. As a condition of eligibility for direct loans, borrowers must be unable to obtain private credit at reasonable rates and terms. As FSA is the "lender of last resort," default rates on FSA direct loans are generally higher than those on private-sector loans. FSA-guaranteed farm loans are made to more creditworthy borrowers who have access to private credit markets. Because the private loan originators must retain 10 percent of the risk, they exercise care in examining the repayment ability of borrowers. The subsidy rates for the direct programs fluctuate largely because of changes in the interest component of the subsidy rate.

The number of loans provided by these programs has varied over the past several years. In 2015, FSA provided loans and loan guarantees to more than 37,000 family farmers totaling $5.7 billion. Direct and guaranteed loan programs provided assistance totaling $2.5 billion to beginning farmers during 2015. Loans for socially disadvantaged farmers totaled $827 million, of which $438 million was in the farm ownership program and $389 million in the farm operating program. The average size of farm ownership loans was consistent over the past two years, with new customers receiving the bulk of the direct loans. The majority of assistance provided in the operating loan program during 2015 was to beginning farmers as well. Overall, demand for FSA loans—both direct and guaranteed—continues to be high. More conservative credit standards in the private sector continue to drive applicants from commercial credit to FSA direct programs. Low grain prices and uncertainty over interest rates continue to cause lenders to force their marginal borrowers to FSA for credit. In the 2017 Budget, FSA proposes to make $6.7 billion in direct and guaranteed loans through discretionary programs, including guaranteed conservation loans. The overall loan level for conservation loans is unchanged from the 2016 requested level of $150 million.

Lending to beginning farmers was strong during 2015. FSA provided direct or guaranteed loans to more than 20,500 beginning farmers. Loans provided under the Beginning Farmer Down Payment Loan Program represented 37 percent of total direct ownership loans made during the year, slightly lower than the previous year. Sixty-four percent of direct operating loans were made to beginning farmers, an increase of 4 percent in dollar volume over 2015. Overall, as a percentage of funds available, lending to beginning farmers was 7 percentage points above the 2014 level, propelled by a 5 percent increase in ownership loans and 9 percent increase in operating loans made to beginning farmers. Lending to minority and women farmers was a significant portion of overall assistance provided, with $827 million in loans and loan guarantees provided to more than 9,200 farmers. This represents an increase of 8 percent in the overall number of direct loans to minority and women borrowers. Outreach efforts by FSA field offices to reach out to beginning and minority farmers and promote FSA funding have resulted in increased lending to these groups.

FSA continues to evaluate the farm loan programs in order to improve their effectiveness. FSA released a new Microloan program to increase lending to small niche producers and minorities. This program has been expanded to include guaranteed as well as direct loans. This program dramatically simplifies application procedures for small loans, and implements more flexible eligibility and experience requirements. The demand for the microloan program continues to grow while delinquencies and defaults remain at or below those of the regular FSA operating loan program. FSA has also developed a nationwide continuing education program for its loan officers to ensure they remain experts in agricultural lending, and it is transitioning all information technology applications for direct loan servicing into a single, web-based application that will expand on existing capabilities to include all special servicing options. Its implementation will allow FSA to better service its delinquent and financially distressed borrowers.

The Farm Credit System (Banks and Associations)

The Farm Credit System (FCS or System) is a Government-sponsored enterprise (GSE) composed of a nationwide network of borrower-owned cooperative lending institutions originally authorized by Congress in 1916. The FCS's mission continues to be providing sound and dependable credit to American farmers, ranchers, producers or harvesters of aquatic products, their cooperatives, and farm-related businesses. In addition, they serve rural America by providing financing for rural residential real estate, rural communication, energy and water infrastructure, and agricultural exports.

The financial condition of the System's banks and associations remains fundamentally sound. The ratio of capital to assets has remained stable at 16.8 percent on September 30, 2015, compared with 16.9 percent on September 30, 2014. Capital consisted of $44.9 billion in unrestricted capital and $4.0 billion in restricted capital in the Farm Credit System Insurance Fund, which is held by the Farm Credit System Insurance Corporation (FCSIC). For the first nine months of calendar year 2015, net income equaled $3.5 billion compared with $3.6 billion for the same period of the previous year. The small decline in net income resulted from a slight increase in noninterest expense.

Over the 12-month period ending September 30, 2015, nonperforming loans as a percentage of total loans outstanding decreased from 0.85 percent to 0.76 percent. System assets moderately grew by 7.1 percent during that period, primarily due to increases in real estate mortgage loans and agribusiness loans. Real estate mortgage loans increased due to continued demand for financing cropland. The increase in agribusiness loans was due to an increase in advances on existing processing and marketing loans.

Over the 12-month period ending September 30, 2015, the System's loans outstanding grew by $18.8 billion, or 9.0 percent, while over the past three years they grew by $41.7 billion, or 23.0 percent. As required by law, borrowers are also stockholder-owners of System banks and associations. As of September 30, 2015, System institutions had 504,568 of these stockholders-owners.

The number of FCS institutions continues to decrease because of consolidation. As of September 30, 2015, the System consisted of four banks and 76 associations, compared with seven banks and 104 associations in September 2002. Of the 80 FCS banks and associations, 76 of them had one of the top two examination ratings (1 or 2 on a 1 to 5 scale) and accounted for 99 percent of gross Systems assets. Three FCS institutions had a rating of 3, and 1 institution was rated a 4.

In 2014, the pace of new lending to young, beginning, and small farmers exceeded the pace in overall farm lending by Farm Credit System institutions. The number of loans made in 2014 to young and beginning farmers increased by 2.0 percent and 1.8 percent from 2013, while overall the number of farm loans made by the System fell 1.8 percent. The number of loans to small farmers declined by 1.4 percent, but because small farmer loans declined less than overall farm loans, the share of small farmer loans increased as well. Loans to young, beginning, and small farmers and ranchers represented 16.9 percent, 21.2 percent, and 40.2 percent, respectively, of the total new farm loans made in 2014.

The dollar volume of new loans made to young and beginning categories rose in 2014 from 2013 by 5.0 percent and 3.2 percent, respectively. The System's overall volume of new farm loans grew by 1.8 percent. Therefore, the share of total System farm loan volume made to these categories rose from that of 2013. Loan volume to small farmers decreased 5.2 percent from 2013. Loans to young, beginning, and small farmers and ranchers represented 11.3 percent, 14.8 percent, and 13.9 percent, respectively, of the total dollar volume of all new farm loans made in 2014. Young, beginning, and small farmers are not mutually exclusive groups and, thus, cannot be added across categories. Maintaining special policies and programs for the extension of credit to young, beginning, and small farmers and ranchers is a legislative mandate for the System.

The System, while continuing to record strong earnings and capital growth, remains exposed to a variety of risks associated with its portfolio concentration in agriculture and rural America. In 2015, downward pressure on grain prices stemmed from large supplies relative to demand following bumper crops in recent years for the major grains. Low grain and oilseed prices have helped control feed costs for livestock, poultry, and dairy farmers, but margins for these subsectors have been squeezed by weaker output prices. The housing sector continues to improve, which should translate into improved credit conditions for the housing related sectors such as timber and nurseries. Overall, the agricultural sector remains subject to risks such as a farmland price decline, which actually occurred in 2015 in the Midwest and other parts of the country, a potential rise in interest rates, continued volatility in commodity prices, weather-related catastrophes, and long-term environmental risks related to climate change.

The FCSIC, an independent Government-controlled corporation, ensures the timely payment of principal and interest on FCS obligations on which the System banks are jointly and severally liable. On September 30, 2015, the assets in the Insurance Fund totaled $4.0 billion. As of September 30, 2015, the Insurance Fund as a percentage of adjusted insured debt was 1.94 percent. This was slightly below the statutory secure base amount of 2 percent. During the first nine months of calendar year 2015, outstanding insured System obligations grew by 2.7 percent.

Federal Agricultural Mortgage Corporation (Farmer Mac)

Farmer Mac was established in 1988 as a federally chartered instrumentality of the United States and an institution of the FCS to facilitate a secondary market for farm real estate and rural housing loans. Farmer Mac is not liable for any debt or obligation of the other System institutions, and no other System institutions are liable for any debt or obligation of Farmer Mac. The Farm Credit System Reform Act of 1996 expanded Farmer Mac's role from a guarantor of securities backed by loan pools to a direct purchaser of mortgages, enabling it to form pools to securitize. In May 2008, the Food, Conservation and Energy Act of 2008 (2008 Farm Bill) expanded Farmer Mac's program authorities by allowing it to purchase and guarantee securities backed by rural utility loans made by cooperatives.

Farmer Mac continues to meet core capital and regulatory risk-based capital requirements. As of September 30, 2015, Farmer Mac's total outstanding program volume (loans purchased and guaranteed, standby loan purchase commitments, and AgVantage bonds purchased and guaranteed) amounted to $15.6 billion, which represents an increase of 11.4 percent from the level a year ago. Of to-

tal program activity, $11.1 billion were on-balance sheet loans and guaranteed securities, and $4.5 billion were off-balance-sheet obligations. Total assets were $14.9 billion, with non-program investments (including cash and cash equivalents) accounting for $3.5 billion of those assets. Farmer Mac's net income attributable to common stockholders ("net income") for the first three quarters of calendar year 2015 was $32.3 million. Net income was stable compared to the same period in 2014 during which Farmer Mac reported net income of $32.6 million.

Farmer Mac's earnings can be substantially influenced by unrealized fair-value gains and losses. For example, fair-value changes on financial derivatives resulted in an unrealized gain of $0.9 million for the first three quarters of 2015, compared with unrealized losses of $12.5 million for the same period in 2014 (both pre-tax). Although unrealized fair-value changes experienced on financial derivatives temporarily impact earnings and capital, those changes are not expected to have any permanent effect if the financial derivatives are held to maturity, as is expected.

Energy and Infrastructure Credit Programs

This Administration is committed to constructing a new foundation for economic growth and job creation, and clean energy is a critical component of that. The general public, as well as individual consumers and owners, benefits from clean energy and well-developed infrastructure. Thus, the Federal Government promotes clean energy and infrastructure development through various credit programs.

Credit Programs to Promote Clean and Efficient Energy

The Department of Energy (DOE) administers two credit programs that serve to reduce emissions and enhance energy efficiency: a loan guarantee program to support innovative energy technologies and a direct loan program to support advanced automotive technologies.

The Energy Policy Act of 2005 authorized DOE to issue loan guarantees for projects that employ innovative technologies to reduce air pollutants or man-made greenhouse gases under the Title 17 loan guarantee program. Congress provided $4 billion in loan volume authority for Title 17 in 2007, and the 2009 Consolidated Appropriations Act provided an additional $47 billion in loan volume authority, allocated as follows: $18.5 billion for nuclear power facilities, $2 billion for "front-end" nuclear enrichment activities, $8 billion for advanced fossil energy technologies, and $18.5 billion for energy efficiency, renewable energy, and transmission and distribution projects. The 2011 appropriations reduced the available loan volume authority for energy efficiency, renewable energy, and transmission and distribution projects by $17 billion and provided $170 million in credit subsidy to support renewable energy or energy efficient end-use energy technologies. In 2015 DOE added $1 billion from existing unallocated mixed-use authority to existing loan solicitations and clarified eligibility for distributed energy projects. The President's 2017 Budget requests $4 billion in mixed-use loan authority.

The American Reinvestment and Recovery Act of 2009 amended the program's authorizing statute to allow loan guarantees on a temporary basis for commercial or advanced renewable energy systems, electric power transmission systems, and leading edge biofuel projects, providing $2.5 billion in credit subsidy for loan guarantees. Authority for the temporary program to extend new loans expired September 30, 2011. DOE provided loan guarantees to 28 projects totaling over $16 billion in guaranteed debt including: 12 solar generation, 4 solar manufacturing, 4 wind generation, 3 geothermal, 2 biofuels, and 3 transmission/energy storage projects. Four projects withdrew prior to any disbursement of funds. From 2014-2015, DOE closed on three loan guarantees totaling approximately $8 billion to support the construction of two new commercial nuclear power reactors. Currently DOE has open solicitations for Renewable Energy and Efficient Energy, Advanced Fossil, and Advanced Nuclear projects.

The Advanced Technology Vehicle Manufacturing (ATVM) Direct Loan program was created to support the development of advanced technology vehicles and associated components in the United States that would improve vehicle energy efficiency by at least 25 percent relative to a 2005 Corporate Average Fuel Economy standards baseline. In 2009, Congress appropriated $7.5 billion in credit subsidy to support a maximum of $25 billion in loans under ATVM. The program provides loans to automobile and automobile part manufacturers for the cost of re-equipping, expanding, or establishing manufacturing facilities in the United States, and for other costs associated with engineering integration.

Electric and Telecommunications Loans

Rural Utilities Service (RUS) programs of the United States Department of Agriculture (USDA) provide loans for rural electrification, telecommunications, distance learning, and telemedicine, and also provide grants for distance learning and telemedicine (DLT).

The Budget includes $6.5 billion in direct loans for electricity distribution, construction of renewable energy facilities, transmission, and carbon capture projects on facilities to replace fossil fuels. The Budget also provides $690 million in direct telecommunications loans, $39 million in broadband grants, and $35 million in DLT grants.

USDA Rural Infrastructure and Business Development Programs

USDA provides grants, loans, and loan guarantees to communities for constructing facilities such as healthcare clinics, police stations, and water systems. Direct loans are available at lower interest rates for the poorest communities. These programs have very low default rates. That coupled with the historically low funding costs for the Government has resulted in negative subsidy rates for these programs.

The program level for the Water and Wastewater treatment facility loan and grant program in the 2017

President's Budget is $1.23 billion. These funds are available to communities of 10,000 or fewer residents.

The Community Facility (CF) Program targets grants and direct loans to rural communities with fewer than 20,000 residents. The 2017 Budget includes $25 million for the CF grants to expand the community facility grant program to address ongoing needs and emerging priorities such as Promise Zones and Strike Force Communities. These funds will allow USDA to be responsive to new needs in communities across rural America and target them in a flexible way. In addition, the Budget includes a direct CF loan level of $2.2 billion.

USDA also provides grants, direct loans, and loan guarantees to assist rural businesses, cooperatives, nonprofits, and farmers in creating new community infrastructure (i.e. educational and healthcare networks) and to diversify the rural economy and employment opportunities. In 2017, USDA proposes to provide $935 million in loan guarantees and direct loans to entities that serve communities of 25,000 or fewer residents through the Intermediary Relending program and to entities that serve communities of 50,000 or fewer residents through the Business and Industry guaranteed loan program and the Rural Microentrepreneur Assistance program. These loans are structured to save or create jobs and stabilize fluctuating rural economies.

The Rural Business Service is also responsible for the Rural Energy for America program for which the Budget includes $68.5 million in funding to support $357 million in loan guarantees and grants to promote energy efficiencies, renewable energy, and small business development in rural communities.

Transportation Infrastructure

Federal credit programs offered through the Department of Transportation (DOT) fund critical transportation infrastructure projects, often using innovative financing methods. The two predominant programs are the program authorized by the Transportation Infrastructure Finance and Innovation Act (TIFIA) and the Railroad Rehabilitation and Improvement Financing (RRIF) program.

Established by the Transportation Equity Act of the 21st century (TEA-21) in 1998, the TIFIA program is designed to fill market gaps and leverage substantial private co-investment by providing supplemental and subordinate capital to projects of national or regional significance. Through TIFIA, DOT provides three types of Federal credit assistance to highway, transit, rail, and intermodal projects: direct loans, loan guarantees, and lines of credit. The 61 TIFIA-assisted loans account for almost $83 billion of infrastructure investment in the United States. Government commitments in these partnerships constitute over $23 billion in Federal assistance with a budgetary cost of approximately $1.5 billion.

TIFIA can help advance qualified, large-scale projects that otherwise might be delayed or deferred because of size, complexity, or uncertainty over the timing of revenues at a relatively low budgetary cost. Each dollar of subsidy provided for TIFIA can provide approximately

$10 in credit assistance, and leverage an additional $20 to $30 in non-Federal transportation infrastructure investment. The Fixing America's Surface Transportation (FAST) Act of 2015 authorizes TIFIA at $275 million in fiscal year 2016, escalating to $300 million by fiscal year 2020.

DOT has also provided direct loans and loan guarantees to railroads since 1976 for facilities maintenance, rehabilitation, acquisitions, and refinancing. Federal assistance was created to provide financial assistance to the financially-challenged portions of the rail industry. However, following railroad deregulation in 1980, the industry's financial condition began to improve, larger railroads were able to access private credit markets, and interest in Federal credit support began to decrease.

Also established by TEA-21 in 1998, the RRIF program may provide loans or loan guarantees with an interest rate equal to the Treasury rate for similar-term securities. TEA-21 also stipulates that non-Federal sources pay the subsidy cost of the loan, thereby allowing the program to operate without Federal subsidy appropriations. The RRIF program assists projects that improve rail safety, enhance the environment, promote economic development, or enhance the capacity of the national rail network. While refinancing existing debt is an eligible use of RRIF proceeds, capital investment projects that would not occur without a RRIF loan are prioritized. Since its inception, $2.7 billion in direct loans have been made under the RRIF program.

The FAST Act included programmatic changes to enhance the RRIF program to mirror the qualities of TIFIA, including broader eligibility, a loan term that can be as long as 35 years from project completion, and a fully subordinated loan under certain conditions. Additionally, in 2016 Congress reprogrammed $1.96 million in unobligated balances to assist Class II and Class III Railroads in preparing and applying for direct loans and loan guarantees.

Financing America's Infrastructure Renewal (FAIR) program

The Budget proposes to establish a Financing America's Infrastructure Renewal (FAIR) program within the Department of the Treasury that would provide direct loans to U.S. infrastructure projects developed through a public-private partnership (P3). The program seeks to reduce the financing cost gap between P3s and traditional procurement, which will level the playing field for P3s and encourage the public sector, including State and local governments, to evaluate the merits of P3s for a given project. While P3s are not a solution to the Nation's overall infrastructure funding needs, which continue to deserve greater Federal investment, they may generate certain public benefits. P3s are a financing and procurement tool that, in some circumstances, can accelerate the delivery of complex projects, leverage the resources and expertise of the private sector, mitigate construction and operational risks to the public sector, and reduce the likelihood of deferred maintenance on a project.

Eligible projects under the program will encompass the transportation, water, energy, and broadband sectors, as well as certain social infrastructure, such as educational facilities, and must meet all applicable environmental and labor standards. The Budget estimates that the FAIR program will provide $15 billion in financing support over the current 10 year budget window (2017-2026), with an average transaction size of $300 million. The proposal differs from the Administration's National Infrastructure Bank (NIB) proposal, described more fully below, because it targets lending at zero financing subsidy and does not require the formation of a new entity. The Budget estimates approximately $2.3 million per year of administrative expenses. This program may ultimately serve as a bridge to the creation of a NIB.

National Infrastructure Bank

To direct Federal resources for infrastructure to projects that demonstrate the most merit and may be difficult to fund under the current patchwork of Federal programs, the President has called for the creation of an independent, non-partisan National Infrastructure Bank (NIB), led by infrastructure and financial experts. The NIB would offer broad eligibility and unbiased selection for transportation, water, and energy infrastructure projects. Projects would have a clear public benefit, meet rigorous economic, technical and environmental standards, and be backed by a dedicated revenue stream. Geographic, sector, and size considerations would also be taken into account. Interest rates on loans issued by the NIB would be indexed to United States Treasury rates, and the maturity could be extended up to 35 years, giving the NIB the ability to be a "patient" partner side-by-side with State, local, and private co-investors. To maximize leverage from Federal investments, the NIB would finance no more than 50 percent of the total costs of any project.

International Credit Programs

Seven Federal agencies—the Department of Agriculture (USDA), the Department of Defense, the Department of State, the Department of the Treasury, the Agency for International Development (USAID), the Export-Import Bank, and the Overseas Private Investment Corporation (OPIC)—provide direct loans, loan guarantees, and insurance to a variety of private and sovereign borrowers. These programs are intended to level the playing field for U.S. exporters, deliver robust support for U.S. goods and services, stabilize international financial markets, enhance security and promote sustainable development.

Leveling the Playing Field

Federal export credit programs counter official financing that foreign governments around the world, largely in Europe and Japan but also increasingly in emerging markets such as China and Brazil, provide their exporters, usually through export credit agencies (ECAs). The U.S. Government has worked since the 1970's to constrain official credit support through a multilateral agreement in the Organization for Economic Cooperation and Development

(OECD). In its current form, this agreement has virtually eliminated direct interest rate subsidies, significantly constrained tied-aid grants, and standardized the fees for corporate and sovereign lending across all OECD ECAs—bringing the all-in costs of OECD export credit financing broadly in line with market levels. In addition to ongoing OECD negotiations, U.S. Government efforts resulted in the 2012 creation of the International Working Group (IWG) on export credits. This group includes China and other non-OECD providers of export credits in discussions on a broader framework that would bring common practices to ECAs throughout the world.

The Export-Import Bank provides export credits, in the form of direct loans or loan guarantees, to U.S. exporters who meet basic eligibility criteria and who request the Bank's assistance. USDA's Export Credit Guarantee Programs (also known as GSM programs) similarly help to level the playing field. Like programs of other agricultural exporting nations, GSM programs guarantee payment from countries and entities that want to import U.S. agricultural products but cannot easily obtain credit.

Stabilizing International Financial Markets

Consistent with U.S. obligations in the International Monetary Fund regarding global financial stability, the Exchange Stabilization Fund managed by the Department of the Treasury may provide loans or credits to a foreign entity or government of a foreign country. A loan or credit may not be made for more than six months in any 12-month period unless the President gives the Congress a written statement that unique or emergency circumstances require that the loan or credit be for more than six months.

Supporting the Nation's International Partners

The U.S. Government, through USAID, can extend short-to-medium-term loan guarantees that cover potential losses that might be incurred by lenders if a country defaults on its borrowings; for example, the U.S. may guarantee another country's sovereign bond issuance. The purpose of this tool is to provide the Nation's sovereign international partners access to necessary, urgent, and relatively affordable financing during temporary periods of strain when they cannot access such financing in international financial markets, and to support critical reforms that will enhance long term fiscal sustainability, often in concert with support from international financial institutions such as the International Monetary Fund. The long term goal of sovereign loan guarantees is to help lay the economic groundwork for the Nation's international partners to graduate to an unenhanced bond issuance in the international capital markets. For example, as part of the U.S. response to fiscal crises, the U.S. Government has extended sovereign loan guarantees to Tunisia, Jordan, and Ukraine to enhance their access to capital markets, while promoting economic policy adjustment.

Using Credit to Promote Sustainable Development

Credit is an important tool in U.S. bilateral assistance to promote sustainable development. USAID's Development Credit Authority (DCA) allows USAID to use a variety of credit tools to support its development activities abroad. DCA provides non-sovereign loan guarantees in targeted cases where credit serves more effectively than traditional grant mechanisms to achieve sustainable development. DCA is intended to mobilize host country private capital to finance sustainable development in line with USAID's strategic objectives. Through the use of partial loan guarantees and risk sharing with the private sector, DCA stimulates private-sector lending for financially viable development projects, thereby leveraging host-country capital and strengthening sub-national capital markets in the developing world.

OPIC mobilizes private capital to help solve critical challenges such as renewable energy and infrastructure development, and in doing so, advances U.S. foreign policy. OPIC achieves its mission by providing investors with financing, guarantees, political risk insurance, and support for private equity investment funds. These programs are intended to create more efficient financial markets, eventually encouraging the private sector to supplant OPIC finance in developing countries.

Ongoing Coordination

International credit programs are coordinated through two groups to ensure consistency in policy design and credit implementation. The Trade Promotion Coordinating Committee (TPCC) works within the Administration to develop a National Export Strategy to make the delivery of trade promotion support more effective and convenient for U.S. exporters.

The Interagency Country Risk Assessment System (ICRAS) standardizes the way in which most agencies that lack sufficient historical experience to budget for the cost associated with the risk of international lending. The cost of lending by these agencies is governed by proprietary U.S. Government ratings, which correspond to a set of default estimates over a given maturity. The methodology establishes assumptions about default risks in international lending using averages of international sovereign bond market data. The strength of this method is its link to the market and an annual update that adjusts the default estimates to reflect the most recent risks observed in the market.

Promoting Economic Growth and Poverty Reduction through Debt Sustainability

The Enhanced Heavily Indebted Poor Countries (HIPC) Initiative reduces the debt of some of the poorest countries with unsustainable debt burdens that are committed to economic reform and poverty reduction.

III. INSURANCE PROGRAMS

Deposit Insurance

Federal deposit insurance promotes stability in the U.S. financial system. Prior to the establishment of Federal deposit insurance, depository institution failures often caused depositors to lose confidence in the banking system and rush to withdraw deposits. Such sudden withdrawals caused serious disruption to the economy. In 1933, in the midst of the Great Depression, a system of Federal deposit insurance was established to protect depositors and to prevent bank failures from causing widespread disruption in financial markets.

Today, the Federal Deposit Insurance Corporation (FDIC) insures deposits in banks and savings associations (thrifts) using the resources available in its Deposit Insurance Fund (DIF). The National Credit Union Administration (NCUA) insures deposits (shares) in most credit unions through the National Credit Union Share Insurance Fund (SIF). (Some credit unions are privately insured.) As of September 30, 2015, the FDIC insured $6.4 trillion of deposits at 6,279 commercial banks and thrifts, and the NCUA insured $940 billion of shares at 6,102 credit unions.

Recent Reforms

Since its creation, the Federal deposit insurance system has undergone many reforms. As a result of the 2008 crisis, several reforms were enacted to protect both the immediate and longer-term integrity of the Federal deposit insurance system. The Helping Families Save Their Homes Act of 2009 (P.L. 111–22) provided NCUA with tools to protect the Share Insurance Fund and the financial stability of the credit union system. Notably, the Helping Families Save Their Homes Act:

- Established the Temporary Corporate Credit Union Stabilization Fund (TCCUSF), allowing NCUA to segregate the losses of corporate credit unions and providing a mechanism for assessing those losses to federally insured credit unions over an extended period of time;

- Provided flexibility to the NCUA Board by permitting use of a restoration plan to spread insurance premium assessments over a period of up to eight years or longer in extraordinary circumstances, if the SIF equity ratio fell below 1.2 percent; and

- Permanently increased the Share Insurance Fund's borrowing authority to $6 billion.

The Dodd-Frank Wall Street Reform and Consumer Protection (Wall Street Reform) Act of 2010 included provisions allowing the FDIC to more effectively and efficiently manage the DIF. The Act requires the FDIC to achieve a minimum DIF reserve ratio (ratio of the deposit insurance fund balance to total estimated insured deposits) to 1.35 percent by 2020, up from 1.15 percent. In addition to raising the minimum reserve ratio, the Wall Street Reform Act also:

- Eliminated the FDIC's requirement to rebate premiums when the DIF reserve ratio is between 1.35 and 1.5 percent;

- Gave the FDIC discretion to suspend or limit rebates when the DIF reserve ratio is 1.5 percent or higher, effectively removing the 1.5 percent cap on the DIF; and

- Required the FDIC to offset the effect on small insured depository institutions (defined as banks with assets less than $10 billion) when setting assessments to raise the reserve ratio from 1.15 to 1.35 percent.

In implementing the Wall Street Reform Act, the FDIC issued a final rule setting a long-term (i.e., beyond 2025) reserve ratio target of 2 percent, a goal that FDIC considers necessary to maintain a positive fund balance during economic crises while permitting steady long-term assessment rates that provide transparency and predictability to the banking sector. This rule, coupled with other provisions of the Wall Street Reform Act, will significantly improve the FDIC's capacity to resolve bank failures and maintain financial stability during economic downturns.

The Wall Street Reform Act also permanently increased the insured deposit level to $250,000 per account at banks or credit unions insured by the FDIC or NCUA.

Recent Fund Performance

After seven consecutive quarters of negative balances, the DIF balance became positive on June 30, 2011, standing at $3.9 billion on an accrual basis, then doubling to $7.8 billion on September 30, 2011. As of September 30, 2015, the DIF fund balance stood at $70.1 billion. The growth in the DIF balance is a result of fewer bank failures and higher assessment revenue. The reserve ratio on September 30, 2015 was 1.09 percent.

As of September 30, 2015, the number of insured institutions on the FDIC's "problem list" (institutions with the highest risk ratings) totaled 203, which represented a decrease of more than 74 percent from December 2010, the peak year for bank failures during the recent crisis. Furthermore, the assets held by problem institutions decreased by nearly 87 percent.

The SIF ended September 2015 with assets of $12.5 billion and an equity ratio of 1.29 percent. If the equity ratio increases above the normal operating level of 1.30 percent, a distribution is normally paid to member credit unions to reduce the equity ratio to the normal operating level. However, the Helping Families Save Their Homes Act requires that the SIF distribution be directed to Treasury for the repayment of any outstanding TCCUSF loans before a distribution can be paid to member credit unions. In 2015, the equity ratio did not exceed 1.30

percent. As of September 30, 2015, the TCCUSF had a $2.3 billion loan outstanding from the Department of the Treasury.

The health of the credit union industry continues to improve. Consequently, the ratio of insured shares in problem institutions to total insured shares decreased to 0.81 percent in September 2015 from a high of 5.7 percent in December 2009. With the improving health of credit unions, NCUA has been steadily reducing SIF loss reserves. As of September 30, 2015, the SIF had set aside $169.5 million in reserves to cover potential losses, a reduction of 31 percent from the $244 million set-aside as of September 30, 2013.

Restoring the Deposit Insurance Funds

Pursuant to the Wall Street Reform Act, the restoration period for the FDIC's DIF reserve ratio to reach 1.35 percent was extended to 2020. (Prior to the Act, the DIF reserve ratio was required to reach the minimum target of 1.15 percent by the end of 2016.) In late 2009, the FDIC Board of Directors adopted a final rule requiring insured institutions to prepay quarterly risk-based assessments for the fourth quarter of CY 2009 and for all of CY 2010, 2011, and 2012. The FDIC collected approximately $45 billion in prepaid assessments pursuant to this rule. Unlike a special assessment, the prepaid assessments did not immediately affect bank earnings; it was booked as an asset and amortized each quarter by that quarter's assessment charge. This prepaid assessment, coupled with annual assessments on the banking industry, provided the FDIC with ample operating cash flows to effectively and efficiently resolve bank failures during the short period in which the DIF balance was negative. Although the FDIC has authority to borrow up to $100 billion from Treasury to maintain sufficient DIF balances, the Budget does not anticipate FDIC utilizing its borrowing authority because the DIF is projected to maintain positive operating cash flows over the entire 10-year budget horizon.

Since 2009 NCUA has successfully restored the reserve ratio of the SIF to the normal operating level. Additionally, NCUA continues to seek compensation from the parties that created and sold troubled assets to the failed corporate credit unions. As of September 30, 2015, NCUA's gross recoveries from securities underwriters total more than $1.9 billion, helping to minimize losses and future assessments on federally insured credit unions. These recoveries have also accelerated repayment of the TCCUSF's outstanding U.S. Treasury borrowings.

Budget Outlook

The Budget estimates DIF net outlays of -$68.0 billion over the current 10-year budget window (2017-2026). Over the previous 10-year window of 2016-2025, net outlays are -$68.2 billion. This $68.2 billion in net inflows to the DIF is $6 billion lower than estimated for the 2016 Mid-Session Review (MSR). The latest public data on the banking industry led to a reduction in bank failure estimates, reducing receivership proceeds, resolution outlays, and premiums necessary to reach the minimum Wall Street Reform Act DIF reserve ratio of 1.35 percent rela-

tive to MSR. On November 6, 2015, the FDIC published a notice of proposed rulemaking (as required by the Wall Street Reform Act) that would lower overall assessments and impose a 4.5 basis point surcharge on large banks, starting in the first quarter after the DIF reserve ratio reaches 1.15 percent and continuing until the reserve ratio reaches 1.35 percent. FDIC expects to collect these surcharges during 2017 and 2018 and the Budget estimates reflect the proposed assessment rates and a DIF reserve ratio of 1.35 percent in 2020.

Pension Guarantees

The Pension Benefit Guaranty Corporation (PBGC) insures the pension benefits of workers and retirees in covered defined-benefit pension plans. PBGC operates two legally distinct insurance programs: single-employer plans and multiemployer plans.

Single-Employer Program. Under the single-employer program, PBGC pays benefits, up to a guaranteed level, when a company's plan closes without enough assets to pay future benefits. PBGC's claims exposure is the amount by which qualified benefits exceed assets in insured plans. In the near term, the risk of loss stems from financially distressed firms with underfunded plans. In the longer term, loss exposure results from the possibility that well-funded plans become underfunded due to inadequate contributions, poor investment results, or increased liabilities, and that the healthy firms sponsoring those plans become distressed.

PBGC monitors companies with underfunded plans and acts to protect the interests of the pension insurance program's stakeholders where possible. Under its Early Warning Program, PBGC works with companies to strengthen plan funding or otherwise protect the insurance program from avoidable losses. However, PBGC's authority to manage risks to the insurance program is limited. Most private insurers can diversify or reinsure their catastrophic risks as well as flexibly price these risks. Unlike private insurers, federal law does not allow PBGC to deny insurance coverage to a defined-benefit plan or adjust premiums according to risk. Both types of PBGC premiums—the flat rate (a per person charge paid by all plans) and the variable rate (paid by some underfunded plans) are set in statute.

Claims against PBGC's insurance programs are highly variable. One large pension plan termination may result in a larger claim against PBGC than the termination of many smaller plans. The future financial health of the PBGC will continue to depend largely on the termination of a limited number of very large plans.

Single employer plans generally provide benefits to the employees of one employer. When an underfunded single employer plan terminates, usually through the bankruptcy process, PBGC becomes trustee of the plan, applies legal limits on payouts, and pays benefits. The amount of benefit paid is determined after taking into account (a) the benefit that a beneficiary had accrued in the terminated plan, (b) the availability of assets from the terminated plan to cover benefits, and (c) the legal maximum benefit level set in statute. In 2015, the maximum annual payment guaranteed under the single-employer program was $60,136 for a retiree aged 65. This limit is indexed for inflation.

PBGC's single-employer program has incurred substantial losses over the past 15 years from underfunded plan terminations. Table 20-1 shows the ten largest plan termination losses in PBGC's history. Nine of the ten happened since 2001.

Multiemployer Plans. Multiemployer plans are collectively bargained pension plans maintained by one or more labor unions and more than one unrelated employer, usually within the same or related industries. PBGC's role in the multiemployer program is more like that of a re-insurer; if a company sponsoring a multiemployer plan fails, its liabilities are assumed by the other employers in the collective bargaining agreement, not by PBGC, although employers can withdraw from a plan for an exit fee. PBGC becomes responsible for insurance coverage when the plan runs out of money to pay benefits at the statutorily guaranteed level, which usually occurs after all contributing employers have withdrawn from the plan, leaving the plan without a source of income. PBGC provides insolvent multiemployer plans with financial assistance in the form of loans sufficient to pay guaranteed benefits and administrative expenses. Since multiemployer plans do not receive PBGC assistance until their assets are fully depleted, financial assistance is almost never repaid. Benefits under the multiemployer program are calculated based on the benefit that a participant would have received under the insolvent plan, subject to the legal multiemployer maximum set in statute. The maximum guaranteed amount depends on the participant's years of service and the rate at which benefits are accrued. In 2015, for example, for a participant with 30 years of service, PBGC guarantees 100 percent of the pension benefit up to a yearly amount of $3,960. If the pension exceeds that amount, PBGC guarantees 75 percent of the rest of the pension benefit up to a total maximum guarantee of $12,870 per year. This limit has been in place since 2011.

In recent years, many multiemployer pension plans have become severely underfunded as a result of unfavorable investment outcomes, employers withdrawing from plans, and demographic challenges. In 2001, only 15 plans covering about 80,000 participants were under 40 percent funded using estimated market rates. By 2011, this had grown to almost 200 plans covering almost 1.5 million participants. While many plans have benefited from an improving economy and will recover, a small number of plans are severely underfunded and, absent any changes, projected to become insolvent within ten years.

As of September 30, 2015, the single-employer and multi-employer programs reported deficits of $24.1 billion and $52.3 billion, respectively. While both programs are projected to be unable to meet their long-term obligations under current law, the challenges facing the multiemployer program are more immediate. In its 2015 Annual Report, PBGC reported that it had just $2 billion in accumulated assets from premium payments made by

Table 20–1.   TOP 10 FIRMS PRESENTING CLAIMS (1975-2014)

Single-Employer Program

Firm	Fiscal Year(s) of Plan Termination(s)	Claims (by firm)	Percent of Total Claims (1975-2014)
1 United Airlines	2005	$7,304,186,216	14.98%
2 Delphi	2009	$6,382,168,004	13.09%
3 Bethlehem Steel	2003	$3,702,771,656	7.59%
4 US Airways	2003, 2005	$2,708,858,934	5.55%
5 LTV Steel*	2002, 2003, 2004	$2,116,397,590	4.34%
6 Delta Air Lines	2006	$1,720,156,505	3.53%
7 National Steel	2003	$1,319,009,116	2.70%
8 Pan American Air	1991, 1992	$841,082,434	1.72%
9 Trans World Airlines	2001	$668,377,105	1.37%
10 Weirton Steel	2004	$640,480,969	1.31%
Top 10 Total		$27,403,488,529	56.19%
All Other Total		$21,368,826,989	43.81%
TOTAL		$48,772,315,518	100.00%

Sources: PBGC Fiscal Year Closing File (9/30/14), PBGC Case Management System, and PBGC Participant System (PRISM).

Due to rounding of individual items, numbers and percentages may not add up to totals.

Data in this table have been calculated on a firm basis and, except as noted, include all trusteed plans of each firm.

Values and distributions are subject to change as PBGC completes its reviews and establishes termination dates.

* Does not include 1986 termination of a Republic Steel plan sponsored by LTV.

multiemployer plans, which it projected would be depleted by 2025. If the program runs out of cash, the only funds available to support benefits would be the premiums that continue to be paid by remaining plans; this could result in benefits being cut much more deeply, to a small fraction of current guarantee levels.

To address the problems facing the multiemployer program and the millions of Americans who rely on those plans for their retirement security, the Congress passed The Multiemployer Pension Reform Act, which was included in the Consolidated and Further Continuing Appropriations Act signed on December 16, 2014. The law includes significant reforms to the multiemployer pension plan system, including provisions that allow trustees of multiemployer plans facing insolvency to apply to the Department of Treasury to reduce benefits by temporarily or permanently suspending benefits. The law does not allow suspensions for individuals over age 80 or for those receiving a disability retirement benefit. A participant or beneficiary's monthly benefit cannot be reduced below 110 percent of the PBGC guarantee. It also increases PBGC premiums from the $13 per person to $26 beginning in 2015. While the legislation is an important first step, it will not be enough to improve PBGC's solvency for more than a very short period of time. PBGC projects that it is likely to become insolvent by 2025, extending its projected insolvency date by three years compared to the 2013 projection.

In addition, Congress enacted premium increases in the single-employer program as part of the Bipartisan Budget Act of 2015 (BBA). By increasing both the flat-rate and variable-rate premiums, the Act will raise as estimated $4 billion over the 10-year budget window. This additional revenue will improve the financial outlook for the single-employer program, which was already projected to see a large reduction in its deficit over the next 10 years.

Premiums. Both programs are underfunded, with combined liabilities exceeding assets by $76 billion at the end of 2015. While the single-employer program's financial position is projected to improve over the next 10 years, in part because Congress has raised premiums in that program several times in recent years, the multiemployer program is projected to run out of funds in 2024. Particularly in the multiemployer program, premium rates remain much lower than what a private financial institution would charge for insuring the same risk and well below what is needed to ensure PBGC's solvency.

To address these concerns, the Budget proposes to give the PBGC Board the authority to adjust premiums. The 2016 Budget proposed to raise premiums by $19 billion, with premiums to be split between the multiemployer and single-employer programs based on the size of their deficits. Given the $4 billion in recent premium increases enacted in the Bipartisan Budget Act (BBA) of 2015 and the single-employer program's improving financial projections, the Budget directs the Board to raise $15 billion in additional premium revenue within the Budget window only from the multiemployer program. The Administration believes additional increases in single-employer premiums are unwise at this time and would unnecessarily create further disincentives to maintaining defined benefit pension plans. This level of additional multiemployer premium revenue would nearly eliminate the risk of the multiemployer program becoming insolvent within 20 years.

The Budget assumes that the Board will raise these revenues by using its premium-setting authority to create a variable-rate premium (VRP) and an exit premium in the multiemployer program. A multiemployer VRP would require plans to pay additional premiums based on their level of underfunding—as is done in the single-employer program. An exit premium assessed on employers that withdraw from a plan would compensate PBGC for the additional risk imposed on it when healthy employers exit.

Disaster Insurance

Flood Insurance

The Federal Government provides flood insurance through the National Flood Insurance Program (NFIP), which is administered by the Federal Emergency Management Agency of the Department of Homeland Security (DHS). Flood insurance is available to homeowners and businesses in communities that have adopted and enforce appropriate floodplain management measures. Coverage is limited to buildings and their contents. At the end of fiscal year 2015, the program had over 5.1 million policies in more than 22,100 communities with $1.23 trillion of insurance in force.

Prior to the creation of the program in 1968, many factors made it cost prohibitive for private insurance companies alone to make affordable flood insurance available. In response, the NFIP was established to make insurance coverage widely available, to combine a program of insurance with flood mitigation measures to reduce the nation's risk of loss from flood, and to minimize Federal disaster-assistance expenditures. The NFIP requires participating communities to adopt certain building standards and take other mitigation efforts to reduce flood-related losses, and operates a flood hazard mapping program to quantify geographic variation in the risk of flooding. These efforts have resulted in substantial reductions in the risk of flood-related losses nationwide. However, structures built prior to flood mapping and NFIP floodplain management requirements, which make up 20 percent of the total policies in force, currently pay less than fully actuarial rates and continue to pose relatively high risk.

A major goal of the National Flood Insurance Program is to ensure that property owners are compensated for flood losses through flood insurance, rather than through taxpayer-funded disaster assistance. The agency's marketing strategy aims to increase the number of Americans insured against flood losses and improve retention of policies among existing customers. The strategy includes:

1. Providing financial incentives to the private insurers that sell and service flood policies for the Federal Government to expand the flood insurance business.

2. Conducting the national marketing and advertising campaign, FloodSmart, which uses TV, radio, print and online advertising, direct mailings, and public relations activities to help overcome denial and resistance and increase demand.

3. Fostering lender compliance with flood insurance requirements through training, guidance materials, and regular communication with lending regulators and the lending community.

4. Conducting NFIP training for insurance agents via instructor-led seminars, online training modules, and other vehicles.

5. Seeking opportunities to simplify and clarify NFIP processes and products to make it easier for agents to sell and for consumers to buy.

These strategies resulted in steady policy growth for many years, peaking in 2008 at 5.62 million policies. From 2009-2013, in the aftermath of the economic recession, policy growth stagnated and total policies in effect ranged between 5.55 million and 5.61 million. In fiscal year 2014, when policy premiums were increased in compliance with the Biggert-Waters legislation, policy counts dropped 4.3% to 5.3 million. Additionally, in fiscal year 2015, when a surcharge on all policyholders was introduced in compliance with the Homeowner Flood Insurance Affordability Act of 2014 (HFIAA), policy counts dropped an additional 3.8% to 5.1 million.

DHS has a multi-pronged strategy for reducing future flood damage. The NFIP offers flood mitigation assistance grants to assist flood victims to rebuild to current building codes, including higher base flood elevations, thereby reducing the likelihood of future flood damage. In particular, flood mitigation assistance grants targeted toward repetitive and severe repetitive loss properties not only help owners of high-risk property, but also reduce the disproportionate drain these properties cause on the National Flood Insurance Fund, through acquisition, relocation, or elevation of select properties. DHS is working to ensure that the flood mitigation grant program is closely integrated with other FEMA mitigation grant programs, resulting in better coordination and communication with State and local governments. Further, through the Community Rating System, DHS adjusts premium rates to encourage community and State mitigation activities beyond those required by the NFIP. These efforts, in addition to the minimum NFIP requirements for floodplain management, save over $1 billion annually in avoided flood damages claims.

Due to the catastrophic nature of flooding, with hurricanes Katrina and Sandy as notable examples, insured flood damages far exceeded premium revenue in some years and depleted the program's reserve account. On those occasions, the NFIP exercises its borrowing authority through the Treasury to meet flood insurance claim obligations. While the program needed appropriations in the early 1980s to repay the funds borrowed during the 1970's, it was able to repay all borrowed funds with interest using only premium dollars between 1986 and 2004. In 2005, however, hurricanes Katrina, Rita, and Wilma generated more flood insurance claims than the cumulative number of claims paid from 1968 to 2004. Hurricane Sandy in 2012 generated $8.3 billion in flood insurance claims. As a result, the Administration and Congress have increased the borrowing authority for the fund to $30.4 billion. On December 31, 2014, the NFIP repaid $1 billion of outstanding borrowing, reducing the program's outstanding debt to $23 billion.

The catastrophic nature of the 2005 hurricane season also triggered an examination of the program, and the Administration worked with the Congress to improve the program. On July 6, 2012, the Biggert Waters Flood Insurance Reform Act of 2012 (BW-12) was signed into law. In addition to reauthorizing the NFIP for 5 years, the bill required the NFIP generally to move to full risk-based premium rates and strengthened the NFIP financially and operationally. BW-12 also required FEMA, in conjunction with the National Academy of Sciences (NAS), conduct a study regarding the affordability of the NFIP to policyholders. In 2013, the NFIP began phasing in risk-based premiums for certain properties, as required by the law. In March 2014, HFIAA was signed into law, further reforming the NFIP and revising many sections of BW-12. Notably, HFIAA repealed many of the largest premium increases introduced by BW-12 and required retroactive refunds of collected BW-12 premium increases, introduced a phase-in to higher full-risk premiums for structures newly mapped into the Special Flood Hazard Area, and created a Flood Insurance Advocate.

In 2015, FEMA initiated a Hurricane Sandy NFIP Claims Review Process to ensure that policyholders impacted by Hurricane Sandy receive every dollar they are entitled to under their policy. In many cases, the review validates that the original payment was correct. In others, the review indicates that additional payment is warranted. FEMA directed insurance companies to issue checks to those who were determined to have been underpaid after the completion of the claim review. Also in 2015, NAS completed two studies related to NFIP affordability, and FEMA now has 18 months to develop an affordability framework that can inform NFIP reauthorization. The current NFIP authorization ends September 30, 2017.

Crop Insurance

Subsidized Federal crop insurance, administered by USDA's Risk Management Agency (RMA) on behalf of the Federal Crop Insurance Corporation (FCIC), assists farmers in managing yield and revenue shortfalls due to bad weather or other natural disasters, and is commonly known as "multi-peril crop insurance" (MPCI). The program is a cooperative partnership between the Federal Government and the private insurance industry. Private insurance companies sell and service crop insurance policies. The Federal Government, in turn, pays private companies an administrative and operating expense subsidy to cover expenses associated with selling and servicing these policies. The Federal Government also provides reinsurance on MPCI policies through the Standard Reinsurance Agreement (SRA) and pays companies an "underwriting gain" if they have a profitable year. However, the private companies also rely on commercial reinsurance for premium retained after reinsurance provided by the SRA. For the 2017 Budget, the payments to the companies are projected to be $2.5 billion in combined subsidies. The Federal Government also subsidizes premiums for farmers as a way to encourage farmers to participate in the program and purchase higher levels of coverage.

The 2017 Budget includes two proposals that are designed to optimize the current crop insurance program so that it will continue to provide a quality safety net at a lower cost:

1. Reduce premium subsidy by 10 percentage points for revenue coverage that includes additional coverage for the price at harvest. This would simplify revenue insurance by reducing indemnity payments based on the higher of the market price right before planting or the harvest price. This would, in turn, reduce the potential for "windfall" profits from this additional coverage. Under this coverage, farmers pay an out-of-pocket premium which more closely matches the market price of the coverage purchased. As a result, the number farmers choosing the more expensive coverage for price hedging will decrease. Over 10 years the government will save $16.9 billion, of which 7.6 percent will be from subsidies that the government pays the insurance companies.

2. Reform the prevented planting program by: eliminating prevented planting optional +5 and +10 coverage, and requiring a 60 percent transitional yield be applied to the producer's Actual Production History (APH) for those who receive a prevented planting payment. This is expected to save $1.07 billion over 10 years and improve the accuracy of the prevented planting coverage as well as promote additional food production.

The most basic type of crop insurance is catastrophic coverage (CAT), which compensates the farmer for losses in excess of 50 percent of the individual's average yield at 55 percent of the expected market price. The CAT premium is entirely subsidized, and farmers pay only an administrative fee. Higher levels of coverage, called "buy-up," are also available. A portion of the premium for buy-up coverage is paid by FCIC on behalf of producers and varies by coverage level - generally, the higher the coverage level, the lower the percent of premium subsidized. The remaining (unsubsidized) premium amount is owed by the producer and represents an out-of-pocket expense.

For 2015, the 10 principal crops, (barley, corn, cotton, grain sorghum, peanuts, potatoes, rice, soybeans, tobacco, and wheat) accounted for over 80 percent of total liability, and approximately 86 percent of the total U.S. planted acres of the 10 crops were covered by crop insurance. Producers can purchase both yield and revenue-based insurance products which are underwritten on the basis of a producer's APH. Revenue insurance programs protect against loss of revenue resulting from low prices, low yields, or a combination of both. Revenue insurance has enhanced traditional yield insurance by adding price as an insurable component. In the current program, the farmer can opt to cover the projected or the harvest price. Traditional revenue insurance only protects against a projected price decline, where the farmer is guaranteed a price at the time of planting. Revenue coverage that protects against the price at the time of harvest guarantees the price to the farmer for the higher of the projected price or the harvest price. The harvest price protection policies are more costly than traditional revenue coverage and therefore more heavily subsidized by the government. Almost all farmers choose the harvest price option because taxpayers pay such a large portion of the extra premium and in some cases, this heavy subsidy results in windfall profits to the farmer.

In addition to price and revenue insurance, FCIC has made available other plans of insurance to provide protection for a variety of crops grown across the United States. For example, "area plans" of insurance offer protection based on a geographic area (most commonly, a county), and do not directly insure an individual farm. Often, the loss trigger is based on an index, such as a rainfall or vegetative index, which is established by a Government entity (for example, NOAA or USGS). One such plan is the pilot Rainfall and Vegetation Index plan, which insures against a decline in an index value covering Pasture, Rangeland, and Forage. These pilot programs meet the needs of livestock producers who purchase insurance for protection from losses of forage produced for grazing or harvested for hay. In 2015, there were 28,779 Rainfall and Vegetation Index policies earning premium, covering about 56 million acres of pasture, rangeland and forage. As of December 2015, there was about $1.2 billion in liability, with $142 million in indemnities paid to livestock producers who purchased coverage.

A crop insurance policy also contains coverage compensating farmers when they are prevented from planting their crops due to weather and other perils. When an insured farmer can't plant the planned crop within the planting time period because of excessive drought or moisture, the farmer may file a prevented planting claim, which pays the farmer a portion of the full coverage level. It is optional for the farmer to plant a second crop on the acreage. If the farmer does, the prevented planting claim on the first crop is reduced and the farmer's APH is recorded for that year. If the farmer does not plant a second crop, the farmer gets the full prevented planting claim, and the farmer's APH is held harmless for premium calculation purposes the following year. USDA recently conducted a study to determine if the prevented planting costs were accurately priced for all crops and have considered policy changes for prevented planting based on the study's findings.

RMA is continuously working to develop new products and to expand or improve existing products in order to cover more agricultural commodities. Under section 508(h) of the Federal Crop Insurance Act, RMA may advance payment of up to 50 percent of expected reasonable research and development costs for FCIC Board approved Concept Proposals prior to the complete submission of the policy or plan of insurance. Numerous private products have been approved through the 508(h) authority, including Downed Rice Endorsement, Machine Harvested Cucumbers, APH Olive, Camelina, Pulse Crop Revenue, Fresh Market Beans, and Louisiana Sweet Potato.

Last, the Agricultural Act of 2014 (2014 Farm Bill) expanded FCIC's authority to approve products developed under the 508(h) process, authorized new plans, and mandated specific research and development priorities. For example, in 2015 RMA implemented the Supplemental Coverage Option for major crops and the Stacked Risk Income Protection for upland cotton. These "area" plans were mandated by the 2014 Farm Bill and supplement an underlying MPCI policy. In addition, in 2015 FCIC approved and implemented a Peanut Revenue plan and a Whole Farm Revenue Protection plan, which were also mandated by the 2014 Farm Bill. RMA also implemented the APH Yield Exclusion option in 2015. Additional Research and Development priorities mandated by the 2014 Farm Bill included biomass and sweet sorghum energy insurance, catastrophic programs for swine and poultry, margin coverage for catfish, and insurance for organic crops. In some instances RMA contracts with qualified entities to develop feasibility studies or develop the products.

For more information and additional crop insurance program details, please reference RMA's web site (*www. rma.usda.gov*).

Insurance against Security-Related Risks

Terrorism Risk Insurance

The Terrorism Risk Insurance Program (TRIP) was authorized under P.L. 107-297 to help ensure the continued availability of property and casualty insurance following the terrorist attacks of September 11, 2001. TRIP's initial three-year authorization enabled the Federal Government to establish a system of shared public and private compensation for insured property and casualty losses arising from certified acts of foreign terrorism. In 2005, Congress passed a two-year extension (P.L. 109-144), which narrowed the Government's role by increasing the private sector's share of losses, reducing lines of insurance covered by the program, and adding a threshold event amount triggering Federal payments.

In 2007, Congress enacted a further seven-year extension of TRIP and expanded the program to include losses from domestic as well as foreign acts of terrorism (P.L. 110-318). For all seven extension years, TRIP maintained a private insurer deductible of 20 percent of the prior year's direct earned premiums, an insurer co-payment of 15 percent of insured losses of up to $100 billion above the deductible, and a $100 million minimum event cost triggering Federal coverage. The 2007 extension also required Treasury to recoup 133 percent of all Federal payments made under the program up to $27.5 billion, and accelerated deadlines for recoupment of any Federal payments made before September 30, 2017.

In January 2015, Congress passed the Terrorism Risk Insurance Extension Act of 2015 (P.L. 114–1), which extended TRIP for six more years, through December 31, 2020 and made several program changes to further reduce Federal liability. Over the first five extension years, the loss threshold that triggers Federal assistance will be increased by $20 million each year to $200 million in 2019, and the Government's share of losses above the deductible will decrease from 85 to 80 percent over the same period. The 2015 extension also requires Treasury to recoup 140 percent of all Federal payments made under the program up to a mandatory recoupment amount which increases by $2 billion each year until 2019 when the threshold will be set at $37.5 billion. Effective January 1, 2020, the mandatory recoupment amount will be indexed to a running three-year average of the aggregate insurer deductible of 20 percent of direct-earned premiums. These programmatic reforms will facilitate, over the longer term, full transition of the program to the private sector. The Budget baseline includes the estimated Federal cost of providing terrorism risk insurance, reflecting the 2015 TRIA extension. Using market data synthesized through a proprietary model, the Budget projects annual outlays and recoupment for TRIP. While the Budget does not forecast any specific triggering events, the Budget includes estimates representing the weighted average of TRIP payments over a full range of possible scenarios, most of which include no notional terrorist attacks (and therefore no TRIP payments), and some of which include notional terrorist attacks of varying magnitudes. On this basis, the Budget projects net spending of $1.4 billion over the 2017–2021 period and $1.2 billion over the 2017–2026 period.

Aviation War Risk Insurance

In December 2014, Congress sunset the premium aviation war risk insurance program, thereby sending U.S. air carriers back to the commercial aviation insurance market for all of their war risk insurance coverage. The non-premium program is authorized through December 31, 2018. It provides aviation insurance coverage for aircraft used in connection with certain Government contract operations by a Department or Agency that agrees to indemnify the Secretary of Transportation for any losses covered by the insurance.

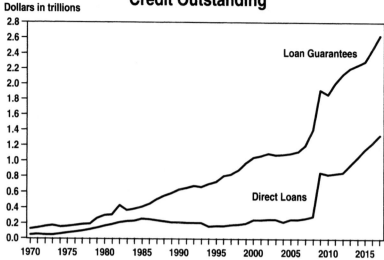

Chart 20-1. Face Value of Federal Credit Outstanding

Table 20–2. ESTIMATED FUTURE COST OF OUTSTANDING DIRECT LOANS AND LOAN GUARANTEES

(In billions of dollars)

Program	Outstanding 2014	Estimated Future Costs of 2014 Outstanding [1]	Outstanding 2015	Estimated Future Costs of 2015 Outstanding [1]
Direct Loans: [2]				
Federal Student Loans	734	–37	839	–26
Education Temporary Student Loan Purchase Authority	84	–13	77	–12
Rural Utilities Service and Rural Telephone Bank	56	2	52	2
Farm Service Agency, Rural Development, Rural Housing	54	6	55	6
Export-Import Bank	22	3	23	2
Advance Technology Vehicle Manufacturing, Title 17 Loans	15	2	16	2
Housing and Urban Development	14	8	19	11
State Housing Finance Authority Direct Loans	9	1	8	1
Transportation Infrastructure Finance and Innovation Act Loans	9	*	11	*
Disaster Assistance	7	1	6	1
International Assistance	5	1	3	1
Public Law 480	4	2	3	2
Troubled Asset Relief Program (TARP) [3]	3	1	1	*
Small Business Lending Fund (SBLF) [3]	3	*	2	*
Other direct loan programs [3]	27	9	29	8
Total direct loans	1,046	–15	1,145	–2
Guaranteed Loans: [2]				
FHA Mutual Mortgage Insurance Fund	1,132	25	1,123	10
Department of Veterans Affairs (VA) Mortgages	398	9	462	10
Federal Student Loan Guarantees	242	*	220	*
FHA General and Special Risk Insurance Fund	153	9	149	6
Farm Service Agency, Rural Development, Rural Housing	124	5	134	6
Small Business Administration (SBA) Business Loan Guarantees [4]	99	2	106	2
Export-Import Bank	63	2	62	2
International Assistance	24	2	24	2
Commodity Credit Corporation Export Loan Guarantees	4	*	3	*
Title 17 Loan Guarantees	3	*	3	*
Government National Mortgage Association (GNMA) [4]	....	*	....	*
Other guaranteed loan programs [3]	11	1	13	1
Total guaranteed loans	2,253	55	2,300	38
Total Federal credit	**3,299**	**40**	**3,445**	**36**

* $500 million or less.

[1] Future costs represent balance sheet estimates of allowance for subsidy cost, liabilities for loan guarantees, and estimated uncollectible principal and interest.

[2] Excludes loans and guarantees by deposit insurance agencies and programs not included under credit reform, such as Tennessee Valley Authority loan guarantees. Defaulted guaranteed loans that result in loans receivable are included in direct loan amounts.

[3] As authorized by the statute, table includes TARP and SBLF equity purchases, and International Monetary Fund (IMF) transactions resulting from the 2009 Supplemental Appropriations Act. Future costs for TARP and IMF transactions are calculated using the discount rate required by the Federal Credit Reform Act adjusted for market risks, as directed in legislation. IMF activity is accounted for on a present value basis beginning in FY 2016 as directed by P. L. 114-113 Consolidated Appropriations Act, 2016. IMF activity will no longer be reflected in this table as of the end of FY 2015.

[4] To avoid double-counting, outstandings for GNMA and SBA secondary market guarantees, and TARP FHA Letter of Credit program are excluded from the totals.

Table 20–3. **DIRECT LOAN SUBSIDY RATES, BUDGET AUTHORITY, AND LOAN LEVELS, 2015–2017**

(Dollar amounts in millions)

Agency and Program Account	2015 Actual			2016 Enacted			2017 Proposed		
	Subsidy rate [1]	Subsidy budget authority	Loan levels	Subsidy rate [1]	Subsidy budget authority	Loan levels	Subsidy rate [1]	Subsidy budget authority	Loan levels
Agriculture:									
Agricultural Credit Insurance Fund Program Account	2.18	49	2,272	0.49	16	2,899	1.24	40	3,097
Farm Storage Facility Loans Program Account	–3.00	–5	180	–1.64	–5	320	–1.33	–5	309
Rural Electrification and Telecommunications Loans Program Account	–5.19	–188	3,644	–3.96	–269	6,817	–4.53	–327	7,190
Distance Learning, Telemedicine, and Broadband Program	....	....	....	22.80	15	65	....	....	....
Rural Water and Waste Disposal Program Account	–0.61	–7	1,106	2.61	36	1,364	4.34	45	1,037
Rural Community Facilities Program Account	–12.41	–213	1,713	–8.04	–177	2,200	–2.56	–56	2,200
Multifamily Housing Revitalization Program Account	53.42	25	47	52.31	22	42	54.49	19	34
Rural Housing Insurance Fund Program Account	8.73	85	968	8.33	84	1,007	8.44	86	1,017
Rural Microenterprise Investment Program Account	12.81	*	2	11.33	1	11	12.40	4	32
Intermediary Relending Program Fund Account	30.80	6	19	27.62	5	19	28.99	6	19
Rural Economic Development Loans Program Account	12.77	5	39	13.39	5	37	14.23	13	89
Commerce:									
Fisheries Finance Program Account	–4.83	–3	57	–3.09	–4	124	–0.33	–*	124
Education:									
Historically Black College and University Capital Financing Program Account	5.94	12	183	6.67	20	302	7.14	20	282
TEACH Grant Program Account	16.57	16	95	13.05	12	95	11.88	12	104
Federal Perkins Loan Program Account	....	....	....	....	....	....	–13.67	–640	4,684
Federal Direct Student Loan Program Account	–2.67	–4,333	162,312	–5.28	–8,365	158,278	–5.08	–8,292	163,161
Energy:									
Title 17 Innovative Technology Loan Guarantee Program	–1.24	–21	1,691	0.34	28	8,200	[2] 0.87	27	3,100
Advanced Technology Vehicles Manufacturing Loan Program Account	7.28	19	259	5.01	170	3,400	[2] 4.75	119	2,500
Health and Human Services:									
Consumer Operated and Oriented Plan Program Contingency Fund	48.22	42	88	....	....	....	....	....	....
Homeland Security:									
Disaster Assistance Direct Loan Program Account	96.35	15	16	91.05	46	50	91.03	46	50
Housing and Urban Development:									
FHA-Mutual Mortgage Insurance Program Account	....	....	....	....	....	5	....	....	5
FHA-General and Special Risk Program Account	–10.83	–11	106	–10.91	–27	250	–11.19	–39	350
State:									
Repatriation Loans Program Account	52.65	1	2	53.18	1	2	53.42	1	2
Transportation:									
Federal-Aid Highways	7.48	223	2,982	6.85	252	3,673	6.73	251	3,736
Railroad Rehabilitation and Improvement Program	–2.09	–21	982	....	....	600	....	....	600
Treasury:									
Community Development Financial Institutions Fund Program Account	–0.87	–3	343	[2] 0.40	3	775	[2] 0.28	3	1,025
Veterans Affairs:									
Veterans Housing Benefit Program Fund	–7.03	–1	8	–24.94	–74	298	–23.01	–92	401
Native American Veteran Housing Loan Program Account	–11.24	–1	6	–14.49	–2	16	–14.86	–2	16
Environmental Protection Agency:									
Water Infrastructure Finance And Innovation Program Account	....	....	....	....	....	....	[2] 1.53	15	980
International Assistance Programs:									
Foreign Military Financing Loan Program Account	....	....	....	[2] 2.34	63	2,700	[2] 5.23	141	2,700
Overseas Private Investment Corporation Program Account	–7.79	–94	1,206	[2] –5.80	–58	1,000	[2] –5.64	–73	1,300
Small Business Administration:									

Table 20–3.   DIRECT LOAN SUBSIDY RATES, BUDGET AUTHORITY, AND LOAN LEVELS, 2015–2017—Continued

(Dollar amounts in millions)

Agency and Program Account	2015 Actual			2016 Enacted			2017 Proposed		
	Subsidy rate [1]	Subsidy budget authority	Loan levels	Subsidy rate [1]	Subsidy budget authority	Loan levels	Subsidy rate [1]	Subsidy budget authority	Loan levels
Disaster Loans Program Account	12.43	36	293	12.10	133	1,100	14.42	159	1,100
Business Loans Program Account	10.12	3	34	8.87	3	35	9.08	4	44
Export-Import Bank of the United States:									
Export-Import Bank Loans Program Account	–8.27	–6	73	....	....	....	....	....	....
National Infrastructure Bank:									
National Infrastructure Bank Program Account	....	....	....	....	....	....	[2] 12.26	123	1,000
Total	**N/A**	**–4,370**	**180,726**	**N/A**	**–8,066**	**195,684**	**N/A**	**–8,392**	**202,288**

N/A = Not applicable

*$500,000 or less

[1] Additional information on credit subsidy rates is contained in the Federal Credit Supplement.

[2] Rate reflects notional estimate. Estimates will be determined at the time of execution and will reflect the terms of the contracts and other characteristics.

Table 20–4. LOAN GUARANTEE SUBSIDY RATES, BUDGET AUTHORITY, AND LOAN LEVELS, 2015–2017

(Dollar amounts in millions)

Agency and Program Account	2015 Actual			2016 Enacted			2017 Proposed		
	Subsidy rate [1]	Subsidy budget authority	Loan levels	Subsidy rate [1]	Subsidy budget authority	Loan levels	Subsidy rate [1]	Subsidy budget authority	Loan levels
Agriculture:									
Agricultural Credit Insurance Fund Program Account	0.35	12	3,407	0.31	11	3,543	0.38	14	3,582
Commodity Credit Corporation Export Loans Program Account	–0.69	–12	1,811	–0.51	–28	5,500	–0.58	–32	5,500
Rural Water and Waste Disposal Program Account	0.59	*	15	0.55	*	16	0.48	*	16
Rural Community Facilities Program Account	4.78	6	135	2.36	6	246	2.24	2	78
Rural Housing Insurance Fund Program Account	–0.61	–115	18,737	–0.17	–31	18,130	–0.79	–161	20,411
Rural Business Program Account	5.11	53	1,044	3.88	59	1,520	4.01	44	1,099
Rural Business Investment Program Account	....	....	....	....	....	....	12.51	3	21
Rural Energy for America Program	10.58	17	161	6.60	16	236	4.64	19	411
Biorefinery Assistance Program Account	40.32	18	45	22.42	45	199	[2] 20.81	42	201
Commerce:									
Economic Development Assistance Programs	....	....	....	....	....	....	7.00	5	70
Health and Human Services:									
Health Resources and Services	....	....	....	2.67	*	9	4.30	*	6
Housing and Urban Development:									
Indian Housing Loan Guarantee Fund Program Account	1.16	9	772	0.63	7	1,151	0.41	5	1,200
Native Hawaiian Housing Loan Guarantee Fund Program Account	0.62	*	11	0.51	*	25	–0.28	–*	23
Native American Housing Block Grant	11.21	2	14	11.46	3	27	11.20	3	27
Community Development Loan Guarantees Program Account	2.42	3	123	....	....	300	....	....	300
FHA-Mutual Mortgage Insurance Program Account	–5.71	–13,085	229,143	–3.49	–7,837	224,438	–4.08	–9,085	222,832
FHA-General and Special Risk Program Account	–4.12	–550	13,334	–3.24	–438	13,555	–3.40	–457	13,410
Interior:									
Indian Guaranteed Loan Program Account	6.68	7	100	5.88	7	114	6.32	7	106
Transportation:									
Minority Business Resource Center Program	2.27	*	1	2.50	*	13	2.36	*	14
Maritime Guaranteed Loan (Title XI) Program Account	6.09	1	12	8.11	42	514	....	....	....
Veterans Affairs:									
Veterans Housing Benefit Program Fund	0.27	405	149,822	0.25	346	138,275	0.51	584	114,493
International Assistance Programs:									
Loan Guarantees to Israel Program Account	....	....	....	....	....	1,000	....	....	1,000
Ukraine Loan Guarantees Program Account	44.65	447	1,000	29.93	299	1,000	....	....	....
MENA Loan Guarantee Program Account	12.37	186	1,500	5.81	29	500	26.08	261	1,000
Development Credit Authority Program Account	6.30	37	581	4.53	50	1,106	4.95	71	1,434
Overseas Private Investment Corporation Program Account	–9.01	–270	3,000	–6.26	–188	3,000	–5.29	–169	3,200
Small Business Administration:									
Disaster Loans Program Account	....	....	....	....	....	....	2.17	1	77
Business Loans Program Account	0.07	26	34,956	....	....	57,500	....	....	58,000
Business Loans Program Account (Legislative Proposal)	....	....	....	....	....	....	[2] 25.00	1,250	5,000
Export-Import Bank of the United States:									
Export-Import Bank Loans Program Account	–2.98	–367	12,311	–4.22	–639	15,140	–5.79	–1,182	20,425
National Infrastructure Bank:									
National Infrastructure Bank Program Account	....	....	....	....	....	....	[2] 14.83	30	200
Total	**N/A**	**–13,171**	**472,035**	**N/A**	**–8,241**	**487,057**	**N/A**	**–8,745**	**474,136**
ADDENDUM: SECONDARY GUARANTEED LOAN COMMITMENT LIMITATIONS									
Government National Mortgage Association:									
Guarantees of Mortgage-backed securities Loan Guarantee Program Account	–0.28	–1,221	435,939	–0.29	–958	330,200	–0.37	–1,328	359,000
Small Business Administration:									
Secondary Market Guarantee Program	....	....	6,236	....	....	12,000	....	....	12,000
Total, secondary guarantee loan commitments	**N/A**	**–1,221**	**442,175**	**N/A**	**–958**	**342,200**	**N/A**	**–1,328**	**371,000**

N/A = Not applicable.

*$500,000 or less

[1] Additional information on credit subsidy rates is contained in the Federal Credit Supplement.

[2] Rate reflects notional estimate. Estimates will be determined at the time of execution and will reflect the terms of the contracts and other characteristics.

Table 20–5. SUMMARY OF FEDERAL DIRECT LOANS AND LOAN GUARANTEES [1]

(In billions of dollars)

	Actual								Estimate	
	2008	2009	2010	2011	2012	2013	2014	2015	2016	2017
Direct Loans:										
Obligations	75.6	812.9	246.0	296.3	191.1	174.4	174.0	181.3	195.7	202.3
Disbursements	41.1	669.4	218.9	186.7	170.0	157.5	155.4	161.4	169.0	182.0
New subsidy budget authority [2]	3.7	140.1	−9.2	−15.7	−27.2	−29.8	−22.4	4.9	−8.1	−8.5
Reestimated subsidy budget authority [2,3]	−0.8	−0.1	−125.1	−66.8	16.8	−19.7	−0.8	10.1	7.9	....
Total subsidy budget authority	**2.8**	**140.0**	**−134.3**	**−82.5**	**−10.4**	**−49.4**	**−23.2**	**15.1**	**−0.1**	**−8.5**
Loan guarantees:										
Commitments [4]	367.7	879.2	507.3	446.7	479.7	536.6	350.8	478.3	499.1	486.0
Lender disbursements [4]	354.6	841.5	494.8	384.1	444.3	491.3	335.6	461.6	454.5	442.1
New subsidy budget authority [2]	−1.4	−7.8	−4.9	−7.4	−6.9	−17.9	−13.7	−11.9	−7.1	−7.5
Reestimated subsidy budget authority [2,3]	3.6	0.5	7.6	−4.0	−4.9	20.8	1.2	−1.1	−13.6	....
Total subsidy budget authority	**2.2**	**−7.3**	**2.7**	**−11.4**	**−11.8**	**2.8**	**−12.5**	**−13.1**	**−20.7**	**−7.5**

[1] As authorized by statute, table includes TARP and SBLF equity purchases, and International Monetary Fund (IMF) transactions resulting from the 2009 Supplemental Appropriations Act.

[2] Credit subsidy costs for TARP and IMF transactions are calculated using the discount rate required by the Federal Credit Reform Act adjusted for market risks, as directed in legislation.

[3] Includes interest on reestimate.

[4] To avoid double-counting, the face value of GNMA and SBA secondary market guarantees and the TARP FHA Letter of Credit program are excluded from the totals.

21.   BUDGETARY EFFECTS OF THE TROUBLED ASSET RELIEF PROGRAM

This chapter reports on the cost and budgetary effects of Treasury's Troubled Asset Relief Program (TARP), consistent with Sections 202 and 203 of the Emergency Economic Stabilization Act (EESA) of 2008 (P.L. 110–343), as amended. The cost estimates in this report reflect transactions as of September 30, 2015, and expected future transactions as reflected in the Budget and required under EESA. Where noted, a descriptive analysis of additional transactions that occurred after September 30, 2015, is provided. For information on subsequent TARP program developments, please consult the Treasury Department's TARP Monthly Reports to Congress. EESA authorized Treasury to purchase or guarantee troubled assets and other financial instruments to restore liquidity and stability to the financial system of the United States while protecting taxpayers. Treasury has used its authority under EESA to restore confidence in U.S. financial institutions, to restart markets critical to financing American household and business activity, and to address housing market problems and the foreclosure crisis. Under EESA, TARP purchase authority was limited to $700 billion in obligations at any one time, as measured by the total purchase price paid for assets and guaranteed amounts outstanding. The Helping Families Save Their Homes Act of 2009 (P.L. 111-22) reduced total TARP purchase authority by $1.3 billion, and in July 2010, the Dodd-Frank Wall Street Reform and Consumer Protection Act (P.L. 111-203) further reduced total TARP purchase authority to a maximum of $475 billion in cumulative obligations. On October 3, 2010, Treasury's authority to make new TARP commitments expired. Treasury continues to manage existing investments and is authorized to expend previously-committed TARP funds pursuant to obligations entered into prior to October 3, 2010. Additionally, in December 2015, the Consolidated Appropriations Act, 2016 (P.L. 114-113) granted Treasury authority to make an additional $2.0 billion in commitments through the TARP Hardest Hit Fund (HHF) and fixed the termination date for new applications under the Making Home Affordable initiative (MHA) as December 31, 2016.

The Administration's current estimate of TARP's lifetime deficit cost for its $454.6 billion in cumulative obligations is $34.5 billion (see Tables 21–1 and 21–6). Section 123 of EESA requires TARP costs to be estimated on a net present value basis, adjusted to reflect a premium for market risk. As investments are liquidated, their actual costs (including any market risk effects) become known and are reflected in reestimates. It is likely that the total cost of TARP to taxpayers will eventually be lower than current estimates as the forecast market risk premiums are replaced by actual costs, but the total cost will not be fully known until all TARP investments have been extinguished.

A description of the market impact of TARP programs, followed by a detailed analysis of the assets purchased through TARP, is provided at the end of this report.

Method for Estimating the Cost of TARP Transactions

Under EESA, Treasury has purchased different types of financial instruments with varying terms and conditions. The budget reflects the costs of these instruments using the methodology as provided by Section 123 of EESA.

The estimated costs of each transaction reflect the underlying structure of the instrument. To date, TARP financial instruments have included direct loans, structured loans, equity, loan guarantees, and direct incentive payments. The costs of equity purchases, loans, guarantees, and loss sharing are the net present value of cash flows to and from the Government over the life of the instrument, per the Federal Credit Reform Act (FCRA) of 1990; as amended (2 U.S.C. 661 et seq.), with an EESA-required adjustment to the discount rate for market risks. Costs for the incentive payments under TARP housing programs, other than loss sharing under the Federal Housing Administration (FHA) Refinance program, involve financial instruments without any provision for future returns and are recorded on a cash basis.[1]

For each of these instruments, cash flow models[2] are used to estimate future cash flows to and from the Government over the life of a program or facility. Each cash flow model reflects the specific terms and conditions of the program, and technical assumptions regarding the underlying assets, risk of default or other losses, and other factors that may affect cash flows to and from the Government. For instruments other than direct incentive payments, projected cash flows are discounted using the appropriate Treasury rates, adjusted for market risks as prescribed under EESA. Risk adjustments to the discount rates are intended to capture a risk premium for uncertainty around future cash flows, and were made using available data and methods. Consistent with the require-

---

[1] Section 123 of the EESA provides the Administration the authority to record TARP equity purchases pursuant to the FCRA, with required adjustments to the discount rate for market risks. The MHA programs and HHF involve the purchase of financial instruments that have no provision for repayment or other return on investment, and do not constitute direct loans or guarantees under FCRA. Therefore these purchases are recorded on a cash basis. Administrative expenses are recorded for all of TARP under the Office of Financial Stability and the Special Inspector General for TARP on a cash basis, consistent with other Federal administrative costs, but are recorded separately from TARP program costs.

[2] The basic methods for each of these models are outlined in Chapter 21 of the *Analytical Perspectives* volume of the 2015 Budget, "Financial Stabilization Efforts and Their Budgetary Effects."

ment under FCRA to reflect the lifetime present value cost, subsidy cost estimates are reestimated every year an instrument is outstanding, with a final closing reestimate once an instrument is fully liquidated. Reestimates update the cost for actual transactions, and updated future expectations. When all investments in a given cohort are liquidated, their actual costs (including any market risk effects) become known and are reflected in final closing reestimates.

subsidy cost of TARP is likely to be lower than the current estimate because projected cash flows are discounted using a risk adjustment to the discount rate as required by EESA. This requirement adds a premium to current estimates of TARP costs on top of market and other risks already reflected in the estimated cash flows with the public. Over time, the added risk premium for uncertainty on future estimated TARP cash flows is returned to the General Fund through subsidy reestimates as actual cash

Table 21-1.   CHANGE IN PROGRAMMATIC COSTS OF TROUBLED ASSET RELIEF PROGRAM
(In billions of dollars)

TARP Programs	2016 Budget		2017 Budget		Change from 2016 Budget to 2017 Budget	
	TARP Obligations [1]	Estimated Cost (+) / Savings (−)	TARP Obligations [1]	Estimated Cost (+) / Savings (−)	TARP Obligations [1]	Estimated Cost (+) / Savings (−)
Equity Programs	336.0	5.7	335.8	5.8	−0.1	*
Structured and Direct Loan Programs	76.2	16.3	76.2	16.7	....	0.4
Guarantee Programs [2]	5.0	−3.9	5.0	−3.9	....	....
TARP Housing Programs [3]	38.4	37.4	37.5	34.7	−0.9	−2.8
Total programmatic costs [4]	**455.6**	**55.6**	**454.6**	**53.2**	**−1.0**	**−2.3**
Memorandum:						
Deficit impact with interest on reestimates [5]		*37.4*		*34.5*		*−3.0*

*$50 million or less.
[1] TARP obligations are net of cancellations.
[2] The total assets supported by the Asset Guarantee Program were $301 billion.
[3] TARP obligations include FHA Refinance Letter of Credit first loss coverage of eligible FHA insured mortgages.
[4] Total programmatic costs of TARP exclude interest on reestimates.
[5] The total deficit impact of TARP as of September 30, 2015 includes $17.43 billion in subsidy cost for TARP investments in AIG. Additional proceeds of $17.55 billion resulting from Treasury holdings of non-TARP shares in AIG are not included.

TARP Program Costs and Current Value of Assets

This section provides the special analysis required under Sections 202 and 203 of EESA, including estimates of the cost to taxpayers and the budgetary effects of TARP transactions as reflected in the Budget.[3] This section explains the changes in TARP costs, and includes alternative estimates as prescribed under EESA. It also includes a comparison of the current cost estimates with previous estimates provided by OMB and by the Congressional Budget Office (CBO).

Table 21-1, above, summarizes the cumulative and anticipated activity under TARP, and the estimated lifetime budgetary cost reflected in the Budget, compared to estimates from the 2016 Budget. The direct impact of TARP on the deficit is projected to be $34.5 billion, down $3.0 billion from the $37.4 billion estimate in the 2016 Budget. The total programmatic cost represents the lifetime net present value cost of TARP obligations from the date of disbursement, which is now estimated to be $53.2 billion, a figure that excludes interest on reestimates.[4] The final

flows become known. TARP's overall cost to taxpayers will not be fully known until all TARP investments are extinguished.

Current Value of Assets

The current value of future cash flows related to TARP transactions can also be measured by the balances in the program's non-budgetary credit financing accounts. Under the FCRA budgetary accounting structure, the net debt or cash balances in non-budgetary credit financing accounts at the end of each fiscal year reflect the present value of anticipated cash flows to and from the public.[5] Therefore, the net debt or cash balances reflect the expected present value of the asset or liability. Future collections from the public—such as proceeds from stock sales, or payments of principal and interest—are financial assets, just as future payments to the public are financial liabilities. The current year reestimates true-up assets and liabilities, setting the net debt or cash balance in the financing account equal to the present value of future cash flows.

Table 21-2 shows the actual balances of TARP financing accounts as of the end of each fiscal year through

---

[3] The analysis does not assume the effects on net TARP costs of a recoupment proposal required by Section 134 of EESA. However, the Budget includes a financial fee proposal that satisfies this requirement (see chapter 12, "Governmental Receipts," in this volume).

[4] With the exception of MHA and HHF, all the other TARP investments are reflected on a present value basis pursuant to FCRA and EESA.

[5] For example, to finance a loan disbursement to a borrower, a direct loan financing account receives the subsidy cost from the program account, and borrows from the Treasury the difference between the face value of the loan and the subsidy cost. As loan and interest payments from the public are received, the value is realized and these amounts are used to repay the financing account's debt to Treasury.

Table 21–2. TROUBLED ASSET RELIEF PROGRAM CURRENT VALUE[1]

(In billions of dollars)

	Actual							Estimate										
	2009	2010	2011	2012	2013	2014	2015	2016	2017	2018	2019	2020	2021	2022	2023	2024	2025	2026
Financing Account Balances:																		
Troubled Asset Relief Program Equity Purchase Financing Account	105.4	76.9	74.9	13.6	6.6	0.9	0.4	0.4	0.4	0.3	0.2	0.1	0.1	0.1	0.1	*	*	*
Troubled Asset Relief Program Direct Loan Financing Account	23.9	42.7	28.5	17.9	3.1	–0.2	–0.1											
Troubled Assets Insurance Financing Fund Guaranteed Loan Financing Account	0.6	2.4	0.8	0.8														
Troubled Assets Relief Program FHA Refinance Letter of Credit Financing Account			–*	–*	–*	–*	–*	–*	–*	–*	–*	–*						
Total Financing Account Balances	129.9	122.0	104.1	32.2	9.7	0.7	0.3	0.4	0.4	0.3	0.2	0.1	0.1	0.1	0.1	*	*	*

* $50 million or less.

[1] Current value as reflected in the 2017 Budget. Amounts exclude housing activity under the Making Home Affordable initiative and the Hardest Hit Fund as these programs are reflected on a cash basis.

2015, and projected balances for each subsequent year through 2026.[6] Based on actual net balances in financing accounts at the end of 2009, the value of TARP assets totaled $129.9 billion. As of September 30, 2015, total TARP net asset value has decreased to $0.3 billion as repayments, repurchases, and other liquidations have reduced the inventory of TARP assets. Estimates in 2016 and beyond reflect estimated TARP net asset values over time, and future anticipated transactions. The overall balance of the financing accounts is estimated to continue falling over the next few years, as TARP investments continue to wind down.

The value of TARP equity purchases reached a high of $105.4 billion in 2009, and has since declined significantly with the wind down of American International Group (AIG) funding and repayments from large financial institutions. In December 2014, TARP finished winding down its equity investments in Ally, leaving remaining equity investments concentrated in only two programs, the Capital Purchase Program and the Community Development Capital Initiative. The value of the TARP equity portfolio is anticipated to continue declining as participants repurchase stock and assets are sold. TARP direct loans were fully liquidated in January 2014. The Asset Guarantee Program concluded with the February 2013 liquidation of trust preferred shares Treasury received from the Federal Deposit Insurance Company (FDIC), following termination of the guarantee on Citigroup assets, and shows no financing account balance as of the end of 2013. The FHA Refinance Letter of Credit financing account reflects net cash balances, showing the reserves set aside to cover TARP's share of default claims for FHA Refinance mortgages over the letter of credit facility which expires in December 2022. These reserves are projected to fall as claims are paid and as TARP coverage expires.

---

[6] Reestimates for TARP are calculated using actual data through September 30, 2015, and updated projections of future activity. Thus, the full impacts of TARP reestimates are reflected in the 2016 financing account balances.

Estimate of the Deficit, Debt Held by the Public, and Gross Federal Debt, Based on the EESA Methodology

The estimates of the deficit and debt in the Budget reflect the impact of TARP as estimated under FCRA and Section 123 of EESA. The deficit estimates include the budgetary costs for each program under TARP, administrative expenses, certain indirect interest effects of credit programs, and the debt service cost to finance the program. As shown in Table 21-3, direct activity under TARP is expected to increase the 2016 deficit by $5.5 billion. This reflects estimated TARP programmatic and administrative outlays of $5.6 billion, offset by $0.2 billion in downward reestimates on TARP investments, including interest on reestimates, and $0.1 billion in interest effects. The estimates of U.S. Treasury debt attributable to TARP include borrowing to finance both the deficit impacts of TARP activity and the cash flows to and from the Government reflected as a means of financing in the TARP financing accounts. Estimated debt due to TARP at the end of 2016 is $25.9 billion.

Debt held by the public net of financial assets reflects the cumulative amount of money the Government has borrowed from the public for the program and not repaid, minus the current value of financial assets acquired with the proceeds of this debt, such as loan assets, or equity held by the Government. While debt held by the public is one useful measure for examining the impact of TARP, it provides incomplete information on the program's effect on the Government's financial condition. Debt held by the public net of financial assets provides a more complete picture of the Government's financial position because it reflects the net change in the Government's balance sheet due to the program.

Debt net of financial assets due to TARP is estimated to be $25.4 billion as of the end of 2016. This is $1.0 billion lower than the projected debt held net of financial assets for 2016 that was reflected in the 2016 Budget. However, debt net of financial assets is anticipated to continue increasing annually, as debt is incurred to finance TARP housing program costs and debt service.

Table 21–3.   TROUBLED ASSET RELIEF PROGRAM EFFECTS ON THE DEFICIT AND DEBT[1]

(Dollars in billions)

	Actual							Estimate										
	2009	2010	2011	2012	2013	2014	2015	2016	2017	2018	2019	2020	2021	2022	2023	2024	2025	2026
Deficit Effect:																		
Programmatic and administrative expenses	151.3	–109.6	–37.3	24.6	–8.5	–3.6	2.9	5.4	4.3	2.7	2.2	1.3	0.8	0.6	0.3	*	*	*
Interest effects[2,3]	*	*	*	*	*	*	*	0.1	0.5	0.8	1.1	1.3	1.4	1.5	1.6	1.6	1.6	1.7
Total deficit impact	**151.3**	**–109.6**	**–37.3**	**24.7**	**–8.5**	**–3.6**	**2.9**	**5.5**	**4.7**	**3.5**	**3.3**	**2.7**	**2.2**	**2.1**	**1.9**	**1.6**	**1.7**	**1.7**
Debt held by the public:																		
Deficit impact	151.3	–109.6	–37.3	24.7	–8.5	–3.6	2.9	5.5	4.7	3.5	3.3	2.7	2.2	2.1	1.9	1.6	1.7	1.7
Net disbursements of credit financing accounts	129.9	–7.9	–17.8	–71.9	–22.5	–9.0	–0.4	0.1	–*	–0.1	–0.1	–*	–*	–*	–*	–*	–*	–*
Total change in debt held by the public	281.2	–117.5	–55.1	–47.2	–31.0	–12.6	2.5	5.7	4.7	3.5	3.1	2.6	2.2	2.1	1.9	1.6	1.7	1.7
Debt held by the public	**281.2**	**163.6**	**108.5**	**61.3**	**30.3**	**17.6**	**20.2**	**25.9**	**30.5**	**34.0**	**37.1**	**39.7**	**41.9**	**44.0**	**45.9**	**47.5**	**49.2**	**50.9**
Debt held by the public net of financial assets:																		
Debt held by the public	281.2	163.6	108.5	61.3	30.3	17.6	20.2	25.9	30.5	34.0	37.1	39.7	41.9	44.0	45.9	47.5	49.2	50.9
Less financial assets net of liabilities	129.9	122.0	104.1	32.2	9.7	0.7	0.3	0.4	0.4	0.3	0.2	0.1	0.1	0.1	0.1	*	*	....
Debt held by the public net of financial assets	**151.3**	**41.6**	**4.4**	**29.0**	**20.5**	**17.0**	**19.9**	**25.4**	**30.2**	**33.7**	**37.0**	**39.6**	**41.8**	**43.9**	**45.8**	**47.4**	**49.1**	**50.9**

* $50 million or less.

[1] Table reflects the deficit effects of the TARP program, including administrative costs and interest effects.

[2] Projected Treasury interest transactions with credit financing accounts are based on the market-risk adjusted rates. Actual credit financing account interest transactions reflect the appropriate Treasury rates under the FCRA.

[3] Includes estimated debt service effects of all TARP transactions that affect borrowing from the public.

Under FCRA, the financing account earns and pays interest on its Treasury borrowings at the same interest rate used to discount cash flows for the credit subsidy cost. Section 123 of EESA requires an adjustment to the discount rate used to value TARP subsidy costs to account for market risks. However, actual cash flows as of September 30, 2015, already reflect the effect of any incurred market risks to that point, and therefore actual financing account interest transactions reflect the FCRA Treasury interest rates, with no additional risk adjustment.[7] Future cash flows reflect a risk adjusted discount rate and the corresponding financing account interest rate, consistent with the EESA requirement. For ongoing TARP credit programs, the risk adjusted discount rates on future cash flows result in subsidy costs that are higher than subsidy costs estimated under FCRA.

Estimates on a Cash Basis

The value to the Federal Government of the assets acquired through TARP is the same whether the costs of acquiring the assets are recorded in the Budget on a cash basis, or a credit basis. As noted above, the Budget records the cost of equity purchases, direct loans, and guarantees as the net present value cost to the Government, discounted at the rate required under FCRA and adjusted for market risks as required under Section 123 of EESA.

Therefore, the net present value cost of the assets is reflected on-budget, and the gross value of these assets is reflected in the financing accounts.[8] If these purchases were instead presented in the Budget on a cash basis, the Budget would reflect outlays for each disbursement (whether a purchase, a loan disbursement, or a default claim payment), and offsetting collections as cash is received from the public, with no obvious indication of whether the outflows and inflows leave the Government in a better or worse financial position, or what the net value of the transaction is.

Revised Estimate of the Deficit, Debt Held by the Public, and Gross Federal Debt Based on the Cash-basis Valuation

The estimated effects of TARP transactions on the deficit and debt, as calculated on a cash basis, are reflected in Table 21–4. For comparison, the estimates in Table 21–3 reflect TARP transactions' effects as calculated consistent with FCRA and Section 123 of EESA.

If TARP transactions were reported on a cash basis, the annual budgetary effect would include the full amount of Government disbursements for activities such as equity purchases and direct loans, offset by cash inflows from dividend payments, redemptions, and loan repayments occurring in each year. For loan guarantees, the deficit would show fees, claim payouts, or other cash transactions associated with the guarantees as they occurred. Updates to estimates of future performance would affect

---

[7] As TARP transactions wind down, the final lifetime cost estimates under the requirements of Section 123 of EESA will reflect no adjustment to the discount rate for market risks, as these risks have already been realized in the actual cash flows. Therefore, the final subsidy cost for TARP transactions will equal the cost per FCRA, where the net present value costs are estimated by discounting cash flows using Treasury rates.

[8] For MHA programs and HHF, Treasury's purchases of financial instruments do not result in the acquisition of assets with potential for future cash flows, and therefore are recorded on a cash basis.

Table 21–4. TROUBLED ASSET RELIEF PROGRAM EFFECTS ON THE DEFICIT AND DEBT CALCULATED ON A CASH BASIS

(Dollars in billions)

	Actual							Estimate										
	2009	2010	2011	2012	2013	2014	2015	2016	2017	2018	2019	2020	2021	2022	2023	2024	2025	2026
Deficit Effect:																		
Programmatic and administrative expenses .	278.4	–122.3	–58.1	–48.9	–31.6	–12.8	2.5	5.6	4.2	2.6	2.0	1.3	0.7	0.5	0.3	*	*	*
Debt service [2]	2.8	4.7	3.0	1.7	0.6	0.2	*	0.1	0.5	0.8	1.1	1.3	1.4	1.5	1.6	1.6	1.6	1.7
Total deficit impact	281.2	–117.5	–55.1	–47.2	–31.0	–12.6	2.5	5.7	4.7	3.5	3.1	2.6	2.2	2.1	1.9	1.6	1.7	1.7

* $50 million or less.

[1] Table reflects deficit effect of budgetary costs, substituting estimates calculated on a cash basis for estimates calculated under FCRA and Sec. 123 of EESA.

[2] Includes estimated debt service effects of all TARP transactions affecting borrowing from the public.

the deficit in the year that they occur, and there would not be credit reestimates.

Under cash basis reporting, TARP would increase the deficit in 2016 by an estimated $5.7 billion, so if this basis was used the 2016 deficit would be $0.2 billion higher than the $5.5 billion estimate now reflected in the Budget. The deficit would be higher because downward subsidy reestimates, which reduce the deficit, are not included under cash basis reporting. Under FCRA, the marginal change in the present value attributable to better-than-expected future inflows from the public would be recognized up front in a downward reestimate, in contrast to a cash-based treatment that would show the annual marginal changes in cash flows. However, the impact of TARP on the Federal debt, and on debt held net of financial assets, is the same on a cash basis as under FCRA. Because debt held by the public and debt net of financial assets are the same on a cash and present value basis, these data are not repeated in Table 21-4.

Portion of the Deficit Attributable to TARP, and the Extent to Which the Deficit Impact is Due to a Reestimate

Table 21–3 shows the portion of the deficit attributable to TARP transactions. The major components of TARP's $5.5 billion deficit effects in 2016 are as follows:

- TARP reestimates and interest on reestimates will decrease the deficit by $0.2 billion in 2016. This includes $0.4 billion in increased subsidy costs for TARP programs, and is reduced by $0.6 billion in interest on reestimates.

- Outlays for TARP housing programs are estimated at $5.3 billion in 2016, which includes outlays under the MHA initiative and HHF. Outlays for TARP housing programs are estimated to increase slightly in the near term as a result of new HHF obligation authority included in P.L. 114-113, before declining gradually through 2024.

- Administrative expense outlays for TARP are estimated at $235 million in 2016, and are expected to decrease annually thereafter as TARP winds down. Outlays for the Special Inspector General for TARP are estimated at $49 million in 2016.

- Interest transactions with credit financing accounts include interest paid to Treasury on borrowing by the financing accounts, offset by interest paid by Treasury on the financing accounts' uninvested balances. Although the financing accounts are non-budgetary, Treasury payments to these accounts and receipt of interest from them are budgetary transactions and therefore affect net outlays and the deficit. For TARP financing accounts, projected interest transactions are based on the market risk adjusted rates used to discount the cash flows. The projected net financing account interest paid to Treasury at market risk adjusted rates is $28 million in 2016 and after a slight increase in 2017, declines over time as the financing accounts repay borrowing from Treasury through investment sale proceeds and repayments on TARP equity purchases and direct loans.

The full impact of TARP on the deficit includes the estimated cost of Treasury borrowing from the public—debt service—for the outlays listed above. Debt service is estimated at $141 million for 2016 and is expected to increase to $1.7 billion by 2026, largely due to outlays for TARP housing programs. Total debt service will continue over time after TARP winds down, due to the financing of past TARP costs.

Analysis of TARP Reestimates

The costs of outstanding TARP assistance are reestimated annually by updating cash flows for actual experience and new assumptions, and adjusting for any changes by either recording additional subsidy costs (an upward technical and economic reestimate) or by reducing subsidy costs (a downward reestimate). The reestimated dollar amounts to be recorded in 2016 reflect TARP disbursements through September 30, 2015, while reestimated subsidy rates reflect the full lifetime costs, including anticipated future disbursements. Detailed information on upward and downward reestimates to program costs is reflected in Table 21–5.

The current reestimate of -$0.2 billion reflects a decrease in estimated TARP costs from the 2016 Budget. This decrease was due in large part to improved market conditions and continued progress winding down TARP investments over the past year.

Table 21–5. TROUBLED ASSET RELIEF PROGRAM REESTIMATES
(In billions of dollars)

TARP Program and Cohort Year	Original subsidy rate	Current reestimate rate	Current reestimate amount	Net lifetime reestimate amount, excluding interest	TARP disbursements as of 09/30/2015
Equity Programs:					
Automotive Industry Financing Program (AIFP) - Equity:					
2009	54.52%	6.48%	*	−6.5	12.5
2010	30.25%	−16.81%	....	−1.6	3.8
Capital Purchase Program (CPP):					
2009	26.99%	−6.82%	−0.1	−65.7	204.6
2010	5.77%	0.47%	−*	−*	0.3
AIG Investment Program (AIG):					
2009	82.78%	21.88%	....	−38.5	67.8
Public-Private Investment Program (PPIP) - Equity:					
2009	34.62%	−20.41%	....	−0.3	0.7
2010	22.97%	−51.02%	*	−3.7	5.5
Targeted Investment Program (TIP):					
2009	48.85%	−8.47%	....	−23.2	40.0
Community Development Capital Initiative (CDCI):					
2010	48.06%	17.61%	−*	−0.2	0.6
Subtotal Equity Programs			**−0.1**	**−139.7**	**335.8**
Structured and Direct Loan Programs:					
Automotive Industry Financing Program (AIFP) - Debt:					
2009	58.75%	21.70%	−0.1	−19.9	63.4
Public Private Investment Program (PPIP) - Debt:					
2009	−2.52%	−0.29%	....	*	1.4
2010	−10.85%	1.84%	....	1.3	11.0
Small Business 7(a) program (SBA 7(a)):					
2010	0.48%	−1.35%	....	−*	0.4
Term-Asset Backed Securities Loan Facility (TALF)[1]:					
2009	−104.23%	−605.59%	....	−0.4	0.1
Subtotal Structured and Direct Loan Programs			**−0.1**	**−18.9**	**76.2**
Guarantee Programs[2]:					
Asset Guarantee Program (AGP)[3]:					
2009	−0.25%	−1.20%	....	−1.4	301.0
FHA Refinance Letter of Credit[4]:					
2011	1.26%	0.37%	−*	−*	0.1
2012	4.00%	1.41%	−*	−*	0.2
2013	2.48%	1.32%	−*	−*	0.2
2015	1.64%	1.82%	*	*	0.1
Subtotal Guarantee Program			**−***	**−1.4**	**301.5**
Total TARP			**−0.2**	**−160.0**	**713.6**

* $50 million or less.

[1] The Term-Asset Backed Securities Loan Facility original subsidy rate reflects the anticipated collections for Treasury's $20 billion commitment, as a percent of estimated lifetime disbursements of roughly $0.1 billion.

[2] Disbursement amounts for Guarantee Programs reflect the face value of the assets supported by the guarantees.

[3] The TARP obligation for this program was $5 billion, the maximum contingent liability while the guarantee was in force.

[4] The FHA Refinance Letter of Credit, which is considered a TARP Housing Program, is also a guarantee program subject to FCRA.

Differences Between Current and Previous OMB Estimates

As shown in Table 21–6, the 2017 Budget reflects a total TARP deficit impact of $34.5 billion. This is a decrease of $3.0 billion from the 2016 Budget projection of $37.4 billion. $2.7 billion of this decrease is due to reduced estimated outlays within TARP housing programs.

The estimated 2017 TARP deficit impact reflected in Table 21–6 differs from the programmatic cost of $53.2 billion in the Budget because the deficit impact includes $18.7

Table 21–6. DETAILED TARP PROGRAM LEVELS AND COSTS
(In billions of dollars)

Program	2016 Budget		2017 Budget	
	TARP Obligations	Subsidy Costs	TARP Obligations	Subsidy Costs
Equity Purchases:				
Capital Purchase Program (CPP)	204.9	–8.4	204.9	–8.4
AIG Investment Program (AIG)	67.8	17.4	67.8	17.4
Targeted Investment Program (TIP)	40.0	–3.6	40.0	–3.6
Automotive Industry Financing Program (AIFP) - Equity	16.3	2.7	16.3	2.8
Public-Private Investment Program (PPIP) - Equity	6.4	–2.5	6.2	–2.5
Community Development Capital Initiative (CDCI)	0.6	0.1	0.6	0.1
Subtotal equity purchases	336.0	5.7	335.8	5.8
Structured and Direct Loan Programs:				
Automotive Industry Financing Program (AIFP) - Debt	63.4	16.7	63.4	17.1
Term Asset-Backed Securities Loan Facility (TALF)	0.1	–0.5	0.1	–0.6
Public-Private Investment Program (PPIP) - Debt	12.4	0.1	12.4	0.1
Small Business 7(a) Program (SBA 7(a))	0.4	*	0.4	*
Subtotal direct loan programs	76.2	16.3	76.2	16.7
Guarantee Programs:				
Asset Guarantee Program (AGP) [1]	5.0	–3.9	5.0	–3.9
Subtotal asset guarantees	5.0	–3.9	5.0	–3.9
TARP Housing Programs:				
Making Home Affordable (MHA) Programs	29.8	29.8	27.8	25.1
Hardest Hit Fund	7.6	7.6	9.6	9.6
Subtotal non-credit programs	37.4	37.4	37.4	34.7
FHA Refinance Letter of Credit	1.0	*	0.1	*
Subtotal TARP housing programs	38.4	37.4	37.5	34.7
Totals	**455.6**	**55.6**	**454.6**	**53.2**
Memorandum:				
Interest on reestimates		–18.1		–18.7
Deficit impact with interest on reestimates [2]		*37.4*		*34.5*

* $50 million or less.
[1] The total assets supported by the Asset Guarantee Program were $301 billion.
[2] Total programmatic costs of TARP exclude interest on reestimates of $18.1 billion in the 2016 Budget and $18.7 billion in the 2017 Budget. Interest on reestimates is an adjustment that accounts for the time between the original subsidy costs and current estimates; such adjustments impact the deficit but are not direct programmatic costs.

billion in cumulative downward adjustments for interest on subsidy reestimates. See footnote 2 in Table 21–6.

Differences Between OMB and CBO Estimates

Table 21–7 compares the OMB estimate for TARP's deficit impact to the deficit impact estimated by CBO in its "Report on the Troubled Asset Relief Program—March 2015."[9]

CBO estimates the total cost of TARP at $28 billion, based on estimated lifetime TARP disbursements of $440 billion. The Budget reflects the total deficit cost at $34 billion, based on current estimates of $455 billion in program obligations. The main difference between OMB and CBO cost estimates is the difference in the estimated cost of TARP housing programs, which stems from divergent demand and participation rate assumptions. The CBO

projects $28 billion in total TARP housing expenditures, while the Budget reflects a $35 billion estimate. Other differences between CBO and OMB cost estimates for TARP have diminished over time as TARP equity programs have wound down and differences in assumptions for the future performance of equity investments in the program have been eliminated.

TARP Market Impact

TARP's support to the banking sector through the Capital Purchase Program, Targeted Investment Program, Asset Guarantee Program, and the Community Development Capital Initiative helped stabilize the financial system and strengthen the financial position of the Nation's banking institutions. With the auto industry profitable and growing again, in December 2014, Treasury sold all its remaining shares of Ally Financial (the successor organization to General Motors Acceptance

[9] Available at: www.cbo.gov/sites/default/files/114th-congress- 2015-2016/reports/50034-TARP.pdf

Table 21–7.   COMPARISON OF CBO AND OMB TARP COSTS

(In billions of dollars)

Program	Estimates of Deficit Impact [1]	
	CBO Cost Estimate [2]	OMB Cost Estimate
Capital Purchase Program	−16	−16
Targeted Investment Program & Asset Guarantee Program	−8	−8
AIG assistance	15	15
Automotive Industry Financing Program	12	12
Term Asset-Backed Securities Loan Facility	−1	−1
Public-Private Investment Programs [3].............................. ...	−3	−3
Other programs [4]	*	*
TARP housing programs [5]	28	35
Total	**28**	**34**

* Amounts round to less than $1 billion.
[1] Totals include interest on reestimates.
[2] CBO estimates from March 2015, available at *www.cbo.gov/sites/default/files/114th-congress-2015-2016/reports/50034-TARP.pdf*
[3] Includes both debt and equity purchases.
[4] "Other programs" reflects an aggregate cost for CDCI and small business programs. In previous Budgets, Other programs included AGP and PPIP.
[5] OMB Cost Estimate for TARP housing programs reflect legislation passed in December 2015.

Corporation (GMAC)), recouping a total of $70.5 billion from the original investment. With this sale, the Automotive Industry Financing Program was effectively wound down. Treasury retains the right to receive proceeds from Chrysler and General Motors (GM) liquidation trusts, and in 2015 received $100.2 million and $8.3 million, respectively, and could continue to receive future cash flows from further liquidation and/or legal proceedings. Sales of TARP assets occurring after September 30, 2015, are not included in the cost analysis provided in this report.

The Administration's housing programs implemented through TARP have helped stabilize the housing market and kept millions of borrowers in their homes. As of December 31, 2015, more than 1.6 million borrowers have received permanent mortgage modifications through the Home Affordable Modification Program (HAMP), which amounts to an estimated $40 billion in realized monthly mortgage payment savings for these homeowners. In addition to helping these borrowers, the Administration's TARP housing programs have been a catalyst for private sector mortgage modifications. Since April 2009, HAMP, FHA, and the private sector HOPE NOW alliance have initiated more than 10 million mortgage modifications, which is nearly double the number of foreclosures completed in the same period. In late 2014, the Administration announced several enhancements to housing programs under MHA designed to motivate borrowers to continue making their modified mortgage payments, strengthen the safety net for homeowners facing continuing financial hardships, and help homeowners in MHA programs build equity in their homes, further stabilizing neighborhoods. Also, in July 2015, the Administration announced a streamlined modification process under HAMP to assist homeowners who are seriously delinquent and have not yet completed a HAMP application. See the "Credit and Insurance" chapter in this volume for more information on the Administration's efforts to support the housing market.

Description of Assets Purchased Through TARP, by Program

Capital Purchase Program (CPP): Pursuant to EESA, Treasury created the CPP in October 2008 to restore confidence throughout the financial system by ensuring that the Nation's banking institutions had a sufficient capital cushion against potential future losses and to support lending to creditworthy borrowers. All eligible CPP recipients completed funding applications by December 31, 2009, and Treasury purchased $204.9 billion in preferred stock in 707 financial institutions under CPP. As of November 30, 2015, Treasury had received approximately $199.6 billion in principal repayments and $27.1 billion in revenues from dividends, interest, warrants, gains/other interest and fees. CPP cash proceeds of $226.6 billion now exceed Treasury's initial investment by $21.7 billion. As of September 30, 2015, $0.3 billion remained outstanding under the program.

Community Development Capital Initiative (CDCI): The CDCI program invested lower-cost capital in Community Development Financial Institutions (CDFIs), which operate in markets underserved by traditional financial institutions. In February 2010, Treasury released program terms for the CDCI program, under which participating institutions received capital investments of up to 5 percent of risk-weighted assets and pay dividends to Treasury of as low as 2 percent per annum. The dividend rate increases to 9 percent after eight years. CDFI credit unions were able to apply to TARP for subordinated debt at rates equivalent to those offered to CDFI banks and thrifts. These institutions could apply for capital investments of up to 3.5 percent of total assets — an amount approximately equivalent to the 5 percent of risk-weighted assets available under the CDCI program to banks and thrifts. TARP capital of $570 million has been committed to this program. As of November 30, 2015, Treasury has received $173 million in cash back on its CDCI investments and $445 million remains outstanding.

Capital Assistance Program (CAP) and Other Programs: In 2009, Treasury worked with Federal banking regulators to develop a comprehensive "stress test" known as the Supervisory Capital Assessment Program (SCAP) to assess the health of the nation's 19 largest bank holding companies. In conjunction with SCAP, Treasury announced that it would provide capital under TARP through the Capital Assistance Program (CAP) to institutions that participated in the stress tests as well as others. Only one TARP institution (Ally Financial) required additional funds under the stress tests, but received them through the Automotive Industry Financing Program (AIFP), not CAP. CAP closed on November 9, 2009, without making any investments and did not incur any losses to taxpayers. Following the release of the stress test results, banks were able to raise hundreds of billions of dollars in private capital.

American International Group (AIG) Investments: During the financial crisis, the Federal Reserve Bank of New York (FRBNY) and Treasury provided financial support to AIG in order to mitigate broader systemic risks that would have resulted from the disorderly failure of the company. To prevent the company from entering bankruptcy and to resolve the liquidity issues it faced, the FRBNY provided an $85 billion line of credit to AIG in September 2008 and received preferred shares that entitled it to 79.8 percent of the voting rights of AIG's common stock. After TARP was enacted, FRBNY and Treasury continued to work to facilitate AIG's execution of its plan to sell certain of its businesses in an orderly manner, promote market stability, and protect the interests of the U.S. Government and taxpayers. As of December 31, 2008, when purchases ended, Treasury had purchased $40 billion in preferred shares from AIG through TARP, which were subsequently converted into common stock. In April 2009, Treasury also extended a $29.8 billion line of credit, of which AIG drew down $27.8 billion, in exchange for additional preferred stock. The remaining $2 billion obligation was subsequently canceled.

AIG executed a recapitalization plan with FRBNY, Treasury, and the AIG Credit Facility Trust in January 2011 that allowed for the acceleration of the Government's exit from AIG. Following the restructuring and AIG's ensuing public offering in May 2011, Treasury had a 77 percent ownership (or 1.45 billion shares) stake in AIG, which represented a 15 percentage point reduction from Treasury's 92 percent ownership stake in January 2011. Throughout 2012, Treasury completed public offerings to further reduce its AIG ownership stake. In December 2012, Treasury sold its remaining balance of AIG common stock in a public offering that reduced Treasury's AIG common stock position to zero, including its shares ac-

quired outside of TARP from FRBNY. With this final sale, Treasury and FRBNY fully recovered all funds committed to stabilize AIG during the financial crisis.[10] In March 2013, Treasury sold its remaining 2.7 million warrants for $25.2 million and has fully exited its investment in AIG. (A summary of the deal terms and transactions can be found in the Financial Stabilization Efforts and their Budgetary Effects Chapter of the *Analytical Perspectives* volume of the 2014 Budget.) In total, TARP's AIG commitments totaled $67.8 billion and, with the program closed, yielded $55.3 billion in total cash back.

Targeted Investment Program (TIP): The goal of TIP was to stabilize the financial system by making investments in institutions that are critical to the functioning of the financial system. Investments made through TIP sought to avoid significant market disruptions resulting from the deterioration of one financial institution that could threaten other financial institutions and impair broader financial markets, and thereby pose a threat to the overall economy. Under TIP, Treasury purchased $20 billion in preferred stock from Citigroup and $20 billion in preferred stock from Bank of America. Treasury also received stock warrants from each company. Both Citigroup and Bank of America repaid their TIP investments in full in December 2009, along with dividend payments of approximately $3.0 billion. In March 2010, Treasury sold all of its Bank of America warrants for $1.2 billion, and in January 2011, Treasury sold Citigroup warrants acquired through TIP for $190.4 million. In total, TARP's TIP commitments totaled $40 billion and, with the program closed, yielded $44.4 billion in total cash back.

Asset Guarantee Program (AGP): The AGP was created to provide Government assurances for assets held by financial institutions that were critical to the functioning of the Nation's financial system. Under the AGP, Treasury and FDIC guaranteed up to $5 billion and $10 billion, respectively, of potential losses incurred on a $301 billion portfolio of financial assets held by Citigroup. In exchange, Treasury received $4 billion of preferred stock that was later converted to trust preferred securities; FDIC received $3 billion in preferred stock.[11] The preferred stock provided an 8 percent annual dividend. On December 23, 2009, in connection with Citigroup's TIP repayment, Citigroup and the Government terminated the AGP agreement. Treasury and FDIC did not pay any losses under the agreement, and retained $5.2 billion of the $7 billion in trust preferred securities that were part of the initial agreement with Citigroup. TARP retained $2.2 billion of the trust preferred securities, as well as warrants for common stock shares that were issued by Citigroup as consideration for the guarantee. Treasury

---

[10] Treasury's investment in AIG common shares consisted of shares acquired in exchange for preferred stock purchased with TARP funds (TARP shares) and shares received from the trust created by FRBNY for the benefit of Treasury as a result of its loan to AIG (non-TARP shares). Treasury collected proceeds of $17.5 billion for its non-TARP shares in AIG.

[11] Trust preferred securities are financial instruments that have the following features: they are taxed like debt; counted as equity by regulators; are generally longer term; have early redemption features; make quarterly fixed interest payments; and mature at face value.

sold the trust preferred securities on September 30, 2010, and the warrants on January 25, 2011. On December 28, 2012, Treasury received $800 million in additional Citigroup trust preferred securities from FDIC and, in 2013, sold them for $894 million. In total, with the program closed, TARP's Citigroup asset guarantees yielded $3.9 billion in total cash back.

In May 2009, Bank of America announced a similar asset guarantee agreement with respect to approximately $118 billion in Bank of America assets, but the final agreement was never executed. As a result, in 2009, Bank of America paid a termination fee of $425 million to the Government. Of this amount, $276 million was paid to TARP, $92 million was paid to FDIC, and $57 million was paid to the Federal Reserve. In total, AGP obligated $5 billion, but never paid a claim, and with the program closed, TARP's AGP guarantees yielded $4.1 billion in total cash back.

Automotive Industry Support Programs: In December 2008, in order to mitigate a systemic threat to the Nation's economy and a potential loss of thousands of jobs, Treasury established several programs to prevent the collapse of the domestic automotive industry. Through the Automotive Industry Financing Program (AIFP), TARP made emergency loans to Chrysler, Chrysler Financial, and GM. Additionally, TARP bought equity in Ally Financial, formerly GMAC, and assisted Chrysler and GM during their bankruptcy proceedings.

Treasury has liquidated its AIFP holdings and AIFP is now closed. In total, of the $12.4 billion committed to Chrysler, TARP was repaid $11.1 billion in total cash back.[12] On December 9, 2013, TARP sold its last remaining shares in GM, recouping $39.0 billion from TARP's $49.5 billion investment in GM.[13] On January 16, 2014, Treasury announced that TARP had sold 410,000 shares of Ally common equity for $3 billion in a private placement offering. Treasury sold Ally common stock as part of Ally's initial public offering on April 15, 2014, for $2.4 billion in additional proceeds and $181 million associated with the over-allotment option that was exercised in May 2014. TARP conducted two trading plans between August 14, 2014, and October 16, 2014, resulting in collections of $464 million. On December 18, 2014, TARP sold its remaining 54.9 million shares of Ally common stock in an underwritten offering, completing the wind down of its remaining investments through the AIFP and recovering $1.3 billion. In total, Treasury recovered $19.6 billion on its investment in Ally, roughly $2.4 billion more than the original investment of $17.2 billion.

Through the Auto Supplier Support Program (Supplier Program) and the Auto Warranty Commitment Program (Warranty Program), Treasury disbursed $1.1 billion in direct loans to GM and Chrysler to support auto parts manufacturers and suppliers. Both the Supplier and

Warranty Programs have closed and, in aggregate, these investments yielded $1.2 billion in total cash back. TARP's AIFP disbursements—including the GM, Chrysler, Ally (GMAC), Supplier, and Warranty Programs—totaled $79.7 billion and, with all programs effectively wound down, AIFP yielded $70.5 billion in total cash back.

TARP maintains an interest in the ongoing bankruptcy proceedings of the automotive entities it invested in. In 2015, TARP received payments of $100.2 million from the Chrysler bankruptcy proceedings and $8.3 million from the GM bankruptcy proceedings. Additional future payments are possible, but not anticipated.

Credit Market Programs: The Credit Market Programs were designed to facilitate lending that supports consumers and small businesses, through the Term Asset-Backed Securities Loan Facility (TALF), the CDCI discussed previously, and the Small Business Administration's guaranteed loan program (SBA 7(a)).

Term Asset-Backed Securities Loan Facility (TALF): The TALF was a joint initiative with the Federal Reserve that provided financing (TALF loans) to private investors to help facilitate the restoration of efficient and robust secondary markets for various types of credit. Treasury provided protection to the Federal Reserve through a loan to TALF's special purpose vehicle (SPV), which was originally available to purchase up to $20 billion in assets that would be acquired in the event of default on Federal Reserve financing. In March 2009 Treasury disbursed $0.1 billion of this amount to the TALF SPV to implement the program. In July 2010, Treasury, in consultation with the Federal Reserve, reduced the maximum amount of assets Treasury would acquire to $4.3 billion, or 10 percent of the total $43 billion outstanding in the facility when the program was closed to new lending on June 30, 2010. In June 2012, Treasury, in consultation with the Federal Reserve, further reduced its loss-coverage to $1.4 billion. Finally, Treasury and the Federal Reserve announced in January 2013 that Treasury's commitment of TARP funds to provide credit protection was no longer necessary due to the fact that the accumulated fees collected through TALF exceeded the total principal amount of TALF loans outstanding. As of November 30, 2015, Treasury had accumulated income of $685 million from TALF.

Small Business 7(a) Program (SBA 7(a)): In March 2009, Treasury and the Small Business Administration (SBA) announced a Treasury program to purchase SBA-guaranteed securities (pooled certificates) to re-start the secondary market in these loans. Through a pilot program, Treasury purchased 31 SBA-guaranteed securities with an aggregate face value of approximately $368 million. Treasury reduced its commitment to the SBA 7(a) Program from $1 billion to $370 million, as demand for the Program waned due to a significantly improved secondary market for these securities following the original announcement of the Program. In January 2012, Treasury completed the final disposition of its SBA 7(a) securities portfolio. The SBA 7(a) Program received total proceeds of $376 million, representing a gain of approximately $8 million to taxpayers.

---

[12] Chrysler repayments of $11.1 billion include $560 million in proceeds from the sale of Treasury's 6 percent fully diluted equity interest in Chrysler to Fiat and Treasury's interest in an agreement with the United Automobile Worker's retiree trust that were executed on July 21, 2011.

[13] This excludes the $884 million loan to GM that was converted to GMAC common stock.

Public Private Investment Program (PPIP): Treasury announced the Legacy Securities Public-Private Investment Partnership (PPIP) on March 23, 2009, to help restart the market for legacy mortgage-backed securities, thereby helping financial institutions begin to remove these assets from their balance sheets and allowing for a general increase in credit availability to consumers and small businesses. Under the Program, Public-Private Investment Funds (PPIFs) were established by private sector fund managers for the purchase of eligible legacy securities from banks, insurance companies, mutual funds, pension funds, and other eligible sellers as defined under EESA. On June 30, 2010, PPIP closed for new funding and as of December 2012 the PPIFs can no longer deploy capital and make new investments. Treasury was authorized to continue to manage these investments for up to five additional years, and as of September 30, 2015, all PPIFs have been terminated. As of November 30, 2015, after obligating $18.6 billion, PPIP investments had yielded $22.5 billion in total cash back.

TARP Housing Programs: To mitigate foreclosures and preserve homeownership, in February 2009 the Administration announced a comprehensive housing program utilizing up to $50 billion in TARP funding. The Government-Sponsored Enterprises: Fannie Mae and Freddie Mac participated in the Administration's programs both as Treasury's financial agents for Treasury's contracts with servicers, and by implementing similar policies for their own mortgage portfolios. These housing programs are focused on creating sustainably-affordable mortgages for responsible homeowners who are making a good faith effort to make their mortgage payments, while mitigating the spillover effects of foreclosures on neighborhoods, communities, the financial system, and the economy. Following the enactment of the 2010 Wall Street Reform Act, Treasury reduced its commitments to TARP housing programs to $45.6 billion. These programs fall into three initiatives:

- Making Home Affordable (MHA);

- Housing Finance Agency (HFA) Hardest-Hit Fund (HHF); and

- Federal Housing Administration (FHA) Refinance Program.[14]

Making Home Affordable (MHA): Programs under MHA include the Home Affordable Modification Program (HAMP), FHA-HAMP[15], the Second Lien Modification Program (2MP), and Rural Development-HAMP.[16] MHA also includes the Home Affordable Foreclosure Alternatives Program, which provides short sale and deed-in-lieu of foreclosure opportunities to borrowers when a modification is not possible, as well as assistance to borrowers who are unemployed or underwater (owe more than their home is worth). Under MHA programs, Treasury contracts with servicers to modify loans or provide other foreclosure alternatives in accordance with the program's guidelines, and to make incentive payments to the borrowers, servicers, and, in some programs, investors for those modifications or other foreclosure alternatives. On June 26, 2014, the Administration announced that the application deadline for MHA would be extended to December 31, 2016. In December 2015, P.L. 114-113 set December 31, 2016 as the termination date for new MHA applications and prohibited further extensions. As of September 30, 2015, TARP has paid $12.24 billion in MHA related incentive payments and an additional $15.54 billion in TARP funds have been obligated but not yet disbursed.

HFA Hardest-Hit Fund (HHF): The $9.6 billion HHF provides the eligible entities of HFAs from 18 states and the District of Columbia with funding to design and implement innovative programs to prevent foreclosures and bring stability to local housing markets. The Administration targeted areas hardest hit by unemployment and home price declines through the program. The flexibility of HHF funds enables states to design and tailor innovative programs to meet the unique needs of their communities. Over the past five years, the Administration has taken key actions to help communities turn the corner to recovery, including working with Alabama, Indiana, Illinois, Michigan, Ohio, South Carolina, and Tennessee to use their HHF funds for blight elimination. In addition, Arizona, Florida, Illinois, Kentucky, North Carolina, and Rhode Island offer Down Payment Assistance Programs, making assistance available to moderate-income homebuyers in counties that continue to demonstrate housing market distress. In December 2015, P.L. 114-113 extended Treasury's authority to incur certain obligations for HHF funds through December 31, 2017; Treasury expects to allocate $2 billion in additional HHF funds to currently participating jurisdictions in early 2016.

FHA Refinance Program: This program, which is administered by the FHA and supported by TARP, was initiated in September 2010 and allows eligible borrowers who are current on their mortgages, but owe more than their home is worth, to refinance into an FHA-guaranteed loan if the lender writes off at least 10 percent of the existing loan. $8.1 billion was originally committed through a letter of credit agreement with Citigroup to cover a share of any losses on the loans and administrative expenses. In 2013, Treasury's commitment to cover a share of any losses under the FHA Refinance Program was reduced from $8.1 billion to $1.0 billion. In March 2015, Treasury's commitment was further reduced from $1.0 billion to $0.1 billion, and the Program was extended through December 31, 2016. As of November 30, 2015, TARP's remaining commitment to the FHA Refinance Program was $0.1 billion.

---

[14] The FHA Refinance Program is run by the Department of Housing and Urban Development (HUD), but is supported by Treasury through TARP with $100 million to cover a share of any losses on these particular FHA Refinance loans. This program has also been referred to as the FHA Short Refinance Program or Option in other reporting.

[15] FHA-HAMP is administered by HUD; Treasury provides incentives for servicers and borrowers who qualify for Treasury FHA-HAMP

[16] For additional information on MHA programs, visit: *www.makinghomeaffordable.gov.*

22. HOMELAND SECURITY FUNDING ANALYSIS

Section 889 of the Homeland Security Act of 2002 requires that a homeland security funding analysis be incorporated in the President's Budget. This analysis addresses that legislative requirement and covers homeland security funding and activities of all Federal agencies, not just those carried out by the Department of Homeland Security (DHS). Since not all activities carried out by DHS constitute traditional homeland security funding (e.g. response to natural disasters and Coast Guard search and rescue activities), DHS estimates in this section do not encompass the entire DHS budget. As also required in the Homeland Security Act of 2002, this analysis includes estimates of State, local, and private sector expenditures on homeland security activities.

The President's highest priority is to keep the American people safe. Homeland security budgetary priorities will continue to be informed by careful, government-wide strategic analysis and review.

Data Collection Methodology and Adjustments, Including for the Department of Defense

The Federal spending estimates in this analysis utilize funding and programmatic information collected on the Executive Branch's homeland security efforts. Throughout the budget formulation process, the Office of Management and Budget (OMB) collects three-year funding estimates and associated programmatic information from all Federal agencies with homeland security responsibilities. These estimates do not include the efforts of the Legislative or Judicial branches. Information in this chapter is augmented by a detailed appendix of account-level funding estimates, which is available on the internet at: www.budget.gov/budget/Analytical_Perspectives and on the Budget CD-ROM.

To compile this data, agencies report information using standardized definitions for homeland security. The data provided by the agencies are developed at the "activity level," which incorporates a set of like programs or projects, at a level of detail sufficient to consolidate the information to determine total Governmental spending on homeland security.

To the extent possible, this analysis maintains programmatic and funding consistency with previous estimates. Some discrepancies from data reported in earlier years arise due to agencies' improved ability to extract homeland security-related activities from host programs and refine their characterizations, as was the case with Department of Defense (DOD) data last year (see paragraph below). As in the Budget, where appropriate, the data is also updated to reflect agency activities, Congressional action, and technical re-estimates. In addition, the Administration may refine definitions or mission area estimates over time based on additional analysis or changes in the way specific activities are characterized, aggregated, or disaggregated.

As reported in the Fiscal Year 2016 President's budget, DOD refined its characterization of homeland security-related activities to report its spending for this purpose more accurately. This effort resulted in an approximately $4 billion reduction in estimated homeland security funding for DOD relative to what was previously estimated for 2014, for example. The majority of this reduction is related to lower estimated Army National Guard and Reserve personnel costs due to a more accurate allocation methodology for estimating National Guardsmen and Reservist assignments. The composition of these assignments changed due to troop withdrawal from Afghanistan and associated reductions in manpower required for pre-deployment training and backfilling troops who were deployed. In addition, DOD previously included some activities focused outside of the continental United States, which have been removed from current homeland security estimates. Examples include overseas activities by the Special Operations Command related to counterterrorism and Marine Corps activities related to countering improvised explosive devices. DOD and OMB worked together to restate past estimates using the refined methodology. The results of this effort are shown in Table 22-10.

During this effort, DOD also identified adjustments necessary to maintain consistency throughout the database. DOD determined that the funding methodology used prior to Fiscal Year 2012 to account for Protecting Infrastructure and Critical Key Assets (PICKA) was different than the current methodology. DOD previously included funding for both domestic and select international activities as PICKA. In this revision, DOD normalized the historical data to reflect the current practice of reporting only the United States-based portion of those activities related to DOD's homeland security mission. DOD is still reporting the same programs over the Fiscal Year 2004-2017 period; however, this revision provides a better accounting of the estimated homeland security funding within those programs prior to Fiscal Year 2012. Therefore, to allow data comparisons, DOD restated PICKA funding data for the Fiscal Year 2004-2011 period, as shown in the other adjustments row.

Further adjustments were also required to correct Prior Year and Budget Year 2012 data entry errors. Net corrections of these errors are shown in the Fiscal Year 2012 column in the other adjustments row.

Federal Expenditures

Total funding for homeland security has grown significantly since the attacks of September 11, 2001. For 2017, the President's Budget includes $70.5 billion of gross budget authority for homeland security activities, a $1.2 billion (1.7 percent) decrease below the 2016 level, attributable, in part, to the non-recurrence of 2014, 2015, and 2016 authority to build a nationwide interoperable public safety broadband network for first responders and related programs. Excluding mandatory spending, fees, and the Department of Defense's (DOD) homeland security budget, the 2017 Budget proposes a net, non-Defense, discretionary budget authority level of $50.4 billion, which is an increase of $5.2 billion (11.5 percent) above the 2016 level (see Table 22–1).

A total of 29 agency budgets include Federal homeland security funding in 2017. Six agencies—the Departments of Homeland Security (DHS), Defense (DOD), Health and Human Services (HHS), Justice (DOJ), State (DOS), and Energy (DOE)—account for approximately $66.4 billion (94.3 percent) of total Government-wide gross discretionary homeland security funding in 2017.

As required by the Homeland Security Act, this analysis presents homeland security risk and spending in three broad categories: Prevent and Disrupt Terrorist Attacks; Protect the American People, Our Critical Infrastructure, and Key Resources; and Respond To and Recover From Incidents.

Prevent and Disrupt Terrorist Attacks

Activities in the areas of intelligence-and-warning and domestic counterterrorism aim to disrupt the ability of terrorists to operate within our borders and prevent the emergence of violent radicalization. Intelligence-and-warning funding covers activities designed to detect terrorist activity before it manifests itself in an attack so that proper preemptive, preventive, and protective action can be taken. Specifically, it is made up of efforts to identify, collect, analyze, and distribute source intelligence information or the resultant warnings from intelligence analysis. It also includes information sharing activities among Federal, State, and local governments, relevant private sector entities, and the public at large; it does not include most foreign intelligence collection, although the resulting intelligence may inform homeland security activities. In 2017, funding for intelligence-and-warning is distributed between DOJ (79 percent), primarily in the Federal Bureau of Investigation ($217.7 million), and National Security Division ($97.3 million) for activities to deny terrorists and terrorist-related weapons and materials entry into our country and across all international borders. Funding includes measures to protect border and transportation systems, such as screening airport passengers, detecting dangerous materials at ports overseas and at U.S. ports-of-entry, and patrolling our coasts and the land between ports-of-entry. Securing our borders and transportation systems is a complex task. Security enhancements in one area may make another avenue more attractive to terrorists. Therefore, our border and transportation security strategy aims to make the U.S. borders "smarter" while facilitating the flow of legitimate visitors and commerce. Government programs do

this by targeting layered resources toward the highest risks and sharing information so that frontline personnel can stay ahead of potential adversaries. The majority of funding for border and transportation security is in DHS ($25.5 billion, or 83.7 percent), largely for U.S. Customs and Border Protection (CBP), the Transportation Security Administration (TSA), the U.S. Coast Guard, and U.S. Immigration and Customs Enforcement (ICE). Other Federal Departments, such as the Department of State ($4.4 billion, or 14.4 percent), also play a significant role. Many of these activities support the Obama Administration's emphasis on reducing the illicit flow of drugs, currency, weapons, and people across our borders as well as targeting transnational criminal organizations operating along the Southwest border and elsewhere.

Funding for domestic counterterrorism contains Federal and Federally-supported efforts to identify, thwart, and prosecute terrorists in the United States. It includes pursuit not only of the individuals directly involved in terrorist activity but also their sources of support: the people and organizations that knowingly fund the terrorists and those that provide them with logistical assistance. In today's world, preventing and interdicting terrorist activity within the United States is a priority for law enforcement at all levels of government. The largest contributors to the domestic counterterrorism goal in 2017 are law enforcement organizations, including DOJ ($3.4 billion or 60.1 percent), largely for the FBI and DHS ($2.2 billion or 38.3 percent), largely for ICE.

Protect the American People, Our Critical Infrastructure, and Key Resources

Critical infrastructure includes the assets, systems, and networks, whether physical or virtual, so vital to the United States that their destruction would have a debilitating effect on national economic or homeland security, public health or safety, or any combination thereof. Key resources are publicly or privately controlled resources essential to the minimal operations of the economy and government whose disruption or destruction could have significant consequences across multiple dimensions, including national monuments and icons.

Efforts to protect the American people include defending against catastrophic threats through research, development, and deployment of technologies, systems, and medical measures to detect and counter the threat of chemical, biological, radiological, and nuclear (CBRN) weapons. Funding encompasses activities to protect against, detect, deter, or mitigate the possible terrorist use of CBRN weapons through detection systems and procedures, improving decontamination techniques, and the development of medical countermeasures, such as vaccines, drugs and diagnostics to protect the public from the threat of a CBRN attack or other public health emergency. The agencies with the most significant resources to help develop and field technologies to counter CBRN threats are: HHS ($2.9 billion, or 43.8 percent) largely for research at the National Institutes of Health (NIH); DOD ($2.1 billion, or 31.7 percent) largely for Research

Development and Testing; and DHS ($1.2 billion, or 18.9 percent) largely for research in science and technology.

Protecting the Nation's critical infrastructure and key resources (CI/KR) is a complex challenge for two reasons: (1) the diversity of infrastructure and (2) the high level of private ownership of the Nation's critical infrastructure and key assets. Efforts to protect CI/KR include unifying disparate efforts to protect critical infrastructure across the Federal Government and with State, local, and private stakeholders; accurately assessing CI/KR and prioritizing protective action based on risk; and reducing threats and vulnerabilities in cyberspace. Securing cyberspace is a top priority of the Obama Administration both to protect Americans and our way of life and as a foundation for continuing to grow the Nation's economy. DOD continues to report the largest share of funding for protecting CI/KR for 2017 ($10.3 billion, or 49.2 percent), which includes programs focusing on physical security and improving the military's ability to prevent or mitigate the consequences of attacks against departmental personnel and facilities. DHS has overall responsibility for prioritizing and executing infrastructure protection activities at the national level and accounts for $5.6 billion (26.7 percent of total 2017 funding). Another twenty-four agencies also report funding to protect their own assets and work with States, localities, and the private sector to reduce vulnerabilities in their areas of expertise.

Respond To and Recover From Incidents

The ability to respond to and recover from incidents requires efforts to bolster capabilities nationwide to prevent and protect against terrorist attacks, and also minimize the damage from attacks through effective response and recovery. This includes programs that help to plan, equip, train, and practice the capabilities of many different response units (including first responders, such as police officers, firefighters, emergency medical providers, public works personnel, and emergency management officials) that are instrumental in their preparedness to mobilize without warning for an emergency. Building this capability encompasses a broad range of agency incident management activities, as well as grants and other assistance to States and localities for first responder preparedness capabilities. For this analysis, spending for response to specific natural disasters or other major incidents, including catastrophic natural events such as Hurricanes Sandy and Katrina, and chemical or oil spills, like Deepwater Horizon, do not directly fall within the definition of a homeland security activity, as defined by section 889 of the Homeland Security Act of 2002. Preparing for terrorism-related threats includes many activities that also support preparedness for catastrophic natural and man-made disasters, however. Additionally, lessons learned from the response to Hurricanes Sandy and Katrina have been used to revise and strengthen catastrophic response planning. The agencies with the most significant participation in this effort are: DHS ($2.2 billion, or 35.9 percent, of the 2017 total); HHS ($1.9 billion, or 31.4 percent of the 2017 total); and DOD ($1.1 billion, or

17.5 percent of the 2017 total). Twenty other agencies include emergency preparedness and response funding. The President's 2017 request reflects a decrease of $1.1 billion (14.6 percent) below the 2016 level, primarily attributable to the non-recurrence of 2014, 2015, and 2016 authority to build a nationwide interoperable public safety broadband network for first responders and related programs.

Continue to Strengthen the Homeland Security Foundation

Preventing and disrupting terrorist attacks; protecting the American people, critical infrastructure, and key resources; and responding to and recovering from incidents that do occur are enduring homeland security responsibilities. For the long-term fulfillment of these responsibilities it is necessary to continue to strengthen the principles, systems, structures, and institutions that cut across the homeland security enterprise and support our activities to secure the Nation. Long-term success across several cross-cutting areas is essential to protect the United States. Engaging with and leveraging the resources of the whole community, including Federal, State, local, tribal, and territorial governments, the non-governmental and private sectors, as well as families and individuals, are essential for effective preparedness and incident response capabilities. While these areas are not quantifiable in terms of budget figures, they are important elements in the management and budgeting processes. As the Administration sets priorities and determines funding for new and existing homeland security programs, consideration must be given to areas such as the assessment and management of risk, which underlie the full spectrum of homeland security activities. This includes decisions about when, where, and how to invest resources in capabilities or assets that eliminate, control, or mitigate risks. Likewise, research and development initiatives promote the application of science and technology to homeland security activities and can drive improvements in processes and efficiencies to reduce the vulnerability of the Nation.

Non-Federal Expenditures[1]

State and local governments and private-sector firms also have devoted resources of their own to the task of defending against terrorist threats. Some of the spending has been of a one-time nature, such as investment in new security equipment and infrastructure; some spending has been ongoing, such as hiring more personnel, and increasing overtime for existing security personnel. In many cases, own-source spending has supplemented the resources provided by the Federal Government.

Many governments and businesses, though not all, place a high priority on, and provide additional resources, for security. A 2004 survey conducted by the National Association of Counties found, that as a result of intergovernmental homeland security planning and funding processes, three out of four counties believed they were

---

[1] OMB does not collect detailed homeland security expenditure data from State, local, or private entities directly.

better prepared to respond to terrorist threats. Moreover, almost 40 percent of the surveyed counties had appropriated their own funds to assist with homeland security. Own-source resources supplemented funds provided by States and the Federal Government. However, the same survey revealed that 54 percent of counties had not used any of their own funds.[2] The survey's findings were based on the responses from 471 counties (15 percent) nationwide, out of 3,140 counties or equivalents.[3]

A March 2009 study conducted by the Heritage Foundation, one of the few organizations to compile homeland security spending estimates from States and localities, provides data on State and local spending in

---

[2] Source: National Association of Counties, "Homeland Security Funding—2003 State Homeland Security Grants Programs I and II."

[3] The National Association of Counties conducted a survey through its various state associations (48), responses were received from 471 counties in 26 states.

Table 22–1.   HOMELAND SECURITY FUNDING BY AGENCY
(Budget Authority in milions of dollars)

	FY2015 Actual	FY2015 Supplemental	FY2016 Enacted	FY2017 Request
Department of Agriculture	452.2	0.0	577.4	544.6
Department of Commerce*	5,389.4	9.8	1,373.9	579.8
Department of Defense—Military Programs**	12,363.0	181.8	13,708.3	13,541.9
Department of Health and Human Services	4,753.2	804.3	5,327.8	5,064.7
Department of the Interior	54.2	0.0	58.1	57.8
Department of Justice	4,080.8	0.0	4,148.5	4,340.4
Department of Labor	29.1	0.0	28.9	29.1
Department of State	3,641.8	0.0	4,344.7	4,503.4
Department of the Treasury	121.8	0.0	122.3	168.3
Social Security Administration	231.1	0.0	256.4	274.2
Department of Education	35.8	0.0	51.5	59.4
Department of Energy	1,930.9	0.0	2,047.5	2,157.0
Environmental Protection Agency	90.7	0.0	90.7	89.5
Department of Transportation	307.6	0.0	342.5	356.4
General Services Administration	370.5	0.0	320.8	371.5
Department of Homeland Security	36,634.5	92.2	37,601.0	36,837.5
Department of Housing and Urban Development	1.1	0.0	1.3	1.3
National Aeronautics and Space Administration	230.8	0.0	251.1	226.2
Department of Veterans Affairs	367.8	0.0	334.8	534.5
Executive Office of the President	9.1	0.0	9.5	13.2
Corps of Engineers—Civil Works	11.3	0.0	11.0	12.0
District of Columbia	13.0	0.0	13.0	15.0
Federal Communications Commission	2.0	0.0	2.0	2.0
National Archives and Records Administration	26.3	0.0	25.2	25.1
National Science Foundation	431.3	0.0	438.9	457.1
Nuclear Regulatory Commission	60.5	0.0	64.3	65.1
Securities and Exchange Commission	7.0	0.0	9.0	9.0
Smithsonian Institution	101.9	0.0	107.1	120.5
United States Holocaust Memorial Museum	11.0	0.0	12.0	12.0
Total, Homeland Security Budget Authority	**71,759.8**	**1,088.1**	**71,679.3**	**70,468.3**
Less Department of Defense	−12,363.0	−181.8	−13,708.3	−13,541.9
Non-Defense Homeland Security BA	**59,396.8**	**906.3**	**57,971.1**	**56,926.5**
Less Discretionary Fee-Funded Homeland Security Programs	−7,764.5	−9.8	−8,605.2	−5,209.1
Less Mandatory Homeland Security Programs	−8,087.4	0.0	−4,152.8	−1,325.2
Net Non-Defense Discretionary Homeland Security BA	**43,544.9**	**896.5**	**45,213.1**	**50,392.1**

* Funding decreases in the Department of Commerce from FY 2015 to FY 2017 reflect the non-recurrence of authority to build a nationwide interoperable public safety broadband network for first responders and related programs.

** DOD homeland security funding for all years prior to 2017 reflects a revised calculation methodology (see Data Collection Methodology and Adjustments, Including the Department of Defense).

support of homeland security activities.[4] The report surveyed 43 jurisdictions that are eligible for DHS' Urban Areas Security Initiative (UASI) grant funds due to the risk of a terrorist attack.[5] These jurisdictions are home to approximately 145 million people or 47 percent of the total United States population. According to the report, the 2007 homeland security budgets for the jurisdictions examined (which include 26 States and the District of Columbia, 50 primary cities, and 35 primary counties) totaled $37 billion, while the same entities received slightly more than $2 billion in Federal homeland security grants.[6] The report further states that from 2000 - 2007, these States and localities spent $220 billion on homeland security activities, which includes increases of three to six percent a year for law enforcement and fire services budgets, and received over $10 billion in Federal grants. California, the most populous State, is also the largest recipient of Federal homeland security funds, having received almost $1.5 billion between 2000 and 2007,

while spending over $45 billion in State and local funding. Over the same time period, the top ten most populous States (including California) spent $148 billion on State and local homeland security related activities.

There is also a diversity of responses in the businesses community. A 2003 survey of 199 corporate security directors conducted by the Conference Board showed that just over half of the companies reported that they had permanently increased security spending post-September 11, 2001.[7] About 15 percent of the companies surveyed had increased their security spending by 20 percent or more.[8] Large increases in spending were especially evident in critical industries, such as transportation, energy, financial services, media and telecommunications, information technology, and healthcare. However, about one-third of the surveyed companies reported that they had not increased their security spending after September 11th.[9] Given the difficulty of obtaining survey results that are representative of the universe of States, localities, and businesses, it is likely that there will be a wide range of estimates of non-Federal security spending for critical infrastructure protection.

---

[4] Source: Matt A. Mayer, "An Analysis of Federal, State, and Local Homeland Security Budgets," A Report of the Heritage Center for Data Analysis, CDA09–01, March 9, 2009, at http://www.heritage.org/Research/HomelandSecurity/upload/ CDA_09_01.pdf. Figures cited in this report have not been independently verified by the Office of Management and Budget.

[5] The Heritage Foundation report's methodology in selecting the states, cities, and counties to include in the report is as follows: the state had to possess a designated UASI jurisdiction and the city and county had to belong to a designated UASI jurisdiction that had received at least $15 million from 2003 to 2007 from the DHS.

[6] The Heritage Foundation report's budget data for homeland security included primary law enforcement agencies, fire departments, homeland security offices, and emergency management agencies. In some cases, state and local emergency management agency budget data was embedded in the fire department budget data and was not separately noted in its own category.

[7] Source: Thomas E. Cavanagh and Meredith Whiting, "2003 Corporate Security Management: Organization and Spending Since 9/11," The Conference Board. R–1333–03-RR. July 2003. This report references sample size of 199 corporate security directors, of which 96 were in "critical industries", while the remaining 103 were in "non-critical industries." In the report, the Conference Board states that it followed the DHS usage of critical industries, "defined as the following: transportation; energy and utilities; financial services; media and telecommunications; information technology; and healthcare."

[8] The Conference Board survey cites the sample size for this statistic was 192 corporate security directors.

[9] The Conference Board survey cites the sample size for this statistic was 199 corporate security directors.

Table 22–2. PREVENT AND DISRUPT TERRORIST ATTACKS

(Budget Authority in millions of dollars)

	FY2015 Actual	FY2015 Supplemental	FY2016 Enacted	FY2017 Request
Department of Agriculture	199.7	0.0	246.2	267.6
Department of Commerce	4.1	1.8	4.6	4.7
Department of the Interior	.5	0.0	.5	.5
Department of Justice	3,553.1	0.0	3,597.7	3,770.2
Department of State	3,520.1	0.0	4,219.0	4,385.2
Department of the Treasury	60.7	0.0	60.9	62.1
Department of Energy	0.0	0.0	11.7	10.5
Department of Transportation	87.9	0.0	116.5	85.1
General Services Administration	315.0	0.0	191.0	248.0
Department of Homeland Security	27,646.6	4.3	28,191.7	27,756.1
Total, Prevent and Disrupt Terrorist Attacks	**35,387.6**	**6.1**	**36,639.7**	**36,590.0**

Additional Tables

The tables in the Federal expenditures section of this chapter present data based on the President's policy for the 2017 Budget. The tables below present additional policy and baseline data, as directed by the Homeland Security Act of 2002. The final table of the chapter shows homeland security funding for DOD as corrected for the 2002-2015 period.

An appendix of account-level funding estimates is available on the Analytical Perspectives CD-ROM.

Table 22-3. PROTECT THE AMERICAN PEOPLE, OUR CRITICAL INFRASTRUCTURE, AND KEY RESOURCES
(Budget Authority in milions of dollars)

	FY2015 Actual	FY2015 Supplemental	FY2016 Enacted	FY2017 Request
Department of Agriculture	189.3	0.0	261.9	218.1
Department of Commerce	266.2	8.0	287.0	301.6
Department of Defense—Military Programs*	11,429.3	181.8	12,741.5	12,463.7
Department of Health and Human Services	2,867.3	395.0	3,283.3	3,127.8
Department of the Interior	48.7	0.0	52.5	52.1
Department of Justice	511.1	0.0	529.4	543.9
Department of Labor	11.8	0.0	11.5	11.6
Department of State	109.5	0.0	101.5	101.5
Department of the Treasury	26.7	0.0	26.9	71.6
Social Security Administration	228.4	0.0	252.9	270.7
Department of Education	34.8	0.0	50.3	58.0
Department of Energy	1,711.4	0.0	1,807.2	1,880.6
Environmental Protection Agency	44.9	0.0	44.4	47.2
Department of Transportation	147.2	0.0	152.9	196.8
General Services Administration	51.5	0.0	125.6	119.2
Department of Homeland Security	6,533.4	87.9	6,923.0	6,870.7
National Aeronautics and Space Administration	230.8	0.0	251.1	226.2
Department of Veterans Affairs	284.9	0.0	250.5	449.9
Executive Office of the President	7.4	0.0	7.7	10.7
Corps of Engineers—Civil Works	11.3	0.0	11.0	12.0
National Archives and Records Administration	25.0	0.0	24.0	23.8
National Science Foundation	431.3	0.0	438.9	457.1
Nuclear Regulatory Commission	60.5	0.0	64.3	65.1
Securities and Exchange Commission	2.0	0.0	3.0	3.0
Smithsonian Institution	101.9	0.0	107.1	120.5
United States Holocaust Memorial Museum	11.0	0.0	12.0	12.0
Total, Protect the American People, Our Critical Infrastructure, and Key Resources	**25,377.4**	**672.7**	**27,821.4**	**27,715.4**

* DOD homeland security funding for all years prior to 2017 reflects a revised calculation methodology (see Data Collection Methodology and Adjustments, Including the Department of Defense).

Table 22–4.   RESPOND AND RECOVER FROM INCIDENTS

(Budget Authority in milions of dollars)

	FY2015 Actual	FY2015 Supplemental	FY2016 Enacted	FY2017 Request
Department of Agriculture	63.3	0.0	69.4	58.9
Department of Commerce	5,119.1	0.0	1,082.3	273.5
Department of Defense—Military Programs*	933.7	0.0	966.7	1,078.2
Department of Health and Human Services	1,885.9	409.3	2,044.5	1,936.8
Department of the Interior	5.0	0.0	5.1	5.3
Department of Justice	16.6	0.0	21.4	26.3
Department of Labor	17.3	0.0	17.4	17.5
Department of State	12.3	0.0	24.2	16.7
Department of the Treasury	34.4	0.0	34.5	34.6
Social Security Administration	2.8	0.0	3.4	3.4
Department of Education	1.0	0.0	1.2	1.4
Department of Energy	219.4	0.0	228.6	265.9
Environmental Protection Agency	45.8	0.0	46.3	42.3
Department of Transportation	72.6	0.0	73.1	74.5
General Services Administration	4.0	0.0	4.1	4.4
Department of Homeland Security	2,454.5	0.0	2,486.3	2,210.7
Department of Housing and Urban Development	1.1	0.0	1.3	1.3
Department of Veterans Affairs	83.0	0.0	84.3	84.6
Executive Office of the President	1.7	0.0	1.8	2.5
District of Columbia	13.0	0.0	13.0	15.0
Federal Communications Commission	2.0	0.0	2.0	2.0
National Archives and Records Administration	1.2	0.0	1.2	1.2
Securities and Exchange Commission	5.0	0.0	6.0	6.0
Total, Respond and Recover from Incidents	**10,994.8**	**409.3**	**7,218.2**	**6,162.9**

* DOD homeland security funding for all years prior to 2017 reflects a revised calculation methodology (see Data Collection Methodology and Adjustments, Including the Department of Defense).

Table 22–5. DISCRETIONARY FEE-FUNDED HOMELAND SECURITY ACTIVITIES BY AGENCY
(Budget Authority in milions of dollars)

	FY2015 Actual	FY2015 Supplemental	FY2016 Enacted	FY2017 Request
Department of Commerce	28.0	9.8	34.4	44.9
Department of Defense—Military Programs*	230.1	0.0	227.0	227.2
Department of Health and Human Services	12.5	0.0	12.5	12.6
Department of Labor	16.2	0.0	16.2	16.2
Department of State**	3,426.8	0.0	4,125.8	1.6
Social Security Administration	231.1	0.0	256.4	274.2
Department of Energy	0.0	0.0	0.0	0.0
General Services Administration	367.8	0.0	318.0	368.8
Department of Homeland Security	3,673.1	0.0	3,831.0	4,479.9
Federal Communications Commission	2.0	0.0	2.0	2.0
Securities and Exchange Commission	7.0	0.0	9.0	9.0
Total, Discretionary Fee-Funded Homeland Security Activities	**7,994.5**	**9.8**	**8,832.3**	**5,436.3**

* DOD homeland security funding for all years prior to 2017 reflects a revised calculation methodology (see Data Collection Methodology and Adjustments, Including the Department of Defense).

** Department of State, Border Security Program, fees previously recorded as offsetting collections in the Diplomatic and Consular Program (D&CP) are reflected in a special fund for Consular and Border Security Programs (CBSP). Given the format of the new account structure, these fees are recorded as budgetary authority rather than offsetting collections, but the program will continue to be fully funded by fee revenue in FY 2017.

Table 22–6. MANDATORY HOMELAND SECURITY ACTIVITIES BY AGENCY
(Budget Authority in milions of dollars)

	FY2015 Actual	FY2016 Enacted	FY2017 Request
Department of Agriculture	166.5	211.4	230.9
Department of Commerce	5,003.0	967.0	168.0
Department of Defense—Military Programs*	273.0	275.5	277.9
Department of Health and Human Services	.2	.2	.4
Department of Labor	2.2	2.3	2.4
Department of Energy	13.0	11.0	11.0
General Services Administration	2.8	2.8	2.8
Department of Homeland Security	2,899.7	2,958.1	909.7
Total, Mandatory Homeland Security Activities	**8,360.4**	**4,428.3**	**1,603.1**

* DOD homeland security funding for all years prior to 2017 reflects a revised calculation methodology (see Data Collection Methodology and Adjustments, Including the Department of Defense).

Table 22–7. BASELINE ESTIMATES—TOTAL HOMELAND SECURITY FUNDING BY AGENCY
(Budget Authority in millions of dollars)

	FY2016	FY2017	FY2018	FY2019	FY2020	FY2021
Department of Agriculture	577	599	654	666	679	694
Department of Commerce	1,374	445	423	431	440	450
Department of Defense—Military Programs	13,708	14,048	14,280	14,643	14,998	15,364
Department of Health and Human Services	5,328	5,437	5,545	5,671	5,798	5,919
Department of the Interior	58	60	61	63	65	66
Department of Justice	4,148	4,271	4,387	4,516	4,650	4,778
Department of Labor	29	30	30	31	32	33
Department of State	4,345	2,545	2,595	2,625	2,678	2,734
Department of the Treasury	122	127	129	134	137	142
Social Security Administration	256	275	280	286	291	297
Department of Education	52	53	54	56	58	60
Department of Energy	2,047	2,092	2,129	2,168	2,220	2,264
Environmental Protection Agency	91	93	95	98	100	103
Department of Transportation	343	228	233	241	248	255
General Services Administration	321	321	327	333	340	347
Department of Homeland Security	37,601	37,712	38,595	39,630	40,686	41,810
Department of Housing and Urban Development	1	1	1	1	2	2
National Aeronautics and Space Administration	251	258	265	272	280	287
Department of Veterans Affairs	335	341	347	354	367	374
Executive Office of the President	9	9	10	10	10	11
Corps of Engineers—Civil Works	11	11	11	12	12	12
District of Columbia	13	13	13	14	14	14
Federal Communications Commission	2	2	2	2	2	2
National Archives and Records Administration	25	26	27	27	28	29
National Science Foundation	439	447	455	464	473	483
Nuclear Regulatory Commission	64	66	68	70	72	74
Securities and Exchange Commission	9	9	9	10	10	10
Smithsonian Institution	107	110	113	117	120	124
United States Holocaust Memorial Museum	12	12	13	13	13	14
Total, Homeland Security Budget Authority	**71,679**	**69,642**	**71,153**	**72,957**	**74,822**	**76,751**
Less Department of Defense	−13,708	−14,048	−14,280	−14,643	−14,998	−15,364
Non-Defense Homeland Security	**57,971**	**55,593**	**56,873**	**58,314**	**59,824**	**61,388**
Less Discretionary Fee-Funded Homeland Security Programs	−8,605	−6,767	−6,910	−6,999	−7,115	−7,253
Less Mandatory Homeland Security Programs	−4,153	−3,160	−3,159	−3,248	−3,341	−3,434
Net Non-Defense Discretionary Homeland Security BA	**45,213**	**45,666**	**46,804**	**48,067**	**49,368**	**50,700**

* DOD homeland security funding for all years prior to 2017 reflects a revised calculation methodology (see Data Collection Methodology and Adjustments, Including the Department of Defense).

Table 22–8. TOTAL HOMELAND SECURITY FUNDING BY FUNCTION
(Budget Authority in millions of dollars)

	FY2015 Actual	FY2016 Enacted	FY2017 Request
Administration of Justice	22,530	22,893	23,465
Agriculture	443	567	534
Commerce and Housing Credit	5,177	1,155	366
Community and Regional Development	2,867	2,883	3,280
Education, Training, Employment, and Social Services	174	195	217
Energy	150	167	169
General Government	1,947	2,007	2,017
General Science, Space, and Technology	755	793	786
Health	5,541	5,312	5,049
Income Security	4	4	4
International Affairs	3,641	4,345	4,503
Medicare	27	27	27
National Defense	17,475	18,878	17,956
Natural Resources and Environment	313	308	293
Social Security	231	256	274
Transportation	11,204	11,553	10,993
Veterans Benefits and Services	368	335	535
Total, Homeland Security Budget Authority	**72,848**	**71,679**	**70,468**
Less Department of Defense	−12,545	−13,708	−13,542
Non-Defense Homeland Security BA	**60,303**	**57,971**	**56,926**
Less Discretionary Fee-Funded Homeland Security Programs	−7,774	−8,605	−5,209
Less Mandatory Homeland Security Programs	−8,087	−4,153	−1,325
Net Non-Defense Discretionary Homeland Security BA	**44,441**	**45,213**	**50,392**

Table 22–9. BASELINE ESTIMATES—TOTAL HOMELAND SECURITY FUNDING BY FUNCTION

(Budget Authority in millions of dollars)

	FY2016	FY2017	FY2018	FY2019	FY2020	FY2021
Administration of Justice	22,893	23,008	23,562	24,229	24,929	25,651
Agriculture	567	588	643	655	667	682
Commerce and Housing Credit	1,155	223	197	202	207	213
Community and Regional Development	2,883	2,896	2,948	3,023	3,076	3,151
Education, Training, Employment, and Social Services	195	200	206	212	218	225
Energy	167	173	177	180	185	191
General Government	2,007	2,026	2,080	2,109	2,134	2,178
General Science, Space, and Technology	793	810	827	845	864	884
Health	5,312	5,421	5,529	5,654	5,781	5,902
Income Security	4	4	5	5	5	5
International Affairs	4,345	2,545	2,595	2,625	2,678	2,734
Medicare	27	28	28	29	30	30
National Defense	18,878	19,340	19,691	20,181	20,679	21,175
Natural Resources and Environment	308	316	323	331	340	348
Social Security	256	275	280	286	291	297
Transportation	11,553	11,447	11,713	12,036	12,369	12,709
Veterans Benefits and Services	335	341	347	354	367	374
Total, Homeland Security Budget Authority	**71,679**	**69,642**	**71,153**	**72,957**	**74,822**	**76,751**
Less Department of Defense	−13,708	−14,048	−14,280	−14,643	−14,998	−15,364
Non-Defense Homeland Security	**57,971**	**55,593**	**56,873**	**58,314**	**59,824**	**61,388**
Less Discretionary Fee-Funded Homeland Security Programs	−8,605	−6,767	−6,910	−6,999	−7,115	−7,253
Less Mandatory Homeland Security Programs	−4,153	−3,160	−3,159	−3,248	−3,341	−3,434
Net Non-Defense Discretionary Homeland Security BA	**45,213**	**45,666**	**46,804**	**48,067**	**49,368**	**50,700**

Table 22–10. DEPARTMENT OF DEFENSE HOMELAND SECURITY REPORTING ADJUSTMENTS
(Budget Authority in millions of dollars)

President's Budget	PB 2004			PB 2005			PB 2006			PB 2007			PB 2008			PB 2009			PB 2010		
	2002 Actual	2003 Enacted	2004 Request	2003 Actual	2004 Enacted	2005 Request	2004 Actual	2005 Enacted	2006 Request	2005 Actual	2006 Enacted	2007 Request	2006 Actual	2007 Enacted	2008 Request	2007 Actual	2008 Enacted	2009 Request	2008 Actual	2009 Enacted	2010 Request
Previous Estimate ..	13,394	12,953	13,918	12,953	13,918	16,108	13,918	16,108	16,440	16,108	16,440	16,698	16,479	16,538	17,559	16,538	17,374	17,646	17,374	19,413	19,303
Special Operations Command	....	....	....	....	....	....	....	....	....	....	....	....	....	....	....	....	....	....	....	....	....
Guard Reserve Personnel Composition ..	....	....	....	....	....	....	....	....	....	....	....	....	....	....	....	....	....	....	....	....	....
USMC Counter Improvised Explosive Devices	....	....	....	....	....	....	....	....	....	....	....	....	....	....	....	....	....	....	....	....	....
Other Adjustments ..	–1,952	–2,000	–2,233	–1,864	–2,233	–3,320	–2,224	–3,320	–3,948	–3,613	–3,948	–3,982	–3,802	–3,894	–4,455	–3,987	–5,069	–4,261	–4,455	–4,647	–4,519
Adjusted Estimate ..	11,442	10,953	11,685	11,089	11,685	12,788	11,694	12,788	12,492	12,495	12,492	12,716	12,677	12,644	13,104	12,552	12,305	13,385	12,920	14,766	14,784

President's Budget	PB 2011			PB 2012			PB 2013			PB 2014			PB 2015		
	2009 Actual	2010 Enacted	2011 Request	2010 Actual	2011 Enacted	2012 Request	2011 Actual	2012 Enacted	2013 Request	2012 Actual	2013 Enacted	2014 Request	2013 Actual	2014 Enacted	2015 Request
Previous Estimate	19,414	19,041	19,103	19,054	17,626	18,102	16,994	17,358	17,955	17,780	17,481	17,360	16,527	16,365	15,762
Special Operations Command ...	–672	–614	–606	–1,455	–1,502	–1,485	–2,039	–1,917	–2,290	–1,531	–1,447	–1,518	–1,237	–1,234	–1,304
Guard Reserve Personnel Composition	....	....	....	405	–2,314	–2,164	–2,188	–2,143	–2,193	–2,134	–2,154	–2,174	–2,189	–2,194	–2,083
USMC Counter Improvised Explosive Devices	....	....	....	115	–8	–4	–9	–6	–82	–12	–66	–3	–403	–246	–188
Other Adjustments	–7,006	–5,796	–6,046	–4,898	....	514	....	....	....	....	....	....	....	....	....
Adjusted Estimate	11,735	12,631	12,450	13,221	13,802	14,963	12,758	13,292	13,390	14,103	13,814	13,665	12,697	12,691	12,187

23. FEDERAL DRUG CONTROL FUNDING

In support of the 2016 National Drug Control Strategy (Strategy), the President requests $31.071 billion in Fiscal Year 2017 to reduce drug use and its consequences in the United States. The Strategy represents a 21st century approach to drug policy that outlines innovative policies and programs and recognizes that substance use disorders are not just a criminal justice issue, but also a major public health concern. Decades of research demonstrate that addiction is a disease of the brain - one that can be prevented, treated, and from which people can recover. The Strategy lays out an evidence-based plan for real drug policy reform, spanning the spectrum of prevention, early intervention, treatment, recovery support, criminal justice reform, effective law enforcement, and international cooperation.

Table 23–1. DRUG CONTROL FUNDING FY 2015–FY 2017

(Budget authority, in millions of dollars)

Department/Agency	FY 2015 Actual	FY 2016 Enacted	FY 2017 President's Budget
Department of Agriculture:			
U.S. Forest Service	12.400	12.300	17.900
Court Services and Offender Supervision Agency for D.C.:	52.602	58.146	58.710
Department of Defense:			
Drug Interdiction and Counterdrug Activities (incl. OPTEMPO and OCO)	1,409.348	1,343.316	1,221.979
Defense Health Program	73.500	75.500	75.500
Total DOD	1,482.848	1,418.816	1,297.479
Department of Education:			
Office of Elementary and Secondary Education	50.249	50.084	50.087
Federal Judiciary:	1,158.887	1,210.620	1,246.704
Department of Health and Human Services:			
Administration for Children and Families	18.560	18.540	60.000
Centers for Disease Control and Prevention	20.000	75.580	85.580
Centers for Medicare and Medicaid Services 2	8,230.000	8,760.000	9,140.000
Health Resources and Services Administration	27.800	129.000	164.000
Indian Health Service	111.345	114.670	140.930
National Institute on Alcohol Abuse and Alcoholism	59.534	54.225	54.225
National Institute on Drug Abuse	1,015.695	1,050.550	1,050.550
Substance Abuse and Mental Health Services Administration 3	2,460.395	2,512.173	2,986.039
Total HHS	11,943.329	12,714.738	13,681.324
Department of Homeland Security4:			
Customs and Border Protection	2,422.994	2,664.943	2,655.711
Federal Emergency Management Agency	8.250	8.250	6.187
Federal Law Enforcement Training Center	46.757	44.100	43.587
Immigration and Customs Enforcement	467.853	485.771	527.037
U.S. Coast Guard	1,265.675	1,616.059	1,269.033
Total DHS	4,211.529	4,819.123	4,501.555
Department of Housing and Urban Development:			
Office of Community Planning and Development	463.490	486.936	589.112
Department of the Interior:			
Bureau of Indian Affairs	9.716	9.716	9.716
Bureau of Land Management	5.100	5.100	5.100
National Park Service	3.300	3.300	3.300
Total DOI	18.116	18.116	18.116

Table 23–1. DRUG CONTROL FUNDING FY 2015–FY 2017—Continued
(Budget authority, in millions of dollars)

Department/Agency	FY 2015 Actual	FY 2016 Enacted	FY 2017 President's Budget
Department of Justice:			
Assets Forfeiture Fund	284.139	238.710	243.103
Bureau of Prisons	3,491.004	3,672.401	3,491.841
Criminal Division	40.043	39.019	39.910
Drug Enforcement Administration	2,373.145	2,426.490	2,485.638
Organized Crime Drug Enforcement Task Force	507.194	512.000	522.135
Office of Justice Programs	260.870	280.220	275.570
U.S. Attorneys	76.838	72.644	75.862
U.S. Marshals Service	270.421	278.118	289.923
Federal Prisoner Detention	498.010	510.037	505.463
Total DOJ	**7,801.664**	**8,029.639**	**7,929.445**
Department of Labor:			
Employment and Training Administration	**6.000**	**6.000**	**6.000**
Office of National Drug Control Policy:			
Operations	22.647	20.047	19.274
High Intensity Drug Trafficking Area Program	245.000	250.000	196.410
Other Federal Drug Control Programs	107.150	109.810	98.480
Total ONDCP	**374.797**	**379.857**	**314.164**
Department of State[4]:			
Bureau of International Narcotics and Law Enforcement Affairs	446.061	434.662	382.373
United States Agency for International Development	95.502	136.155	131.920
Total DOS	**541.563**	**570.817**	**514.293**
Department of the Transportation:			
Federal Aviation Administration	30.670	31.470	31.610
National Highway Traffic Safety Administration	2.688	11.488	11.488
Total DOT	**33.358**	**42.958**	**43.098**
Department of the Treasury:			
Internal Revenue Service	**60.257**	**60.257**	**95.821**
Department of Veterans Affairs:			
Veterans Health Administration [5]	**671.810**	**682.430**	**707.602**
Total Federal Drug Budget	**28,882.899**	**30,560.837**	**31,071.410**

[1] Detail may not add due to rounding.

[2] The estimates for the Centers for Medicare & Medicaid Services reflect Medicaid and Medicare benefit outlays for substance abuse treatment; they do not reflect budget authority. The estimates were developed by the CMS Office of the Actuary.

[3] Includes budget authority and funding through evaluation set-aside authorized by Section 241 of the Public Health Service (PHS) Act.

[4] The FY 2015 funding level represents the FY 2016 President's Budget request.

[5] VA Medical Care receives advance appropriations; FY 2017 funding was provided in the Consolidated Appropriations Act 2016.

24. FEDERAL BUDGET EXPOSURE TO CLIMATE RISK

No challenge poses a greater threat to future generations than climate change. This past year was the planet's warmest on record. The 15 warmest years on record have all fallen in the first 16 years of this century. Across the American landscape, the impact of climate change is undeniable. Along our Eastern seaboard, a number of cities now flood regularly at high tide. The vast majority of the largest wildfires in modern U.S. history have occurred since 2000. In parts of the Midwest, higher temperatures will increase irrigation demand and exacerbate current stresses on agricultural productivity. And in the Mississippi and Missouri River Basins, numerous studies indicate increasing severity and frequency of flooding, leading to potential disruptions to the Nation's inland water system, as seen most recently in the devastating and widespread flooding in the interior of the United States. The imprint of climate change on the Federal budget is increasingly apparent—in the escalating costs of disaster response and relief, flood and crop insurance, wildland fire management, Federal facility management, and a host of other Federal programs that are vulnerable to the impacts of climate change. For this reason, understanding the Federal Government's exposure to climate change risks is increasingly critical for policymakers charged with making sound investment decisions and stewarding the Federal budget over the long term.

The Third National Climate Assessment (NCA) concludes that climate change is already affecting every region of the country and key sectors of the U.S. economy. The report was developed over four years by a team of more than 300 of the Nation's top climate scientists and technical experts, guided by a 60-member Federal Advisory Committee, and extensively reviewed by the public and experts including the National Academy of Sciences. Key findings of the NCA include the following:[1]

- Heavy downpours are increasing nationally, and this trend in extreme precipitation is projected to continue for all U.S. regions.

- Floods and droughts are increasing in some regions. Drought in the Southwest is projected to increase. Heat waves have become more frequent and intense, and this trend is projected to continue as average temperatures rise.

- The intensity, frequency, and duration of North Atlantic hurricanes and the number of strongest storms (Category 4 and 5) all increased in the last few decades. Hurricane intensity and rainfall are projected to increase with further climate change.

- Winter storms have increased in frequency and intensity since mid-20th Century, and their tracks have shifted northward.

- Global sea level has risen by about 8 inches since reliable record keeping began and is projected to rise another 1 to 4 feet by 2100.

- Oceans are becoming more acidic as they absorb a quarter of the carbon dioxide emitted annually, forming carbonic acid and thereby putting marine ecosystems at risk.

The Federal Government has broad exposure to escalating costs and lost revenue as a direct or indirect result of a changing climate. For example, the Federal Government plays a critical role in helping American families, businesses, and communities recover from the impacts of catastrophic events. As economic damages from such events grow, so does the liability for the Federal budget. At the same time, the Federal Government is directly at risk from extreme weather impacts to Federal facilities nationwide and the growing incidence of fire on Federal lands.

While existing climate change-related expenditures can be identified for a number of Federal programs, it is inherently difficult to isolate climate change-related expenditures for many other programs across the Federal Government. Even in these cases, however, the directional impact on the Budget of expected climatic changes is clear.

Identifiable Costs

Over the last decade, the Federal Government has incurred over $357 billion in direct costs[2] due to extreme weather and fire alone, including for domestic disaster response and relief ($205 billion), flood insurance ($23 billion), crop insurance ($67 billion), wildland fire management ($34 billion), and maintenance and repairs to Federal facilities and Federally managed lands, infrastructure, and waterways ($28 billion). Additional costs have been incurred for international disaster response and relief in the wake of extreme events like droughts, floods, and storms. While it is not possible to identify the portion of these costs incurred as a result of human-

---

[1] Melillo, Jerry M., Terese (T.C.) Richmond, and Gary W. Yohe, Eds., 2014. Climate Change Impacts in the United States: The Third National Climate Assessment. U.S. Global Research Program, 841 pp. doi:10.7930/J0Z31WJ2.

[2] This figure is revised from the estimate in the FY 2016 President's Budget. The difference is largely attributable to improved estimation, rather than increased costs in 2015. This estimate does not include some categories of spending, such as international disaster response and relief, military spending, direct healthcare costs, as well as some Federal property and resource management costs. As a result, this estimate potentially significantly understates actual direct Federal costs due to extreme weather and fire.

Chart 24-1. National Flood Insurance Program
Paid Losses & Total Exposure

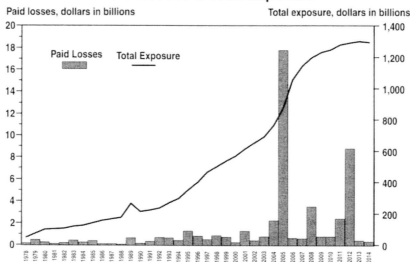

Paid losses, dollars in billions

Total exposure, dollars in billions

induced climate change, costs for each of these Federal programs have been increasing, are inherently sensitive to the effects of climate change, and can therefore be expected to continue to rise as the impacts of climate change intensify.

Domestic Disaster Response and Relief

The Federal Emergency Management Agency (FEMA) has incurred roughly $90 billion in costs for domestic, extreme weather-related disaster response and relief over the last decade. Over that time period, other Federal agencies received appropriations of roughly $99 billion for domestic disaster relief efforts, largely related to the 2005 Gulf Coast hurricanes and Superstorm Sandy. An additional $16 billion in tax expenditures were incurred between 2006 and 2015 for tax relief associated with the 2005 Gulf Coast hurricanes, according to the Congressional Budget Office (CBO) and the Joint Committee on Taxation.[3]

Climate models predict that climate-driven changes, such as higher sea levels and stronger hurricanes, as well as increases in extreme precipitation, are likely to magnify damages due to extreme weather and associated needs for disaster response and relief.[4] For example, the National Climate Assessment found that the amount of rain falling in very heavy precipitation events since 1991 has increased in the Northeast, Midwest, and upper Great Plains by more than 30 percent above the 1901-1906 average. This has caused an increase in costly flooding events in the Northeast and Midwest in particular, such as the most recent flooding in the Mississippi River Basin. This trend towards increased heavy precipitation events is expected to continue, threatening levees and other infrastructure and the communities that depend on them. In the coastal environment, a review by the Government Accountability Office of 20 scientific studies found a predicted increase of 14-47 percent in inflation-adjusted U.S. hurricane losses by 2040, attributable to changes in the severity of storms. By 2100, losses are projected to grow by 54 to 110 percent. Accounting for the combination of projected sea-level rise and changes in hurricane activity, hurricane losses could more than quadruple by the year 2100.[5]

Historically, the cost of Federal action following a major disaster has averaged roughly a third of total economic losses.[6] If this share of total losses continues, Federal disaster response and relief costs can be expected to rise proportionally with projected increases in total economic losses. However, this type of linear extrapolation may underestimate the true exposure of the Federal budget given that a major event or series of major events could, for example, affect the solvency of an industry, municipality, or State.

Flood Insurance

In addition to its disaster response activities, FEMA manages the National Flood Insurance Program (NFIP), established in 1968. NFIP is designed to provide an insurance alternative to disaster assistance to meet the escalating costs of flood damage. While the program is designed to offset paid losses with premium collections, catastrophic events in any given year can have outsized impacts on NFIP. Due largely to Hurricane Katrina in

---

[3] Congressional Budget Office, 2007. The Federal Government's Spending and Tax Actions in Response to the 2005 Gulf Coast Hurricanes. Prepared for the House Budget Committee.

[4] Kopp, Robert, and Solomon Hsiang, 2014: American Climate Prospectus. Economic Risks in the United States. Rhodium Group, LLC.

[5] U.S. Government Accountability Office, 2014. Climate Change: Better Management of Exposure to Potential Future Losses Is Needed for Federal Flood and Crop Insurance. GAO 15-28: Published October 29, 2014.

[6] Cummins, J. David, Michael Suher, and George Zanjani. 2010. Federal Financial Exposure to Natural Catastrophe Risk in Lucas, D. (ed.) Measuring and Managing Federal Financial Risk. National Bureau of Economic Research. University of Chicago Press.

2005 and Superstorm Sandy in 2012, the program incurred substantial paid losses in excess of premiums collected, incurring approximately $23 billion in debt to the U.S. Treasury as of June 2015. The figure above details the program's historical paid losses and total exposure—the total value of property insured by the program. NFIP's total exposure has quadrupled over the last two decades to $1.3 trillion due to an increase in the number of insured properties, as well as the value of those properties.

Nationwide, the Special Flood Hazard Area—the land area subject to a one percent or greater chance of flooding in any given year—is projected to increase by 40-45 percent by 2100 (with large regional variations), driven predominantly by the effects of climate change, according to a FEMA study.[7] In the coastal environment, this projected increase is a result of rising sea levels and increasing storm intensity and frequency. In the riverine environment, less than one-third of the increase in typical areas is attributable to population growth and associated impacts on stormwater runoff, while more than two-thirds is attributable to the influence of climate change. As a result of the projected increase in the flood hazard area, the average loss cost per policy[8] in today's dollars is estimated to increase approximately 50-90 percent by 2100, with a 10-15 percent increase as soon as 2020. These increases will be compounded by projected growth in the total number of policyholders participating in NFIP—approximately 80-100 percent through 2100 as a product of population growth and also the expansion of the flood hazard area. These projected increases in loss cost per policy are median estimates; catastrophic events in any

given year could have much larger impacts on NFIP and the Federal budget.[9]

The expected implications of climate change for hurricane-related damage is supported by preliminary CBO findings. CBO modeled increases in expected storm damage in 2075 due to coastal development and climate change. Both factors were found to exacerbate storm damage. However, while the damage due solely to coastal development was found to grow more slowly than gross domestic product (GDP), the damage due to the combined effect of coastal development and climate change was found to grow more rapidly than GDP.[10]

Crop Insurance

The United States Department of Agriculture's Risk Management Agency (RMA) provides crop insurance to American farmers and ranchers through the Federal Crop Insurance Corporation (FCIC). Federal crop insurance policies cover loss of crop yields from natural causes including drought, excessive moisture, freeze, disease, and hail. The Federal Government incurs costs for crop insurance in the form of subsidized premiums, losses associated with any claims paid in excess of collected premiums, and costs for program administration and operation—a total of $67 billion between 2005 and 2014. Costs can increase sharply in years affected by extreme weather. For example, droughts caused the surge in costs in 2011 and 2012 shown above. The Federal Government's total exposure for crop insurance is currently about $120 billion, up from $67 billion in 2007.

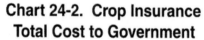

Chart 24-2. Crop Insurance Total Cost to Government

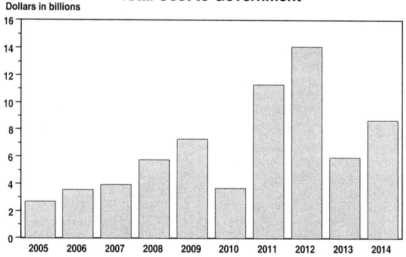

[7] AECOM, 2013. The Impact of Climate Change and Population Growth on the National Flood Insurance Program through 2100. Prepared for Federal Emergency Management Agency.

[8] Loss cost is a measure of expected loss payments per $100 of insured building value.

[9] AECOM, 2013. The Impact of Climate Change and Population Growth on the National Flood Insurance Program through 2100. Prepared for Federal Emergency Management Agency.

[10] Dinan, Terry, 2015. Hurricane Damage: Effects of Climate Change and Coastal Development. Congressional Budget Office.

Wildland Fire Management

The U.S. Forest Service (USFS) and Department of the Interior (DOI) manage wildland fire to protect human life and property. Climate change is contributing to an increase in wildland fire frequency and intensity across the western United States and Alaska.[11] The majority of the largest fires in modern U.S. history have occurred in just the last two decades. On average, firefighting appropriations grew 25 percent per year over that period, adjusted for inflation. At the USFS, appropriations for wildland fire management grew from 16 percent of the agency's total budget in 1995 to 52 percent in 2015. These budget increases are due to a number of factors, including population growth in the wildland-urban interface, a legacy of aggressive fire suppression, and climatic factors. For example, in the Southwest, increased warming, drought, and insect outbreaks, all caused by or linked to climate change, are creating chronic forest stress and increased tree mortality rates, increasing the risk for wildfire and its impacts to people and ecosystems. Fire models project more wildfire and increased risks to communities across extensive areas.[12] Increasing temperatures may contribute to increased fire frequency, intensity, and size in parts of the Southeastern United States, and notably Florida, as well.[13]

Federal Property and Resource Management

Federal facilities are directly at risk from the extreme weather events that are being influenced by climate change. At this time, there is no government-wide total cost estimate for these impacts because Federal agencies do not separately track facility-related expenditures that are incurred as a consequence of extreme weather events. However, the last decade has provided a long list of examples of costly damage to Federal facilities. Those facilities damaged by major events have often required significant supplemental appropriations to repair those damages—roughly $19 billion throughout the last decade to agencies as diverse as NASA, the Coast Guard, the National Park Service, the Federal Bureau of Prisons, and the National Cemetery Administration. An additional $8 billion was appropriated in the wake of major storms to agencies that manage land, infrastructure, and waterways.

While these costs were associated with large events like the 2005 Gulf Coast hurricanes and Superstorm Sandy, smaller events and ongoing impacts of climate change also have cost and mission implications. For example:

- An Army installation in the Southwest incurred $64 million in damages due to extreme torrential downpours. Within an 80-minute period, the installation experienced as much rain as typically falls over the course of a year. The flooding caused by the storm damaged 160 facilities, 8 roads, 1 bridge, and 11,000 linear feet of fencing.

- At Cape Lisburne Air Station on the Alaskan coastline, home to a vital early-warning radar site, erosion of the stone seawall due to increased coastal flooding is putting the installation's airstrip at risk. The Air Force recently began a $41 million project to protect the runway, the primary avenue for resupplying the installation and its Airmen.

- Record-breaking rainfall and severe flash flooding in 2010 overwhelmed man-made drainage systems at the Department of Energy's Pantex Plant—the Nation's only nuclear weapons assembly and disassembly facility. Since the incident, the facility has invested in improved drainage, response plans, and procedures to better prepare for flash flooding events.

Under Executive Order 13653, Federal agencies must continue to update comprehensive adaptation plans that indicate how the agency will integrate climate resilience into agency actions, such as supply chain management, real property investments, and capital equipment purchases. Such consideration could include updating agency policies for leasing, building upgrades, relocation of existing facilities and equipment, and construction of new facilities. Under Executive Order 13690, which establishes a Federal Flood Risk Management Standard, Federal agencies are directed to integrate current and future flooding considerations into their investments, where relevant. In addition, Executive Order 13693 directs Federal agencies to convene regional interagency workshops to address water resource management and drought response opportunities, and climate change preparedness and resilience planning in coordination with State, local, and tribal communities. Finally, under Executive Order 13677, agencies with international development programs are now systematically factoring climate-resilience considerations into new international development investments, including planning and managing overseas facilities.

Other Direct and Indirect Costs

The Federal Government's climate risk exposure extends well beyond disaster response, flood and crop insurance, wildland fire management, and Federal property management. For example, the Federal Government will likely incur additional direct and indirect costs for health care, national security, and species recovery efforts as a result of climate-driven changes across sectors of the economy. However, it is inherently difficult in these areas to identify current expenditures that are related to climatic factors such as extreme weather and rising temperatures.

Health Care

Climate change threatens the health and well-being of Americans in a number of ways, including increasing impacts from extreme weather events, wildland fire, decreased air quality, and illnesses transmitted by food, water, and disease carriers such as mosquitoes and ticks. While the economic literature on the current and project-

---

[11] Melillo, Jerry M., Terese (T.C.) Richmond, and Gary W. Yohe, Eds., 2014. Climate Change Impacts in the United States: The Third National Climate Assessment. U.S. Global Research Program, 841 pp. doi:10.7930/J0Z31WJ2.

[12] Ibid.

[13] Ibid.

ed health costs associated with climate change is limited, a number of studies have found substantial health costs due to climate-related events.[14] The Federal Government is the Nation's largest purchaser of health care services—spending nearly $900 billion in 2015 on Medicare, Medicaid, and the Children's Health Insurance Program. These programs provide health care for those most vulnerable to the health-related impacts of climate change: children, the elderly, and low-income individuals.

National Security

National security, diplomacy, and development agencies expect that climate change will intensify the challenges of global instability, hunger, poverty, conflict, emerging disease, disputes over water, food, and energy resources, and destruction by natural disasters. The Department of Defense (DOD) refers to climate change as a "threat multiplier" because it can exacerbate many challenges, including population migration and global instability. Climate change will impact the Department's military readiness, personnel training, stationing, environmental compliance and stewardship, and infrastructure protection and maintenance. DOD is conducting vulnerability assessments at major military installations to consider current and projected climate impacts, and to assess and manage risks to man-made and natural infrastructure. The Department will incorporate climate change considerations in its natural resource management, historic preservation, design and construction standards, asset management, encroachment management, utility systems, and emergency management operations. Climate impacts may adversely influence the frequency, scale, and complexity of future operational missions, and may increase the need for defense support to civil authorities. Climate impacts may affect supply chains and critical equipment replenishment needs. These impacts could be a burden on the Federal budget as costs increase for military and humanitarian operations.

DOD has taken several concrete steps to improve its ability to mitigate the risks climate change poses to its mission. DOD issued its Climate Change Adaptation and Resilience Directive in January 2016. The Directive establishes policies and assigns responsibilities to various departmental offices to assess and manage risks associated with climate change. For example, the Directive requires DOD organizations to consider climate change and resiliency when developing installation plans, making basing decisions, and determining acquisition strategies.

DOD also has three pilot projects with local communities to address common, region-specific climate change impacts. One of the DOD pilots is at Mountain Home Air Force Base in Idaho. The Base is working with nearly 50 stakeholders, including city, county, and state governments, as well as tribal, academic, and nonprofit organizations and other Federal agencies to develop a regional Action Plan for climate change and

resilience. The plan, which is expected to be completed in 2016, will include partner roles and responsibilities, establish milestones for actions, as well as specify other opportunities for developing climate risk partnerships.

In the Hampton Roads/Norfolk, VA area, White House offices and Federal partners, led by the Department of Defense, are participating with State, local, and academic officials to support an Intergovernmental pilot project addressing sea level rise in that area. The pilot is a two-year project to develop a regional "whole of government" and "whole of community" approach to sea level rise preparedness and resilience planning in Hampton Roads that also can be used as a template for other regions.

Species Recovery

Climate change is expected to fundamentally alter ecosystems in ways that are costly to those systems and the people who depend upon and value them. For example, a changing climate is expected to cause rapid shifts in habitat and species ranges and to exacerbate the non-climatic stressors (e.g., habitat loss, overutilization, invasive species) that affect plants and animals, leading to potential reductions in biodiversity through the local or global loss of species.

For example, climate change appears to be a key driver causing a mismatch between the life cycle of the Edith's checkerspot butterfly and the timing of the flowering plants it depends on, causing the butterfly's population to crash along its southern range. Similarly, warming and reduced stream flows due to declining snowmelt are affecting salmon species. A small increase in water temperature can cause coho salmon eggs to hatch weeks early, leading to a mismatch between the time the salmon reach the ocean and the abundance of their prey.[15] Researchers estimate that up to 90 percent of species may be displaced from their current range and forced into new areas or to go extinct.[16]

The Intergovernmental Panel on Climate Change (IPCC), in its recent Fifth Assessment Report, found that a large fraction of terrestrial, freshwater and marine species face increased extinction risk due to climate change during and beyond the 21st century, especially as climate change interacts with other stressors.[17] These and other ecosystem impacts are likely to pose significant costs, though it is difficult to monetize the precise value of lost species and ecosystem services. In addition to costs to private citizens and industry, the expected decline in species may increase the costs of Federal species recovery efforts.

---

[14] Kopp, Robert, and Solomon Hsiang, 2014: American Climate Prospectus. Economic Risks in the United States. Rhodium Group, LLC.

[15] National Fish, Wildlife and Plants Climate Adaptation Partnership. 2012. National Fish, Wildlife and Plants Climate Adaptation Strategy, Association of Fish and Wildlife Agencies, Council on Environmental Quality, Great Lakes Indian Fish and Wildlife Commission, National Oceanic and Atmospheric Administration, and U.S. Fish and Wildlife Service. Washington, DC.

[16] Lawler, J. et al., 2009: Projected Climate-Induced Faunal Change in the Western Hemisphere. Ecology, 90(3), 2009, pp. 588–597.

[17] IPCC, 2014: Climate Change 2014: Synthesis Report. Contribution of Working Groups I, II and III to the Fifth Assessment Report of the Intergovernmental Panel on Climate Change [Core Writing Team, R.K. Pachauri and L.A. Meyer (eds.)]. IPCC, Geneva, Switzerland, 67.

Lost Revenue

Unabated climate change is projected to hamper economic production in the United States and across the globe. Economic loss in the United States means lost revenue for the Federal Government. Projections by the IPCC include a warming range of about 3.5 to 5.5 degrees Celsius (6.3 to 9.9 degrees Fahrenheit) over preindustrial levels by 2100 if recent global emissions are allowed to continue along IPCC's high-end scenario.[18] Available economic assessments of warming of four degrees Celsius indicate economic damages of more than four percent of global GDP each year by 2100.[19]

There are a number of factors that may affect the accuracy of this estimate. For example, the estimate does not account for important factors that are inherently difficult to quantify or monetize, such as biodiversity loss, increased ocean acidification, changes in weather related to changes in ocean circulation, catastrophic events, irreversibility of climate change impacts, tipping points leading to non-linear changes to the climate, and heightened political instability as a result of climate impacts. In addition, current models factor in economic damages over time but treat rate of growth exogenously. Yet, there is some evidence that climate losses may also undermine the rate of GDP growth.[20] As a result, this four percent estimate could understate the potential economic impact on global GDP.

The uncertainty of economic loss projections is compounded when attempting to estimate the associated

potential for lost Federal revenue in the United States. For illustrative purposes only, assuming the underlying economic loss projection is accurate, that the United States incurs a share of global losses proportional to its current share of global GDP, and that Federal revenue as a share of U.S. GDP remains constant, lost revenue could be as high as 0.7 percent of U.S. GDP in 2100. Today, a loss of that magnitude would translate to $120 billion in lost tax revenue. It should be noted that this example does not take into account the fact that a portion of the projected economic losses include non-market losses that may not directly translate into lost revenue.

The Need for Action

The exposure of the Federal budget to climate risks provides yet another call to action for policymakers. How we respond to one of the most significant long-term challenges that our country and our planet faces speaks volumes about our values. It speaks to who we are as policymakers—if we embrace the challenge of developing pragmatic solutions. It speaks to who we are as Americans—if we seize this moment and lead. It speaks to who we are as parents—if we take responsibility and leave our children a safer planet.

The President has set the United States on an ambitious course and provided leadership that helped secure a strong global agreement to tackle emissions and prepare our communities for the effects of climate change not only because he believes we have a moral obligation, but also because climate action is an economic and fiscal imperative. For this reason, the President's Budget invests in building a climate-smart economy, creating a 21st Century Clean Transportation System, doubling our clean energy research and development, implementing common sense standards for carbon pollution, partnering with communities to tackle climate risk, and continuing leadership in international efforts to cut carbon pollution and enhance climate change resilience.

---

[18] IPCC, 2014: Climate Change 2014: Synthesis Report. Contribution of Working Groups I, II and III to the Fifth Assessment Report of the Intergovernmental Panel on Climate Change [Core Writing Team, R.K. Pachauri and L.A. Meyer (eds.)]. IPCC, Geneva, Switzerland, 67.

[19] Nordhaus, William, 2007. Dynamic Integrated Climate and Economy (DICE), as presented in the Technical Support Document: Social Cost of Carbon for Regulatory Impact Analysis Under Executive Order 12866. Interagency Working Group on Social Cost of Carbon, United States Government.

[20] Burke, M., H. Solomon, and E. Miguel, 2015. Global Non-Linear Effect of Temperature on Economic Production. Nature. 527: 235-9.

TECHNICAL BUDGET ANALYSES

25. CURRENT SERVICES ESTIMATES

Current services, or "baseline," estimates are designed to provide a benchmark against which budget proposals can be measured. A baseline is not a prediction of the final outcome of the annual budget process, nor is it a proposed budget. It can be a useful tool in budgeting, however. It can be used as a benchmark against which to measure the magnitude of the policy changes in the President's Budget or other budget proposals, and it can also be used to warn of future problems if policy is not changed, either for the Government's overall fiscal health or for individual tax and spending programs.

Ideally, a current services baseline would provide a projection of estimated receipts, outlays, deficits or surpluses, and budget authority reflecting this year's enacted policies and programs for each year in the future. Defining this baseline is challenging because funding for many programs in operation today expires within the 10-year budget window. Most significantly, funding for discretionary programs is provided one year at a time in annual appropriations acts. Mandatory programs are not generally subject to annual appropriations, but many operate under multi-year authorizations that expire within the budget window. The framework used to construct the baseline must address whether and how to project forward the funding for these programs beyond their scheduled expiration dates.

Since the early 1970s, when the first requirements for the calculation of a "current services" baseline were enacted, the baseline has been constructed using a variety of concepts and measures. Throughout the 1990s, the baseline was calculated using a detailed set of rules enacted through amendments to the Balanced Budget Emergency Deficit Control Act of 1985 (BBEDCA) made by the Budget Enforcement Act of 1990 (BEA). The BBEDCA baseline rules lapsed after the enforcement provisions of the BEA expired in 2002, but even after the lapse they were largely adhered to in practice until they were officially reinstated through amendments to BBEDCA enacted in the Budget Control Act of 2011 (BCA).

The Administration believes adjustments to the BBEDCA baseline are needed to better represent the deficit outlook under current policy and to serve as a more appropriate benchmark for measuring policy changes. The next section provides detailed estimates of an adjusted baseline that corrects for some of the shortcomings in the BBEDCA baseline.

Table 25–1. CATEGORY TOTALS FOR THE ADJUSTED BASELINE

	2015	2016	2017	2018	2019	2020	2021	2022	2023	2024	2025	2026
Receipts	3,250	3,336	3,477	3,615	3,783	4,006	4,204	4,400	4,593	4,801	5,012	5,247
Outlays:												
Discretionary:												
Defense	583	595	601	606	620	633	644	682	711	733	752	771
Non-defense	581	627	614	604	607	614	626	660	685	703	720	738
Subtotal, discretionary	1,165	1,223	1,215	1,210	1,227	1,246	1,270	1,342	1,396	1,437	1,472	1,509
Mandatory:												
Social Security	882	924	967	1,025	1,089	1,157	1,224	1,297	1,373	1,454	1,538	1,626
Medicare	540	589	602	611	674	725	781	879	912	936	1,046	1,114
Medicaid and CHIP	359	382	392	412	429	450	475	502	530	561	594	638
Other mandatory	520	593	605	615	667	686	715	757	761	763	787	865
Subtotal, mandatory	2,301	2,487	2,565	2,663	2,860	3,018	3,196	3,434	3,577	3,713	3,966	4,243
Disaster costs [1]	....	2	6	8	8	9	9	10	10	10	10	10
Net interest	223	240	304	390	473	547	609	669	729	783	838	901
Total, outlays	3,688	3,952	4,089	4,270	4,568	4,820	5,085	5,455	5,713	5,943	6,286	6,662
Unified deficit(+)/surplus(–)	438	616	612	655	785	814	881	1,055	1,120	1,143	1,273	1,415
(On-budget)	(466)	(623)	(608)	(634)	(741)	(737)	(788)	(939)	(972)	(966)	(1,064)	(1,179)
(Off-budget)	(–27)	(–7)	(4)	(21)	(45)	(77)	(93)	(116)	(148)	(176)	(210)	(236)
Memorandum:												
BBEDCA baseline deficit	438	615	636	719	875	917	994	1,121	1,167	1,185	1,325	1,440
Adjustments for provisions contained in the Budget Control Act	....	....	–27	–67	–89	–97	–102	–52	–32	–26	–33	–5
Remove non-recurring emergency costs	....	....	–2	–3	–6	–8	–8	–8	–8	–9	–9	–9
Add placeholder for future emergency costs	....	2	6	8	8	9	9	10	10	10	10	10
Related debt service	....	*	–*	–1	–4	–8	–12	–15	–17	–18	–20	–21
Adjusted baseline deficit	438	616	612	655	785	814	881	1,055	1,120	1,143	1,273	1,415

*$500 million or less.

[1] These amounts represent the probability of major disasters requiring Federal assistance for relief and reconstruction. Such assistance might be provided in the form of discretionary or mandatory outlays or tax relief. These amounts are included as outlays for convenience.

Table 25–1 shows estimates of receipts, outlays, and deficits under the Administration's adjusted baseline for 2015 through 2026.[1] The estimates are based on the economic assumptions described later in this chapter. The table also shows the Administration's estimates by major component of the budget. Estimates of the deficit based on the BBEDCA baseline rules are shown as a memorandum in the table.

Conceptual Basis for Estimates

Receipts and outlays are divided into two categories that are important for calculating the baseline: those controlled by authorizing legislation (receipts and direct spending) and those controlled through the annual appropriations process (discretionary spending). Different estimating rules apply to each category.

Direct spending and receipts.—Direct spending includes the major entitlement programs, such as Social Security, Medicare, Medicaid, Federal employee retirement, unemployment compensation, and the Supplemental Nutrition Assistance Program (SNAP). It also includes such programs as deposit insurance and farm price and income supports, where the Government is legally obligated to make payments under certain conditions. Taxes and other receipts are like direct spending in that they involve ongoing activities that generally operate under permanent or long-standing authority, and the underlying statutes generally specify the tax rates or benefit levels that must be collected or paid, and who must pay or who is eligible to receive benefits.

The baseline generally—but not always—assumes that receipts and direct spending programs continue in the future as specified by current law. The budgetary effects of anticipated regulatory and administrative actions that are permissible under current law are also reflected in the estimates. The Administration's adjusted baseline incorporates further exceptions to produce a more realistic deficit outlook. Exceptions in BBEDCA and in the Administration's adjusted baselines are described below:

- Consistent with BBEDCA, expiring excise taxes dedicated to a trust fund are assumed to be extended at the rates in effect at the time of expiration. During the projection period of 2016 through 2026, the taxes affected by this exception are taxes deposited in the Airport and Airway Trust Fund, which expire on March 31, 2016; taxes deposited in the Highway Trust Fund, the Leaking Underground Storage Tank Trust Fund, and the Sport Fish Restoration and Boating Resources Trust Fund, which expire on September 30, 2022; the Heavy Vehicle Use Tax, which expires on September 30, 2023; taxes deposited in the Oil Spill Liability Trust Fund, which expire on December 31, 2017; and taxes deposited in the Patient-Centered Outcomes Research Trust Fund, which expire on September 30, 2019.

- BBEDCA requires expiring authorizations for direct spending programs that were enacted before

the Balanced Budget Act of 1997 to be extended if their current year outlays exceed $50 million. For example, even though the National Flood Insurance program, which was authorized before the Balanced Budget Act of 1997, is scheduled to expire at the end of 2017, the baseline estimates assume continuation of this program through the projection period, because the program's current year outlays exceed the $50 million threshold.[2]

Discretionary spending.—Discretionary programs differ in one important aspect from direct spending programs: the Congress provides spending authority for almost all discretionary programs one year at a time. The spending authority is normally provided in the form of annual appropriations. Absent appropriations of additional funds in the future, discretionary programs would cease to operate after existing balances were spent. If the baseline were intended strictly to reflect current law, then a baseline would reflect only the expenditure of remaining balances from appropriations laws already enacted. Instead, the BBEDCA baseline provides a mechanical definition to reflect the continuing costs of discretionary programs. Under BBEDCA, the baseline estimates for discretionary programs in the current year are based on that year's enacted appropriations.[3] For the budget year and beyond, the spending authority enacted in the current year is adjusted for inflation, using specified inflation rates.[4] The definition attempts to keep discretionary spending roughly level in real terms. The Administration's adjusted baseline makes the following modifications to the BBEDCA baseline:

- The adjusted baseline includes allowances to comply with the discretionary "caps" enacted in BBEDCA, which limit the amount of discretionary budget authority that can be provided through the annual appropriations process. The current caps were initially established by the BCA and later amended for 2013 by the American Taxpayer Relief Act of 2012 (ATRA).

---

[1] The estimates are shown on a unified budget basis; i.e., the off-budget receipts and outlays of the Social Security trust funds and the Postal Service Fund are added to the on-budget receipts and outlays to calculate the unified budget totals.

[2] For programs enacted since the Balanced Budget Act of 1997, programs that are explicitly temporary in nature expire in the baseline as provided by current law even if their current year outlays exceed the $50 million threshold. In contrast, if commodity price support programs typically funded in the Farm Bill expire at the time the baseline is prepared, they are assumed to continue to operate in the same way they operated immediately before the expiration, because these programs were enacted prior to the Balanced Budget Act of 1997 and their current year outlays exceed the $50 million threshold.

[3] When current year appropriations have not been enacted BBEDCA requires the baseline estimates for discretionary spending and collections for the current year to be based on the levels provided in a full-year continuing resolution or the annualized level of a part-year continuing resolution.

[4] The Administration's baseline uses the same inflation rates for discretionary spending as required by BBEDCA, despite the fact that this allows for an overcompensation for Federal pay inherent in the BBEDCA definition. At the time the BEA was enacted, it failed to account for the nearly contemporaneous enactment of the Federal Employees Compensation Act of 1991 that shifted the effective date of Federal employee pay raises from October to January. This oversight was not corrected when the baseline definition was reinstated by the BCA amendments to BBEDCA. Correcting for this error would have only a small effect on the discretionary baseline.

The caps for 2014 and 2015 were amended by the Bipartisan Budget Act of 2013 while the caps for 2016 and 2017 were amended by the Bipartisan Budget Act of 2015. (Chapter 9 of this volume, "Budget Concepts," provides more information on the effects of BBEDCA, as amended by the BCA and subsequent legislation.)

- The BBEDCA caps allow for adjustments to the discretionary caps for disaster relief spending, emergency requirements, Overseas Contingency Operations (OCO), and program integrity.

  o Disaster relief and emergency requirements. — The adjusted baseline does not reflect funding under the disaster relief or emergency cap adjustments beyond what has already been enacted for 2016. While the BBEDCA baseline projects forward the $7.1 billion of enacted disaster relief funding for the Departments of Agriculture, Homeland Security, and Housing and Urban Development in 2016, increased by the BBEDCA inflation rates, the adjusted baseline removes this extrapolation. This same treatment is given to the $0.8 billion of enacted emergency funding provided to the Departments of Agriculture (Forest Service) for wildland fire suppression activities and the International Monetary Fund (IMF) for the IMF quota to protect global financial security and prevent and manage financial crises.

  o OCO. — The adjusted baseline for OCO is identical to the BBEDCA baseline, reflecting 2016 enacted funding for OCO inflated at the BBEDCA inflation rates.

  o Program integrity. — The adjusted baseline assumes full funding for the enacted cap adjustment levels, and inflates those amounts after the cap adjustments expire in 2021. These amounts are not the equivalent of the BBEDCA baseline, because the allowable cap adjustment amounts vary from year to year and Congress does not always provide the full allowable adjustment under current law. Additionally, the adjusted baseline assumes savings from enacting the program integrity cap adjustments at their full levels.

Reclassification of transportation spending. — To provide an appropriate baseline for assessing the budgetary impact of the Administration's surface transportation proposal, the adjusted baseline reclassifies certain surface transportation accounts from discretionary to mandatory. The reclassification is a zero-sum shift of both BA and outlays from the discretionary category to the mandatory category.

Disaster funding. — An allowance for the possible costs of major natural or man-made disasters during the remainder of 2016 and in subsequent years is assumed in the adjusted baseline to make budget totals more realistic. Baselines would be more meaningful if they did not project forward the amount of any disaster funding provided

in the current year. Rather, baselines should replace the projection of enacted current-year funding—which might be unusually low or unusually high—with plausible estimates of future costs.

Joint Committee Enforcement. — Because the Joint Select Committee process under Title IV of the BCA did not result in enactment of legislation that reduced the deficit by at least $1.2 trillion, the BCA stipulated that, absent intervening legislation, enforcement procedures would be invoked on an annual basis to reduce the levels of discretionary and mandatory spending to accomplish deficit reduction. The BBEDCA baseline includes the effects of the across-the-board reductions ("sequestration") already invoked by Joint Committee sequestration orders for 2013 through 2016, as well as the mandatory sequestration order for 2017 issued with the transmittal of the 2017 Budget.[5] Further Joint Committee enforcement—consisting of mandatory sequestration and discretionary cap reductions for 2018 through 2021—is reflected as adjustments to the BBEDCA baseline in the form of an allowance in the amount of the required reductions. Pursuant to subsequent legislation, the adjusted baseline also includes the extension of mandatory sequestration through 2025 at the rate required for 2021 by the BCA.[6]

Economic Assumptions

As discussed above, an important purpose of the baseline is to serve as a benchmark against which policy proposals are measured. However, this purpose is achieved only if the policies and the baseline are constructed under the same set of economic and technical assumptions. For this reason, the Administration uses the same assumptions—for example, the same inflation assumptions—in preparing its current service estimates and its Budget. These assumptions are based on enactment of the President's Budget proposals.

The economy and the budget interact. Changes in economic conditions significantly alter the estimates of tax receipts, unemployment benefits, entitlement payments that receive automatic cost-of-living adjustments (COLAs), income support programs for low-income in-

[5] The effects of past sequestration reductions are reflected in the detailed schedules for the affected budget accounts, while the 2017 reductions are reflected in an allowance due to the timing of the preparation of the detailed budget estimates and the issuance of the 2017 sequestration order.

[6] The Bipartisan Budget Act of 2013 (P.L. 113-67) extended mandatory sequestration through 2023, at the rate required for 2021 by the BCA. This Act also specified for 2023 that, notwithstanding the 2 percent limit on Medicare sequestration in the BCA, the Medicare reduction should be 2.90 percent for the first half of the sequestration period and 1.11 percent for the second half of the period. The Military Retired Pay Restoration Act (P.L. 113-82) extended mandatory sequestration through 2024. The Protecting Access to Medicare Act of 2014 (P.L. 113-93) specified for 2024 that the Medicare reduction should be 4.0 percent for the first half of the sequestration period and zero for the second half of the period. The Bipartisan Budget Act of 2015 (P.L. 114-74) further extended mandatory sequestration through 2025. This Act also reset the Medicare reduction to a constant 2 percent through 2024 and specified for 2025 that the Medicare program should be reduced by 4.0 percent for the first half of the sequestration period and zero for the second half of the period.

dividuals, and interest on the Federal debt. In turn, Government tax and spending policies influence prices, economic growth, consumption, savings, and investment. Because of these interactions, it would be reasonable, from an economic perspective, to assume different economic paths for the baseline projection and the President's Budget. However, this would diminish the value of the baseline estimates as a benchmark for measuring proposed policy changes, because it would then be difficult to separate the effects of proposed policy changes from the effects of different economic assumptions. Using the same economic assumptions for the baseline and the President's Budget eliminates this potential source of confusion. The economic assumptions underlying the Budget and the Administration's baseline are summarized in Table 25–2. The economic outlook underlying these assumptions is discussed in greater detail in Chapter 2, "Economic Assumptions and Interactions with the Budget," of this volume.

Major Programmatic Assumptions

In addition to the baseline adjustments described earlier in this chapter, a number of programmatic assumptions must be made to calculate the baseline estimates. These include assumptions about annual cost-of-living adjustments in the indexed programs and the number of beneficiaries who will receive payments from the major benefit programs. Assumptions about various automatic cost-of-living-adjustments are shown in Table 25–2, and assumptions about baseline caseload projections for the major benefit programs are shown in Table 25–3. These assumptions affect baseline estimates of direct spending for each of these programs, and they also affect estimates of the discretionary baseline for a limited number of programs. For the administrative expenses for Medicare, Railroad Retirement, and unemployment insurance, the discretionary baseline is increased (or decreased) for changes in the number of beneficiaries in addition to the adjustments for inflation described earlier.[7]

It is also necessary to make assumptions about the continuation of expiring programs and provisions. As explained above, in the baseline estimates provided here, expiring excise taxes dedicated to a trust fund are extended at current rates. In general, mandatory programs with spending of at least $50 million in the current year are also assumed to continue, unless the programs are explicitly temporary in nature. Table 25–4, available on the Internet at *www.budget.gov/budget/Analytical_Perspectives* and on the Budget CD-ROM, provides a listing of mandatory programs and taxes assumed to continue in the baseline after their expiration.[8] Many other important assumptions must be made in order to calculate the baseline estimates. These include

---

[7] Although these adjustments are applied at the account level, they have no effect in the aggregate because discretionary baseline levels are constrained to the BBEDCA caps.

[8] All discretionary programs with enacted non-emergency, non-disaster appropriations in the current year and the 2016 costs for overseas contingency operations in Iraq and Afghanistan and other recurring international activities are assumed to continue, and are therefore not presented in Table 25-4.

Table 25–2. SUMMARY OF ECONOMIC ASSUMPTIONS
(Fiscal years; in billions of dollars)

	2015	2016	2017	2018	2019	2020	2021	2022	2023	2024	2025	2026
Gross Domestic Product (GDP):												
Levels, in billions of dollars:												
Current dollars	17,803.4	18,472.0	19,302.8	20,129.6	21,012.6	21,921.4	22,875.2	23,872.2	24,912.4	25,994.8	27,123.0	28,300.9
Real, chained (2009) dollars	16,264.1	16,665.8	17,103.3	17,524.4	17,938.4	18,351.0	18,773.0	19,204.8	19,646.6	20,098.4	20,560.7	21,033.6
Percent change, year over year:												
Current dollars	3.6	3.8	4.5	4.3	4.4	4.3	4.4	4.4	4.4	4.3	4.3	4.3
Real, chained (2009) dollars	2.5	2.5	2.6	2.5	2.4	2.3	2.3	2.3	2.3	2.3	2.3	2.3
Inflation measures (percent change, year over year):												
GDP chained price index	1.1	1.2	1.8	1.8	2.0	2.0	2.0	2.0	2.0	2.0	2.0	2.0
Consumer price index (all urban)	0.3	1.2	2.1	2.0	2.2	2.2	2.3	2.3	2.3	2.3	2.3	2.3
Unemployment rate, civilian (percent)	5.5	4.8	4.5	4.6	4.6	4.7	4.7	4.8	4.8	4.9	4.9	4.9
Interest rates (percent):												
91-day Treasury bills	*	0.4	1.6	2.4	3.0	3.3	3.4	3.4	3.3	3.3	3.3	3.3
10-year Treasury notes	2.2	2.7	3.4	3.8	4.1	4.2	4.2	4.2	4.2	4.2	4.2	4.2
MEMORANDUM:												
Related program assumptions:												
Automatic benefit increases (percent):												
Social security and veterans pensions	1.7	....	0.8	2.2	2.1	2.3	2.2	2.3	2.3	2.3	2.3	2.3
Federal employee retirement	1.7	....	0.8	2.2	2.1	2.3	2.2	2.3	2.3	2.3	2.3	2.3
Supplemental Nutrition Assistance Program ...	2.8	....	1.0	2.2	2.0	2.3	2.2	2.3	2.3	2.3	2.3	2.3
Insured unemployment rate	1.7	1.7	1.6	1.6	1.6	1.6	1.6	1.6	1.6	1.7	1.7	1.7

* 0.05 percent or less.

assumptions about the timing and substance of regulations that will be issued over the projection period, the use of administrative discretion provided under current law, and other assumptions about the way programs operate. Table 25–4 lists many of these assumptions and their effects on the baseline estimates. It is not intended to be an exhaustive listing; the variety and complexity of Government programs are too great to provide a complete list. Instead, some of the more important assumptions are shown.

Current Services Receipts, Outlays, and Budget Authority

Receipts.—Table 25–5 shows the Administration's baseline receipts by major source. Table 25-6 shows the scheduled increases in the Social Security taxable earnings base, which affect both payroll tax receipts for the program and the initial benefit levels for certain retirees.

Outlays.—Table 25–7 shows the growth from 2015 to 2016 and average annual growth over the five-year

Table 25–3. BASELINE BENEFICIARY PROJECTIONS FOR MAJOR BENEFIT PROGRAMS
(Annual average, in thousands)

	Actual 2015	Estimate										
		2016	2017	2018	2019	2020	2021	2022	2023	2024	2025	2026
Farmers receiving Federal payments	1,159	1,153	1,147	1,141	1,135	1,129	1,123	1,117	1,111	1,105	1,099	1,093
Federal direct student loans	9,746	9,666	9,891	10,135	10,434	10,735	11,067	11,420	11,798	12,198	12,618	13,055
Federal Pell Grants	7,670	7,679	7,750	7,894	8,102	8,248	8,410	8,552	8,724	8,908	9,095	9,217
Medicaid/Children's Health Insurance Program [1]	73,090	74,451	76,367	76,994	76,288	77,541	78,279	78,939	79,580	80,222	80,770	81,291
Medicare-eligible military retiree health benefits	2,311	2,342	2,374	2,403	2,430	2,460	2,492	2,524	2,554	2,554	2,554	2,554
Medicare [2]												
Hospital insurance	54,633	56,328	58,031	59,749	61,540	63,407	65,308	67,230	69,120	70,963	72,810	74,635
Supplementary medical insurance:												
Part B	50,382	51,743	53,164	54,684	56,249	57,916	59,601	61,310	63,016	64,650	66,297	67,946
Part D	41,449	42,975	44,529	45,844	47,149	48,552	49,991	51,444	52,878	54,274	55,676	57,063
Prescription Drug Plans and Medicare:												
Advantage Prescription Drug Plans	39,113	41,089	43,030	44,661	46,215	47,656	49,068	50,496	51,903	53,274	54,650	56,013
Retiree Drug Subsidy	2,336	1,886	1,499	1,183	934	896	922	949	975	1,000	1,026	1,051
Managed Care Enrollment [3]	17,206	18,300	19,295	20,228	21,147	21,864	22,615	23,467	24,319	25,131	25,917	26,684
Railroad retirement	534	523	520	517	512	508	502	496	488	481	473	465
Federal civil service retirement	2,638	2,650	2,663	2,678	2,696	2,714	2,733	2,753	2,773	2,787	2,802	2,819
Military retirement	2,271	2,286	2,299	2,311	2,322	2,333	2,345	2,358	2,370	2,401	2,407	2,412
Unemployment insurance	6,676	6,422	6,585	6,801	6,897	7,026	7,125	7,173	7,195	7,259	7,278	7,252
Supplemental Nutrition Assistance Program (formerly Food Stamps)	45,767	45,537	44,482	42,828	41,507	38,793	36,968	35,690	34,751	33,598	32,289	31,527
Child nutrition	34,741	36,099	36,875	37,269	37,639	37,956	38,278	38,605	38,937	39,275	39,619	39,968
Foster care, adoption assistance and guardianship assistance	633	647	671	695	717	739	761	784	808	833	859	885
Supplemental security income (SSI):												
Aged	1,100	1,106	1,111	1,118	1,127	1,140	1,153	1,168	1,186	1,206	1,229	1,253
Blind/disabled	7,073	7,113	7,126	7,136	7,146	7,171	7,181	7,195	7,220	7,254	7,294	7,323
Total, SSI	8,173	8,219	8,237	8,254	8,273	8,311	8,334	8,363	8,406	8,460	8,523	8,576
Child care and development fund [4]	2,081	2,117	2,096	2,073	2,028	1,985	1,946	1,910	1,874	1,838	1,805	1,771
Social security (OASDI):												
Old age and survivors insurance	48,338	50,060	51,766	53,486	55,253	57,035	58,637	60,277	61,924	63,561	65,116	66,637
Disability insurance	10,899	10,888	11,006	11,119	11,226	11,319	11,438	11,543	11,635	11,704	11,788	11,858
Total, OASDI	59,237	60,948	62,772	64,605	66,479	68,354	70,075	71,820	73,559	75,265	76,904	78,495
Veterans compensation:												
Veterans	4,062	4,245	4,427	4,585	4,728	4,862	4,989	5,112	5,232	5,348	5,461	5,571
Survivors (non-veterans)	386	395	405	417	430	444	459	475	492	510	527	546
Total, Veterans compensation	4,448	4,640	4,832	5,002	5,157	5,306	5,448	5,587	5,724	5,858	5,989	6,117
Veterans pensions:												
Veterans	298	296	297	298	299	301	302	303	304	306	307	308
Survivors (non-veterans)	208	207	210	212	214	216	218	221	223	225	227	230
Total, Veterans pensions	506	503	507	510	513	517	520	524	527	531	534	538

[1] Medicaid enrollment excludes territories.

[2] Medicare figures (Hospital Insurance, Part B, and Part D) do not sum to total Medicare enrollment due to enrollment in multiple programs.

[3] Enrollment figures include only beneficiaries who receive both Part A and Part B services through managed care.

[4] These levels include children served through CCDF (including Temporary Assistance for Needy Families (TANF) transfers) and through funds spent directly on child care in the Social Services Block Grant and TANF programs.

and ten-year periods for certain discretionary and major mandatory programs. Tables 25–8 and 25–9 show the Administration's baseline outlays by function and by agency, respectively. A more detailed presentation of these outlays (by function, category, subfunction, and program) is available on the Internet as part of Table 25–12 at *www.budget.gov/budget/Analytical_Perspectives* and on the Budget CD-ROM.

Budget authority.—Tables 25–10 and 25–11 show estimates of budget authority in the Administration's baseline by function and by agency, respectively. A more detailed presentation of this budget authority with program-level estimates is also available on the Internet as part of Table 25–12 at *www.budget.gov/budget/Analytical_Perspectives* and on the Budget CD-ROM.

Table 25–5. RECEIPTS BY SOURCE IN THE PROJECTION OF ADJUSTED BASELINE

(In billions of dollars)

	2015 Actual	Estimate										
		2016	2017	2018	2019	2020	2021	2022	2023	2024	2025	2026
Individual income taxes	1,540.8	1,627.8	1,724.1	1,793.0	1,878.1	1,987.6	2,095.0	2,205.2	2,318.8	2,436.6	2,559.4	2,688.3
Corporation income taxes	343.8	292.6	342.7	364.0	400.7	454.0	461.3	466.8	470.9	478.0	485.8	494.5
Social insurance and retirement receipts	1,065.3	1,100.8	1,139.1	1,184.8	1,232.5	1,279.2	1,344.9	1,409.0	1,469.4	1,537.5	1,604.6	1,684.6
(On-budget)	(294.9)	(303.1)	(312.4)	(320.9)	(333.2)	(345.5)	(362.1)	(378.2)	(394.0)	(410.9)	(428.2)	(448.7)
(Off-budget)	(770.4)	(797.7)	(826.8)	(863.9)	(899.3)	(933.8)	(982.8)	(1,030.8)	(1,075.4)	(1,126.6)	(1,176.4)	(1,235.8)
Excise taxes	98.3	96.8	86.5	105.3	105.8	108.5	113.6	116.7	120.1	123.9	128.3	133.5
Estate and gift taxes	19.2	21.1	22.4	23.7	25.1	26.4	28.1	29.7	31.5	33.5	35.6	37.9
Customs duties	35.0	36.7	39.5	42.2	44.1	45.8	47.6	49.4	51.1	52.7	54.3	56.1
Miscellaneous receipts	147.5	159.7	122.5	101.5	97.0	103.9	113.3	123.2	130.9	138.5	144.5	152.1
Total, receipts	**3,249.9**	**3,335.5**	**3,476.8**	**3,614.5**	**3,783.2**	**4,005.5**	**4,203.9**	**4,400.0**	**4,592.8**	**4,800.7**	**5,012.4**	**5,247.0**
(On-budget)	(2,479.5)	(2,537.9)	(2,650.0)	(2,750.7)	(2,883.9)	(3,071.7)	(3,221.1)	(3,369.2)	(3,517.5)	(3,674.1)	(3,836.0)	(4,011.2)
(Off-budget)	(770.4)	(797.7)	(826.8)	(863.9)	(899.3)	(933.8)	(982.8)	(1,030.8)	(1,075.4)	(1,126.6)	(1,176.4)	(1,235.8)

Table 25–6. EFFECT ON RECEIPTS OF CHANGES IN THE SOCIAL SECURITY TAXABLE EARNINGS BASE

(In billions of dollars)

	2017	2018	2019	2020	2021	2022	2023	2024	2025	2026
Social security (OASDI) taxable earnings base increases:										
$118,500 to $126,000 on Jan. 1, 2017	3.9	9.8	10.6	11.5	12.7	13.9	15.2	16.7	18.2	19.9
$126,000 to $129,300 on Jan. 1, 2018	....	1.7	4.3	4.6	5.1	5.6	6.1	6.7	7.3	8.0
$129,300 to $133,200 on Jan. 1, 2019	....	....	2.0	5.1	5.7	6.2	6.8	7.4	8.1	8.9
$133,200 to $137,700 on Jan. 1, 2020	....	....	....	2.4	6.1	6.7	7.3	8.0	8.8	9.6
$137,700 to $143,100 on Jan. 1, 2021	....	....	....	....	2.9	7.4	8.1	8.9	9.7	10.7
$143,100 to $148,800 on Jan. 1, 2022	....	....	....	....	....	3.1	7.9	8.7	9.4	10.4
$148,800 to $154,800 on Jan. 1, 2023	....	....	....	....	....	....	3.3	8.4	9.2	10.0
$154,800 to $161,100 on Jan. 1, 2024	....	....	....	....	....	....	....	3.5	8.8	9.7
$161,100 to $167,700 on Jan. 1, 2025	....	....	....	....	....	....	....	....	3.6	9.3
$167,700 to $174,600 on Jan. 1, 2026	....	....	....	....	....	....	....	....	....	3.8

Table 25–7. CHANGE IN OUTLAY ESTIMATES BY CATEGORY IN THE ADJUSTED BASELINE
(In billions of dollars)

	2016	2017	2018	2019	2020	2021	2022	2023	2024	2025	2026	Change 2016 to 2017		Change 2016 to 2021		Change 2016 to 2026	
												Amount	Percent	Amount	Average annual rate	Amount	Average annual rate
Outlays:																	
Discretionary:																	
Defense	595	601	606	620	633	644	682	711	733	752	771	6	1.0%	49	1.6%	176	2.6%
Non-defense	627	614	604	607	614	626	660	685	703	720	738	−14	−2.2%	−1	−0.0%	110	1.6%
Subtotal, discretionary	1,223	1,215	1,210	1,227	1,246	1,270	1,342	1,396	1,437	1,472	1,509	−8	−0.7%	47	0.8%	286	2.1%
Mandatory:																	
Farm programs	18	21	21	16	15	18	18	18	18	18	18	2	13.7%	*	0.2%	−*	−0.2%
GSE support	−19	−22	−21	−19	−19	−18	−16	−15	−14	−14	−13	−3	15.6%	1	−1.3%	5	−3.3%
Medicaid	367	377	398	424	444	469	496	525	555	589	632	9	2.5%	102	5.0%	265	5.6%
Other health care	98	119	136	150	159	168	177	185	194	202	211	21	21.5%	69	11.3%	112	7.9%
Medicare	589	602	611	674	725	781	879	912	936	1,046	1,114	13	2.2%	193	5.8%	526	6.6%
Federal employee retirement and disability	145	144	143	152	157	162	172	172	172	183	189	−1	−1.0%	17	2.2%	44	2.7%
Unemployment compensation ...	32	32	33	35	36	38	39	41	43	44	46	−*	−1.1%	5	3.1%	13	3.5%
Other income security programs	283	280	275	283	284	287	297	298	298	305	318	−3	−1.1%	4	0.3%	35	1.2%
Social Security	924	967	1,025	1,089	1,157	1,224	1,297	1,373	1,454	1,538	1,626	43	4.7%	301	5.8%	702	5.8%
Veterans programs	109	106	102	114	121	128	144	143	141	160	168	−3	−2.5%	18	3.2%	59	4.4%
Other mandatory programs ...	41	48	41	39	38	42	38	34	29	19	55	6	15.5%	*	0.1%	13	2.8%
Undistributed offsetting receipts	−101	−108	−102	−97	−100	−103	−106	−109	−111	−124	−120	−7	7.1%	−2	0.4%	−19	1.7%
Subtotal, mandatory	2,487	2,565	2,663	2,860	3,018	3,196	3,434	3,577	3,713	3,966	4,243	78	3.1%	709	5.1%	1,756	5.5%
Disaster costs [1]	2	6	8	8	9	9	10	10	10	10	10	4	193.3%	8	38.0%	8	18.2%
Net interest	240	304	390	473	547	609	669	729	783	838	901	64	26.5%	369	20.5%	661	14.1%
Total, outlays	3,952	4,089	4,270	4,568	4,820	5,085	5,455	5,713	5,943	6,286	6,662	137	3.5%	1,133	5.2%	2,710	5.4%

*Less than $500 million.

[1] These amounts represent the probability of a major disaster requiring federal assistance for relief and reconstruction. Such assistance might be provided in the form of discretionary or mandatory outlays or tax relief. These amounts are included as outlays for convenience.

Table 25–8. OUTLAYS BY FUNCTION IN THE ADJUSTED BASELINE
(In billions of dollars)

Function	2015 Actual	Estimate										
		2016	2017	2018	2019	2020	2021	2022	2023	2024	2025	2026
National Defense:												
Department of Defense—Military	562.5	576.3	579.8	585.0	599.2	610.8	622.6	658.0	686.5	707.4	725.3	744.6
Other	27.1	28.1	29.7	29.5	29.6	30.2	30.0	32.3	33.6	34.4	35.1	35.9
Total, National Defense	589.6	604.5	609.5	614.5	628.8	641.1	652.6	690.3	720.1	741.8	760.4	780.5
International Affairs	48.6	46.4	56.9	61.0	61.2	61.3	61.3	61.1	61.9	62.9	64.0	65.5
General Science, Space, and Technology	29.4	30.8	31.8	32.5	33.1	33.8	34.7	35.5	36.5	37.3	37.9	38.7
Energy	6.8	7.5	6.8	5.5	4.3	4.9	4.8	4.5	3.5	2.8	2.6	4.9
Natural Resources and Environment	36.0	42.6	45.0	45.7	46.1	47.2	48.2	49.1	50.0	50.8	51.7	52.6
Agriculture	18.5	25.6	27.5	27.3	23.0	21.6	25.3	25.5	25.6	25.6	25.8	25.9
Commerce and Housing Credit	–37.9	–26.1	–21.2	–20.4	–16.7	–16.1	–10.4	–10.0	–10.1	–11.8	–13.0	–13.4
On-Budget	(–36.2)	(–27.6)	(–24.7)	(–20.7)	(–17.0)	(–16.4)	(–10.7)	(–10.3)	(–10.4)	(–12.1)	(–13.3)	(–13.8)
Off-Budget	(–1.7)	(1.5)	(3.5)	(0.3)	(0.3)	(0.3)	(0.3)	(0.3)	(0.3)	(0.3)	(0.3)	(0.3)
Transportation	89.5	92.4	96.1	96.4	97.2	98.0	99.6	102.0	104.2	106.4	108.6	112.6
Community and Regional Development	20.7	27.9	19.1	16.9	15.6	13.0	13.0	13.0	12.9	13.1	13.4	13.7
Education, Training, Employment, and Social Services	122.1	113.9	104.8	111.1	116.8	120.3	123.4	125.1	126.8	129.0	131.6	135.1
Health	482.2	525.9	558.1	597.1	636.4	667.0	701.9	739.3	777.1	818.0	861.3	915.5
Medicare	546.2	595.3	608.6	617.5	681.4	732.3	788.7	886.4	919.9	943.6	1,054.2	1,122.6
Income Security	508.8	528.2	526.5	522.6	541.3	550.4	560.7	584.3	588.7	592.0	613.2	635.0
Social Security	887.8	929.4	972.6	1,031.2	1,095.3	1,163.3	1,230.9	1,303.4	1,380.3	1,461.1	1,545.2	1,633.5
On-Budget	(31.0)	(32.8)	(39.3)	(42.9)	(46.7)	(50.7)	(54.7)	(59.2)	(63.9)	(68.9)	(74.3)	(80.1)
Off-Budget	(856.8)	(896.7)	(933.3)	(988.3)	(1,048.7)	(1,112.6)	(1,176.2)	(1,244.3)	(1,316.4)	(1,392.2)	(1,470.9)	(1,553.4)
Veterans Benefits and Services	159.7	178.2	182.7	181.0	195.2	204.4	213.7	232.4	234.0	234.3	256.0	267.2
Administration of Justice	51.9	64.4	68.9	66.0	63.4	63.7	65.2	66.9	68.5	70.2	72.1	78.5
General Government	21.0	24.5	24.0	24.9	25.8	26.5	26.9	27.4	28.2	29.2	30.1	30.4
Net Interest	223.2	240.0	303.7	390.0	472.9	546.8	609.3	668.8	729.5	783.3	837.9	900.6
On-Budget	(319.1)	(330.7)	(392.0)	(475.7)	(559.2)	(629.6)	(689.9)	(745.7)	(800.7)	(850.1)	(899.5)	(956.9)
Off-Budget	(–96.0)	(–90.7)	(–88.3)	(–85.7)	(–86.3)	(–82.8)	(–80.6)	(–76.9)	(–71.2)	(–66.8)	(–61.6)	(–56.3)
Allowances	....	1.9	–24.0	–48.7	–55.4	–59.5	–62.0	–43.5	–36.2	–34.8	–43.8	–17.4
Undistributed Offsetting Receipts:												
Employer share, employee retirement (on-budget)	–65.1	–67.5	–71.0	–71.4	–72.9	–74.4	–76.1	–78.0	–80.0	–82.1	–84.2	–86.9
Employer share, employee retirement (off-budget)	–16.0	–16.9	–17.3	–18.0	–18.8	–19.5	–20.3	–21.2	–21.9	–22.6	–23.6	–26.1
Rents and royalties on the Outer Continental Shelf	–4.6	–3.8	–4.5	–5.1	–5.8	–6.1	–6.2	–6.9	–6.5	–6.7	–6.9	–7.1
Sale of major assets	....	....	....	....	....	....	....	....	....	....	....	....
Other undistributed offsetting receipts	–30.1	–12.9	–15.5	–7.7	....	–0.4	–0.4	–0.4	–0.3	....	–8.8	....
Total, Undistributed Offsetting Receipts	–115.8	–101.2	–108.3	–102.2	–97.5	–100.4	–103.1	–106.5	–108.7	–111.5	–123.5	–120.1
On-Budget	(–99.8)	(–84.3)	(–91.0)	(–84.2)	(–78.6)	(–80.9)	(–82.7)	(–85.3)	(–86.8)	(–88.9)	(–99.9)	(–94.0)
Off-Budget	(–16.0)	(–16.9)	(–17.3)	(–18.0)	(–18.8)	(–19.5)	(–20.3)	(–21.2)	(–21.9)	(–22.6)	(–23.6)	(–26.1)
Total	**3,688.3**	**3,951.9**	**4,088.9**	**4,269.9**	**4,568.4**	**4,819.5**	**5,084.8**	**5,455.0**	**5,712.7**	**5,943.3**	**6,285.7**	**6,661.9**
(On-Budget)	(2,945.2)	(3,161.3)	(3,257.7)	(3,385.0)	(3,624.5)	(3,809.0)	(4,009.3)	(4,308.5)	(4,489.1)	(4,640.2)	(4,899.7)	(5,190.6)
(Off-Budget)	(743.1)	(790.6)	(831.1)	(884.9)	(943.8)	(1,010.6)	(1,075.5)	(1,146.5)	(1,223.6)	(1,303.1)	(1,386.0)	(1,471.3)

Table 25–9. OUTLAYS BY AGENCY IN THE ADJUSTED BASELINE
(In billions of dollars)

Agency	2015 Actual	Estimate										
		2016	2017	2018	2019	2020	2021	2022	2023	2024	2025	2026
Legislative Branch	4.3	4.7	4.7	4.8	5.0	5.1	5.2	5.4	5.5	5.7	5.8	6.0
Judicial Branch	7.1	7.7	7.7	7.9	8.2	8.4	8.7	8.9	9.2	9.5	9.7	10.0
Agriculture	139.1	153.8	153.8	155.2	151.8	149.6	153.9	155.5	157.6	159.2	160.2	161.8
Commerce	9.0	10.5	10.4	10.7	11.8	12.0	12.3	11.7	11.3	11.5	11.8	12.1
Defense—Military Programs	562.5	576.3	587.2	601.4	620.1	634.3	647.3	651.7	667.2	683.2	698.8	715.9
Education	90.0	79.1	69.9	76.3	81.6	84.6	87.1	88.2	89.3	90.8	92.9	95.7
Energy	25.4	27.4	30.2	30.4	30.1	30.9	30.1	30.3	29.8	29.9	30.3	33.2
Health and Human Services	1,027.5	1,110.4	1,133.9	1,159.4	1,240.9	1,314.6	1,398.3	1,525.4	1,589.5	1,646.2	1,792.5	1,906.8
Homeland Security	42.6	51.8	44.8	43.5	44.5	43.5	44.2	45.3	46.4	47.5	48.8	56.2
Housing and Urban Development	35.5	28.7	39.9	39.0	37.4	36.7	36.9	36.8	36.8	36.9	37.2	37.7
Interior	12.3	14.0	14.5	14.8	15.2	15.8	16.1	16.4	16.6	16.7	17.0	17.3
Justice	26.9	39.1	41.9	39.1	36.2	35.9	36.9	37.8	38.6	39.5	40.5	41.5
Labor	45.2	43.5	45.3	45.9	45.9	48.6	50.4	52.9	55.5	58.3	57.0	67.0
State	26.5	30.9	30.3	31.6	32.4	32.8	33.3	33.2	33.7	34.3	35.0	35.7
Transportation	75.4	77.8	81.0	81.0	81.4	81.8	83.2	85.1	86.8	88.4	90.1	92.0
Treasury	485.6	540.4	617.5	717.5	828.5	912.0	986.9	1,058.2	1,126.3	1,190.4	1,248.8	1,306.1
Veterans Affairs	159.2	177.6	182.1	180.4	194.7	203.9	213.2	232.0	233.5	233.8	255.5	266.7
Corps of Engineers—Civil Works	6.7	6.7	7.4	7.8	7.8	7.7	7.7	7.7	7.8	7.9	7.9	8.0
Other Defense Civil Programs	63.0	63.7	59.6	57.1	63.7	65.2	66.9	75.3	72.1	68.4	78.5	84.7
Environmental Protection Agency	7.0	8.3	8.4	7.7	8.0	8.4	8.7	9.1	9.4	9.6	9.9	10.1
Executive Office of the President	0.4	0.4	0.4	0.4	0.4	0.4	0.5	0.5	0.5	0.5	0.5	0.5
General Services Administration	-0.9	-0.7	-0.5	-0.1	0.3	0.1	0.1	-0.0	-0.0	-0.0	-0.1	-0.1
International Assistance Programs	21.0	16.0	26.0	28.9	28.0	27.4	26.9	26.6	26.9	27.3	27.6	28.4
National Aeronautics and Space Administration	18.3	19.2	19.7	20.0	20.5	20.9	21.4	21.9	22.2	22.8	23.3	23.8
National Science Foundation	6.8	6.9	6.9	7.5	7.6	7.7	8.0	8.2	8.8	9.0	9.1	9.3
Office of Personnel Management	91.7	93.6	95.3	101.3	105.6	109.9	113.2	117.2	121.6	126.6	131.2	136.6
Small Business Administration	-0.7	-0.4	1.0	0.9	0.9	1.0	1.0	1.0	1.0	1.1	1.1	1.1
Social Security Administration	944.1	991.6	1,031.6	1,087.1	1,157.3	1,226.9	1,296.1	1,375.4	1,449.4	1,526.8	1,618.2	1,708.7
On-Budget	(87.4)	(94.9)	(98.3)	(98.8)	(108.6)	(114.3)	(119.9)	(131.2)	(132.9)	(134.6)	(147.4)	(155.3)
Off-Budget	(856.8)	(896.7)	(933.3)	(988.3)	(1,048.7)	(1,112.6)	(1,176.2)	(1,244.3)	(1,316.4)	(1,392.2)	(1,470.9)	(1,553.4)
Other Independent Agencies	14.2	23.6	25.1	22.3	25.0	25.8	33.3	34.1	35.0	33.5	32.6	32.3
On-Budget	(15.9)	(22.1)	(21.6)	(22.0)	(24.7)	(25.5)	(33.0)	(33.8)	(34.7)	(33.1)	(32.3)	(32.0)
Off-Budget	(-1.7)	(1.5)	(3.5)	(0.3)	(0.3)	(0.3)	(0.3)	(0.3)	(0.3)	(0.3)	(0.3)	(0.3)
Allowances	---	1.9	-31.7	-66.0	-77.4	-84.0	-87.7	-36.6	-15.6	-9.3	-16.0	12.7
Undistributed Offsetting Receipts	-257.6	-252.6	-255.7	-243.9	-245.0	-248.4	-255.2	-259.9	-259.8	-262.4	-270.1	-256.1
On-Budget	(-145.6)	(-145.1)	(-150.0)	(-140.2)	(-139.9)	(-146.0)	(-154.3)	(-161.8)	(-166.7)	(-173.0)	(-185.0)	(-173.7)
Off-Budget	(-112.0)	(-107.6)	(-105.7)	(-103.7)	(-105.1)	(-102.4)	(-101.0)	(-98.1)	(-93.1)	(-89.4)	(-85.2)	(-82.4)
Total	**3,688.3**	**3,951.9**	**4,088.9**	**4,269.9**	**4,568.4**	**4,819.5**	**5,084.8**	**5,455.0**	**5,712.7**	**5,943.3**	**6,285.7**	**6,661.9**
(On-Budget)	(2,945.2)	(3,161.3)	(3,257.7)	(3,385.0)	(3,624.5)	(3,809.0)	(4,009.3)	(4,308.5)	(4,489.1)	(4,640.2)	(4,899.7)	(5,190.6)
(Off-Budget)	(743.1)	(790.6)	(831.1)	(884.9)	(943.8)	(1,010.6)	(1,075.5)	(1,146.5)	(1,223.6)	(1,303.1)	(1,386.0)	(1,471.3)

Table 25–10.   BUDGET AUTHORITY BY FUNCTION IN THE ADJUSTED BASELINE
(In billions of dollars)

Function	2015 Actual	Estimate										
		2016	2017	2018	2019	2020	2021	2022	2023	2024	2025	2026
National Defense:												
Department of Defense—Military	570.9	587.1	591.2	590.3	604.0	618.5	633.3	700.9	717.8	735.0	752.7	771.7
Other	27.5	28.3	28.3	28.5	29.1	29.7	30.3	33.3	34.0	34.7	35.4	36.2
Total, National Defense	598.4	615.4	619.5	618.8	633.1	648.2	663.6	734.2	751.8	769.7	788.1	807.9
International Affairs	63.3	59.4	59.7	45.4	48.4	52.1	55.4	58.5	61.3	63.4	65.2	67.1
General Science, Space, and Technology	29.9	31.5	32.1	32.8	33.5	34.2	34.9	35.7	36.5	37.3	38.1	38.9
Energy	6.4	8.1	7.0	5.1	4.1	5.0	4.7	4.7	3.7	3.0	2.9	5.1
Natural Resources and Environment	35.7	41.1	43.1	43.9	44.8	46.0	47.0	48.1	49.2	50.2	51.2	52.4
Agriculture	16.9	33.4	26.6	23.0	22.1	24.2	25.9	26.1	26.2	26.4	26.5	26.8
Commerce and Housing Credit	–2.2	2.8	–3.5	2.3	4.2	5.8	6.7	9.1	10.3	11.8	12.9	14.0
On-Budget	(–2.2)	(3.0)	(–3.8)	(2.0)	(4.0)	(5.5)	(6.4)	(8.8)	(10.0)	(11.4)	(12.6)	(13.7)
Off-Budget	....	(–0.1)	(0.3)	(0.3)	(0.3)	(0.3)	(0.3)	(0.3)	(0.3)	(0.3)	(0.3)	(0.3)
Transportation	85.4	90.4	92.6	94.4	96.6	99.0	100.0	101.1	102.2	103.3	104.5	106.0
Community and Regional Development	17.5	18.3	13.2	13.2	13.8	14.3	14.7	15.0	15.3	15.7	16.1	16.4
Education, Training, Employment, and Social Services	119.6	112.0	109.1	112.7	118.9	122.2	125.3	127.2	129.0	131.3	134.0	137.5
Health	496.1	524.8	564.5	588.0	634.8	677.0	702.5	740.9	778.3	819.1	862.5	916.8
Medicare	547.6	601.6	608.9	617.5	681.4	732.3	788.8	886.5	920.0	943.8	1,054.4	1,122.8
Income Security	515.6	525.9	527.4	534.3	550.2	559.5	571.4	589.2	598.7	607.9	626.2	640.0
Social Security	892.0	932.9	976.3	1,036.0	1,100.5	1,168.9	1,236.2	1,309.2	1,386.4	1,467.5	1,551.9	1,640.5
On-Budget	(30.9)	(32.7)	(39.3)	(42.9)	(46.7)	(50.7)	(54.7)	(59.2)	(63.9)	(68.9)	(74.3)	(80.1)
Off-Budget	(861.1)	(900.2)	(937.0)	(993.2)	(1,053.8)	(1,118.2)	(1,181.4)	(1,250.0)	(1,322.5)	(1,398.6)	(1,477.6)	(1,560.4)
Veterans Benefits and Services	161.0	164.4	182.5	185.7	198.4	207.7	217.1	227.3	237.8	248.6	261.1	272.5
Administration of Justice	60.4	56.9	71.3	61.0	62.5	64.0	65.7	67.3	69.0	70.8	72.6	78.9
General Government	21.8	25.4	25.3	26.0	26.7	27.3	27.9	28.6	29.3	29.9	30.7	31.5
Net Interest	223.2	240.0	303.7	389.9	472.9	546.8	609.3	668.8	729.5	783.3	837.9	900.6
On-Budget	(319.2)	(330.7)	(392.0)	(475.6)	(559.2)	(629.6)	(689.9)	(745.6)	(800.7)	(850.1)	(899.5)	(956.9)
Off-Budget	(–96.0)	(–90.7)	(–88.3)	(–85.7)	(–86.3)	(–82.8)	(–80.6)	(–76.9)	(–71.2)	(–66.8)	(–61.6)	(–56.3)
Allowances	....	7.5	–37.1	–57.8	–58.2	–60.4	–62.9	–30.6	–32.4	–33.8	–46.6	–10.3
Undistributed Offsetting Receipts:												
Employer share, employee retirement (on-budget)	–65.1	–67.5	–71.0	–71.4	–72.9	–74.4	–76.1	–78.0	–80.0	–82.1	–84.2	–86.9
Employer share, employee retirement (off-budget)	–16.0	–16.9	–17.3	–18.0	–18.8	–19.5	–20.3	–21.2	–21.9	–22.6	–23.6	–26.1
Rents and royalties on the Outer Continental Shelf	–4.6	–3.8	–4.5	–5.1	–5.8	–6.1	–6.2	–6.9	–6.5	–6.7	–6.9	–7.1
Sale of major assets	....	....	....	....	....	....	....	....	....	....	....	....
Other undistributed offsetting receipts	–30.1	–12.9	–15.5	–7.7	....	–0.4	–0.4	–0.4	–0.3	....	–8.8	....
Total, Undistributed Offsetting Receipts	–115.8	–101.2	–108.3	–102.2	–97.5	–100.4	–103.1	–106.5	–108.7	–111.5	–123.5	–120.1
On-Budget	(–99.8)	(–84.3)	(–91.0)	(–84.2)	(–78.6)	(–80.9)	(–82.7)	(–85.3)	(–86.8)	(–88.9)	(–99.9)	(–94.0)
Off-Budget	(–16.0)	(–16.9)	(–17.3)	(–18.0)	(–18.8)	(–19.5)	(–20.3)	(–21.2)	(–21.9)	(–22.6)	(–23.6)	(–26.1)
Total	**3,772.7**	**3,990.6**	**4,113.9**	**4,269.9**	**4,591.2**	**4,873.8**	**5,131.1**	**5,540.3**	**5,793.6**	**6,037.7**	**6,366.9**	**6,745.5**
On-Budget	(3,023.6)	(3,198.1)	(3,282.3)	(3,380.1)	(3,642.2)	(3,857.7)	(4,050.4)	(4,388.1)	(4,563.9)	(4,728.2)	(4,974.2)	(5,267.2)
Off-Budget	(749.1)	(792.5)	(831.6)	(889.8)	(949.0)	(1,016.1)	(1,080.8)	(1,152.2)	(1,229.7)	(1,309.5)	(1,392.7)	(1,478.4)
MEMORANDUM												
Discretionary Budget Authority:												
National Defense	585.9	606.9	610.9	609.9	624.2	639.5	654.8	725.8	743.2	761.2	779.5	798.3
International Affairs	54.2	54.7	55.7	56.7	57.9	59.0	60.3	61.6	62.9	64.2	65.6	67.0
Domestic	472.5	501.5	475.5	471.8	484.9	496.8	508.8	556.6	570.3	584.5	599.0	613.8
Total, Discretionary	1,112.5	1,163.0	1,142.1	1,138.4	1,166.9	1,195.3	1,223.9	1,343.9	1,376.4	1,409.9	1,444.0	1,479.1

Table 25–11. BUDGET AUTHORITY BY AGENCY IN THE ADJUSTED BASELINE
(In billions of dollars)

Agency	2015 Actual	Estimate										
		2016	2017	2018	2019	2020	2021	2022	2023	2024	2025	2026
Legislative Branch	4.5	4.6	4.7	4.9	5.0	5.1	5.3	5.4	5.6	5.7	5.9	6.0
Judicial Branch	7.4	7.6	7.8	8.0	8.3	8.5	8.8	9.0	9.3	9.6	9.9	10.1
Agriculture	142.5	164.0	157.9	155.5	155.9	157.2	159.6	161.1	163.3	165.0	165.9	167.8
Commerce	13.8	10.1	9.9	10.1	10.3	10.6	10.8	11.1	11.4	11.7	12.0	12.3
Defense—Military Programs	570.9	587.1	602.7	613.7	628.7	643.5	659.0	674.4	690.8	707.3	724.5	742.1
Education	87.3	78.0	74.5	77.9	83.4	86.2	88.7	90.0	91.2	92.7	94.8	97.6
Energy	25.4	28.9	29.3	28.9	29.2	30.2	30.1	30.6	30.1	30.2	30.8	33.7
Health and Human Services	1,045.2	1,116.8	1,141.1	1,149.8	1,239.8	1,323.8	1,398.4	1,526.5	1,590.4	1,647.2	1,793.4	1,908.3
Homeland Security	45.3	46.9	42.2	42.9	44.2	45.6	46.8	48.0	49.2	50.5	51.9	59.2
Housing and Urban Development	44.1	47.9	47.0	48.0	49.2	50.9	52.0	53.1	54.2	55.4	56.5	57.7
Interior	12.5	14.0	14.1	14.7	14.9	15.4	15.7	16.0	16.4	16.5	16.8	17.3
Justice	29.4	35.0	44.2	34.3	35.2	36.1	37.0	37.9	38.7	39.7	40.7	41.7
Labor	46.0	46.8	46.8	48.5	49.8	51.8	53.5	55.4	57.1	59.3	61.2	62.9
State	29.1	29.5	30.1	30.7	31.3	32.0	32.7	33.4	34.1	34.9	35.6	36.4
Transportation	71.9	75.8	77.6	79.1	81.0	82.8	83.4	84.0	84.5	85.1	85.8	85.1
Treasury	486.0	530.5	614.5	715.1	827.3	911.6	987.3	1,058.8	1,127.0	1,191.0	1,249.2	1,306.9
Veterans Affairs	160.5	163.9	181.9	185.2	197.9	207.2	216.6	226.8	237.3	248.1	260.6	272.0
Corps of Engineers—Civil Works	5.5	5.9	6.1	6.2	6.3	6.5	6.6	6.8	6.9	7.1	7.3	7.4
Other Defense Civil Programs	62.6	59.0	59.7	61.8	63.9	65.4	67.2	69.9	72.2	74.4	78.8	85.0
Environmental Protection Agency	7.8	8.1	8.4	8.5	8.7	8.9	9.1	9.3	9.5	9.8	10.0	10.3
Executive Office of the President	3.5	0.4	0.4	0.4	0.4	0.5	0.5	0.5	0.5	0.5	0.5	0.5
General Services Administration	-0.5	0.6	0.2	0.2	0.2	0.3	0.3	0.3	0.3	0.3	0.3	0.3
International Assistance Programs	32.7	30.1	28.5	13.6	15.9	18.8	21.4	23.6	25.6	27.0	28.0	29.0
National Aeronautics and Space Administration	18.0	19.3	19.7	20.1	20.5	21.0	21.5	22.0	22.5	23.0	23.5	24.0
National Science Foundation	7.5	7.6	7.7	7.8	8.0	8.2	8.3	8.5	8.7	8.8	9.0	9.2
Office of Personnel Management	92.4	93.7	96.7	103.4	107.5	111.9	115.9	120.4	124.8	129.6	134.4	139.6
Small Business Administration	-0.7	-0.5	0.9	0.9	0.9	1.0	1.0	1.0	1.0	1.1	1.1	1.1
Social Security Administration	950.4	994.8	1,032.0	1,092.2	1,162.4	1,232.5	1,301.4	1,380.9	1,455.5	1,533.5	1,625.0	1,715.7
On-Budget	(89.3)	(94.6)	(95.0)	(99.0)	(108.6)	(114.3)	(120.0)	(130.9)	(133.0)	(134.9)	(147.4)	(155.3)
Off-Budget	(861.1)	(900.2)	(937.0)	(993.2)	(1,053.8)	(1,118.2)	(1,181.4)	(1,250.0)	(1,322.5)	(1,398.6)	(1,477.6)	(1,560.4)
Other Independent Agencies	29.5	29.4	32.2	33.6	33.7	35.3	37.4	38.4	39.2	39.9	40.5	41.2
On-Budget	(29.5)	(29.6)	(31.9)	(33.3)	(33.5)	(35.0)	(37.1)	(38.1)	(38.8)	(39.5)	(40.2)	(40.9)
Off-Budget	....	(-0.1)	(0.3)	(0.3)	(0.3)	(0.3)	(0.3)	(0.3)	(0.3)	(0.3)	(0.3)	(0.3)
Allowances	....	7.5	-49.1	-82.2	-83.9	-86.4	-89.6	-2.8	-4.0	-4.7	-16.9	20.8
Undistributed Offsetting Receipts	-257.6	-252.6	-255.7	-243.9	-245.0	-248.4	-255.2	-259.9	-259.8	-262.4	-270.1	-256.1
On-Budget	(-145.6)	(-145.1)	(-150.0)	(-140.2)	(-139.9)	(-146.0)	(-154.3)	(-161.8)	(-166.7)	(-173.0)	(-185.0)	(-173.7)
Off-Budget	(-112.0)	(-107.6)	(-105.7)	(-103.7)	(-105.1)	(-102.4)	(-101.0)	(-98.1)	(-93.1)	(-89.4)	(-85.2)	(-82.4)
Total	**3,772.7**	**3,990.6**	**4,113.9**	**4,269.9**	**4,591.2**	**4,873.8**	**5,131.1**	**5,540.3**	**5,793.6**	**6,037.7**	**6,366.9**	**6,745.5**
(On-Budget)	(3,023.6)	(3,198.1)	(3,282.3)	(3,380.1)	(3,642.2)	(3,857.7)	(4,050.4)	(4,388.1)	(4,563.9)	(4,728.2)	(4,974.2)	(5,267.2)
(Off-Budget)	(749.1)	(792.5)	(831.6)	(889.8)	(949.0)	(1,016.1)	(1,080.8)	(1,152.2)	(1,229.7)	(1,309.5)	(1,392.7)	(1,478.4)

26. TRUST FUNDS AND FEDERAL FUNDS

As is common for State and local government budgets, the budget for the Federal Government contains information about collections and expenditures for different types of funds. This chapter presents summary information about the transactions of the two major fund groups used by the Federal Government, trust funds and Federal funds. It also presents information about the income and outgo of the major trust funds and a number of Federal funds that are financed by dedicated collections in a manner similar to trust funds.

The Federal Funds Group

The Federal funds group includes all financial transactions of the Government that are not required by law to be recorded in trust funds. It accounts for a larger share of the budget than the trust funds group.

The Federal funds group includes the "general fund," which is used for the general purposes of Government rather than being restricted by law to a specific program. The general fund is the largest fund in the Government and it receives all collections not dedicated for some other fund, including virtually all income taxes and many excise taxes. The general fund is used for all programs that are not supported by trust, special, or revolving funds.

The Federal funds group also includes special funds and revolving funds, both of which receive collections that are dedicated by law for specific purposes. Where the law requires that Federal fund collections be dedicated to a particular program, the collections and associated disbursements are recorded in special fund receipt and expenditure accounts.[1] An example is the portion of the Outer Continental Shelf mineral leasing receipts deposited into the Land and Water Conservation Fund. Money in special fund receipt accounts must be appropriated before it can be obligated and spent. The majority of special fund collections are derived from the Government's power to impose taxes or fines, or otherwise compel payment, as in the case of the Crime Victims Fund. In addition, a significant amount of collections credited to special funds is derived from certain types of business-like activity, such as the sale of Government land or other assets or the use of Government property. These collections include receipts from timber sales and royalties from oil and gas extraction.

Revolving funds are used to conduct continuing cycles of business-like activity. Revolving funds receive proceeds from the sale of products or services, and these proceeds finance ongoing activities that continue to provide products or services. Instead of being deposited in receipt accounts, the proceeds are recorded in revolving fund expenditure accounts. The proceeds are generally available for obligation and expenditure without further legislative action. Outlays for programs with revolving funds are reported both gross and net of these proceeds; gross outlays include the expenditures from the proceeds and net program outlays are derived by subtracting the proceeds from gross outlays. Because the proceeds of these sales are recorded as offsets to outlays within expenditure accounts rather than receipt accounts, the proceeds are known as "offsetting collections."[2] There are two classes of revolving funds in the Federal funds group. Public enterprise funds, such as the Postal Service Fund, conduct business-like operations mainly with the public. Intragovernmental funds, such as the Federal Buildings Fund, conduct business-like operations mainly within and between Government agencies.

The Trust Funds Group

The trust funds group consists of funds that are designated by law as trust funds. Like special funds and revolving funds, trust funds receive collections that are dedicated by law for specific purposes. Many of the larger trust funds are used to budget for social insurance programs, such as Social Security, Medicare, and unemployment compensation. Other large trust funds are used to budget for military and Federal civilian employees' retirement benefits, highway and transit construction and maintenance, and airport and airway development and maintenance. There are a few trust revolving funds that are credited with collections earmarked by law to carry out a cycle of business-type operations. There are also a few small trust funds that have been established to carry out the terms of a conditional gift or bequest.

There is no substantive difference between special funds in the Federal funds group and trust funds, or between revolving funds in the Federal funds group and trust revolving funds. Whether a particular fund is designated in law as a trust fund is, in many cases, arbitrary. For example, the National Service Life Insurance Fund is a trust fund, but the Servicemen's Group Life Insurance Fund is a Federal fund, even though both receive dedicated collections from veterans and both provide life insurance payments to veterans' beneficiaries.

The Federal Government uses the term "trust fund" differently than the way in which it is commonly used. In common usage, the term is used to refer to a private fund that has a beneficiary who owns the trust's income and may also own the trust's assets. A custodian or trustee

---

[1] There are two types of budget accounts: expenditure (or appropriation) accounts and receipt accounts. Expenditure accounts are used to record outlays and receipt accounts are used to record governmental receipts and offsetting receipts. For further detail on expenditure and receipt accounts, see Chapter 9, "Budget Concepts," in this volume.

[2] See Chapter 13 in this volume for more information on offsetting collections and offsetting receipts.

Table 26–1. RECEIPTS, OUTLAYS AND SURPLUS OR DEFICIT BY FUND GROUP

(In billions of dollars)

	2015 Actual	Estimate					
		2016	2017	2018	2019	2020	2021
Receipts:							
Federal funds cash income:							
From the public	2,468.4	2,506.9	2,776.6	2,963.0	3,108.6	3,316.8	3,477.3
From trust funds	1.5	1.1	1.4	1.4	1.3	1.4	1.4
Total, Federal funds cash income	2,469.9	2,508.1	2,778.0	2,964.4	3,109.9	3,318.2	3,478.8
Trust funds cash income:							
From the public	1,297.5	1,338.9	1,401.1	1,468.8	1,533.0	1,602.1	1,689.5
From Federal funds:							
Interest	141.8	151.5	147.3	141.8	148.0	149.0	154.0
Other	513.2	639.2	584.4	637.8	697.6	727.8	763.9
Total, Trust funds cash income	1,952.5	2,129.5	2,132.9	2,248.3	2,378.6	2,478.9	2,607.3
Offsetting collections from the public and offsetting receipts:							
Federal funds	–348.8	–337.7	–350.3	–341.6	–346.3	–359.3	–367.5
Trust funds	–823.8	–964.4	–916.9	–972.6	–1,047.2	–1,092.0	–1,146.6
Total, offsetting collections from the public and offsetting receipts	–1,172.5	–1,302.1	–1,267.2	–1,314.1	–1,393.5	–1,451.4	–1,514.1
Total, unified budget receipts	3,249.9	3,335.5	3,643.7	3,898.6	4,095.1	4,345.7	4,572.0
Federal funds	2,121.1	2,170.3	2,427.8	2,622.9	2,763.6	2,958.8	3,111.3
Trust funds	1,128.7	1,165.2	1,216.0	1,275.8	1,331.4	1,386.9	1,460.7
Outlays:							
Federal funds cash outgo	3,019.9	3,310.6	3,391.9	3,553.0	3,769.3	3,927.7	4,094.2
Trust funds cash outgo	1,840.9	1,942.8	2,022.5	2,113.3	2,268.5	2,403.5	2,544.1
Offsetting collections from the public and offsetting receipts:							
Federal funds	–348.8	–337.7	–350.3	–341.6	–346.3	–359.3	–367.5
Trust funds	–823.8	–964.4	–916.9	–972.6	–1,047.2	–1,092.0	–1,146.6
Total, offsetting collections from the public and receipts	–1,172.5	–1,302.1	–1,267.2	–1,314.1	–1,393.5	–1,451.4	–1,514.1
Total, unified budget outlays	3,688.3	3,951.3	4,147.2	4,352.2	4,644.3	4,879.8	5,124.2
Federal funds	2,671.1	2,972.9	3,041.6	3,211.5	3,423.0	3,568.3	3,726.7
Trust funds	1,017.2	978.4	1,105.6	1,140.8	1,221.3	1,311.5	1,397.5
Surplus or deficit(–):							
Federal funds	–550.0	–802.6	–613.9	–588.6	–659.4	–609.5	–615.4
Trust funds	111.6	186.8	110.4	135.0	110.1	75.4	63.2
Total, unified surplus/deficit(–)	–438.4	–615.8	–503.5	–453.6	–549.3	–534.1	–552.3

Note: Receipts include governmental, interfund, and proprietary, and exclude intrafund receipts (which are offset against intrafund payments so that cash income and cash outgo are not overstated).

manages the assets on behalf of the beneficiary according to the terms of the trust agreement, as established by a trustor. Neither the trustee nor the beneficiary can change the terms of the trust agreement; only the trustor can change the terms of the agreement. In contrast, the Federal Government owns and manages the assets and the earnings of most Federal trust funds and can unilaterally change the law to raise or lower future trust fund collections and payments or change the purpose for which the collections are used. Only a few small Federal trust funds are managed pursuant to a trust agreement whereby the Government acts as the trustee; even then the Government generally owns the funds and has some ability to alter the amount deposited into or paid out of the funds.

Deposit funds, which are funds held by the Government as a custodian on behalf of individuals or a non-Federal entity, are similar to private-sector trust funds. The Government makes no decisions about the amount of money placed in deposit funds or about how the proceeds are spent. For this reason, these funds are not classified as Federal trust funds, but are instead considered to be non-budgetary and excluded from the Federal budget.[3]

The income of a Federal Government trust fund must be used for the purposes specified in law. The income of some trust funds, such as the Federal Employees Health Benefits fund, is spent almost as quickly as it is collected. In other cases, such as the Social Security and Federal civilian employees' retirement trust funds, the trust fund income is not spent as quickly as it is collected. Currently, these funds do not use all of their annual income (which includes intragovernmental interest income). This surplus of income over outgo adds to the trust fund's balance, which is available for future expenditures. The balances

---

[3] Deposit funds are discussed briefly in Chapter 10 of this volume, "Coverage of the Budget."

are generally required by law to be invested in Federal securities issued by the Department of the Treasury.[4] The National Railroad Retirement Investment Trust is a rare example of a Government trust fund authorized to invest balances in equity markets.

A trust fund normally consists of one or more receipt accounts (to record income) and an expenditure account (to record outgo). However, a few trust funds, such as the Veterans Special Life Insurance fund, are established by law as trust revolving funds. Such a fund is similar to a revolving fund in the Federal funds group in that it may consist of a single account to record both income and outgo. Trust revolving funds are used to conduct a cycle of business-type operations; offsetting collections are credited to the funds (which are also expenditure accounts) and the funds' outlays are displayed net of the offsetting collections.

Income and Outgo by Fund Group

Table 26–1 shows income, outgo, and the surplus or deficit by fund group and in the aggregate (netted to avoid double-counting) from which the total unified budget receipts, outlays, and surplus or deficit are derived. Income consists mostly of governmental receipts (derived from governmental activity, primarily income, payroll, and excise taxes). Income also includes offsetting receipts, which include proprietary receipts (derived from business-like transactions with the public), interfund collections (derived from payments from a fund in one fund group to a fund in the other fund group), and gifts. Outgo consists of payments made to the public or to a fund in the other fund group.

Two types of transactions are treated specially in the table. First, income and outgo for each fund group exclude all transactions that occur between funds within the same fund group.[5] These intrafund transactions constitute outgo and income for the individual funds that make and collect the payments, but they are offsetting within the fund group as a whole. The totals for each fund group measure only the group's transactions with the public and the other fund group. Second, outgo is calculated net of the collections from Federal sources that are credited to expenditure accounts (which, as noted above, are referred to as offsetting collections); the spending that is financed by those collections is included in outgo and the collections from Federal sources are subsequently subtracted from outgo.[6] Although it would be conceptually correct to

add interfund offsetting collections from Federal sources to income for a particular fund, this cannot be done at the present time because the budget data do not provide this type of detail. As a result, both interfund and intrafund offsetting collections from Federal sources are offset against outgo in Table 26–1 and are not shown separately.

The vast majority of the interfund transactions in the table are payments by the Federal funds to the trust funds. These payments include interest payments from the general fund to the trust funds for interest earned on trust fund balances invested in interest-bearing Treasury securities. The payments also include payments by Federal agencies to Federal employee benefits trust funds and Social Security trust funds on behalf of current employees and general fund transfers to employee retirement trust funds to amortize the unfunded liabilities of these funds. In addition, the payments include general fund transfers to the Supplementary Medical Insurance trust fund for the cost of Medicare Parts B (outpatient and physician benefits) and D (prescription drug benefits) that is not covered by premiums (or, for Part D, transfers from States).

In addition to investing their balances with the Treasury, some funds in the Federal funds group and most trust funds are authorized to borrow from the general fund of the Treasury.[7] Similar to the treatment of funds invested with the Treasury, borrowed funds are not recorded as receipts of the fund or included in the income of the fund. Rather, the borrowed funds finance outlays by the fund in excess of available receipts. Subsequently, any excess fund receipts are transferred from the fund to the general fund in repayment of the borrowing. The repayment is not recorded as an outlay of the fund or included in fund outgo. This treatment is consistent with the broad principle that borrowing and debt redemption are not budgetary transactions but rather a means of financing deficits or disposing of surpluses.[8]

Some income in both Federal funds and trust funds consists of offsetting receipts.[9] Offsetting receipts are not considered governmental receipts (such as taxes), but they are instead recorded on the outlay side of the budget. Expenditures resulting from offsetting receipts are recorded as gross outlays and the collections of offsetting receipts are then subtracted from gross outlays to derive net outlays. Net outlays reflect the government's net transactions with the public.

As shown in Table 26-1, 35 percent of all governmental receipts were deposited in trust funds in 2015 and the remaining 65 percent of governmental receipts were de-

---

[4] Securities held by trust funds (and by other Government accounts), debt held by the public, and gross Federal debt are discussed in Chapter 4 of this volume, "Federal Borrowing and Debt."

[5] For example, the railroad retirement trust funds pay the equivalent of Social Security benefits to railroad retirees in addition to the regular railroad pension. These benefits are financed by a payment from the Federal Old-Age and Survivors Insurance trust fund to the railroad retirement trust funds. The payment and collection are not included in Table 26–1 so that the total trust fund income and outgo shown in the table reflect disbursements to the public and to Federal funds.

[6] Collections from non-Federal sources are shown as income and spending that is financed by those collections is shown as outgo. For example, postage stamp fees are deposited as offsetting collections in the Postal Service Fund. As a result, the Fund's income reported in Table 26–1 includes Postage stamp fees and the Fund's outgo is gross disbursements, including disbursements financed by those fees.

[7] For example, the Unemployment trust fund is authorized to borrow from the general fund for unemployment benefits; the Bonneville Power Administration Fund, a revolving fund in the Department of Energy, is authorized to borrow from the general fund; and the Black Lung Disability Trust Fund, a trust fund in the Department of Labor, is authorized to receive appropriations of repayable advances from the general fund, which constitutes a form of borrowing.

[8] Borrowing and debt repayment are discussed in Chapter 4 of this volume, "Federal Borrowing and Debt," and Chapter 9 of this volume, "Budget Concepts."

[9] Interest on borrowed funds is an example of an intragovernmental offsetting receipt and Medicare Part B's premiums are an example of offsetting receipts from the public.

Table 26-2. COMPARISON OF TOTAL FEDERAL FUND AND TRUST FUND RECEIPTS TO UNIFIED BUDGET RECEIPTS, FISCAL YEAR 2015

(In billions of dollars)

Gross Trust fund receipts	1,938.6
Gross Federal fund receipts	2,280.0
Total, gross receipts	4,218.6
Deduct intrafund receipts (from funds within same fund group):	
Trust fund intrafund receipts	–6.0
Federal fund intrafund receipts	–24.0
Subtotal, intrafund receipts	–30.0
Total Trust funds and Federal Funds cash income	4,188.5
Deduct other offsetting receipts:	
Trust fund receipts from Federal funds:	
Interest in receipt accounts	–141.8
General fund payments to Medicare Parts B and D	–263.5
Employing agencies' payments for pensions, Social Security, and Medicare	–73.9
General fund payments for unfunded liabilities of Federal employees' retirement funds	–112.1
Transfer of taxation of Social Security and RRB benefits to OASDI, HI, and RRB	–51.6
Other receipts from Federal funds	–12.1
Subtotal, Trust fund receipts from Federal funds	–655.0
Federal fund receipts from Trust funds	–1.5
Proprietary receipts	–252.7
Offsetting governmental receipts	–29.5
Subtotal, offsetting receipts	–938.6
Unified budget receipts	3,249.9

Note: Offsetting receipts are included in cash income for each fund group, but are deducted from outlays in the unified budget.

posited in Federal funds, which, as noted above, include the general fund. As noted above, most outlays between the trust fund and Federal fund groups (interfund outlays) flow from Federal funds to trust funds, rather than from trust funds to Federal funds. As a result, while trust funds account for 28 percent of total 2015 outlays, they account for 34 percent of 2015 outlays net of interfund transactions.

Because the income for Federal funds and trust funds recorded in Table 26–1 includes offsetting receipts and offsetting collections from the public, offsetting receipts and offsetting collections from the public must be deducted from the two fund groups' combined gross income in order to reconcile to total governmental receipts in the unified budget. Similarly, because the outgo for Federal funds and trust funds in Table 26–1 consists of outlays gross of offsetting receipts and offsetting collections from the public, the amount of the offsetting receipts and offsetting collections from the public must be deducted from the sum of the Federal funds' and the trust funds' gross outgo in order to reconcile to total (net) unified budget outlays. Table 26–2 reconciles, for fiscal year 2015, the gross total of all trust fund and Federal fund receipts with the receipt total of the unified budget.

Income, Outgo, and Balances of Trust Funds

Table 26–3 shows, for the trust funds group as a whole, the funds' balance at the start of each year, income and

outgo during the year, and the end-of-year balance. Income and outgo are divided between transactions with the public and transactions with Federal funds. Receipts from Federal funds are divided between interest and other interfund receipts.

The definitions of income and outgo in this table differ from those in Table 26–1 in one important way. Trust fund collections that are offset against outgo (offsetting collections from Federal sources) within expenditure accounts instead of being deposited in separate receipt accounts are classified as income in this table, but not in Table 26–1. This classification is consistent with the definitions of income and outgo for trust funds used elsewhere in the budget. It has the effect of increasing both income and outgo by the amount of the offsetting collections from Federal sources. The difference was approximately $47 billion in 2015. Table 26–3, therefore, provides a more complete summary of trust fund income and outgo.

The trust funds group ran a surplus of $112 billion in 2015, and is expected to continue to run surpluses over the next several years. The resulting growth in trust fund balances continues a trend that has persisted over the past several decades. The size of these balances is largely the consequence of changes in the way some trust funds (primarily Social Security and the Federal retirement funds) are financed.

Because of these changes and economic growth (both real and inflationary), trust fund balances increased from $205 billion in 1982 to $4.7 trillion in 2015. The current balances are estimated to increase by approximately 14 percent by the year 2021, rising to $5.4 trillion. Almost all of these balances are invested in Treasury securities and earn interest. The balances represent the value, in current dollars, of the unspent portion of (1) taxes and fees received by the Government and dedicated to trust funds and (2) intragovernmental payments (from the general fund and from agency appropriations) to the trust funds.

Until the 1980s, most trust funds operated on a pay-as-you-go basis as distinct from a pre-funded basis. Taxes and fees were set at levels sufficient to finance current program expenditures and administrative expenses, and to maintain balances generally equal to one year's worth of expenditures (to provide for unexpected events). As a result, trust fund balances tended to grow at about the same rate as the fund's annual expenditures.

For some of the larger trust funds, pay-as-you-go financing was replaced in the 1980s by full or partial advance funding. The Social Security Amendments of 1983 raised payroll taxes above the levels necessary to finance current expenditures. Similarly, in 1985, a new system took effect that funded military retirement benefits on a full accrual basis and, in 1986, full accrual funding of retirement benefits was mandated for Federal civilian employees hired after December 31, 1983. The two retirement programs now require Federal agencies and employees together to pay the trust funds that disburse Federal civilian and military retirement benefits an amount equal to those accruing retirement benefits. Since many years will pass between the time when benefits are earned (or accrued) and when they are paid, the trust funds will accumulate substantial balances over time.

From the perspective of the trust fund, these balances represent the value, in today's dollars, of past taxes, fees, and other income that the trust fund has received in excess of past spending. Trust fund assets held in Treasury bonds are legal claims on the Treasury, similar to bonds issued to the public. Like all other fund assets, these are available to the fund for future benefit payments and other expenditures.

However, from the perspective of the Government as a whole, the trust fund balances do not represent net additions to the Government's balance sheet. The trust fund balances are assets of the agencies responsible for administering the trust fund programs and liabilities of the Department of the Treasury.[10] These assets and liabilities cancel each other out in the Government-wide balance sheet. When trust fund holdings are redeemed to fund the payment of benefits, the Department of the Treasury finances the expenditure in the same way as any other Federal expenditure—by using current receipts if the unified budget is in surplus or by borrowing from the public if it is in deficit. Therefore, the existence of large trust fund balances, while representing a legal claim on the Treasury, does not, by itself, determine the Government's ability to pay benefits. From an economic standpoint, the Government is able to pre-fund benefits only by increasing saving and investment in the economy as a whole,

---

[10] The effects of Treasury debt held by trust funds and other Government accounts are discussed further in Chapter 4 of this volume, "Federal Borrowing and Debt."

which increases future national income and, as a result, strengthens the Nation's ability to support future benefits. This can be accomplished by simultaneously running trust fund surpluses while maintaining an unchanged Federal fund surplus or deficit, so that the trust fund surplus reduces the unified budget deficit or increases the unified budget surplus.

This demonstrates the need to follow a fiscal policy that is consistent with the Government's obligation to repay the bonds when needed to pay benefits in the future. This means saving more now before the obligations become due and pursuing policies that will increase long-run growth and national income. Otherwise, the Nation will have fewer resources available in the future to meet its obligations and will face more difficult choices among cutting spending, raising taxes, or borrowing from private credit markets.

Table 26–4 shows estimates of income, outgo, surplus or deficit, and balances for 2015 through 2021 for the major trust funds. With the exception of transactions between trust funds, the data for the individual trust funds are conceptually the same as the data in Table 26–3 for the trust funds group. As explained previously, transactions between trust funds are shown as outgo of the fund that makes the payment and as income of the fund that collects it in the data for an individual trust fund, but the collections are offset against outgo in the data for the trust fund group as a whole.

As noted above, trust funds are funded by a combination of payments from the public and payments from Federal funds, including payments directly from the

Table 26–3.   INCOME, OUTGO, AND BALANCES OF TRUST FUNDS GROUP
(In billions of dollars)

	2015 Actual	Estimate					
		2016	2017	2018	2019	2020	2021
Balance, start of year	4,603.2	4,702.4	4,881.4	4,991.8	5,126.8	5,236.9	5,312.3
Adjustments to balances	0.2	....	....	....	....	....	....
Total balance, start of year	4,603.4	4,702.4	4,881.4	4,991.8	5,126.8	5,236.9	5,312.3
Income:							
Governmental receipts	1,128.7	1,165.2	1,216.0	1,275.8	1,331.4	1,386.9	1,460.7
Offsetting governmental	18.7	13.0	13.4	7.4	*	*	*
Proprietary	150.1	159.0	170.9	184.7	200.6	214.3	227.8
From Federal funds:							
Interest	142.5	154.2	149.6	144.5	150.9	152.1	157.6
Other	559.9	688.2	637.0	692.2	754.5	787.4	826.3
Total income during the year	1,999.9	2,179.5	2,186.8	2,304.6	2,437.5	2,540.7	2,672.5
Outgo (–)	–1,888.4	–1,992.7	–2,076.4	–2,169.6	–2,327.4	–2,465.4	–2,609.3
Change in fund balance:							
Surplus or deficit(–):							
Excluding interest	–30.9	32.6	–39.2	–9.5	–40.8	–76.8	–94.4
Interest	142.5	154.2	149.6	144.5	150.9	152.1	157.6
Subtotal, surplus or deficit (–)	111.6	186.8	110.4	135.0	110.1	75.4	63.2
Borrowing, transfers, lapses, & other adjustments	–12.6	–7.8	*	....	....	....	....
Total change in fund balance	99.0	179.0	110.4	135.0	110.1	75.4	63.2
Balance, end of year	4,702.4	4,881.4	4,991.8	5,126.8	5,236.9	5,312.3	5,375.4

* $50 million or less.

NOTE: In contrast to table 26-1, income also includes income that is offset within expenditure accounts as offsetting collections from Federal sources, instead of being deposited in receipt accounts.

general fund and payments from agency appropriations. Similarly, the fund outgo amounts in Table 26-4 represent both outflows to the public—such as for the provision of benefit payments or the purchase of goods or services— and outflows to other Government accounts—such as for reimbursement for services provided by other agencies or payment of interest on borrowing from Treasury.

Because trust funds and Federal special and revolving funds conduct transactions both with the public and with other Government accounts, the surplus or deficit of an individual fund may differ from the fund's impact on the surplus or deficit of the Federal Government. Transactions with the public affect both the surplus or deficit of an individual fund and the Federal Government surplus or deficit. Transactions with other government accounts affect the surplus or deficit of the particular fund. However, because that same transaction is offset in another government account, there is no net impact on the total Federal Government surplus or deficit.

A brief description of the major trust funds is given below; additional information for these and other trust funds can be found in the Status of Funds tables in the *Budget Appendix.*

- Social Security Trust Funds: The Social Security trust funds consist of the Old Age and Survivors Insurance (OASI) trust fund and the Disability Insurance (DI) trust fund. The trust funds are funded by payroll taxes from employers and employees, interest earnings on trust fund balances, Federal agency payments as employers, and a portion of the income taxes paid on Social Security benefits. The 2014 and 2015 Social Security Trustees' reports projected that on a stand-alone basis, the DI trust fund would be unable to pay full benefits under current law starting in 2016. The Bipartisan Budget Act of 2015 included a provision to bolster the DI fund by reallocating a portion of Social Security payroll taxes from the OASI trust fund to the DI trust fund in calendar years 2016 through 2018. Similar reallocation measures have been taken in the past to prevent depletion of the DI fund. The Social Security trustees project that this change will extend the ability of the DI trust fund to pay full benefits until the second half of calendar year 2022.

- Medicare Trust Funds: Like the Social Security trust funds, the Medicare Hospital Insurance (HI) trust fund is funded by payroll taxes from employers and employees, Federal agency payments as employers, and a portion of the income taxes paid on Social Security benefits. The HI trust fund also receives transfers from the general fund of the Treasury for certain HI benefits. In addition, the Budget proposes that the HI trust fund receive income taxes attributable to taxes on net investment income as

an additional dedicated financing source. The other Medicare trust fund, Supplementary Medical Insurance (SMI), finances Part B (outpatient and physician benefits) and Part D (prescription drug benefits). SMI receives premium payments from covered individuals, transfers from States toward Part D benefits, and transfers from the general fund of the Treasury for the portion of Part B and Part D costs not covered by premiums or transfers from States. In addition, like other trust funds, these two trust funds receive interest earnings on their trust fund balances.

- Transportation Trust Fund: The Budget proposes to replace the existing Highway Trust Fund with a new Transportation Trust Fund. The existing Highway Trust Fund is financed by the gasoline tax and, in recent years, by general fund transfers as those taxes have proven inadequate to support current levels of investment. Under the Budget's 21st Century Clean Transportation Plan, the Transportation Trust Fund would also receive a portion of a new oil fee of $10.25 per barrel, along with a portion of transition revenues from business tax reform, to improve infrastructure condition and performance, expand clean, reliable, and safe transportation options like transit and rail for American families, and provide sustainable levels of revenue for future surface transportation spending. This proposal is discussed in more detail in Chapter 11, "Budget Process," in this volume.

- Unemployment Trust Fund: The Unemployment Trust Fund is funded by taxes on employers, payments from Federal agencies, taxes on certain employees, and interest earnings on trust fund balances.

- Civilian and military retirement trust funds: The Civil Service Retirement and Disability Fund is funded by employee and agency payments, general fund transfers for the unfunded portion of retirement costs, and interest earnings on trust fund balances. The Military Retirement Fund likewise is funded by payments from the Department of Defense, general fund transfers for unfunded retirement costs, and interest earnings on trust fund balances.

Table 26-5 shows income, outgo, and balances of two Federal funds that are designated as special funds. These funds are similar to trust funds in that they are financed by dedicated receipts, the excess of income over outgo is invested in Treasury securities, the interest earnings add to fund balances, and the balances remain available to cover future expenditures. The table is illustrative of the Federal funds group, which includes many revolving funds and special funds.

Table 26–4. INCOME, OUTGO, AND BALANCE OF MAJOR TRUST FUNDS
(In billions of dollars)

	2015 Actual	Estimate					
		2016	2017	2018	2019	2020	2021
Airport and Airway Trust Fund							
Balance, start of year	14.2	14.1	14.3	15.4	17.2	19.4	22.2
Adjustments to balances	....	....	....	....	....	....	....
Total balance, start of year	14.2	14.1	14.3	15.4	17.2	19.4	22.2
Income:							
Governmental receipts	14.3	14.4	15.1	15.6	16.1	16.8	17.3
Offsetting governmental	....	....	....	....	....	....	....
Proprietary	*	*	*	*	*	*	*
Intrabudgetary:							
Intrafund	....	....	....	....	....	....	....
Interest	0.3	0.3	0.3	0.4	0.5	0.6	0.8
Other intrabudgetary	*	*	*	*	*	*	*
Total income during the year	14.6	14.7	15.4	16.1	16.7	17.4	18.1
Outgo (–)	–14.7	–14.5	–14.3	–14.3	–14.4	–14.7	–14.7
Change in fund balance:							
Surplus or deficit(–):							
Excluding interest	–0.4	–0.1	0.8	1.4	1.7	2.2	2.7
Interest	0.3	0.3	0.3	0.4	0.5	0.6	0.8
Subtotal, surplus or deficit (–)	–0.1	0.2	1.1	1.8	2.2	2.8	3.4
Borrowing, transfers, lapses, & other adjustments	–*	....	....	....	....	....	....
Total change in fund balance	–0.1	0.2	1.1	1.8	2.2	2.8	3.4
Balance, end of year	14.1	14.3	15.4	17.2	19.4	22.2	25.6
Civil Service Retirement and Disability Fund							
Balance, start of year	857.2	871.9	888.7	903.5	916.6	929.2	941.2
Adjustments to balances	–*	....	....	....	....	....	....
Total balance, start of year	857.2	871.9	888.7	903.5	916.6	929.2	941.2
Income:							
Governmental receipts	3.6	3.8	4.2	4.5	4.8	5.1	5.5
Offsetting governmental	....	....	....	....	....	....	....
Proprietary	....	....	....	....	....	....	....
Intrabudgetary:							
Intrafund	....	....	....	....	....	....	....
Interest	29.2	29.2	27.8	27.7	28.2	29.0	29.8
Other intrabudgetary	63.7	66.6	67.8	68.8	70.4	71.9	72.7
Total income during the year	96.6	99.6	99.8	100.9	103.4	105.9	108.0
Outgo (–)	–81.9	–82.8	–84.9	–87.8	–90.8	–94.0	–97.1
Change in fund balance:							
Surplus or deficit(–):							
Excluding interest	–14.6	–12.4	–12.9	–14.6	–15.6	–17.0	–18.9
Interest	29.2	29.2	27.8	27.7	28.2	29.0	29.8
Subtotal, surplus or deficit (–)	14.7	16.8	14.8	13.1	12.6	12.0	10.9
Borrowing, transfers, lapses, & other adjustments	....	....	....	....	....	....	....
Total change in fund balance	14.7	16.8	14.8	13.1	12.6	12.0	10.9
Balance, end of year	871.9	888.7	903.5	916.6	929.2	941.2	952.1

Table 26–4. INCOME, OUTGO, AND BALANCE OF MAJOR TRUST FUNDS—Continued
(In billions of dollars)

	2015 Actual	Estimate					
		2016	2017	2018	2019	2020	2021
Employees and Retired Employees Health Benefits Funds							
Balance, start of year	23.6	23.0	24.0	24.5	25.3	25.7	26.2
Adjustments to balances	....	....	....	....	....	....	....
Total balance, start of year	23.6	23.0	24.0	24.5	25.3	25.7	26.2
Income:							
Governmental receipts	....	....	....	....	....	....	....
Offsetting governmental	....	....	....	....	....	....	....
Proprietary	13.9	15.1	16.1	16.9	17.9	18.9	20.0
Intrabudgetary:							
Intrafund	....	....	....	....	....	....	....
Interest	0.2	0.5	0.6	0.7	0.8	1.0	1.0
Other intrabudgetary	33.7	35.6	37.7	39.8	42.0	44.5	47.0
Total income during the year	47.9	51.2	54.4	57.5	60.7	64.4	68.0
Outgo (–)	–48.4	–50.2	–53.8	–56.7	–60.3	–63.9	–67.3
Change in fund balance:							
Surplus or deficit(–):							
Excluding interest	–0.8	0.4	–*	*	–0.4	–0.5	–0.2
Interest	0.2	0.5	0.6	0.7	0.8	1.0	1.0
Subtotal, surplus or deficit (–)	–0.5	1.0	0.5	0.7	0.4	0.5	0.7
Borrowing, transfers, lapses, & other adjustments	....	....	....	....	....	....	....
Total change in fund balance	–0.5	1.0	0.5	0.7	0.4	0.5	0.7
Balance, end of year	23.0	24.0	24.5	25.3	25.7	26.2	26.9
Foreign Military Sales Trust Fund							
Balance, start of year	21.7	25.7	32.4	31.8	29.0	26.7	25.1
Adjustments to balances	....	....	....	....	....	....	....
Total balance, start of year	21.7	25.7	32.4	31.8	29.0	26.7	25.1
Income:							
Governmental receipts	....	....	....	....	....	....	....
Offsetting governmental	....	....	....	....	....	....	....
Proprietary	32.4	36.0	37.4	36.0	34.1	31.7	29.7
Intrabudgetary:							
Intrafund	....	....	....	....	....	....	....
Interest	....	....	....	....	....	....	....
Other intrabudgetary	....	....	....	....	....	....	....
Total income during the year	32.4	36.0	37.4	36.0	34.1	31.7	29.7
Outgo (–)	–28.4	–29.3	–38.0	–38.8	–36.4	–33.3	–30.5
Change in fund balance:							
Surplus or deficit(–):							
Excluding interest	4.0	6.6	–0.6	–2.8	–2.3	–1.6	–0.7
Interest	....	....	....	....	....	....	....
Subtotal, surplus or deficit (–)	4.0	6.6	–0.6	–2.8	–2.3	–1.6	–0.7
Borrowing, transfers, lapses, & other adjustments	....	....	....	....	....	....	....
Total change in fund balance	4.0	6.6	–0.6	–2.8	–2.3	–1.6	–0.7
Balance, end of year	25.7	32.4	31.8	29.0	26.7	25.1	24.3

Table 26–4. INCOME, OUTGO, AND BALANCE OF MAJOR TRUST FUNDS—Continued
(In billions of dollars)

	2015 Actual	Estimate					
		2016	2017	2018	2019	2020	2021
Medicare: Hospital Insurance (HI) Trust Fund							
Balance, start of year	202.4	196.1	190.1	192.4	224.9	279.3	334.9
Adjustments to balances	....	....	....	....	....	....	....
Total balance, start of year	202.4	196.1	190.1	192.4	224.9	279.3	334.9
Income:							
Governmental receipts	234.7	244.3	254.6	266.2	278.4	289.5	304.8
Offsetting governmental	....	....	....	....	....	....	....
Proprietary	8.5	9.8	10.0	10.3	10.5	10.8	11.0
Intrabudgetary:							
Intrafund	....	....	....	....	....	....	....
Interest	8.6	8.1	8.1	7.8	7.7	7.6	7.3
Other intrabudgetary	25.4	29.6	32.3	58.8	90.4	97.5	104.8
Total income during the year	277.2	291.8	305.0	343.0	387.0	405.4	427.9
Outgo (–)	–283.5	–297.7	–302.8	–310.5	–332.6	–349.8	–370.8
Change in fund balance:							
Surplus or deficit(–):							
Excluding interest	–14.9	–14.0	–5.8	24.7	46.7	48.0	49.8
Interest	8.6	8.1	8.1	7.8	7.7	7.6	7.3
Subtotal, surplus or deficit (–)	–6.3	–5.9	2.3	32.5	54.4	55.6	57.1
Borrowing, transfers, lapses, & other adjustments	–*						
Total change in fund balance	–6.3	–5.9	2.3	32.5	54.4	55.6	57.1
Balance, end of year	196.1	190.1	192.4	224.9	279.3	334.9	392.0
Medicare: Supplementary Insurance (SMI) Trust Fund							
Balance, start of year	71.3	69.1	80.3	71.2	84.7	88.0	90.6
Adjustments to balances	....	....	....	....	....	....	....
Total balance, start of year	71.3	69.1	80.3	71.2	84.7	88.0	90.6
Income:							
Governmental receipts	3.0	3.0	4.0	4.1	2.8	2.8	2.8
Offsetting governmental	....	....	....	....	....	....	....
Proprietary	85.8	91.9	100.9	114.8	131.3	146.1	160.2
Intrabudgetary:							
Intrafund	....	....	....	....	....	....	....
Interest	2.5	1.9	2.1	1.3	1.3	1.5	2.8
Other intrabudgetary	263.5	313.7	297.0	315.7	340.5	362.2	387.8
Total income during the year	354.7	410.5	403.9	436.0	475.9	512.7	553.6
Outgo (–)	–357.0	–399.3	–413.1	–422.5	–472.6	–510.0	–551.6
Change in fund balance:							
Surplus or deficit(–):							
Excluding interest	–4.7	9.3	–11.3	12.2	2.1	1.1	–0.8
Interest	2.5	1.9	2.1	1.3	1.3	1.5	2.8
Subtotal, surplus or deficit (–)	–2.2	11.2	–9.2	13.5	3.3	2.6	2.1
Borrowing, transfers, lapses, & other adjustments	....	....	....	....	....	....	....
Total change in fund balance	–2.2	11.2	–9.2	13.5	3.3	2.6	2.1
Balance, end of year	69.1	80.3	71.2	84.7	88.0	90.6	92.7

Table 26–4.   INCOME, OUTGO, AND BALANCE OF MAJOR TRUST FUNDS—Continued
(In billions of dollars)

	2015 Actual	Estimate					
		2016	2017	2018	2019	2020	2021
Military Retirement Fund							
Balance, start of year	478.1	525.9	589.0	656.5	727.1	799.2	875.4
Adjustments to balances	....	....	....	....	....	....	....
Total balance, start of year	478.1	525.9	589.0	656.5	727.1	799.2	875.4
Income:							
Governmental receipts	....	....	....	....	....	....	....
Offsetting governmental	....	....	....	....	....	....	....
Proprietary	....	....	....	....	....	....	....
Intrabudgetary:							
Intrafund	....	....	....	....	....	....	....
Interest	3.1	18.9	18.0	16.1	20.8	23.6	28.0
Other intrabudgetary	101.4	105.6	107.7	109.5	112.5	115.7	119.1
Total income during the year	104.6	124.5	125.7	125.5	133.2	139.2	147.2
Outgo (–)	–56.7	–61.5	–58.2	–54.9	–61.2	–63.0	–65.0
Change in fund balance:							
Surplus or deficit(–):							
Excluding interest	44.7	44.1	49.5	54.6	51.3	52.6	54.2
Interest	3.1	18.9	18.0	16.1	20.8	23.6	28.0
Subtotal, surplus or deficit (–)	47.9	63.0	67.5	70.6	72.1	76.2	82.2
Borrowing, transfers, lapses, & other adjustments	....	....	....	....	....	....	....
Total change in fund balance	47.9	63.0	67.5	70.6	72.1	76.2	82.2
Balance, end of year	525.9	589.0	656.5	727.1	799.2	875.4	957.6
Railroad Retirement Trust Funds							
Balance, start of year	23.2	21.9	21.2	20.1	19.4	18.6	17.9
Adjustments to balances	0.1	....	....	....	....	....	....
Total balance, start of year	23.3	21.9	21.2	20.1	19.4	18.6	17.9
Income:							
Governmental receipts	5.9	5.9	6.0	6.1	6.3	6.5	6.6
Offsetting governmental	....	....	....	....	....	....	....
Proprietary	....	....	....	....	....	....	....
Intrabudgetary:							
Intrafund	4.7	4.6	4.3	4.7	4.7	4.9	4.8
Interest	–0.3	1.7	0.8	0.9	0.9	0.9	0.9
Other intrabudgetary	0.9	0.9	0.9	0.9	0.9	1.0	1.0
Total income during the year	11.1	13.0	12.0	12.6	12.9	13.2	13.4
Outgo (–)	–12.6	–13.7	–13.0	–13.4	–13.7	–14.0	–14.2
Change in fund balance:							
Surplus or deficit(–):							
Excluding interest	–1.1	–2.3	–1.9	–1.6	–1.7	–1.7	–1.8
Interest	–0.3	1.7	0.8	0.9	0.9	0.9	0.9
Subtotal, surplus or deficit (–)	–1.4	–0.7	–1.1	–0.7	–0.8	–0.7	–0.8
Borrowing, transfers, lapses, & other adjustments	*	....	....	....	....	....	....
Total change in fund balance	–1.4	–0.7	–1.1	–0.7	–0.8	–0.7	–0.8
Balance, end of year	21.9	21.2	20.1	19.4	18.6	17.9	17.1

Table 26–4.   INCOME, OUTGO, AND BALANCE OF MAJOR TRUST FUNDS—Continued

(In billions of dollars)

	2015 Actual	Estimate					
		2016	2017	2018	2019	2020	2021
Social Security: Old Age, Survivors, and Disability Insurance (OASDI) Trust Funds							
Balance, start of year	2,782.6	2,808.2	2,816.7	2,816.2	2,795.1	2,749.9	2,672.4
Adjustments to balances	–*	....	....	....	....	....	....
Total balance, start of year	2,782.6	2,808.2	2,816.7	2,816.2	2,795.1	2,749.9	2,672.4
Income:							
Governmental receipts	770.4	797.7	826.9	863.3	898.2	931.9	980.2
Offsetting governmental	....	....	....	....	....	....	....
Proprietary	0.1	0.1	0.1	0.1	0.1	0.1	0.1
Intrabudgetary:							
Intrafund	....	....	....	....	....	....	....
Interest	96.0	90.7	88.3	85.7	86.3	82.8	80.6
Other intrabudgetary	59.0	62.0	70.2	74.3	79.2	84.1	89.2
Total income during the year	925.5	950.4	985.5	1,023.4	1,063.7	1,098.9	1,150.2
Outgo (–)	–899.9	–941.8	–986.0	–1,044.5	–1,108.9	–1,176.4	–1,243.6
Change in fund balance:							
Surplus or deficit(–):							
Excluding interest	–70.4	–82.1	–88.9	–106.8	–131.5	–160.3	–174.0
Interest	96.0	90.7	88.3	85.7	86.3	82.8	80.6
Subtotal, surplus or deficit (–)	25.6	8.6	–0.5	–21.1	–45.2	–77.5	–93.4
Borrowing, transfers, lapses, & other adjustments	*	....	....	....	....	....	....
Total change in fund balance	25.6	8.6	–0.5	–21.1	–45.2	–77.5	–93.4
Balance, end of year	2,808.2	2,816.7	2,816.2	2,795.1	2,749.9	2,672.4	2,579.0
Transportation Trust Fund							
Balance, start of year	14.8	11.9	71.0	76.7	80.8	77.6	65.5
Adjustments to balances	....	....	....	....	....	....	....
Total balance, start of year	14.8	11.9	71.0	76.7	80.8	77.6	65.5
Income:							
Governmental receipts	40.8	41.3	47.5	55.8	63.6	71.5	79.2
Offsetting governmental	*	*	*	*	*	*	*
Proprietary	0.1	....	....	....	....	....	....
Intrabudgetary:							
Intrafund	....	0.1	0.1	0.1	....	....	....
Interest	*	*	*	*	*	*	....
Other intrabudgetary	8.2	70.4	19.4	20.4	14.4	6.5	0.4
Total income during the year	49.1	111.8	67.0	76.3	78.0	78.0	79.6
Outgo (–)	–52.0	–52.7	–61.3	–72.2	–81.2	–90.1	–96.5
Change in fund balance:							
Surplus or deficit(–):							
Excluding interest	–2.9	59.1	5.7	4.0	–3.2	–12.0	–16.8
Interest	*	*	*	*	*	*	....
Subtotal, surplus or deficit (–)	–2.9	59.1	5.7	4.1	–3.2	–12.0	–16.8
Borrowing, transfers, lapses, & other adjustments	*	....	....	....	....	....	....
Total change in fund balance	–2.9	59.1	5.7	4.1	–3.2	–12.0	–16.8
Balance, end of year	11.9	71.0	76.7	80.8	77.6	65.5	48.7

Table 26–4. INCOME, OUTGO, AND BALANCE OF MAJOR TRUST FUNDS—Continued

(In billions of dollars)

	2015 Actual	Estimate					
		2016	2017	2018	2019	2020	2021
Unemployment Trust Fund							
Balance, start of year	15.2	31.6	46.1	58.5	69.7	81.5	92.9
Adjustments to balances	....	....	....	....	....	....	....
Total balance, start of year	15.2	31.6	46.1	58.5	69.7	81.5	92.9
Income:							
Governmental receipts	51.2	49.9	50.3	51.8	52.8	54.4	55.6
Offsetting governmental	....	....	....	....	....	....	....
Proprietary	*	*	*	*	*	*	*
Intrabudgetary:							
Intrafund	....	....	....	....	....	....	....
Interest	1.1	1.3	1.4	1.5	1.8	2.3	2.8
Other intrabudgetary	0.8	0.8	0.7	0.7	0.7	0.8	1.0
Total income during the year	53.1	51.9	52.4	54.1	55.4	57.5	59.4
Outgo (–)	–36.7	–37.4	–40.0	–42.9	–43.6	–46.0	–47.9
Change in fund balance:							
Surplus or deficit(–):							
Excluding interest	15.3	13.3	11.0	9.6	10.0	9.1	8.6
Interest	1.1	1.3	1.4	1.5	1.8	2.3	2.8
Subtotal, surplus or deficit (–)	16.5	14.5	12.4	11.1	11.8	11.4	11.5
Borrowing, transfers, lapses, & other adjustments	–*	....	....	....	....	....	....
Total change in fund balance	16.5	14.5	12.4	11.1	11.8	11.4	11.5
Balance, end of year	31.6	46.1	58.5	69.7	81.5	92.9	104.4
Veterans Life Insurance Funds							
Balance, start of year	7.5	6.7	5.9	5.1	4.4	3.7	3.0
Adjustments to balances	....	....	....	....	....	....	....
Total balance, start of year	7.5	6.7	5.9	5.1	4.4	3.7	3.0
Income:							
Governmental receipts	....	....	....	....	....	....	....
Offsetting governmental	....	....	....	....	....	....	....
Proprietary	0.2	0.2	0.2	0.1	0.1	0.1	0.1
Intrabudgetary:							
Intrafund	....	....	....	....	....	....	....
Interest	0.3	0.3	0.2	0.2	0.2	0.1	0.1
Other intrabudgetary	....	....	....	....	....	....	....
Total income during the year	0.5	0.4	0.4	0.3	0.3	0.3	0.2
Outgo (–)	–1.3	–1.2	–1.2	–1.1	–1.0	–0.9	–0.8
Change in fund balance:							
Surplus or deficit(–):							
Excluding interest	–1.1	–1.0	–1.0	–1.0	–0.9	–0.8	–0.7
Interest	0.3	0.3	0.2	0.2	0.2	0.1	0.1
Subtotal, surplus or deficit (–)	–0.8	–0.8	–0.8	–0.8	–0.7	–0.6	–0.6
Borrowing, transfers, lapses, & other adjustments	....	....	....	....	....	....	....
Total change in fund balance	–0.8	–0.8	–0.8	–0.8	–0.7	–0.6	–0.6
Balance, end of year	6.7	5.9	5.1	4.4	3.7	3.0	2.4

Table 26–4.   INCOME, OUTGO, AND BALANCE OF MAJOR TRUST FUNDS—Continued

(In billions of dollars)

	2015 Actual	Estimate					
		2016	2017	2018	2019	2020	2021
All Other Trust Funds							
Balance, start of year	91.5	96.2	101.6	119.7	132.8	138.2	145.0
Adjustments to balances	0.1	....	....	....	....	....	....
Total balance, start of year	91.6	96.2	101.6	119.7	132.8	138.2	145.0
Income:							
Governmental receipts	4.9	5.0	7.5	8.4	8.4	8.5	8.7
Offsetting governmental	18.6	12.9	13.4	7.4	*	*	*
Proprietary	9.1	6.0	6.2	6.4	6.5	6.5	6.6
Intrabudgetary:							
Intrafund	0.1	0.1	0.1	0.1	0.2	*	*
Interest	1.3	1.4	1.9	2.3	2.5	2.7	3.3
Other intrabudgetary	3.2	3.0	3.2	3.3	3.4	3.3	3.4
Total income during the year	37.3	28.5	32.4	27.9	21.0	21.0	22.0
Outgo (–)	–20.0	–15.4	–14.2	–14.9	–15.5	–14.2	–14.3
Change in fund balance:							
Surplus or deficit(–):							
Excluding interest	15.9	11.7	16.2	10.7	3.0	4.1	4.4
Interest	1.3	1.4	1.9	2.3	2.5	2.7	3.3
Subtotal, surplus or deficit (–)	17.3	13.1	18.2	13.0	5.5	6.8	7.7
Borrowing, transfers, lapses, & other adjustments	–12.6	–7.8	*	....	....	....	....
Total change in fund balance	4.6	5.4	18.2	13.0	5.5	6.8	7.7
Balance, end of year	96.2	101.6	119.7	132.8	138.2	145.0	152.6

* $50 million or less.

Table 26–5.   INCOME, OUTGO, AND BALANCE OF SELECTED SPECIAL FUNDS
(In billions of dollars)

	2015 Actual	Estimate					
		2016	2017	2018	2019	2020	2021
Abandoned Mine Reclamation Fund							
Balance, start of year	2.8	2.8	2.7	2.7	2.6	2.5	2.3
Adjustments to balances	....	....	....	....	....	....	....
Total balance, start of year	2.8	2.8	2.7	2.7	2.6	2.5	2.3
Income:							
Governmental receipts	0.2	0.2	0.2	0.2	0.3	0.3	0.3
Offsetting governmental	....	....	....	....	....	....	....
Proprietary	....	....	....	....	....	....	....
Intrabudgetary:							
Intrafund	....	....	....	....	....	....	....
Interest	*	*	*	0.1	0.1	0.1	0.1
Other intrabudgetary	....	....	....	....	....	....	....
Total income during the year	0.2	0.2	0.3	0.3	0.3	0.3	0.4
Outgo (–)	–0.2	–0.3	–0.3	–0.4	–0.5	–0.5	–0.6
Change in fund balance:							
Surplus or deficit(–):							
Excluding interest	–*	–0.1	–0.1	–0.2	–0.2	–0.3	–0.3
Interest	*	*	*	0.1	0.1	0.1	0.1
Subtotal, surplus or deficit (–)	–*	–0.1	–*	–0.1	–0.2	–0.2	–0.2
Borrowing, transfers, lapses, & other adjustments	....	....	....	....	....	....	....
Total change in fund balance	–*	–0.1	–*	–0.1	–0.2	–0.2	–0.2
Balance, end of year	2.8	2.7	2.7	2.6	2.5	2.3	2.1
Department of Defense Medicare-Eligible Retiree Health Care Fund							
Balance, start of year	198.9	204.3	212.8	220.6	227.9	235.3	243.8
Adjustments to balances	....	....	....	....	....	....	....
Total balance, start of year	198.9	204.3	212.8	220.6	227.9	235.3	243.8
Income:							
Governmental receipts	....	....	....	....	....	....	....
Offsetting governmental	....	....	....	....	....	....	....
Proprietary	....	....	....	....	....	....	....
Intrabudgetary:							
Intrafund	11.2	10.2	8.4	8.8	9.2	9.7	10.2
Interest	4.2	8.6	9.6	9.3	9.5	10.4	11.2
Other intrabudgetary	....	....	....	....	....	....	....
Total income during the year	15.4	18.7	18.1	18.1	18.7	20.1	21.4
Outgo (–)	–10.0	–10.2	–10.3	–10.8	–11.3	–11.7	–12.3
Change in fund balance:							
Surplus or deficit(–):							
Excluding interest	1.3	–0.1	–1.8	–2.0	–2.1	–2.0	–2.1
Interest	4.2	8.6	9.6	9.3	9.5	10.4	11.2
Subtotal, surplus or deficit (–)	5.5	8.5	7.8	7.3	7.4	8.4	9.1
Borrowing, transfers, lapses, & other adjustments	....	....	....	....	....	....	....
Total change in fund balance	5.5	8.5	7.8	7.3	7.4	8.4	9.1
Balance, end of year	204.3	212.8	220.6	227.9	235.3	243.8	252.9

* $50 million or less.

27. COMPARISON OF ACTUAL TO ESTIMATED TOTALS

In successive budgets, the Administration publishes estimates of the surplus or deficit for a particular fiscal year. Initially, the year appears as an outyear projection at the end of the budget horizon. In each subsequent budget, the year advances in the estimating horizon until it becomes the "budget year." One year later, the year becomes the "current year" then in progress, and the following year, it becomes the just-completed "actual year."

The Budget is legally required to compare budget year estimates of receipts and outlays with the subsequent actual receipts and outlays for that year. This chapter meets that requirement by comparing the actual receipts, outlays, and deficit for 2015 with the current services estimates shown in the 2015 Budget, published in March 2014.[1] It also presents a more detailed comparison for mandatory and related programs, and reconciles the actual receipts, outlays, and deficit totals shown here with the figures for 2015 previously published by the Department of the Treasury.

---

[1] The current services concept is discussed in Chapter 25, "Current Services Estimates." For mandatory programs and receipts, the March 2014 current services estimate was based on laws then in place, with specified adjustments for current policy - for example relief from scheduled reductions under the Medicare Sustainable Growth Rate mechanism and extension of certain expiring tax provisions. For discretionary programs the current services estimate was based on the discretionary spending limits enacted in the Budget Control Act of 2011 (BCA). Spending for Overseas Contingency Operations, was estimated based on annualizing the amounts provided in the 2014 appropriations and increasing for inflation. The current services estimates also reflected the effects of discretionary and mandatory sequestration as required by the BCA following failure of the Joint Select Committee on Deficit Reduction to meet its deficit reduction target. The current services estimates published in the 2015 Budget re-classified a large number of surface transportation programs as mandatory. The published estimates for nondefense discretionary outlays and mandatory outlays were $543 billion and $2,405 billion, respectively. This proposal was not subsequently enacted, so the applicable costs are shown as discretionary in this chapter for comparability. For a detailed explanation of the 2015 estimate, see "Current Services Estimates," Chapter 25 in *Analytical Perspectives, Budget of the United States Government, Fiscal Year 2015.*

Receipts

Actual receipts for 2015 were $3,250 billion, only $1 billion less than the $3,251 billion current services estimate in the 2015 Budget, which was published in March 2014. As shown in Table 27–1, this decrease was the net effect of legislated tax changes and economic conditions that differed from what had been expected, which were almost completely offset by technical factors that resulted in different tax liabilities and collection patterns than had been assumed.

Policy differences. Legislated tax changes enacted after March 2014 reduced 2015 receipts by a net $83 billion relative to the 2015 Budget current services estimate. Legislation that extended certain expiring tax provisions and made other modifications to the Internal Revenue Code, which was signed into law by President Obama on December 19, 2014, accounted for almost all of this net reduction in receipts, reducing 2015 receipts by an estimated $82 billion.

Economic differences. Differences between the economic assumptions upon which the current services estimates were based and actual economic performance reduced 2015 receipts by a net $40 billion below the March 2014 current services estimate. Corporations were less profitable than initially projected, which reduced receipts $30 billion below the March 2014 estimate and accounted for 75 percent of the net reduction in receipts attributable to economic differences. Different economic factors than those assumed in March 2014 had a much smaller effect on other sources of receipts, reducing collections by a net $10 billion.

Technical factors. Technical factors increased receipts by a net $122 billion relative to the March 2014 current services estimate. These factors had the greatest effect on individual income taxes, increasing collections by $73 billion. Increases in corporation income taxes of $12 billion, social insurance and retirement receipts of $16 billion, and miscellaneous receipts of $18 billion accounted for most of the remaining net increase in 2015

Table 27–1. COMPARISON OF ACTUAL 2015 RECEIPTS WITH THE INITIAL CURRENT SERVICES ESTIMATES
(In billions of dollars)

	Estimate (March 2014)	Changes			Total Changes	Actual
		Policy	Economic	Technical		
Individual income taxes	1,498	–30	–1	73	42	1,541
Corporation income taxes	412	–50	–30	12	–68	344
Social insurance and retirement receipts	1,055	....	–6	16	10	1,065
Excise taxes	99	–3	–1	3	–1	98
Estate and gift taxes	18	....	–*	2	2	19
Customs duties	38	–1	*	–2	–3	35
Miscellaneous receipts	131	*	–2	18	16	147
Total receipts	3,251	–83	–40	122	–1	3,250

* $500 million or less

receipts attributable to technical factors. The models used to prepare the March 2014 estimates of individual and corporation income taxes were based on historical economic data and then-current tax and collections data that were all subsequently revised and account for the net increase in these two sources of receipts attributable to technical factors. These revisions in the individual and corporation income tax models indicated that: (1) sources of income that are not part of the economic forecast, but subject to tax, such as capital gains and pensions, differed from what was expected at the time the March 2014 estimates were prepared; (2) for most sources of income subject to individual and corporation income taxes, both the percentage that was subject to tax and the effective tax rate on the portion subject to tax differed from what was anticipated; and (3) the timing of the payment of tax liability was different from what had been assumed. The $16 billion increase in social insurance and retirement receipts attributable to technical factors reflected a $24 billion increase in Social Security and Medicare payroll taxes that was partially offset by an $8 billion reduction in unemployment insurance receipts. The $24 billion increase in Social Security and Medicare payroll taxes was attributable in large part to models based on historical economic data and then-current data from employer returns that underestimated the percentage of wages and salaries and self-employment earnings subject to payroll taxes. The $8 billion reduction in unemployment insurance receipts reflected lower-than-anticipated deposits by States to the unemployment insurance trust fund. Changes in the size and composition of the investments of the Federal Reserve System accounted for $11 billion of the $18 billion increase in miscellaneous receipts attributable to technical factors. Penalties and forfeitures related to large settlement agreements that were not reflected in the March 2014 estimates of 2015 receipts accounted for most of the remaining increase in miscellaneous receipts.

Outlays

Outlays for 2015 were $3,688 billion, $124 billion less than the $3,812 billion current services estimate in the 2015 Budget. Table 27–2 distributes the $124 billion net decrease in outlays among discretionary and mandatory programs and net interest.[2] The table also shows rough estimates according to three reasons for the changes: policy; economic conditions; and technical estimating differences, a residual.

Policy differences. Policy changes are the result of legislative actions that change spending levels, primarily through higher or lower appropriations or changes in authorizing legislation, which may themselves be in response to changed economic conditions. For 2015, policy changes increased outlays by $14 billion relative to the initial current services estimates, which included the impacts of sequestration and discretionary cap reductions as part of the Joint Committee enforcement provisions of the Budget Control Act of 2011. Final 2014 discretionary appropriations were enacted as the 2015 Budget was being prepared, so the March 2014 estimate of discretionary outlays assumed rates that were lower than the final enacted appropriations allowed. The combined policy changes from final 2014 and 2015 appropriations, including Overseas Contingency Operations, increased discretionary outlays by $3 billion. Policy changes increased mandatory outlays by a net $11 billion above current law. Much of this increase was the result of changes in the Medicare program enacted primarily in 2015 that increased 2015 outlays by $6 billion. Debt service costs associated with all policy changes increased outlays by less than $1 billion.

---

[2] Discretionary programs are controlled by annual appropriations, while mandatory programs are generally controlled by authorizing legislation. Mandatory programs are primarily formula benefit or entitlement programs with permanent spending authority that depends on eligibility criteria, benefit levels, and other factors.

Table 27–2. COMPARISON OF ACTUAL 2015 OUTLAYS WITH THE INITIAL CURRENT SERVICES ESTIMATES
(In billions of dollars)

	Estimate (March 2014)	Changes Policy	Changes Economic	Changes Technical	Total Changes	Actual
Discretionary:						
Defense	606	–10	....	–13	–23	583
Nondefense	602	13	....	–30	–17	585
Subtotal, discretionary	1,208	3	....	–42	–40	1,169
Mandatory:						
Social Security	896	....	2	–17	–15	882
Other programs	1,450	11	–38	–9	–36	1,414
Subtotal, mandatory	2,346	11	–36	–26	–51	2,296
Allowance for disaster costs [1]	6	....	....	–6	–6	....
Net interest	251	*	–34	6	–28	223
Total outlays	3,812	14	–70	–68	–124	3,688

* $500 million or less

[1] These amounts were included in the 2015 Budget to represent the statistical probability of a major disaster requiring federal assistance for relief and reconstruction. Such assistance might be provided in the form of discretionary, or mandatory outlays or tax relief. These amounts were included as outlays for convenience.

Economic and technical factors. Economic and technical estimating factors resulted in a net decrease in outlays of $139 billion. Technical changes result from changes in such factors as the number of beneficiaries for entitlement programs, crop conditions, or other factors not associated with policy changes or economic conditions. Increases in discretionary outlays due to legislation, as discussed above, were partially offset by a $42 billion decrease in net outlays resulting from technical changes. Outlays for mandatory programs decreased $62 billion due to economic and technical factors. There was a net decrease in outlays of $36 billion as a result of differences between actual economic conditions versus those forecast in March 2014. Outlays for Social Security were $15 billion lower than anticipated in the 2015 Budget largely due to lower-than-estimated number of beneficiaries. Unemployment compensation and food and nutrition assistance programs outlays were a combined $15 billion lower. Remaining changes were in other health and assistance programs. Outlays for net interest were $28 billion lower due to economic and technical factors, primarily lower interest rates than originally assumed.

Deficit

The preceding two sections discussed the differences between the initial current services estimates and the actual amounts of Federal government receipts and outlays for 2014. This section combines these effects to show the net deficit impact of these differences.

As shown in Table 27–3, the 2015 current services deficit was initially estimated to be $561 billion. The actual deficit was $438 billion, which was a $123 billion decrease from the initial estimate. Receipts were $1 billion lower and outlays were $124 billion less than the initial estimate. The table shows the distribution of the changes according to the categories in the preceding two sections. The net effect of policy changes for receipts and outlays increased the deficit by $97 billion. Economic conditions that differed from the initial assumptions in March 2014 decreased the deficit by $30 billion. Technical factors decreased the deficit by an estimated $190 billion.

Comparison of the Actual and Estimated Outlays for Mandatory and Related Programs for 2015

This section compares the original 2015 outlay estimates for mandatory and related programs in the current services estimates of the Budget with the actual outlays. Major examples of these programs include Social Security

and Medicare benefits, Medicaid and unemployment compensation payments, and deposit insurance for banks and thrift institutions. This category also includes net interest outlays and undistributed offsetting receipts.

A number of factors may cause differences between the amounts estimated in the Budget and the actual mandatory outlays. For example, legislation may change benefit rates or coverage, the actual number of beneficiaries may differ from the number estimated, or economic conditions (such as inflation or interest rates) may differ from what was assumed in making the original estimates.

Table 27–4 shows the differences between the actual outlays for these programs in 2015 and the current services estimates included in the 2015 Budget.[3] Actual outlays for mandatory spending and net interest in 2015 were $2,296 billion, which was $51 billion less than the current services estimate of $2,346 billion in March 2014.

As Table 27–4 shows, actual outlays for mandatory human resources programs were $2,416 billion, $17 billion less than originally estimated. This decrease was the net effect of legislative action, differences between actual and assumed economic conditions, differences between the anticipated and actual number of beneficiaries, and other technical differences. Most significantly, outlays for Social Security, income security, and other health programs decreased by $69 billion due to economic, legislative and technical factors. Mandatory outlays for programs in functions outside human resources were $12 billion less than originally estimated.

Outlays for net interest were $223 billion, or $28 billion less than the original estimate. As shown on Table 27–4, interest payments on Treasury debt securities decreased by $25 billion. Interest earnings of trust funds increased by $5 billion, further reducing net outlays, while net outlays for other interest rose by $2 billion.

Reconciliation of Differences with Amounts Published by the Treasury for 2015

Table 27-5 provides a reconciliation of the receipts, outlays, and deficit totals for 2015 published by the Department of the Treasury in the September 2015 Monthly Treasury Statement (MTS) and those published in this Budget. The Department of the Treasury made adjustments to the estimates for the Combined Statement of Receipts, Outlays, and Balances, which decreased receipts by $22 million and decreased outlays by $26 million. Additional adjustments for the 2017 Budget increased receipts by $1,184 million and increased outlays

---

[3] See footnote 1 for an explanation of the current services concept.

Table 27–3. COMPARISON OF THE ACTUAL 2015 DEFICIT WITH THE INITIAL CURRENT SERVICES ESTIMATE

(In billions of dollars)

	Estimate (March 2014)	Changes			Total Changes	Actual
		Policy	Economic	Technical		
Receipts	3,251	–83	–40	122	–1	3,250
Outlays	3,812	14	–70	–68	–124	3,688
Deficit	561	97	–30	–190	–123	438

Note: Deficit changes are outlays minus receipts. For these changes, a positive number indicates an increase in the deficit.

by $690 million. Most of these adjustments are for financial transactions that are not reported to the Department of the Treasury but are included in the Budget, including those for the Public Company Accounting Oversight Board, the Affordable Housing Program, the Securities Investor Protection Corporation, the Electric Reliability Organization, the United Mine Workers of America benefit funds, the payment to the Standard Setting Body, and the Federal Retirement Thrift Investment Board program expenses. There is also an adjustment for the National

Railroad Retirement Investment Trust (NRRIT) which relates to a conceptual difference in reporting. NRRIT reports to the Department of the Treasury with a one-month lag so that the fiscal year total provided in the Treasury Combined Statement covers September 2014 through August 2015. The Budget has been adjusted to reflect transactions that occurred during the actual fiscal year, which begins October 1. The Budget also reflects agency adjustments to 2015 outlays reported to Treasury after preparation of the Treasury Combined Statement.

Table 27–4. COMPARISON OF ACTUAL AND ESTIMATED OUTLAYS FOR MANDATORY AND RELATED PROGRAMS UNDER CURRENT LAW

(In billions of dollars)

	2015		
	Estimate	Actual	Change
Mandatory outlays:			
Human resources programs:			
Education, training, employment, and social services:			
Higher Education	1	26	25
Other	8	7	–1
Total, education, training, employment, and social services	9	33	24
Health:			
Medicaid	331	350	18
Other	116	77	–39
Total, health	447	426	–21
Medicare	529	540	11
Income security:			
Retirement and disability	147	146	–1
Unemployment compensation	41	32	–9
Food and nutrition assistance	100	98	–2
Other	171	168	–3
Total, income security	458	443	–15
Social security	896	882	–15
Veterans benefits and services:			
Income security for veterans	79	76	–3
Other	14	16	1
Total, veterans benefits and services	94	92	–1
Total, mandatory human resources programs	2,433	2,416	–17
Other functions:			
Agriculture	12	12	1
International	–3	–3	–*
Mortgage credit	–23	–21	2
Deposit insurance	–9	–13	–4
Other advancement of commerce (includes the Troubled Asset Relief Program)	14	8	–6
Other functions	17	12	–5
Total, other functions	7	–5	–12
Undistributed offsetting receipts:			
Employer share, employee retirement	–84	–79	4
Rents and royalties on the outer continental shelf	–8	–5	4
Other undistributed offsetting receipts	–2	–32	–30
Total, undistributed offsetting receipts	–94	–116	–22
Total, mandatory	2,346	2,296	–51
Net interest:			
Interest on Treasury debt securities (gross)	455	430	–25
Interest received by trust funds	–153	–158	–5
Other interest	–51	–48	2
Total, net interest	251	223	–28
Total, outlays for mandatory and net interest	2,598	2,519	–79

Table 27–5. RECONCILIATION OF FINAL AMOUNTS FOR 2015

(In millions of dollars)

	Receipts	Outlays	Deficit
Totals published by Treasury (September MTS)	3,248,723	3,687,622	438,899
Miscellaneous Treasury adjustments	–22	–26	–4
Totals published by Treasury in Combined Statement	3,248,701	3,687,596	438,895
National Railroad Retirement Investment Trust	....	–126	–126
Public Company Accounting Oversight Board	228	245	17
Affordable Housing Program	319	319	....
Securities Investor Protection Corporation	425	163	–262
Electric Reliability Organization	100	100	....
United Mine Workers of America benefit funds	25	25	....
Federal Retirement Thrift Investment Board Program Expenses	....	–30	–30
Standard Setting Body	26	26	....
Risk Adjustment program	61	61	....
Intelligence Community Management Account	....	–95	–95
Other	1	8	7
Total adjustments, net	1,185	696	–489
Totals in the Budget	3,249,886	3,688,292	438,406
MEMORANDUM:			
Total change since year-end statement	1,163	670	–493